The Early Lectures of

Ralph Waldo Emerson

VOLUME III

1 8 3 8 – 1 8 4 2

THE EARLY LECTURES OF
Ralph Waldo Emerson

VOLUME III

1838–1842

Edited by

Robert E. Spiller and Wallace E. Williams

THE BELKNAP PRESS

OF HARVARD UNIVERSITY PRESS

Cambridge, Massachusetts

1972

© 1972 by the President and Fellows of Harvard College

Distributed in Great Britain by Oxford University Press, London

Library of Congress Catalog Card Number 59–5160

SBN 674–22152–4

Typography by Burton Jones

Printed in the U.S.A.

Preface

The third and final volume of this edition of *The Early Lectures of Ralph Waldo Emerson* was originally planned to include all of the previously unpublished lecture manuscripts that could be reproduced with reasonable accuracy up to the time of Emerson's first lectures in England in 1847. Closer study of the manuscripts, however, supported by the publication of the full texts of the important *Journals and Miscellaneous Notebooks* of this period, has led to a better understanding of the editorial problems involved as they are related to newly discovered and interpreted biographical facts. With the completion of Emerson's final winter series of lectures on "The Times" at the Masonic Temple in Boston in January 1842, and with the publication of *Essays, Second Series* in 1844, Emerson's approach to the whole process of written and oral composition underwent a profound change. The editorial problems involved in the rescue and reconstruction of the later manuscripts, both published and unpublished, therefore call for a basically different editorial policy from that applied to the lectures of the previous decade. The new problems begin to appear in the series on "New England" in 1843, which were specifically written for library companies and other groups in New York, Philadelphia, and Baltimore, and were offered to them individually, in combination, or in series, before any of the lectures were repeated in New England or elsewhere. It is before this point, therefore, that the present edition of *The Early Lectures* has been terminated and the way opened for a projected edition of all the remaining unpublished lecture manuscripts surviving from Emerson's later career.

Although Stephen E. Whicher shared in much of the editorial planning which has resulted in this volume and did some of the preliminary work on the series on "Human Life" (which was originally planned for the second volume), it would not be fair to his memory to hold him accountable in any way for the volume as it now appears. His colleagues, therefore, accept this responsibility with profound gratitude for the inspiration and wisdom that he provided.

It is reassuring to note that Wallace E. Williams, who joined the project as research assistant for the first volume, has carried the main editorial burdens of this, the third, and will emerge as the principal editor of the projected edition of the later lectures, which is already in an advanced state of preparation.

The editors are indebted to the late Edward W. Forbes and the Ralph Waldo Emerson Memorial Association and to the President and Fellows of Harvard College for permission to publish the texts of these lectures from manuscripts in the Houghton Library. For the assistance, encouragement, and unfailing courtesy at Houghton Library the editors express their appreciation to the late William A. Jackson, to his successor as Librarian, William H. Bond, to Carolyn Jakeman, and to the library staff.

The sharing of a common workshop in Houghton Library with the editors of *The Journals and Miscellaneous Notebooks of Ralph Waldo Emerson,* the exchange of information common to the annotation of their edition and this, and other important help have again created an indebtedness, hereby acknowledged with gratitude, to William H. Gilman, Alfred R. Ferguson, Merton M. Sealts, Harrison Hayford, Ralph H. Orth, Arthur W. Plumstead, and James E. Parsons.

The editors were fortunate again in having an excellent typescript made by Elizabeth C. Tompkins. To James H. Justus, Alex M. Baumgartner, Thornton F. Jordan, and George L. Miljanich the editors are grateful for their generous aid at various stages in the preparation of this volume.

Finally, acknowledgment must once more be made to the faculty research committees of Indiana University, the University of Pennsylvania, and Cornell University for special grants in aid to the several editors.

R.E.S.

CONTENTS

Introduction   *xi*

I   *HUMAN LIFE*   *1*

     1. *Doctrine of the Soul*   5
     2. *Home*   23
     3. *The School*   34
     4. *Love*   51
     5. *Genius*   68
     6. *The Protest*   85
     7. *Tragedy*   103
     8. *Comedy*   121
     9. *Duty*   138
     10. *Demonology*   151

II   *THE PRESENT AGE*   *175*

     1. *Introductory*   185
     2. *Literature* [*first lecture*]   202
     3. *Literature* [*second lecture*]   224
     4. *Politics*   238
     5. *Private Life*   248
     6. *Reforms*   256
     7. *Religion*   271
     9. *Education*   286
     10. *Tendencies*   302

III   *ADDRESS TO THE PEOPLE OF EAST LEXINGTON*   *319*

     (*On the Dedication of Their Church,*
         15 January 1840)

CONTENTS

IV THE TIMES   335
    3. The Poet   347
    8. Prospects   366

    BIBLIOGRAPHY OF PRINCIPAL
        SOURCES   385

    TEXTUAL NOTES AND VARIANT
        PASSAGES   387

    ANALYTICAL INDEX TO THE
        THREE VOLUMES   527

Several manuscript pages are reproduced
following page 326

INTRODUCTION

Introduction

IN March 1838, five weeks after ending his Boston series on "Human Culture," Emerson wrote to his brother William that he had given up his charge at the church in East Lexington and would "not preach more except from the Lyceum." The series, read also at Lowell, Framingham, and Cambridge, had been financially successful, and Emerson thought that henceforth he might "live by lecturing which promises to be good bread" (*L*, II, 120). The confidence implied here doubtless sustained him in delivering four months later, on July 15, 1838, to the senior class at the Divinity School, the address which effectively severed him from the good graces of the Unitarian establishment. This marks the height of his first popularity, and he was in demand as an occasional speaker, partly owing to the success of his Phi Beta Kappa oration the previous summer, which was now in its second edition. During 1838 he also read a lecture in March in the series sponsored in Boston by the American Peace Society, later printed as "War," and on July 25 before the literary societies of Dartmouth College an oration, published at the time and later collected as "Literary Ethics." It was with confidence then that Emerson might rely on his profession as a lecturer. Particularly he could, as he had done the previous two winters, offer a private lecture series, announcing his own topics, renting the Masonic Temple in Boston, selling tickets at his own risk, and then engaging to repeat all or some of the lectures at nearby towns. The lectures in this volume are the means whereby Emerson produced virtually all his earned income from 1838 to 1842.

The sureness of his profession as a lecturer is reflected in other aspects of his busy life. He was settled well in Concord with a growing family. The death of his oldest child, Waldo, did not occur until after the close of the lectures on "The Times" in

January 1842; Ellen was born in February 1839; Edith in November 1841. The household also consisted of his wife, his mother, and for two years, from April 1841, Henry Thoreau. Elizabeth Hoar, because of her engagement to Charles, almost a member of the family, lived near at hand, and the Bronson Alcotts, whom Emerson once charitably hoped to add to his household, at least lived in Concord from the spring of 1840. His concern for domestic affairs is suggested not only by physical improvements to his house and small acreage, but also by the unsuccessful attempt in 1841 to include the cook and maid at table. The Concord family was in close touch with the family of Emerson's brother William in New York, both by frequent visits and extensive correspondence. His only other surviving brother, the retarded Bulkeley, Emerson cared for, if not usually at home, at least by placing him with farming families and by sharing expenses for him with William. He also undertook for a while to employ a boy, Alexander McCaffery, who was the child of William's maid, and paid for the education of Hillman Sampson, whose father had been a friend of Emerson. There were increasing responsibilities managed with ordinary efficiency. In all, the Concord household was busy and happy. Though far from wealthy, Emerson could extend an offer of hospitality not only to the Alcotts, but to the Carlyles, who also declined. Increasingly Emerson's home was a center for those interested in "the newness"; he particularly enjoyed in these years a select band of intimate friends, Margaret Fuller, Caroline Sturgis, Anna Barker, and Samuel Gray Ward, but there were other, older friends, members of "Hedge's Club," newer ones as diverse as James Russell Lowell and Charles King Newcomb, and many itinerant transcendentalists and reformers, "monotones" and "goodies."

Meanwhile, Emerson was busily engaged in other literary activities. He was deeply involved in the American publishing affairs of Thomas Carlyle, acting as "banker and attorney" in successful efforts to secure for his friend financial returns for editions of *The French Revolution, Miscellanies*, and *Chartism*, all of which involved him not only in intricate matters of business, promotion, accounting, and transmission of money, but also for a while put a severe strain on his finances since he had to advance money to pay printing and publishing costs. Although he did not actually become editor of it until the spring of 1842, Emerson was also much engaged in the affairs of *The Dial* from its planning in the fall of 1839 through the two years of Margaret Fuller's editorship. Not only did he provide liberal contributions of his own, but he also became a combination talent scout and chief editorial consultant. These two literary enterprises left him little time for writing the book of essays which he was determined to make out of his growing mass of lecture manuscripts.

The book was already in the back of his mind as an attractive alternative when on August 31, 1838, he reflected on the disfavor into which he had fallen over the Divinity School address: "My resources are far from exhausted. If they will not hear me lecture, I shall have leisure for my book which wants me" (D, 87–88). Emerson had cause to be worried: he was responsible for the printing costs of *The French Revolution,* and he had borrowed in order to help William while he was building a house on Staten Island. By the end of September, he was concerned that if he offered another course of lectures he might not even meet expenses; yet he had no real alternative to trying. His fears were not borne out, however, and the new series on "Human Life," given at the Masonic Temple in Boston in the winter of 1838–39, was successful, though, perhaps because he had given many complimentary tickets, "that I may not have labored in vain" (L, II, 172), it did not bring in so much net profit as "Human Culture." Despite bad health which caused him to end the Boston readings earlier than he had planned, Emerson partially repeated the new series in Concord and gave two lectures from it in Plymouth. For the Mechanics' Apprentices' Association in Boston he read an unidentified lecture called "Intellectual Integrity" on March 6, 1839, and in November of that year gave two more lectures, both old ones, in the Concord Lyceum. It may well be that Emerson was less in demand for repetitions of his lectures or for occasional addresses, but it is also true that as early as April 1839 he was working on *Essays;* he wrote to Alcott: "I have been writing a little and arranging old papers more, and by and by, I hope to get a shapely book of Genesis" (L, II, 194). He wanted to complete the book by autumn and reported progress in the completion of at least three essays, but by September he had postponed the book and had begun to plan on "one more course of lectures in Boston" (*L*, II, 224).

The series on "The Present Age," given in the winter of 1839–40 in Boston, shows a sharp decline in financial returns. He took two lectures to the Salem Lyceum and nine lectures from the new course to the Concord Lyceum for a series interrupted by a trip to New York, where he read two of the new lectures and an old one at the Mercantile Library, and a stay at Providence, Rhode Island, where he read old and new lectures in a series announced as "Human Life" before the Franklin Lyceum. The trip to New York and Providence made the lecture season financially successful and allowed Emerson to turn by mid-April to the completion of *Essays,* even while he continued reading "The Present Age" to the Concord audience. Despite distractions, Emerson was able to finish *Essays,* but he gave no regular lecture series in the winter of 1840–41. He sent the manuscript to press on New Year's Day and read proofs in late January and February. The book was published in mid-March 1841. Meanwhile he was beginning to recover some of the money he had advanced for Carlyle's American editions. He wrote to William in December 1840: "No I don't lecture any where. No body asks me, Sir" (*L*, II, 372) — but the statement is not literally true, for he read single lectures, doubtless old ones, at Waltham, Worcester, Concord, and perhaps two at Billerica between November 14 and January 1, and on January 25 he read "Man the Reformer" for the Mechanics' Apprentices' Library Association in the Masonic Temple. This was perhaps the lecture he also read as "Reform" before the Concord Lyceum on March 10, since he had got it ready for publication in the April number of *The Dial.* Unexpectedly a request for an occasional address came from Waterville College, Maine, and he delivered there in August 1841 "The Method of Nature."

Perhaps in part because of his financial plight, a result of the failure of his bank to pay dividends, Emerson planned another private lecture series in Boston for the winter of 1841–42. Apprehensive about his diminishing success there, he thought in September that he might have to carry the course to "the West End of New York or of Philadelphia, or, as I have lately been challenged to do, of Baltimore" (*L*, II, 454). The series of eight lectures on "The Times," read at the Masonic Temple in December and January, brought him greater net profit per lecture there than any since "Human Culture," but it still fell short of his needs. Despite the death of Waldo, Emerson carried his new series first to Providence and then to New York, marking the end of the annual private lecture series at the Masonic Temple. From now on the professional lecturer would return to the lyceum series and individual lectures, relying on the demand for him expressed by others. More important, he had found an audience outside eastern New England: he would be drawn first to the Middle Atlantic states, then to England, and finally to the West.

Furthermore, the publication of *Essays* freed Emerson for new topics. He had made his statements on the important general topics of "The Philosophy of History," "Human Culture," "Human Life," and partially of "The Present Age" — "History," "Self-Reliance," "The Over-Soul," "Compensation," "Spiritual Laws" — in the book, and it is not surprising to find him moving now into different subject matter. "The Present Age" is built upon a theme which he had anticipated, though with a different emphasis, in a lecture in "The Philosophy of History" and which is still undeveloped in the essay "History." The insight into the future, based on the "movement party" of the present, is an emerging theme, and he pursued it from the lectures on "The Present Age" and "The Times" through "The Young American" and the lectures of 1848–50, "Mind and Manners of the Nineteenth Century." Another important development in this period was Emerson's new role as "observer" or "reporter." He had recognized his two voices — teacher and reporter — in reviewing his lecture manuscripts for *Essays*, and had finally embodied the dominant one in his lecture on "The Poet" — the expresser. He had moved from the pulpit-inspired rhetoric of "The Philosophy of History" and "Human Culture" to the "portrait gallery" of "The Times."

The intricate reworking of his prose from the lectures and journals into essays had sharpened his prose style, but the increasing use of whole lectures as essays, instead of the mosaic work of the 1841 volume, suggests that the stylistic distinction between the two public forms of his prose expression was diminishing. The periodical publication of three lectures on "The Times" shows the way to his later practice, as in *Representative Men, Seven Lectures;* but even in "The Poet" and "Prospects," two lectures published here for the first time, there is a maturing of prose style, which by 1842 closely approximated the voice of the lecturer.

Too much has been made of the seeming formlessness of Emerson's writing. In the lectures — even allowing for the freedom of the form which he claimed and for lacunae in the surviving manuscripts (caused partly by his publishing habits) — formlessness is not a characteristic. The sentence is not the unit of composition, as many critics have held. While often the structure of a lecture is perfunctory or lacks proportion, there is nevertheless an organization which bears a significant relation to what he is trying to say. Emerson's outlines, when they survive, are not so much heads as indexes to passages of prose from his journals. Ordinarily the diction and sentence structure are improved upon — condensed, expanded, reordered; characteristically the personal allusions, irrelevant circumstances, and the immediate or personal context are partially depersonalized or generalized; but often the application, the point, or the inference is changed. Emerson the artist deals in passages of prose — not in ideas alone.

Emerson recognized a "lapidary style" in his *Essays* (1841) and thought that a corrective might be the spoken word (cf. p. 338). In his lectures he hoped for what he called "ecstacy" and the "clean & permeable" transmission. His aspiration for eloquence in the lecture hall was high when in July 1839, taking time out from work on essays, he wrote in his journal: "A lecture is a new literature, which leaves aside all tradition, time, place, circumstance, & addresses an assembly as mere human beings, — no more — It has never yet been done well . . . But only then is the orator successful when he is himself agitated & is as much a hearer as any of the assembly. In that office you may & shall (please God!) yet see the electricity part from the cloud & shine from one part of heaven to the other" (D, 336). With his determination to live by lecturing alone, Emerson recognized the artistic, as earlier he had assumed the hortatory, possibilities of

eloquence and the potentialities of the secular pulpit — the lyceum lectern. Characteristically he accepts this new phenomenon
not only as an expressive cultural fact but also as his own medium. The journals are studded with references to the lyceum,
its appeals both high and low, its receptive audiences, its contributions to the newness and the democratic ideal. An extensive
entry on a loose sheet laid in before the entry of October 11,
1839, emphasizes the aesthetic potentialities of the lyceum, particularly as Emerson himself might realize them: "Here is all the
true orator will ask, for here is a convertible audience, & here are
no stiff conventions that prescribe a method a style a limited quotation of books & an exact respect to certain books persons or
opinions. No, here everything is admissible, philosophy, ethics,
divinity, criticism, poetry, humor, fun, mimicry, anecdotes, jokes,
ventriloquism, all the breadth & versatility of the most liberal
conversation personal local topics, all are permitted, and all may
be combined in one speech; it is a panharmonicon, — every note
on the longest gamut, from the explosion of cannon, to the tinkle
of a guitar. Let us try if Folly, Custom, Invention & Phlegm cannot hear our sharp artillery. Here is a pulpit that makes other
pulpits tame & ineffectual — with their cold mechanical preparation for a delivery the most decorous, — fine things, pretty things,
wise things, but no arrows no axes no nectar, no growling no
transpiercing no loving no enchantment. Here he may lay himself
out utterly, large, enormous, prodigal, on the subject of the hour.
Here he may dare to hope for ecstacy & eloquence" (E, vi$_a$) By
1842 Emerson had found his new vocation. He was laying himself
out utterly on the varied issues of his time without becoming personally involved in any specific causes, and his effectiveness was
being attested by audiences far and near. Lecturing was indeed
his vocation.

The lectures in this volume show Emerson as the mature, accomplished lecturer, directing himself toward that highest eloquence, that ecstasy, to which he aspired. In the first volume of
the three we saw his apprenticeship, the effort to find a vocation
other than the Unitarian ministry; in the second we saw him attempting to free himself further by means of the private lecture
series, managed at his own risk, in the Masonic Temple in Boston.

But in this third, he has established himself. After 1842 the private series in Boston can no longer contain him, and he launches confidently into further ventures.

Most of the manuscripts of these lectures, like those of the preceding volumes, are generally complete and legible; a few are wholly missing, presumably because they served as printer's copy or perhaps were destroyed after fair copy had been made; and a few are fragmentary. The explanation for this fragmentation seems to lie in Emerson's use of the lectures for his essays rather than from any more general factor. No attempt has been made to approximate the missing parts by printing material from the journals or works, though we have provided clues, when they exist, about the missing parts and have attempted explanations of Emerson's use of the material.

Somewhat more has had to be done in this volume than in the earlier ones "to restore the text itself to the form in which it was first heard by an audience," though we have taken care not to reject Emerson's revisions except in the case of obvious and verifiable alterations made for subsequent readings. The explanations for all such restorations are in the headnotes to the lectures, and a full record is preserved in the textual notes. While it is relatively easy to reject inserted introductions for subsequent readings and to reject certain other modifications made for a later time and another place, or a series of adjustments resulting from restructuring, resewing, and renumbering pages, it is impossible to discriminate among the many small verbal insertions and cancellations whether in ink or pencil. Most of these were undoubtedly made before the first reading of the lecture, but there is no certainty that all were made before even the final reading. As in the earlier volumes of this edition, we have accepted all such minor revisions which cannot with certainty be ascribed to later versions of the lecture.

Most of the passages used in the essays were cancelled by James Elliot Cabot or Edward Emerson in blue or black pencil. In his economy of prose, taking care not to use passages already in print, Emerson also cancelled many such passages to remind himself that they had been used. His cancellations for this purpose are sometimes ink and sometimes pencil marks and are often not with certainty distinguishable from genuine cancellations of passages not to be read. Our principle has been to leave a passage in the text unless we found an obvious reason, like duplication elsewhere in the manuscript, to accept the mark as an authentic cancellation rather than a use mark. In all except a very few cases the application of this principle has been confirmed by discovery of the printed version occasioning the use mark. The task has been greatly simplified by Edward Emerson's extensive annotation of the manuscripts, identifying used passages generally by volume and page numbers in the Riverside Edition. We have modified our principle, however, to the extent of omitting from the text some short cancelled passages too unimportant to have been taken for essay use and not found in the essays. The problem of Emerson's cancellations is further complicated by his occasional enclosure of words and short passages in brackets or parentheses. In a few cases it has been difficult to determine whether the latter signify possible cancellation or are genuine marks of punctuation. We have in such cases left the passage, with parentheses, in the text. It is likely that brackets sometimes indicate *possible* deletion, deletion in subsequent readings, or revision for use elsewhere. Nevertheless, with the exception of such self-explanatory bracketing as annotation of sources and headings which presumably would not be read, bracketed passages not otherwise cancelled have generally been retained in the text, though the brackets themselves have been removed and recorded in the textual notes.

Because the new edition of *The Journals and Miscellaneous Notebooks of Ralph Waldo Emerson* is replacing *The Journals of Ralph Waldo Emerson* (1909–14), this volume continues to use the system of referring to journal passages by name and *manuscript* page number, thus: B, 300; E, 29; F No. 2, 10; Encyclopedia, 30; Φ, 27; Notebook Ψ, 80, etc. As the new edition retains these designations of journal and page, it will probably be the more convenient to use as the volumes are published; but the older edition can also be used for those passages to be found in it because within the chronological order it groups its selections according to manuscript journal source. A complete listing of all journals is given at the end of the first volume of the new edition.

All journal readings are from the manuscript rather than any printed text.

This volume contains the lectures and addresses of Emerson from December 5, 1838, to January 20, 1842, as listed by Cabot in Appendix F of his *Memoir* (Boston, 1887), II, 737–748, with the exception of "Man the Reformer," read to the Mechanics' Apprentices' Library Association in Boston on January 25, 1841; "The Method of Nature," read at Waterville College, Waterville, Maine, on August 11, 1841; "Introduction," "The Conservative," "The Transcendentalist," "Manners," "Character," and "Relation of Man to Nature" from "The Times" series read in Boston between December 2, 1841, and January 13, 1842; and the eighth lecture in "The Present Age' series, called "Ethics" when it was read on January 29, 1840. No manuscripts survive for these lectures, and all except the last four were collected by Emerson in *Nature, Addresses, and Lectures* in 1849, reprinted from *The Dial* or, in the instance of "The Method of Nature," from pamphlet publication. There are no known manuscripts surviving for three addresses read earlier in 1838, but these have also been printed elsewhere: the address delivered at the Divinity School on July 15 and the one at Dartmouth College on July 25 were printed in separate pamphlets in October 1838 and collected by Emerson in *Nature, Addresses, and Lectures* as "An Address to the Senior Class in Divinity College, Cambridge, July 15, 1838" and "Literary Ethics"; the address Emerson read to the American Peace Society in Boston on March 12, 1838, was printed in *Aesthetic Papers*, edited by Elizabeth Peabody (Boston, 1849), and collected as "War" in *Miscellanies* (1883). All other named lectures from this period which are listed by William Charvat in *Emerson's American Lecture Engagements* (New York, 1961) can with reasonable certainty be identified as readings of the lectures printed in this volume, or of earlier lectures, with the exception of "Intellectual Integrity," read to the Mechanics' Apprentices' Association in Boston on March 6, 1839.

The text of these lectures is that of the manuscripts preserved in whole or in part in the collections of the Ralph Waldo Emerson Memorial Association in the Houghton Library of Harvard University. Because of the fragmentary nature of a few of these lectures it has been necessary to rearrange the leaves of the manuscripts in more cases than in the two earlier volumes of this edition. Deviations from what is now a permanently established order in the manuscripts have been noted and explained in the textual notes. The manuscript which Cabot summarized as the eighth lecture of the series on "The Present Age" has been reidentified as the concluding lecture of "The Times" on the basis of evidence argued in our headnote to the lecture.

The forthcoming edition of *Nature, Addresses, and Lectures*, the first volume in a projected new edition of Emerson's works, has made it impractical to supply from printed sources missing lectures on "The Times"; otherwise the editorial policies remain the same as in our second volume and are repeated here for convenience.

Modern editorial practice is not intractable with respect to alterations in punctuation, spelling, and capitalization. In preparing this text for printing, we have therefore:

(1) Expanded those contractions and abbreviations which are ordinarily expanded in modern printing practice.

(2) Regularized the use of quotation marks, except that Emerson's habit of using quotes around indirect speech has been retained where it occurs.

(3) Retained or supplied capitalization at the beginnings of sentences and for proper nouns, and retained it also, where it occurs, for certain emphatic abstractions ("Nature," "Spirit," etc.) or other words where such emphasis seems clearly intended; but we have eliminated possible capitalization where it seems merely an eccentricity of orthography. Emerson's practice is thoroughly inconsistent in this matter; in fact it is often impossible to determine from the manuscript whether he intends a capital or not.

(4) Supplied periods, question marks, exclamation points, commas, dashes, colons, and semicolons where they are unquestionably needed, as at the end of sentences or to separate items in a series, to introduce quotations, or to set off appositional or subordinate phrases and clauses where the construction requires.

(5) Added a minimum of further punctuation for clarity, all instances of this sort being recorded in the textual notes. We have constantly reminded ourselves of the word "minimum," even

when the result may take a little concentration to read, believing that editorial help can easily become officious in these matters. We have made a special point of not arbitrarily removing ambiguities of interpretation. No effort has been made to point the text in the style Emerson would have used if he had prepared it himself for publication. His own manuscript punctuation, even when eccentric, has rarely been altered, and the few such instances are all recorded in the textual notes.

(6) Regularized the forms of printing dates and numbers. With the former, we have been guided by Emerson's own practice when he edited the lecture "Michel Angelo Buonaroti" for publication, this representing presumably the way he was accustomed to read dates aloud before an audience. We have therefore replaced the usual manuscript form "15 March, 1572" with the form "the 15th of March, 1572" in all cases. With numbers, we have followed modern press style.

(7) Corrected accidental misspellings. When in doubt we have followed the manuscript.

(8) Followed the manuscript for compound and hyphenated words but, reserving the right to use common sense, we have more freely regularized Emerson's hyphenation in this volume than in the first. Eccentricity here is relatively meaningless, especially as Emerson's omission of many hyphens seems to have been more a matter of penmanship than policy. His practice in the matter of compounds and hyphens is inconsistent and in a number of cases his intention is not clear.

(9) Used our judgment in paragraphing, since Emerson's manuscript practice is often not suited to the printed page.

With these minimum changes, the text follows Emerson's manuscript with no further attempt to eliminate his numerous inconsistencies and idiosyncrasies.

The following editorial marks have been used:

A. In the text:

(1) Square brackets [ ] indicate matter inserted by the editors. Matter in roman type within brackets forms part of Emerson's text; italics indicate editorial comments.

(2) Three dots indicate Emerson's omissions.

B. In the textual and other notes:

INTRODUCTION

(1) Angle brackets ⟨ ⟩ indicate cancelled material; square brackets [ ], editorial comments; small braces { }, Emerson's brackets.

(2) Arrows ↑ ↓ indicate inserted material.

(3) A single slanted line / marks a page division in the manuscript.

(4) Three dots indicate editorial omissions.

(5) The symbol [E] in the footnotes means that all the preceding matter in the note is a marginal note or something similar transcribed from Emerson's manuscript.

The following abbreviations are used throughout the editorial notes:

Cabot — James Elliot Cabot, *A Memoir of Ralph Waldo Emerson* (1887).

Charvat — William Charvat, *Emerson's American Lecture Engagements: A Chronological List* (1961).

CEC — *The Correspondence of Emerson and Carlyle*, ed. Joseph Slater (1964).

EWE — Edward Waldo Emerson, literary executor and editor of *Works*, Centenary Edition (1903–04) and *Journals* (1900–14).

J — *The Journals of Ralph Waldo Emerson*, ed. Edward Waldo Emerson and Waldo Emerson Forbes (1909–14).

JMN — *The Journals and Miscellaneous Notebooks of Ralph Waldo Emerson*, ed. William H. Gilman, Alfred R. Ferguson, and others (1960–   ).

Kronman — Jeanne Kronman, ed., "Three Unpublished Lectures of Ralph Waldo Emerson," *The New England Quarterly*, XIX (March 1946), 98–110.

L — *The Letters of Ralph Waldo Emerson*, ed. Ralph L. Rusk (1939).

Lectures — *The Early Lectures of Ralph Waldo Emerson*, ed. Stephen E. Whicher, Robert E. Spiller, and Wallace E. Williams (vol. I, 1959; vol. II, 1964).

Letters . . . to a Friend — *Letters from Ralph Waldo Emerson to a Friend, 1838–1853*, ed. Charles Eliot Norton (1899).

Life — Ralph L. Rusk, *The Life of Ralph Waldo Emerson* (1949).

Parnassus — *Parnassus*, ed. Ralph Waldo Emerson (1875).

Reading — Kenneth W. Cameron, *Ralph Waldo Emerson's Reading* (1941).

Scudder — Townsend Scudder III, "A Chronological List of Emerson's Lectures on his British Lecture Tour of 1847–1848," *PMLA*, LI (March 1936), 243–248.

Uncollected Writings — Uncollected Writings . . . by Ralph Waldo Emerson, ed. Charles C. Bigelow (1912).

W — The Complete Works of Ralph Waldo Emerson, Centenary Edition, ed. Edward Waldo Emerson (1903–04).

The analytical index at the end of this volume is comprehensive and incorporates the indexes in the two earlier volumes.

I

HUMAN LIFE

Mr. EMERSON's course of lectures, on *Human Life,* will commence on WEDNESDAY EVENING, 5th December, at 7 o'clock, at the Masonic Temple.

Tickets to the Course, or to the single Lecture, may be had at C. C. Little & James Brown's, No 112, and at James Munroe & Co's, 134, Washington Street.   dec 3

[Newspaper announcement in the *Boston Daily Advertiser and Patriot,* December 3, 1838]

THE success of the lectures on "Human Culture" pointed inevitably to a new series during the following winter and would account for the general high spirits of the journals for the balance of 1838 and well into 1839 in spite of Emerson's uncertain health and the disillusioning experience of the controversy over the Divinity School address of the previous July. At home the baby Waldo and his mother continued to be sources of constant delight, and walks and talks with friends such as Alcott, Thoreau, Elizabeth Hoar, and the occasional house guests Margaret Fuller, Caroline Sturgis, and Jones Very, gave him much to think about. Meetings of the "Symposium" or "Hedge's Club" continued fairly regularly, but otherwise Emerson avoided evening parties and kept as close as possible to his Concord home. His reading during this year was somewhat less in philosophy and history and more in general literature than it had recently been. His journals quote passages from the works of the German philosopher-historian, Arnold H. L. Heeren (1760–1842) (D, 80–83; cf. L, II, 154), but most of his references are to old friends like Montaigne, Shakespeare, and Goethe, to Elizabethan poetry and plays, to contemporaries like Wordsworth, Landor, Scott, and Byron, and to the writings of his friends and intimates.

The new series of lectures was undertaken somewhat reluctantly because of his concern that the controversy over the Divinity School address might scare away his audiences (L, II, 172). Sleepless nights caused the postponement of at least one lecture (D, 244), but apparently his worries were ill-founded as the audiences were better than ever, the reception excellent, and the financial returns reasonably gratifying. Seven of the lectures were repeated in a series at the Concord Lyceum from March to May and two, with one from the previous season, in Plymouth (Charvat, pp. 17–18; D, 245). In the spring of 1840, he journeyed to Providence, Rhode Island, and repeated two or more of them in

1

a series before the Franklin Lyceum, but for some reason he was not in nearly so great demand as in the previous season, or his health was such that he could not undertake so heavy a schedule (*L*, II, 266).

For topic, he picked up where the "Human Culture" series had left him. "It may be stated as the end of Culture to teach us to Be," he had said (*Lectures*, II, 298). The new lectures started with the "Doctrine of the Soul," the chief lesson of culture, and then proceeded to relate this doctrine to some of the leading aspects of daily living. The general purpose, as he set it down in his workbook Φ, was to describe "Man related to the Universe" — almost exactly the topic of the last lecture of the previous series, which he had called in his notes "Position of man in nature." Inevitably he found himself going over much of the same ground as in his previous two series, under an even more general title and with a less strongly controlling purpose.

In its planning stages the new series was vague. Emerson's preliminary announcement in the *Daily Advertiser* gave the title and indicated that the course of "ten or more Lectures" would "embrace a circle of topics in Literature, History, and the Conduct of Life, esteemed most interesting and useful in the present state of society, and with a special aim at the development and illustration of principles" (October 22 and 26, 1838; printed in *JMN*, VII, 124, footnote 362). This was little more than what he had done before, though there is an unfulfilled suggestion that he would now bring his perceptions to a sharp focus, resulting in an articulated culmination, perhaps, of the previous courses. Reflecting a week later on the undertaking, he wrote: "And I am to seek to solve for my fellows the problem of human Life, in words . . . Well, boy, what canst thou say? Knowest thou its law? its way? its equipoise, its endless end?" (D, 180). These questions suggest that Emerson had not yet any very concrete thesis for the new lectures.

His notes show that a simple biographical organization for the early lectures in the series, from home and childhood, to school, to love, and so on, occurred to him early, as soon as he had set down his first trial list of topics, but a direction for the course thereafter was harder to set. "We are all very well," he wrote his brother William on November 16, 1838, while in the thick of composition, "I floating drifting far & wide in the sea of 'Human Life' without port without chart & even a glass so thick over the compass that it is only once in a while I can sharply see where it points" (*L*, II, 175). At various times he jotted down trial lists — "Love, Study, Poetry, Duty, Condition," or "Love, Duty, Beauty, Society, Condition, Church, New Life," or "Love, Genius, Duty, Society, Church," or "Society, Duty, Church, Sorrow," — only to abandon them all. Although "Demonology" and "Comic" occur among possible topics (with "Tragedy" hinted in the above "Sorrow"), the evolution of his final list is not clearly traceable in his notes.

Its rationale is explained in the summary he appended to his tenth lecture (pp. 170–171), where it appears that poor health forced him to drop two intended lectures on "Condition" and "Prospects," for which intention there is some but not much evidence in the working journal. So completed and so explained, his scheme is by no means formless, but it retains a certain improvised character not found in the previous two series. His struggle with organization, while successful, led him to take up a number of topics not wholly congenial to him. One suspects that the strain of writing these lectures had something to do with his decision to break off the course. For the first time in his work the representative or descriptive principle was competing with the prophetic or inspirational, with results he himself may have found confusing. Thereafter the "reporter" or "observer" increasingly took over from the teacher in his lecturing, until he could call his 1841–42 series on "The Times" a "portrait gallery."

As it stands, this truncated series lacks something of the enthusiastic conviction and purpose — and therefore of the rhetorical buoyancy — of the previous two. It is likely that the steady demand for new lectures (some seventy in five years, not counting *Nature*) was beginning to make itself felt. The accumulated riches of past journals were showing signs of exhaustion, even though he was not yet repeating himself to any great extent, and new reading and meditation — however broad and vital — was insufficient to fully restore the sources. The ill-health that forced him to cancel his last two lectures also took its toll. Nevertheless, his audiences were large and responsive and the lectures retain today much of their original creative life, some being among his best. Emerson the lecturer was still at the crest of his first power.

1

Doctrine of the Soul

This opening lecture of Emerson's third series under his own management was delivered at the Masonic Temple in Boston on December 5, 1838. It probably was not the first lecture of the abbreviated course announced as "Human Life" which began on March 20, 1840, before the Franklin Lyceum at the Masonic Hall in Providence, Rhode Island (see *L*, II, 266), nor does it seem to have been read elsewhere. Except for two leaves which do not belong with it, the manuscript, which is complete, was once sewn and the pages are numbered consecutively in pencil. A large part of this lecture was revised for "The Over-Soul," and a long passage was used for "History."

I PROPOSE to continue the Course of Lectures delivered by me last winter in this hall on Human Culture by a new series on such parts and topics in the problem of Human Life as are familiar to me. In approaching this subject I have been led into the great question of primary philosophy, Who lives? What is the Life? I shall endeavor in the present lecture to give some general account of the doctrine of the Soul, and what historical appearances have attended its recent activity and what that Doctrine is. In subsequent lectures, I shall perhaps consult better the taste of my audience as well as my own strength, in surveying its modified activity in the various domains of youth, of gaiety, [of] tenderness, of danger, of security as man marches with divine omens and guidance on his unknown road.

The thought that is now awakening the minds of all men and appearing in all the arts, in the laws, in the manners, countenances, and actions of men is a faith in the Soul. Men are possessed with the belief that Man has not had justice done him by himself. A new spirit characterises the men and works of this age.

It stands in strong contrast to the spirit of antiquity. It is said that the ancients contented themselves with what happened; we inquire what is thought and felt.[1] The ancients observed the fact; we observe its effect upon the mind. The whole of modern history has an ethical character. Even in its outbreaks of ferocious passion it is the assertion of the moral sentiments of justice and freedom.

I see with joy a certain deeper thought shared by thousands and thousands and which appears in the new consequence which religion, literature, and philosophy, enjoy in the world. The indications of it are not always agreeable facts. I know very well that the first information we have of great movements comes from some quite external sign very remote from the heart as the first vegetable life in the spring appears in the extreme buds. And we are so often pointed to movements of charity, of education, of religion, which are quite external and end in nothing that many thoughtful persons are apt to overlook the fact that they had their origin in some deeper truth whereof they were a very modified and imperfect expression but which they do yet presignify and announce.

The movement of which I have spoken and which we all share is marked as is all modern history with a deep religious tinge, and at times wears an exclusively religious aspect. But this is not permanent. A religious history which is only religious does not satisfy the whole mind of man. It only meets one sentiment. True history will be religious but it will not be a religious history. Yet I gladly hail the appearance of that element as everywhere the true friend and benefactor of man. It always indicates the presence of man and not of the brute, whilst the perfection of the arts of war, trade, of luxury, may indicate only the perfection of the appetites.

That I may illustrate a little in particular the apparent growth of the thought of which I speak let me select a few facts in civil and literary history for nearer remark. And first some notices of that epoch of the English Commonwealth which as is often said

---

[1] Johann Wolfgang von Goethe, *Winckelmann und sein Jahrhundert* in *Werke*, 55 vols. (Stuttgart and Tübingen, 1828–33), XXXVII, 21; T, 211; *Lectures*, II, 168.

emerges every year into more consequence as one of the most important dates in the spiritual history of mankind. "About this time there were abundance of people in England who having searched all sects could nowhere find satisfaction for their hungry souls. And these now understanding that God by his light was so near in their hearts began to take heed thereunto." [2] About the same time was given by Milton the following testimony to the interior character of the period. He describes the city of London in the time of the Long Parliament, "Behold now this vast city; a city of refuge, the mansion house of liberty encompassed and surrounded with his protection; the shop of war hath not there more anvils and hammers waking to fashion out the plates and instruments of armed justice in defence of beleaguered truth than there be pens and heads there sitting by their studious lamps, musing, searching, revolving new motions and ideas wherewith to present as with their homage and their fealty the approaching reformation; others as fast reading, trying all things, assenting to the force of reason and convincement." Then see further the reason with which he persuades himself of the good issue to humanity of the Civil War. "When a city shall be as it were besieged and blocked about, her navigable river infested, inroads and incursions round, defiance and battle oft rumored to be marching up even to her walls and suburb trenches, that then the people or the greater part more than at other times, wholly taken up with the study of highest and most important matters to be reformed, should be disputing, reasoning, reading, inventing, discoursing, even to a rarity and admiration, things not before discoursed or written of, . . . it betokens a people destined to become great and honorable in these latter ages." [3]

This is history and not the skeleton of history, the catalogue of names which so many volumes are. I find in it good auguries and itself is a great fact, for the revelation that there is not only an Assyrian Empire and Roman Empire but a human race, that there is a great responsible Thinker and Actor moving wherever moves a man, — is itself almost a discovery of modern times; and

[2] William Sewel, *The History of the Rise, Increase, and Progress of the Christian People Called Quakers,* 2 vols. (Philadelphia, 1823), I, 147; *Lectures,* I, 459.
[3] John Milton, "Areopagitica," *A Selection from the English Prose Works,* 2 vols. (Boston, 1826), II, 60, 63.

certainly far the greatest discovery that was ever made.[4] So in the pause which Lord Clarendon makes in the thread of his narrative at the death of Lord Falkland, feeling that history should stop when such an event transpires, that it may describe the perfections of such a man. "But I must here take leave (a little longer) to discontinue this narration; and if the celebrating the memory of eminent and extraordinary persons and transmitting their great virtues for the imitation of posterity be one of the principal ends and duties of history, it will not be thought impertinent in this place to remember a loss which no time will suffer to be forgotten, and no success or good fortune could repair. In this unhappy battle was slain the lord Viscount Falkland."[5]

The subsequent history of western Europe and of America has been the slow unfolding of the higher elements of the human nature. Its value is in their literature and their laws. Much of the external activity of the people, their trades, their policies, their domestic life, is very unsatisfactory to the philosopher, as it exhibits, for the most part, a half-consciousness of the new thought, aiming to use the old and bad elements, and is by these corrupted and defeated. But in literature, whilst many masters sung a vulgar strain, and talent was perverted as ever, yet over all has brooded a certain higher melody, now retiring, now prevailing, and constraining at last all jarring notes which sought at first to drown it, to fall into unison with it, or to cease. The prodigious growth and influence of the genius of Shakspeare in the last one hundred fifty years, is itself a fact of the first importance. It almost alone has called out the genius of the German nation into an activity which spreading from the poetic into the scientific, religious, and philosophical domains has made theirs now at last the paramount intellectual influence of the world, reacting with great energy on England and America.[6] And if it will not be esteemed an indecorum to introduce the name of the living between

[4] Cf. "Self-Reliance," W, II, 60; below, pp. 188, 242.

[5] "History of the Rebellion Vol III p. 1518" [E]; cf. C, 105. Emerson is citing Edward Hyde, 1st Earl of Clarendon, *The History of the Rebellion and Civil Wars in England,* 6 vols. (Boston, 1827).

[6] "But in literature . . . England and America" (below, p. 208); "The prodigious growth . . . England and America" ("Thoughts on Modern Literature," W, XII, 312).

whom and us the broad Atlantic roars, I will say that the fame of Wordsworth is one of the most instructive facts in modern literature when it is considered how utterly hostile his genius at first seemed to the reigning taste, and I may add with what feeble poetic talents his great and steadily growing dominion has been established. More than any poet his success has been not his own but that of the Idea or principle which possessed him and which he has rarely succeeded in adequately expressing. His inspiring genius is as he has said the still, sad music of humanity.[7] It is the human soul in these last ages striving for a just publication of itself through priest and legislator and poet which is the subject of history and the author of revolutions.[8] It strives to give account of itself to itself in all places, in all modes. Irresistibly it opens itself to the day, and lo! all men are sensible of its uprise and give sign of the same perception. Its first revelation is of course the trial and condemnation of that which is not true. It exposes differences. It craves realities. The old say, the young are not like them. The young say, You have nothing that satisfies. Whilst we stand still here we had as lief not be. We must obey this call sounding louder, clearer, and more musical than ever, and follow whithersoever it may lead us. Every part of life shows the dominion of a new spirit. Men have become introversive and speculative even to embarrassment and fear. The very child in the nursery says strange things and doubts and philosophizes. A wild striving to express more inward and infinite sense characterises the works of every art. The music of Beethoven is said by those [who] understand it to labor with vast[er] conceptions and aspirations than music has attempted before.[9] The science is introversive like the philosophy. The microscope is carried to perfection and Geology looks no longer in written histories but opens the crust of the earth to study organic remains and strata that the core of the globe like a sort of material conscience may tell its own tale.[10] This democratic element which so rages when pent and obstructed, which gains steadily on the monarchical and aris-

---

[7] "Lines Composed a Few Miles above Tintern Abbey," line 91.
[8] "the fame of Wordsworth . . . of revolutions" (cf. "Thoughts on Modern Literature," W, XII, 320–321; below, pp. 217–218).
[9] "The very child . . . attempted before" (below, p. 217).
[10] "The science . . . own tale" (D, 162).

tocratical institutions is the first fruits of reflection. The plentiful crop of new projects, of temperance, of peace, of suffrage, the denunciation of oaths, of capital punishment, of disqualifying opinions, which keep the good public in perpetual alarm and will not let it sleep nor a king nor a bishop so much as sleep in England or America, is based on the same. These turbulent movements are disagreeable as is the felling of the forest and the noise and piles of board and brick and the scaffolding that attend the rising of a new city but pondered deeply and seen as signs of that which shall be, they may be seen without sadness.

Nor ought it to give a wise spirit any uneasiness, [the] too conscious, self-analysing temper which marks the period and movement of which we speak. I do not accept this complaint of the morbidness of this age of consciousness or introversion. I do not think there is any treachery in nature. I think the spirit will be true to itself in every emergency.[11] Undoubtedly this has its foolish and canting side. New thoughts will always introduce a crop of new words and these are all that the foolish will get. There will be fools on both sides whenever party begins. This crisis or state is as natural as any state; must be foreseen, and forearmed, and forebalanced, and undoubtedly has its own checks and good fruit. Indeed I joy to think how much in the most worn, pedantic, criticising self-tormentor's life is incalculable by him, unforeseen, unimaginable altogether. What am I? What has my will done to make me that I am? Nothing. I have been floated into this thought, this hour, this connexion of events, by might and mind sublime, and my little ingenuities and wilfulnesses have not thwarted, have not aided to an appreciable degree.[12] I shall presently have occasion to advert with great distinctness to the fact that the whole tendency of our time is in the submission it enjoins to the Unconscious and Infinite.

And what do the ages say? What do the present times and movements portend; and what lights are yet given to solve today the old problem of Human Life? Ever the attempt to explain it goes directly to the Nature of Man. All history is the biography

---

[11] "I do not accept . . . every emergency" (D, 17).
[12] "This crisis or state . . . appreciable degree" (D, 17); "Indeed I joy to think . . . appreciable degree" ("Intellect," W, II, 328).

of a few men around whose persons while living, around whose memory when dead, our sociable race by thousands and millions has clustered.[13]

And beautiful is Man; beautiful even in its tragic dangers his lot. See him newborn in his world beginning all as all had never been. Around him stand the same potentates to drop gifts of love and doom into his cradle as all the heroes and half gods had before him. They bring him the wondrous gift of Day and Night; of Sleep; of Labor; Laughter; Society; Religion; Beauty; Opportunity; and Death. And over all and around all the dread constitution of things, now terrible to him under the name of fate, now blessed and blessing, under the name of God. Here in the old walls of Nature and Circumstance, under the old conditions of Want, Climate, Health, Society, our young philosopher is trying his fortune anew. Related by his form to the whole world, and by his soul to the whole universe, with faculties buried in time and space, but animated by a soul that dwells out of time and space, behold this lover, scholar, laborer, fighter passing through what a scale of powers and merits from reptile sympathies with the earth to enthusiasm and ecstacy!

And graceful and gifted as he lies in nature so also is his history unpleasing. Man has encumbered himself with aged errors, with usages and ceremonies, with law, property, church, customs, and books until he is almost smothered under his own institutions. Yet still beautiful is his nature the ornament of the world when it emerges in any strong character, in any noble action. Man is good though men are bad.[14] Man is dear to us and the reason why we love our friend so well is because he and not the fool represents to us the race.

Something of worth and beauty always attaches to the persons and natures of accomplished men. Always we are filled with joy at every appearance of intrinsic worth in a man. How grateful in poetry, in history, in actual society are always those traits which attract love and veneration to the individual and not to his circumstances and make us feel that he is not the ball of fortune

[13] Cf. "Self-Reliance," W, II, 61.
[14] Cf. D, 268, *Lectures*, I, 359, and Encyclopedia, 16, where Emerson attributes a similar quotation to Rousseau.

but fortune is his follower and minister. How noble in Homer is the perception of individual merit by which he signalizes his heroes and wins our admiration. Always it is a memorable event to him, the meeting with a great man and he dwells with pleasure on his personal attributes.

When Helen sits on the walls of Troy and points out to Antenor the leaders of the Greeks he seizes the occasion to show Ulysses:

" 'Tell me dear child who is that? Shorter by a head than Agamemnon son of Atreus, but he seems broader in his shoulders and breast. His arms lie on the earth, but he like a leader walks about the bands of men. He seems to me like a stately ram who goes as a master through the flock.'

"Him answered Helen daughter of Jove. 'This is the wise Ulysses son of Laertes who was reared in the state of craggy Ithaca, knowing all wiles and wise counsels.'

"To her the prudent Antenor replied again, 'O woman, you have spoken a true word. For once the godlike Ulysses came hither on an embassy with Menelaus beloved by Mars. I received them and entertained them at my house. Of both I learned to know the genius and the prudent judgments. When they mixed with the congregated Trojans and stood, the broad shoulders of Menelaus rose above the other but both sitting, Ulysses was more majestic. When they conversed and interweaved stories and opinions with all, Menelaus spoke succinctly, few but very sharp words, since he was not talkative nor exceeding in speech, and was the younger. But when the wise Ulysses arose and stood and looked down, fixing his eyes on the ground and moved his sceptre neither backward nor forward but held it still like an awkward person you would say it was some fool and simple man; but when he sent his great voice forth out of his breast, and words like to the winter snows, not then would any mortal compare with Ulysses; and we rejoice not in beholding the countenance of Ulysses here.' " [15]

And what is there which to an able man has such attraction as a great and good soul in another man? Every great man knows the exceeding worth of a man. Milton calls Scipio "the height of

[15] *Iliad*, III, 191–224; "Eloquence," W, VII, 71–72.

Rome." [16] Napoleon, after seeing the prodigious force of character exhibited by one of his marshals in the disasters of the Russian Campaign, said, "I have two hundred millions in my coffers, and I would give them all for Ney." [17] And every generous spirit understands well this excellency and feels the dignity of personal attributes, feels the superiority that follows him who when he gives his hand, gives endurance and perseverance and immaculate honor.

And yet if history were complete, if history exhausted the possibilities of our nature, if human life were not haunted by hope and faith, — the problem of human life would not remain still to be solved, nor could we entertain the lofty thoughts which the soul feels justified in indulging. If history were all, — then we could not reply to those objections which resound in low society and among the half wise of every age. Mighty fine theories, exclaims the man of the world, but unhappily experience has made me acquainted with Men. Genius is rare. Good sense is as rare. Virtue, for the most part, is a name. There are few beautiful. Perseverance is a fine word, but no man acts on a grand design ten days together. We live as we can and say the best things we know about it. Sir Robert Walpole thought every man had his price and most men could be bought for a dinner.[18] And Fontanes, the worthy President of the legislative body in France in 1804, in his address to the First Consul praying him to assume the imperial power, declared, that "the desire of perfection is the worst disease that can afflict the human mind." [19] Be it so. With all the godlike knowledge and godlike virtue we can find in history, we can spare it all.

[16] *Paradise Lost,* IX, 510; "Self-Reliance," W, II, 61; D, 143, 271; see below, p. 243.

[17] Count Emmanuel Augustin Dieudonné de Las Cases, *Mémorial de Sainte Hélène. Journal of the Private Life and Conversations of the Emperor Napoleon at Saint Helena,* 4 vols. (Boston, 1823), IV, vii, 123; "Napoleon," W, IV, 244; C, 348; D, 10.

[18] The first part of this maxim is widely attributed to Sir Robert Walpole (1676–1745), British prime minister during the Whig Ascendancy, but cf. William Coxe, *Memoirs of the Life of Walpole, Earl of Orford,* 3 vols. (London, 1798), I, 757, and letter of Horace Walpole to Sir Horace Mann, dated August 26, 1785.

[19] Review of A. C. Thibaudeau's *Mémoirs sur le consulat . . .* and *Le Consulat et l'empire . . .* in *The Foreign Quarterly Review,* American Edition, XVII (July 1836), 196; "Napoleon," W, IV, 228; B, 300.

Frankly we give up the Past to the objector.[20] He may find what matter for sneers and for tears in it he will. Beautiful as is man's intellect and kind and glorious as is the physical and metaphysical nature in which he lies, there is something better within him unrealized at which all this progress points, there is that in hope which reduces to contempt all that is gone. What is the reason of this uneasiness of ours? of this great Discontent? What is the reason that all souls feel that the natural history of man has never been written, but always he is leaving behind what you have said of him, and it becomes old; and books of metaphysics, worthless? [21] Six thousand years have not searched the chambers and magazines of the soul.

Philosophy has been unable to satisfy us that we can do no more than others. In all its experiments there has always remained in the last analysis a residuum which it could not resolve.[22] And here the central hope of nature is on that somewhat miraculous and divine which always remains in man. Always there is in man somewhat incalculable, a presiding, overseeing, imparting, unexhausted soul. I could forgive the man of calculation his want of faith if he had knowledge of the uttermost that man could be and do, if arithmetic could predict the last possibilities of instinct. But men are not made like boxes, a hundred, a thousand to order and all exactly alike, of known dimension and all their properties known. No; they come into nature through a nine months' astonishment and of a character each one incalculable and of extravagant possibilities. Out of darkness and the awful Cause they come, to be caught up into this vision of a seeing, partaking, acting, and suffering life. Not foreknown, not fore-measurable, but slowly or speedily they unfold new, unknown, most subtile powers; no boxes, but alive, agitated, fearing, sorrowing, resolving machines.[23]

More therefore than the most exact and self-satisfied calculator we always welcome the inexact, extravagant spirits who set routine and etiquette at defiance and drawing their impulse from some

[20] Cf. F No. 2, 49.
[21] D, 241.
[22] "Frankly we give up . . . could not resolve" ("The Over-Soul," W, II, 267–268, condensed).
[23] "I could forgive . . . machines" (D, 216).

profound thought appear in society as its accusers, its prophets and however repelled and discredited by the people of influence and station have a certain secret to make their commission felt in the heart and soul of the common hearer. Such persons though oft imperfect men without adequate results and ending ill perhaps do us yet a high service. They flash on us beams out of the heart of heaven. If you give them the freedom of your inner house, they shall make you wise to the extent of their own uttermost receivings. What if they be, as often such are, monotonous and called men of one idea? Yet is the partial action of such a mind in one direction, a telescope for the objects on which it is pointed, and as we know that every single path we take is but a radius of our sphere, and we may dive as deep in every other direction as we have in that, a far insight of one evil suggests instantly the immense extent of that revolution that must be wrought in our condition and so by implication suggests the magnitude of that perfection for which we are made.[24]

The upward movement in society dating from the beginning of the world and including in it, as a concert of a thousand tongues, every inspired man, and every beneficent revolution has for its end to teach the Doctrine of the Soul: Who it is that lives this human life and to what unaccomplished end. If we consider what happens in conversation, in reveries, in remorse, in times of passion, in times when any affecting incident surprises us from our habits of prudence and inaction, the instructions of dreams wherein often we see ourselves in masquerade, in wild masquerade and yet ourselves, the droll disguises only magnifying and enhancing a real element and forcing it on our distinct notice — we shall catch many hints that will gradually broaden and lighten into perfect knowledge.

All goes to show that a higher reverence than yet has been paid is due to that which is called the Soul in man; which is not an organ but which animates and exercises all the organs; which is not a function like the power of the memory, of calculation, of comparison, — but which uses these as hands and feet; which is not a faculty but a Light; which is not the Intellect or the Will but the master of the Intellect and the Will — the vast back-

[24] D, 168.

15

ground of our being in which they lie; an immensity not possessed and that cannot be possessed.

From within or from behind I may say a light shines through us upon things and makes us aware that we are nothing but the Light is all. A man is the least part of himself. A man is but the façade of a temple wherein all wisdom and all good abide. I mean that the part of man most known to us — the eating, drinking, planting, counting, speaking man does not, as we know him, represent himself, but misrepresents himself. Him we do not respect, but the Soul whose organ he is — would he let it appear through his action — would make our knees bend. It is yet the life of every man: when it breathes through his intellect, — it is genius. When it breathes through his will, it is virtue. And the whole evil of the Intellect is when the Intellect would be something of itself and not simply the organ of the soul. The whole evil of the Will is when the Individual would be something of himself and not simply the child of the Soul. All Reform aims in some one particular to break down this busy Interference and to let the great Soul have its way through us; in other words to live simply and obey.[25]

It shines for all. There is a certain wisdom of humanity which is common to the greatest men with the lowest and which our ordinary education often labors to silence and obstruct. We owe a good many valuable observations to people who are not very acute or profound and who say the thing without effort which we want and have been long hunting in vain.[26]

And truly the action of the soul is oftener in that which is felt but left unsaid than in that which is said in any conversation. It broods over every society and they unconsciously and incessantly seek for it in each other.[27] It perceives truth. We know truth when we see it, let skeptic and scoffer say what they choose. The soul looks with a lofty defiance on all such as ask that foolish question, "But how do you know it is truth and not an error of your own?" We know truth when we see it, from opinion, as we know, when we are awake, that we are awake. It was a grand sentence of Emanuel Swedenborg which would alone indicate

[25] "If we consider what happens . . . and obey" ("The Over-Soul," *W*, II, 270–271).
[26] "We owe a good many . . . in vain" (D, 190).
[27] "It shines for all . . . in each other" ("The Over-Soul," *W*, II, 277–278).

the greatness of his perception: — "It is no proof of a man's understanding to be able to confirm whatever he pleases, but to be able to discern that what is true is true, and that what is false is false, — this is the mark and character of intelligence." [28] In the book I read, the good thought returns to me the image of the soul. To the bad thought which I find in it, the same soul becomes a discerning, separating sword and lops it away.

We are wiser than we know. If we will not interfere with our thought but will act entirely or see how the thing stands in God we know the particular thing and every thing and every man. For the Maker of all things and all persons stands behind us and casts his dread omniscience through us over things.[29]

I have expressed the opinion that the fame of Shakspeare was an important fact in detecting the true history of our time, and among the existing generation the poet Wordsworth. For Mr. Wordsworth almost alone among the contemporary poets is pervaded with a reverence for somewhat higher than (conscious) thought.[30] There is in all great poets a wisdom of humanity which is superior to any talents they exercise. It is the wisest part of Shakspeare and of Milton. The author, the wit, the partisan, the fine gentleman does not take place of the man. Humanity smiles in Homer, in Chaucer, in Spenser, in Shakspeare, in Milton. They are content with truth; they use the positive degree. They seem frigid and phlegmatic to those who have been spiced with the frantic passion and violent coloring of the Byrons, Shelleys, and Hugoes of today.[31]

For they are poets by the free course which they allow to the informing soul which through their eyes beholdeth again and blesseth the things which it hath made. Before it all particular thoughts shrink into subaltern and partial worth. It includes them all. The soul is superior to its knowledge; wiser than any of its

---

[28] Caleb Reed, "The Nature and Character of True Wisdom and Intelligence," *The New Jerusalem Magazine*, III (January 1830), 151. In T, 61, this passage is given along with its source in Swedenborg, *The Doctrine of the New Jerusalem Respecting the Sacred Scripture*, chapter X, section 91. "The soul looks . . . of intelligence" (D, 167).

[29] "It perceives truth . . . over things" ("The Over-Soul," W, II, 279–280); "In the book . . . over things" (D, 178).

[30] "Thoughts on Modern Literature," W, XII, 321; below, p. 218.

[31] "They are content . . . Hugoes of today" (C, 179).

works. The great poet makes us feel our own wealth and then we think less of all he has done. His greatest communication to our mind is to teach us to despise all he has done. Shakspeare carries us to such a lofty strain of intelligent activity as to suggest a wealth which beggars his own and we then feel that the splendid works which he has created and which in other hours we extol as a sort of self-existent poetry, take no stronger hold of real nature than the shadow of a passing traveller on the rock.[32] The inspiration which uttered itself in Hamlet and Lear could utter things as good from day to day, forever. Why then should I make account of Hamlet and Lear as if we had not the soul from which they fell as syllables from the tongue? [33]

By the same Soul, serene, impersonal, perfect, which shines and shines until it shall dissolve all things into mere waves and surges of an Ocean of Light, we see and know each other and what spirit each is of. Who can tell the grounds of his knowledge of the character of the several individuals in his circle of friends? No man. Yet their acts and words do not disappoint him. In that man though he knew no ill of him, he put no trust. In that other though they had seldom met yet authentic signs had passed to signify that he might be confided in as one who had interest in his own character.[34] There is a natural connexion of opinion which is a practical metaphysics and is called knowledge of human nature by which a knowing man predicts with great confidence from a few opinions of any man the general circle of his thoughts, or if not what they are now yet what they certainly will be when he shall have carried his tendencies fully out. Contemporary souls understand each other very well as they watch the rising of the same waters in their own and another's cistern. There is confession in the glances of our eyes, in our smiles, in salutations, and the grasp of hands.[35] We know of each other very well which of us has been just to himself and so whether that we teach or behold, is only an aspiration or our honest effort also.

The truth is, we are all discerners of spirits. That diagnosis

---

[32] D, 102.

[33] "There is in all great poets . . . from the tongue" ("The Over-Soul," W, II, 288–289). See "Thoughts on Modern Literature," W, XII, 321; below, p. 218.

[34] "By the same soul . . . own character" ("The Over-Soul," W, II, 285).

[35] "Spiritual Laws," W, II, 159.

lies aloft in our life or unconscious power, not in the understanding. The whole intercourse of society, its trade, its religion, its friendships, its quarrels is all one wide judicial investigation of character. In full court or in small committee, or confronted face to face, accuser and accused — people are always offering themselves to be judged. Against their will they are ever exhibiting those decisive trifles by which character is read. But who judges and what? Not our understanding. We do not read them by learning or craft. The wisdom of the wise man consists herein that he does not judge them, he lets them judge themselves and merely records in his memory the verdict.[36]

And as it perceives truth and discerns spirits, so it commands the prospect of all action. The sense of shame — has any man asked himself what that is when in the petty act he meditates he suddenly comes full upon this great light in himself and flees before it and hides himself? Perhaps the most extraordinary fact in our experience is the deep joy that attends the stings of remorse[37] — for it is the acknowledgment that this higher Judgment seat is also ours.

We know better than we do. We do not yet possess ourselves and know at the same time that we are much more. I feel the same truth how often in my merely trivial conversation or dealing with my neighbors that somewhat higher in each of us overlooks this by-play and Jove nods to Jove from behind each of us. Men descend to meet.[38] They seem to me to resemble those Arabian sheikhs who dwell in mean houses and affect an external poverty to escape the rapacity of the Pacha and reserve all their display of wealth for their interior and guarded retirements.[39]

A man is not a man until he gives up to his soul and suffers it to publish itself through all his words and actions. He and he alone is great who apprehends and obeys this truth. All the men who have by their names made the cities in which they dwelled famous and beautiful to us, have had some sense of this fact. The

[36] "We know of each . . . the verdict" ("The Over-Soul," W, II, 285–286); "The truth is . . . the verdict" (D, 225, expanded).
[37] Cf. D, 167.
[38] Cf. below, p. 96.
[39] "We know better . . . guarded retirements" ("The Over-Soul," W, II, 278–279; D, 208–209).

same difference divides society today. The great difference between educated men is that one class acknowledge an ideal standard, and the other class do not. We demand of an intellectual man, be his defects what they may, and his practice what it may, faith in the possibilities of man. And this will every man have, the moment he is made sensible of a Divine Presence which as soon as he ceases to put up bars and impediments will flow through him in floods of wisdom. It is the essential condition of that perception to suggest an infinite scope to his spirit. Not a hope but a knowledge that instead of a few possessions for a short time, entire existence is his. From that inspiration he comes back with a changed tone. He does not talk with men any more with an eye to their opinion. He tries them. The infallible index of true progress is found in the tone the man takes. Neither his age, nor his breeding, nor company, nor books, nor actions, nor talents, nor all together, can hinder him from being deferential to a higher spirit than his own. If he have not found his home in God, his manners, his forms of speech, the construction of his sentences, the build — shall I say? — of all his opinions will involuntarily confess it, let him brave it out how he will. If he have found his centre, the commanding God will shine through him, through all the disguises of modesty, of ignorance, of ungenial temperament. The tone of seeking is one, and the tone of having is another.[40]

I am very sensible that I am quite unable to illustrate with clearness a doctrine so high as this, that the Unconscious Nature is the grandeur of man; that it is the great Reformer; it upheaves society, it appears and reappears, and its will must be done. I have only hoped that by naming a few of those facts in which we are made aware of it I might suggest the majestic Presence to the soul. Take this out and we are beasts or boxes at once. Own this and no hope is too daring for man.

The wise man will perceive the presence of this element in all intellectual activity in the calmest and commonest life. Every grave action supposes it and it is this great, common, universal nature which gives worth to particular men and actions. This is

[40] "The infallible index . . . is another" ("The Over-Soul," W, II, 286–287; D, 231).

what we read in history. This is what we honor in enacting a law.

Human life as containing this seems to us a sacred and inviolable thing and we hedge it round with penalties and shames. Property also holds of the soul, covers great spiritual facts, and instinctively therefore we at first hold to it with swords and laws and vast and complex combinations. Because of this we always read as superior beings. Universal History, the poets, the romancers, do not in their stateliest pictures, in the sacerdotal, the imperial, the royal palaces, in the triumphs of will or of genius anywhere lose our ear, anywhere make us feel that we intrude, that this is for our betters, but rather is it true that in their grandest strokes there we feel most at home. All that Shakspeare says of the king, — the reader, the humblest boy feels to be true of himself.[41]

We sympathize in the great moments of history, in the great discoveries, the great resistances, the great prosperities of men because there law was enacted, the sea was searched, the land was found, or the blow was struck for us as we ourselves there in that place would have done or applauded. So is it in respect to condition and character. We honor the rich because they have externally the freedom, power, and grace which we feel to be proper to man, proper to us. So all that is said of the wise man by stoic or oriental or modern essayist describes to each man his own ideal, describes himself, his unattained but attainable self.[42] All literature writes the character of the wise man. All books, monuments, pictures, conversation are portraits in which the wise man finds the lineaments he is forming, he has formed. The silent and the loud praise him and accost him and he is stimulated wherever he moves as by personal allusions.[43] A wise and good soul therefore never needs look for allusions personal and laudatory in discourse. He hears the commendations not of himself but — more sweet — of that character he seeks, in every word that is said concerning character, yea further in every fact that befals, in the running river and the rustling corn. Praise is looked, homage tendered, love flows from mute nature, from the mountains

---

[41] "This is what we honor . . . true of himself" (D, 205, 211).
[42] "We honor the rich . . . attainable self" (D, 211).
[43] "All literature . . . personal allusions" (C, 121).

21

and the lights of the firmament.[44] With such siding champions he can well afford to meet vexations and disasters when they fall.[45]

The presence of this element is constant creation. Combined with each individual's distinguishing genius it is character; flashing through his intellect it is truth; ruling his will it is virtue. The end of all Culture is to establish its dominion by removing checks and impediments from it. Our busy intellect, our bribing senses interfere: *they* will speak; they will enjoy; and hinder our beatitude. Let us see what rays it will throw on the several stages and departments of human life; let us see if we can detect the footsteps of this august visitant in nature and in art, in literature and society, at home and in travels, in the works and in the pleasures, in the mysteries of time, and in the disappearance of man out of nature.

[44] "Every grave action supposes it . . . of the firmament" ("History," W, II, 5–7).

[45] "A wise and good . . . they fall" (D, 89).

2

Home

This lecture, which establishes a central metaphor in the course, was first delivered in the Masonic Temple, Boston, on December 12, 1838; repeated at Plymouth, Massachusetts, on February 1, 1839 (D, 245); and again as the opening lecture of the "Human Life" series at the Concord, Massachusetts, Lyceum on March 20. Although it was announced as "Domestic Life," this was doubtless the lecture read on March 23, 1840, as second in the series before the Franklin Lyceum in Providence, Rhode Island (see *L*, II, 266), but it is probably not the "Domestic Life" read in New York on February 28, 1843, in Hartford, Connecticut on March 8, 1843, sixteen times in Northern England, Glasgow, and London from November 15, 1847, to June 27, 1848 (Scudder, pp. 245–247; *L*, IV, 84 n), and before the Parker Fraternity in Boston on November 13, 1859. These were probably readings of the "ancient MS. Lecture . . . long ago familiar to Lyceums" (*L*, V, 221) which was sent to Moncure Conway for publication in the Cincinnati *Dial*, I (October 1860), 585–602, and later collected in *Society and Solitude* (1870). That lecture may have been the writing on the subject of "Domestic Life" reported by Emerson in the summer of 1840 (*L*, II, 322). Perhaps not more than five of the leaves now missing from the present manuscript of "Home" were incorporated into it to survive into the printed essay "Domestic Life." Another four of the missing leaves may have gone into "Self-Reliance."

There are many cancellations and omissions in the body of the lecture, but what remains intact is in good order. The leaves, with the exception of one not belonging with the lecture, were once sewn together and are paginated in ink; some are labelled "Home." The opening paragraph is written on the verso of the cover, and the surviving text begins on page 12. For a pencilled introduction, apparently for another lecture, see the textual notes. Since the lecture is incomplete, it has been supplemented in the textual notes with the working notes from journal Φ.

In MY last Lecture I attempted a sketch of the spirit which characterises the recent movements of society and which appears in history, in letters, in art, in the manners and way of thinking of the people. It was shown as the indication of a more sincere and intelligent reception of the Doctrine of the True Nature of Man than has been before known. And some very general statements were then made of the Doctrine of the Soul with a view to suggest what truth lies already in each mind respecting the Nature that inhabits this world, that lives this human life.[1]

.　　.　　.

A household is the school of power.[2] Not only angels and muses resort thither, but thither come the elves and gnomes and whatsoever lower ministers aid in the Culture of man. I look upon a house I confess with great respect as upon a state, a little world, a several Olympus where all the gods repair, if Jove and Apollo, so Ceres, Mercury, and Vulcan also. What relations from that centre radiate over all the land! Who keeps a house opens an office, a shop in the heart of all trades, professions, and arts so that upon him these shall all play. By keeping house I go to a universal school where all liberal and all useful knowledges are taught me and the price of my tuition is my annual expenditure whether it be a hundred or a thousand dollars. To set up my stove I happen to want a piece of sheet iron thirty-one inches by thirty-three. Now if it happen as it does that I am profoundly ignorant on that head, that want entitles me to call on the professors of tin and iron in the village and learn of them the kind of iron best adapted for my purpose, the cost of production of a pound of cast or wrought metal, and any other related information they possess and furthermore to see my question answered in the practical experiment of the use of their apparatus for the benefit of my fun-

[1] Five manuscript leaves are missing at this point. The working notes in journal Φ (see textual notes, p. 400) indicate a relationship between what is missing here and what is now printed in "Domestic Life," *W*, VII, 103–105.
[2] "Education," *W*, X, 128.

nel and blower, and all the beautiful rules and contrivances that facilitate the working in iron. All which they courteously teach for a very moderate fee. In like manner the wants of each day shall make a chemist of you with ashes, soap, beer, vinegar, medicines; the naturalist with flowerpot, trees, shrubs, hens, pigs, cows, horses, fishes, bees, cankerworms; the politician with the select man, the assessor, the town meeting, and the jury box.[3]

One of the uses of Home not to be neglected by earnest and laborious characters is its recreation. It is indispensable to the health of the soul that it should have some free playground where it can unbend and repose itself; and where better than on the proverbial affection of aunts and cousins? Louis XIV was so studious of dignity that he never showed himself without his wig to his valet. And in the children's books, we used to see pictures of kings and queens lying in bed with their crowns on, and sceptres in their hands. And in real life we now and then see men in buckram, whose forms have absorbed the substance, whose dignity has usurped the man, who walk stilted and harnessed up to every trifle. But to all men there must be the boundless charter of innocence somewhere where is no duty but kindness. Every employment too long persisted in is sickly, studies, handiworks, arts, trade, politics; — and the garden, the house, and the old and new familiar faces therein contained are a balsam. There is health in table talk and nursery play.[4] The cords which we wove in play often hold us in earnest. The affections which were our recreation once become our dearest attraction to life and so Home is to most men the fact which gives all its vigor and sinew to their patriotism and their love of Man. And the most sublime consequences acting to the limits of our being, flow out of these spontaneous and earthborn attachments.

But I will not further expand the consideration of particular benefits.[5]

Every appearance covers a fact; every fact covers a principle. And what is the philosophy of Home? What principle is covered

---

[3] "Who keeps a house . . . jury box" (D, 108). See textual notes for an alternate introduction which appears at this point, apparently not for this lecture.
[4] "Every employment . . . nursery play" (cf. C, 298).
[5] One manuscript leaf (possibly blank) is missing at this point.

up under this universal fact? The circumstances which we call Home, which do not essentially vary, whether the house in which the child is born, is a palace or a covered wagon, seem to correspond invariably to an invariable instinct of the human nature. There is in the mind a subjective or inward sense of stability and repose, which demands some outward or objective type of the same. To the infant, — the mother, the bed, the furniture of the chamber, the walls, supply this object. His spirit rests on them as a fixture. If a table or chair falls or is moved, the child is agitated, because it has been his object of stability. Presently his mother is gone from him: new faces pass: he finds that the furniture is changed: and he enters into new apartments, he leaves the house, and goes in his basket coach into the street. So changes — so enlarges the object which corresponds to his subjective stability. Home becomes a large presence of several persons, — of a whole house, — a yard, a garden, a street. By and by, the boy finds the house is to be pulled down; the family removes. He is not related then to these primeval walls! He and they can part and he remain whole! Home is not one house, but any house where a few related persons are. By and by, these grow old; he goes to school; to college; to his trade. He finds new inmates of his expanding circle. The old ties are fading; the father, the mother have grown old, and are dead. What! and neither are these essential to his reposed being! He can live without them too! The brothers are scattered; and their faces acquire a sort of strangeness; new ties are found: new faces have smiled on him: new hands have grasped and labored with his own. The warm affections, the ardent intellect of youth open, and together find a higher home than before, — not in house walls, not in a fenced garden, not in a town, but in souls that give back a true image of his own; and the dear friendships and loves of youth seem a sufficient asylum and hearth if all old places and old faces should perish. But sad changes come over these. Yet the man meantime has transferred his affection to his cause; to his trade and profession; to his connexion in society; to his political, religious, literary parties. The cultivated soul soars higher yet; disdains all local, temporary connexions, and says with Milton, "Our country is where we can live as we ought." [6] Or with an earlier philosopher, Where I am well, there I am at home. [7]

The instinct of the mind requires ever some permanent thing — permanent as itself — to be its outward object; to be its home, and as fast as one and another are seen to be impermanent and fleeting, it transfers its regard. To very many persons in whom the course of thought is slow and phlegmatic, places remain an object of superstitious regard; the houses in which they have done and suffered the few memorable facts of their lives; the names and bodies of their friends, — though the habits of thought are gone, and so the affections that bound them to them have perished long ago; yet, as ghosts round charnel houses, they cleave unto dead men; dead to the dead. Nor do such persons ever find their town, their country, much less the earth, and nature, unfit resting places for the spirit, and hence the anomaly so frequent now in the world, of death of the body before the will of the dying is reconciled to the change. In a true life of man it seems certain the outward and the inward event would ever coincide, so that when in the Universal Order, it behoved that the individual should pass out of time, his own instincts would advertise him, his own connexion and loving cooperation with the Universe would have brought his own will into a perfect consent and he would depart out of this world as gladly as he had worked in it.

But persons of a more lively thought in their conversation with nature and men do speedily find that what is in them has a permanence which is wanting in these external objects. Nature which looks so brute and still to the clownish eye is detected by them to be in endless flux and the spirit fluttering like a bird to find somewhere a resting place refuses to plant itself on the ticklish and unsteady plank. Whither shall it go for a foothold?

It receives from all things an impression of stable causation. In the most diverse changes in nature there is always somewhat resembling, as all the parts of a plant are only transformations of

[6] Letter to Peter Heimbach (August 15, 1666), trans. in Charles Symmons, ed., *The Prose Works of John Milton,* 7 vols. (London, 1806), VII, 456.
[7] Cf. Blotting Book I, 35, and Encyclopedia, 30, for "Bolingbroke's motto" in Latin. Perhaps the reference here is to Cicero, *Tusculanarum Disputationum,* book V, chapter 37, section 108, or other early source.

a leaf. Every day resembles every other day though the sky, the light, the landscape, the temperature differ. Nature is not a wild, chaotic series but though variegated endlessly, yet a perfect Order, the Revolution of all the parts being precisely fulfilled.

Quickly therefore the spirit learns to discern stability at the heart of agitation and Law riding sure through wild and prodigious motion. It finds in this Law the natural counterpart to its own spiritual fixedness, and is at home in Law. This is not a voluntary thinking. It is the unconscious riches of experience and perception gathered from year to year in every place. He does not state it to himself in propositions. But I think in all men in the progress of Culture the rest or Home of the mind comes to be in the perceived Order and Perfection of Nature as the great fact which all changes do publish, and which is the external fact corresponding to the Divine Soul in which its own being is seen to lie.

The individual whilst he is merely an individual has in him no assurance of permanence or eternity, and therefore when he comes to assume his manly vows, he seeks with passion and above all things symbols of endurance. A castle, a city, a mountain, intelligent man, a family whose love does not wear out, seem to him to have that security and duration in them. But presently he detects insecurity in all these. What permanency is there in things which are in perpetual flux nor remain the same one moment though the pile were Andes or the town were London? And what security can he find in the affections of a few mortals as soon as he discovers that they like him are groping for some immoveable foundation which they have not found? But he is attended wherever he goes, by that which he seeks. He is instructed by his consciousness that within the Individual is that which is not individual but Universal; that which is nearer than the nearest; that which looked out upon him from the eyes that loved his infancy; that to which all nature answers; that whose work all nature is. Here is Unity which sees itself throughout infinite variety, and so in the Divine Soul, he finds the rest which in so many types he had sought.

All places are alike to him for in all appear that law and order which certify him of co-nature with his own constitution more than do the lineaments which resemble his own which he sees in his own house. Having found his Home in that which affirms itself to be the Cause of all, all his knowledge and moral growth go to domesticate him in every fact and event that transpire in nature. All places are alike to him for that which is with him constitutes place. He is place and whatsoever is not with him in spirit is abroad and vagabond.

It is plain that the more inward the principle of association is the more permanent will it be and the more indifference will the man exhibit in his behaviour to trifles. As the house, the village, the towns and mountains in which once he thought all that was dear to him was found dwindle and disappear in the greatness of his horizon, as he finds a home wherever truth, love, and justice and the symbolic laws of nature are found, his nature and his efficiency increase. Now first he can go abroad with impunity for he carries his household god with him. He is at home in markets, in senates, in battles, at home with Man, at home with God, and learns to look at sea and land, at nations and globes, as the moveables and furniture of the City of God.

This ready domestication which though only in the highest minds is perfectly completed and understands itself yet exists in every degree is always a trait of great men, that whilst ordinary men are disconcerted and wear a look of utter helplessness the moment they are taken out of their routine and miss their usual meal, their fireside corner, their desk and slippers, the able man whose life is not lodged in these things, but in laws which he greets reappearing wherever he goes, finds nature still, and so himself, in untrodden wilds; in terrific dangers; in shipwrecks; in conflagration; in mobs; in his own deathbed; and is not possibly to be lifted off his feet, — is not possibly disconcerted. It is the secret of perfect Heroism. His face indicates that he feels himself at home, and so infuses a confidence in him and obedience to his genius in all the bystanders.

Not less is the same instinct the spring and motive of all intellectual research. If it be seen a little deeper all growth, all progress is a constant endeavor of the Soul to find that which is within without there in nature; to answer its question; Itself is a Question, and Nature is the Answer; to produce a unity within and

29

without; to find a Home. So that Philosophy has been called with the highest Propriety, the Homesickness of the Soul. I wish to see my own nature in every fact. All inquiry into antiquity, all curiosity respecting the pyramids, the excavated cities, Stonehenge, the Ohio Circles, Rome, Memphis, is simply and at last the desire to do away this wild savage and preposterous There or Then and introduce in its place the Here and the Now. It is to banish the Not Me and supply the Me. It is to abolish difference and restore unity.

Belzoni digs and scratches and climbs and gropes in the mummy pits and pyramids of Thebes until he can see the end of the difference between the monstrous work and himself. When he has satisfied himself in general and in detail that it was made by such a person as himself, so armed, and so motived; and to ends to which he himself in given circumstances should also have worked, the problem is then solved; his Me lives along the whole line of temples and sphinxes and catacombs, — passes through them all, like a creative soul, with satisfaction, and they live again to the mind, or are Now.[8] And this is also the aim in all science, in the unprofitable abysses of entomology, in the gigantic masses of geology, and spaces of astronomy, simply to transport our consciousness of cause and effect into those remote and by us uninhabited members, and see that they all proceed from causes related to our cause, from causes now in operation, from Our Cause, from One Mind.[9] To what end else is the learned classification of botany, of natural history, to what end except as an aid to bring the object to me in its place and connexion so that I may clearer see its relation to me and to the Cause of Me? I do not wish to know that what I have been contented to call a shell is by you called a strombus or a buccinum nor that what I have been content to call a butterfly is a Vanessa, but I wish to unite the shell and the moth to my being.[10]

---

[8] "All inquiry into antiquity . . . are Now" ("History," W, II, 11). Cf. the passage Emerson copied into T, 55–56, from Giovanni Belzoni (1778–1823), *Narrative of the Operations and Recent Discoveries within the Pyramids, Temples, Tombs, and Excavations, in Egypt and Nubia,* 3rd ed., 2 vols. (London, 1822), I, 236; he had withdrawn the two volumes from the Boston Athenaeum in October 1838 (*Reading,* p. 24).

[9] "All inquiry into antiquity . . . One Mind" (D, 160).

[10] D, 99; also cf. D, 160.

The constant progress of Culture is to a more interior life, to a deeper Home. As it proceeds, it roots a man the faster to principles and so makes it ever the more indifferent in what places his lot may fall or how often he changes his place. But the progress of true Culture is yet to be felt in public and private Education, [and] will give a gravity and domestic rest to the educated classes in this country. We shall not always travel over seas and lands with light purposes and for pleasure, as we say. It is for want of Culture and home that the idol [11]

.   .   .

I have said that a true Culture goes to make man a citizen of the world, at home in Nature. It is the effect of this domestication in the All to estrange the man in the particular. Having learned to know the depth of peace which belongs to a home in the Soul, he becomes impatient and a stranger in whatsoever relation or place is not like it eternal. He who has learned by happy inspiration that his home and country are so wide that not possibly can he go forth out of it, immediately comes back to view his old private haunts, once so familiar as to seem part and parcel of himself, under an altered aspect. They look strange and foreign. Now that he has learned to range and associate himself by affinities and not by custom he finds himself a stranger under his own roof. And so the uniform language of the philosopher and of the saint in every age has signified their sense as Pilgrims in nature. It was a highly philosophic and poetic mind which under the rude form of the Saxon Witan advised King Edwin in the Seventh Century to entertain the Christian missionaries:

"Man's life, O king, is like a sparrow that during one of your winter feasts enters at a window, flutters a while around the warm house, and flies out at another and none knoweth whence he came or whither he goes. If these strangers can give us tidings of it, let them have cheerful reception from us." [12]

[11] Four manuscript leaves are missing at this point. Cf. "Self-Reliance," W, II, 80; and D, 163–164, for continuation. The working notes in journal Φ provide clues to the missing passage (see textual notes, pp. 400–401).
[12] Probably a paraphrase derived from Sharon Turner, *The History of the Anglo-Saxons*, 2nd ed., 2 vols. (London, 1807), II, 439. Cf. *Lectures*, I, 251; "Immortality," W, VIII, 323; B, 56.

The advancing spirit sees how unworthy it is to be immersed in such poor considerations as its bed and board, and to be wounded in every foolish injury that befals these, and to die daily in the perishing of property and merely local and temporary personal relations. It sees it to be far nobler to hold itself off on cooler terms, and survey the moving drama of life aloof and alone. Then he comes with new rights and with new curiosity into his house to his family, to his household tasks, and relations. Now Home becomes to him a school of constant education. Now is he guest in Nature, a guest in his own house, a stranger to his wife and children, a stranger in his own body. He learns that he has lived in the outside of his world. A nearer intimacy has shown him how much a stranger he is there. For if love and thought be nearness, our bodies are not near us. Open the skin, the flesh, enter the skeleton, touch the heart, liver, or brain of the man, and you have come no nearer to the man than when you were still outside. All this is as strange and foreign to him as to you. You have almost as much property in his body as he has. So in the family in which he had supposed a perfect understanding and intimate bonds subsisted he finds with surprise that in proportion to the force of character existing all are in a degree strangers to and mutually observant of each other's acts.[13]

Let him value and keep his new position. Let him not be cheated out of his eyes by fondness and be the fool of affection but let him use his eyes, see his friend, his son, his wife, his parents impartially as he is truth's friend more than theirs. Natural affection so called, the relation of father, mother, brother, sister, wife, child, is merely opportunity, no more. All men are at heart good and wise; we know it only of those nearest us. Let my brother live and die in Japan, — all intercourse forborne — his virtues, affections, and qualities quite unknown to me, — I should not yield him one tear. A child, — every child, — is infinitely beautiful; but the father alone by position and duty is led to look near enough to see and know. He looks with microscope at his own. We love our wives, our mothers, our children better than strangers, not because they are the best people in the world, nor

[13] "He learns . . . other's acts" (B, 228, condensed).

that we think them so, but because we can see nearer and know the talents, graces, virtues that are in them.[14]

And so let the student, having learned how to use the household as his school, value it above all things. There, behind the curtain let him learn the tragicomedy of human life. Here is the sincere thing, the wondrous composition for which Day and Night go round. Here in the lowly household routine spring the sacred relations, the passions that bind and sever. Here he shall learn poverty and all the rich wisdom that its hated necessities can teach. Here labor drudges. Here affections glow. Here the last secrets of character are told; the guards of man; the guards of woman; the sublime compensations which like angels of Justice pay every debt, keep exact balance in all the actions of man; the opium of custom whereof all drink and go mad and lead thereafter a slipshod life of miserable shifts, unplanned, unreasoned, unhoping, and unblessed. Learn how much Will and how little Wisdom or invocation of the Soul attendeth there. There is Glee and Hospitality and Frankness and Calamity and Death.[15]

He is not yet a man if he have not learned the Household Laws, if he have not learned how in some way to labor for the maintenance of himself and others and the hard precepts of economy and how to reconcile these with the promptings of partial love and of friendship and of humanity. Nor has he seen its secret until he has found through it an open way to all the splendors and sanctities of nature. A wise man can better spare all the marts and temples and galleries and statehouses and libraries of the world than afford to exclude himself from this key and alphabet that deciphers them all.

[14] "Natural affection . . . in them" (D, 102, modified).
[15] "And so let the student . . . Calamity and Death" (cf. "Education," W, X, 128).

3

The School

Delivered in the Masonic Temple, Boston, on December 19, 1838, this lecture apparently was not repeated. The manuscript is complete and in good condition; it remains sewn and the pages are numbered in ink. A number of passages in this lecture were used in *Essays* (1841), particularly in "Self-Reliance," "Spiritual Laws," and "The Over-Soul," and Cabot drew heavily on this early lecture for the essay "Education," which was published posthumously in 1883.

HAVING in former lectures considered the nature of the soul who lives the human life, and the Home and domestic relations in which it is born, predicting the true Home to which its tendencies and aspirations point, I proceed now to enumerate the agencies which combine in his nurture and breeding. It may be a fault to undertake in a single discourse the sketching of agencies so large and which so minutely subdivide themselves in actual experience, and some of which it will be necessary to examine nearer. But the School of Man seemed to stand next in natural order to his Cradle and Home.

In the present lecture I proceed to describe Man as the pupil of God and of the world, a relation so obvious in all his structure and all his position, in all his action and in the very expression of his countenance, (for his eye habitually asks or inquires,) that it becomes very easy and natural to consider the world and distribute the parts of nature under that aspect.

And first that I may enumerate in their order his teachers, they are the Instincts, Condition, Persons, Books, Facts.

I. Instincts. And first and supreme is Instinct his teacher. I use this old and popular word in the twofold sense in which we continually use it in conversation, first in the sense of *sentiments,*

34

and secondly in the sense of instincts of organization. There is a fitness in using the same word notwithstanding its double sense, inasmuch as it indicates the superior, the supreme activity in the first instance flowing into the Individual mind and overawing the will and in the second instance flowing into his organization.

And in the high sense of instinct it may be called our primary Teacher in so great a latitude as almost to exclude all other teaching. For that sentiment of essential life, the sense of being which in calm hours rises, we know not how, in the soul, is not diverse from things, — from the sky, from light, from time, from man, but one with them and proceedeth obviously from the same source whence their life and being also proceedeth[1] and so we owe it an infinite reverence, for in our condition, and in the natures of men and things around us, we only see the secondary or modified effects of the one Soul. All men are taught of this and hence our uniform belief in the unlimited possibilities of every man. For when I see the doors by which God entereth into the mind and that there is no sot nor fop nor ruffian, nor pedant, into whom thoughts do not enter by passages which the individual never left open, I can expect any revolution in character.[2] The co-presence of the living soul is essential to all teaching. The informations of the soul are so great in amount that, (where they are received and obeyed,) they degrade all the other teachings into mere organs and apparatus. For, this mighty nature works through all conditions alike, and delights in equalising the greatest disadvantages of condition by larger infusions of itself. It cares not for costly apparatus, but makes for the docile man an apparatus out of society, nature, books, churches, property, vocation.

This instruction makes all other instruction nugatory (where this is not declined) by its predominating determining quality. For this contains in itself the world of intellect and that of conscience. And we distinguish this primary wisdom as *Intuition,* whilst all subordinate teachings are *tuitions.*[3]

In the first place, this is the source of the intuitions which

---

[1] "Self-Reliance," W, II, 64.
[2] "Education," W, X, 133; B, 86.
[3] "Self-Reliance," W, II, 64.

make all the grand moments of any life, and whatever is grand in any moment. The doctrine of the proper inspiration of man is, I know, denied, — but to me, to deny it seems impiety and strict atheism. Here we lie in the lap of immense intelligence which createth us, createth all, and makes us organs of its activity and receivers of its truth. When we discern justice, when we discern truth, we seem to me to do nothing of ourselves, but to give way to its inspirations. If we ask whence this comes, if we seek to pry into the soul that speaketh, — all metaphysics, all philosophy is at fault.[4] "It is not lawful," said Plotinus, speaking of the intuitive knowledge, "to inquire whence it sprang, as if it were a thing subject to place and motion; for it neither approached hither, nor again departs from hence to some other place; but, it either appears to us, or it does not appear."[5] Every man discerns between the voluntary acts of his mind and his *involuntary perceptions*. And to his involuntary perceptions, he knows, a perfect respect is due. He may err in his expression of them, but he knows that these things are so, like day and night, not to be disputed,[6] and therefore when he affirms what was thus his involuntary perception, he feels the insufferable impertinence of contradiction from the unthinking as if he had uttered a private opinion or caprice, when in truth he was the while a bare pipe for better wisdom to flow through.

In the next place, this in its primary and mysterious combination with the nature of the Individual makes what we call distinctively the *genius* of the man or the peculiar quality that differences him from every other; — a susceptibility to one class of influences; — a selection of what is fit for him; a rejection of what is unfit. And this evidently determines for each soul the character of the Universe.[7] As a man thinketh, so is he; and as a man chooseth, so is he, and so is Nature. A man is a method; a progressive arrangement; a selecting principle, gathering his like to

---

[4] "The doctrine of the proper . . . at fault" ("Self-Reliance," W, II, 64–65).

[5] Plotinus, *Enneads*, V, v, as quoted in Coleridge, *Biographia Literaria*, 2 vols. in 1 (New York, 1834), pp. 144–145; B, 113; cf. *Lectures*, I, 226, and *Nature*, W, I ,34.

[6] "Every man discerns . . . to be disputed" ("Self-Reliance," W, II, 65).

[7] "the *genius* of the man . . . of the Universe" ("Spiritual Laws," W, II, 143–144).

him wherever he goes.[8] He takes only his own out of the multiplicity that sweeps and circles round him. He is like one of those nets or frames that are set out from the shore on rivers to catch driftwood, etc. or like the loadstone amongst splinters of steel.[9] In the midst of action and thought God sets down these perceivers and recorders. And each only hears and announces that note of the thousand-voiced harmony to which his own ear is strung.[10]

Hence arises that mysterious emphasis which certain facts, thoughts, characters, faces, have for each man, of which he can give no account, but which make them impressive on his affections and so on his memory quite without any effort of his will, and determine all his tastes, associates, and pursuits. Here comes in the preponderance of nature over will in every life. There is less intention in history than we ascribe to it. We impute deep-laid, far-sighted plans to Caesar and Napoleon, but the best of their power was in nature not in them.[11] And so in the intellectual culture "We only row, we are steered by fate." [12] Our will never gave the images in the mind the rank they now take there. The regular course of studies, the years of academical or professional education have not yielded the man so many grand facts as some idle books under the bench at school. What we do not call education is vastly more precious than that which we do call so. We form no guess at the time of receiving a thought of its comparative value.[13] And Education often wastes its effort in attempts to thwart and baulk this natural magnetism which with sure discrimination selects its own.[14]

Those facts, words, and persons which dwell in a man's memory without his being able to say why, remain because they have a relation to him not less real for being as yet unapprehended. They are symbols of value to him as they can interpret parts of his consciousness which he would vainly seek words for in the

[8] B, 125; cf. *JMN*, V, 114, footnote 347.
[9] "A man is a method . . . splinters of steel" ("Spiritual Laws," *W*, II, 144).
[10] "a selecting principle . . . is strung" (D, 68–69).
[11] "Here comes in . . . not in them" ("Spiritual Laws," *W*, II, 134; B, 104, 276).
[12] Samuel Butler, *Hudibras*, I, i, 874; also quoted in *Lectures*, II, 343.
[13] "Our will never gave . . . comparative value" (B, 104, 276).
[14] "Our will never gave . . . its own" ("Spiritual Laws," *W*, II, 133).

conventional images of books and other minds. What therefore attracts my attention shall have it, as I will go to the man who knocks at my door, whilst a thousand persons as worthy, go by it, to whom I give no regard.[15] It is sufficient that these particulars speak to me. A few anecdotes, a few traits of character, manners, face, a few incidents, have an emphasis in your memory out of all proportion to their apparent significance, if you measure them by the ordinary standards. Do not for a moment doubt their value to you. They relate to your peculiar gift. Let them have all their weight, and do not reject them and cast about for illustration and facts more usual in Literature.[16] Respect them, for they have their origin in deepest nature. What your heart thinks great is great. The soul's emphasis is the true one.[17] [Every day will show you] that time and space are always yielding to the abiding instincts of the soul. In our real education magnitude and duration make a classification for beginners introductory to the real classification of cause and effect as the Linnean Botany gives way to the natural classes of Jussieu.[18] Let every object lie in your mind for what it is worth to you. Let it take its own rank. Time is nothing in the presence of spirit. See how the deep divine thought demolishes centuries and millenniums and makes itself present through all ages.

Is the teaching of Christ less effective now than it was when first taught? The emphasis of facts and persons to my soul has nothing to do with Time.[19] And so always the soul's scale of things is one; the scale of the senses and understanding, is another. Before the great revelations of the soul, — Time, Space, and Nature shrink away. In ordinary speech, in ordinary life we refer all things to Time as we habitually refer the immensely sundered stars to one concave sphere. And so we say that the Judgment is distant or near, that the Millennium approaches, and the like,

---

[15] "Those facts, words . . . no regard" (C, 249).

[16] "A few anecdotes . . . in Literature" (D, 234).

[17] "Those facts, words . . . true one" ("Spiritual Laws," W, II, 144–145).

[18] D, 207. Emerson probably refers to Antoine Laurent de Jussieu (1748–1836), who continued and elaborated the botanical work of his uncle, Bernard de Jussieu (1699–1777). The system of classification in his *Genera plantarum secundum ordines naturales disposita, juxta methodum in horto regio Parisiensi exaratam, anno MDCCLXXIV* replaced the more artificial botanical classifications of Linnaeus (1707–1778).

[19] "Time is nothing . . . with Time" (D, 178).

when we should simply affirm that in the nature of things one of the facts we contemplate is ephemeral and fugitive and the other is permanent and connate with the soul. The things we now esteem fixed shall one by one detach themselves like ripe fruit, from our experience, and fall; the wind shall blow them none knows whither. The landscape, the figures, Boston, London, are facts as fugitive as any institution past or any whiff of mist or smoke and so is society and the world. The soul goes steadily forwards creating a world alway before her and leaving worlds alway behind her. She has no dates nor rites nor persons nor specialties nor men. The soul knows only the soul. All else is idle weeds for her wearing.[20]

These high primary instincts are the perception of truth in thought; and the [love] of truth in action, which is justice; the faith in unity of mind, which is love, or the instinct of society; the sentiment of hope, or, I should rather say, what seems to me far nobler and profounder than Hope, an absolute trust, which can spring only from the beholding of everlasting elements.

These sentiments are the supreme teachers of the highborn pupil. They lie around him like the deep vault of the firmament, sometimes partly, sometimes wholly overcast and hid, but still reappearing in whole or in part to the wanderer in nature. In the docile soul such heed is given to them, so steadfastly are they watched and loved that these celestial lights shine more and more inward, the curtain of clouds is absorbed, and in deep eternal peace the heaven orbs itself in the soul.

And so, as the weapons of this lordly intelligence, are the secondary instincts that proceed from this organization our teachers. This apparatus of wants and faculties, this craving body, whose organs ask all the elements and all the functions of nature for their satisfaction and teach the wondrous creature which they satisfy with light, with heat, with water, with wood, with bread, with wool. The necessities imposed by this most irritable and all-related texture have taught man hunting, pasturage, agriculture, commerce, weaving, joining, masonry, geometry, astronomy.[21]

[20] "See how the deep . . . her wearing" ("The Over-Soul," W, II, 273–274); "we refer all things . . . her wearing" (D, 171).
[21] "This apparatus of wants . . . geometry, astronomy" ("Education," W, X, 127–128).

II. [Condition.] His condition is the next tutor, — in which is included Nature, or the laws of the world, whereby his being is conditioned; Space and Time, the sun and moon, climate, want, sleep, the law of Dualism or Polarity that runs through things, Growth and Death. There revolve, to give bound and period to his being on all sides, [the sun and moon, the great formalists,] in the sky: here lies stubborn Matter, above, around, below, and will not swerve a hairsbreadth from its chemical routine. Here is a planted world pierced and belted with natural laws, and fenced and planted externally with civil partitions, and properties which all impose new restraints on the young inhabitant.[22] He too must come into this magic circle of relations, and know health, and sickness; the charm of riches; the charm of power; the charm of circumstance; the fear of injury, the desire of external good.[23] Everyone has a trust of power, every man, every boy a jurisdiction if it be only over a cow or a rood of a potato field or a fleet of ships or the laws of a state.[24]

He tills his acre, he plants his tree, and sees with joy the visits of heat and moisture to his trees, and pleases himself with the idea of possession. By this act of ownership he strangely mixes himself with nature; and the Universal Power works, buds, and blooms in his garden and orchard. He seems to himself in this planting and owning an enchanter who by some rune or mystic gesture compels the service of superior beings, or as one who by constructing a canal, compels the flood of a great river to labor for him. But the instant he separates the image of possession from the tree and the potato field, and no longer says "my own" — it loses its piquancy. He presently sees that he also is but an instrument like the tree and in the same hands, — a reagent. The tree was to grow; he was to transplant and water it; not for him, not for it, but for all.[25] What activity the desire of power inspires! what toils it sustains! how it educates the senses, and stores the memory with facts, sharpens the perceptions! [26]

[22] "His condition is . . . young inhabitant" ("Prudence," W, II, 224–225). See textual notes for last two sentences.

[23] "Here is a planted . . . external good" ("Education," W, X, 128).

[24] "Education," W, X, 128–129; B, 214.

[25] "He tills his acre . . . but for all" (expanded from C, 63, where Emerson uses the first person).

[26] "Education," W, X, 129.

The education we receive from things, from the frame of the world, its order, are the theme of poetry, the wonder of philosophy. By the permanence of nature, minds are trained alike and made intelligible to each other. In our condition are the roots of language and communication and these instructions we never exhaust.[27] We all have an innate belief that every thing we have seen, admits of being seen nearer; is nearer related to us than we know: we have intimations of our riches much more than possession, as is the lot of other heirs. Every object suggests in certain moods a dim anticipation of profound meaning as if by and by it would appear to us why the apple tree, why the meadow, why the sea, why the land, stand there and what they signify to us.

What is true of our general condition in nature is true of the particulars of our condition. From our temperament, from our personal circumstances, our natural powers and defects and all that we call fortune, solid wisdom is always passing into the open mind. But this is subsidiary to the teaching of Instinct, to the the teaching of the soul: yields to that. He who opens himself to the sublime admonitions of the soul, is always demolishing the feeble structures of condition; for the soul makes all condition one, in its everlasting effort.

> Were it the will of heaven an osier bough
> Were vessel safe enough the seas to plough,[28]

and the sentiment of Unity at the Heart of things destroys for feeble man the most massive differences of Nature and Fortune.

III. Persons. Another of my teachers is the incarnation of the spirit in a form, — in forms, — like my own. I live in society: — with persons who answer to thoughts in my own mind, or do outwardly express to me a certain obedience to the great instincts to which I live. I see its presence in them. I am certified of a common nature; and so these other souls, these separated selves have a witchcraft for me that nothing else has. They stir in me the new emotions we call passion; of love, hatred, fear, admiration, pity;

[27] "By the permanence . . . never exhaust" ("Education," W, X, 131).
[28] Translation of Pindar in Plutarch, "Why the Pythian Priestess Ceases Her Oracles in Verse," *Morals*, trans. "several hands," 5th ed., 5 vols. (London, 1718), III, 123; T, 185; A, 167; NQ, 44; Morals, 162.

thence comes conversation, competition, persuasion, cities, and war.[29]

What influences can rival this of Persons? These are the pungent instructors who thrill the heart of each of us and make all other teaching formal and cold. How I follow them with aching heart, with pining desire! I count myself nothing before them. I would die for them with joy. They can do what they will with me. How they lash us with those tongues! How they make the tears start, and make us blush, and turn pale, and lap us in Elysium with soothing dreams, and castles in the air! By tones of triumph; of dear love; by threats; by pride that freezes, these have the skill to make the world look bleak and inhospitable, or seem the nest of tenderness and joy. I do not wonder at the miracles which poetry attributes to the music of Orpheus, when I remember what I have experienced from the varied notes of the human voice.[30] All these forms in all these ways and each with the force of all his acquisitions and character act perpetually upon us. The world is a system of mutual instruction. Every man is for his hour or his minute my tutor. Can I teach him something? as surely can he me. The boy in the road side of whom I inquire my way, is my tutor; knows that I do not, and I cannot forego his tuition.[31] The curiosity that beams in each face in rotation in every group, as the conversation takes new turns, evinces this. Every man knows somewhat I do not: — carries about in him a piece of me: — and, as soon as I am made aware of it, I am perforce his follower and suitor. He is my brother. I must feel that he is pleading my cause, — that he is also a missionary of the great soul from whom also I draw my warrant. We learn most from those nearest. I think we learn as much from the sick as from the sound, from the morbid as from the sane. Deal kindly and truly with every man and you convert him instantly into an invaluable teacher of *his* science, and every man has a science.[32]

Yet is it easy to see and maturer years are always showing us

[29] "Another of my teachers . . . and war" ("The Over-Soul," W, II, 276–277).

[30] "These are the pungent . . . human voice" ("Lecture on the Times," W, I, 262–263).

[31] "Every man is . . . tuition" (C, 192).

[32] "I think we learn . . . a science" (D, 166).

that persons are only supplementary to this primary teaching of
the Soul. It is in youth that we are mad for persons. Childhood
and youth do see, as I have said, all the world in them. But the
larger experience of man discovers the identical nature appearing
through them all. Persons themselves acquaint us with the Impersonal. In all conversation between two persons, tacit reference is
made as to a third party, to a common nature. That third party or
common nature is not social; it is impersonal; is God.[33] And so in
groups wherever debate is earnest and especially on great questions of thought the company become aware of their unity; that
the thought rises to an equal height in all bosoms, that all have
a spiritual property in what was said as well as the sayer. They
all wax wiser than they were. It arches over them like a Temple,
this Unity of thought in which every heart beats with nobler
sense of power and duty, and thinks and acts with unusual solemnity.[34] All are conscious of attaining to a higher self-possession.[35]
But in our experience how transitory is this elevation! From that
high colloquy, the parties go away and forget what manner of
men they were, and if a man suffer himself to forget his guiding
sentiment or to depend on persons in any other way than as con-
firming and refreshing its oracles he will become deaf and blind.
Persons are for sympathy and not for guidance. Thyself must be
thy guide. Persons unless they be of commanding excellence do
not rejoice heads as old as mine like thoughts. Persons I labor at
and grope after and experiment upon, — make continual effort at
sympathy which sometimes is found and sometimes is missed,
but I tire at last, and the fruit they bring to my intellect or affection, is oft small and poor. But a thought has its own proper motion which it communicates to me, not borrows of me, and on its
winged back I override and overlook the world.[36]

IV. Books. Another great and unestimable fund of influence
and information to the pupil is the record of the past thinking of
mankind, which however variously offered us, comes to us chiefly
through Books. In my thought, I have my present; in my Condi-

[33] "In all conversation . . . is God" (D, 94).
[34] "And so in groups . . . unusual solemnity" (D, 147).
[35] "persons are only supplementary . . . higher self-possession" ("The Over-
Soul," W, II, 277).
[36] "Persons unless they be . . . the world" (C, 300–301).

tion, the Universal Organization; in persons, I have myself repeated and modified in a thousand conditions so that from all these I deduce a certain immutable and pure man; in Books I have history; or, the energy of the past; its thought; its tendency; its result. Angels they are to me of entertainment, of sympathy, of provocation. With them many of us spend the most of our life, these silent wise, these tractable prophets, historians, and singers whose embalmed life is the highest feat of art, who now cast their bland illumination over desolate hours, solitary chambers, and fallen fortunes. "Reading," Montaigne complained, "was a languid pleasure." [37] Be it so, yet the vast extent of this resource and its perfect tameness — coming and going, like a dog at our bidding, compensate the quietness and contrast with the slowness and sternness of the lessons of *Condition,* with the waywardness and oft inaccessibleness of *Persons,* and however in relation to the primary infusions of the high *Instinct* we may slight this great Magazine of its infusions for all ages, yet none can fail to see how sublime is the invention and how deep and salutary the working. The best souls in the world love books the best.

But Books are not only History, they are uttermost achievements of the human intellect. That Nature which we all share has not been vouchsafed to us in like measures. We are only the prophecy of that we shall be. Here is this great Tragedy, shall I call it, of More and Less; though robbed of all its bitterness in the great compensations of the whole.[38] But my great brothers have seen that which I have not seen, which I cannot see; they have created that which I can understand and enjoy and the book is their depository of the treasure. The book whilst it gives us the joy makes us sensible of our defect.

Impotent creatures that we are, stung by this desire for thought we run up and down into booksellers' shops, into colleges, into athenaeums, into the studies of learned men. The moment we receive a thought, it is the identical thing we had before, with a new mask, and therefore hailed as authentic; yet as soon as we have received it, we desire another new one; we are

[37] Cf. "Of Books," *Essays,* trans. Charles Cotton, 3 vols. (vols. I, III, 2nd ed. [London, 1693]; vol. II, 3rd ed. [London, 1700]), II, 125; "Books," *W,* VII, 197; below, p. 209.
[38] Cf. "Compensation," *W,* II, 123.

not really enriched.[39] Give me, said the sick and dying Herder, a new thought wherewithal I may refresh myself.[40] I have known another accomplished person who said if he could have his wish it should be that he might always have a great thought shining before him. And when we receive it we are beatified for the time. We seem to be capable of all thought. We are on a level then with all Intelligences. We cast all books and teachers behind us. What have I to do with means when I am in the presence of the Infinite Light?[41]

How comes it then that any one book, any one record of a few particular thoughts should be able to remain a hundred, a thousand years of equal value when ten hundred thousand souls are always opening themselves to the exercises and discoveries of this inexhaustible intellectual world? One would think that all old books, old records would be waste paper beside the thinking of today. And yet familiar as that state of mind is the books of Aristotle, Tully, Bacon, of Leibnitz still retain their value from age to age. And why? Because so impassable is at last that thin, imperceptible boundary between *perception* and *creation;* between perfect understanding of the author, perfect fellowship with him, quasi-consciousness of the same gifts — *and the faculty of subordinating that rapture to the Will in such degree as to be able ourselves to conjoin and record our states of mind.*[42]

The fame of Homer, of Shakspeare too plainly declares that only once in an age is the man born that has that faculty.

The fame of a poet, these million repeatings of his name, like the price of some masterpieces of art which are reckoned at the price of states and dukedoms are facts of much import. The price of the picture indicates the common sense of men in regard to the chance there is for the appearance of equal genius. The chances are millions to one that no new Raphael is born today and therefore pictures as great as the actual Raphael painted express that chance in their nominal value.[43] And as the price of the picture

[39] "Impotent creatures . . . really enriched" (D, 238; cf. "Intellect," W, II, 341).
[40] Cf. Johannes von Müller, letter to Johann Georg Müller (Jan. 25, 1804), in *Sämmtliche Werke,* 27 vols. (Tübingen, 1810–19), VII, 113.
[41] "And when we receive . . . Infinite Light" (D, 238).
[42] "And yet familiar . . . *of mind*" (D, 238).
[43] "The price of the picture . . . nominal value" (D, 56).

indicates the odds that exist against the appearance of a genius pure as Raphael or Angelo; so is the glory of the name of Shakspeare, Bacon, Milton an index of the exceeding difficulty with which the reader who perfectly understands what they say and sees no reason why he should not continue the same sentence — overleaps that invisible barrier and continues the sentence. Whilst he reads, the drawbridge is down; nothing hinders that he should pass with the author. When he assays to write, lo suddenly! the draw is up, and will not down.[44]

Meantime let him not forget — (it is dangerous to forget) that he can and should make this passage: that in his lifetime already somehow somewhere he has made it: that it is the constant oracle of the soul, "what man has done thou canst do;" and if he will be true to the spirit which animates him, he shall have and do and be all things.

And therefore notwithstanding the noble solace and excitement which books furnish us, if we truly consider them, — their profusion and their use must be esteemed excessive. The reliance upon them will be inversely to the activity of the intuitions. A wise man will need less. Always in proportion to the creative faculty is the reliance on learning less. Not by books are great poets made. Somewhat — much — he unquestionably owes to his books but you could not find in his circumstances the history of his poem. It was made without hands in his invisible world. A mightier magic than any learning, the deep logic of cause and effect he studied: its roots were cast so deep; therefore it flung out its branches so high.[45] And so always the greater is the man the less are books to him. Day by day he lessens the distance betwixt him and his authors and soon finds very few to whom he can pay so high a compliment as to read them.[46]

Again it may be said in abridgment of the value of books, there must be somewhat unfair in entire literature. For every writer avoids of course saying what all think and say around him. It is his endeavor in every sentence to say that which others omit to think and say. Because it was *not* said, therefore Cicero, there-

[44] "And as the price of the picture . . . will not down" (D, 238–239).
[45] "Not by books . . . so high" (D, 209).
[46] "And so always . . . read them" (D, 114).

fore Horace said it. Of course that which they skipped is precisely that which it now concerns us to know. He shunned the things of garish day and gave us the shades. He shunned the obvious and seized the rare and recondite.[47]

And of books it must also be said that they underlie the same defect as all attempts to preserve and perpetuate the past utterance of thought. In the moment when it is spoken it is alive; when you gather it up and write it in firm letters of black and white in vellum or on iron stereotypes it has already lost its best life. Always when man has made him a weapon he abates somewhat of his natural energy; if he uses a crutch his muscles lose their strength. And so it fares with the teaching of books universally that they are suffered to intervene between the man and the original spirit that gave them forth.

V. [Facts.] But beside Instinct, Condition or general laws, Persons, and Books, there is another tuition which follows us from the dawn of consciousness: Facts or Events. Nature which is One in Law falls upon us in showers of subdivision in Facts. These never give us pause but awaken our curiosity every day and by their infinite variety distract the undisciplined intellect. Between them as a confounding, distracting force and the Unity of the Soul our being is suspended. If we yield to them they twitch us by the sleeve, now on this hand, now on that, and we live as slaves, ever in a hurry, with no unity, but weave ever patch work. Yet without giving them our attention a man would not live in nature, could not give force and reality to his existence.

With all the extreme attention that we give to every day's events their philosophical import we do not scrutinize. Day creeps after day, each full of facts, dull, strange, despised things that we cannot enough despise, call heavy, prosaic, and desart. The time we seek to kill. The attention it is elegant to divert from things around us. And presently the aroused intellect finds gold and gems in one of these scorned facts, then finds that the day of facts is a rock of diamonds, that a fact is an Epiphany of God,[48] that on every fact of his life he should rear a temple of wonder and joy; that in going to eat meat, to buy or to sell; to meet a friend

---

[47] "there must be somewhat . . . recondite" (D, 101).
[48] "Day creeps after day . . . Epiphany of God" ("Education," W, X, 132).

or thwart an adversary, to communicate a piece of news or to give a gift he celebrates the arrival of an inconceivably remote purpose and law at last on the shores of Being and into the ripeness and domain of Nature and because nothing chances but all is locked and wheeled and chained in Law, in these motes and dust he can read the writing of the true Life and of a startling sublimity.[49]

Our life is indeed nothing but an endless procession of facts or events like the pulsations of the heart or the beats of the pendulum. In swarms, in splendid variety these changes come all putting questions to the human spirit. We have our theory of life, our religion, our philosophy and the event of each moment, the harvest, the shower, the steam-boat disaster, the bankruptcy, the riot, the passing of a beautiful face, the apoplexy of your neighbor are all tests to try your theory, your Truth, the approximate result you call truth and reveal its defects. These come all asking honest questions of the pupil soul. If I have renounced the search of truth, if I have come into the port of some pretending dogmatism, some new church or old church, some Schelling or Cousin, I have died to all use of these new events that are born out of prolific time into multitude of life every hour. I am as a bankrupt to whom brilliant opportunities offer in vain. He has just foreclosed his freedom, tied his hands, locked himself up and given the key to another to keep.[50] And this, it seems to me, is the true explanation of that old fable of the Sphinx, who was said to sit in the roadside and put riddles to every passenger. If the man could not answer, she swallowed him alive. If he could solve the riddle, the Sphinx was slain. And so men who cannot answer these questions of Time, these facts, by a superior wisdom, serve them. Facts encumber them, tyrannize over them, and make the men of routine, the men of understanding, the men of sense, in whom a literal obedience to facts has extinguished every spark of that light by which man is truly man. But if the man is true to his higher Instincts or sentiments and refuses the dominion of facts as one that comes of a higher race, dwells with the soul and sees the principle

[49] "Day creeps after day . . . startling sublimity" (D, 36).
[50] "We have our theory . . . to keep" ("Education," W, X, 132–133); "and the event . . . to keep" (D, 43).

then the facts fall aptly and supple into their places; they know their master; and the meanest of them glorifies him.[51]

It is only by the sallies of the Soul into the facts that we can come to a piercing inquisition, a right administration of them. The facts are like numerical ciphers or like letters of the alphabet which have no value but what place gives them. The soul opening its eyes, and seeing, — the fact obeys, and takes its true place, and then first is beautiful. The place of the fact is always the value of it. The detached fact is ugly. Replace it in its series of cause and effect, and it is beautiful. Putrefaction is loathsome; but putrefaction seen as a step in the circle of nature, pleases. A mean or malicious act vexes me: but if I can raise myself to see how it stands related to past and future in the biography of the doer, it becomes comic, pleasant, fair, and prophetic. The laws of disease are the laws of health masked.[52]

And as they take their place to the seeing soul, so to it is no great, no small. The least fact to its eye is full of meaning. The vulgar would hear with scorn on what slight single observations Kepler and Newton and Bradley had inferred those laws which they promulgated, and which the world receives with respect, and writes down as the canons of nature. A flute heard out of a village window, a prevailing strain of a village maid will teach a susceptible man as much as others learn from the orchestra of the Academy.[53]

But do not imagine that the astronomer or the naturalist has a monopoly of the riches of facts or that scientific significance is the measure of their value. We walk amidst wonders in every thing we see and do. In what is small and common not less than in the great, the prophet recognises the footstep of Deity, and scorns not to sympathise with the homely song of Bunyan,

> The dunghill-raker, spider, hen,
> The chicken, too, to me
> Have taught a lesson; let me then
> Conformed to it be.

[51] "And this, it seems to me . . . glorifies him" ("History," W, II, 32–33).
[52] "The detached fact . . . health masked" (D, 114). For the last sentence, cf. "Spiritual Laws," W, II, 155; C, 340; below, p. 130.
[53] "The vulgar . . . the Academy" (D, 101).

The butcher, garden, and the field
The Robin and his bait
Also the rotten tree, doth yield
Me argument of weight.[54]

A renouncement of all pride of opinion, a willingness to be taught, a pious beholding of that wisdom which is inscribed all over life, beaming from every trifle scarcely less than from great events and remarkable persons, will qualify us to learn. And an open ear is the most commanding claim upon the Spirit of Wisdom.

[54] *The Pilgrim's Progress,* part II, the parable of the hen and chickens in the Interpreter's house. Also quoted in C, 237.

4

Love

This lecture was first read at the Masonic Temple, Boston, December 26, 1838, and was repeated as the fourth lecture of the series at Concord, Massachusetts, on April 10, 1839. As third in the series at Providence, Rhode Island, it was read on March 25, 1840.

In June 1840 Emerson notes, "I finish transcribing this morning my old essay on Love" (E, 162); if this refers to making a copy from this manuscript for *Essays* (1841), the lecture manuscript was no longer useful to Emerson. He gave it to Elizabeth Peabody, who attached a note: "to be sent to Mrs Edith Emerson Forbes if I die." A wrapper which once enclosed the lecture bears Edith Forbes' notation: "R.W.E. Lecture on 'Love.' Miss Elizabeth Peabody asked to borrow it to read to the young girls of her School. He gave it to her & told her she might keep it. She gave it to me in her old age — & I was most glad to have it." It may not have been in Edward Emerson's possession when he was preparing his edition since it has none of his characteristic marginal notations, but he perhaps relied on Cabot's extant transcription of manuscript passages not used in the printed essay. Cabot dismissed it without a summary and with the note: "Printed almost entire" (Cabot, II, 740). Much of it, but not all, was revised for "Love" in *Essays* (1841). Because it presumably was not in the hands of Emerson's editors and because he apparently revised from a copy, the manuscript does not have the usual use marks for passages used elsewhere. It has been carefully preserved and remains sewn; the pencilled page numbers are not Emerson's. There also survives with the manuscript an extensive miscellany which contains notes, quotations, and brief passages related to the topic.

H AVING in the foregoing lectures considered the nature o[f] the soul, its nurture amidst the protecting and fostering influences of Home; and, in a general way, the tuition it owes to the five sources, of Instinct; of Condition; of Persons; of Books; and of Facts; — I proceed to the enumeration and inspection, according to our skill, of the pupil's own activity and cooperation in his growth with God and nature.

I come now with a mingled feeling of diffidence and joy to describe the great enchantment of life, which, like a certain divine rage and enthusiasm, seizes on man at one period, and works a revolution in his soul and body, unites him to his race, pledges him to the domestic and civic relation, carries him with new sympathy into nature; enhances the power of the senses; gives him new eyes, and new ears, — so much does it exalt the force of the old; awakens new and finer susceptibilities to poetry, music, art; adds to his character the heroic and even the sacred attributes; establishes marriage; and gives permanence to human society;[1] and then at last proves only introductory to more expansive and divine affection.

The power of Love is indeed the great poem of nature which all brute matter does seem to predict from the affinities of chemistry — and of crystals, upward. The dualism which in human nature makes sex, in inorganic matter strives and works in polarity, showing itself in elective affinities, in explosion, in flame, in new products. In the vegetable kingdom it solemnizes in the springtime the marriage of the plants, with the splendid bridal apparel of those sons and daughters of beauty, in whose sibylline leaves we read the approach of man. At the same season all the senses apprise us of a stimulated life and wide jubilee throughout the inferior creation. Suddenly birds arrive and the silent woods tinkle and swell with melody. In spring new life appears brisk and jocund in the animal tribes.

In the temperate zones, since immemorial time, men have celebrated these welcome changes on the morning of May. One of Wordsworth's latest lays is dedicated to the May day:

> All nature welcomes her whose sway
> Tempers the year's extremes,
> Who scattereth lustres o'er noonday
> Like morning's dewy gleams
> While mellow warble, sprightly trill,
> The tremulous heart excite

[1] "Love," W, II, 169.

And hums the balmy air to still
   The balance of delight.

    .   .   .

Yet where love nestles, thou canst teach
   The soul to love thee more;
Hearts also shall thy lessons reach
   That never loved before.
Stript is the haughty one of pride
   The bashful freed from fear
While rising like the ocean tide
   In flows the joyous year.[2]

These gay physical influences are celebrated by an old poet three centuries ago:

May makes the cheerful sure; May breeds
   and brings new blood
May marcheth throughout every limb; May
   makes the merry mood.[3]

This seems pardonable and a good-natured condescension in the poets to attribute the gay influences of the forest and field to cold and even tempered man who sees surely in these that which symbolizes his own life and affections, but whose own life is not annual but eternal and whose affections are not bound by laws so humble and brute. In the polar winter his flames glow as genially as in the Italian spring; his heart, the citizen of every country and the lover of every month, can tinge the snowdrifts and glaciers with rosy light, and warm the alpine cabins of New Hampshire and the cellars of the Fins and Laps with tenderness and personal truth as readily as the mansions of England and the sunny pastures of Spain.

And yet the natural association of the sentiment of Love with the heyday of the blood leads me to say that in order to describe it in vivid tints which every youth and maid should confess to be true to their throbbing experience, one must not be too old. The delicious images of youth reject the least savor of a mature philosophy, as chilling with age and pedantry their purple bloom. And

[2] "Ode, composed on May Morning," lines 9–16, 49–56 (misquoted). The poem was first published in 1835.
[3] "Richard Edwards" [E], "May," lines 7–8 (misquoted); D, 26.

therefore I know well, I incur the risque of criticism of being unnecessarily hard and stoical from those whom I would willingly persuade to ennoble their affections. But from these formidable censors I shall appeal to my seniors. For it is to be considered, on the other side, that this passion of which we speak, though it begin with the young, yet forsakes not the old, or rather suffers no one who is truly its servant to grow old, but makes the aged participators of it, not less than the tender maiden, though in a different and nobler sort.

For it is a fire that kindling its first embers in the narrow nook of a private bosom, caught from a wandering spark out of another private heart, does glow and enlarge until it warms and beams upon multitudes of men and women, upon the universal Heart of All, and so lights up the whole world and all nature with its generous flames. It matters not therefore whether we attempt to describe the passion at twenty, thirty, or eighty years; he who paints it at the first period will miss some of its later, he who paints it at the last some of its earlier traits. Only it is to be hoped that by patience and the Muses' aid, we may attain to that inward view of the law which shall describe a truth ever young, ever beautiful, so central that it shall commend itself to the eye at whatever angle beholden.

And the first condition is that we must leave a too close and lingering adherence to the actual, to facts, and seek to study this sentiment in its ideal manifestation. For it is the nature of man that each man always sees his own life defaced and disfigured as the life of man is not to his imagination. If you will forgive the expression every man sees over all his own experience a certain slime of error whilst that of other men looks fair and ideal. Let any man go back to those delicious relations which make the beauty of his life, which have given him sincerest instruction and nourishment, he will shrink and shrink. Alas I know not why, but infinite compunctions embitter in mature life all the recollections of budding sentiment and cover every beloved name.

Everything is beautiful seen from the point of the intellect, or, as truth. But all is sour if seen as experience in nature. Details are always melancholy. The plan is seemly and noble. It is strange how painful is the actual world, — the painful kingdom of time

54

and place. There dwells care and canker and fear. With thought, with the ideal, is immortal hilarity; the rose of joy. Round it, all the Muses sing: but with names and persons and the partial interests of today and yesterday is grief.[4] I hate history; I hate names and dates. Let them fall, forget the *you* and *me*, converse with things as the irresponsible picture that sails in beauty before your eye and you may deal with all Creation — things nearest and coarsest, never naming names, never giving you the glooms of a recent date or relation but hang there in the heaven of letters unrelated, untimed, a joy and a sign, an autumnal star.

The strong bent of nature is seen in the proportion which this topic of personal relations usurps in the conversation of society. What do we wish to know of any person so much as how they have sped in the history of this sentiment? See then the attractiveness of all stories true or false of which love is the theme. What books in the circulating libraries circulate? How we glow over these novels when told with any spark of truth and nature! And what fastens the attention in the intercourse of life like any passage betraying affection between two parties? It matters not how strange they are to us: we never saw them before, and never shall see them again. But we see them exchange a glance, or betray a deep emotion, and we are no longer strangers to them. We understand them thoroughly, and take the warmest interest in the development of the romance. The earliest demonstrations of complacency and kindness are winningest pictures of nature.[5] In the country and in the middle classes where the manners are freer, this is very prettily seen in the engaging, half-artful, half-artless ways of school girls who go into the shops to buy a skein of silk, a sheet of paper, and talk half an hour about nothing with the broad-faced, good-natured shop boy. In the village they are on a perfect equality which Love delights in, and without any coquetry the happy, affectionate nature of woman flows out in this pretty gossip. The girls have little beauty yet plainly do they establish between them and the good boy the most agreeable,

---

[4] "And yet the natural association . . . yesterday is grief" ("Love," W, II, 169–171); "It is strange . . . yesterday is grief" (D, 95).

[5] "Insert 'Village Love' D256" [E]. The passage referred to is incorporated in "Love," W, II, 172–173; it was written March 8, 1839, after the Boston reading of this lecture.

confiding relations what with their fun and their earnest about Edgar and Jonas and Almira and who was invited and who danced at the dancing school and when the singing school would begin, and other nothings concerning which the parties cooed. By and by that boy wants a wife and very truly and heartily will he know where to find a sincere, sweet mate without any risk such as Milton deplores as incident to scholars and great men.[6]

In strict philosophy there is a quite infinite distance between our knowledge of our own existence and the evidence we have for the existence of nature including that of persons. In Logic the position of the Idealist is inexpugnable who persists in regarding men as appearances and phantoms merely which represent to him his own ideas in the masquerade of forms like his own. But when we treat of Human Life and its several departments we must descend from this high ground of absolute science and converse with things as they appear.

I said in my last lecture somewhat of the part Persons play in the education of us all. I own I shrink already to think of some disparaging words that fell from me in that connexion in relation to the imperfect, unsatisfying influence of Persons. For Persons are love's world; and the coldest philosopher cannot recall the debt of the young soul wandering here in nature to the power of love, without putting a new value instantly on the social relation and tempting him to unsay as treasonable to nature aught derogatory to the social instincts. For though the celestial rapture falling out of heaven seizes only upon those of tender age, and although a beauty overpowering all analysis or comparison and putting us quite beside ourselves, we can seldom see after thirty, yet the remembrance of these visions outlasts all other remembrance and is a wreath of flowers on the oldest brows.

What I am going to say may sound strange, yet I shall say it. It may seem to many men in revising their experience that they have no fairer page in their life's book than the delicious memory of some passages when affection contrived to give a witchcraft surpassing even the deep attraction of its own truth, to a parcel of accidental and insignificant circumstances. In looking back-

[6] "The strong bent of nature . . . great men" ("Love," W, II, 172–173, with alterations); "In the country . . . great men" (D, 236).

ward, they may find, that, several things which were not the
charm, have more reality to this groping memory, than the charm
itself which illuminated them.

> Passing sweet
> Are the domains of tender memory.[7]

Who has ever forgotten the visitations of that Power to his heart
and brain which created all things new; which was the dawn in
him of Music, of Poetry, of Art; which made the face of Nature
radiant with purple light; the morning and the night varied en-
chantments; when a single tone of one voice could make the heart
beat and the most trivial circumstance associated with one form
is put in the amber of memory; when we became all eye when
one was present, and all memory when one was gone; when the
youth becomes a watcher of windows and studious of a glove, a
veil, a ribbon, or the wheels of a carriage; when no place is too
solitary and none too silent for him who has richer company and
sweeter conversation in his new thoughts than any old friends,
though best and surest, can give him: for the figure, the motions,
the words of the beloved object, even the slightest, are not like
other images written as in water but enamelled in fire and make
the study of midnight?

> Thou art not gone, being gone; where'er thou art,
> Thou leav'st in him thy watchful eyes, in him thy loving heart.[8]

Who but throbs at the recollection of days when happiness was
not happy enough but must be drugged with the relish of pain
and fear; for he touched the secret of the matter who said of love,

> All other pleasures are not worth his pains:[9]

and when the day was not long enough but the night too must be
consumed in keen recollections: when the head boiled all night

[7] "It may seem to many men . . . tender memory" (cf. B, 6); Wordsworth,
"To the Same" ["Poems of Sentiment and Reflection," XXVI], lines 50–51.

[8] Donne, "Epithalamion," stanza IX (punctuation supplied).

[9] Quoted in Charles de Marguetel de Saint-Denis de St. Évremond, *The
Works*, 3 vols. (London, 1700–1705), I, 398, where it is attributed to Charleval,
"Ballade." Also in Blotting Book Ψ, 88; Encyclopedia, 105.

on the pillow with the generous deed it resolved upon: when the moonlight was a pleasing fever, and the stars were letters, and the flowers ciphers, and the air was coined into song: when all business seemed an impertinence and all the men and women running to and fro in the street, mere pictures?

The passion operates a revolution in the youth. It quickens all things, and makes all things significant. Nature grows conscious. The bird who sung unheeded yesterday on the boughs of the tree, as the boy whistled by, — himself as gay as the bird, sings now to his heart and soul. Almost the notes are articulate. The clouds almost have faces, as he looks on them. The waving bough of the forest, the undulating grass beneath, and the peeping flowers have grown sympathetic; and almost he fears to trust them with the secret which they seem to invite.

Yet nature soothes and sympathises. In the green solitude he finds a dearer home than with men.

> Fountain heads and pathless groves,
> Places which pale passion loves,
> Moonlight walks when all the fowls
> Are warmly housed save bats and owls,
> A midnight bell, a passing groan,
> These are the sounds we feed upon.[10]

Lo now there in the wood is the fine madman; he is a palace of sweet sounds and sights. He dilates. He is twice a man; he walks with arms akimbo. He soliloquizes; he accosts the grass and the trees. He feels the blood of the violet, the clover, and the buttercup in his veins,[11] and he talks with the brook that wets his foot. The causes that have sharpened his perceptions to natural beauty have made him love music and verse. It is a fact often observed that men have written good verses under the inspiration of passion who cannot write well under any other circumstances.[12] I believe we can never grow quite indifferent to the sweet elegiac strains that once were the breath of joy and harmony.

[10] William Strode, "A Song in Praise of Melancholy" in John Fletcher, *The Nice Valour*, III, iii.

[11] "he is a palace . . . in his veins" (D, 6, where Emerson uses the first person).

[12] "I said in my last lecture . . . other circumstances" ("Love," W, II, 173–177, with alterations).

Our English speech if harsh and hissing is full of pathetic and tender strains which have worthily celebrated the sorrows and the triumphs of love. There are many cadences and verses of a deep inward power speaking to emotion and not to thought which are the property and creation of this sentiment and which are often found in the newspapers and magazines, in corners which the eye fails not to visit, more affecting as it seems to me than those which by the purer thought and perfect literary merit do attain a classic rank and go down for some ages. The like force has passion over all the nature of man; it expands the sentiment. It makes the clown gentle and gives the coward heart. Into the most fitful and abject breast it will infuse a heart and courage to defy the world so only it have the countenance of the beloved object. In giving him to another it still more gives him to himself. The lover says — "I am not what I was since I beheld her." He has new perceptions, new and keener purposes, a religious solemnity of character and aims. He does not longer appertain to his family and society. *He* is something. *He* is a person. He is a soul.

And here let us examine a little nearer the nature of that influence which is thus potent over the human youth. Let us approach and admire Beauty, whose revelation to man we now celebrate — Beauty, welcome as the sun wherever it pleases to shine, which pleases everybody with it and with themselves.[13] (Brandt had weak eyes but it did not hurt them to look into the eyes of Emma ever so long.)[14]

Beauty is ever that divine thing the ancient[s] esteemed it. It is, they said, the flowering of virtue.[15] It would be hard to analyze the nameless charm which glances from one and another face and form. We are touched with emotions of tenderness and complacency but we cannot find whereat this dainty emotion, this wandering gleam point[s]. It is destroyed for the imagination by any attempt to refer it to the organization. Nor does it point to any relations of friendship or love that society knows and has, but, as it seems to me, to a quite other and unattainable sphere, to re-

[13] "The like force . . . with themselves" ("Love," W, II, 177–178, which paraphrases the quotation); for last sentence cf. C, 203.
[14] Cf. "Beauty," W, VI, 297; D, 31.
[15] Cf. Plutarch, "Of Love," *Morals,* IV, 297; Sermons and Journal, 44; *Lectures,* II, 264, 275.

lations of transcendant delicacy and sweetness; a true faerie land; to what roses and violets hint and foreshow. We cannot get at beauty. Its nature is like opaline dovesneck lustres, hovering and evanescent.[16]

And so it resembles the selectest things we know, which all have this rainbow character defying all attempts at appropriation and use. I have never heard anything better said of music than the saying of Jean Paul: "Away! away! thou speakest to me of things which in all my endless life I have found not and shall not find." [17] And so with every work of the plastic arts. The statue is then beautiful when it begins to be incomprehensible, when it is passing out of criticism and can no longer be described by one compass and measuring wand but demands an active imagination to go with it and to say what it is in the act of doing. It is always represented in a transition *from* that which is representable to the senses, *to* that which is not. Then first it ceases to be a stone. And the same remark holds of painting. And of poetry, Landor finely asks, "Whether it is not to be referred to some purer state of sensation and existence?" [18] So must it be with Beauty. Then first is it charming and itself, when it dissatisfies us with any end; when it becomes a story without an end; when it suggests gleams and visions, and not earthly satisfactions; when it seems "too bright and good for human nature's daily food." [19] When it makes the beholder feel his unworthiness: when he cannot feel his right to it though he were Caesar; he cannot feel more right than to the firmament and the splendors of a sunset.

And this agrees well with the high philosophy of beauty which the ancient writers delighted in; for, they said, that the soul of man embodied here on earth went wandering everywhere to seek that other world of its own out of which it came into this, but was soon stupefied by the light of the natural sun, and unable to see any objects but those of this world, which are but shadows

[16] "Beauty is ever that divine thing . . . and evanescent" (C, 34).
[17] D, 203; quotation of Jean Paul Richter in *Memorials of Mrs. Hemans,* ed. Henry F. Chorley, 2 vols. (New York, 1836), I, 231; also in C, 99, and Encyclopedia, 216.
[18] Cf. Walter Savage Landor, "Duke de Richelieu, Sir Fire Coats, and Lady Glengrin," *Imaginary Conversations,* [First Series], 3 vols. (vols. I, II, 2nd. ed. [London, 1826]; vol. III [London, 1828]), III, 206; cf. B, 45.
[19] Cf. Wordsworth, "She was a Phantom of delight," lines 7–8.

of real things. And, as geometers are not able to present to their scholars the ideal circle and solids without the aid of diagrams, so the Divine Love avails itself of beautiful bodies as aids to the soul's recollection of the eternally fair and good, and the man beholding such a person runs to her and finds the highest joy in contemplating the form, movement, and intelligence of such an one because it suggests to him the presence of that which indeed is within the beauty and the cause of the beauty.

But if from too much conversing with material objects, the soul was gross and sought to find its satisfaction in the body, it reaped nothing but sorrow, body being unable utterly to fulfil the promise that beauty holds out; but if, accepting the hint of these visions and suggestions that beauty makes to his mind, he passes through the body and falls to admire manners and dispositions, and the lovers converse together and contemplate one another in their discourses and their actions (the Beauty of the visible body being but an organ of the memory,) then they pass to the true mansion of beauty, more and more inflame their love of it, and mounted upon the wings of chaste desire become pure and hallowed; and by conversation with that which is in itself excellent, magnanimous, lowly, and just, the lover comes to a warmer love of these celestial traits and a quicker apprehension of them; so he passes from loving them in one to love them in all and so is the one beautiful soul only the door through which he enters to the society of all true and pure souls. So comes he in the particular society of his mate to a clearer sight of any spot, any taint which her beauty has contracted from this world and is able to point it out and this with mutual joy that they are now able without offence to point out blemishes and hindrances in each other and give each other all help and comfort in curing the same.

And beholding in many souls the traits of the divine Beauty and separating in each soul that which is divine from the taint which they have contracted in the world the lover ascends ever to the highest beauty, to the love and knowledge of the Divinity, by steps on this ladder of created souls.

Somewhat like this thought have all the truly wise told us of Love, in all ages. This doctrine is not old, nor is it new. If Plato, Plutarch, and Apuleius taught it, so have Petrarch, Angelo, and

Milton. The soul teaches it in every time, in opposition and rebuke to that subterranean prudence which talks of marriage with words that take hold of the upper world, whilst one eye is eternally down cellar, so that its gravest discourse has ever a slight savor of bacon and soapbarrels. Base when the snout of this influence touches the education of young women, and withers the blessed affection and hope of human nature by teaching that marriage is nothing but housekeeping and that woman's life has no other aim.[20] The soul teaches this doctrine again in rebuke to that worse depravation of the libertine. There is no deeper dupe than he. He dreams that he has the sparkle and the color of the cup and the chaste society of marriage the dregs. They see him in the base court without a glimpse of the good he desires, mocked by joyless riots, with the hounds and wolves and snakes of Nemesis close behind him in dread and fatal pursuit.[21]

Marriage unites the severed halves and joins characters which are complements to each other. Man represents Intellect whose object is Truth, Woman Love whose object is goodness. Man loves Reality, woman order; man power, woman grace. Man goes abroad into the world and works and acquires. Woman stays at home to make the house beautiful. For whilst man represents the Intellect, whilst man excels in understanding, in woman is always affection and therein somewhat sacred and oracular and nearer to the Divinity.[22]

Woman in very unfriendly condition, very unfriendly to a finer culture, is found the spontaneous adviser of noble courses. The sentiment which the man thinks he came unto gradually through the events of years, to his surprise he finds woman dwelling there in the same as in her natural home. Each with its powers has corresponding weakness and temptations which find their fortress in the other. Man mighty in his faculties and resources, impelled ever to action and experiments, makes experiment of the bad as well as of the good. The woman inclines to virtue. But woman with her tenderness and finer susceptibility is keenly alive to suffering; tears are always near her eye; anguish near her

[20] "Beauty is ever that divine thing . . . no other aim" ("Love," W, II, 179–183).
[21] "The soul teaches . . . fatal pursuit" (C, 38, modified).
[22] Cf. *Lectures,* II, 102.

heart. Man's acuteness is prone to degenerate into injustice: his courage and sufficiency into selfishness. Woman's taste and love of order into a trivial tyranny; her love into an unprogressive jealousy. They must balance and redress each other. The man must not be offended at the superfluous, supererogatory order and nicety of the housewife. He must bear with little extremities and flourishes of a quality that makes comfort for all the senses throughout his house. He must look at a virtue whole and not only at the skirt of its garment where it gathers up a little dust.[23] Nor let the roughness of man accuse the softness of the wife and blind him to a grandeur in the same soul, namely, that sensibility which is the costliest of attributes, which gives the person who hath it, an universal life, and mirrors all nature in her face.

Meantime the woman must not yield to that sweet inaction which has such charms for [her] kindly nature. The rare women that charm us are those happily constituted persons who take possession of society wherever they go, and give it its form, its tone. If they sit as we sit to wait for what shall be said, we shall have no Olympus. To their genius elegance is essential. It is enough that we men stammer and mince words, and play the clown and pedant alternately; they must speak as clearly and simply as a song. This is a happiness that kindness and the culture of what is noble will bestow. Neither will the Graces suffer their daughter in conversation to *run on,* as it is called — a great vice. A fine woman keeps her purpose, and maintains her ground with integrity of manner whilst you censure or rally her. If she is disconcerted and grieved the game is up and society a gloom.[24]

But not to expand at present these trite ethics of society, let us inspect a little more narrowly the progress of the affections and see how friendship is transformed into charity, into an universal benevolence. In the procession of the soul from within outward it enlarges its circles ever like the pebble thrown into the pond or the light proceeding from an orb. The rays of the soul alight first upon things nearest, — upon every utensil and toy; upon nurses and domestics, upon the house and yard and passengers, upon the circle of acquaintance, upon politics and geog-

[23] "The man must not . . . little dust" (C, 159).
[24] "Neither will the Graces . . . society a gloom" (C, 298).

raphy and history. But things are ever grouping themselves according to higher or more interior laws. Neighborhood, names, magnitude, glitter, soon cease to draw us. Cause and Effect, real affinities, the high, progressive, idealizing instinct, these predominate later and ever the step backward from the higher to the lower relations is impossible.

Thus even Love which is the deification of persons must become more impersonal every day.[25] Of this at first it gives no hint. Little think the youth and maiden who are glancing at each other across crowded rooms with eyes so full of mutual intelligence, little think they of the precious fruit long hereafter to proceed from this new, quite external stimulus. The work of vegetation begins first in the irritability of the bark and leafbuds. From exchanging glances they advance to acts of courtesy, of gallantry, then to fiery passion, to plighting troth and marriage.[26] Passion beholds its object as a perfect unit. The soul is wholly embodied and the body is wholly ensouled.

> Her pure and eloquent blood
> Spoke in her cheeks and so distinctly wrought
> That one might almost say her body thought.[27]

Romeo if dead should be cut up into little stars to make the heavens fine. Life with this pair has no other aim — asks no more than Juliet, than Romeo. Night, day, studies, talents, riches, kingdoms, religion — are latent all in this form full of soul, — in this soul which is all form. The lovers delight in endearments, in avowals of love, in comparisons of their regards. When alone, their happiness is in the imagination of the other. Does that other see the same star; the same melting cloud; read the same book; feel the same emotion, that now delight me? They love alone to try and weigh their affection and by enumerating those advantages which they have most prized, friends, prospects in life, property, to discover that willingly, joyfully they would give all as a ransom for the beautiful, the beloved head, not one hair of

---

[25] "In the procession of the soul . . . every day" (D, 120).
[26] "Little think the youth . . . and marriage" (C, 27–28).
[27] Donne, "Of the Progress of the Soul: The Second Anniversary," lines 244–246; C, 89.

which shall be harmed.[28] But the lot of humanity is on these children. Danger, sorrow, and pain impend to them as to all. Love prays. It makes covenants with the Creator in behalf of this dear mate. The union which is thus effected and which bathes the soul in sweetest emotions which find expression in every delicate form and tint of matter is yet a temporary state. Not always can flowers, pearls, poetry, protestations, nor even home in another heart content the awful soul that dwells in clay. It arouses itself at last from these endearments as toys and puts on the harness and aspires to vast and universal aims.[29] The soul which is in the soul of each, craving for a perfect beatitude, detects incongruities, defects, disproportion in the behaviour of the other; hence arises surprise and expostulation and pain. But that which drew them at first was signs of loveliness, signs of virtue. And these virtues are there however eclipsed. They appear and reappear and continue to attract, but the regard changes, quits the sign and attaches to the substance. This repairs the wounded affection. Meantime as life wears on it proves a game of permutation and combination of all possible positions of the parties to extort all the resources of each and acquaint each with the whole strength and weakness of the other.[30]

For it is the nature and end of this relation that they should represent as it were the human race to each other. All that is in the world which is and ought to be known are cunningly wrought into the texture of man, of woman.

> The person love does to us fit
> Like manna has the taste of all in it.[31]

All the angels that inhabit this temple of the body appear at the windows and all the gnomes and vices also. By all the virtues they are more united. If there is virtue all the vices are known as such, confess and flee.[32] Their once flaming regard is sobered by time

[28] "Passion beholds . . . shall be harmed" (D, 120–121, without the quotation).
[29] "Love prays . . . universal aims" (D, 121).
[30] "The soul . . . of the other" (C, 28).
[31] Abraham Cowley, "Resolve to be Beloved" (in *The Mistress*), lines 23–24; C, 89.
[32] "All the angels . . . confess and flee" (cf. C, 28; for first sentence cf. *Lectures*, II, 283).

in either breast; losing in violence what it gains in extent, it becomes confidence, a perfect mutual understanding. They resign each other without complaint to the good offices which man and woman are severally appointed to discharge in time and exchange the passion which once could not lose sight of its object for a cheerful, disengaged furtherance whether present or absent of each other's designs.[33] At last they discover that all which at first drew them together was wholly deciduous, had merely a prospective end like the scaffolding by which the house was built and the unsuspected and wholly unconscious growth of principles from year to year is the real marriage foreseen and prepared from the first but wholly above their consciousness.[34] When I see the grandeur and immense extent of those aims for which two persons, a man and a woman, so variously and correlatively gifted, are shut up in one house to spend in the nuptial society forty or fifty years, I cease to wonder at the emphasis [with] which the creator points out this crisis from early infancy, at the splendor with which the instincts decorate the nuptial bower and all Nature and all Intellect and Art emulate one another in the gift and in the melody they bring to the Epithalamium.[35]

They educate each other to that worth which prizes a grain of Being over all the seeming of Europe and America; the Yes and No of truth, above a tempest of professions; they educate each other to know and love the core of character; to see the infinite superiority of simpleness to the highest glitter of accomplishments without it; to prize a word that is sacred as Fate; and to prize over all partialities and all fading charms a justice that neither yields to kindness nor to fear nor to self-indulgence and that never forgets. Present or absent; in danger and persecution, or in sunshine and troops of friends; living, or dying; that one can be relied on as the axis of the world. What perturbations and questionings have they forever dismissed! They are to teach each other by experiment the whole law of Ethics, the whole domain of thought, the whole domain of deed; to share and so to learn the ornaments of man and woman; the joyous troop of jests and rail-

[33] "Their once flaming regard . . . other's designs" (D, 121).
[34] "At last they discover . . . consciousness" (C, 28).
[35] "In the procession of the soul . . . to the Epithalamium" ("Love," W, II, 183–188).

lery, of games and humors, the cheerful and the merry mood; the plain song of labor, and household economy; the love and skill to meet the emergencies of social life, of charity to the poor and sick; the tenderness to soften the ragged hours of calamity when they come and front unterrified and endure unhurt the tragedy of life. And to uplift day by day and year by year the heart and mind of each by opening the whole nature to every thought as a privilege, — to every virtue as the incoming and visitation of God. By strictest dependence they rear each other to independence. Thus they form each in the other the perfect man, the perfect woman and attain a regard from which everything personal is at last utterly excluded; they have called out in each other all the faculties not only of John and of Joan but all of Adam and of Eve and meet as nations should meet, perfect, spiritual, self-sufficing, eternal.

Thus are the great objections and antagonisms reconciled. Thus are we put in training of a love which knows not sex nor person nor partiality but which loveth virtue and wisdom everywhere to the end of increasing virtue and wisdom. We are by nature observers and so learners. That is our permanent state. The affections are subordinated to the soul. Though slowly and with pain the objects of the affections change as the objects of thought do. There are moments when the affections rule and absorb the man but they are only moments. In health the mind is presently seen again — its overarching vault bright with galaxies of fires; and the warm loves and fears that swept over us as clouds must lose their finite character and blend with God [36] to attain their own perfection. But we need not fear that we can lose any thing by the progress of the soul. The soul may be trusted to the end. That which is so beautiful and attractive as these relations, must be succeeded and supplanted only by what is more beautiful, and that forever.[37]

[36] "We are by nature . . . blend with God" (D, 112).
[37] "Thus are we put . . . and that forever" ("Love," W, II, 188).

5

Genius

This lecture was delivered in Boston at the Masonic Temple on January 9, 1839, and repeated at Plymouth, Massachusetts, on January 31 (D, 245). On March 27 it was read as the second lecture in the abbreviated course on "Human Life" before the Concord, Massachusetts, Lyceum. The manuscript is complete and in good condition; it was once sewn together and the sheets are labelled, sometimes with subheadings. Pencilled page numbers begin after the cover verso, on which the first paragraph is written. Passages have been used in various essays: "History," "Self-Reliance," "The Poet," "Intellect," "Art."

IN MY last lecture I considered the subject of Love which diffuses a light so dazzling over the morning of life, whose heats and lustres subside however in all healthy minds into a calm daylight and vital heat which are of the substance of the soul. Let us pass now to some analysis of the great brother element in the substance of the soul; from the enchantment of the affection to the enchantment of the intellect.

What is Genius? Genius — which in its various manifestations all men reverence, that which attracts from the interior of their soul wonder and joy and presentiments of still higher good, which constrains us to attribute to the possessor a rare and splendid nature, — to believe, that, as was said of Alexander, he had the eyes of a god and a fragrance as of flowers exhaled from his skin, so that when once known and acknowledged every one — from the highest to the meanest in an entire nation, — delights in his name, feels a strict relation to him, welcomes him to all hospitality, gives him the freedom of institutions, houses, yea of the road, and the stage-coach, and begs a hair of him for memory; and when the clay which it animated, and made beloved and illustrious among men, — a mark and harbinger of respect and festivity wheresoever it went, — is forsaken by it, and the man departed to God, a still more deep and reverent hospitality awaits him among men. All nations adorn their walls with his bust and picture. His name becomes a proverb in fair and learned mouths; and that he said or did thus or thus, is thought an argument for ages not only against the contrary opinion but even against the truth itself. But with this external shew of honor there goes a finer compliment. The select souls of that man's nation and then in due time of other nations are stung by his words or works so that they cannot sleep and cannot sit. They talk with his ghost in solitude; they catch with hungry ear, every new opinion, practice, act, trait, that any book or stranger reports to them of this master and write it in light in their memories. These sing a sweet music in their brain. By these as fixed points they arrange all their knowledge; from these cardinal points map out the world of men and things in their memory; and from these recollections clustered into form, they measure men and things, and draw their estimate of life, and the possibilities of the soul. If you look over the pages of chronology, you will see that each nation has a few names that have long ago acquired an ideal brightness and have become indefinitely potent in forming the character of the succeeding generations, by constituting all that influence which every man concedes to authority.

The life of Moses, it will be admitted, was not without influence on the Hebrew people; the life of Numa, of Scipio, of Caesar, among the Romans; the life of Lycurgus, of Homer, of Socrates, Plato, Pericles, Alexander, among the Greeks.

The Venetian, Florentine, and Roman masters do still as it were paint heads and landscapes through the hands and on the easels of other men, and, in lands which they never saw. And why name the gods of our English Parnassus which outshine in our memory all foreign images? These are the synonyms of Genius in our minds and by them we interpret that word. See the infinite pain with which every arm, head, or trunk mutilated and abraded by weather, ascribed to the hand of Phidias — is excavated, restored, modelled, copied in engravings, and exhibited in every museum of the world; and then for Shakspeare we have libraries of editors and commentators and illustrators and translators — an edition every year — his mulberry, his will, and the parish registers of London and Stratford, and now we have got so far that I see on the bookseller's counter a fair volume entitled "Insects Mentioned by Shakspeare." [1]

And what is this Genius whose hand is so strong, which pours this deep infusion into every man's cup of human life, so that he goes about the willing adorer of one or another of his fellows, dead or living, as if they were not his fellows but the inhabitants of some superior sphere? It is because they are his fellows, and live from his own superior sphere, that he pays them this respect. To speak somewhat paradoxically, they are more himself than he is. They hold of the Soul, as he also does, but they more.

The essence of Genius is Spontaneity. It is, as it were, the voice of the Soul, of the Soul that made all men, uttered through a particular man; and so, as soon as it is apprehended it is accepted by every man as a voice proceeding from his own inmost self.

It is wonderful into what deep considerations any definition will carry us of trivial things, as well of great and stately. It is an easy thing to say Spontaneity, — but not so easy to enter the dim infinity, which all spontaneous action implies. In all works, books, acts, manners, words, to which this sacred emphasis of Genius attaches, it is not mere man, but more than man that worketh. The energy is not a knack, a habit, a skill of practice, a working by a rule, nor any empirical skill whatever; it is not anything the man can handle and describe and communicate, can even do or not do, but always a power which overawes himself, always an enthusiasm not subject to his control, which takes him off his feet, draws him this way and that, and is the master, not the slave.

But before we proceed further, it is proper to observe that this fact of Spontaneity is the link between the two established senses of the word Genius in our tongue.

1. Genius, a man's natural bias or turn of mind, as when we say, consult the boy's genius in choosing his trade or work; where it signifies the spontaneous turning of every mind to some one

---

[1] Robert Patterson, *Letters on the Natural History of the Insects Mentioned in Shakspeare's Plays* (London, 1838).

class of things and relates to practice. And, in like manner, we say the *Genius* of a certain institution, code of laws, or department of literature as history, the drama, etc., or of a tribe or nation of men, meaning thereby the spontaneous or unconscious quality by which quite above the intention of the author or authors or parties, the thing or class makes a certain impression on the mind.

2. The second and popular sense of Genius is the intellect's spontaneous perception and exhibition of truth. Its subject is truth, its object a creation of truth without, — whether in a temple, a song, an argument, a steamboat, a Copernican system of astronomy.

Genius is the spontaneous perception and exhibition of truth. Its object is Truth. They err who think Genius converses with fancies and phantoms; has anything in it fantastic and unreal. Genius is the truest soul; the most articulate, precise of speakers; hating all delusion and words; loving things. Common literature seems to be mere paraphrase and imitation; but when genius arrives, the good human soul speaks because it has something to say. Genius seems to consist in trueness of sight, — in using such words as show that the man was an eyewitness of the fact, and not a mere repeater of what was told. Thus the poor girl who having overheard an account of the inclination of the axis of the earth to the plane of its orbit repeating the information in her own way said the earth was *a-gee*, evinced her perception not less than Lord Bacon when he calls exploding gunpowder "a fiery wind blowing with expansive force."[2]

It evinces its realism or worship of truth by this that it pauses never but gives new matter with every word. And it utters things *for the things.* There is no halfness about genius. It utters things for their own worthiness because they must be said: and what it saith therefore always justifies the saying.

But here is the reason why Genius is taxed with loving falsehood, playing with moonshine, and building air castles; namely, because its sight is piercing and pauses not like other men's at the surface of the fact, but looks through it for the causal thought.

[2] "Genius seems to consist . . . expansive force" (B, 38). Cf. Francis Bacon, *Works*, 10 vols. (London, 1824), I, 258 (*Natural History*, cent. I, par. 30); VIII, 152 (*Novum Organum*, lib. II, aph. xxxvi); IX, 18 (*Historia Densi et Rari*).

Whilst other men give undivided heed to the fact Genius has been startled out of its propriety by perceiving the fact to be a mere appearance, a mask, and detecting eyes that peer through it to meet its own. It knows that facts are not ultimates. Through them it seeks the soul. A state of mind is the ancestor of every thing. Now common sense stops at a fact; to it a fact is sacred; it will not go behind this; and it reckons mad all who do. Yet *is* there somewhat higher than common sense.

There is at the surface infinite variety of things. At the centre, there is simplicity and unity of cause. How many are the acts of one man in which we recognize the same character! Let me illustrate this remark by adverting to the perfectness of our information in respect to the Greek genius. Thus at first we have the *civil history* of that people as Herodotus, Thucydides, Xenophon, Plutarch have given it to us: a very sufficient account of what manner of persons they were and what they did. Then we have the same soul expressed for us again in their *literature;* in their poems, drama, and philosophy: a very complete form. Then we have it once more in their *architecture:* — the purest sensual beauty: the perfect medium never overstepping the limit of charming propriety and grace. Then we have it once more in *sculpture;* "the tongue on the balance of expression:" [3] those forms in every action, at every age of life, ranging through all the scale of condition from god to beast, and never transgressing the ideal serenity, but in convulsive exertion the liege of Order and of law.

Thus we have for one remarkable people, a four-fold representation of the same genius in History, in Literature, in Architecture, and in Sculpture, the most various expression of one moral thing, and each of these do give back the same thought to the mind. Yet what is more unlike to the senses than an ode of Pindar and a marble centaur; the peristyle of the Parthenon and the last actions of Phocion? Who then can doubt that these varied external expressions proceed from one spiritual cause?

In like manner, every one must have observed faces and forms which without any one resembling feature make yet a like im-

[3] Cf. August Wilhelm von Schlegel, *A Course of Lectures on Dramatic Art and Literature,* trans. John Black (Philadelphia, 1833), p. 50, where the same definition is of beauty and is ascribed to Johann Joachim Winckelmann; cf. *Lectures,* I, 348; B, 17, 117; Encyclopedia, 143; D, 90.

pression on his mind. Further have you not found that a particular picture or copy of verses will awaken in your mind if not the same train of images yet superinduce the same frame of thought as some wild walk, perhaps into lonely and somewhat savage solitudes, although the resemblance is nowise obvious to the senses but is occult and out of the reach of the understanding? [4] It is the spirit and not the fact that is identical. What is to be inferred from these facts but this; that, in a certain state of thought is the common origin of very diverse works; and that by descending far down into the depths of the soul, and not primarily by a painful acquisition of many manual skills, you shall attain the power of awakening other souls to a given activity? Thus it has been greatly said that, "common souls pay with what they do; nobler souls, with that which they are." And why? because a soul living from a great depth of being, awakens in us by its actions and words, by its very looks and manners, the same power and beauty that a gallery of sculpture or of pictures enkindle[s] in me.[5]

Truth is the subject of genius: not truth of facts, of figures, dates, measures, — which is a poor, low, sensual truth, — but Ideal truth, or, the just suggestion of the thought which caused the thing. Therein is the inspiration: there the dart that rankles goads him with noble desire to express this beauty to men. That is what art aims ever to say — the truth of thought, and not a mere copy of the fact.

The sculptor sees hovering over all particular human forms a fairer and so a truer form than any actual beautiful person, and copies it with desire in marble: and so we have the Theseus; the Apollo; which with wonder all men allow, is truer than nature.

In landscape, the painter's aim is not surely to give us the enjoyment of a real landscape; for, air, light, motion, life, heat, dampness, and actual infinite space, he cannot give us — but the suggestion of a better, fairer creation than we know. He collects a greater number of beautiful effects into his picture than coexist in any real landscape: the details — the prose of nature, he omits, and gives us only the spirit and splendor, so that we should find

[4] "There is at the surface . . . of the understanding" ("History," W, II, 14–15).
[5] "It is the spirit . . . enkindle[s] in me" ("History," W, II, 17).

73

his landscape more exalting to the inner man, than any actual lake or hill-side.[6]

And now having illustrated from these arts of design the object of genius let me indicate from them also the mystery of its subjective power. It is by its spontaneity that genius is rich. And who knows the resources that lie in the vast bosom of the soul? If you would feel poor, reckon the things you have and those you can choose to do. If you would feel rich, resign yourself to Nature, and do its commandment. Not by any conscious imitation of particular forms are the grand strokes of the painter executed, but by repairing to the fountainhead of all forms in his mind. Consider who is the first drawing-master, — only in humble aid of whom our earthly drawing-master comes. Whence had you those primary lessons in drawing, — the elements on which all practical skill must be based? — Without instruction we know very well the ideal of the human form. A child knows at once if an arm or a leg be distorted in a picture, if the attitude be natural, be grand, or mean, though he has never received any instruction in drawing, nor heard any conversation on the subject, nor can himself draw with correctness a single feature of the body. A good form strikes all eyes pleasantly long before they have any science on the subject.[7] And a beautiful face sets twenty hearts in palpitation prior to all consideration of the mechanical proportions of the features and head. We may owe to Dreams some light on the fountain of this skill; for, as soon as we let our will go, and let the unconscious states ensue, — see what cunning draughtsmen we are. We entertain ourselves with wonderful forms of men, of women, of animals, of gardens, woods,[8] and of monsters and the mystic pencil wherewith we then draw has no aukwardness or inexperience, has no meagreness and poverty, it can design well and group well, its composition is full of art, its colours are well laid on, and the whole canvas which it paints is lifelike and apt to touch us with terror, with tenderness, with desire, and with grief.[9]

Genius is the activity which repairs the decays of things. Na-

[6] "In landscape . . . lake or hill-side" (D, 88; cf. "Art," W, II, 351).
[7] "Without instruction . . . science on the subject" (C, 251).
[8] "We may owe . . . of gardens, woods" (D, 211).
[9] "Not by any conscious . . . with grief" ("Intellect," W, II, 336–338).

ture through all her kingdoms insures herself. Nobody cares for planting the poor fungus: so she shakes down from the gills of one agaric, countless spores, any one of which, being preserved, transmits new billions of spores tomorrow or next day. The new agaric of this hour has a chance which the old one had not. This atom of seed is blown into a new place not subject to the accidents which destroyed its parent two rods off.

She makes a man; and having brought him to ripe age, she will no longer run the risk of losing this wonder at a blow: but she detaches from him a new self, that the work may be safe from accidents to which the single individual is exposed. So when the soul of the poet has come to the ripeness of thought, it detaches from itself and sends away from it its poems or songs, a fearless, sleepless, deathless progeny which is not exposed to the accidents of the weary kingdom of time. A fearless, vivacious offspring, clad with wings, (such was the virtue of the soul out of which they came) which carry them fast and far and infix them irrecoverably into the hearts of men. These wings are the beauty of the poet's soul. The songs thus flying immortal from their mortal parent are pursued by clamorous flight of censures which swarm in far greater numbers and threaten to devour them; but these last are not winged. At the end of a very short leap, they fall plump down and rot, having unfortunately received from the souls out of which they came no beautiful wings. But the melodies of the poet ascend and leap and pierce into the deeps of infinite time.[10]

Equally manifest in every form of art, of action, of speech it elevates and informs our life. The few memorable hours of life are the few strokes of genius that have been dealt upon us. Some Napoleon has struck the thunder strings which vibrate through the world; or some wise mechanic has thought out a toy coach to roll on a bar, and Europe and America are striped with iron roads; a poet in his walk has mused on the Supreme Cause and (written out) *that* shall be theology for the next age. Some chemist has detected a subtle affinity that instantly to his eye shoots its roots through Nature. It is a few thoughts that carve out this

[10] "Genius is the activity . . . infinite time" ("The Poet," W, III, 22–24); "Nature through all . . . infinite time" (D, 123).

vast business which the world so bustles in with endless craftsmen and clerks and books. A few men invented the works which all do.

Except in fortunate hours we do not even apprehend genius, much less exercise it. Our eye rests on the multiplicity of the details and does not pierce to the simplicity and grandeur of the Cause. Yet as soon as we do enter into the causes we sympathise with it; we see that it is aloof from everything artificial, low, and old: that it is pure and fresh as childhood and morning: its words and works affirm their own right to exist: in short, that it is allied to God. A tree, a flower, an animal, a mountain need no apology: their own constitution is the reason why they are. If we see a house, a boat, an implement we have no *a priori* reason why it should be. Experience is to make that good: but a work of genius, mechanical, plastic, literary, or active does in being vindicate itself. That is the prerogative of a masterpiece, — the kindred emotion which it awakens with that awakened by works of nature. That apprises us how deep in thought is its origin, how near to God it was. The identity of their origin at the fountain head, we augur with a thrill of joy.

And of this great pedigree whence these impulses come, another proof is furnished in the perfect analogy that is between virtue and genius. One is ethical; the other is intellectual creation.[11] The work of genius implies and is a species of worship of the supreme Being, — an earnest of his favor and nearer communion — and, in like manner, the expression of the religious sentiment, wherever it is perfectly simple, strikes us with the same surprise and deep contentment as genius.

And proportionate to this dignity of its origin, is the date of its success. The work of genius is not perishable: it has immortal youth: it appeals to eternity. Verses that were made in the beginning of the world, we still read and imitate. Statues and buildings that were the earliest efforts of men at carving and building, are known to all the boys in the civilized world. We talk of old times; but the Apollo, the Venus, the Phidian marbles, are our emblems of youth; yet they are older than the oldest times that we know much of. To this purpose let me read you a sentence of Sir Chris-

[11] "another proof . . . intellectual creation" (C, 91).

topher Wren: "An architect ought to be jealous of novelties, in which fancy blinds the judgment and to think his judges as well those that are to live five centuries after him, as those of his own time. That which is commendable now for novelty, will not be a new invention to posterity, when his works are often imitated, and when it is unknown which was the original; but the glory of that which is good of itself, is eternal." [12] And the reason why the work of genius fits the wants of all ages, is because that which is spontaneous is not local or individual but flows from that internal soul which is also the soul of every man.

1. To analyze a little this wonderful energy — not to take it to pieces, for it is essentially one and whole, but to see successively features which in it are entire — and to enumerate a few of the conspicuous traits, I will say, first, Genius captivates us by its self-reliance. To believe your own thought, — that is genius.[13] The voice of society sometimes, and the writings of great geniuses always are so noble and prolific that it seems justifiable to follow and imitate; but it is better to be an independent groom than to be the player of a King. In every work of genius, you recognize your own rejected thoughts. Here as in science the true chemist collects what every body else throws away. Our own thoughts come back to us in unexpected majesty.[14] We are admonished to hold fast our trust in our instincts another time. What self-reliance is shown in every poetic description! Trifles so simple and fugitive that no man remembers the poet seizes and by force of them hurls you instantly into the presence of his joys.

Let me adorn my discourse with an example of the manner in which a poet seizes a circumstance so trivial that an inferior writer would not have trusted himself to detach and specify, from Wordsworth's picture of skating:

> So through the darkness and the cold we flew
> And not a voice was idle: with the din
> Meanwhile the precipices rang aloud;
> The leafless trees and every icy crag

[12] [H. B. Ker], "Sir Christopher Wren" in *Lives of Eminent Persons* (London, 1833), p. 30; B, 255; T, 41–42.
[13] "Self-Reliance," W, II, 45; B, 185.
[14] "The voice of society . . . unexpected majesty" (B, 102); "In every work . . . unexpected majesty" (cf. "Self-Reliance," W, II, 45–46).

Tinkled like iron: while the distant hills
Into the tumult sent an alien sound
Of melancholy not unnoticed, while the stars
Eastward were sparkling clear, and in the west
The orange sky of evening died away.

    Not seldom from the uproar I retired
Into a silent bay, — or sportively
Glanced sideway, leaving the tumultuous throng
To cross the bright reflection of a star,
Image that flying still before me gleamed
Upon the glassy plain: and oftentimes
When we had given our bodies to the wind,
And all the shadowy banks on either side
Came sweeping through the darkness, spinning still
The rapid line of motion, then at once
Have I, reclining back upon my heels,
Stopped short; yet still the solitary cliffs
Wheeled by me — even as if the earth had rolled
With visible motion her diurnal round.
Behind me did they stretch in solemn train
Feebler and feebler, and I stood and watched
Till all was tranquil as a summer sea.[15]

The reason of this trust is indeed very deep for the soul is sight, and all facts are hers; facts are her words with which she speaketh her sense and well she knoweth what facts speak to the imagination and the soul. For always the dignity is in the thought not in the thing; and an Assyrian empire, a kingdom of Britain, is a fact no more material to it than the tint of a fading violet. To the soul all facts are sacred as they are expressive. It is the senses that creep and measure with balances and yardsticks, and sidereal years. To the soul Andes is not large nor is grass seed small and the only duration is the depth of the thought.

And well may the soul rely on itself and speak in a firm tone, assuring itself of a welcome in all hearts; for it asks nothing but welcome; it is rich, it is strong, it is good itself, and it leans on God. Rare indeed in this world is the voice of genius but when it cometh it can say all things. It raises immediately the apprehension of inexhaustible fertility. When genius does arrive, it

[15] "Works, Vol. 1 p. 29." [E]. "Influence of Natural Objects . . ." lines 38–63; *The Poetical Works,* 4 vols. (Boston, 1824), I, 30; C, 269.

writes itself out in every word and deed and manner as truly and selfsame as in its elaborate masterpiece. In our purest hours nature appears to us one with Art; art perfected; the work of genius and the fertility of both is alike. In nature a leaf in the forest or a field lily is a precious tablet on which the united energies of the creation have writ their perfect mind and if these two things were brought alone to the detached and hermit soul, would administer the same gratification and the same culture which we draw now from the treasuries of art and nature. But what a profusion of leaves in the vast forest! — of flowers, in the five zones! Not less opulent is genius. As many things as exist, so many things doth it ennoble; for what it looketh upon, instantly shines with wisdom. Let a man of lively parts and profoundness only name his subject and we begin to see it under his point of view. Its subtle infusions nothing can resist. Every work of genius makes us for the moment idealists. It dissipates this block of earth into shining ether.[16]

2. And being spontaneous, the work of genius is never predictable. It always surprises. It is the distinction of genius that it is always inconceivable: once and ever a surprise.[17] Itself unsurprised, — itself doing the most natural thing in the world, it astonishes and exalts by every pulse. A strange influence! Michel Angelo in his seventh sonnet describing to his mistress the effect of her beauty on him speaks thus (if you will allow me to render into literal prose his mystic song):

"I know not if it be the reflected light of its author which the soul perceives, or if from the memory, or from the mind, any other beauty shines through into the heart; or if in the soul yet beams and glows a bright ray of its preexistence, leaving of itself I know not what burning, which leads me to complain. That which I feel, and that which I see, and that which guides me, is not with me; nor know I well where to find it in me, and it seems as if another showed it to me. This, lady, befel me when I first beheld you, that a bitter sweet, a yes and no moved me." [18]

This ambiguity which touches the springs of wonder in the

---

[16] "Every work of genius . . . shining ether" (B, 136).
[17] D, 18.
[18] Cf. Emerson's translation in A, 132–133, from *Rime di Michelagnolo Buonarroti il Vecchio* . . . ed. Giambattista Biagioli (Paris, 1821), p. 7.

soul at the contemplation of beauty; this feeling of *relationship* to that which is at the same time new and strange; this confusion which at the same time says, It is my own, and, It is not my own — is not less remarkable in regard to the works of genius. Talent draws and experiments and the soul says, That is brave, but not right: You have great merit, no doubt, but I know you not: you help me not: you speak not to me. Genius grasps the pencil, and with sure audacity goes daring, daring on, new and incalculable ever, and the Soul attentive greets each stroke with entire welcome, and says, That is it: It is true; It is true. Its tone, its deed, its song none can predict, not even genius itself. Shakspeare we cannot account for. No history, no "life and times," solves the insoluble problem. I cannot slope things to him so as to make him less steep and precipitous; so as to make him one of many. Inferior poets who give us pleasure, we can see, wrote things which we might and should also write, were we a little more favored by time and circumstance; a little cleverer. But Shakspeare, as Coleridge says, is as unlike his contemporaries as he is unlike us.[19] His style is his own. And so is genius ever total, and not mechanically composable. It stands there, a beautiful, unapproachable whole, like a pinetree or a strawberry, alive, perfect, yet inimitable, nor can we find where to lay the first stone, which given, we could build the arch. Phidias and the great Greeks who cut the Elgin marbles and the Apollo and Laocoon, belong to the same exalted category with Shakspear and Homer.[20]

3. As one more sign of the deep aboriginal nature of genius and its perfect accord with all the highest elements of spirit, another trait is its *love*. Genius is always humane, affectionate, sportful. Always it is gentle. It has been observed that there is always somewhat feminine in the face of men of genius. Hence the perfect safety we feel whenever genius is entrusted with political or ecclesiastical power. There is no fanaticism as long as there is the creative muse. Genius is a charter of illimitable freedom and as long as I hear one graceful modulation of wit I know the genial soul and do not smell fagots. The Bunyan, the Behmen is

[19] Cf. *Specimens of the Table Talk of the Late Samuel Taylor Coleridge*, 2 vols. in 1 (New York, 1835), II, 64, 150–152.
[20] "Shakspeare we cannot . . . and Homer" (D, 18–19, where Goethe is cited instead of "Inferior poets who give us pleasure").

nearer far to Rabelais and Montaigne than to Bloody Mary and Becket and the Inquisition.[21] It is a just saying of Scaliger: "Never was a man a poet, or a lover of the works of poets who had not his heart in the right place." [22] They are not tainted by the worst company. Genius hath an immunity from the worst times and drawing its life from that which is out of time and place is serene and glad amid bigots and juntoes. I think if literary history be observed it will be found that the most devout persons [are] the freest speakers in reference to divine things, as Luther, Melancthon, More, Fuller, Herbert, Milton, whose words are an offence to the pursed mouths which make formal prayers; and beyond the word they are freethinkers also. We trust genius; we trust its integrity. Its praise is praise; its religion, sincere. And so we prize the devotion, the moral sentiment which flames aloft even amid licence and nonsense in Chaucer, and in Shakspeare's broadest comedy. I believe that we shall often find a covert, unexpressed association in our own minds of names that minister to Faith, that would shock the squeamish ear of men that judge by appearance. And this will no wise appear strange to any one who considers what I may here affirm as the highest statement at which we can arrive concerning genius, that every work of pure genius will satisfy the demands of Taste, Virtue, and Science, or, in other words, is charged with the elements of beauty, goodness, and truth. If it lack either of these elements so much genius does it lack.

4. To add one more to these traits of this brave spontaneous life I may say that Genius is always representative. The men of genius are watchers set on the towers to report of their outlook to you and me. Do not describe him as detached and aloof: if he is, he is no genius. Genius is the most communicative of all things: the man of genius the most frank and sincere confessor of all his experience. The man of genius apprises us not of his wealth but of the commonwealth.[23] And so I think all worthy men feel a

---

[21] "There is no fanaticism . . . Inquisition" (C, 295). Jakob Böhme (1575–1624), a German mystic, is described by Emerson in *Lectures*, II, 92, as a shepherd and cobbler who led a contemplative life after seeing visions.

[22] T, 59, in French. *JMN*, VI, 341, footnote 66, cites *Scaligerana*, 2 vols. (Amsterdam, 1740), II, 140. Joseph Justus Scaliger (1540–1609) was a French scholar and critic.

[23] Cf. "The Poet," W, III, 5.

warm brotherhood to the seers that are left in the land. If Collins,
if Burns, if our American painter and our American poet is in the
world we have more tolerance and more love for the changing
sky, the mist, the rain, the bleak, overcast day, the indescribable
sunrise, and the immortal stars. If we believed no poet survived
on the planet nature would sometimes be tedious.[24] The very
highest merit of the poet is always his profounder sympathy with
human nature than ours. The reason why he is alone; why we are
slow to share his thought; is, because he deserts our customs and
conventions to drink deeper of the thought which as yet we have
hardly tasted. He commends it to our lips. When we have learned
its wholesomeness and life, we shall do him justice. The true bard
has always this consolation in his pursuits, that if they do not interest all men now, yet they will sooner or later. However alone,
or in what small minority he may now stand, every man will, one
day, recall his image with grateful and honorable remembrance.
The best verse I think that Shelley has written is that which
paints the skylark,

> Like a poet hidden
> In the light of thought
> Singing hymns unbidden
> Till the world is brought
> To sympathy with hopes and fears it heeded not.[25]

Whose wit was Homer's? and whose Virgil's? Whose was Bunyan's, Defoe's and Cervantes' and Newton's? Whose was it not?
To whom in the swarming nations did not the joy and music and
perception of these masters belong?

I know no more striking instance of the representative character of genius than we have in the rare fact of genuine eloquence.
The orator masters us by being our tongue. By simply saying what
we would but cannot say, he tyrannises over our wills and affections. The high exercises of this power are indeed rare; but a
quite analogous example is familiar to us in our popular assemblies. As it was happily said of Sir James Scarlett, that the reason
of his extraordinary success with juries was that "there were

---

[24] "If Collins . . . be tedious" (B, 16, modified).
[25] "To a Skylark," lines 36–40; C, 22.

twelve Scarletts in the jury-box,"[26] so he who can say without hitch or hindrance that which is boiling in the bosom of all men, is the poet and master of the crowd. We have all read this lesson at Faneuil Hall time and again. Join the dark, irregular, thickening groups that gather in the old house when fate hangs on the vote of the morrow. As the crowd grows and the hall fills behold that solid block of life; few old men: mostly young and middle aged, with shining heads and swoln veins. Much of the speaking shall no doubt be slovenly and tiresome but this excited multitude predominates; is all the time interlocutor; and the air grows electric; and the bucket goes up and down according to the success of the speaker. The pinched, wedged, elbowed, sweltering assembly, as soon as the speaker loses their ear by the tameness of his harangue, feel sorely how ill-accommodated they are, and begin to forget all politics and patriotism, and attend only to themselves and the coarse outcries made all around them. Each man in turn is lifted off his feet as the press sways now this way, now that. They back, push, resist and fill the hall with cries of tumult. The speaker stops; the moderator persuades, commands, entreats. The speaker gives way. At last the chosen man rises, the soul of the people, in whose bosom beats audibly the common heart. With his first words he strikes a note which all know; his word goes to the right place; as he catches the light spirit of the occasion his voice alters, vibrates, pierces the private ear of every one; the mob quiets itself somehow, — every one being magnetized, — and the house hangs suspended on the lips of one man. Each man whilst he hears thinks he too can speak; and in the pauses of the orator bursts forth the splendid voice of four or five thousand men in full cry, the grandest sound in nature. If a dull speaker come again, instantly our poor wedges begin to feel their pains and strive and cry.[27]

And as the humblest hearer feels under that spell that he too could speak, so it is always the effect of genius to communicate

[26] In C, 145, Emerson attributes this statement to Fonblanque, presumably the editor of the London *Examiner*, Albany Fonblanque. James Scarlett, 1st baron Abinger (1769–1844), had a highly successful career as a lawyer before entering politics.

[27] "Join the dark . . . strive and cry" (C, 227–228, modified, where Emerson records his visit to a political rally at Faneuil Hall in November 1837).

its life to our torpid powers, to inspire a boundless confidence in the resources of the human mind. But for them we should be cowards and sleepers. To them we owe the great facts, and the laws, and the works of art, and the sweet and sublime songs that establish, instruct, and decorate this human life. Genius gave us astronomy, and navigation, the arts, and the bible. But to all her gifts genius adds one which makes all the rest of no esteem: An infinite hope. Genius counts all its miracles poor and short. Its own idea genius never executed. The Iliad, the Hamlet, the Doric column, the Roman arch, the Gothic minster, the Beethoven anthem, when they are ended, the master casts behind him impatient and ashamed. How sinks the song in the waves of melody that the Universe pours over his soul! Before that gracious infinite, out of which he drew these few strokes, how poor and thin and dead they look, though the praises of the world attend them. From the triumphs of his art the master turns with his heart and soul to this greater defeat. Let those admire who will. With deep homage and joy he sees himself to be capable of a beauty which eclipses all that his hands have done, — all that human hands have done. Immense is now his ambition: immense his trust. What he did, was given him to do; he wist not of it; but lo! before him, all Nature awaits, and will give itself unto him.

6

The Protest

Delivered in Boston at the Masonic Temple on January 16, 1839, and as the third lecture in the Concord, Massachusetts, series on April 3, this lecture seems not to have been read elsewhere. The manuscript is still sewn and in good condition. The pencilled page numbers are not Emerson's. The opening paragraphs and another leaf are on different paper, and there are numerous corrections, including the final paragraph, in pencil. For an alternate opening, probably never used, see textual notes. Little of this anticipation of "Circles" and "The Transcendentalist" has been printed elsewhere.

DR. JOHNSON thought there were no men of entirely sane mind; that every man was tainted with some vein of extravagance which spoiled the harmony of his character.[1] We hear this remark confirmed in common opinion and conversation every day. How few sanities! how few well-principled, well-balanced characters! Yet is every man and every woman in the planet a new experiment, to be and exhibit the full and perfect soul, and so we may count near a thousand million contemporary experiments. For notwithstanding the extreme paucity of men who meet our judgment, our conscience, and our aspirations, — every thing testifies our instinctive belief that this grand hope proposes itself to every individual; that all men live from the same soul, and that each is prompted unceasingly to represent in his life all its will.

We analyse Genius and portray it as known to us in a few men who have suffered the great Intellect, which gives to all what thought they have, to speak through them unobstructed. But this very love and admiration which they draw after them, indicates

---

[1] Cf. *Rasselas*, chapter XLIV.

the presence of the same divine energy in each of us. What is this love of genius, but genius imperfect? We understand it, because it is our own. Here and there it finds a purer organ and it speaks out intelligible to every ear and arouses mankind with its creative teaching. All men hearken; all men greet it; it creates and establishes its own modes, tastes, schools. What it does is called good; what it hates is called evil; and its empire is despotic for a thousand years.

This is the history of the few who are emphatically separated from others as men of genius, those, that is, who from a finer organization, yield freer passage to the universal soul, those who have succeeded, who have not only sought but found. But what is the history of the remainder; of the immense majority; of men and women who have not yet made their mark; in whom unfavorable organization, unfavorable circumstance, hereditary disease, or sensual indulgence block up the channels through which the soul pours itself in full stream to its objects? These are fired with the same thought but it is too ineffectual a flame.

Then arise new and painful appearances. The soul prompts them also to create their usages and words and works. But the world resists them at every step. The law of the mind is one: the law of the members is another. God the Soul says one thing; the whole world says or seems to say another. Then arises War. The prophets call the word of the Lord that was given them a Burden. How shall it not be said? Yet how shall it be said to deaf and unwilling ears?

Hence arises how much of the tragedy of life! There is heaviness on the brow of youth and its heart is heavy. There is ill-concealed diversity of aim, of religion, of theory of life between every newly arrived soul and the existing population of the planet and it is always breaking out afresh. And the nature and limits of this Dissension I shall endeavor to expose.

The dissonance of which I speak is involuntary and necessary. It is a necessity flowing from the nature of things. What is the front the world always shows to the young spirit? Strange to say, The Fall of Man. The Fall of Man is the first word of history and the last fact of experience. In the written annals or in the older

tradition of every nation this dark legend is told of the depravation of a once pure and happy society. And in the experience of
every individual somewhat analogous is recognized.

In all our reasonings respecting society this is assumed, that
there has been violation and consequent penalty and loss, to
bring things into the confessedly bad pass where they are. What
is the account to be given of this persuasion that has taken such
deep root in all minds? What but this that it is an universal fact
that man is always in his actual life lapsing from the Commandments of the Soul? His enemy is indeed very near him as the co-
hort of angels in the Garden of Eden detected the Snake "squat
close by the ear of Eve." [2] There is somewhat infirm and retreating in every action; a pause of self-praise; a second thought. He
has done well and he says I have done well and lo! this is the beginning of ill. He is encumbered by his own past. His past hour
mortgages the present hour. Yesterday is the enemy of Today.
His deed hinders him from doing, his thought from thinking; his
former virtue is apt to become an impediment to new virtue. The
life of the soul in men is ordinarily not continuous and sustained
but impulsive. But the life of the senses is continuous and usurping.

Each individual is born sane. [His] instincts are true. His affections pure. His senses are keen; his intellect curious; he tastes
the knowledge of good and evil. But he finds in society a nurture
for his vice which it does not offer to his virtue. His vice is bribed.
His virtue sad and unsaluted in society. His virtue accuses
their customs. The fact is very strange and the cause of it perhaps
too deep in our constitution and too subtle to be explored, to
know why we are such slaves of Custom; why it is so much easier
to repeat an old, than to invent a new act; why we decline creation; why we dread to speak our own speech; and even to pray
our own prayer; and had rather find a proverb to express our
thought, or a text as the vehicle of our worship. Why, with the
world before us, we slip into the narrowest lane or path already
cut, though it lead through the back side of cities and common
sewers, rather than incur the toil of choosing our own, though we

[2] Milton, *Paradise Lost*, IV, 800.

might walk on mountain and woodland by the cataract and the seashore.

But always we crutch ourselves on other men's thinking; on the accepted virtues; rather than obey those youthful impulses which prompt us to write our own law. So we go back to the deed we have done; to the virtue we have known; to the word we have said; rather than venture again into new action. You must not invite the veteran soldier to the breach once more. He is counting his old scars and slaying the long ago slain. You must not propose new thoughts to the old scholar: he has fought his literary quarrels; labelled and ticketed all his opinions. You must not propose strenuous self-denial and the regeneration of society to the saint of sixty years; he cannot understand what you mean; he is so busy with preserving the dignity and reputation of those same virtues of the last century, of which the world somehow seems to be getting unmindful. He must write his memoirs.

It seems as if it would be a blessing if you could steep the man in the waters of some river of oblivion, — get this crotchet of something he has done, fairly out of his head, and there would be some hope for his humility and his vigor. It is just the same in letters. Things to be said are infinite yet as soon as we begin to write, we imitate some old thing. "The Classics," "the Classics"! forsooth; as if there were only twenty or fifty books to be called books to set the pitch for all thought, and as if every man was not a new world and his thinking new, entire, and perfect. Ah me! Is there any tragedy so dire as this deliquium, of this falling back, this epilepsy, this old age? that virtue should pause; and intellect pause, and decease out of the body, *it* remaining to drivel on for the pleasure of the senses. See that all that has been done in the planet was done by young men. We mislead ourselves by talking of the ancients till we almost think they were bearded Methusalems. They were young men too. It is said the great geniuses have done their best things before thirty. Alexander, Scipio, Raphael, Sidney, Napoleon, are all that occur to me but I have seen a longer list.[3] After thirty a man begins to feel the walls of his condition which before the soul did overflow — asks himself if he have not done something that he may sit down and enjoy. He would enjoy

[3] "See that all . . . longer list" (D, 244, expanded).

his fame. By looking outward at things, his small action looks large; by comparing his acts with the acts of others, and not with the commandment of Reason.

This pause is fatal. Sense pauses: the soul pauses not. In its world is incessant movement. Genius has no retrospect. Virtue has no memory. And that is the law for man. Live without interval: if you rest on your oars, if you stop, you fall. He only is wise who thinks now; who reproduces all his experience for the present exigency; as a man stands on his feet only by a perpetual play and adjustment of the muscles. A dead body or a statue cannot be set up in the upright posture without support.[4] You must live even to stand.

Well now magnify this by seeing the same influence on millions with the same result, and you will have the aspect which society exhibits at any one moment to the young soul. Society loves the past; society desponds; sneers; serves; sits; it talks from the memory or from the senses and not from the soul. It is poor-spirited; it cannot bear freedom; it craves a rider for its neck and says like the old French noblesse in the service of the new imperial court, "You know one must serve somebody."[5] It pillows itself in usages and forms until the man is killed with kindness. Its tediousness is torture to a masculine and advancing temper. Poor Napoleon home at Paris from his fierce Italian campaigns to be crowned emperor could scarce sustain the ennui and insipidity of the coronation and did nothing but gape all day.[6]

This old age; this ossification of the heart; this fat in the brain; this degeneracy; is the Fall of Man.

But somehow or other Life will live; soul does not die; God still is; still bright, still new, springs evermore the fresh ray of thought, the bounding pulse of virtue. The old, halt, numb, bed-rid world must ever be plagued with this incessant soul. In the eternal soul lives the central protest against every abomination and whatsoever be the last crime or folly in which society falls, instantly out of some one heart a wild denouncing voice is heard to condemn.

[4] "Live without interval . . . without support" (D, 163).
[5] Cf. D, 46.
[6] Cf. C, 258.

By resistance to this strong Custom and strong Sense, — by obedience to the soul, is the world to be saved. The Redemption from this ruin is lodged in the heart of Youth. The Saviour is as eternal as the harm. The heart of Youth is the regenerator of society; the perpetual hope; the incessant effort of recovery. To every young man and young woman, the world puts the same question, "Wilt thou become one of us?" And to this question the soul in each one of them says heartily, No. Well for it if it can abide by its Protest. It is the voice of virtue. It is the breath of Hope; it is the pledge of God. The world has no interest so deep as to cherish that resistance. No matter though this young heart do not yet understand itself; do not know well what it wants; knows nothing but that it is ill at ease, sorely pinched by your conventions, and does not like Dr. Fell; and so contents itself with saying No; No; No; to unamiable tediousness; — or breaks out into sallies of extravagance; cherish it nevertheless. There is hope in extravagance; there is none in Routine.[7]

There is indeed no heart to which in some form this great question does not come home and to most in smitings of sorrow and pain. To one the crisis is veiled in an exclusively religious form, and he calls it a profession of religion and a renunciation of the world. To another it comes as to Bacon, Newton, Galileo, in a philosophical Reform, a war against Ignorance and Rules, and a manifesto for Nature. To another in a political form when despotism of some sort has so driven men to the wall that all the religion of the Heart seems to consist in the love of liberty. To another in the question of choice of pursuit or the preference of poverty to dishonest gain; to another in some practical abuse against which he takes up arms.

Look around society at any period and see where the youth, the pith, and heart of life is. Is it with, or is it against the institutions? Look at the unfolding of every young man and young

---

[7] D, 25. John Fell (1625–1686), Dean of Christ Church, Oxford, was the subject of the well-known translation by Tom Brown (1663–1704) of Martial, *Epigrams*, I, 32:

> I do not love you, Dr. Fell,
> But why I cannot tell;
> But this I know full well,
> I do not love you, Dr. Fell.

woman in whom any eminent degree of moral and intellectual force appears. In proportion to that degree — more or less, you shall find them in what the world calls a false position; you shall find them contending actively or passively against the opinions, practices, standards, that are current in the community. The institutions of society come across each ingenuous and original soul in some different point. One feels the jar in property; one in marriage; one in money; one in social conventions; one in the church; one in slavery; one in war. One assails alcohol, one animal food, [one] domestic hired service. Each feels it in some one and a different point according to his own circumstance and history, and for a long time does not see that it is a central falsehood which he is contending against, and that his protest against a particular superficial falsehood, will surely ripen with time into a deeper and universal grudge.[8]

Every reformer is partial and exaggerates some one grievance. You may even feel that there is somewhat ridiculous in his tenacious oppugnation of some one merely local and as it were cutaneous disorder as if he dreamed, good simple soul, that were this one great wrong righted a new era would begin. For men are not units but poor mixtures. They defend for a long time doctrines wholly foreign from their nature and connexion of opinions and which whilst for moments and externally they espouse — from year to year and in life and soul they reject and abominate. They accept how weary a load of tradition from their elders and more forcible neighbors.[9]

Nevertheless respect the great central impulse of reform even in weak and single and shameful hands. If the reformer is earnest; if there is a little virtue at the bottom of the heart, he will cleanse himself as he cleanses society. By and by as the divine effort of creation, of growth, begins in them, new loves, new aversions take effect, — the first radiation of their own soul amidst things. Yet each of these outbursts of light which make the epochs of growth is partial and leaves abundance of traditions still in force. Each soul hath its own idols, and by an Idol I mean any thing which a man honors, which the constitution of his mind does not

[8] "The institutions of society . . . grudge" (D, 231).
[9] "For men are not units . . . forcible neighbors" (D, 163).

necessitate him to honor. But each new influx from the centre shall classify more facts and will show us idols in how many things which now we esteem part and parcel of our constitution and lot in nature. Property, Government, Books, Systems of Education, and of Religion, successively detach themselves from the growing Spirit.[10]

Let us look a little nearer at the exercises of the unfolding man and see how he applies himself to the facts which the world offers to all.

How generous and noble is the position of the young! Who does not respect it? Who could excuse another spirit? this sovereign freedom, this nonchalance of genius, this entire independence of all mean obligations, this as yet uncommitted hand, unpledged vote, this unconquered power. What shall we not expect from it, when it is put forth? To what good do they not feel a right? They alone have dominion of the world, for they walk in it with a free step; they look dominion and their claims have never yet been rebuked and denied. Each young soul looks with a kind of commiseration on the proprietors of the land in which he walks, as the tenantry who keeps his grounds productive and beautiful. Haughty and graceful they seek in the woods or on the seashore or in the throngs of the town only the verification of the songs, the poems, the romances, and the philosophy of their private study. He represents the Soul and nothing less. He holds cognisance of every thing human and divine. He is of no party, but is the patron of every just cause, of every liberal opinion. He is pledged to himself to make his life an image in every part beautiful. He desires to exhibit what is beautiful to a community besotted with the procuring of the useful. He is very little solicitous like the artisan or even like the successful artist to finish an admirable production that may stand as the document of his skill and genius. He is solicitous only to be whole and true and fair himself, and strangely negligent of producing anything. He fears lest the artist be formed at the expense of the man.[11]

And is he not just in his view? All literature, all art is really

[10] "By and by as the divine . . . growing Spirit" (D, 163–164).
[11] "Each young soul . . . of the man" (cf. D, 212–213, where the "young soul" is identified as Thoreau).

below and not above the aspirations of the youth. Nothing that is done satisfies him. He wishes the perfect, the illimitable. He finds in it instantly the bonds of the Finite. What you have done is well but he likes his imagination better. He wishes to receive his thought today from the great God, and not record it, nor paint it, nor build it, nor in any manner mar its fair proportion, nor husband it as if it were the last birth of time, but in a full confidence that there are new thoughts for tomorrow also, and the next day, and an opening immensity for all such as greatly live. And hence, as the poets say, in the first age, the sons of God printed no epics, carved no stone, painted no canvas, built no railroad, for the sculpture, the poetry, the music and architecture were in the man. Bolts and bars do not seem to him the most exalted or exalting of our institutions. And what other spirit reigns in our intellectual works? We have literary property. The very recording a thought betrays a distrust that there is any more or much more as good for us. If we felt that the Universe was ours, that we dwelled in Eternity and advanced into all wisdom we should be less covetous of these sparks and cinders. Why should we covetously build St. Peters if we had the seeing eye which beheld all the radiance of beauty and majesty in the matted grass and the overarching boughs? Why should a man spend years in carving an Apollo, who looked Apollos into the landscape with every glance he threw? [12] And are there not men whose manners have the same essential splendor as the simple and awful sculpture on the friezes of the Parthenon? [13]

These and such as these are the thoughts of the young, the new pupil of the world as he compares your boasted masterpieces of art or your best action with the wild and unconfinable excellence. Alas that this graceful and dignified self-trust and trust in others, should be doomed to so prompt a downfall that this free and noble creature, — son of God though he be, should stop presently to be a hack of society; the mean fellow of mean men; should forget the dreams of his youth, first, in succumbing to the sins of others; and then, in practising the same.

[12] "And hence . . . he threw" (D, 213).
[13] "History," W, II, 16; D, 206; see also C, 124.

Alas too that friends, companions, and society at large should look so sourly on these blameless aspirations.

Is it not the interest of mankind that to such a rare soul as is made to see beauty and announce it, some charter should be given and not the same culture applied and the same demands made as are made on the crowd? Is not a beholder of beauty and a lover of the infinite as much wanted as a scribe or a seamstress?

Besides; this impatient youth, impatient of the ways and forms and works around him, will not remain inactive, a dreamer. This grand idea that lies like the sky around the soul tends ever to organize itself in institutions to create social systems, laws, religions, customs, arts, professions, books, and ceremonies that shall truly express it. So much the more he suffers in his first rude comparisons of the unshackled Ideal with the strait prison-like limits of the Actual. How galled is he by the first infractions of his right. He meets in sharp terms presently the claims of property. And who, he asks with indignation, are these proprietors who compel me, to whom as much as any the whole world belongs, to walk in a strip of road and crowd me out of all the rest of God's earth? I must not get over the fence? but to the building of that fence, I was no party. Suppose some great proprietor, before I was born, had bought up the whole globe. So had I been hustled out of nature. He will not listen to the explanations of the political economist who would show him that the existing arrangements go to secure to every man what he can earn.[14] He forthwith resolves, as soon as he comes into the counsels of power, to divide the globe anew. So is it with the choice of a pursuit. The prudent, wrinkled friends admire when this long holiday of books and walks and young company is to end and John is to choose his employment and settle down to it. Employment! I am now employed in the gravest and most universal manner. I shall never desist from doing these same things you see me now do. But your living, my son: How will you earn that? You do not wish to owe your bread to another, any longer. Oh no, but a very little will suffice. I can go without all your fine things. Bread and water will content me, and the garret I would not exchange for a palace.

[14] "He meets . . . can earn" (D, 213, which is an account of an exchange between Emerson and Thoreau during a walk to Walden Pond in November 1838).

Only let me convince you that my plans are not ridiculous; are possible; are wise; wiser than yours.

The world of life, of society, of charity, of trade, of manufacture, the handicrafts, the professions, it is very plain ought to stand in such coincidence with the faculties and whole nature of man, that each youth and maiden could readily enter the press and assume at once tasks which taxed their powers without violating their integrity. But whether it be that the world only takes thought for the already existing facts, and each new soul is a quite new and unprecedented energy; or, whether the organization of society consults for the senses only, — it is too plain, that, each good soul that enters nature, if it be of great activity and virtue, finds itself one too many, an unlooked-for guest and that [it] is not easy to put itself in harmony with men and things and find a labor quite adapted to its genius, but is fain, instead, to do, for the most part, somewhat not congenial, for its bread, — and make itself amends by going quite apart from its day-labor to other works for its solace.

With the like proud discontent does our young Hamlet refuse the opportunities of society. Society, he says, should be a congress of sovereigns, without the pride, but with the power.[15] If people were all true, we should see in society the half-gods whose traces are yet left us in poetry and in art, — not yet quite obliterated; those sacred forms careering in contest or in love, in the still grand remains of Greek art.[16] But now there is no grandeur in character and of course none in association. Conversation is ceremonial, no more. If people were all true we should feel that all persons were infinitely deep natures. But now in a crowd of company you have no variety of persons, only one person. Say what you will, to whom you will, — all shall render one and the same answer, without thought, without heart, quite aloof from the experience of the parties, a conversation of the lips.[17] If people would live extempore nobody would be uninteresting, but they live and talk from their memory instead of from their impulses.[18] Put me not, he says, in society where I know every word they will

[15] D, 192.
[16] D, 38.
[17] "If people were all true we should feel . . . of the lips" (D, 192).
[18] D, 118.

say: have heard them say it forty times: can say it by heart.[19] Society cheers not me: only dispirits and suffocates. They meet only on low grounds, for low ends, for sport, for feasting, for idleness, not for provocation and emulous love. They are less together, than they are apart. They descend to meet.[20] In proportion to the nobleness of men nowadays, are they solitary, and in proportion to their virtue are they negligent of the charities of the day. Why should you descend to their measure, instead of raising them up to yours?[21] The great make me great. If we lived with heroes, what would be more natural, easy, and agreeable, to every body, than to live with majesty, silence, and sacrifice? But we have fallen amidst gossips; and good nature ensnares us not to seem wiser than the whole world; and, finding that we have the same capacity of attention to trifles with others, we will consider them since they please to, and magnify them and slide into infatuation.[22] You say, I go too much alone. Yes, but Heaven knows it is from no disrelish for love and fellow working. I shun society to the end of finding society. I quit a society which is no longer one. I repudiate the false out of love of the true.[23] I go alone that I may meet my brother as I ought. I would I could tell you with what joy I hear in the midst of society some word that nothing but austerest solitude and conversation with God, with love, and death, could ever have uttered. Such too is the sincerest joy of fine assemblies to meet in its princes and princesses some authentic token of the Eternal Beauty.[24]

But beside this unanswerable appeal to consciousness, do you not yourselves betray the same discontent. Behold in the most unexpected quarters confirmation is supplied to these flourishes of the idealists. For see that your hard, trenchant man of the world whose heart is a millstone in the ways of trade, as soon as he leaves his ledger and shop behind him, pleases himself with establishing the most generous and self-sacrificing relations of a gentleman with gentlemen. He bids his friend command his

[19] D, 16.
[20] Cf. "The Over-Soul," W, II, 278; D, 208; above, p. 19.
[21] "In proportion to the nobleness . . . up to yours" (D, 186).
[22] "If we lived . . . infatuation" (D, 61).
[23] "You say, I go . . . of the true" (D, 25, modified).
[24] "I would I could . . . Eternal Beauty" (D, 138).

house, his servants, his horses, all that he has, and puts his pride in establishing with a certain number precisely those relations which the visionary philanthropist would establish betwixt all. And always the great-hearted children of fortune, the Caesars, Cleopatras, Alcibiadeses, Essexes, and Sidneys, within their own proud pale, have treated fortune and the popular estimates with a certain defiance and contempt. Irregular glimpses they had of the real Good and Fair which added a more than royal loftiness to their behavior and to their dealing with houses and lands.[25]

Presently come to the youth the questions of opinion. And he reads in many books but cannot find his own opinion in any. Neither in philosophy, neither in religon. Behold, he says, a man comes now into the world a slave; he comes saddled with twenty or forty centuries. Asia has arrearages and Egypt arrearages not to mention all the subsequent history of Europe and America. He is not his own man but the hapless bondman of time with these continents and aeons of prejudice to carry on his back. It is grown so bad that he cannot carry the mountain any longer and be a man. There must be a revolution. Let it come and let one come free into the earth to walk by truth alone.[26] The men that made the books were such as I. Obviously too the whole value of the books is their fidelity to my nature. For only that book can we read which recites to me something that is already in my mind. Why then do you so overestimate a book? You are yourself the book's book. Its worth is always your worth. It is but an echo, a mirror, a shadow. I will read myself and there find the libraries.

In the like spirit he slights all the accepted means and modes of knowledge and action. Opposing one and the same argument, his own unsatisfied Idea — to all the parts in the structure of society, to the forms of law, of religion, charity, of education, of social intercourse.

And truly these fantastic young persons might find a friend in each one of us, might find in the experience of every old stager of society the tally of his own. For consider this love of nature, this passion for the picturesque, this passion for art, this love of travelling. Pray what do they all denote? What is the passionate

[25] "And always the great-hearted . . . and lands" (D, 165–166).
[26] "Behold, he says . . . truth alone" (C, 287).

love of nature that distinguishes all men of a poetic and susceptible constitution but an accusation of Society? In the garden the
eye watches the flying cloud and the distant woods but turns
from the village. The statesman, the jurist, the merchant, weary
of the routine of business and of towns, hides himself in the country. It is a refreshment to the eyes to look at a poultry yard. He
hears the hen cluck and sees her stepping round with perfect
complacency but mark him if a man goes by: his countenance
changes; there seems a shade of sorrowful feeling. If a friend, if
a man of genius or virtue, if a hero passes, then he rejoices and
can no longer see hens. Children are beautiful but few men are.[27]
The truth is Nature is loved by what is best in us. It is loved as
the city of God although or rather because there is no citizen. If
there were good men there would never be this rapture in nature.
If the king is in the palace nobody looks at the walls. It is when
he is gone and the house is filled with gipsies that we turn from
the people with haste to find relief in the splendid men that are
suggested by the pictures and architecture.[28] Carlyle and others
who complain of the sickly separation of the beauty of nature in
this age from the thing to be done do not see that our hunting of
the picturesque is inseparable from our protest against false society. Man is fallen but Nature is unfallen.[29] When history awakens
such emotion as the landscape does now we shall say never a
word of the landscape. "John Thelwall," says Coleridge at table,
"had something very good in him. We were once sitting in a
beautiful recess in the Quantocks when I said to him, 'Citizen
John, this is a fine place to talk treason in.' 'Nay, Citizen Samuel,'
replied he, 'it is rather a place to make a man forget that there is
any necessity for treason.' " [30]

In the actual business and conflicts of life few men are entirely at ease. Few feel that they are doing what is commensurate
with their powers and what they should always desire to do. Most

[27] "It is a refreshment . . . men are" (C, 298, modified).
[28] "The truth is Nature . . . and architecture" (D, 185).
[29] "The truth is Nature . . . is unfallen" ("Nature," W, III, 178); "Carlyle and others . . . is unfallen" (D, 230).
[30] *Table Talk*, I, 129; D, 230. John Thelwall (1764–1834) was tried, with Horne Tooke, for high treason in 1794 and acquitted.

men are looking beyond to something else which they at some time shall be at liberty to embrace — or are casting longing glances aside to some dear asylum when this unfit turmoil is over. One to nature, to science, to gardens, to astronomy; one to music; one to libraries and poetry.

It seems as if a natural life might combine with its daily tasks such enjoyments as these, and the consciousness of this infirmity of purpose in their own life should qualify the condemnation which they bestow on the discontent and the wild theories of youth.

Now this hostile attitude of young persons toward society is nowise pleasant to society. Nay often it makes them very undesireable companions to their friends: querulous, opinionative, impracticable; and, furthermore, it makes them unhappy in their own solitude. If it continue too long, it makes shiftless and morose men. Yet is it, though not universally yet for the most part, an unavoidable preliminary to vigorous and effective action in any sort. For it is a temporary state. It endures only whilst society seems a thing worthy of great respect, whilst it retains an excess of influence and daunts the youth by insisting with all its authority upon his adhesion, — whilst his soul points another and contrary way. Astonished at this irreconcileable diversity, he stands for a time suspended, and is only able to resist society with his sturdy negative. After a brief period, he renounces his opposition and overcome by the multitude of voices, by his own treacherous senses, he compromises. He gets weary of struggling against the stream alone; he postpones for a time hostilities. He gets amused and busy with a trade, a calling, politics or pleasure. He makes a feebler and feebler refusal and at last decides that his opposition was very youthful and unadvised and gives in his adhesion to Old Times and the wisdom of our ancestors, and goes down stream to darkness and to death.

On the other hand if the warlike defence he has attempted is made good by new impulses from within, if he give place to the soul and worship it, if he will not be preached nor cajoled out of his position of perpetual inquiry, if praise from the young on his accomplishments, and taunts from the old on his inefficiency, his homelessness, his pride of opinion, are equally lost on him, in his hushed adoration of that oracle more sacred, more grand, forever dear which speaks in the silence of the passions, and rebukes the babblers of puny taste and of false religion; if he suffers no horizon to fall on the illimitable space; but before the awful power which so slowly uncovers his nature and hope to his curiosity and faith covenants himself to keep in lowliness the law: to bow the knee to no Baal, fine with what jewels, mystic with what poetry soever, but to keep erect the head which was given him, erect against the physical and metaphysical terrors of the universe: then he has immortal youth.[31] This heart will be warm under the frosts of a thousand winters, and apt to warm others as long and longer. Then it is presently revealed to him how he should live and work. Quite naturally his own path opens before him; his object appears; his aim becomes simple and, losing his dread of society which kept him dumb and paralytic, he begins to work according to his faculty. He has done protesting: now he begins to affirm: all art affirms: and with every new stroke with greater serenity and joy.

Such has been the uniform history of genius.

Michel Angelo was reduced to the dilemma of genius when he had procured fresco painters from Florence to execute his designs in the Sistine Chapel (he not understanding the art of laying the colors in mortar). But after he had suffered much mortification day after day from their imperfect and dwarf execution he got into the Chapel early one morning and bolted them all out and tore down all their picture. The painters came to the door, knocked, and waited and complained aloud but Michel would not hear, would not relent. Neither afterwards could they get admission to his house, and they at last returned to Florence full of indignation. Thus he greatly said *No.* He could not help it. Then he went to work and affirmed all over the wall in grand strokes which are there still the wonder of the world.[32]

Luther's mighty No growled through Christendom with longer

[31] "but before the awful power . . . immortal youth" (D, 43).
[32] "Michel Angelo was reduced . . . the world" (D, 16). For the anecdote, recorded in A, 128, see Richard Duppa, *The Life of Michael Angelo Buonarroti,* 2nd ed. (London, 1807), p. 52.

reverberation than the pontifical bolts, and then the stout monk in Eisenach Castle planted himself down to say his own Yes, and unlocked the Bible into the vernacular tongue.[33] Columbus argued sadly wise from court to college against the geography of his time and at last wrote his grand Yes on the furrows of the Ocean with the keel of his galley sailing steadily west day after day, week after week against the prayers, the oaths, and the threats of his mutineers, the only man of his opinion in the world.

As soon as the disappointment at the want of sympathy of society has given place to his increased trust in the justness and perfectness of his own Idea, and in place of looking for help and comfort abroad he has learned to take his own thought for better, for worse as his portion, and to know that though the wide universe is full of good, no kernel of nourishing corn can come to him but through his toil bestowed on that spot of ground which is given him to till; then speedily all rights itself with him.[34] Friendly faces look over the wall into his acre; laborers in all divers crafts show him that they also have one purpose with him, and their works forward each other. His work itself has greater worth and invites him to enlarge its scope, to carry it out on every side to ideal extent, to deck it with poetry, to hallow it with religion, to warm it with love. The more sturdily he adheres to his guiding thought, which of course has its source in central nature and must be true, and discovers each day its fair and smiling fruitage, the more allowance the world gives him. For it is an universal maxim worthy of all acceptation that a man may have that allowance he takes. Take the place and attitude to which you see your unquestionable right and all men acquiesce.[35] The world must be just. It always leaves every man with profound unconcern to set his own rate. Hero or driveller, it meddles not in the matter. It will certainly accept your own measure of your doing and being, whether you sneak about and deny your own name, or

[33] In 1521, after refusing to recant at the Diet of Worms, Luther was held in protective custody for ten months at the Wartburg, overlooking Eisenach. Here he quickly translated the Greek New Testament into German, but his translations of the Old Testment and the Apocrypha were not completed for several years.
[34] Cf. "Self-Reliance," W, II, 46.
[35] "For it is an universal . . . men acquiesce" (D, 87).

101

whether you see your work in the concave sphere of the heaven one with the revolution of the stars.[36] Then dies around him the opposition which looked so formidable. It had no root in things and no stability. He is sure of his point; he is fast rooted. But this when analyzed is made up of such timidities, uncertainties, and no opinions that it is not worth dispersing.[37]

On the whole, then, we think that this crisis in the life of each earnest man, which comes in so forbidding and painful aspect, has nothing in it that need alarm or confound us. It is the inevitable result of the relation of the soul to the existing corruption of society. It puts to the man the question, Will you fulfil the demands of the soul or will you yield yourself to the conventions of the world? In some form the question comes to each. None can escape the challenge. But why need you sit cowering there pale and pouting or why with such a mock tragic air, affect such a discontent and superiority?

There is nothing to fear. If you would obey the soul, obey it. Do your own work, and you shall have leave to do it. The bugbear of society is only such until you have accepted your own law. Then all omens are good; all stars auspicious; all men your allies; all parts of life take order and beauty.

[36] "For it is an universal . . . of the stars" ("Spiritual Laws," W, II, 151); "It always leaves . . . of the stars" (cf. D, 245).
[37] "Then dies around him . . . worth dispersing" (cf. D, 87).

7

Tragedy

This lecture was read in Boston at the Masonic Temple on January 23, 1839, and again at Concord, Massachusetts, on April 24 as the fifth lecture in the series there. The manuscript is complete and still sewn except for three loose leaves of later paper which do not belong with the lecture as read. These perhaps found their way into the manuscript as a result of Emerson's preparation of an extensive selection printed as "The Tragic" in *The Dial*, IV (April 1844), 515–521, and reprinted in 1893 in *Natural History of Intellect* (*W*, XII, 405–417). The pencilled pagination, which includes the loose leaves, is not Emerson's. Aside from the passages in "The Tragic," a brief passage was used in "Compensation" and another in "The Fortune of the Republic." The lecture also contains a poem by Emerson which was published in *The Dial* and collected in *Poems*, 1847, but not printed in *Selected Poems*, 1876, or subsequent collections.

W E HAVE examined in foregoing lectures the outset of the pupil Man, his early teaching, the discipline of the affections, the sallies of the intellect, and the antagonism that appears always to the unfolding of the soul in the actual state of the world, formidable in appearance but tractable and obedient to valor and self-trust.

There remains to be considered the shades of the picture; the nocturnal side of nature. He has seen but half the Universe who never has been shown the House of Pain. It would even seem that this is the flagrant obtrusive side, that as the salt sea covers more than two thirds of the surface of the globe so Sorrow encroaches in Man on Felicity. Care sits close on every mature face; and the conversation of men is a mixture of regrets and apprehensions.

> And who the fool that doth not know
> How bloom and beauty come and go

And how disease and pain and sorrow
May chance today, may chance tomorrow
Unto the merriest of us all? [1]

The common complaint is of the dulness of life. I do not know but it must be confessed that the glance we give at things in a leisure hour is melancholy.[2] With names, and persons, and today's interests, is grief. It does seem too as if history gave no intimation of any society in which despondency came so readily to heart as we see it and feel it in ours. As we see and know it, melancholy cleaves to the English mind in both hemispheres as closely as to the strings of an Aeolian harp. Young men, young women at thirty and even earlier have lost all spring and vivacity and if they fail in their first enterprizes there seems to be no remedial force in nature, no Roman recovery, but the rest of life is rock and shallow.[3]

And whether we are more or less vulnerable, who can without levity or a stony heart slight the audible moanings of the human spirit, victim of so many disasters? No theory of life can have any solidity which leaves out of account the value of Vice, Pain, Disease, Poverty, Insecurity, Disunion, Affection, Fear, and Death.[4]

In the dark hours our existence seems to be a defensive war; a struggle against the encroaching All, which threatens with certainty to engulf us soon, and seems impatient of our little reprieve. How slender is the possession that yet remains to us; how faint the animation! How the spirit seems already to contract its domain, to retire within narrower walls by the loss of memory, leaving what were its planted fields, to erasure and annihilation. Already our own thoughts and words have an alien sound. There is a simultaneous diminution of Hope and of Memory. Projects that once we laughed and leaped to execute, find us now sleepy and preparing to lie down in the snow.[5] And in the bright hours we

---

[1] Ascribed to Byron in CR, 77; under the title "Hurts of Time" these lines are subjoined to six lines from "The Seige of Corinth" and ascribed to Byron in *Parnassus*, p. 138.

[2] "He has seen . . . is melancholy" (cf. "The Tragic," W, XII, 405); "The common complaint . . . is melancholy" (C, 166).

[3] "It does seem too . . . rock and shallow" ("The Fortune of the Republic," W, XI, 532, condensed; D, 103; cf. also C, 166, and B, 117).

[4] "It does seem too . . . and Death" (cf. "The Tragic," W, XII, 406).

[5] "In the dark hours . . . in the snow" (B, 28).

have no courage to spare. We cannot afford to let go any advantages. The riches, the powers of body and mind that we do not need today, are the resources for the calamity that may arrive tomorrow.[6]

Let us then enumerate the tragic elements in our constitution and see what commentary they themselves suggest.

And the first and highest conceivable element of tragedy in life is the belief in Fate or Destiny; that the Order of nature and events is constrained by a law not adapted to man nor man to that, but which holds on its way to the end, blessing him if his wishes chance to lie in the same course, — crushing him if his wishes lie contrary to it, — and careless whether it cheers or crushes him. This is the terrible idea that lies at the foundation of the old Greek tragedy and makes the poor Oedipus and Antigone and Orestes the objects of such hopeless commiseration. They must perish and there is no over god to call to account this hideous Enginery that grinds and thunders and takes them up into its terrific jaws. The same idea is found in India; and any of my audience who read Southey's Curse of Kehama when they were young will perhaps remember the paralyzing terror with which that mythology haunts the imagination. The same thought makes the terror of those pictures from the Bhagavad Gita which have been brought to light by the French savans.[7] The same thought is the Predestination of the Turk.[8] The Arabians tell us that as Solomon, whom they supposed a magician from his superior wisdom, was one day walking with a person in Palestine, his companion said to him with horror, "What hideous spectre is that which approaches us? I don't like his visage. Send me I pray thee to the remotest mountain of India." Solomon complied; and the very moment he was sent off, the spectre arrived. "Solomon," said he, "how came that fellow here? I was to have fetched him

[6] "In the dark hours . . . arrive tomorrow" (cf. "The Tragic," W, XII, 405–406).

[7] Emerson apparently knew the *Bhagavadgita* from the résumé and extracts in Victor Cousin, *Cours de philosophie* (Paris, 1828), and H. G. Linberg's translation of the same book, *Introduction to the History of Philosophy* (Boston, 1832), both of which he owned. He did not see the complete *Bhagavadgita* until 1845. See L, I, lix–lxi, 322; III, 288, 290; VI, 246.

[8] "Let us then enumerate . . . of the Turk" (cf. "The Tragic," W, XII, 406–407).

from the remotest mountain of India." Solomon answered; "Angel of Death, thou wilt find him there." [9] And I think we discover in uneducated, unreflecting persons on whom too the religious sentiment exerts little force, traits of the same superstition, as all the nursery fables betray. If you count the stars you will fall down dead, if you spill the salt, if your fork sticks upright in the floor, if you say Pater Noster backwards, and so on, a several penalty nowise grounded in the nature of the thing but an arbitrary will.

But this terror which deserves the name, and might well benumb the active powers of man into stupid passiveness, can not coexist with reflection; it disappears with civilization and can no more be reproduced than the fear of ghosts which can never go beyond the region of boys and nurses. It is contradistinguished from the doctrine of Philosophical Necessity (it is important to observe) herein; that the last is an Optimism; and therefore the suffering individual finds his good consulted in the good of All, of which he is a part.

But in Destiny, it is not the good of the Whole or the Best Will that is enacted, but only *one particular Will*. Destiny in reality is not a Will at all; but an Immense Whim. And this seems to be the only possible ground of Terror and Despair in the rational mind and of Tragedy in literature. Hence the antique Tragedy which was founded on this faith can never be reproduced.

The next tragic element in life is the hindrance of our private satisfaction by the laws of the world. The law which consults for the race and for nature continually baulks and thwarts the purposes of the individual, and this in the particulars of Disease, Want, Insecurity, Disunion.[10]

Sickness is mean and dispiriting. That the organ should not answer to the impulses of the soul and should be unseasonably lame or languid or aching and a great man be baulked by the weakness of an eye or an eardrum, by an indigestion or a fever! Health is our sound relation to external objects; our sympathy with external being. We prize in our great contemporaries an answering body as in Goethe; and Napoleon; and Humboldt and

---

[9] Dugald Stewart, *Works*, 7 vols. (Cambridge, Mass., 1829), V, 597. Stewart calls it an "Arabian tale, which I quote from the late Mr. Harris." Emerson in Σ,1, ascribes it to "Harris."

[10] "And I think we . . . Disunion" (cf. "The Tragic," *W*, XII, 407–408).

Scott. What tough bodies answered to their unweariable minds! Proportionally annoying is it that man may not in this climate sit down in the grass nor yet on the stone wall in a night of June to see the racing of the liquid lights in the nearing heavens because he has consumption in his side, rheumatism in his shoulder.[11] The swift penalty of torture acute or chronic on each abuse of the organs produces a very large proportion of the suffering in the world.

Want. The radical tragedy of nature seems to be the distinction of More and Less. How can Less not feel the pain? How not feel indignation or malevolence toward More? Look at those who have less faculty and one feels sad and knows not well what to make of it. Almost he shuns their eye; almost he fears they will upbraid God. What should they do? Yet the answer is plain. The basis of all men is divine and if I feel overshadowed and outdone by great neighbors I can yet love. I can still receive. Beside, my turn will come. This Better is a plain token that my lustrum of silence is not yet complete. Why should I intrude into the guild of the workmen before I receive a sign? I will retreat into the solitudes of ability and love. He that loveth maketh his own the grandeurs he loves.[12] Consider again that each can do somewhat which he was made for. A true man can never feel rivalry. All men are ministers to him, servants to bring him materials, but none nor all can do what he must do. He alone is privy, nor even is he yet privy to his own secret. They can never know until he has shown them what that is. Let them mind their own.[13]

Much less is to the individual the sincerity of pain in wanting external goods. The advantage of riches seems to be in the skin or not much deeper. The rich man need not purse up his mouth in dreadful expectation of meeting a patron, a great man, an employer. He need not consult any worse man's or any odd man's humor. He is no man's man. He commands his hours and his goings and comings. And this freedom makes a state of preparation for his work. If he is poor and goes up and down under compulsion he feels a certain irritability as much in the skin as in the

---

[11] "We prize in our great . . . shoulder" (D, 21).
[12] "The radical tragedy . . . grandeurs he loves" ("Compensation," W, II, 123–124; D, 48–49).
[13] "A true man . . . their own" (D, 57).

mind that pesters and hinders him. If he is rich enough to control the circumstances he rids himself of this and so he will. If he have more soul, more will, less skin, — he can do without riches.[14] Let him have a little more nerve and resolution and he is the rich man. The effeminate capitalist in gloves and surtout on the cold spring day says by his shrug that he fears the earth will not yield man bread this year. The hard-faced farmer looks on contented and fearless. He has fronted the year cold and grim. He knows the virtue that resides in the hoe, the ox yoke, and the ploughtail long ago and knows that the hardest year that ever blew afforded to such straining and sweating as his milk, rye, potatoes, turnips, pork, and beef and he does not think of famine any more than a sailor rowing to a ship mistrusts at all of sinking before he gets there; he rows and goes: landsmen may do the doubting and fearing if they like it.[15]

The brave man will always be rich in the best sense; he will do the dictates of his character and genius, will do substantially the same things whether rich or poor, will make the same impression.

The ghastly brother of Disease and Want is Insecurity. The dances of Paris over the catacombs and under the guillotine aptly illustrate the state of menace in which our keenest enjoyments tremble. The highest gifts are not secure; Genius and madness; Love and Sorrow; Piety and fanaticism; how strictly are these words married in the ear and expectation of men. What purer efflux of the Godhead than the ray of the moral sentiment? Yet it comes before me so pure as to consent in language to all the tests we can apply, and yet is it morbid, painful, unwise. My faith is perfect that what is from God shall be more wise, more fair, more gracious, more manifold, more rejoicing than aught the soul had already. How sad to behold aught come in that name which gives no light, which confounds only, which shines on nothing, affirming that it is all light, does nothing, affirming that it does all.[16]

And here interposes the spectre Death, as it breaks up all the

---

[14] "The advantage of riches . . . without riches" (cf. C, 281).
[15] "The effeminate capitalist . . . they like it" (C, 294).
[16] "The highest gifts . . . does all" (D, 174, expanded).

fittest partnerships of life and the habits of mutual leaning and furtherance, to say nothing of all the imaginary hopes it shivers. I speak not of our own death. With that properly we have nothing to do.[17] It seems the impertinence of folly to suffer from the fear of death. My soul advertises me of none. If it concerned me the soul would apprise me of it. I can see very well how gloomy is to me the death of others, but with my own I have no more to do than with providing myself with coffin and sexton. My call is to live. But whilst I see the rude disappointments occasioned by death they seem to me to be made ruder by ourselves. The imagination makes the largest part: and indolence, the senses, and custom find in these disasters a ready and lasting apology for duties omitted and faculties rusted; for narrowness and sleep.

The next tragic element in life is the hindrance of private felicity by vice.

The senses would make things of all persons for our behoof. Our enjoyments are cruel. Our enjoyments do rob, kidnap, and kill. We separate ourselves from the human family and from remembrance of debt above us, and say, "shall I not take mine ease in mine inn?" [18] So are we devils. Only that good which we taste with all doors open: not separate, but *in the chain of beings;* so that the spark freely passes; makes all happy as well as us; — only that is godlike. Other enjoyments, — enjoyments sought for enjoyment, — are false, and degrade all the partakers and ministers.[19] The particular act makes no difference: that depends on mere fortune; on mere circumstance. Obedience and disobedience make the difference in Man. We read Lear and hate the unkind daughters. But meantime our fathers and mothers find us hard and forgetful as the civility of the times will allow. We swell the cry of horror at the slaveholder and we treat our laborer or farmer or debtor as a thing; women; children; the poor; and so we do hold slaves.[20] In the base hour, we become slaveholders. We use persons as things and we think of persons as things.[21]

[17] "I speak not . . . nothing to do" (cf. C, 206, 247).
[18] Shakespeare, *Henry IV, Part I,* III, 3:91.
[19] "Our enjoyments are . . . partakers and ministers" (D, 186).
[20] "The particular act . . . slaves" (D, 206).
[21] "In the base hour . . . persons as things" (D, 186).

But the essence of tragedy does not seem to me to lie in any list of particular evils. After we have enumerated famine, fever, siege, onslaught, mutilation, palsy, the rack, madness, and loss of friends, we have not yet included the proper tragic element, which is, Terror, — and does not consist in definite evils, but in indefinite; an ominous spirit which haunts the afternoon and the night; idleness, and solitude, ignorance, and vice. A low haggard sprite sits by our side, casting the fashion of uncertain evils; a sinister presentiment; gloom on the brow; weight at the heart; — a certain looking for calamity; a power of the imagination to dislocate things orderly and cheerful, and show them in startling disarray. Hark! what sounds in the night wind, the cry of murder in that friendly house; see these marks of stamping feet; of hidden riot; the whisper overheard; the detected glance; that glare of malignity. Ungrounded fears, suspicions, half knowledge, and mistakes darken the brow and chill the heart of men. And accordingly it is in natures not clear, not of quick and steady perceptions but in imperfect character from which somewhat is hidden that all others see who suffer most from these causes.

Look at those persons who move the profoundest pity; tragedy seems to consist in temperament, not in events. There are people who have an appetite for grief. Pleasure is not strong enough and they crave pain as morbid stomachs crave alcohol and sulphuric acid. There are natures so doomed that no prosperity can soothe their ragged and dishevelled desolation.[22] They mishear; and misbehold; they suspect; and dread. They seize every rose by the thorn and in every meadow tread on the snake. Perverse solicitors of woe.

> O how feeble is man's power
> That if good fortune fall
> Cannot add another hour
> Nor a lost hour recall.
> But come bad chance
> And we add to it our strength
> And we teach it art and length
> Itself o'er us to advance.[23]

[22] "tragedy seems . . . desolation" (D, 244, expanded).
[23] Donne, "Song" ["Sweetest love, I do not goe"], lines 17–24; C, 90.

If you would have me speak frankly the instructions of the soul on this head it is necessary to say that all sorrow dwells in a low element, that it is superficial: for the most part fantastic, or in the appearance, and not in things. It is full of illusions. Tragedy is in the eye of the observer, and not in the heart of the sufferer. It seems an insupportable load with which earth moans aloud: but analyse it; it is not I; it is not you; it is always another person that is tormented. If a man says, Lo I suffer, it is apparent that he suffers not, for Grief is dumb. It is so distributed as not to destroy. That which would rend you falls on tougher textures. That which seems intolerable reproach or bereavement does not take from the accused or bereaved man or woman appetite or sleep. Some men are above grief, and some below it.[24] Few are capable of affection. In phlegmatic natures, the calamity is unaffecting. In shallow natures it is rhetorical. That only is deep sorrow, that only is tragedy, which I can respect. A querulous habit is not tragedy. A panic such as frequently in ancient or savage nations has put a troop or an army to flight without an enemy; a fear of ghosts; a terror of freezing to death that seizes a man in a winter midnight on the moors; a fright at uncertain sounds heard by a family at night in the cellar on the stairs — these are terrors unaffected and withering that make the knees knock and the teeth chatter, but these are no tragedy, any more than seasickness which may also destroy life.

It is full of illusion. As it comes, it has its support. The most exposed classes that have had the rudest stripes, — soldiers, sailors, paupers, are nowise destitute of animal spirits. The spirit is true to itself and finds its own support in any condition; learns to live in what is called calamity as easily as in what is called felicity as the frailest glass bell will support a weight of a thousand pounds of water at the bottom of a river or sea, if filled with the same.[25]

All this sorrow and fear are the result of pure spiritual laws. The wants of men explain instantly their use: they make power

[24] D, 185.
[25] "But the essence of tragedy . . . with the same" (cf. "The Tragic," W, XII, 408–411).

and benefit. The evils that come to us from general laws, give us more than they take. They are the Angels of Knowledge that make wise. The evils that come to us from vice are Punishers; they threaten with skinny forefinger; assert eternal justice and so are our outward consciences and benefactors. The horrors of the Middle Passage are the ulcers that admonish us that a violation of nature has preceded. We should not, the nations would not know of the extremity of the wrong but for the terrors of the retribution.[26]

The attitude that befits a man is composure. He should not commit his tranquillity to things, but keep as much as possible the reins in his own hands, rarely giving way to extreme emotion of joy or grief. It is observed that the first works of the art of sculpture are countenances of sublime tranquillity. The Egyptian sphinxes that still sit as they sat when the Greek came and viewed them and departed and as the Roman came and viewed them and departed, and as they will still sit when the Turk, the Frenchman, and the Englishman, who visit them now shall have passed by, with their stony eyes fixed on the East and on the Nile, — are observed to have all a countenance expressive of complacency and tranquillity, an expression of health, deserving their permanency and verifying the primeval observation of history on that permanency of that people.[27] "Their strength is to sit still." [28] To this architectural stability of the human form, the Greek genius added an ideal beauty yet never overstepping the limits of composure and grace; permitting no violence of mirth or wrath or suffering. How true was this to human nature. For in life actions are few, opinions even few, prayers few; loves, hatreds, or any emissions of the soul. All that life demands of us through the greater part of the day is composure, an equilibrium, a readiness, open eyes and ears and free hands, a sympathy. Society asks this and Truth and Love and the Genius of our Life. There is a fire in many men which demands an outlet in some vigorous action. They betray their impatience of quiet in an irregular Catilinarian walk; in irregular, faltering, disturbed speech too emphatic for

---

[26] "The horrors of the Middle Passage . . . retribution" (C, 151).
[27] Cf. D, 89.
[28] Isaiah 30:7; D, 80.

the occasion. They do trifles with a tragic air. This is not beautiful. Let them split wood and work off this superabundant irritability. When a man meets a man in the highway, strangers to each other, all that each demands of the other is that the aspect should show a firm mind ready for any event of good or ill; prepared alike to give death or give life as the emergency of the next moment may require.[29] We must walk as guests in nature here for education; not impassioned but cool and disengaged. A man should try time. His face should wear the expression of a patient judge who has nowise made up his opinion, who fears nothing and even hopes nothing, but who puts nature and fortune on their merits. He will hear the case out and then decide.[30] I plead for no superficial tranquillity, a front of marble masking a boiling and passionate soul. I say only that all melancholy as all passion belongs to the exterior life, that so long as a man is subject to terror or to rage he is not yet grounded in the soul. For lack of these natural roots he clings by tendrils of affection to society, mayhap to what is best and greatest in it, and in calm times it will not appear that he is adrift and not moored, but let any disorder take place in society, any revolution of custom, of law, of opinion, and instantly his whole type of permanence is rudely shaken. In the disorder of society universal disorder seems to him to take place, chaos is come again,[31] and his despair takes at first the form of rage and hatred against the act or actor which has broken the seeming peace of nature. But the fact is he was already a driving wreck before the wind arose which merely revealed to him his vagabond state. If a man is at one with the soul and in all things obeyeth it, life and fortune and society become to him at once a fair show and reflection of that which he knoweth beforehand in himself. If any man, neighbor or stranger, in his presence does anything foolish, wild, or shocking, or if any perversity or profligacy appear in the whole society, he will see it for what it is and grieve for it as a man and a member of society but it will not touch him with resentment or fear, it will not cast one shadow over the lofty brow of the soul. The soul will not grieve; the soul sits behind there in

[29] "How true was this . . . may require" (D, 90–91).
[30] "A man should try . . . then decide" (D, 78, where Emerson is referring to Samuel Hoar).
[31] Shakespeare, *Othello*, III, 3:92.

a serene peace; no jot or tittle of its Convictions can be either shaken or confirmed. It sees already in the ebullition of sin the simultaneous remedy arising. This is the city which hath foundations whose builder and maker is God.[32]

And now let me show the several reliefs which fit themselves to these several evils.

Time the Consoler, Time the rich bringer of all changes, drugs us with forgetfulness by ever obtruding new figures, new costumes, new roads on our eye, new voices on our ear. How soon, too soon, the golden joy that yesterday possessed us is dimmed in the haze of the days and months. As the west wind lifts up again the heads of the wheat which were bent down and lodged in the storm, and combs out the matted and dishevelled grass as it lay in night locks on the ground, so we let in Time as a drying wind into the seedfield of thoughts which are dank and wet and low bent.[33] Time restores to them temper and elasticity. How fast we forget the blow that seemed to cripple us for life. Nature will not lie still: the faculties will do somewhat: new hopes are born: new affections twine and the broken is whole again.

In the next place Temperament is the relief. To the evil to be borne Nature supplies sufficient resistance. Our human being is wonderfully pliant and plastic: if it cannot win this satisfaction here it makes itself amends by running out there and winning that. It is like a stream of water which if dammed up on one bank overflows the other and flows equally to its own convenience over sand or mud or marble. Hence a vast deal of suffering is only apparent; it seems suffering from our point of view; the patient has his own compensations. A tender American girl doubts of Divine Providence whilst she reads the horrors of the middle passage. And they are bad enough. But to such as she these crucifixions do not come. They come to the obtuse and barbarous to whom they are not horrid, but only a little worse than the old sufferings. They exchange a cannibal war for the stench of the hold. They have gratifications which would be none to the civilized girl. The market man never damned the lady because she had not paid her bill,

[32] "so long as a man is subject . . . maker is God" (D, 240). For the last sentence see Hebrews 11:10
[33] D, 49.

but the good Irish woman has that to suffer once a month. She in return never feels weakness in her back because of the slave trade.[34]

Especially is this self-adapting strength seen in disease. "It is my daily duty," says Sir Charles Bell, "to visit certain wards of the hospital where there is no patient admitted but with that complaint which most fills the imagination with the idea of insufferable pain and certain death. Yet these wards are not the least remarkable for the composure and cheerfulness of their inmates. The individual who suffers has a mysterious counterbalance to that condition which to us who look on her appears to be attended with no alleviating circumstance."[35] It is not otherwise with those whose character leads into vast exertions of body and mind. Napoleon said to one of his friends at St. Helena, "Nature seems to have calculated that I should have to endure great reverses, for she has given me a temperament like a block of marble. Thunder cannot move it; the shaft merely glides along. The great events of my life have slipped over me without producing any impression on my moral or physical nature."[36]

Another relief which nature provides us is in the just application of the intellect to the facts, so investigating the real nature and extent of the calamity and removing all imaginary parts; then in suggesting resources and diversions; and lastly by invoking the only true and perfect succour, that of the soul, the perception of our true place, duty, and being which at once rights us by exposing the low and limitary nature of these perturbations and redeems us from them by a single leap into the region of pure thought, of eternal life.

The intellect may fairly come in to check the extravagance of sympathy. It may ask the question, Why should we grieve for those things befalling another which would not cause us grief befalling us? We receive so much daily benefit from our sym-

[34] "A tender American girl . . . slave trade" (cf. C, 151, which refers to Lidian Emerson).

[35] Sir Charles Bell, *The Hand, Its Mechanism and Vital Endowments, as Evincing Design* (Philadelphia, 1833), p. 128; Blotting Book IV [A], 20.

[36] "He should not commit . . . physical nature" (cf. "The Tragic," W, XII, 411–416). For the last quotation cf. Las Cases, *Journal,* II, iii, 133, and IV, vii, 120; C, 314, 348.

pathetic structure that we can easily expect to suffer some detriment from its untimely action.

> The rain has spoiled the farmer's day;
> Shall sorrow put my books away?
> Thereby are two days lost.
> Nature will speed her own affairs,
> I will attend my proper cares,
> Come rain or sun or frost.[37]

Reason admonishes him of the simplicity of his task. He is responsible for playing the game well for nothing else, not for his convenience the while, not for the final success, only to play his game the best he can. A great man escapes out of the kingdom of time; he puts time under his feet. He does not look at his performance and say, I am twenty, I am thirty, I am forty years old and must therefore accomplish somewhat conspicuous. See Alexander at twenty-six. See what Sidney had done before thirty. He says rather, Is this that I do genuine and fit? Then it contributes no doubt to immortal and sublime results; no doubt it partakes of the same lustre itself. Dark though the hour be and dull the wit no flood of thoughts, no lovely pictures in memory or in hope, only heavy, weary duty moving on cart wheels along the old ruts of life. The wisest men have owed their wisdom to the common day. I will still trust. Was not Luther's Bible, Shakspeare's Hamlet, Paul's epistle a deed as notable and far-reaching as Marengo or the dike of Arcola?[38] Yet these were written by dint of flagging spirits. Sobs of the heart and dull, waste, unprofitable hours taught the master how to write to apprehensive thousands the tragedy of these same.[39]

Reflection acquaints us with our resources. That is said to be the best condition which has the most outlets. But a man with the vast range of his susceptibilities of pleasure seems infinitely rich. Extreme enduring grief we cannot forgive him. Always

[37] B, 228; printed as "Suum Cuique" in *The Dial*, I (January 1841), 347, and in Emerson's *Poems* (Boston, 1847), p. 128, but omitted in *Selected Poems* (Boston, 1876), the Riverside Edition, and *W*, IX. All end-line punctuation supplied from *The Dial*.

[38] At Arcola and Marengo, villages in northern Italy, Napoleon gained important victories over the Austrians in 1796 and 1800.

[39] "Teachers D32" [E]. "A great man . . . of these same (C, 324–325).

Beauty invites him. Why do we seek this lurking beauty in skies, in woods, in poems, in drawings? Ah, because there we are safe; there we neither sicken nor die. I think we fly to Beauty as an asylum from the terrors of finite nature. We are made immortal by this kiss. We are immortal at once by the contemplation of beauty.[40]

Nature is the beautiful asylum to which we look in all the years of striving and conflict as the assured resource when we shall be driven out of society by ennui or chagrin or persecution or defect of character. I say as I go up the hill and through the wood and behold the soliciting plants — I care not for you mosses and lichens! and for you fugitive birds or secular rocks! Grow, fly, or sleep there in your order which I know is excellent though I perceive it not. I am content not to perceive it. Now have I entertainment enough with things nearer, homelier. Things wherein passion enters and hope and fear have not yet become too dangerous, too insipid for me to handle. But by and by if men shall drive me out, if books shall become stale, I see gladly that the door of your palace of magic stands ajar

> and my age
> Shall find the antique hermitage,
> The hairy gown and mossy cell
> Where I may sit and rightly spell
> Of every star that heaven doth show
> And every herb that sips the dew.[41]

Yes, "of every star that heaven doth show." Astronomy is sedative to the human mind. It seems to me a simple in the highest pharmacopia, the anodyne and balsam of the intellect. In skeptical hours when things go whirling and we doubt if all is not an extemporary dream; the remote calm and secular character of astronomical facts composes us to a sublime peace.[42]

And as natural science always stands open to us and in the conflict with the common cares we throw an affectionate glance

---

[40] "Why do we seek . . . contemplation of beauty" (D, 6).
[41] Milton, "Il Penseroso," lines 167–172 (misquoted). "Nature is the beautiful . . . mossy cell" (D, 117).
[42] "Astronomy . . . sublime peace" (C, 287, expanded).

at lichen and fungus, barometer and microscope as cities of refuge to which we can one day flee if the worst come to the worst, so another asylum is the exercise of the fancy whether in the rich treasuries of the reading of poets or in the original activity of the same faculty. Puck and Oberon, Tam O'Shanter and Lili's Park,[43] the Troubadours and the old ballads are bowers of joy that beguile us of our woes, catch us up into brief heavens, and drown all remembrance and that too without a death tramp of the Eumenides being heard close behind as behind other revels. Better still is it to soar into the heaven of invention and coin fancies of our own, weave a web of dreams as gay and beautiful as any of these our brothers have done, and learn by bold attempt your own riches. As the body is rested and refreshed by riding in the saddle after walking and by walking again after the saddle, or as new muscles are called into play in climbing a hill and then in descending or walking on the plain, an analogous joy and strength flows from this exercise. Let no man despise these entertainments as if they were mere luxury and the drunkard's bowl. These airy realms of perpetual joy are also in nature, and what they are may well move the deepest wonder and inquisition of the coldest and surliest philosopher.[44]

But chiefly in moral activity, in the growth of the interior life, in the development of the slow but precious fruit of character, is the final relief and emancipation to be sought and found. Solitude is full of fears because in it the man is disjoined from men and the more if he is appropriating and not imparting. In society he feels safe because in sympathy with men he is joined again to the universe. Idleness is coward for the soul is not therein. Labor is cheerful. Property is timid for it dwells wholly in the finite. Charity is brave for it flows out of the infinite. It is all the difference of the presence or the absence of the soul. "The honorable man," said Confucius, "is serene and enlarged in mind; the low man is always anxiously fearing. Chee koong asked concerning sundry persons, Were they discontented? The sage replied, They

[43] Goethe's poem, "Lili's Park" (*Werke*, II, 90–95), figures the poet as a bear, captive in the fanciful menagerie of his beloved Lili (Anna Elizabeth Schönemann).

[44] "And as natural science . . . surliest philosopher" (D, 202).

sought and attained complete virtue. How then could they be discontented!"[45]

The one resource of beneficent activity remains always a certain medicine for a soul diseased with apprehensions or crippled by calamities. It seems to me that we should load our shoulders with love till we bend, kneel, and lie down under the burden. Why need we think afar off of one or two acts of good will as you pay thirty dollars to constitute you a life member of the Charities? Go to it man. Set down your shoulder with a Yeo heave O! of labor and understand well without mincing the matter there are you to sweat and drudge and toil forever. Condition, your private condition of riches or relations or talents or seclusion, what difference does that make? It is not other people's wants but your own wants that crave your devotion. You will find, be your condition what it may, that the world, your native world, is a poor beggar, naked, cold, starving, sick, whom you must clothe, warm, feed, and restore. Unless you kill yourself you cannot get out of the sight of its wants nor out of the hearing of its piteous moanings. You are rich, you are literary, have taste, your connexion of society detaches you, you lament you have not the helping hand. I think no wise man will ever be rich; none that is will have anything at his disposal for unless he had the riches of nature at hand he could not supply all the needs that look to him for relief. Friends near and friends afar, brothers, cousins, parents, virtuous men unkindly used by the world, bereaved women and children, beside that creative charity which will never let us be, but as if out of wantonness and ingenuity of goodness is contriving objects and inventing subscription papers. The richest man needs to economize his cloth, his hay, his harvest, his house labor and wear the white seam, the soiled hat of his fellow's need if not of his own. I must regard the old coat, the dusty shoes, the weary limbs of the man frugal from benevolence as luminous points that ray out glory to all the sundered friends he loves and serves. The call comes. Death and rates, men say, are sure. These poor-rates are surest of all. They knock at every door: they go to every closet:

[45] *The Works of Confucius,* trans. Joshua Marshman (Serampore, 1809), pp. 507, 452–453; T, 189.

they levy a poll-tax. Fool, you will not decline it! O no! for see a little onward when this sturdy beggar takes off his foul disguise and behold who and what he is. God looked through his eyes. God held out that asking hand. This sturdy beggar went before to all the heroes and whilst he took substance and time and pleasure, — with the other hand he enriched them by every thing he seemed to take; he gave them learning and wit and sympathy and insight and noble manners and the blessing of every eye that saw, of every ear that heard them. How came that great heart to such a huge compass of love? How but because it has loved and served so many that it is now charged with the life of thousands, of countries, of races.[46]

[46] "It seems to me . . . countries, of races" (C, 326–327, modified).

8

Comedy

This lecture was first read in Boston at the Masonic Temple on January 30, 1839, and repeated in Concord, Massachusetts, on May 1 as the sixth in the series there. Except for the opening paragraphs and a few other scattered passages, this lecture was printed in full, with substantial revision, under the title "The Comic" in *The Dial,* IV (October 1843), 247–256, and was reprinted in 1875 in *Letters and Social Aims* (*W*, VIII, 155–174). The manuscript is still sewn, complete, and in good condition. The pencilled page numbers are not Emerson's.

IN MY last lecture, I attempted an enumeration of the tragic elements in [man's] life and endeavored to indicate their ulterior value in his culture; to indicate the inferior region in his nature which they affect; the perpetual effort of the soul to place itself in equilibrium; and the several reliefs which come in aid of man against the several afflictions.

There remains for our consideration the foolish side of life: the perception of the ridiculous, the phenomenon of laughter, and the various objects and relations in ordinary life which give occasion to the emotion of mirth and the activity of the risible muscles.

There is as much place for comedy as for tragedy in nature. We walk ever on the confines of both. It is a nail of pain and pleasure which fastens the body to the mind. In any collection of men in the market, the courthouse, the church, see the wistful human history written out in the faces. The silent assembly thus talks very loud. The sailor carries on his face the tan of tropic suns, and the record of rough weather. The merchant's face is sharpened with forty years of thrift and calculation. The old farmer carries palpable in his face, stone walls, rough wood-lots, the meadows, and the barnyard. The old doctor is a fragrant gallipot of virtues; the carpenter still measures feet and inches with his eye and the licensed landlord mixes liquors yet in motionless pantomime. And if beauty, softness, and faith in female form have their own influence, vices even in slight degree are thought to improve the expression; malice and scorn add to beauty. You shall see eyes set too near; and limited faces, — faces of one marked and invariable character. How the busy fancy inquires into their biography and relations. They pique but must tire. Compared with universal faces, countenances of a general humane type, which pique less, they look less safe.

In such a study one is irresistibly reminded of other figures and other modes of being than heroes and sages. In the silentest and motionless meeting the eye reads plainly in these manifold persons the plain prose of life, timidity, caution, appetite, ignorance, old houses, musty savors, stationary, retrograde faculties puttering round (to borrow a country phrase) in paltry routines from January to December.[1]

It seems but reasonable in our circle of topics to include the comic and, though I do it with extreme reluctance (as conscious of a deficiency in the organ of representing these parts of nature), to inquire into the essence and limits of the comic in life.

A very curious subject. Man is the only joker in nature. All nature, he alone excepted, is very grave. The rocks, the plants, the worms, the beasts, the birds, neither do anything ridiculous, nor betray the least perception of anything absurd done in their presence by any other. Nor are these things the subject of laughter. As thus the lower nature never jests neither does the highest.

On the other side neither does the soul receive the perception of the ludicrous. The soul affirms Yea or Nay with an omniscience but meddles never with degrees or fractions; and it is in comparing fractions with essential integers or wholes, that laughter begins.[2] It was in this feeling that Alexander answered the priests of Ammon who told him he was a god, that, "sleep and laughter

---

[1] "It is a nail of pain . . . to December" (cf. notes to "The Comic," W, VIII, 395–396); "In any collection . . . to December" (D, 9, modified).

[2] "A very curious subject . . . laughter begins" (cf. "The Comic," W, VIII, 157).

convinced him he was a man."[3] Man is the only jester in nature and the only jest.

Mr. Coleridge in his excellent Essay on Wit has cited [Aristotle's] definition of the ridiculous, as, "what is out of time and place, without danger."[4] If there be pain and danger, it becomes tragic; if not, comic. I confess this definition does not quite satisfy me; does not say all we know. The essence of all jokes, of all comedy, seems to be Halfness; a non-performance of what is pretended to be performed, at the same time that one is giving loud pledges of performance. The baulking of the intellect, the frustrated expectation, the break of continuity, *in the intellect,* is what we call comedy, and it embodies itself physically in the pleasant convulsions or spasms we call *laughter.*

Until the appearance of Man in nature there is no rebellion, no seeming, no halfness. Unconscious creatures do the whole will of Wisdom. An oak, a pine, a palm, undertake no function they cannot execute; or if there are facts in botany which we call abortions, yet the abortion is a function of Nature too, and assumes to the intellect the like completeness with the other function to which in other circumstances it had attained. The same remark holds of the animal creation. Dr. Turner observes, that the entire activity of animals is marked by a strong good sense. They do precisely what unerring good sense would do under the limitations of their organization.[5]

But in man first appears the Reason: Reason, which is essentially whole; which must be or not be; which a man has or has lost; obeys or disobeys; but which cannot be disunited, or halved, or diminished, or increased. By his access to Reason, a man is capable of the perception of a whole and a part. *That* is the whole; and whatsoever is not that, is a part. The whole of Nature is agreeable to this whole of thought, or to the Reason: but separate any part of nature and attempt to look at it as a Whole

[3] Cf. Plutarch, "How to Know a Flatterer from a Friend," *Morals,* II, 133.
[4] *The Literary Remains of Samuel Taylor Coleridge,* ed. H. N. Coleridge, 4 vols. (London, 1836–39), I, 132–133: "I think Aristotle has already excellently defined the laughable, τὸ γελοῖον, as consisting of, or depending on, what is out of its proper time and place, yet without danger or pain."
[5] Cf. Sharon Turner, *The Sacred History of the World,* 3 vols. (New York, 1832–38), [I], 268 (Letter XII); cf. *Lectures,* II, 34.

by itself, and the perception of the ridiculous begins. The perpetual game of Humour is to look with considerate, condescending good nature at every object in existence *aloof* as a man might look at a mouse, comparing it with the eternal Whole; enjoying the figure which each self-satisfied particular creature cuts in the unrespecting All; and dismissing it with a benison. If you separate any object whatever, a particular bodily man, a horse, a pine-board, an umbrella, a broom, from the connexion of things and contemplate it alone standing there in absolute nature it instantly becomes comic; no useful, no amiable, no respectable qualities can redeem it from the ludicrous.

In virtue of man's access to Reason, or the Whole, — the form of man is a pledge of a Whole: suggests to our imagination the perfection of truth or goodness; and shows, by contrast, any halfness or imperfection. The appearance of the human form, announces the arrival of Truth and Virtue. We have an *a priori* association between perfectness and this form. But the facts that transpire when John and Joshua enter, do not make good this original anticipation; — a discrepancy, which instantly is detected by the intellect; and the outward sign is the muscular irritation of laughter.

Reason does not joke; and men of reason do not; a prophet, in whom the moral sentiment predominates; or a philosopher in whom the love of truth predominates; — these do not joke. They however bring the standard, the whole, — exposing all actual defect; and therefore, the best of all jokes is, the sympathetic contemplation of things by the understanding from the philosopher's point of view. There is no joke so true and deep in actual life as when some pure idealist goes up and down among the institutions of society attended by a man of acute understanding, that is, a man who knows the world, and who sympathizing with the philosopher's question sympathizes with the confusion and indignation of the detected skulking institutions. His perception of difference, his eye wandering perpetually from the rule to the crooked, lying, thieving fact makes the eyes run over with laughter.

This is the radical joke of life and then of literature. The tacit presence of the ideal of right and of truth in all action makes the

124

yawning delinquencies of practice painful to the conscience; tragic to the interest; but droll to the intellect.

The activity of our sympathies may for a time hinder our perceiving the fact intellectually and so deriving mirth from it. But it is worthy of remark that all falsehoods, all vices seen at sufficient distance, seen from the point where our moral sympathies do not interfere, become ludicrous. The comedy, the fun is in the intellect's perception of discrepancy. And whilst the tacit presence of the ideal exposes the difference, the comedy is always enhanced if that ideal is embodied or represented visibly in a man.[6] Hence Don Quixote represents Reason though with the one notion of knight errantry, Sancho the Understanding.

Falstaff in Shakspeare is the broadest comedy, giving himself unreservedly to his senses, deliberately ignoring the reason, invoking however all the time its name, pretending to patriotism and to parental virtues not with any intent to deceive but only to make the fun perfect by seeing himself, as well as we, the inconsistency betwixt reason and the negation of reason, in other words, the rank rascaldom he is calling by her name. Prince Hal stands by as the acute understanding who sees the Right, and sympathises with it, and in the heyday of youth feels also the full attractions of pleasure; and is thus eminently qualified to appreciate the joke. At the same time, he is to that degree under the Reason that it does not amuse him as much as it does another spectator.

If it be true that the essence of the comic be the contrast in the intellect between somewhat pretended to be done, and the idea, the reason appears why we should be so deeply affected by the exposure. We have no deeper interest than our integrity, and that we should be made aware by joke and by stroke of any lie that we still harbour. We are therefore instructed by laughter as well as by tears in truth. Besides a perception of the comic seems to be a balance wheel in the metaphysical structure of man. It seems an essential element in a fine character, a perception of the comic. Wherever the intellect is constructive, this will be. We feel it as a defect in the noblest, most oracular soul that it should not have this perception of difference. It insulates the man, cuts down all

[6] "[Aristotle's] definition . . . in a man" (cf. "The Comic," W, VIII, 157–160).

bridges between him and other men. The perception of this comic is a tie of sympathy with other men. The perception of the comic is a pledge of sanity. And it is a protection from those perverse tendencies and gloomy insanities into which fine intellects sometimes lose themselves. Every man with the perception of the ludicrous is still convertible. If that is lost, his fellowmen can do little for him.[7]

And so the ancients held the jest to be a legitimate weapon of the philosopher. Hear Plutarch. "Men cannot exercise their rhetoric unless they speak; but their philosophy, even whilst they are silent, or jest merrily; for as it is the highest degree of injustice not to be just and yet seem so, so it is the top of wisdom to philosophize, yet not appear to do it, and in mirth to do the same with those that are serious and seem in earnest; for as in Euripides the Bacchae though unprovided of iron weapons and unarmed, wounded their invaders with the boughs of trees they carried, thus the very jests and merry talk of true philosophers move those that are not altogether insensible, and unusually reform." [8]

It is one of the trustiest weapons of the intellect, a true shaft of Apollo, and travels everywhere heralded and harbingered by smiles and greetings. It hath the freedom of every city, of every circle, of every mind, unless a dumpish or a mystic soul. Wit makes its own welcome.

Wit is a leveller that mocks at all distinctions but his own. No dignity, no learning, no force of character can make any stand against good wit. It is like ice on which no beauty of form, no majesty of carriage can plead any exemption; they must walk gingerly according to the laws of ice or down they must go dignity and all. It says to them with Sir Toby, "Dost thou think because thou [art virtuous, there shall be no more cakes and ale?"] [9]

And yet because it is the index of Halfness and a latent lie, Wit and Comedy are celebrated ever by those strange and hoarse

[7] "Falstaff in Shakspeare . . . little for him" (cf. "The Comic," *W*, VIII, 160–162).

[8] "Plutarch's Symposiacs," *Morals*, III, 229; C, 131; "And so the ancients . . . unusually reform" (cf. "The Comic," *W*, VIII, 163–164).

[9] Shakespeare, *Twelfth Night*, II, 3:124; "It is one of the trustiest . . . cakes and ale" (cf. "The Comic," *W*, VIII, 163).

explosions which men call laughter. This is their sign and cognisance. So painfully susceptible are some men to these impressions, that if a man of wit come into the room where they are, it seems to take them out of themselves with violent convulsions of the face and sides, and obstreperous roarings of the throat. And when such receiving like a willing martyr the whispers into his ear of a man of wit, the person who has just received the discharge, if in a solemn company, has the air very much of a stout vessel which has just shipped a heavy sea, and though it does not split it, the poor bark is for the moment critically staggered. The peace of society and decorum of companies seems to require that next to a notable wit should always be posted a phlegmatic, bolt upright man able to stand without movement of muscle whole broadsides of this Greek fire.[10]

Let me now illustrate this theory of the comic by considering its application to the great parts of life. In all cases we shall see that the occasion of laughter is some great seeming, some keeping of the word to the ear and eye whilst it is broken to the soul.

Thus as the religious sentiment is the highest sentiment in man, and at once raises and transports into new life whatsoever it approaches, communicating glory as by the touches of the God to every action and sentiment in which it appears, in proportion is it abhorrent to our whole nature when in the lack of the sentiment, the act or word or officer volunteers to stand in its stead. To the sympathies, — this is shocking; and occasions deep grief, a painful disappointment. Not so to the intellect; the lack of the sentiment gives it no pain; merely it compares incessantly the sublime idea with this bloated nothing which stands or squats there pretending to be it, and the perception of the disproportion is comedy. And as the religious sentiment is the most real and earnest thing in nature, being a mere rapture, the vitiating this, is the greatest lie or an attempt at an impossibility. Therefore the oldest gibe of literature as of life is the perpetual ridicule of false religion. This is the joke of jokes: you cannot open a book but there is some fling at hypocrisy and superstition.

The comedy is here. The religious sentiment is religion. The

[10] "And yet because . . . Greek fire" (cf. "The Comic," *W*, VIII, 162–163); "The peace of society . . . Greek fire" (C, 9).

sentiment is all. The rite, the form, nothing. But the inactivity of men inclines them, when the sentiment sleeps, to imitate that thing it did; it goes through the ceremony, the whole truth being out of it; makes the mistake of the wig for the head; the clothes for the man. The older this mistake is, the older the particular form is, the more ridiculous to the intellect. This makes the exquisite fun of the step taken by Captain John Smith, the discoverer of New England. When the Society in London who had contributed their means to convert the savages, hoping doubtless to see the Keokuks, Blackhawks, Roaring Thunders and Walk the Waters of that day, converted into churchwardens and deacons at the least; pestered the gallant rover with frequent solicitations in letters out of England as to the conversion of the Indians and enlargement of the Church, Smith in his perplexity how to satisfy the London churches, sent out a party, caught an Indian, and sent him home in the first ship to London, telling the society they might convert one themselves.[11]

The satire reaches its climax when the actual church is set in direct contradiction to the dictates of the religious sentiment, as in the famous account of our Puritan politics in Hudibras.

> Our brethren of New England use
> Choice malefactors to excuse
> And hang the guiltless in their stead
> Of whom the Churches have less need;
> As lately it happened. In a town
> There lived a cobler, and but one,
> That out of doctrine could cut use,
> And mend men's lives, as well as shoes.
> This precious brother having slain
> In times of peace an Indian;
> Not out of malice, but mere zeal

[11] Emerson may have based this anecdote on Smith's complaint that the London Virginia Company neglected him and the Jamestown settlers, sent them incompetent and treacherous men, and then, motivated wholly by a desire for immediate profit, but "making Religion their colour," criticized them: "Much they blamed us for not converting the Savages, when those they sent us were little better, if not worse, nor did they all convert any of those we sent them to *England* for that purpose. So doating of Mines of gold, and the South Sea, that all the world could not have devised better courses to bring us to ruine than they did themselves . . ." (*Advertisements for the Unexperienced Planters of New-England, or Any Where* [London, 1631], reprinted in *Collections of the Massachusetts Historical Society*, 3rd series [Cambridge, Mass., 1833], III, 10–11).

Because he was an infidel;
The mighty Tottipotimoy
Sent to our elders an envoy
Complaining sorely of the breach
Of league held forth by brother Patch
Against the articles in force
Between both Churches, his and ours;
For which he craved the saints to render
Into his hands, or hang the offender.
But they maturely having weighed
They had no more but him of the trade, —
A man that served them in the double
Capacity to teach and cobble;
Resolved to spare him; yet to do
The Indian Hogan Mogan too
Impartial justice, in his stead did
Hang an old weaver that was bed-rid.[12]

From the universal presence in all minds of the religious sentiment and the facility with which the form can be compared with it, it comes that the joke at sacred things is so prompt and cheap. In one form it is especially easy, where the persons and acts reverenced in the popular theology, are actualised or degraded by taking them out of their imaginative and poetic element and viewed as plain historical persons, which is done in Lord Byron's Vision of Judgment. It makes us laugh, to be sure, but it degrades the jester. Such jests can be made by sheets, by volumes; and every boatswain and street boy can make the same.

In science, the jest at pedantry (and ignorance) is precisely analogous to that in Religion that lies against hypocrisy and superstition. Thus a nomenclature, a classification used by the Scholar as a help to the memory, or a bare illustration of his present perception of the law of nature, the memorandum only of his last lesson, and, in the face of it, merely a makeshift; merely momentary; a landing place on the staircase, a bivouac for a night, and implying a march, a progress, a conquest tomorrow, becomes, through the indolence or absence of the mind, a barrack, a stronghold, an obstacle; in which the man settles down immoveable, insane, obstinate; mistaking his means for his end; his bivouac

---

[12] Samuel Butler, *Hudibras*, II, ii, 409–436. "Let me now illustrate . . . bedrid" (cf. "The Comic," *W*, VIII, 164–166).

for the promised land; and requires your respect to this whimsy as to truth itself.[13] Hence the wit of the remark of Alphonso, king of Leon and Castile, who when the astronomers had shown him the Ptolemaic scheme of the heavens with the cycle and epicycle orb on orb by which they patched their system to make it comply with each new discovery, replied, that, "if that was the structure of the heavens, he thought — if he had been present at the creation, he could have given some useful advice." [14]

This influence by which the secondary takes the place of the primary, the end is lost sight of in the means, is the root of all the wit that is flung at men of science. The celebrated physiologist Camper freely owns the dislocation that his own studies had operated in his ordinary associations. "I have been employed for six weeks upon the Cetacea; I understand actually the osteology of the head of all these monsters. I have made the combination with the human head so well that everybody now appears to me narwhale, porpoise, or marsouin. Women, the prettiest in society, and those whom I find less comely, they look all either narwhales or marsouines to my eyes." [15]

It happened to me once a good while ago to fall in with an odd illustration of the remark I had heard that the laws of disease are as beautiful as the laws of health.[16] As I was hastening to visit an honoured friend, an old man, who had been represented to me as in a dying condition, I met his physician, who accosted me in great spirits with joy sparkling in his eyes. "And how is my friend?" I asked. "O, I have not seen him today, but it is the most correct apoplexy I have ever seen; face and hands livid; breathing stertorous; and all the symptoms perfect!" and he rubbed his hands with delight, for it would seem in the country we cannot

[13] "In science . . . truth itself" (cf. "The Comic," *W*, VIII, 166–167).

[14] Carlyle (*History of Frederick the Great*, book II, chapter 7) identifies this as the only one of the many sayings of Alfonso the Wise (1221–1284) which people remember. Nor is he better remembered for the Alfonsine Tables, a revision of the Ptolemaic planetary calculations, completed by his astronomers in 1252.

[15] *Briefe an Johann Heinrich Merck von Göthe, Herder, Wieland und andern bedeutenden Zeitgenossen*, ed. Karl Wagner (Darmstadt, 1835), p. 485; C, 30. Emerson is translating, with abridgement, from the French of Pieter Camper (1722–1789), Dutch physician and comparative anatomist.

[16] C, 340, where Emerson ascribes the saying to Dr. Charles T. Jackson, his brother-in-law, who was a geologist and one of the discoverers of ether as an anesthetic; "Spiritual Laws," *W*, II, 155; cf. D, 114; above, p. 49.

find every day a case that complies with the diagnosis of the books.[17]

Indeed I am inclined to suspect a great deal of malice in a very trifling story which goes about from mouth to mouth, and which I should not take any notice of, if I did not suspect it to contain some satire upon my brothers of the Natural History society. It is that of the boy that was learning his alphabet. That letter is A; said the teacher. A — drawls the boy. That is B; said the teacher. B — drawled the boy; and so on. That letter is W; says the teacher. The Deuce! cries the boy, is that W?[18] It seemed to be aimed at the lady who had shells and knew no better than to call them cowries, cockles, muscles, and snails. By and by the learned Dr. Botherwell came by and he informed her that these were the cypraea maculata, the nerita formosa, and the trochus nodosus, that the buttercup was ranunculus bulbosus, and the mayweed anthemis cotula. The lady heard the new names with great reverence and could not help querying whether any alteration for the better had taken place in her mantel piece or even in her mind.

The pedantry of literature belongs to the same category. In both cases there is a lie when the mind seizing a classification to help it to a sincerer knowledge of the facts stops in the classification; or learning languages to the end of a better acquaintance with man, stops in the languages; in both the learner seems to be wise and is not.

The same falsehood, the same utter confusion of the sympathies because a pretension is not made good, points the perpetual satire of which poverty is the occasion. According to the famous verse of the Latin moralist which has been rendered into English doggrel

> Poverty does nothing worse
> Than to make man ridiculous.[19]

[17] In C, 340, the anecdote is told, identifying the "honoured friend" as Dr. Ezra Ripley, minister of the First Church in Concord and Emerson's step-grandfather, and the physician as "Dr. Hurd," probably Dr. Isaac Hurd of Concord.

[18] "The celebrated physiologist . . . is that W" (cf. "The Comic," W, VIII, 167–168). The last anecdote is ascribed in A, 42, to George P. Bradford.

[19] Juvenal, *Satires*, III, 152–153; Encyclopedia, 89, gives both the Latin lines and, without ascription, this English version.

In this case, the halfness will appear if it be considered that the point of all ridiculous things quoted on this subject, is, in the pretension of the parties to some consideration on account of their condition. If the man is not ashamed of his poverty there is no joke. The poorest man who stands on his manhood, on his virtue, destroys the jest. The poverty of the saint, of the rapt philosopher, of the naked Indian, is not comic; nor the poverty of man; but only of the pretender. Here the lie is in the surrender of the man to his appearance; as if a man should neglect himself and treat his shadow on the wall with marks of infinite respect. It affects us oddly as to see things turned upside [down] or to see a man in a high wind running after his hat, which is always droll;[20] the relation of the parties is inverted, Hat being for the moment master. The immense extent and multiplication of artificial wants and expenses in civilized life and the exaggeration of all trifling forms, present obviously innumerable occasions for this discrepancy to expose itself.[21] Thus the story that is told of one of the smaller West Indian islands that when the Governor came out from England and was waited on by the principal inhabitants, he remarked with some surprise that they came one at a time and dressed with great uniformity, until fixing his eye upon a remarkable button on the coat of a gentleman he found the same button on every coat; indeed that there was but one good coat on the isle which all the neighbors wore in turn.[22]

So the story related in the life of Northcote of the painter Astley who going out of Rome one day with a party for a ramble in the Campagna, and the weather proving warm refused to take off his coat when his companions threw off theirs, but sweltered on; which, exciting remark, his comrades playfully forced off his coat, — and behold on the back of his vest, a gay cascade was thundering down the rocks with foam and rainbows, a picture of his own with which the poor painter had been fain to piece his vest.[23] The same inversion, the same lie, the same astonishment

---

[20] Cf. C, 86.

[21] "The pedantry . . . expose itself" (cf. "The Comic," W, VIII, 168–169).

[22] D, 158, alludes to the story, identifying the island as St. Lucie.

[23] The anecdote, alluded to in Encyclopedia, 89, and Φ, 27, 31, is told in James Northcote, *The Life of Sir Joshua Reynolds*, 2nd ed., 2 vols. (London, 1818), I, 44. The then impecunious John Astley (1730?–1787) was an early friend of Reyn-

of the intellect at the disappearance of the man out of nature, truth and virtue, that is, bowed out of creation by the clothes they wore, is the occult fact in all the fun that is circulated true or false of Beau Brummell or Beau Nash and in like manner of the gay Rameau of Diderot who believes in nothing but Hunger and that the single end of all art, of all virtue, of all poetry is to put something for mastication between the upper and lower mandibles.[24]

To this class belong all those fears which respect the loss of property. They said in the French Revolution there was a Comte whose ruling passion was the fear of being guillotined. Civil life may show many men whose ruling passion is the fear of being robbed. The love of their spoons hinders them from sleep.[25] The same preference of the shell to the kernel makes the ridicule of all fear. I knew a man scared by the rustle of his own hat band [26] and heard of one who apprehended a conflagration from the fire flies or lightning bugs as there was a pile of shavings between the meadow and his house in a dry time. Alike in all these cases the majesty of man is violated. He whom all things should serve is made a means to some paltry end.

In fine pictures the head subordinates the limbs and gives them all the expression of the face.[27] In Raphael's picture, for example, of the angel driving out Heliodorus from the temple the crest of the angel's helmet is so remarkable that but for the extraordinary energy of the face it would draw the eye too much; but the countenance of the celestial messenger subordinates it, and we see it not.[28] In poor pictures, the limbs and trunk degrade the face. So in the street among the fair promenaders, you shall see one whose bonnet and dress are one thing, and the lady her-

---

olds and Northcote, who called him "as poor in purse, as he ever was as an artist." He later married wealth.

[24] The satiric dialogue of Denis Diderot (1713–1784) between himself and a fictional variation on Jean-François Rameau, nephew of the famous composer, was published in French as *Le Neveu de Rameau* (1821), but Emerson doubtless knew Goethe's earlier translation from manuscript into German, *Rameau's Neffe, ein Dialog von Diderot* (1805), which is reprinted in *Werke*, XXXVI, 1–151. Cf. "Worship," *W*, VI, 210, for last clause.

[25] "They said in the French . . . from sleep" (D, 48).

[26] C, 103.

[27] D, 70.

[28] D, 64.

self quite another, and wearing withal an expression of meek submission to her bonnet and dress; another, whose dress obeys and heightens the expression of her form.[29]

Another form of the same weakness that makes the meat more than the life, is the consideration of personal appearance of face and form and manners, with all which the wise have simply nothing to do. No fashion is the best fashion, for all those matters which will take care of themselves. The diversion of the man to the study of all things is again the respect to his own shadow. And this weakness is the fair game of so much merriment in modern society. This is the butt of all those jokes of the Paris drawing rooms which Napoleon pronounced tremendous, of which I suppose a fair specimen was one lately given in the Memoirs of Queen Hortense, that when a certain lean lady of high rank had given the Countess Dulauloy the nickname of "Le Grenadier tricolore," in allusion to her tall fine figure, as well as to her republican opinions, the Countess retaliated by calling Madame "the Venus of the Père la Chaise," a compliment to her skeleton which did not fail to circulate.[30]

The Persians have a pleasant story of Tamerlane which relates to the same particulars. "Timur was an ugly man; he had a blind eye, and a lame foot. When, one day, Chodscha was with him, Timur scratched his head since the hour of the barber was come, and commanded that the barber should be called. Whilst his head was shaven, the barber gave him as usual a looking glass in his hand. Timur saw himself in the mirror, and found his face quite too ugly. Thereupon began he to weep: also Chodscha set himself to weep, and so they wept for two hours. On this, some courtiers began to comfort Timour and entertained him with strange stories in order to make him forget all about it. Timour ceased weeping; but Chodscha ceased not, but began now first to weep amain and in good earnest. At last, said Timour to Chodscha, 'Hearken! I have looked in the mirror and have seen myself ugly. Thereat I grieved, because although I am Caliph, and have

---

[29] D, 70.
[30] "This is the butt . . . fail to circulate" (C, 45). Cf. Las Cases, *Journal*, II, iii, 61; review of Mlle. Cochelet's *Mémoirs sur la Reine Hortense et la Famille Impériale* in *The Foreign Quarterly Review*, American Edition, XXI (July 1838), 169. The Père Lachaise is a large cemetery in Paris, first opened in 1804.

also much wealth and many wives yet still am I so ugly: therefore have I wept. But thou — why weepest thou without ceasing?'
Chodscha answered, 'If thou hast only seen thy face once and at
once seeing it hast not been able to contain thyself but hast wept,
what should we do, we who see thy face every day and night. If
we weep not, who should weep! Therefore have I wept.' Timour
almost split his sides with laughing." [31]

The like pretension provokes the like satire in our vulgar politics. What is nobler than the expansive sentiment of patriotism
that would find brothers in a whole nation and would love them
more than its own gain or life? But when the intellect perceives
all this incorruptible enthusiasm ending in the very intelligible
maxims of trade, so much for so much, the intellect feels again
the half man.[32] Or when patriotism merges itself in parties. We
would execute our philanthropic projects by means of the enginery of delegated governors. Instantly on the appearance of candidates, the great designs of the moral sentiment and of the
understanding are postponed to growing predilections for these
persons until presently the designs for which alone they are important are dropped and forgotten in the insignificant strife,
which person I like best. In every ward-room and bar-room the
dictators of our rural jacobins teach their little circle of gapers
their political lessons. And here, says the philosopher, is one who
loves what I hate; here is one wholly reversing a true code. I hate
persons who are nothing but persons. I hate numbers. This man
cares for nothing but numbers and persons. All the qualities of
man, all his accomplishments, affections, enterprises, except solely
the ticket he votes for, are nothing to this philosopher. Numbers
of majorities are all he sees in the newspaper. Fair shines the sun
on the noble Alleghany ridge and the rolling silver of the Father
of Waters and beautiful over the broad land fall the shadows of
night. All in Georgia, Alabama, Pennsylvania, or New England
that this man considers is what is the relation of Mr. Henry or Mr.
Martin to those mighty mountain chains, those vast fruitful
champaigns, those expanding nations of instructed men. What an

[31] Goethe, *Noten und Abhandlungen zu besserem Verständniss des West-östlichen Divans* in *Werke*, VI, 146–147.
[32] "So the story related . . . again the half man" (cf. "The Comic," *W*, VIII,
169–173).

existence this to have no home, no heart, but to feed on the very refuse and old straw and chaff of man, numbers, and names of towns and voters.[33]

But I will not push into more particulars the analysis of the foolish and laughable things we poor mortals do. It is but tearing off the bandage from our yawning wounds and exposing our shame. In fact if it be narrowly considered we do nothing that is not laughable whenever we quit our instinct or spontaneous sentiment. All our deeds on which we pride ourselves, all our great plans, managements, houses, poems, all our constructions of any kind, if compared with the nature and tendencies of pure wisdom and love which man represents, are equally imperfect and all ridiculous.

But to us mortal men, scholars here on the first forms of the Dame's school, who cannot afford to part with any advantages, it seems fittest to learn by laughter as well as by tears and terrors, those of us who can, to get fat thereby, and all of us to grow wiser.

It seems the part of wisdom to explore the whole of nature, to see the kitchen, the cellars, and the stables as well as the chapels and pinnacles of our house, to see the farce and buffoonery in the yard below as well as to listen to the voice of poets and philosophers above, to get the rest and refreshment of hearty laughter and the wild flow of the animal spirits not to be always pumping our brains for wise reasons, but when we have no more to say be content to lie by, to let mirth and wit have ample privilege and gladly serve their turn.

> Let Hercules himself do what he may,
> The cat will mew, and dog will have his day.[34]

Another day will come and another duty. The comic is one lesson and a refreshment and replenishment of the strength. But it has its own speedy term. It is not our home. It is as ill a home as a garden summerhouse would be for a dwelling in the months of rain and snow. We are sharply admonished by the sense of hol-

---

[33] "In every ward-room . . . and voters" (D, 142, where the original of "Mr. Henry or Mr. Martin" reads "Mr Clay or of Mr Van Buren"). The third from last sentence is not in the journal source.

[34] Shakespeare, *Hamlet*, V, 1:314–315.

lowness and shame which follows intemperate and continued mirth. It then seems as if the man would die of inanition, as, it is said, some persons have been put to death by tickling. The same scourge whips the joker as the enjoyer of the joke. When Carlini was convulsing Naples with laughter a patient waited on a physician in the city to seek some remedy for excessive melancholy which was rapidly consuming his life. The physician endeavored to cheer his spirits and advised him to go to the theatre and see Carlini. "I am that Carlini;" said the wretched man.[35] On the whole, then, it will be seen, Comedy like Tragedy is an inferior region of man. Neither in wails nor in merry peals is his voice sublime but in its even, articulate tone. Simplicity disarms wit and makes laughter die in the throat which formed it. Truth is never ludicrous. A spontaneous act or word or thought is divine, and takes rank with the gravity of vegetation, with the perfect order of the animal tribes. It is above that, it is accordant with the mind that made them.

[35] "But I will not push . . . the wretched man" (cf. "The Comic," W, VIII, 173–174). The anecdote of Carlini is in Encyclopedia, 86. Carlo-Antonio Bertinazzi (1710–1783), known as Carlino and Carlin, was the best of the many harlequins on the Italian stage before coming in 1742 to the Comédie-Italienne in Paris for a long and celebrated career.

9

Duty

The only recorded reading of this lecture was in the original series at the Masonic Temple in Boston on February 6, 1839. The manuscript, though once sewn and numbered in ink, is fragmentary. A double sheet now filed with "Tendencies" in the series on "The Present Age" (1839–40) is here printed at the beginning of the extant manuscript, where because of paper, numbering, sewing marks, and context it belongs. With this and the restoration of a double sheet now laid in journal Σ, the text begins with page 23 of the manuscript and runs continuously to the conclusion. Many of the surviving passages have been used in "Compensation," "Spiritual Laws," and "Self-Reliance," and it is reasonable to suppose the leaves now missing may have been used in those essays. A small double sheet and a small single leaf quoting journal passages of 1848 have been rejected and placed in the textual notes.

WE FOOLISHLY think that those actions only are great which already have long had the praise and wonder of men and do not perceive that any thing man can do may be divinely done. We think greatness entailed or organized in some places or duties in certain offices or occasions and do not see that Paganini will draw celestial beauty out of a fiddle; and Eulenstein out of a Jews harp; and a nimble boy out of shreds of paper with his scissors; and Landseer out of swine;[1] and the hero out of the pitiful habitation and company in which he was hidden. The truth is, what we call obscure condition or vulgar society, is that condition and society whose poetry is not yet written, but which you shall

[1] Niccolò Paganini (1782–1840), Italian violinist and composer, was celebrated for his brilliant innovations in performance; Charles Eulenstein (1802–1890), German Jew's harp and guitar player, became a celebrity in England after 1827; Sir Edwin Landseer (1802–1873), was noted for his drawings of animals (see D, 296–297).

presently make as enviable and renowned as any.[2] Accept your genius and act it out. Forevermore say what you think, instead of being a brute echo. If people say the spring is beautiful think whether it is or is not, before [you] duck to the remark with a paraphrastic yes. So in all estimates, most are foolish. The parts of hospitality, the connexion of families, the impressiveness of death, and a thousand other things royalty makes its own new estimate of and a royal mind will. We defer all along to the great importance of family events which may really be of none would we see and act anew. To make habitually a new estimate that is elevation.[3] Let not the *name* of goodness be a barrier to you.[4]

Consent to accept the place the Divine Providence has found for you, the society of your contemporaries; the connexion of events. Live in the new age and be the passive organ of its idea. Great men have always done so and confided themselves to the genius of their age. This is an obscure perception of the great philosophy that the Eternal is stirring at my heart, working through my hands and predominates and will predominate in all my being. And we are now men and must accept in the highest mind the same transcendant destiny and not pinched in a corner, not cowards fleeing before revolution, but pious aspirants to be noble clay, plastic in the almighty effort, we must advance and advance into Chaos and the Dark.[5]

Deeply considered all Virtue leads us into the presence of that sublime Vision of the Right which always lies before the mind, imposing on it a perfect obligation. We have nothing to do but to obey piously to follow. Why need you choose? Certainly there is a possible right for you that precludes the need of balance and wilful election.[6] For you there is a reality, a fit place, and congenial duties. Place yourself in the middle of the stream, the stream of power and wisdom which flows into you, as Life; place yourself in the full centre of that flood; then you are without effort impelled to truth, to right, and a perfect contentment. Then

[2] "We think greatness . . . renowned as any" (C, 317, modified).

[3] "We foolishly think . . . is elevation" ("Spiritual Laws," W, II, 142–143, condensed).

[4] "Forevermore say . . . to you" (C, 311).

[5] "Consent to accept . . . the Dark" ("Self-Reliance," W, II, 47, modified); "the connexion of events . . . the Dark" (D, 10).

[6] "Why need . . . wilful election" (below, p. 281).

you put all gainsayers in the wrong; then you are the world; the measure of right, of truth, of beauty.[7]

In this fact, that virtue must be spontaneous, I find the explanation of our dislike to mechanical aids. This is the objection to covenants and pledges that bind men to the performance of some duty. The obligation was perfect before. To sign a pledge, is to add an imperfect obligation, and is thereby to commit a treason and act of high dishonor against virtue itself. Are not its resources sufficient for its needs? My whole being is to be my pledge and declaration and not a signature of ink. The act if done, tomorrow, for the sake of the pledge is no longer virtue.

In like manner it is dangerous to transfer our respect for the sentiment to any rites or acts. The gods, said Cyrus, make those very bad who talk much about them.[8] Goodness that scolds, undoes itself. A little electricity of virtue lurks here and there in kitchens, and among the obscure, chiefly in the heart of women, that flashes out occasional light, and makes the existence of the thing still credible. But one had as lief be a sinner as guilty of this odious religion that watches the food you eat and watches the orbit of the pitcher at table; that shuts the mouth hard at any remark it cannot twist or wrench into a sermon; and preaches as long as itself and its hearer is awake. Goodies make us very bad. We will almost sin to spite them.[9]

But beside pledges and the overgood religionist there is still another mechanical aid that is thrust upon the soul, namely creeds and classifications. Every new mind is a new classification. If it proved a mind of rare activity and power, a Locke, a Wilberforce, a Bentham, a Spurzheim, it imposes its classification on other men and lo! a new system. In proportion always to the depth of the thought and to the number of the objects it touches and brings within the reach of the scholar is the complacency of the pupil. But chiefly is this apparent in the creeds and churches which are also classifications of some powerful mind acting on

[7] "Why need you choose . . . of beauty" ("Spiritual Laws," *W*, II, 139; D, 128).

[8] Landor, "Xenophon and Cyrus the Younger, *Imaginary Conversations*, [First Series], III, 358; B, 28; Encyclopedia, 99. It is Xenophon who says something similar to this.

[9] "Goodness that scolds . . . to spite them" (D, 41).

the great elemental thought of Duty and man's relation to the Highest. Such is Calvinism, Quakerism, Swedenborgianism. The pupil takes the same delight in subordinating everything to the new terminology that a girl does who has just learned Botany, in seeing a new earth and new seasons thereby, which she does. It will happen for a time that the pupil will feel a real debt of spiritual progress to the teacher, — will find his intellectual power has grown by the study of his writings. This will continue until he has exhausted his master's mind. But in all the unbalanced minds (and whose is not so?) the classification is idolized, passes for the end, and not a speedily exhaustible means so that the walls of the system blend to their eye in the remote horizon with the walls of the universe and they cannot think how you aliens have any right to see, — how you can see. It must be somehow that you stole the light from us. They do not yet perceive that light, unsystematic, indomitable, will break into any cabin, even into theirs. Let them chirp awhile and call it their own. If they are honest and do well, presently their neat new pinfold will be worm-eaten and will lean, will rot, and vanish, and the Immortal light all young and joyful, million-orbed, million-colored, will beam over the Universe as on the first morning.[10]

Society is so timid and suspicious, so inapt to refer to principles, to ponder the awful fact, that it seems necessary to expand this statement. I would make it felt how pure and exclusive the relations of the soul are to the Divine Spirit, and how profane it is to interpose helps in that relation. It must be from everlasting and from the infinitude of God, that when God speaketh, he should then and there exist; should fill the world with his voice; should scatter forth light, nature, time, souls, from the centre of the present thought; and new date and new create the whole. Whenever therefore a soul is true, is simple; and, expelling all wilfulness, consents to God and receives the soul of the soul into itself then old things pass away, then means, teachers, texts, temples, fall; it lives now and not from the past. The present hour is the descending God, and all things obey. All the past exists to it as subordinate. All the future is contained in it. All things are

[10] "Every new mind . . . on the first morning" ("Self-Reliance," W, II, 79–80; D, 35, expanded).

made sacred by relation to it, one thing as much as another. It smooths down the mountainous differences of appearance and breathes one life through creation from side to side. All things are dissolved to their centre by the glory of the Cause, and in the universal miracle petty and particular miracles disappear. This is and must be. Do not then be deceived by any false annunciations of the presence of God. If a man claims to know and speak of God and carries you backward as the only road to the phraseology of some old mouldered nation in another country, in another world, believe him not.[11] The stricken soul will greet with joy every sympathetic word and so what was said by devotion thousands of years ago will come up as prophecy fulfilled. But the primary word will be that now spoken. This should be plain enough. Yet see how great and vivacious souls with grand truths in their keeping, do lack faith to utter directly from God that which he would give them to say, but rather wrench to their present wants the old Hebrew language, borrow of David, Jeremiah, and Paul, and disbelieve that God who maketh the stars and stones sing can speak our English tongue in Massachusetts and give as deep and glad a melody to it as shall make the whole world and coming ages ring with the sound. We shall not always set so great a price on a few texts, on a few lives. When we were young, we repeated by rote the words of our grandames, of our tutors, and as we grew older, of the men of talents and character we met: we painfully recollected and recited the exact words they spake. But as we advanced and came into the self-same point of view which they had when they uttered these sayings, we understand them perfectly, and are willing at once to let the words go; for, at any time, we can use words as good, when occasion comes. So will it continue to be, if we proceed. If we live truly, we shall see truly. It is as easy for the strong man to be strong as it is for the weak to be weak. With new perception we shall disburthen our memory of all its hoarded treasures as old rubbish, when we can create. When a man lives with God, his voice shall be as sweet as is now the murmur of the brook and the rustle of the corn.[12]

---

[11] "I would make it felt . . . believe him not" ("Self-Reliance," W, II, 65–66); "It must be from everlasting . . . believe him not" (D, 220).
[12] "This should be plain . . . of the corn" (D, 220–221).

And now, at last, the highest truth on this subject remains unsaid; probably, cannot be said; for, all that we say, is the far off description merely of the awful truth which in moments of life flashes on us and bids us go months and years feeding on the remembrance of that light, and assaying to tell what we saw. That thought, by what I can now nearest approach to say it, is this. When good is near you, when you have life in yourself, it is not by any known or appointed way; you shall not discern the footprints of any other; you shall not see the face of man; you shall not hear any name; the way, the thought, the good, shall be wholly strange and new. It shall exclude all other being. You take the way *from* man not *to* man.[13] All persons that ever existed, are but its perishable ministers. There shall be no fear in it. Fear and Hope are alike beneath it. It asks nothing. There is somewhat low even in Hope.[14]

We are then a vision. There is nothing that can be called gratitude, nor properly joy. The soul is raised over passion. It seeth nothing so much as Identity. It is a perceiving that Truth and Right *are*. Hence it becomes a Tranquillity out of the knowing that all things will go well. Vast spaces of nature; the Atlantic Ocean; the South Sea; — vast intervals of time, years; centuries; are annihilated to it. This which I think and feel, underlay that former state of life and circumstances, as it does underlie my present, and will always all circumstance, and what is called life and what is called death.[15]

When we look at life and see the snatches of thought, the gleams of goodness here and there, amid the wide and wild madness, — does it not seem to be a god dreaming? When shall we awake and dissipate these fumes and phantoms![16] We all complain of the feeble influence of thought on life, — a ray as pale and ineffectual as that of the sun in our bleak winter. They seem to lie — the actual life and the intellectual intervals, — in parallel lines, and never meet; (as we glow over tales of romantic virtue and then skulk, drivel, and sin among our own duties). Yet

[13] "And now, at last . . . not *to* man" (D, 222).
[14] D, 199.
[15] "This should be plain enough . . . called death" ("Self-Reliance," W, II, 67–69); "We are then a vision . . . called death" (C, 289).
[16] "When we look . . . and phantoms" (D, 186).

we doubt not, they act and react ever; that one is even cause of the other; that one is causal, and one servile; a mere vesture. Yet it takes a great deal of elevation of thought to produce a very little elevation of life. How slowly the highest raptures of the intellect break through the trivial forms of habit! Yet imperceptibly they do. Gradually in long years, we bend our living towards our idea but we serve seven years and twice seven for Rachel.[17]

This then is the best account of virtue at which we are at present able to arrive, that, it is the spontaneity of the will, bursting up into the world as a sunbeam out of the aboriginal cause. This is Virtue. And what is Duty? It is the endeavor of man to obey this light: the voluntary conforming our action to the whole; to the inward sentiment never quite absent; the uniform preference of the whole to the particular.

Duty is the application of the sentiment of virtue to the varying events of every day, in making which, all greatness consists. The measure of the force of the principle is of course in the temptations of the sense. And Character is the cumulative force of the Will acquired by the uniform resistance of temptation and the habit of obeying the sovereign instinct.

You see then the reason why in order to present the bare idea of virtue it is necessary to go quite out of our circumstance and custom else it will be instantly confounded with the poor decency and inanition, the poor ghost that wears its name in good society. Therefore it is that we fly to the pagans and use the name and relations of Socrates, of Confucius, Menu, Zoroaster, not that these are better or as good as Jesus and Paul, (for they have not uttered so deep moralities) but because they are good algebraic terms not liable to confusion of thought like those we habitually use. So Michel Angelo's sonnets to Vittoria Colonna we see to be mere rhapsodies to Virtue and in him, a savage artist, they are as unsuspicious, uncanting as if a Spartan or an Arab spoke them.[18]

If it were possible to speak to the virtue in each of our friends in perfect simplicity then would society instantly attain its perfection. If I could say to the young man, the young woman whom

---

[17] "We all complain . . . seven for Rachel" (C, 319, 340). Cf. Genesis 29:15–30.

[18] "You see . . . spoke them" (D, 150).

I meet in company, "Your countenance, your behaviour assure me. I discover in you the sparkles of a right royal virtue. I entreat you to revere its sublime intimations;" and this could be heard by the other party with a perfect trust, then instantly a league is struck between souls that makes life grand, and suffering and sorrow musical. Who would pine under the endurance of the many heavy hours of incapacity and mere waiting that creep over us, if once his soul had been challenged, his virtue recognized and he was assured that a Watcher followed him ever with inexhaustible affection? What then if many simple souls studious of science, of botany, of chemistry, natural history; lovers of all learning and scorners of all seeming should freely say to me — "God keep you, brother, — let us worship Virtue;" — by what a heavenly guard I should feel myself environed. But you see it is indispensable they should say it as men would; they must say it out of the pure sentiment, and not out of the catechism. They may be lovers of Christ, be sure, but they must love him because they cannot help it. For if there be the least smoothness and passive reception in them, then all their talk is cant, and we quit the room if they speak to us.[19]

Having offered these sketches or suggestions of this essence as it is a sentiment let us now look one moment at the outside of it as it is a law. From within we can feel its inspirations. Out there in history, we can see its fatal strength. It alone hath omnipotence. All nature feels its grasp. It enacts itself in time and space. It is in the world and the world was made by it. All nature is an illustration of the moral sentiment. All nature seems to execute it. A perfect equity adjusts its balance in all parts of life. Every secret is told; every crime is punished; every virtue rewarded; every wrong redressed in silence and certainty.[20] Every thing must come round and be told in season. The wild murder which terrified a hundred families, we learn later was an exact revenge.[21] Punishment is a fruit that unsuspected ripens within the very flower of the pleasure that conceals it. Cause and effect; means and ends; seed and fruit; cannot be severed for the

[19] "If it were possible . . . to us" (D, 149).
[20] "From within . . . and certainty" ("Compensation," W, II, 102, with modification).
[21] Cf. D, 141.

effect already blooms in the cause; and the end preexists in the means; the fruit in the seed.[22] Life is full of the most affecting illustrations of this truth.

> Bad counsel so the gods ordain
> Is most of all the adviser's bane.[23]

Every opinion reacts on him who utters it. An opinion is not the safest ware to deal in. It is a cotton ball thrown at a mark, but the other end remains in the thrower's bag. Or rather it is a harpoon thrown at the whale and if the harpoon is not good or not well thrown it will go nigh to cut the steersman in twain or sink the boat.[24]

A like Nemesis presides over all intellectual works. The effect of any composition is mathematically measurable by its depth of thought. How much water does it draw? If it awaken you to think, if it lift you from your feet with the great voice of eloquence, then the effect is to be wide, slow, permanent, over the minds of men; if the pages instruct you not, they will die like flies in an hour.[25]

Not less certain is the law as it touches all conditions. Let a man go ever so far, live ever so long, the same law rules his hundredth year as the first or tenth.

All people seek to be great, they would have offices, wealth, power, and fame. They think that to be great, is to get only one side of nature, the sweet, without the other side, the bitter. But he who by force of will or of thought is great, and overlooks thousands, has the responsibility of overlooking. With every influx of light comes new danger. Has he light? he must bear witness to the light and hate father, mother, wife, and child. Has he all that the world loves, admires, and covets? he must cast behind him their admiration and afflict them by faithfulness to his truth and

[22] "Punishment is a fruit . . . in the seed" ("Compensation," *W*, II, 103).
[23] Plutarch, "Concerning such whom God is slow to punish," *Morals*, IV, 158, ascribed to Hesiod; C, 130.
[24] "Every opinion reacts . . . sink the boat" ("Compensation," *W*, II, 110; C, 34).
[25] "A like Nemesis presides . . . in an hour" ("Spiritual Laws," *W*, II, 152–153); "The effect of any composition . . . in an hour" (D, 141).

become a byword and a hissing.[26] If riches increase, they are increased that use them. If the gatherer gathers too much, nature takes out of the man what she puts into his chest, swells the estate but kills the man. Or is a man too strong and fierce for society and by temper and position a bad citizen? Look at both sides of the account. See the back door as well as the front door; the export as well as the import. Your neighbor is an audacious, morose ruffian; a bad citizen; a dash of the pirate in him: people fear and hate him. What has made him civil? Nature sends him a troop of pretty sons and daughters who are getting along in the dame's classes at the village school; and to win regard for them he has smoothed his grim scowl. Thus nature contrives to intenerate her granite and felspar, — takes the boar out, and puts the lamb in, and keeps her balance true.[27]

This view of the Genius of the divine Providence was especially the study of the Greeks who have left us many memorable examples of it. Herodotus relates that in Lacedaemon lived Glaucus son of Epycides famous amongst his countrymen for his integrity. A Milesian came to Sparta drawn by his reputation and told him that he had come to be benefitted by his justice. " 'I have compared,' he said, 'the insecure condition of Miletus with the tranquillity of Peloponnesus, and seeing that by the chances of war my countrymen lose their wealth, I have converted half of my property into money, which I propose to deposit in your hands. Take it, therefore, and with it these private marks. To the person who shall convince you that he knows them, you will return it.' Glaucus accepted the money of the Milesian, on these conditions. After many years, the sons of this man came to Sparta, presented themselves to Glaucus, produced the test agreed on, and claimed the money. He however rejected the application with anger, and assured them, he remembered nothing of the matter. 'If,' said he, 'I should hereafter be able to recollect the circumstance you mention, I will certainly do you justice, and restore that which you say I have received. If on the contrary,

[26] "All people seek . . . and a hissing" (D, 180); "But he who by force . . . and a hissing" ("Compensation," W, II, 99–100).
[27] "If riches increase . . . balance true" ("Compensation," W, II, 98–99); "Look at both sides . . . balance true" (D, 136).

your claim has no foundation, I shall avail myself of the laws of Greece against you. I therefore invite you to return to me after a period of four months.' The Milesians departed in sorrow, considering themselves cheated of their money. Glaucus (on the other hand) went to consult the oracle at Delphi. On his inquiring whether he might absolve himself from returning the money by an oath, the priestess made him this reply; —

> Glaucus, thus much by swearing you may gain, —
> Through life the gold you safely may retain;
> Swear then, remembering that the awful grave
> Confounds alike the honest man and knave.
> But still an Oath a nameless offspring bears,
> Which, though no feet it has, no arm uprears,
> Swiftly the perjured villain will o'ertake,
> And of his race entire destruction make,
> Whilst their descendants who their oath regard,
> Jove never fails to favor and reward.

On this reply, Glaucus entreated the deity to forgive him: but he was told by the priestess that the intention and the action were alike criminal. Glaucus then sent for the Milesians, and restored the money. At the present day, no descendant of Glaucus nor any traces of his family are to be found: they are utterly extirpated from Sparta." [28]

Life is constituted with inevitable conditions which the unwise seek to dodge, which one and another brags that he does not know, — brags that they do not touch him; — but the brag is on his lips, the conditions are on his soul. If he escapes them in one part they attack him in another more vital part; if he has escaped them in form and in the appearance it is because he has resisted the Spirit there and fled from himself and the deep retribution makes the conditions good by banishing his soul this very hour from life.[29]

We are apt to feel defrauded of the retribution due to evil acts because the criminal goes his way, adheres to his vice and con-

---

[28] "Herodotus Book VI" [E], chapter LXXXVI. Emerson owned *Herodotus,* trans. William Beloe, 3 vols. (London, 1830), from which he quotes here, with some modification, III, 52–54.

[29] "Life is constituted . . . from life" ("Compensation," W, II, 105; D, 180).

tumacy — you adhere to your virtue but he does not come to a crisis or judgment anywhere in visible nature. There is no stunning confutation of his nonsense before men and angels. Be it so. Do not think therefore that he outwitted nature; but see him again with wiser eyes. Learn to make the witness of the Spirit in us what it is, a verdict of the Universe. Find the punishment in the act. Learn that the malignity and lie of the offender are the shadows of death creeping over him; that so far is he deceasing from nature; that in a virtuous action, I properly *am;* in a virtuous act I extend myself into real nature and see the darkness receding on the limits of the horizon.[30] The house praises the carpenter. "The reward of a good action is to have done it." [31]

> Minds that are great and free
> Do not on fortune pause
> 'Tis crown enough to virtue still her own applause.[32]

Experienced men of the world know very well that it is always best to pay scot and lot as they go along and that a man often pays dear for a small frugality. A wise man will extend this lesson to all parts of life and know that it is always the part of prudence to face every claimant and pay every just demand on your time, your talents, your feelings. Always pay, for first or last you must pay your entire expense. Persons and events may stand for a time between you and justice but it is only postponement, you must pay at last your own debt. If you are wise you will dread a prosperity which only loads you with more.[33] Benefit is the end of nature.[34] But for every one which you receive a tax is demanded. He is great who confers the most benefits. He is base — and that is the one base thing in the universe — to receive favors and render none.

In the order of nature we cannot render benefits to those from

---

[30] "We are apt to feel . . . of the horizon" (C, 323–324; cf. "Compensation," W, II, 121–122).

[31] Cf. C, 9, Φ, 11, a similar quotation attributed to Seneca but doubtless taken from Montaigne, "Of Glory," *Essays,* II, 488, where it is also attributed to Seneca, perhaps *De Vita Beata,* IX, 4.

[32] Ben Jonson, "An Ode. To himselfe," lines 16–18 (misquoted); last line only in Encyclopedia, 264.

[33] "Always pay . . . with more" (D, 214).

[34] D, 84.

whom we receive them or only seldom. But the benefits we receive must be rendered again line for line, deed for deed, cent for cent to somebody.[35] Beware of too much good staying in your hand. It will fast corrupt and worm worms. Pay it fast away in some sort.[36] A political victory, a rise of rents, the recovery of your sick, or the return of your absent friend, or some other quite external event raises your spirits and you think easy days are preparing for you. Do not believe it. It can never be so. Nothing can ever bring you peace but yourself. Nothing can bring you peace but the attainment of principle.[37]

By a force as perfect is every action possible to man pervaded.

[35] "He is great . . . to somebody" (D, 84).
[36] "Experienced men of the world . . . in some sort" ("Compensation," W, II, 112, 113).
[37] "A political victory . . . attainment of principle" ("Self-Reliance," W, II, 89–90; D, 214).

10

Demonology

The last of the "Human Life" course, this lecture was read at the Masonic Temple in Boston on February 20, 1839, and as the seventh and last lecture of the shorter series for the Concord, Massachusetts, Lyceum on May 15. Emerson's apology for not continuing the course beyond t   the end of this lecture a   ice, though it is on separe   good condition; it is num   except for one leaf in a   d sheet headed "Demonc   s.

Thoug   n February 11, 1843, ask   record that he read it th   ere until March 21, 1871,   by transcribing this old o   re in his second series on   Hall, Harvard Universit   that Cabot prepared for   d in the *North American*   collected posthumously   (*W*, X, 3–28).

T HI   y seem rather to shun   pher, have in every ma   times and in some mir   the direction of life. I   Coincidences, Luck, So   cts which are supposed   , unacknowledged ele   , if not violation of, t   obscure facts under the   ch individual

has usually in a lifetime two or three hints of this kind that are extraordinarily impressive to him, for this and for the light they throw on our constitution, they crave our consideration.

Let us consider first that with which we are familiar, the necromancy of sleep, the soft enchantress whose witchcraft divides with solid fact the empire of our lives; how strange this alien despotism that visits two children lying locked in each other's arms and carries them asunder by wide spaces of land and sea and wide intervals of time.[1] Yet this is the lot of all.

> There lies a sleeping city. God of dreams!
> What an unreal and fantastic world
> Is going on below!
> Within the sweep of yon encircling wall,
> How many a large creation of the night,
> Wide wilderness and mountain, rock, and sea,
> Peopled with busy transitory groups,
> Finds room to rise, and never feels the crowd! [2]

It is odd to consider it so, — the dreams of multitudes; but the astonishment remains that *one* should dream; that we should resign so fearlessly this deifying Reason, and become the theatre of delirious shows; and time, space, persons, cities, animals, should dance before us in this merry and mad confusion; sometimes the gravest secrets of thoughts should be told; sometimes the forgotten, the beloved, the youthful should be recalled —

> They come in dim procession led.
> The cold, the faithless, and the dead,
> As warm each hand, each brow as gay,
> As if they parted yesterday — [3]

a delicate creation outdoing the prime and flower of daily life; that antic comedy should alternate with gloomy and horrid pictures, transcending all waking experience or record; that we should be so earnestly busied as it seems for hours and days in peregrinations over seas and lands, in earnest dialogues, strenu-

[1] B, 131.
[2] Sir Henry Taylor, *Philip van Artevelde: A Dramatic Romance, in Two Parts,* 2 vols. in 1 (Cambridge and Boston, 1835), I, 169 (part I, IV, 1).
[3] Sir Walter Scott, *The Lady of the Lake,* I, xxxiii, 21–24; Blotting Book I, 38.

ous actions, for nothings and absurdities; cheated by spectral jokes and waking suddenly with our ghastly laughter to be rebuked by the cold, lonely, silent midnight, and gathering up with confusion in memory the gibbering nonsense as the occasion of this contemptible cachinnation.[4] Meantime that this spawn and limbo and dusthole of thought should be presided over by a certain nature and reason too; that we should recognize therein ourselves; that we should owe to sleep and dreams a certain divination and wisdom.[5]

A dislocation seems to be the foremost trait of the Dream. A painful imperfection almost always attends them. The fairest forms and the most noble and excellent persons are deformed by some pitiful and insane circumstance. The very landscape and scenery in dreams seem not to fit us, but, like a cloak or coat of some other person, to overlap and encumber the wearer; so is the ground, the road, the house in dreams too long or too short, and if it served no other purpose, would show us how accurately nature fits man awake.[6]

There is one memory of waking and another of sleep. In our dreams the same scenes and fancies are many times associated, and that, too, it would seem, for years.[7] One shall meet a whole crew of boarders at some dream house, of which gentlemen and ladies he can trace no shadow of remembrance in any waking experience. In sleep he shall travel certain roads in stage coaches or gigs which he recognizes as familiar and has dreamed that ride a dozen times; or shall walk alone in fields and meadows; which road, or which meadow, in waking hours, he never looked upon.[8] This feature of dreams deserves the more attention from its singular resemblance to that obscure yet startling experience which almost every person confesses in daylight, that particular passages of conversation and action have occurred to him in the same order before, whether dreaming or waking, — a suspicion that they have been with precisely these persons in precisely this

[4] "Let us consider . . . contemptible cachinnation" ("Demonology," W, X, 3–4.
[5] Cf. "Demonology," W, X, 7.
[6] "Demonology," W, X, 5; C, 258.
[7] "There is one memory . . . for years" ("Demonology," W, X, 5).
[8] "There is one memory . . . looked upon" (C, 10, where Emerson uses first person).

room, and heard precisely this dialogue at some former hour, they know not when.[9]

Another singular trait in dreams, is, that they have their own Fauna. Animals have been called "the dreams of nature." [10] Perhaps we go to our own dreams for a conception of their consciousness. In a dream we have the same instinctive obedience, the same torpidity of the highest power, the same unsurprised assent to the monstrous as these metamorphosed men exhibit.[11] Our thoughts in a barn or in a menagerie on the other hand, may well remind us of our dreams. What a compassion do these limitary forms occasionally awaken. You may catch the glance of a dog sometimes which seems to lay a kind of claim to sympathy and brotherhood. What! somewhat of me down there? Does the dog know it? Can he too, as I, go out of himself, see himself, perceive relations? We fear lest they should catch a glimpse of their forlorn condition. What a calamity if they should see for one moment the tough limitations of the organization which imprisons them!

The glance that suggests this strange melancholy, at once explains those ancient fables in which antiquity delighted, of the metamorphosis of men into beasts; and the transmigration of souls; for we see that this is our own thought carried out. What keeps those wild tales so long in circulation from ear to ear, from eye to eye, hundreds and thousands of years, what but the wild fact itself to which they suggest some approximation of theory?

Nor is the fact quite solitary, for in varieties of our own species where organization seems to predominate over the genius of man, — in Calmuc, or Malay, or African, or Flathead Indian, we are sometimes pained by the same feeling; and sometimes too the sharpwitted, prosperous white man awakens it. You think, — could he overlook his own condition, he could not be restrained from suicide.

Our dreams have a poetic integrity and truth. Their extravagance from nature is yet within a higher nature.[12] They are like

[9] "In sleep he shall travel . . . know not when" ("Demonology," W, X, 5–6).
[10] Madame de Staël, *Germany*, 3 vols. in 2 (New York, 1814), II, 322.
[11] "Animals have been . . . men exhibit" (A, 54).
[12] "Animals have been called . . . a higher nature" ("Demonology," W, X, 6–7).

monstrous formations, (for example, the toes that occasionally show themselves in a horse's hoof,) and note the generic law.[13] Wise and sometimes terrible hints shall in them be thrown to the man out of a quite unknown intelligence. He shall be startled two or three times in his life by the justice as well as the significance of the intimations of this phantasmagoria. Once or twice the conscious fetters of the spirit shall seem to be unlocked, and a freer utterance attained.

They pique us by independence of us. My dreams are not *me*. They are not Nature, or the *Not Me*. They are both: they have a double consciousness: at once *sub* and *ob*jective. I call the phantoms that rise the creation of my fancy; but they act like mutineers, — and fire on their commander, showing that every act, every thought, every cause is bipolar, and in the act is contained the counter-action. If I strike, I am struck; if I chase, I am pursued.[14]

A prophetic character in all ages has haunted them.[15] Our dreams show like the sequel of waking knowledge. The visions of the night bear some kindred to the visions of the day.[16] They are the maturation often of knowledge which we possessed the elements of, but had not consciously carried out to statements. Thus, when awake, I know the character of Rupert, but do not think what he may do. In dreams, I see him engaged in certain actions which seem preposterous, out of all fitness. He is hostile, he is cruel, he is frightful, he is a poltroon. It turns out a prophecy, a year later. But it was already in my mind as character, and the Sibyl of dreams merely embodied it in a fact.[17] We learn from the same dark Interpreter the shades of our own character. Hideous dreams are only exaggerations of the sins of the day. We see our own evil affections embodied in frightful physiognomies. On the Alps, the traveller sometimes sees a singular phenomenon, his own shadow magnified to a giant so that every gesture of his

---

[13] C, 300.

[14] "they have a double . . . pursued" (C, 300).

[15] "Wise and sometimes terrible . . . haunted them" ("Demonology," W, X, 7–8, rearranged).

[16] "Our dreams . . . of the day" ("Spiritual Laws," W, II, 148); first sentence in C, 134.

[17] "They are the maturation . . . in a fact" ("Demonology," W, X, 8–9; cf. C, 134–135).

hand is terrific. "My children," said an old man to his boys scared by a figure in the dark entry, "My children, you will never see anything worse than yourselves." [18]

We are let by this experience into the high region of Cause, and acquainted with the identity of very unlike seeming effects. [We learn] that actions whose turpitude is very differently reputed proceed from one and the same affection. Sleep takes off the costume of circumstance, arms us with a terrible freedom, so that every will rushes to a deed. A man amused himself in destroying the name and character of one of his neighbors in an evening circle; and at night he saw the vision of murder and a murderer's face grinning and gibbering over him with devilish intelligence.[19]

Dreams, however monstrous and grotesque their apparitions, have a substantial truth. The same remark may be extended to the omens, coincidences, presentiments which may chance to have astonished any person once in a while in the course of his life. Of all it is true that the reason of such an appearance is latent in the life of the individual. Why should not symptoms, auguries, forebodings be, and the moanings of the spirit?

The soul contains in itself the event that shall presently befal it, — for the event is only the actualizing of its thoughts.[20] "A man's destiny," it has been said, "is his temper." [21] More truly a man's fortune is in his character. As in dreams, so in the scarcely less fluid events of the world, every man sees himself in colossal, without knowing that it is himself that he sees. The good that he sees compared to the evil that he sees, is as his own good to his own evil. Every quality of his mind is represented in magnifico in some one acquaintance, and every emotion of his heart in some one. He is like a quincunx which counts *five* east, west, north, or south, or an initial medial and terminal acrostic.[22] And why not?

---

[18] "Hideous dreams . . . than yourselves" ("Spiritual Laws," W, II, 148); in Scotland and England, 7, the "old man" is identified as "my Grandfather," perhaps Ezra Ripley.

[19] B, 123.

[20] "Dreams, however monstrous . . . of its thoughts" ("Demonology," W, X, 9, rearranged); "Why should not . . . of its thoughts" (C, 135, in different order, and with the phrase "the moanings of the spirit" ascribed to Hedge).

[21] Cf. Benjamin Disraeli, *Vivian Grey*, book VI, chapter VII; Blotting Book II, 9.

[22] Cf. B, 216, 291.

His peculiar character leads him to increase his acquaintance with one person and neglect another according to their likeness or unlikeness to himself, so that he is truly seeking himself in his associates, and moreover in his trade, and habits, and gestures, and meats, and drinks; and comes finally to be faithfully represented by any view you take of his circumstances.[23]

Therefore it is no wonder, if the affairs in which a man engages, the words spoken by him and to him, the events, greater or less, that befal, should in a marked manner express his character and the legitimate issues of that character: it is no wonder that particular dreams, omens, coincidences, should fall out, and be prophetic, because all are prophetic. The fallacy consists in selecting a few insignificant hints when all are inspired with the same sense.

Every man goes through the world attended by innumerable facts prefiguring (yes, distinctly announcing) his fate — if only eyes of sufficient heed and illumination were fastened on the sign. The sign is always there, if only the eye were also, just as, under every tree, in the speckled sunshine and shade, no man notices that every spot of light is a perfect image of the sun, until in some hour the moon eclipses the luminary, and then first we notice that the spots of light have become crescents or annular, and correspond with the changed figure of the sun. Things are significant enough, Heaven knows, but the seer of the sign, where is he? We doubt not a man's fortune may be read in the lines of his right hand by palmistry, — in the lines of his face by physiognomy, in the outlines of the skull by craniology: the lines are all there, but where is the reader? [24]

The long waves indicate to the instructed mariner that there is no near land in the direction from which they come. Belzoni describes the three marks which led him to dig for a door to the Pyramid of Ghizeh. What thousands had beheld the same spot for so many ages and seen no three marks.[25] Is not the whole

[23] "As in dreams . . . of his circumstances" ("Spiritual Laws," W, II, 148–149).

[24] Cf. B, 216.

[25] "The long waves . . . no three marks" (D, 161). Giovanni Belzoni was the first to penetrate into the second pyramid at Giza, the entrance to which he discovered by observing three marks on the wall, which had previously gone unnoticed. See Belzoni, *Narrative,* I, 398 ff.

world instinct with life, and a man can go nowhither, and do nothing, that shall not instantly betray who and what he is, and tell the whole history of the world in every act. A man reveals himself in every glance he throws, in every step and movement and rest. Every part of nature represents the whole.

> Head with foot hath private amity,
> And both with moons and tides.[26]

Not a mathematical axiom but is a moral rule.[27] The jest and by-word to an intelligent ear extends its meaning to the Soul, and to all time. Indeed all productions of man are so anthropomorphous, that not possibly can he invent any fable that shall not have a deep and universal moral, and be true in senses and to an extent never intended by the inventor. Thus all the idlest fables of Homer and the poets, the modern poets and philosophers can explain with profound judgment, of law, and state, and Ethics. Lucian has an idle tale that Pancrates, journeying from Memphis to Coptus, and wanting a servant, took a door-bar, and pronounced over it some magical words, and it stood up and brought him water, and turned a spit, and carried bundles, doing all the work of a slave. What is this but a prophecy of the progress of art? For Pancrates read Fulton or Watt, and for magical word read steam, and do they not make an iron bar and half a dozen wheels do the work not of one, but of a thousand skilful mechanics? [28]

The universe is pervaded with secret analogies that tie together its remotest parts as the atmosphere of a summer morning is filled with innumerable gossamer threads running in every direction but revealed by the beams of the rising sun.[29]

And in those times and countries where the human mind gave the most faith to these fancies and whimsies, they were always

---

[26] George Herbert, "Man," lines 17–18.

[27] Cf. de Staël, *Germany*, II, 195; *Nature, W,* I, 33; *Lectures,* I, 25, 290; Encyclopedia, 189.

[28] "Lucian has an idle tale . . . skilful mechanics" (*Lectures,* I, 259–260; cf. Lucian, "The Lover of Lies, or the Doubter," 33–35).

[29] "it is no wonder that particular dreams . . . rising sun" ("Demonology," *W,* X, 9–12, with alteration and rearrangement); "Head with foot . . . rising sun" (Blotting Book Ψ, 102–103, expanded).

met and rebuked by the grave spirit of Reason and humanity. When Hector is told that the omens are unpropitious, he replies,

> One omen is good — to die for one's country.[30]

In the same spirit is the line of Lucan —

> Dire is the omen when the valiant fear.[31]

Euripides said, "He is not the best prophet who guesses well and he is not the wisest man whose guess succeeds well in the event, but he who, whatever the event be, takes reason and probability for his guide." [32] "Swans, horses, dogs and dragons," says Plutarch, "we distinguish as sacred, and vehicles of the divine foresight, and yet we cannot believe that men are sacred and favourites of Heaven." [33] The poor shipmaster discovered a true theology underneath the cover of a false, when in the storm at sea, he made his prayer to Neptune; "O God! thou mayest save me if thou wilt; and if thou wilt, thou mayest destroy me; but, however, I will steer my rudder true." [34] Let me add one more example of the same good sense, in a story quoted out of Hecateus of Abdera.

"As I was once travelling by the Red Sea there was one among the horsemen that attended us named Masollam, a brave and strong man and according to the testimony of all the Greeks and barbarians a very skilful archer. Now while the whole multitude was on the way, an augur called out to them to stand still; and this man inquired the reason of their halting. The augur showed him a bird, and told him, 'If that bird remained where he was, it would be better for them all to remain; if he flew on, they might proceed; but if he flew back, they must return.' The Jew said nothing, but bent his bow and shot the bird to the ground.

[30] Cf. *Iliad*, XII, 243; translation corrected in "Demonology," W, X, 13; variously in Greek in No. XVIII [A], ix; Blotting Book I, 39; Blotting Book II, 45; Blotting Book III, 17, 61; Encyclopedia, 37; Q, 1.

[31] *Pharsalia*, VII, 340–341 (Nicholas Rowe's translation); Blotting Book I, 35; Encyclopedia, 37.

[32] Plutarch, "Why the Oracles cease to give Answers," *Morals*, IV, 47.

[33] "A Discourse concerning Socrates's Daemon," *Morals*, II, 411.

[34] Montaigne, "Of Glory," *Essays*, II, 482; Encyclopedia, 167.

This act offended the augur, and some others, and they began to utter imprecations against the Jew. But he replied, 'Wherefore? Why are you so foolish as to take care of this unfortunate bird? How could this fowl give us any wise directions respecting our journey, when he could not save his own life? Had he known anything of futurity, he would not have come here to be killed by the arrow of Masollam the Jew.' " [35]

It is not the tendency of our times to ascribe importance to the whimsical pictures of sleep or to omens. But the faith in peculiar and alien power takes another form in the modern mind, much more resembling the ancient doctrine of the guardian genius. [36]

The ancients held that a genius or good Daemon presided over every man, leading him, whenever he suffered himself to be led, into good and successful courses; that this genius might even in some cases be preternaturally heard and seen; — when seen, appearing as a star immediately above the head and attached to the head of the person whom it guided. If of an evil and vicious man, then was the Daemon so immersed in his body that the light became dim as of a quenched star; if of a wise and divine person, the star was a pure splendor floating free over him and illumining the way before him. But rarely seen by the eyes of man, they rather waited to hear it as a voice, which at times became sensible and commanding to the astonished ears of the individual, and even of other men; but oftener, was only perceptible to the single ear of divine and extraordinary men. "For, as a stroke upon a brazen shield when the noise ariseth out of a hollow, is heard only by those who are in a convenient position and not perceived by others, so the speeches of the Daemon though indifferently applied to all, yet sound only to those who are of a quiet temper and sedate mind, and such as we call holy and divine men." In like manner, its instructions were oftener perceived by men in sleep; because, whilst we sleep, "the body is quiet and undisturbed, and the soul apt for finer advertisements than it can ap-

---

[35] "Hecateus of Abdera apud *Jahn, Heb. Com.* p. 215" [E]. Johann Jahn, *History of the Hebrew Commonwealth,* trans. Calvin E. Stowe (Andover, 1828), p. 215; Σ, 1–2.

[36] "And in those times . . . guardian genius" ("Demonology," *W,* X, 13–15).

prehend in the hurry of distracting business and tumultuous passions in which it serves the body when awake." [37]

This doctrine is a faint disguise of the most familiar and universal facts in human nature passed presently into the doctrine of a private and exclusive fortune such as that described in the conversation between Antony and the soothsayer in Shakspeare.

> *Antony.* Whose fortunes shall rise higher, Caesar's or mine?
> *Soothsayer.* Caesar's.
> > Therefore, O Antony, stay not by his side:
> > Thy dacmon, that's thy spirit which keeps thee, is
> > Noble, courageous, high, unmatchable,
> > Where Caesar's is not; but, near him, thy angel
> > Becomes a Fear, as being o'erpowered; therefore
> > Make space enough between you.
>
> .   .   .
>
> > If thou dost play with him at any game,
> > Thou art sure to lose, and of that natural luck
> > He beats thee 'gainst the odds; thy lustre thickens,
> > When he shines by. I say again, thy spirit
> > Is all afraid to govern thee near him;
> > But, he away, 'tis noble.[38]

An opinion equivalent to this almost all men entertain with more or less fulness. The belief that particular individuals are attended by a certain good fortune which makes them desireable associates in any enterprize of uncertain success, is I believe very prevalent not only among those who take part in great political and military projects, but in the ordinary speculations of commerce, internal improvements, and the mechanic arts. Corresponding to this is the firm assurance in the individuals themselves so distinguished, who meet and justify the expectation of others by a boundless self trust. "I have a lucky hand, sir;" said Bonaparte to his hesitating chancellor; "those on whom I lay it are fit for any thing." [39]

A thousand proverbs and common facts will attest the exist-

[37] "Plutarch" [E]; cf. "A Discourse concerning Socrates's Daemon," *Morals*, II, 403–409, for the whole paragraph.
[38] Shakespeare, *Antony and Cleopatra*, II, 3:16–24, 26–31.
[39] Las Cases, *Journal*, I, ii, 171; C, 314.

ence of this faith in different degrees. Especially it is familiar in one form, — that, often a certain abdication of prudence and fore-sight is an element of success; that children and young persons come off safe from casualties that would have been dangerous to wiser persons. We do not think the young will be forsaken. But he is always approaching the age when the sub-miraculous external protection and leading is withdrawn, and he is committed to his own care. The young man takes a leap in the dark, alights safe, and finds no harm. He remembers incidents and connexions of person and event that seem as he looks at them now to have been supernaturally deprived of injurious influence on him. His eyes were holden that he could not see.[40] Having ventured once, he ventures again. By and by he learns that such risks he may no longer run. He is oppressed by the melancholy discovery not that he incurs misfortunes here and there but that his genius whose invisible benevolence was tower and shield to him is not longer present or active.[41]

This supernatural favoritism is allied with a large class of su-perstitions; with the revelations of ghosts which are a selecting tribe speaking to one and avoiding millions; with the traditions respecting fairies, angels, and saints, scarcely less partial; the agents and the means of magic, as magicians and amulets. This faith in a partial power, so easily sliding into the popular belief every where, and in the particular of lucky days and fortunate persons as common in Boston today as the faith in incantations and philtres was in ancient Rome, or in the beneficent potency of the sign of the Cross in modern Rome; this supposed power crosses the ordinary and acknowledged powers natural and moral which science and religion and philosophy reverence and explore. This power heeded in many actions and partnerships, is not the power to which we build churches or dedicate Sabbaths nor that which is expounded by college professors of moral or metaphysi-cal science; but a different nature.[42] Accordingly Walter Scott, that Doctor of Demonology, has made the White Lady reply to the Monk's inquiry, "who and what she is?" —

[40] Cf. Luke 24:16; "Spiritual Laws," *W*, II, 147; see below, p. 211.
[41] "We do not think . . . present or active" (B, 46).
[42] "The belief that particular individuals . . . different nature" ("Demonol-ogy," *W*, X, 15–17).

"That which is neither ill nor well,
That which belongs not to Heaven nor to hell
A wreath of the mist, a bubble of the stream
Twixt a waking thought and a sleeping dream
A form that men spy
With the half shut eye
In the beams of the setting sun am I." [43]

In like manner a man of extraordinary insight, Goethe, has in his own autobiography recorded speculations upon the same topic, which are well worth citing.

"I believed that I discovered in nature animate and inanimate, intelligent and brute, somewhat which manifested itself only in contradiction, and therefore could not be grasped by a conception, much less by a word. It was not godlike, since it seemed unreasonable; not human, since it had no understanding; not devilish, since it was beneficent; not angelic, since it is often a marplot. It resembled Chance since it showed no sequel. It resembled Foresight since it pointed at connexion. All which limits us, seemed permeable to that. It seemed to strive with the necessary elements of our constitution; it shortened time and extended space. Only in the impossible seemed it to delight, and the possible to repel with contempt.

"This which seemed to insert itself between all others, to sever them, to bind them, I named the *Demoniacal*, after the example of the Ancients and of those who had observed something similar. I sought to redeem myself from this fearful being, whilst, as usual, I fled behind an image.

"Although every demoniacal property can manifest itself in the corporeal and the incorporeal, yes, in beasts too, in a remarkable manner, yet it stands in strictest relations with men, and forms in the moral world, though not an antagonist, yet a transverse element so that the former may be called the warp; the latter, the woof.

"For the phenomena which hence originate are there countless names: since all philosophies and religions have attempted in prose or in poetry this riddle to solve and to settle the thing

[43] *The Monastery*, chapter IX.

163

once for all which yet remained for them henceforward just where it was.

"Most fearful appears this element when it appears sometimes in a predominating man. In the course of my life I have been able to observe several such, some near, some farther off. They are not always the most distinguished men either in genius or in talents seldom recommending themselves through goodness of heart, but a monstrous power goes out from them and they exert an incredible force over all creatures, and even over the elements; and who shall say how far such an influence will extend? All united moral powers avail nothing against them. In vain that the more intelligent part of men will discredit them as deceived or as betrayer, the mass is attracted by them. Seldom or never find they their match among contemporaries, and they are not to be conquered by anything but the Universe itself, with which they begun the battle; and out of such observations doubtless arose [that] monstrous proverb, 'Nobody against God but God.' " [44]

It will be very easy in political history of every time to furnish examples of this inexplicable success. We certainly may find among those who figure in these contests men who have a certain force which, without virtue, and without eminent talents, yet makes them strong and prevailing. No equal appears in the field against them. A force goes out from them which draws all men and events into their favor. The crimes they commit, the exposures that follow, and which would ruin any other cause, are strangely overlooked, or do more strangely turn to their advantage. Lies and truth, crimes and mistakes seem equally to turn to their account.

I relate these things as I find them but however attractive or poetic these twilights of thought, I confess I like broad daylight better, and I think there is somewhat wilful, — some play of hide and seek — when men as wise as Goethe talk mysteriously of the demonological. The insinuation is that the known external laws of morals and of matter are sometimes corrupted or eluded by this lurking gypsy principle, this Mother power, that chooses fa-

[44] "Goethe; Nachgelassene Werke; Vol. 8 p. 178" [E], i.e., *Dichtung und Wahrheit,* part IV, book XX, in *Werke,* XLVIII, 175–179.

vorites, and works in the dark of the Universe for their behoof.[45] I will tell you what I think of it, — that philosophically considered the Demonological principle is nothing but a great name for a very common and well known tendency of the mind, — an exaggeration, namely, of the Individual, of the personal bodily man which nature steadily postpones.[46] In nature the race never dies, — the individual is never spared. And all truly great men have felt that they are so, by sacrificing their private and individual desires, and falling back upon what is general and human; in renouncing family, town, clan, country, and every sort of exclusive and local connexion, and beating with the pulse, and breathing with the lungs of nations and of Man. A highland chief, an Indian sachem, or a feudal baron may easily imagine that the mountains and the lakes were made specially for him Donald, or for him Tecumseh, that the one question fit for all history to discuss is the pedigree of his house, and the one problem for the future ages to enhance if they can, its dignity and renown. Such a person very easily extends the pretensions of his foolish individuality beyond even these — beyond all bounds, — into the domain of the infinite and universal; he assumes that he has a powerful guardian angel; that he is not in the roll of common men, but obeys a great family Destiny; when he acts, unheard of success will evince the presence of rare agents; what befals him, omens and coincidences will foreshow; and when he is to die, ghosts will announce the fact to the kinsman in foreign parts. What more easy and vulgar than to project this exuberant selfhood into the region where the individuality is forever bounded by generic and cosmical laws.[47]

Traces of the same exaggeration are found in the popular religious creeds, whenever they intrude the element of a limited personality into the high place which nothing but spiritual energy can fill; introducing names and persons where a will is an intrusion into growth, repentance, and reformation.[48]

If we please, we can no doubt look strange on the matter, and

[45] "In like manner a man . . . their behoof" ("Demonology," W, X, 17–19).
[46] Cf. "Demonology," W, X, 20.
[47] "And all truly great men . . . cosmical laws" ("Demonology," W, X, 21–22).
[48] "I will tell you . . . and reformation" (D, 248, expanded).

say, in beholding one who is called a fortunate man, "What lucky star presides over him!" but the law of the Universe is one for each, and one for all; — and there is as precise and as describable a reason for every fact occurring to him, as for any occurring to any man; that every fact in which the moral elements intermingle, is not the less under the dominion of fatal law, than the properties of light, or water, or salt, or sugar. Lord Bacon uncovers the magic when he says, "Manifest virtues procure reputation, occult ones fortune." [49] The so-called fortunate man is one who has some rare properties of character, as for example is one who though not peculiarly gifted to speak eloquently or to act gracefully or even understandingly to great ends, — is yet one who in actions of a low and common pitch relies on his instincts and simply does not act when he should not, but waits his time, and without effort acts when the need is: so that he is in a particular circle and knot of affairs not so much his own man as the hand of nature and of time. Whereas the fault of most men is that they are busy bodies, that they do not wait the simple movements of the soul but perpetually interfere and cross and thwart the instructions of their own minds. If to this you add a fitness to the society existing around him, you have the elements of fortune.[50]

And this is the reason too why the young may sometimes venture when the old may not; for, in youth, the instinct has much more perfectness and strength, and the impulses of the young have their origin in that and may be trusted often when the understanding has not been employed on the facts, and is not satisfied; but afterwards when the ripe man has learned to overpower the suggestions of instinct by the perpetual activity of the understanding, — the man of the senses, the man of calculation; the instinct is less true and distinct and when on an occasion he acts in neglect or in defiance of his understanding, he may find that he has mistaken a whim, a caprice, for the suggestion of the high instinct.

So it may be said of those bodily risks incurred by children and by thoughtless and giddy persons which give occasion to the

---

[49] Bacon, *De Augmentis Scientiarum* (lib. VI, cap. III, ex. XI), in *Works*, VII, 321; Encyclopedia, 35.

[50] "If we please . . . elements of fortune" ("Demonology," *W*, X, 22–23, with some alteration).

saying that "Fortune favors fools," that they do habitually rely more than others upon the instinct which is more active in such, than in men whom more knowledge and the habits of the world have accustomed to disuse these original lights.

But here when we speak of the instinct that saves us in bodily risks, as also in what was said before concerning dreams, we are touching another topic that ought to be carefully distinguished from what is said of spiritual laws. I mean the subject of structure. A large proportion of the facts called demonological are not questions of theology or of metaphysics, but semi-medical questions, respecting our structure, very fit to be explored doubtless, and ranging themselves with the wonders of organization; but nowise entitled to be ranked in the category of the supernatural. Such for example is the curious power many persons possess of waking from sleep at a given hour, where the understanding seems to make an appointment with the unconscious, instinctive nature which the latter keeps. So with the influence of the eye; and with many facts of sympathy and antipathy.

To the same category belong the facts which have attracted in the last half century so much notice to Animal Magnetism. The interest of Animal Magnetism turns on the light it may throw on structure, as for example its experiments go to show that we can do that by deputy in another self, which we cannot do in our own. But all these facts are the phenomena of Disease; all these facts are of so fuliginous, nocturnal, and typhoid a character, as to repel rather than invite.[51]

And this is not the least remarkable fact which the adepts have developed. Men who had never wondered at anything, who had thought it the most natural thing in the world that they should exist in this orderly and replenished world, have been unable to suppress their amazement at the disclosures of the somnambulist. The peculiarity of the history of Animal Magnetism is that it drew in as inquirers and students a class of persons never on any other occasion known as students and inquirers. Of course the inquiry is pursued on low principles. Animal Magnetism peeps.[52] It becomes in such hands a black art. The uses of the

[51] Cf. C, 160.
[52] D, 36.

167

thing, the commodity, the power, at once come to mind and direct the course of inquiry. It seemed to open again that door which was open to the imagination of childhood — of magicians and fairies and lamps of Aladdin, the travelling cloak, the shoes of swiftness and the sword of sharpness that were to satisfy the uttermost wish of the senses without danger or a drop of sweat. But as Nature can never be outwitted, as in the Universe no man was ever known to get a cent's worth without paying in some form or other the cent, so this prodigious promiser ends always and always will as sorcery and alchemy have done before in very small and smoky performance.[53]

I speak this of course to the popular idea and pursuit of it. It remains to the physician a legitimate inquiry though I think of exaggerated interest. It is a maxim of reading that he who reads all books may read any book and to the man of science nature sets no bound.

This obscure class of facts have great interest for some minds. They run eagerly into this twilight and cry to the unwilling beholder. There's more than is dreamed of in your philosophy.[54] Certainly these facts are interesting and are not explained. They deserve to be considered. A theory of them is greatly to be desired. But they are entitled only to a share of our attention and that not a large share.[55] The fallacy is in supposing these to be wonders and every thing else truly grand and perfect not wonders, but things of course, as if one should exhaust his astonishment on the economy of his thumbnail, and overlook the central causal miracle of his being — a man! [56]

Besides let their value as exclusive subjects of attention be judged of by the infallible test of the state of mind in which much notice of them leaves us. They savor of nothing great or noble. Read Homer and Plato and Milton; or read Cuvier and Davy or the still more modern inquirers into astronomy, geology, comparative anatomy, and our views are expanded and our sentiments

[53] "And this is not . . . smoky performance" ("Demonology," W, X, 24–25; cf. D, 241).
[54] Cf. Shakespeare, *Hamlet*, I, 5:166–167.
[55] "This obscure class . . . large share" ("Demonology," W, X, 23–24; *Lectures*, I, 332; B, 45, expanded).
[56] Cf. "Demonology," W, X, 10, and B, 160.

ennobled. Read Cornelius Agrippa or the Dream Book or Colquhoun's Report[57] and you are bewildered and brought into low and noisome alleys and blind lanes that lead nowhere. We grope and stumble. They who love them say they shall reveal to us a world of unknown and unsuspected truths. No doubt; all nature is rich but these are her least valuable and productive parts. If a diligent collection and study of these occult facts were made, they could never do much for us. They are merely physiological, opening to our curiosity glimpses of how we live, but throwing no light and no aid on the superior problem why we live and what we do.[58] It is a false view to couple them in any manner with the religious nature and sentiments and a dangerous superstition to raise them to the lofty place of motives and sanctions. This is to prefer haloes and rainbows to the sun and moon.[59]

Meantime far be from me the impatience which can not brook the supernatural, the vast: far be from me the lust of explaining away all which appeals to the imagination, and the great presentiments which haunt us. Willingly I too say — Hail! to the unknown awful powers which transcend the ken of the understanding. And the attraction which this topic has had for me and which induces me to unfold its parts before you is precisely because I think the numberless forms in which this superstition has re-appeared in every time and every people indicates the inextinguishableness of wonder in man; betrays his conviction that behind all your explanations and all your theories, is a vast and potent living nature inexhaustible and sublime which you cannot explain. He is sure no book, no man has told him all. He is sure the great Instinct, the circumambient soul which flows into him as into all,

[57] Henry Cornelius Agrippa von Nettesheim (1486–1535), *De Occulta Philosophia* (1531); *Report of the Experiments on Animal Magnetism, Made by a Committee of . . . the French Royal Academy of Sciences*, trans. John C. Colquhoun (Edinburgh, 1833). The "Dream Book" may refer to Artemidorus Daldianus (fl. 2nd cent.), *Oneirokritica* (1518), which went through many subsequent editions (one in 1805, e.g.) and translations. The English version, reprinted a number of times, has variant titles: *The Judgement, or Exposition of Dreames* (London, 1606) and *The Interpretation of Dreames* (London, 1644).

[58] "Besides let their value . . . what we do" ("Demonology," *W*, X, 24); "Read Cornelius Agrippa . . . what we do" (B, 45).

[59] "Besides let their value . . . sun and moon" (*Lectures*, I, 332); "It is a false . . . sun and moon" ("Demonology," *W*, X, 26); last sentence only, cf. B, 116, and Plutarch, "Why the Pythian Priestess Ceases her Oracles in Verse," *Morals*, III, 134.

and is his life, has not been searched. He is sure that intimate relations subsist between his character and his fortunes, between him and his world; and until he can adequately tell them, he will tell them wildly and fabulously. Demonology is the Shadow of Theology.

The whole world is an omen and a sign. Why look so wistfully in a corner? Man is the Image of God. Why run after a ghost or a dream? The voice of divination resounds everywhere and runs to waste unheard, unregarded as the mountains echo with the bleatings of cattle.[60]

It is with regret that I find myself compelled by the present state of my health to bring to a somewhat abrupt termination this course of lectures. When I began to prepare the lecture I have just read it was fully my intention to attempt to give some completeness to the series by two discourses more: on the Limitations of human activity by the laws of the world, — which would have given scope for a better consideration of the facts of Time, Space, Dualism, Alternation, Climate, and other boundaries that wall us in, and which I had only named in the sketches of the debt of man to his condition in the third Lecture; I desired also to add another Discourse on the intrinsic activity and resources of our nature, its great tendencies and prospects, so far as now we dare cast its horoscope.

At present we have attempted *in the first* lecture to read a line of the Doctrine of the Soul, to indicate the worth of human life by denoting some of the facts that betray a power and virtue the most august and commanding within man; *in the next,* to describe the circumstance and to deduce the law of Home, or the primary condition of the human soul; *then,* to sketch its School or its teaching by the Instincts, Condition, Persons, Books, Facts; *then,* in the two following lectures, to sketch the natural history of Affection, and of Intellect; *then,* to describe the position of antagonism in which each new man finds himself in respect to society and the protest that the soul imposes; *then,* to consider

[60] "Meantime far be from me . . . of cattle" ("Demonology," W, X, 27–28); "Demonology is . . . of cattle" (Φ, 132).

the shades of life, the value and place of the tragic element; *then,* the nature of the Comic; *then,* the grand element of Virtue; and, *tonight,* the alleged exception to the law.

The execution of these plans I find myself constrained to postpone. But what difference does it make? Two or two hundred of our sketches of nature would never make our copy complete. Ever nature mocks our imperfection with her perfection. After a thousand artists have lived and wrought, her secret remains untold, and not begun to be told. And yet this one fact, — that Nature is thus rich, — we are able to say and to repeat. This, I will hope, is the one lesson which these lectures have taught, and confirmed to all brave and open minds, one man's belief that his words and all words are nothing but the confession of ignorance in the presence of Truth and Goodness and Beauty that overhang and environ us all. I shall hope that you have heard through every sentence I speak — "Be it known to you there is higher teaching." And to this progress there is no bound. It is the privilege of man, that, soar as high as he will, there is always a higher. And as in doctrine so in life. I would inspire the love of grandeur of character. Naked simplicity is the perfectness of man. Plain dealing the summit of benevolence and wisdom. Nor can this exist in any mind until he has no self-will, but obeys with a child's trust the power which creates and renews him forever and ever.

II

THE PRESENT AGE

☞ MR. EMERSON'S Course of Lectures on the Present Age, commences TOMORROW EVE- NING, at 7 o'clock, at the *Masonic Temple.*

Tickets to the course or to the single lecture may be had of C. C. Little and James Brown, No. 112; and of James Munroe & Co. 134, Washington street

dec 3

[Newspaper announcement in the *Boston Daily Ad- vertiser and Patriot,* December 3, 1839]

EMERSON reluctantly postponed work on *Essays* (1841) in order to give a new course of lectures in Boston in the winter of 1839–40. His lecturing the previous winter had been a satisfactory enterprise though not financially so successful as in 1837–38: returns had fallen off slightly in Boston and there had been virtually no engagements for money elsewhere. He was gratified at least to know that even after his address at the Divinity School he could still summon an audience and to know, as he wrote Carlyle, that he could not hurt himself — "that no polemical mud" could stick to him (*CEC*, p. 217) — but this pleasure was doubtless qualified by the strain of completing the course, or at least ending it, in bad health. In the summer of 1839 he was still financially overextended, partly because of his publishing ventures on Carlyle's behalf. It was presumably for this reason that by August 17 he saw "plainly I shall have no choice about lecturing next winter; I must do it" (*L*, II, 217–218, 233, 256). On December 4, 1839, then, Emerson began his new course of ten lectures on "The Present Age" at the Masonic Temple in Boston and, except for Christmas, read them on successive Wednesday evenings to the conclusion on February 12.

Again there were diminished returns from the Boston readings, though he increased his income for the season by giving two lectures (probably only one from the new series) at the Salem Lyceum in February and for the first time by carrying regular lectures southward out of Massachusetts. Before the new course had been planned Emerson had agreed to give in March "two or three" lectures at the Mercantile Library in New York, but it was after considering the receipts from the Boston series that he accepted an offer from the Franklin Lyceum in Providence, Rhode Island, for "five or six lectures" to be read on his return from New York (*L*, II, 218–219, 256, 258). Of the three lectures read in New York (March 10, 13, and 17) two came from "The Present Age," though one of these was a condensation of the two lectures on "Literature." The series of six lectures read at Providence between March 20 and April 1, though it was announced as "Human Life," seems to have been drawn in two or more instances from "The Present Age" (*L*, II, 266; Charvat, p. 18). He was notably successful in both Providence and New York, an important indication of his future possibilities, but the failure of the Atlantic Bank to pay a dividend left him financially pretty nearly where he was before. Though he could have remained at Providence to give a course of private lectures, he preferred not to do so (*L*, II, 264, 266, 272). At the beginning of April he returned to continue the reading, which he had begun on March 4, of the new course to his neighbors in Concord, and within the month he was back at work on *Essays* and much involved in *The Dial* (*L*, II, 275–284; *CEC*, p. 267).

Though the financial gain was not great, Emerson derived pleasure from the lecture season of 1839–40. At the end of the Boston course he wrote that he had "spent a happy winter. I meet some old friends. I have made some new ones & my relations to my fellow creatures become more easy & agreeable" (*L*, II, 256). In Providence to his amusement he was a celebrated Transcendentalist and the center of much attention (*L*, II, 266–267). In New York he wrote, "the young people are so attentive & out of the hall ask me so many questions, that I assume all the airs of Age & sapience" (*CEC*, p. 261). Emerson could not but be assured that he had an audience beyond Boston as he concluded the lecture season and turned again to his book.

Emerson's reluctant decision to lecture in the winter of 1839–40 came before he had decided upon a subject. He had materials, though much of them must already have been used up in the work he had done on *Essays,* which, contrary to earlier optimistic expectations, seems to have languished since July because of hot weather, visitors, a vacation trip to the New Hampshire mountains, and indifferent health. He wrote to William on September 26, 1839: "I have just decided, unwillingly somewhat, to read one more course of lectures in Boston next winter but their tenor & topics float yet far off & undefined before me, . . . [I] am as usual neither sick nor well, but, for aught I see, as capable of work as ever, let once my subject stand like a good ghost palpable before me" (L, II, 224). Extensive writing in his journal between September and November suggests that Emerson was groping after a subject; the result of this serious work is a course of lectures more highly unified in theme than his earlier courses. This one did not become the "gay rag bag" he had earlier called his courses by way of illustrating to Frederic Henry Hedge how he sought "the amplest cloak of a name whose folds will reach unto & cover extreme & fantastic things" (L, II, 121). It is of course true that on one level the new course, like the previous three, teaches, as Emerson wrote in April, 1840, "one doctrine, namely, the infinitude of the private man" and, whatever its title, a lecture is "only the application of the same truth . . . to a new class of facts (E, 124). But it is also true that regardless of basic doctrine there is more coherence of theme here than in earlier series. The proportion of material incorporated from journals written after he planned the course is high, suggesting not only that he had exhausted some of his early journal resources, but more significantly that he had a new topic and was writing toward it in his journals.

If near the end of September the "tenor & topics float yet far off & undefined," he at least had a title by November 4, when he wrote to Elizabeth Hoar: "I have advertised my new Course & call it the Present Age, but alas it is still Future Age to me" (L, II, 231). In early October he may have found the topic, though not the tenor; the early suggestion he entered in his journal is quite different from what he actually developed in the course: "The Woes of the time, — is not that topic enough? He that can enumerate their symptoms expose their cause & show how they contain their remedies comes to men from heaven with a palm branch in his hand" (D, 379). From this and "the Dangers of Commerce" as a deserving question (E, 4) it is a considerable shift to his statement in late October: "Trust thy time also. What a fatal prodigality to contemn *our* Age. One would say we could well afford to slight all other Ages if only we value this one . . . He who shall represent the genius of this day, he who shall standing in this great cleft of Past & Future understand the dignity & power of his position so well as to write the laws of Criticism of

Ethics of History will be found an age hence neither false nor unfortunate but will rank immediately & equally with all the masters whom we now acknowledge" (E, 12). Once having got this clue, Emerson quickly developed many of the ideas which would go into the new lectures until, at the end of October, he formulated his plans, warning himself now not to be too narrow in his subject: "Shall I not explore for the subject of my new lectures the character, resources, & tendencies of the Present Age? Such an argument will include what speculations I may have to offer on all my favorite topics. Nor will it cripple me by confining to any local or temporary limits discussions which I should rather extend to universal aims & bearings. For the Age — what is it? It is what the being is who uses it, — a dead routine to me, and the vista of Eternity to thee. One man's view of the Age is confined to his shop & the market, and another's sees the roots of Today in all the Past & beneath the past in the Necessary & Eternal. Let us not dwell so fondly on the characteristics of a single Epoch as to bereave ourselves of the permanent privileges of Man" (E, 29).

When he wrote Elizabeth Hoar that his proposed course on "The Present Age" was to him, alas, "still Future Age," he, perhaps unknowingly, hit upon the central interest the subject held for him. Certainly he was playing with his new-found ideas in the facetious remarks he wrote to Margaret Fuller on November 14: "I must turn again to this woebegone Age. How came I guilty of such condescension to limits? Shall I not even yet escape & announce in the Morning Post Lectures on Eternity?" (L, II, 236). The day before he wrote this letter he recorded in his journal a theme which, while it makes apparent his mock fear of limitations in subject, sets forth at the same time a new and informative theme for the series: "The source of information on which I most rely for unlocking for me the secret of the age is the acceptance of the nearest suggestion & the most faithful utterance of all that which is borne in upon my mind. I cast myself upon the Age & will not resist it. Passive I will think what it thinketh & say what it saith. All my hope of insight & of successful reporting lies in my consciousness of fidelity & the abdication of all will in the matter. Whilst those whom I see around me consulting the same auguries are first enamored of their own opinion or of some past man's opinion or of some institution or of some favorite measure & are striving to do something with the Age, to make their mill go, to persuade the Vast Ocean of the Time to convert itself into a mill stream to turn their nice wheel, & to corrupt if it were possible the incorruptible Wind" (E, 55–56). A central and important position is defined here and gives personal significance to its reappearance in the lectures. On the same day that he wrote to Margaret Fuller, another journal passage, also lifted into the first lecture, defines "The Present Age" so that it docs incorporate "Lectures on Eternity": "We cannot overvalue our Age. All religious considerations lead us to prefer it. Then it is our all. It is the World. As the wandering sea bird which crossing the Ocean alights on some rock or islet to rest for a moment its wings & to look back on the wilderness of waves behind & forward to the wilderness of waters before, so stand we perched on this rock or shoal of time arrived out of the Immensity of the Past & bound & roadready to plunge into immensity again" (E, 56). Under the modest irony of Emerson's statements about "the Present Age" seems to lie authentic excitement about the new lectures.

This excitement, once he had found his topic, affected his attitude about lecturing again. Nearly a month after he had "decided, unwilling somewhat, to read one more course of lectures in Boston," he wrote in his journal, attempting to get started on an as yet undefined subject: "In these golden days it behoves me once more to make my annual inventory of the world. For the five last years I have read each winter a new course of lectures in Boston, and each was my creed & confession of faith. Each told all I thought of the past the present & the future. Once more I must renew my work and I think only once in the same form though I see that he who thinks he does something for the last time ought not to do it at all. Yet my objection is not to the thing but to the form; & the concatenation of errors called *society* to which I still consent, until my plumes be grown, makes even a duty of this concession also. So I submit to sell tickets again" (E, 8). A few pages later, having found excitement in a new subject, his old enthusiasm for the possibilities of lecturing returned, and he wrote that he looked "upon the Lecture room as the true church of today & as the home of a richer eloquence than Faneuil Hall or the Capitol ever knew" (E, 18). This reflects the potential he saw in lectures as "a new literature," which had not yet been successfully exploited, as he had written the previous July; in the office of the orator "You may & shall (please God!) yet see the electricity part from the cloud & shine from one part of heaven to the other" (D, 336).

After having begun the course "with the old experience" that when the first lecture "was done, & the time had come to read it, I was then first ready to begin to write" (E, 91), Emerson still retained his excitement. The third lecture had been read, though the remainder of the course was still not precisely fixed, when he wrote to Margaret Fuller on December 23, expressing some fears about the "treadmill gait" his course threatened to fall into but adding an aspiration which is at variance with his initial reluctance to undertake the lectures: "But truly I would not be frivolous or conventional in this attempt however slight at expounding the spirit & tendency of my day. Let us in the one golden hour allowed us be great & true, be shined upon by the sun & moon, & feel in our pulse circulations from the heart of nature. We shall be more content to be superseded some day, if we have once been clean & permeable channels" (L, II, 246).

If Emerson's enthusiasm for this course grew as he found a subject, he nevertheless experienced a disappointment at the end of the Boston readings. Clearly the disappointment derives from exceedingly high expectations. To William he wrote, "I pleased myself before I began with saying, — I will try this thing once more because I have not yet done what I would with it. I will agitate men being agitated myself. I who rail at the decorums & harness of society why should I not speak very truth, unlimited, overpowering? But now unhappily the lectures are ended — ten decorous speeches & not one extacy, not one rapture, not one thunderbolt. Eloquence therefore there was none" (L, II, 255–256). The dissatisfaction has nothing to do with either the form of the private lecture — Emerson still holds the "new theatre," the "new art," in high regard — or the specific subject of his "Present Age" series. The dissatisfaction is personal and physical — a feeling that he lacks what he calls the "constitutional vigor" necessary to "lay [himself] out utterly" in the preparation of his lectures. Practically, he can spend no more than twenty-one hours on each lecture. "Could I spend sixty hours on each, or what is better, had I such energy that I could rally the lights & mights of sixty hours into twenty, I should hate myself less . . ." (E, 119). One must judge the self-deprecations within the context of what Emerson meant by "clean & permeable channels," "extacy," and "rapture." Certainly, in any ordinary sense, these are eloquent lectures. Even he could admit to William a kind of satisfaction in the public reception of "The Present Age": "As the audience however were not parties to my intention or hope, they did not complain of my failure" (L, II, 256).

There is more to Emerson's expectations for this course than his demanding criteria in oratory. The newness of the subject engaged him more than "Human Life" did. If "A man's subject always lies in his recent thought & habits" (E, 42), the age was an appropriate subject for Emerson. Personally he seemed in 1839 concerned with his own enlarged role in the world, with his involvement on the forward edge of the present: "With the Past as past I have nothing to do, nor with the Future as future. I live now, & will verify all past history in my own moments" (D, 355). Moreover, there is a growth in what he has to say, resulting perhaps from his effort in reworking his earlier material into essays.

To be sure the age, as subject, characteristically opened itself to a series of topics all of which in some form or other Emerson had used before: the course most closely resembles "The Philosophy of History" with which it shares three lecture titles in addition to the course title, used in the 1836–37 course as an individual lecture title. There is, however, in the extant manuscripts of the new course only trifling repetition from earlier lectures. A comparison of the earlier lecture "The Present Age" with the new course shows a marked shift in his ideas. The lecture from "The Philosophy of History" mechanically exposes those traits of the age commonly thought to be advances over the past: in sum, "This is the unfavorable side of the picture." At the end Emerson avoids the "gloomy view" and, characteristic of "The Philosophy of History," destroys his nominal topic: "It is pedantry to insist much upon distinctions so evanescent and unphilosophical as those of mere time." This is introduction for the next lecture, "The Individual," which is the conclusion toward which Emerson had been working. Without in the least slighting "whatsoever abuses mark the existing forms," Emerson's emphasis in the 1839–40 course is on the reform and regeneration heralded amidst them. Emerson defines his method thus: the character of the age is "not to be learned by enumeration of all the traits [which would include the *débris* of the past] but by the eminency of some." The eminent traits are "those elements which are new and operative and by their activity now detaching the future from the past and exposing the decays of the corpse they consume." As the title of the concluding lecture suggests, the emphasis in "The Present Age" is prospective: the present is examined for the seeds of the future.

To mitigate the newness of what Emerson says in "The Present Age" is to postpone and heighten an observable difference between "Human Life" and "The Times," an attractive break in Emerson's thought because of the intervening publication of *Essays* (1841). It is true that much of "The Present Age" went into that volume and is mingled harmoniously with passages from earlier lectures. To emphasize the similarity between "The Present Age" and "The Times" is to strengthen the continuity of Emerson's thought: to find a new emphasis in his work during the fall of 1839 and thus to associate the development of new ideas with the process of reconsideration of earlier material and revision of it for *Essays*. The shift in subject matter is accompanied by a shift in method. "In correcting old discourses to retain only what is alive," Emerson, at the time he was preparing "The Present Age," had learned something about his writing: he found "a good deal of matter which a strong common sense would exclude." The new course is marked by a transitional ambivalence between the reporter and the preacher: "I love facts & so erase this preaching. But also I venerate the Good, the Better & did therefore give it place" (D, 373). The "condescension" to the limits of the age as subject holds Emerson to facts for which he is not assuming responsibility as a preacher of the ideal, but of course Emerson cannot leave his subject there in the realm of mere dead fact. The resultant tension is not characteristic of "Human Culture" and "Human Life" and foreshadows the more explicit reportorial method of later lectures.

Because it has a more palpable subject matter than "Human Culture" and "Human Life," "The Present Age" is more unified than those. Its structure is topical, simple, and seems to conceal no arrangement significant in itself. The undated lists of lectures for the course in Blotting Book Ψ suggest nothing more than topics Emerson found available and appropriate to the exposition of his subject. An extensive draft of the first lecture (Δ, 27–32) and the substantial revisions of the lecture manuscript indicate that Emerson planned a general thesis statement to be illustrated in successive specific topics. That these subsequent lectures remained indefinitely fixed and were written during the Boston course is suggested by the letter Emerson wrote to Margaret Fuller on December 23, after three of the lectures had been read (L, II, 246). He seems never to have broken the habit of weekly preparations in the course of a lecture series, and one suspects that this habit was not uncongenial to his temperament. Nevertheless, because of its straightforward introduction to the thesis, its illustration by various classifications, and its résumé, restatement, and hortatory inference at the end, "The Present Age" is free from the mixed organization of "Human Culture" or the collapse of the scheme of "Human Life." The résumé which begins "Tendencies" is more convincing than the summary added to "Demonology," though we must remember that the latter was an expedient ending because of Emerson's health. Although "The Present Age" is somewhat belabored in its thesis, the resulting unity amidst a variety of topics suggests that Emerson sustained throughout an excitement about his subject.

That the series is fragmentary is a loss for the reader. The lecture "Ethics" was missing or unidentifiable when Cabot listed the manuscripts (see headnote, p. 271) and remains lost; it it possible that it was wholly used up in Essays (1841) or Essays, Second Series (1844) or in another lecture. Only fragments remain of "Private Life" and "Politics" because both manuscripts were used extensively, and their leaves probably served either as printer's copy or were destroyed after fair copy had been made. After considerable reconstruction of manuscripts which are now rearranged, there still remain lacunae. Yet, even with these losses the series is a substantial and important statement; its development beyond the lectures of 1836–39 prefigures such series as "The Times," "New England," and "Mind and Manners of the Nineteenth Century."

1

Introductory

The 1839–40 winter series at the Masonic Temple, Boston, opened with this lecture on December 4, 1839. A lecture at the Salem, Massachusetts, Lyceum on February 26 or 27, 1840, entitled "Analysis, the Character of the Present Age," and the second lecture in a brief series at the New York Mercantile Library on March 13, 1840, announced as "The Character of the Present Age," were doubtless this lecture. It was also repeated to introduce the series on "The Present Age" at the Concord, Massachusetts, Lyceum on March 4, 1840, and at the Franklin Lyceum at Providence, Rhode Island, on March 20, 1840, it was the first in the series announced as "Human Life" but which drew also on the lectures from "The Present Age" series (*L,* II, 266).

At the top of the first leaf after the cover Emerson wrote "Read at the Masonic Temple 4 Dec. 1839 P.A. Lect. 1." No title was announced for the Boston reading and the title chosen here comes from a final listing in Emerson's workbook after he had in incomplete lists used "Age" and "The Age" for the first lecture (Notebook Ψ, 163, 166) and from the list he entered in his journal to note the conclusion of the Boston series (E, 118).

The manuscript was once sewn and the pages numbered in ink (the order followed in this text) and partially in pencil, indicating minor subsequent rearrangement of material. A single leaf now with the manuscript does not belong with it and is printed in its proper place in the ninth lecture of this series, "Education." Five leaves are missing from the manuscript, leaving small gaps in the text at three points. It is a fat manuscript, with much cancelled repetition, reorganization, and cutting, but the revision seems largely done during composition rather than for subsequent readings and suggests that Emerson had much to say on this fruitful topic. A later introduction written in pencil on the verso of the cover (also transcribed in another hand on a loose leaf now with the manuscript) and a few small and obvious revisions for a later reading outside New England, though within a year of the first reading, have been rejected and put in the textual notes.

The lecture seems not to have been used for essays except for passages which found their way into the posthumously published

"Historic Notes of Life and Letters in Massachusetts" and "Boston,"
though in both cases the material passed through other lectures. Much
of this lecture was recast for an existing lecture manuscript of the
1850's variously called "The Spirit of the Times" and "The Spirit of
the Age" (see Kronman, pp. 105–109, for summary of a reading)
which was itself probably a revision of a missing manuscript read in
Scotland in February 1848 called "The Spirit of the Times" and "The
Genius of the Present Age" (Scudder, p. 247). There were doubtless
other uses of the material in later lectures, but the present manuscript
seems to have been read only in 1839–40.

IN LOOKING around for some topic sufficiently general to
include the various thoughts which from time to time occur to
the mind of a retired scholar and which seemed to him fit to be
imparted, and sufficiently definite to promise some convenient
method, I found none so proper as the Character, Resources, and
Tendencies of the Present Age. I hope it will not appear that I
have selected a subject too little or too great. In the first place, I
would not by directing my attention on the interests of the Day
exclude myself from those treasures of past literature and history
nor from those questions of philosophy to which each man ought
to guard his access as the high privilege of a rational being. And
I need not. For what is the Age? It is what the being is who beholds it. It is transparent to every man according to the powers of
his eye. To one man it is the price current and the newspaper;
and another sees the roots of Today in the past centuries and
beneath the past in the Necessary and Eternal. I shall endeavor
not to dwell so fondly on the characteristics of an Epoch as to
bereave myself of the contemplation of the permanent privileges
of man.[1]

On the other hand, neither will this topic if properly handled
seem too vague and extensive to admit of being reduced within
just limits. We set out on the inquiry of the character of the age.
But this is not to be learned by enumeration of all the traits but
by the eminency of some. If everything contemporary is to
characterise the Age, from the markets of Liverpool and New

[1] "In looking around . . . of man" (E, 29, modified).

York, the wealth of London, the learning of Germany, the army of Russia, the despotism of Turkey, the pastures of Tartary, the petty activity and immoveable polity of China and Japan, the creepings of European civility into Australasia, and all the immensity of details which coexist and interact under these broad names, it is plain that nothing could be comprehended of such an inextricable confusion. No foregoing age but has left some residue and relic of itself. In that view it seems as if we could find in modern society no peculiar genius but the specimens of every mode of life and thought which has anywhere prevailed. As if modern society was composed of the *débris* of the foregone structures of religion and politics, a mixed mass just as the soil we till is made up of the degraded mountains of the elder world.[2] But if the age is to be characterised only by those elements which are new and operative and by their activity now detaching the future from the past and exposing the decays of the corpse they consume, then we may hope within reasonable limits to denote the powers of the present epoch and the causes of that which is to follow.

It seems at first impossible to seek to give names and assign causes to things so multiplex and evanescent as the spirit of the time. What is the soul of the age? Why here are many souls — contemporary; many activities; many unlike ends. But there are two parties to one of which all men belong. The party of the Past and the party of the Future. Men range themselves here and elsewhere and everywhere either with the Movement Party or with the Establishment. This schism is the subtlest in all history. It runs under the world and appears in all unexpected quarters. It is in Literature, in Philosophy, in Church, in State, in Social Customs. It seems a war betwixt the Intellect and the Affection. It seems a crack in nature which has split every Church, be its creed what it may — Christendom into Papal and Protestant; Calvinism into old and new schools; Quakerism into old and new;[3] Methodism into old and new. England into Conservers and Reformers; America into Whig and Democrat; Philosophy into Material and

---

[2] "No foregoing age . . . elder world" (E, 64).
[3] "But there are two parties . . . old and new" (see "Historic Notes of Life and Letters in New England," W, X, 325–326).

187

Spiritual. It has reached even into the immoveable East. Constantinople is divided in its opinion whether the Janissaries shall wear coats and the Sultan learns to sit in a chair.

In the attempt to explore the genius of the Age, I fasten my regard on the second of these parties. They are the Age. If we can appreciate their activity and its causes, we can well spare all attention to the other class except as illustrative of this.

The key to the period is the knowledge that in recent times men have been animated with a faith in the Soul. The whole of modern history has an ethical character. There is in it the revelation that there is not only circumstance but man; that there is not only an Assyrian Empire and Roman Empire but a human race; that there is a great responsible Thinker and Actor moving wherever moves a man.[4] The former generations acted under the belief that a shining social prosperity was the aim of men: and sacrificed uniformly individuals to the nation. The modern mind teaches that the nation exists for the Individual, — for the guardianship and education of every man. This idea writes itself out coarsely in all the revolutions and public movements. In the mind of the philosopher [it] has far more precision, and is attaining a depth and splendor.

In the eye of the philosopher the individual has ceased to be regarded as a part and has come to be regarded as a whole. He is the world. The individual learns his access to the Universal Mind, is inspired by the sentiment of a deep and total union with Nature.

This perception is a sword such as was never drawn in the world before. It divides and detaches bone and marrow, soul and body, yea, almost the man from himself. This is the Age of Severance, of Dissociation, of Freedom, of Analysis, of Detachment. It is the age of the first person singular. The man steadily sunders himself more and more from his holdings. Every man for himself. The public speaker disclaims speaking for any other; he answers only for himself. It is All Souls' Day. The social sentiments are weak. The sentiment of patriotism is weak. Veneration is low. The natural affections feebler than they were. People grow philosophical about native land and parents and relatives. There is an

[4] Cf. "Self-Reliance," W, II, 60; also see above, p. 7, and below, p. 242.

universal resistance to ties and ligaments once supposed essential to civil society, the new race is stiff, heady, and rebellious: they are fanatics in freedom; they hate tolls, taxes, turnpikes, banks, hierarchies, yes, almost laws. They have a neck of unspeakable tenderness; it winces at a shadow. They rebel against mediation or saints or any nobility in the Unseen. It tends to solitude. The association of the time is accidental and momentary; the detachment intrinsic and progressive. The association is for power merely, for means; the end is the enlargement and independency of the individual. Anciently society was in the course of things: there was a Sacred Band, a Theban Phalanx. There can be none now. College classes, military corps, or Trades' Unions may fancy themselves indissoluble for a moment over their wine, but it is a painted hoop and has no girth.[5] But two parties endure, the party of the Past and the party of the Future.

But whilst [the] great fact I have mentioned, the uprise of the Soul, remains underneath as the master spring of all the activity we witness it has as yet come very imperfectly to light in small minorities, in a few individuals as a conscious fact. By far the largest proportion of acts and persons are the organs of another school and system of thought; namely, of Analysis, or the exercise of the Understanding. The still reigning school we may call.the epoch of Analysis. The coming era that of the Soul. So that almost all the signs of the time are of destruction rather than of creation. The old leaf, the ripe fruit falls from the plant because it is pushed off by a new leaf bud below.[6]

And here in order to make plain what I shall have to say in the sequel, I must advert to [a] metaphysical distinction. The power by which [man] contemplates the Necessary, the True, the Good, or what we call absolute truth stands in a wonderful antagonism with the power by which he apprehends particular facts, and applies means to ends. The former holds the latter in contempt. When the latter is most active, the former is most withdrawn. The former we call Reason or Sentiment or the Soul; the latter we call the Understanding. Now the world consents to

---

[5] "The former generations . . . has no girth" ("Historic Notes of Life and Letters in New England," *W*, X, 326–327, with some omissions).
[6] Cf. *E*, 169.

acknowledge him the greatest man and that age the happiest era, when the first power has been most active; when the sentiments of the Good, the Beautiful, and the True have predominated; when a sentiment has led his active powers, and not his activity overpowered his sentiment. Man is whole as long as the active powers are directed by the Soul. A nation governed by the religious sentiment, or by the parental sentiment, by the love of military glory, (which is only an impure love of greatness), or by the love of art, is still capable of extraordinary deeds. But an activity of the lower powers once absolved from the dominion of these sentiments, makes life and man mean. It is aimless bluster. All religion departs. Analysis is the understanding taking a step forward of the soul; and so it has the freedom of an evil spirit.

Analysis is, at first, the simple detachment of an object into its parts, to see it for what it is. It is done in obedience to the highest sentiment. We do not wish to be mastered by anything. We wish things to obey us. But the activity of this power absorbs the man; weans him from the sentiments which make his greatness and surrounding him with the fruits of its own industry makes him at once proud and poor.

That which characterises recent history is the extreme activity of the understanding without the check of the sentiments.[7]

·　　·　　·

Commerce is only a single fruit of the new habit of thought. Yet such is the predominance that belongs to Trade and its consequences, at the present day, that viewed superficially the age might easily be designated as the age of Commerce. Commerce removes from nature that mystery and dread which in the infancy of society defend man from profanation before yet his prudence and his conscience are enlightened. At this day amidst the grandeur of Commerce the philosopher may well occupy himself with the price of its gifts. There is nothing more important in the culture of man than to resist the dangers of Commerce. An admirable servant, it has become the hard master. It seems to realize to the senses the sovereignty which the Soul claims.

Commerce has no reverence. Prayer and prophecy are irrele-

[7] One leaf is missing at this point.

vant to its bargain. It encroaches on all sides. "Business before friends" is its byword. The end, *to be rich,* infects the whole world, shoves by the state so that the state becomes subordinate and only an office of trade, one department of Commerce filled with virtual merchants who are there to be rich and conscious of their parentage or filled with the spirit of the time. Government is administered for the protection of trade. Law is interpreted and executed on the same principle, that a man's enjoyment of his estate is its main end. Education is degraded. It aims to make good citizens on this foundation; and Religion even is a mere lever out of the spiritual world to work upon this. Commerce, dazzling us with the perpetual discovery of new facts, of new particulars of power, has availed so far to transfer the devotion of men from the soul to that material in which it works.

See what structures of old faiths in every department of society a few centuries have sufficed [to] destroy. Astrology, Magic, and Palmistry are gone. The very last ghost is laid. Demonology is on its last legs. Prerogative fails every day.[8] There is nothing left but newspapers. If you count ten stars you will fall down dead. Let us see, saith a rosy Analyst, of six years 1, 2, 3, 4, 5, 6, 7, 8, 9, 10, and laughs aloud. If you spill the salt, if you cross your knife and fork, if you make hay on Sunday, if [you] baulk water — Behold, they have done all these unscathed. "God created the sun and the moon," said Moses, "that is," said the Prelates of Pope Boniface VIII, "the Pope and the Emperor." [9] But the Emperor has been driven out of Italy and the Pope out of England, France, and Germany. The king is anointed of God and God punishes treason like impiety, was the doctrine in which our grandfathers were bred. Let us try, said the analysts. They insulted, restrained, imprisoned, and beheaded the king and the whole land ate and slept as well as usual.[10]

.   .   .

Of course, this is most evident and most deplorable in the highest sentiment, that is, the *religious.* Who can read the fiery

[8] "See what structures . . . every day" ("Historic Notes of Life and Letters in New England," W, X, 327).
[9] Jeremy Taylor, *Titles of the Ten Sermons,* Sermon X, in *The Whole Works,* ed. Reginald Heber, 15 vols. (London, 1822), V, 517; Blotting Book II, 31.
[10] Two leaves are missing at this point.

ejaculations of St. Augustine, a man of as clear a sight as almost any other, of Thomas A Kempis, of Milton, of Jeremy Taylor, without feeling how rich and expansive a culture — not so much a culture as a higher life — they owed to the ceaseless and grand promptings of this sentiment; and without contrasting their immortal heat with the cold complexion of our recent wits? Who can read the pious diaries of the Englishmen in the time of the Commonwealth and later without a sigh that we write no diaries today? [11]

Sir Thomas Browne in his diary (which has just now been printed for the first time) sets down his resolution:

"To pray and magnify God in the night and my dark bed when I could not sleep, to have short ejaculations whenever I awaked, and when the four o clock bell awoke me or my first discovery of the light, to say the collect of our liturgy, Eternal God who hath safely brought me to the beginning of this day etc. . . .

"To pray in all places where privacy inviteth; in any house, highway or street; and to know no street or passage in this city which may not witness that I have not forgot God and my saviour in it, and that no parish or town where I have been may not say the like. . . . Upon sight of beautiful persons, to bless God in his creatures, to pray for the beauty of their souls, and to enrich them with inward graces to be answerable to the outward. Upon sight of deformed persons to send them inward graces and enrich their souls and give them the beauty of the resurrection." [12] Even Dr. Johnson, the biographer of Browne, was not born too late for these celestial influences, as his Diary and Prayers may attest. Who can read without emotion a note of his resolutions formed at Church? "During the usual time of meditation I considered the Christian duties under three principles of soberness, righteousness, and godliness; and purposed to forward godliness by the annual perusal of the bible, righteousness by settling something for charity, and soberness by early hours." [13]

[11] "Who can read the fiery . . . diaries today" ("Boston," *W*, XII, 194).

[12] "*Works*. Vol. IV. p. 420." [E], i.e., pp. 420–421. Emerson is citing Sir Thomas Browne, *Works, Including His Life and Correspondence*, ed. Simon Wilkin, 4 vols. (London, 1835–36).

[13] "*Works* Vol IX p. 522." [E]; Blotting Book II, 5. Emerson is citing Samuel Johnson, *Works*, New Edition, 12 vols. (London, 1806).

How richly this old stream of antique faith descended into New England the remembrances of the elder portion of my audience I am sure will bear witness. This country forty or fifty years ago was imbued with a certain normal piety, a levitical education which falling on fit subjects gave often advantages which only rarely devout genius could countervail. It still stands in contrast with the comparatively cold instruction of the theological institutions like a religion in the blood. The depth of the religious sentiment as it may still be remembered in individuals imbuing all their genius and derived to them from hoarded family traditions, from so many godly lives and godly deaths of sainted kindred was itself an Education. It raised every trivial incident to a religious and celestial dignity. I heard with awe in my youth of the pale stranger who at the time one of these fathers in God lay on his deathbed, tapped at the window and asked to come in. The dying man said, "Open the door;" but the family were timid. Immediately he breathed his last, and they said one to another, "It was the angel of death." Another of these elect souls when near his end had lost the power of speech, and his minister came to him and said, If the Lord Christ is with you hold up your hand; and he stretched both arms aloft and died. In every town in Maine you may still hear of the charities and of the commanding administration of his holy office, of Father Moody of Agamenticus. When the offended parishioners, wounded by his pointed preaching, would rise to go out of Church, he cried out, "Come back you graceless sinner, come back." And when his parishioners began to fall into ill customs and ventured into the alehouse on a Saturday night the valiant pastor went in after them, collared the sinners, dragged them forth, and sent them home with rousing admonitions. Charity then went hand in hand with Zeal. They gave alms profusely and the barrel of meal wasted not.[14] One of this venerable line, the minister of Malden, Massachusetts, whilst his house was burning, stood apart with some of his church and sang, "There is a house not made with hands." His successor was wont to go into the road whenever a traveller passed on Sunday, and entreat him to tarry with him during holy time, himself furnishing food for man and beast. Religion was their occupation

[14] Cf. I Kings 17:14.

and the prophetic and apocalyptic ejaculations of these worthies still colour the language of devotion in the American Churches. In the departure of this faith a vast body of religious writings which came down to this generation as an inestimable treasure, — the whole body I mean of English and early American sermons and practical divinity, — have been suddenly found to be unreadable and consigned to remediless neglect.[15]

Art languishes because society is unbelieving, honey combed, and hollow. By our processes of thought the world is stripped of love and terror. The sun and the moon, the mountains and the sea, the harvest and the animals awaken no astonishment. Once, every day had its saint; every unusual occurrence its supernatural ties. Here came the other night an Aurora so wonderful, a curtain of red and blue and silver lustre that in any other century it would have moved the awe and wonder of men and mingled with the profoundest sentiments of religion and love. And we all saw it with cold, arithmetical eyes; we counted the colors; the number of degrees it extended; the number of hours it lasted and of this celestial flower we beheld nothing more — a primrose by the brim of the river of time.[16] Shall we not wish back again the Seven Whistlers, the Flying Dutchman, Eric's cap, St. Elmo's light, the lucky and unlucky days, and the terrors of the day of doom? [17] The decays of piety beget the decay of learning.

The Genius of the Age does not tend to Erudition. The learning of Scaliger and Bentley, of Cudworth and Johnson was the natural fruit of the traditional age in philosophy and religion. Our age tends continually to ask for the sufficient reason, to demand that the author make out his case on its merits; the jury of readers take the *law and the fact* into their judgment and will not be bothered with lexicons. The fine geniuses of the day decry books.

---

[15] "This country forty . . . remediless neglect" (adapted from C, 65–66, where Emerson recollects these anecdotes of his Aunt Mary Moody Emerson). Father Moody was his great-great-grandfather, the Reverend Samuel Moody of York, Maine; the minister of Malden was Emerson's great-grandfather, the Reverend Joseph Emerson (cf. Genealogy, 5). A few small emendations in this paragraph and one in the next have been rejected as obvious revisions for a later reading outside New England, probably in New York on March 13, 1840. See textual notes.

[16] Cf. Wordsworth, "Peter Bell, a Tale," lines 248–250.

[17] "Here came . . . day of doom" (D, 351–352).

It is not strange then, though it deserves notice, that in America, where as I believe all the tendencies of the time may be seen in an exalted state, this whim takes the offensive form. I am sorry to notice a disposition ostentatiously [to] disclaim the knowledge of languages, antiquities, and art.[18] Our self-made men, as the newspapers call them, of whom we have so large a crop, have the whim in public speeches of explaining to the assembly how little they are indebted to Colleges and Latin Schools.[19]

.   .   .

[Napoleon had frequently to harangue at the markets,] in the streets, in the sections, in the faubourgs and insisted that he always found the faubourg St. Antoine, in which the poorest and lowest of the population are found, the most ready to listen to reason, and the most susceptible of a generous impulse.[20]

Let not the abuse of the power discredit the power. It has wrought unhallowed by the Soul. But it is the trusty servant of the Soul.

Analysis thus infinitely busy with its experiments on matter, on society, on labor, on thought, and on action, is inevitable. Analysis is as much in nature as synthesis. Every stone has an upper and an under side. It seems as if analysis were legitimate to the poetic soul. I find analysis I think not less poetical than synthesis but it must be analysis into elements and not mechanical division. If I can detect nature converting water into hydrogen and oxygen, two beautiful and perfect wholes, I see not that it is less grand than when she recomposes water, a new whole. Mechanical analysis picks the lock; Right analysis produces the key.[21] Is not the sublime felt in an analysis as well as in a creation? It seems very impertinent in us to fear a hurt in this tendency as if the gastric juices were beginning to dissolve the stomach and so the stomach eat up the man. Rather expect immense discoveries and a magazine of new elements to enrich the

---

[18] Cf. D, 99.
[19] "The fine geniuses . . . Latin Schools" (cf. E, 351). Two leaves are missing at this point.
[20] Las Cases, *Journal,* I, ii, 95; cf. C, 314.
[21] "It seems as if . . . produces the key" (D, 312).

combinations of the philosopher and the man in the next centuries.[22]

Let us be just to this wonderworker and see its results, the prodigious expansion of trade. It was Commerce that settled this country, however Religion may have mixed on one or two conspicuous occasions therewith. American Commerce alone is already worthy of a history. The coasting trade; the whale trade; the ice trade; the China Trade; the Russia trade; the Northwestern Coast inland trade; steamboat trade; the army of our travellers. See the roads shooting like the crystals of congealing water in every direction so that the rail cars shall skate over all the land. See the mechanical inventions. Now look higher: see the defiance of law, the fanaticism of freedom. Now see the fruitful crop of social reforms: Peace, Liberty, Labor, Wealth, Love, Churches of the Poor; Rights of Women; all ethical, — and sought not by the malignant but by the good.

These all, it may be, see not what they point at. They tend to ends whereof they yet dream not, and which the zealots, who work in these reforms, if suddenly shown, would defy. But the heart and the hand go forward to a better heaven than they know. What a task lies evidently before us and at no great distance to inform with new and holier life Government, Education, Religion, and Social Modes.

Meantime along with the activity of mere commodity of which I have spoken appears ever and anon and now more steadily, as I have intimated, a new agent. These reforms are ethical, religious, humane. Men ask for pure truth; and in practice for simple equity. The age is characterised by a certain yearning or aspiration which has given a new element to poetry and is called the Feeling of the Infinite. This new love of the Vast which was native in Germany, which was imported into France by De Stael, which appeared in England in Coleridge, Wordsworth, Byron, Shelley, Felicia Hemans, which finds a most genial climate in the American taste[23] and may now be noted in every copy of verses or college exercise, what is it but the breathing and sobbing of the long imprisoned but now escaping Soul? Pardon it if it is

---

[22] "Is not the sublime . . . next centuries" (E, 62).
[23] Cf. "Thoughts on Modern Literature," W, XII, 318; below, p. 217; E, 82.

impatient of our schools and books. Do not turn from it, if it propose strange and incredible changes. On man has dawned a hope to make him wild with joy. Wait a little and it will subside into deep peace.

Side by side with this analysis remains the surviving Tradition, the old state of things in Church, State, College, and social forms, numbering in its train multitudes composed of those in whom affection predominates over intellect; of those in whom talent predominates over character; of those who are inactive and indisposed to the exertion which novelty of position demands; and lastly of those who have found good eating under the shadow of the institutions and therefore hate any change. The *inertia* of the Community, that is the Laws, the Property, the Usages, the aged population, and whatever weakness, sickness, or preoccupation of mind with private matters — all this numerous vote goes for Tradition.

The Colleges and all monied foundations of learning or religion are usually found on the side of Tradition; for two reasons; I. Because to answer their permanent wants they must rely on dynamical means, for the government and excitation of large numbers, as Classes, Textbooks, Prizes, and not on means rare and extraordinary as on the teaching of Poets and men of Genius; II. Because such institutions always must call in merchants or bankers to take care of their property and these persons inevitably give a conservative or property direction, to the institutions.

On the other hand an advantage shines ever on the movement party that these philanthropists really feel no clog, no check from authority, no discord, no sore place in their own body which they must keep out of sight or tenderly touch. People just out of the village or the shop reason and plead like practised orators such scope the subject gives them and such stimulus to their affections. The reason is glad to find a question which is not, like the dogmas of the pulpit or the statehouse, bound around with so many traditions and usages that every man is forced to argue unfairly, but one on which he may exhaust his whole love of truth — his heart and his mind. The cause educates the man. Each man feels suddenly the strength of a principle and finds himself greater than he was, greater than all men who do not

197

receive it. Never is a good cause long at loss for an ideal equipment. It shows its nearness to nature presently by awakening the Imagination. Poets are born for it. Young Eloquence nourishes itself gladly on its overflowing truth; and philosophers of the purest sight give it a sacred authority by reconciling it with whatever is just and grand.

Whilst the tradition is every day assailed, in their sorrow at the loss of the objects of the sentiment, men go back to the old books, reprint them, repair the old monuments, celebrate ancient anniversaries, praise that which is old though it was never good, and in new buildings copy the elder architecture and in modern poetry and fiction reproduce the antique or the middle age. Roxburgh Clubs are founded, Shakspeare Societies, Camden Societies, Cheetham Societies; the Retrospective Reviews, Percy's Reliques, and the entire effort of Walter Scott's genius designate our time; Ellis's Letters, Froissart, and Joinville are reprinted; then the recovery of a vast body of archives, correspondence, and history of the Elizabethan Age and of the English Commonwealth.

This dilettantism is a certain sign that a revolution is on foot. This holding back betrays the fact that the general movement is forward. The retreat on the old literature is a sort of truce and sacred game, in which eminent persons of both parties take a part, as nations delight to mitigate the horrors of war by celebrating in weeds of peace, friends mixed with foes, a religious festival. The analysts take part in this movement. They see in the life of these splendid periods new argument to convict the degeneracy of the age, and even the ablest reformer has relentings of common sympathy which make him glad to find a sort of expiation for the shock he occasions in his admiration of the genius of the Past.

But, whilst the cause is not defended on its merits but as all great movements of the human mind have been on some petty and accidental points, the movement party steadily and daily gains; not as far as any one can discern by the light which men or masses contribute but as by the movement of the world itself. The great Idea which gave hope to their hearts and articulation to their tongues creeps on the world like the advance of morning twilight and they have no more part in it than the watchman who announced the daybreak. It takes friends and foes by surprise and refuses to give its glory to a man.

The whole hope and vigor of the period centres in the new importance of the individual man. In the faith, that he represents not a private but a universal interest, that no expediency, no laws, no numbers, no property, no state, no church, are or can be equivalent to a man; much less that he is to be sacrificed to them. He is greater than all the geography and all the governments of the world, standing, whilst he is true and simple, for Reason itself, representing in his person in virtue of his possible perfection all nature and all thought. This faith once admitted, all the movements of the day follow, of course; the attack upon War, upon Slavery, upon Government, upon the systems of Education and the religious Traditions; the inferior estimate in which old literature and old art even, come to be held, — in short a disesteem of the whole Past, a breaking up of all manner of old Idols, out of a supreme reverence of the possibilities of man, an unfaltering Hope, say rather, a perfect Trust in the infinite resources of the soul.

The problem which belongs to us to solve is new and untried. Born in the age of calculation and criticism we are to carry it with all its triumphs and yield it captive to the Universal Reason. Educated in the shop and mill, taught that nature exists for use and for the raw material of art, conveyed, clothed, fed by steam; bred in traditions, and working in state, in church, in education, and charities, by mechanical methods, we are yet made to hear the auguries and prophecies of the soul, which makes light of all these proud mechanisms and calls us to the Holy and the Eternal not by men but alone, not by Bibles but through thought and lowliness. I see already this effort in eminent individuals. They are renouncing that which had been their pride; they encounter scorn and live with scorned men. They acquire a serener heavenlier eye and brow. They avow and defend what yesterday they contradicted, and gain daily a reliance on principles and the habit of reposing childlike on the lap of the incessant soul.[24]

Let us receive the benefits of the Time. What if it be as you

[24] "The problem which belongs . . . incessant soul" (E, 39).

say subjective? What if it act on thought? Must we therefore bewail the Dark Ages? Trust the time. What a fatal prodigality to contemn *our* age.[25] We cannot overvalue it. All religious motions lead us to prefer it. It is our All. It is the World. As the wandering sea bird which crossing the ocean alights on some rock or islet to rest for a moment its wings, and to look back on the wilderness of waves behind, and onward to the wilderness of waters before, so stand we perched on this rock or shoal of time, arrived out of the immensity of the Past and bound and roadready to plunge into immensity again.[26] One would say we could well afford to slight all other ages if only we value this one. Not for nothing it dawns out of everlasting Peace, this pretty discord, this great discontent, this self accusing Reflection.

What apology, what praise can equal the fact that here it is; therefore, certainly, in the vast optimism, here it ought to be. The great will seize with eagerness this novel crisis, when the old and the new stand front to front and reflection is for a time possible, and faith in the eternal stands in close neighborhood to an exhausting use of the economical. The very time sees for us, thinks for us. It is a microscope such as philosophy never had. Insight is for us which was never for any. Wondering we came into this lodge of watchmen, this office of espial. We wonder at the results, but let us not retreat astonished and ashamed. Let us go out of the hall door, and doubt never but a good genius brought us in and will carry us out. He who shall represent the genius of this day; he who shall, standing in this great cleft of Past and Future, understand the dignity and power of his position so well as to write the laws of Criticism, of Ethics, of history, will be found an age hence neither false nor unfortunate, but will rank immediately and equally with all the masters whom we now acknowledge.[27]

And what is the daily work and noblest aspiration of each of us but his study of this problem?

Besides as I stand hovering over this gloom and deep of the Future, and consider earnestly what it forebodes, I cannot dis-

---

[25] "Trust the time . . . *our* age" (E, 12).
[26] "We cannot overvalue . . . immensity again" (E, 56).
[27] "One would say . . . now acknowledge" (E, 12).

miss my joyful auguries. For I will not and cannot see in it a fiction or a dream. It is a reality arriving. It is to me an oracle that I cannot bring myself to undervalue. It is the cloudy temple of the Highest. Meantime it is dear. I look not at the work of its hand. I follow ever its eye with mine. I see the age in the persons it forms — a fair and sacred choir; in my friends; in those to whom I speak and in those who speak to me. Far wider in the noble, the unpledged, and the brave; in those who conceive magnificent hopes, and who can fail in no fortune for they are sure of themselves. The source of information on which I rely for unlocking for me the secret of the age is my love of it, is the acceptance of the nearest suggestion and the most faithful utterance of all that which is borne in on my mind. I cast myself upon the Age and will not resist it. Passive I will think what it thinketh and say what it saith. All my hope of insight and successful reporting lies in my consciousness of fidelity and the abdication of all will in the matter.[28]

Come on then, high Daughter of God! Right onward with new wisdom, O Age unborn! We stand waiting in the white robe of noviciate, — for all are children to thee, — and calm and sympathetic expect thine instruction. There is none mightier among the stars than thou. Teeming with life thou comest; thy pall is lined with beautiful faces, and multitudes of eyes still more friendly and mighty peer out behind them. Thy endowments we read by the hopes that now burn in all hearts. A choir of voices have sung various goodwill to man and these were thy harbingers. Not always shall the hope of man be disappointed; thou openest with wonderful key the door to greatness. His life yet shall be clean and honest, his aim yet unperplexed and sublime. Faith shall be possible and Society possible when once thou hast shown him the infinitude of himself.

[28] "The source of information . . . in the matter" (E, 55).

2

Literature [*first lecture*]

The second lecture in this series was first delivered in the Masonic Temple, Boston, on December 11, 1839, and was followed a week later by another on the same subject. The two were combined into one for the third lecture in the New York Mercantile Library series on March 17, 1840, and repeated as the second of the Concord, Massachusetts, series on April 8. As early as May 1840 Emerson was making a transcription of the combined lecture for an essay which he intended for the first number of *The Dial* though it did not appear until the second number as "Thoughts on Modern Literature," *The Dial*, I (October 1840), 137–158 (see *L*, II, 298, 303–305, 308). Since the essay contains much, though not all, of this lecture and the next with considerable reordering and addition, little was left for use elsewhere. Most of "Thoughts on Modern Literature" was reprinted in 1893 in *Natural History of Intellect* (W, XII, 309–336) with further parts of the *Dial* essay restored in the notes to the Centenary Edition.

The combined lecture, the present sewing of this manuscript, consists of the entire first lecture on "Literature," through Emerson's page 70, a single leaf of transition, and those leaves from the second lecture on "Literature" which Emerson had originally paginated 25–54. The text printed here restores the Boston reading by printing the transitional leaf in the textual notes, removing the leaves belonging to the second lecture, and rejecting certain obvious emendations, including a few passages inserted from the first twenty-four pages of the second lecture on "Literature." All emendations are recorded in the textual notes and a reconstruction of the combined lecture is possible.

THERE is no better illustration of the laws by which the world is governed than Literature. There is no luck in it. It proceeds by Fate. Every scripture is given by the inspiration of God. Every composition proceeds out of a greater or less depth of thought. And in exact proportion to that depth is the amount of its effect. The very highest class of books are those which express the moral element, the next, works of imagination, and the next, works of sciences — all dealing in realities: what ought to be, what really is, and what appears. These, in proportion to the truth and beauty they involve, remain: the rest perish. They proceed out of the silent, living mind, to be heard again by the living mind. Those books which are for all time, are written indifferently at any time. For high genius is a day without [night,] a beautiful ocean which hath no tides. And yet literature, this magical man-provoking talisman, is in some sort a creature of time. It is begotten by Time on the Soul.[1] Always the oracular soul is the source of thought but always the occasion is administered by the low antagonisms of circumstance. Religion, Love, Ambition, War, some fierce antagonism, or it may be some petty annoyance must break the round of perfect circulation or no spark, no joy, no event can be. As good not be. In the country the lover of nature dreaming through the forest would never awake to thought if the scream of an eagle, the cries of a crow or a curlew near his head did not break the continuity. Nay the finest lyrics of the poet come of this unequal parentage: the imps of matter beget such child on the soul, fair daughter of God.[2] Nature mixes Facts with thought to yield a poem. But the gift of immortality is of the mother's side. In the spirit in which they are written is the date of their duration and never in the magnitude of the facts. Every thing lasts in proportion to its beauty. In proportion as it was not polluted by any wilfulness of the writer but flowed from his mind after the divine order of Cause and Effect, it was not his but nature's and shared the sublimity of the sea and sky.

And yet men imagine that books are dice and have no merit in their fortune, that the Trade and the favor of a few critics can get one book into circulation and defeat another, and that in the production of these things the author has chosen and may choose to do thus and so.

Society wishes to assign subjects and method to its writers. But neither reader nor author may intermeddle. You cannot reason at will in this and that other vein but only as you must.

---

[1] "Those books . . . on the Soul" (E, 1–2, condensed).
[2] "Religion, Love . . . daughter of God" (E, 10).

You cannot make quaint combinations and bring to the crucible and alembic of truth things far-fetched or fantastic or popular, but your method and your subject are foreordained in all your nature and in all nature, or ever the earth was, or it has no worth. All that gives currency still to any book advertised in today's newspaper in London or Boston, is, the remains of faith in the breast of men, that not adroit bookmakers but the inextinguishable soul of the Universe reports of itself in articulate discourse today as of old. The ancients strongly expressed their sense of the unmanageableness of these words of the God by saying that the God made his priest insane, took him hither and thither as leaves are whirled by the tempest. But we sing as we are bid. Our inspirations are very manageable and tame. Death and sin have whispered in the ear of the wild horse of Parnassus and he has become a dray and a hack.[3] The fact holds forever and ever that the soul does so speak and that the law of literature giving its exact worth to every ballad and spoken sentence is thus transcendant and self contained.[4]

Literary accomplishments, skill in grammar and rhetoric, knowledge of books can never countervail the want of things that demand voice. Literature is but a poor trick when it busies itself to make words pass for things. The most original book in the world is the Bible. This old collection of the ejaculations of love and dread, of the supreme desires and contritions of men proceeding out of the region of the Grand and Eternal by whatsoever different mouths spoken and through a wide extent of times and countries, seems, (especially if you add to our canon, the kindred sacred writings of the Hindoos, the Persians, and the Greeks,) the alphabet of the nations, and all posterior literature either the chronicle of facts under very inferior Ideas or when it rises to sentiment the combinations, analogies, or degradations of this. The elevation of this book may be measured by observing how certainly all elevation of thought clothes itself in the words and forms of speech of that book. I speak of the fact, not of what should be. Whatever is majestically thought in great moral ele-

[3] "There is no better . . . and a hack" (notes to "Thoughts on Modern Literature," W, XII, 465–467).
[4] "Society wishes to assign . . . and self contained" (E, 2–3).

ment instantly approaches this old Sanscrit. It is in the nature of things that the highest originality must be moral. The only person who can be entirely independent of this fountain of literature and equal to it must be a prophet in his own proper person. Shakspeare, the first literary genius of the world, the highest in whom the moral is not the predominating element, leans on the Bible: his poetry supposes it. If we examine this brilliant influence — Shakspear — as it lies in our minds we shall find it reverent, deeply indebted to the traditional morality, in short, compared with the tone of the prophets, *secondary*.[5] One of the most ingenious and self-centred minds I ever knew and one to whom the learning of antiquity lay all open in considering one day what single book he should choose if condemned to dwell in a solitude, with one volume, told me that of course his choice must lie between Milton, Shakspeare, and the Bible. He could soon drop Milton from the candidates if there must be but one; and then as quickly Shakspeare, because he could better supply Shakspeare to himself than the austere inimitable verdicts of the Hebrew muse.[6]

Shakspeare, as I said, is indebted to this. On the other hand the prophets do not imply the existence of Shakspeare or Homer — advert to no books or arts, — only to dread Ideas and emotions. People imagine that the place which the Bible holds in the world, it owes to miracles. It owes it simply to the fact that it came out of a profounder depth of thought than any other book and the effect must be precisely proportionate. Gibbon fancied that it was combinations of circumstances that gave Christianity its place in history. But in nature it takes an ounce to balance an ounce.[7]

The same necessity which prescribes the form and the style of the work measures its success. There is no luck in literary reputation. They who make up the final verdict upon every book are not the partial and noisy readers of the hour when it appears, but a court as of angels, a public not to be bribed, not to be entreated, and not to be overawed decides upon every man's title to fame.

---

[5] "Literary accomplishments . . . prophets, *secondary*" (E, 70–71).
[6] "One of the most ingenious . . . Hebrew muse" (cf. B, 156, recording a conversation with Charles Chauncy Emerson).
[7] "On the other hand . . . balance an ounce" (E, 71). For last sentence see *Lectures*, I, 319, 382, II, 79.

Only those books come down which deserve to last.[8] All the gilt edges and vellum and morocco, all the presentation copies to all the libraries will not preserve a book in circulation beyond its intrinsic date. It must go with all Walpole's noble and royal authors[9] to its fate. Blackmore, Pollok, and Bulwer may endure for a night, but Moses and Homer last forever. There are not in the world at any one time more than a dozen persons who read and understand Plato, never enough to pay for an edition of his works.[10] Yet to every generation these come duly down for the sake of those few persons as if God brought them in his hand. No book, said Bentley, was ever written down by any but itself.[11] And so with all sterling books their permanence is fixed by no effort friendly or hostile but by their own specific gravity or the intrinsic importance of their contents to the constant mind of man.[12]

Nature cannot be cheated. Life alone can impart life. That only profits which is profitable and though we burst we can only be valued as we make ourselves valuable.

In looking at modern literature we see abundant example of this fact how quickly all books are forgotten which do not appeal to the Vast in Nature. Science, the Imagination, Morals, what is writ to them, endures. Always we wish to know what really is in Nature and man, — a story of facts, of men or countries or things — which is told in simple heed to make them known as they are. That which is truly told Nature herself takes in charge against the whims and injustice of men. For ages Herodotus was reckoned a fabulist in his descriptions of Africa, and now the sublime, silent desert testifies through the mouths of Bruce, Lyon, Cailliaud, Burckhardt, Belzoni, to the truth of the calumniated Herodotus.[13]

[8] Cf. D, 126; "Books," W, VII, 195.
[9] Horace Walpole's *Catalogue of Royal and Noble Authors*, printed at the Strawberry Hill Press, 1758.
[10] Cf. E, 350; "New England Reformers," W, III, 259.
[11] For something similar, see Encyclopedia, 186. Richard Bentley (1662–1742), English divine and classical scholar; opponent of Swift in the famous "Battle of the Books."
[12] "The same necessity . . . mind of man" (*Lectures*, II, 65–66, which is expanded from *Lectures*, I, 212); "There is no luck . . . mind of man" ("Spiritual Laws," W, II, 154–155).
[13] Notes to "Thoughts on Modern Literature," W, XII, 466–467; D, 130. James

Then all books of Imagination endure, all which ascend to that power of thought that the writer sees Nature as subordinate to the soul and uses it as his language. Every sentence, every verse indicating this superiority or health is memorable and will take care of its own immortality. And lastly the edicts of the moral sentiment, the lessons of the good, the alway desireable. But no circumstance can keep alive anything else. A man apparently foolish and helpless, with nothing magnetic in him, who is a churl in a saloon, an ideot in the legislature, hides himself from the pride and pity of men in his chamber and writes a poem which when at last it is published is at first neglected then hissed, and it pushes all potentates from their thrones, changes the course of affairs in a few years, and actually wipes out the memory of that triumphant state of things under which he suffered when he existed.

And lo what numberless volumes of records, political, personal, ecclesiastical, critical, what travels, what fictions, what farces, what jokes, which get into light which the soul never wrote and which therefore the soul never reads — perish untimely. See what acres of printed paper every day pass into the fire because no high purpose inspired the composition.

In looking at the library then of the present age we are struck with the fact of so immense a miscellany. It can hardly be characterised by any species of book for every opinion old and new, every hope and fear, every whim and folly has an organ. It prints a vast carcass of tradition every year with as much solemnity as a new revelation. These serve

With beads and prayer books for the toys of age.[14]

Along with these it vents books that breathe of new morning, that seem to heave with the life of millions, books for which men and women peak and pine, books which take the rose out of the cheek of him that wrote them and give him to the midnight a

---

Bruce (1730–1794), Captain George Francis Lyon (1795–1832), Frédéric Cailliaud (1787–1869), and John Lewis Burckhardt (1784–1817), like Giovanni Belzoni, published accounts of their travels in North Africa, to the upper Nile, or in the Near East.

[14] Pope, *An Essay on Man*, II, 280, modified.

sad, solitary, diseased man, which leave no man where they found him but make him better or worse, and which work dubiously on society and seem to inoculate it with a venom before any healthy result appears.

In order to any complete view of the literature of the day our examination ought to include what it quotes, what it writes, [and] what it wishes to write.

I. In the first place it has all books. The wisdom of the world, it has not let die. And here let us with grateful heart acknowledge the gift of the spiritual nature to whose works no date is fixed. How can we be truly said to live confined to one age, who, by virtue of books, live in all ages? How can the age be a bad one which gives me Plato and Paul and Plutarch, St. Augustine, Marlow, and Beaumont and Fletcher, Donne and Sir Thomas Browne beside its own riches?

See our presses groaning with every year new editions of all the choice pieces of the first of mankind, — meditations, history, opinions, epics, lyrics, fancies, which the age adopts by quoting them.[15] In literature whilst many masters sung a vulgar strain, and talent was perverted as ever, yet over all has brooded a certain higher melody, now retiring, now prevailing, and constraining at last all jarring notes which sought at first to drown it, to fall into unison with it, or to cease. The prodigious growth and influence of the genius of Shakspeare in the last one hundred fifty years is itself a fact of the first importance. It almost alone has called out the genius of the German nation into an activity which, spreading from the poetic into the scientific, religious, and philosophical domains, has made theirs now at last the paramount intellectual influence of the world, reacting with great energy on England and America.[16]

And here since I have heretofore fallen into a way of thinking that seemed to disparage books and am likely to offend still more deeply in my next Lecture let me distinctly declare my conviction of my debt to these mute benefactors. In hours of great activity

[15] "In looking at the library . . . by quoting them" ("Thoughts on Modern Literature," W, XII, 310–311).
[16] "Lecture on the Doctrine of ye Soul" [E]; "In literature whilst . . . and America" (see above, p. 8); "The prodigious growth . . . and America" ("Thoughts on Modern Literature," W, XII, 312).

of mind we think little of a book. A book is a cold and languid pleasure.[17] In the statements we make so freely that books are for idle hours and when we flout all particular books as initial merely, we truly express the privilege of spiritual nature but, alas, not the fact and fortune of this low Massachusetts and Boston, of these humble Decembers and Januaries of mortal life. Our souls are not self-fed, but do eat and drink of chemical water and wheat. We go musing into the vault of day and night, no star shines, no muse descends, the stars are white points, the roses brick-colored leaves, and frogs pipe, mice cheep, and wagons creak along the road. We return to the house and take up Plutarch or Augustine and read some sentences, and lo! the air swarms with life, the front of heaven is full of fiery shapes, secrets of magnanimity and grandeur invite us on every hand. Life is made up of them. Such is our debt to literature. Observe moreover that we ought to credit literature with much more than the just word it gives us. I have just been reading poems which shine with a certain steady, autumnal light. That is not in them which they give me. Over every true poem lingers a certain wild beauty immeasureable; a happiness, lightsome and delicious, fills the heart and brain as they say every man walks environed by his proper atmosphere extending to some distance around him. Well this beautiful result must be credited to literature also in casting its account.[18]

Once more circumstance goes into the value of a book. A good sentence, a noble verse which I meet in my reading are an epoch in my life. From month to month, from year to year they remain fresh and memorable. Yet when we once in our writing come out into the free air of thought we seem to be assured that nothing is easier than to continue this communication at pleasure indefinitely. Up, down, around, the kingdom of thought has no enclosures but the Muse makes us free of her city. Well the world has a million writers. One would think then that good thought would be as familiar as the air and water and the gifts of each

---

[17] Cf. Montaigne, "Of Books," *Essays*, II, 125; "Books," W, VII, 197; above, p. 44.

[18] "In the statements . . . its account" (E, 16–17); "when we flout . . . its account" ("Thoughts on Modern Literature," W, XII, 309–310). The poems Emerson had "just been reading" are identified in the journal as poems by "C.," probably William Ellery Channing, the younger.

new hour exclude the repetition of those of the last. Yet we can count all our great treasures. Nay, I remember any beautiful verse for twenty years.[19]

I proceed to say that beside the entire mass of what may be called the permanent literature of the human race from Moses and Homer down, which every age reprints, our age has sought out with avidity the history of civil liberty, explored every monument of Anglo-Saxon history and law, and eminently in the period of the English Commonwealth. It has out of England devoted much thought and pains to the history of philosophy. It has groped in all nations where was any literature for the early poetry, not only dramatic, but for the popular sort, the ballads, the songs, for the Nibelungen Lied and Hans Sachs in Germany, for the Cid in Spain, for the ruder verse of the interior nations of Europe, and in England for the ballads of Scotland and Robinhood.

II. To pass now to the consideration, *what the age writes.* Not many great names have been added to the procession of the Wise since the present century came in. Chiefly the time is marked by the multitude of writers. Soldiers, sailors, nobles, princes, women write books.[20] Of course in the mass the great proportion is imitation, custom, fear, want, and amusement.

A vast number of books are written in quiet imitation of the old civil, ecclesiastical, and literary history; of these we need take no account. They are written by the dead to be read by the dead. The materials are so multiplied by the opulence of libraries and by the improved science of Bibliography that a passable and laudable book can be very easily written without any thought. But what good will it do? It is not history. Until history is interesting, it is not yet written,[21] and it is very easy to see that one example of a history has come into light that will affect the character of every history that shall hereafter be written.[22]

All facts are clearly exposed; the age is not to be trifled with; it wishes to know who is who, and what is what. Let there be no

---

[19] "A good sentence . . . twenty years" ("Intellect," W, II, 338; E, 54).

[20] "Chiefly the time . . . women write books" (notes to "Thoughts on Modern Literature," W, XII, 468).

[21] "Art and Criticism," W, XII, 298; D, 61.

[22] Probably refers to Carlyle's *The French Revolution,* the American edition of which Emerson arranged to have published in December 1837.

ghost stories more. Send Mr. Parry to learn if there be a North-west passage to America and Mr. Lander to learn the true course of the Niger. Pückler Muskau will go to Algiers and Sir Francis Head to the Pampas and the Brunnens of Nassau.[23] Then let us have our charts true, and our gazetteers correct. We will know where Babylon stood and settle the topography of the Roman Forum. We will know whatsoever is to be known of South America, of Russia, of Persia, of Egypt, of Palestine, of Turkey.[24]

Knowledge is made easy. Immense diffusion, a mechanical diffusion by tracts, by appendixes, by cheap editions, by circulating libraries and book clubs. This to be sure is not the highest sort of diffusion, the way in which an original genius works and spreads himself. It seems as if the Petrarch could not be admired, could not even be seen until his living, conversing, and writing had diffused his spirit into the young and acquiring class so that he had multiplied himself into a thousand sons, a thousand Petrarchs and so *understands himself*.[25]

Our books are characterised by their decorum. An eminent propriety, the consequence of the immense multitude of writers and readers and the flight of every species of information by mail and circulating library and railroad travelling. The age is well bred, knows the world, has no nonsense and herein is well distinguished from learned ages that preceded ours. There's no fool like your wise fool, is a maxim plentifully illustrated in the history or the writings of the English or European scholars of the twelfth, fourteenth, sixteenth centuries; it seems as if their eyes were holden that they could not see.[26] The best heads of their time,

---

[23] Sir William E. Parry (1790–1855), English Arctic explorer, published *Journal of a Voyage to Discover a North-west Passage* (London, 1821) and other accounts of his subsequent explorations; Richard L. Lander (1804–1834), English explorer, and his less famous brother, John Lander (1807–1839), reported their travels in *Journal of an Expedition to Explore the Course and Termination of the Niger* (London, 1832); the travels of Herman von Pückler-Muskau (1785–1871) were translated as *Semilasso in Africa; Adventures in Algiers, and Other Parts of Africa* (London, 1837), a year after their German publication; Sir Francis Head (1793–1875), English soldier and traveler, published *Rough Notes Taken during Some Rapid Journeys across the Pampas and among the Andes* (London, 1826) and *Bubbles from the Brunnens of Nassau* (London, 1835).

[24] "All facts are clearly . . . of Turkey" (notes to "Thoughts on Modern Literature," W, XII, 468–469).

[25] D, 175, where the example is Shakespeare. See textual notes.

[26] Cf. Luke 24:16; "Spiritual Laws," W, II, 147; above, p. 162.

they accept such cardhouse theories of religion, politics, and natural science that a clever boy would blow away. What stuff in Kepler, in Cardan, Lord Bacon. Montaigne with all his French wit is no better.[27] A sophomore would wind him round his finger. Some of the Medical Remains of my Lord Bacon out of the book for his own use of the prolongation of life will move a smile in the unpoetical practitioner of modern times. They remind us of the drugs and practice of the leeches and enchanters of Eastern romance.

Thus his Collection of Astringents is whimsical enough: "A stomacher of scarlet cloth; whelps or young healthy boys applied to the stomach; hippocratic wines so they be made of austere materials."

"8. To remember masticatories for the mouth.

"9. And orange flower water to be smelt or snuffed up.

"10. In the third hour after the sun is risen to take in air from some high and open place with a ventilation of rosae moschatae and fresh violets and to stir the earth with infusion of wine and mint. . . .

"17. To use once during supper time wine in which gold is quenched. . . .

"26. Heroic desires. . . .

"28. To provide always an apt breakfast.

"29. To do nothing against a man's genius." [28]

It is curious to find a good deal of pretty nonsense concerning the virtues of the ashes of a hedgehog, the heart of an ape, the moss that groweth upon the skull of a dead man unburied, and the comfort that proceeds to the system from wearing beads of amber, coral, and hartshorn, rings of seahorse teeth worn for cramp, to find all this masses of moonshine side by side with the gravest and most valuable observations.

Sir Thomas Browne recommends as empirical medicines for the gout:

"Wear shoes made of a lion's skin.

"Give poultices taken from the part to dogs.

"Try the magnified amulet of Muffetus of spiders' legs worn

---

[27] "the history or . . . no better" (B, 105, modified; see also B, 304).
[28] Bacon, *Works*, II, 222, 224–225. Emerson modifies the order.

in a deer's skin or of tortoises' legs cut off from the living tortoise and wrapped up in the skin of a kid." [29]

Burton in the Anatomy of Melancholy states some facts concerning the spiritual world that would hardly find place in the Nineteenth Century. "The air," he says, "is not so full of flies in summer as it is at all times of invisible devils. . . . They counterfeit suns and moons and sit on ship masts. . . . They cause whirlwinds on a sudden and tempestuous storms which though our meteorologists generally refer to natural causes yet I am of Bodine's mind they are more often caused by those aerial devils in their several quarters." Cardan gives much information concerning them. "His father had one of them, an aerial devil bound to him for eight and twenty years. As Agrippa's dog had a devil tied to his collar some think that Paracelsus had one confined in his sword pommel. . . . Others wear them in rings. . . . At Hammel in Saxony the devil in the likeness of a pied piper carried away one hundred thirty children that were never after seen." [30]

All this sky full of cobwebs are now forever swept clean away. Another race is born. Malthus and Basil Hall, Humboldt and Herschel have arrived. If I were called upon to name a writer as a representative of the last, Horace Walpole whose letters circulate in the libraries represents much more truly the spirit of recent literature. He has taste, common sense, love of facts, impatience of humbug, love of history, love of splendor, love of justice, and the sentiment of honor among gentlemen; — but no life whatever of the higher faculties, no faith, no hope, no aspiration, no question touching the secret of nature.[31]

The poetry and the speculation of the age are marked by a certain philosophic turn which discriminates them from the works of earlier times. The poet is not content to see how "fair hangs the apple from the rock," what melody "a sunbeam awoke

[29] "(Vol 4 p. 398)" [E], in Works.

[30] Robert Burton, The Anatomy of Melancholy, 2 vols. (London, 1804), I, 63–74. These sentences, including the paraphrased fourth sentence, are gleaned from part. I, sect. 2, mem. 1, subs. 2, "A Digression on the Nature of Spirits."

[31] "The age is well-bred . . . secret of nature" (notes to "Thoughts on Modern Literature," W, XII, 469–470); "Horace Walpole . . . secret of nature" (E, 1, where Emerson says that he had read Walpole's letters "attentively in the past summer").

in the groves," nor of Hardiknute "how stately stepped he east the way, and stately stepped he west," [32] but he now revolves what is the apple to me? and what the birds to me? and what is Hardiknute to me? and what am I? And this is called *subjectiveness*, as the eye is withdrawn from the object in nature and fixed on the subject or mind.

I readily concede that a resolute and steadfast tendency of this sort appears in the modern literature. It is the new consciousness of the One Mind (to which all have a potential access and which is the Creator) which predominates in Criticism. It is the uprise of the soul and not a decline. It is the road to good and to beauty though not to the same beauty we admire in Homer and Chaucer.

It is founded in that insatiable demand for unity — to recognize one nature in all the variety of objects — which always characterizes a genius of the first order. Accustomed alway to behold the presence of the Universe in every part, the soul will not condescend to look at any new part as a stranger, but saith, "I know all already, and what art thou? Show me thy relations to me to all, and I will entertain thee also."

There is a pernicious ambiguity in the use of the term *subjective*.[33] We say in accordance with the general view I have stated, that the individual soul feels its right to be no longer confounded with numbers but itself to sit in judgment on history and literature, and to constrain all facts and parties to stand their trial before it. And in this sense the mind is subjective.

But in all ages and now more, the narrow minded have no interest in any thing but its relation to their personality. What will help them to be delivered from some burden, eased in some circumstance, flattered, or pardoned, or enriched, what will help to marry, or to divorce them, to prolong or sweeten life is sure of their interest, and nothing else. Whatever subject is referred to them they behold it in this most partial light or darkness of intense selfishness until we hate their being. And this habit of intel-

---

[32] The first and third quotations are, respectively, from William Hamilton, "The Braes of Yarrow," and Elizabeth, Lady Wardlaw, "Hardyknute." The other is not located.

[33] Cf. E, 86.

lectual selfishness has acquired in our day the fine name of sub-jectiveness.

Nor is the distinction between these two habits to be found in the circumstance of using the first person singular or reciting facts and feelings of personal history. A man may say *I*, and never refer to himself as an individual; and a man may recite passages of his life with no feeling of egotism. Nor need a man have a vicious subjectiveness because he delights in abstract propositions.

But the criterion is the tendency; whether they lead us to Nature or to the person of the writer. The great always introduce us to facts; small men introduce us alway to themselves. The great even whilst he relates a private fact personal to him is really leading us away from him to an universal experience. Their own affection is in Nature, in *What is*, and of course all their communication leads outward to it starting from whatsoever point. The great never with their own consent become a load on the minds they instruct. The more they draw us to them the farther from them or more independent of them we are, because they have brought us to the knowledge of somewhat deeper than both them and us. The great never hinder us; for as the Jews had a custom of laying their beds North and South, founded on the opinion that the path of God was East and West, and they would not desecrate by the infirmities of sleep the divine circuits, so the activity of the good is coincident with the axle of the world, with the sun and moon, with the course of the rivers and of the winds, with the stream of laborers in the street, and with all the activity and well-being of the race. The autobiography of the good is the autobiography of God.[34]

The great lead us to Nature and in our age to Metaphysical Nature, to the invisible, awful facts, to moral abstractions, which are not less Nature than are a river or a coal-mine — nay, they are far more Nature — but its heart and soul.

But the weak and evil, led also to analyse, saw nothing in thought but luxury. Thought for the selfish became selfish. They invited us to contemplate nature and showed us an abominable self. Would you know the genius of the writer do not enumerate

[34] "The great always introduce . . . autobiography of God" (E, 86).

his talents or his feats but ask thyself — What spirit is he of? Does gladness and hope and fortitude flow from his page into thy heart? Has he led thee to Nature because his own soul was too happy in beholding her power and love;[35] or, has he only shown you stars and mountains, woods and lovely forms as his house; bribing you by the wild splendor of his abode to come and see *him?* I fear we hear too clearly out of all the poems of Lord Byron this plain prose Burden: *I am Byron the noble poet who am very clever but am not popular in London.* The water we wash with never speaks of itself. Nor does fire or wind or tree. Neither does the noble Natural man: he yields himself to your occasion and use but his act expresses a reference to universal good.[36] The little can see nothing in nature but their own stake and their most discursive regards are still economical. And in their habitual return to their private triviality we are reminded of Scaliger's petulant criticism on Montaigne's gossipping confession that he likes red wine but never drinks white — "Who the devil wants to know what colored wine you drink?" [37]

It is not to be contested that a selfish commerce and government have caught the eye and possessed themselves of the hand of the masses. We do not deny that selfishness and the senses write the Laws under which we live, and that the street seems to be built and the men and women in it moving not out of reference to pure and grand ends but rather to very short and sordid ones. Perhaps no considerable minority, perhaps no one man leads a quite clean and lofty life. What of that? We concede in sadness the fact. But we say that these low customary ways are not all that survives in human beings. There is that in us which mutters and that which groans and that which chaunts and that

---

[35] "The poetry and the speculation . . . her power and love" ("Thoughts on Modern Literature," W, XII, 312–316, with omissions).

[36] "The water we wash . . . universal good" ("Thoughts on Modern Literature," W, XII, 316).

[37] "But the weak and evil . . . wine you drink" (E, 86–87). Emerson wrote in the back of his copy of Montaigne, *Essays*, III: " 'M. de Montagnes. Son pere etoit vendeur de harenc. La grande fadaise de Montagne, qui a écrit qu'il aimoit mieux le vin blanc. M du Puy disoit, Que diable a-t-on à faire de savoir ce qu'il aime? Ceux de Geneve ont été bien impudens d'en oter plus d'un tiers.' *Scaligerana.*" JMN, VII, 320, footnote 165, quotes the anecdote of Joseph Justus Scaliger from *Scaligerana, ou Bons Mots* . . . (Cologne, 1695), p. 269.

which aspires. There are other facts on which men of the world superciliously smile which are worth all their trade and politics, the impulses, namely, which drive young men into gardens and solitary places and cause extravagant gestures, starts, distortions of the countenance, and passionate exclamations,[38] sentiments which find no aliment or language for themselves on the wharves or in the shop or in the courts but do find a home in silence, in darkness, in the pale stars, and in the presence of Nature. All over the modern world the educated and susceptible have betrayed this discontent with the limits of our municipal life and with the poverty of our dogmas of religion and philosophy. They betray this impatience by fleeing for resource to the love of nature — of nature which is courted in a certain moody and exploring spirit as if they expected a more intimate union of man with nature than has yet been known. Those who cannot tell what they wish or expect still sigh and struggle with indefinite thoughts and vast wishes.

The very child in the nursery says strange things and doubts and philosophizes. A wild striving to express more inward and infinite sense characterises the works of every art. The music of Beethoven is said by those who understand it, to labor with vaster conceptions and aspirations than music has attempted before.[39] This Feeling of the Infinite has deeply colored the poetry of the period. This new love of the vast was native in Germany; was imported into France by De Stael; appeared in England in Coleridge, Wordsworth, Byron, Shelley, Felicia Hemans, and finds a most genial climate in the American mind.[40]

The fame of Wordsworth is one of the most instructive facts in modern literature when it is considered how utterly hostile his genius at first seemed to the reigning taste, and I may add with what feeble poetic talents his great and steadily growing dominion has been established. More than any poet his success has been not his own but that of the Idea or principle which possessed him and which he has rarely succeeded in adequately expressing. His

[38] "It is not to be contested . . . exclamations" (E, 27, expanded).
[39] "The very child . . . attempted before" (see above, p. 9).
[40] "It is not to be . . . American mind" ("Thoughts on Modern Literature," W, XII, 317–318); for last sentence, cf. E, 82, and above, p. 196.

inspiring genius is as he has said, the still sad music of human-ity.[41] It is the human soul in these last ages striving for a just publication of itself through priest and legislator and poet which is the subject of literature.[42] More than any contemporary poet he is pervaded with a reverence for somewhat higher than (conscious) thought. There is in all great poets a wisdom of humanity which is superior to any talents they exercise. It is the wisest part of Shakspeare and of Milton. For they are poets by the free course which they allow to the informing soul which through their eyes beholdeth again and blesseth the things which it hath made. The soul is superior to its knowledge, wiser than any of its works.[43]

Scott and Crabbe who formed themselves on the past had none of it, their poetry is objective. The effect of this poetry is not attractive; it seems vague and wild, the critic is not sure the writer understands himself.[44] In Byron it predominates, but in Byron it is blind, it sees not its true end — an infinite good, alive and beautiful. His will is perverted and in the midst of nature he thinks of himself.

Nothing establishes the prevalence of this taste in the people more than the circulation of the volume, one would say most incongruously united by some bookseller, Coleridge, Shelley, and Keats.[45] Its only unity is in the subjectiveness and aspiration common to the three writers.

Shelley is never a poet. His mind is uniformly imitative; all his poems composite. A fine English scholar he is, with taste, ear, and memory, but Imagination, the original authentic fire of the bard, he has not. He is clearly modern and shares with Richter, Chateaubriand, Manzoni, and Wordsworth the feeling of the Infinite which so labors for expression in their different genius. But all his lines [are] arbitrary, not necessary.[46] When we read poetry the mind asks, — was this verse one of twenty which the author at

---

[41] Cf. "Lines Composed a Few Miles above Tintern Abbey," line 91.

[42] "The fame of Wordsworth . . . of literature" (see above, p. 9).

[43] "The fame of Wordsworth . . . any of its works" ("Thoughts on Modern Literature," W, XII, 320–321); see "The Over-Soul," W, II, 288–289; above, pp. 17–18.

[44] "Scott and Crabbe . . . himself" (cf. E, 82).

[45] Emerson may be referring to The Poetical Works of Coleridge, Shelley, and Keats (Paris: A. and W. Galignani, 1829), reprinted in Philadelphia, 1831.

[46] "Shelley is never . . . necessary" (E, 81).

the moment might have written as well; or, is this what that man was created to say? But whilst every line of the true poet will be genuine he is in a boundless power and freedom to say a million things. And the reason why he can say one thing well is because his vision extends to the sight of all things, and so he describes each as one who knows many and all.[47]

But of all men he who has united in himself, and that in the most extraordinary degree, the tendencies of the time is the German poet, naturalist, and philosopher, Goethe. All that we have seen in the time we find in him. He has owed to Commerce and to the victories of the Understanding all their wealth. Such was his capacity that the magazines of the world's ancient or modern wealth which arts and intercourse and skepticism could command, — he wanted them all. Had there been twice so much, he could have used it as well. Geologist, mechanic, merchant, chemist, king, radical, painter, composer, all worked for him. A thousand eyes looked through his. He learned as readily as other men breathe. Of all the men of this time, not one has seemed so much at home in it as he.

And in him this encyclopaedia of facts wrought its effect. He was knowing; he was brave; he was clean from all narrowness; he has the most perfect propriety and taste, — a quality by no means common to the German writers. It did more. It made him that resolute realist he is, gave him that sturdy determination to see things for what they are. Of all men there was never an observer before. What sagacity! What industry of observation! To read Goethe, is an economy of time for you shall find no word that does not stand for a thing, and he is of that comprehension to see the value of truth.[48] His love of nature has seemed to give a new meaning to that word. There was never man more domesticated in this world than he. And he is an apology for the analytic spirit of the period because, of his analysis, always wholes were the result. All conventions, all traditions, he rejected. And yet he felt his entire right and duty to stand before and try and judge every fact in nature. He thought it necessary to dot round as it were

[47] "Scott and Crabbe . . . and all" ("Thoughts on Modern Literature," W, XII, 318–320); "When we read . . . and all" (E, 82).
[48] "Of all men . . . value of truth" (B, 147).

with his own pen the entire sphere of knowables and for many of his stories, this seems the only reason — viz., Here is a piece of humanity I had hitherto omitted to sketch — Take this. He does not say so in syllables. Yet a sort of conscientious feeling he had to be up to the Universe, is the best account and apology for many of them.

He shared also the subjectiveness of the Age, and that too in both the senses I have discriminated. With the sharpest eye for form, colour, botany, engraving, medals, persons, and manners, he never stopped at surface, but pierced the purpose of a thing, and studied to reconcile that purpose with his own being. What he could so reconcile was good, what he could not, was false. Hence a certain greatness encircles every fact he treats, for to him it has a soul, an eternal reason why it was so and not otherwise. This is the secret of that deep realism which went about among all objects he beheld to find the cause why they must be what they are. It was with him a favorite work to give a theory of every institution, art, work of art, custom which he observes. Thus his explanation of the Italian mode of reckoning the hours of the day, as growing out of the Italian climate; of the Obelisk of Egypt, as growing out of a common natural fracture in the granite parallelopiped in Upper Egypt; of the Doric Architecture, and the Gothic; of the Venetian music of the gondolier originating in the habit of the fishers' wives of the Lido singing to their husbands on the sea; of the Amphitheatre which is the natural cup that forms round every spectacle in the street; of the colouring of Titian and Paul Veronese which one may see in daylight in Venice day by day; of the Carnival at Rome; of the domestic rural architecture in Italy.[49]

But also that other vicious subjectiveness, that vice of the time, infected him also. I am provoked with his Olympian self-complacency, the patronizing air with which he vouchsafes to tolerate the genius and performances of other mortals, "the good Hiller," "our costly Kant," "the friendly Wieland," etc., etc. Excellent of this kind is his account of his own philosophy in relation to the Kantian, that it was an analogon of that by the con-

[49] "It was with him . . . in Italy" (B, 146–147; cf. "Art," W, VII, 54–55; and "Thoughts on Art," *The Dial*, I [January 1841], 377).

fession of the Kantists.[50] There is a good letter from Wieland to Merck, in which Wieland describes Goethe's reading of his journal of a tour in Switzerland with the Grand duke and their passage through Valais over the Furka and St. Gothard. It was, "as good as Xenophon's Anabasis. The piece is one of his most masterly productions and thought and written with the great mind peculiar to him. The fair hearers were enthusiastic at the Nature in this piece; I liked the sly Art in the composition, whereof they saw nothing, still better. It is a true poem so concealed is the art also. But what most remarkably in this as in all his other works distinguishes him from Homer and Shakspeare, is that the Me, the Ille Ego, every where glimmers through, although without any boasting and with an infinite fineness." [51]

This subtle element of Egotism in Goethe certainly does not seem to deform his compositions, but to lower the moral influence of the man. He differs from all the great in the total want of frankness. Whoso saw Milton, whoso saw Shakspeare saw them do their best and utter their whole heart manlike among their brethren. No man was permitted to call Goethe brother. He hid himself and worked always to astonish, which is an Egotism and therefore little.[52]

His thinking, as far as I read him, is of great altitude and *all level*. Dramatic power I think he has very little. The great felicities, the miracles of poetry, he has never. It is all design with him, just thought and instructed expression, analogies, allusion, illustration, which knowledge and correct thinking supply, but of Shakspeare and the transcendant muse, no syllable.[53] But I claim for him the praise of truth, of fidelity to his intellectual nature. He is the king of all scholars.[54] In these days and in this country where the scholars are few and idle, where men read easy books and sleep after dinner, it seems as if no book could so safely be put in the hands of young men as the letters of Goethe

[50] "I am provoked . . . of the Kantists" (B, 147–148). For the last sentence, cf. Goethe, *Einwirkung der neuern Philosophie* in *Werke*, L, 50–54, and the passage Emerson translated in Z, 9–10.

[51] *Briefe an . . . Merck*, pp. 235–236; "There is a good letter . . . infinite fineness" (C, 31).

[52] "He differs from all the great . . . little" (C, 38).

[53] "His thinking . . . no syllable" (C, 25–26).

[54] "But I claim for him . . . all scholars" (B, 148).

which attest the incessant activity of this man to eighty years in an endless variety of studies with uniform cheerfulness and greatness of mind. They cannot be read without shaming us into an emulating industry. I claim for him the praise of truth. We think when we contemplate the stupendous glory of the world that it were life enough for one man merely to lift his hands and cry κοσμος! Beauty! Well this he did. Here was a man who in the feeling that the thing itself was so admirable as to leave all comment behind, went up and down from object to object, lifting the veil from every one, and did no more. What he said of Lavater I may better say of him, that "it was fearful to stand in the presence of one before whom all the boundaries within which nature has circumscribed our being were laid flat." [55] His are the bright and terrible eyes which meet you in every sacred and every public enclosure.[56] His thoughts acquaint us with our own.[57]

It is to me very plain that no recent genius can work with equal effect on mankind to Goethe for no intelligent young man can read him without finding his own compositions are immediately modified by his new knowledge.[58] More than any writer he unlocks the faculties of the artist. What a wonderful eye was his for the measure of things, the choice of topics, the mark of a master. Perhaps he overvalues Byron, yet in Byron he has grasped all the peculiarities; but who has seen Shakspeare so truly? Paper money, Periods of Belief, Cheerfulness of the Poet, French Revolution, how just are his views of these trite things! What a multitude of opinions and how few blunders! though his estimate of Sterne I suppose to be one.[59] He is a pledge that the antique force of nature is not spent and it is gay to think what men shall yet be.

In considering then under these two heads, what the age quotes and what it writes, I find very few geniuses of the clear upper sky. I find much doubt, much resolute study, much prepa-

---

[55] Cf. *Dichtung und Wahrheit*, part IV, book XIX, in *Werke*, XLVIII, 146; cf. A, 108

[56] "But of all men . . . every public enclosure" ("Thoughts on Modern Literature," W, XII, 322–328, modified).

[57] "I claim for him the praise of truth. We . . . with our own" (B, 148). For last sentence, cf. A, 127: "Wordsworth, 'whose thoughts acquaint us with our own,'" identified there as from Ebenezer Elliott, "The Village Patriarch," IV, 32.

[58] C, 52.

[59] "What a wonderful eye . . . to be one" (C, 51).

ration, but I find not often the announcement of Ideas, the pae-ans of devotion, or the clarion of the Epic Muse. Still Nature is never poor. Of those who already belong to the irreversible Past I find two or three names of the last and present century which seem still of unexhausted virtue and mainly those of Swedenborg, of Kant, and of Goethe, three original, vast, eternal men who have looked absolute nature in the face and been drawn to her bosom and yet with the widest difference of character and genius and as the ages have yet to show with the most unequal result.

With the memory of these great masters we must close at present this part of our subject and postpone to another lecture the third consideration: What the Age wishes to write.

3

Literature [second lecture]

This, the third lecture in the series, is a continuation of the previous lecture on "Literature," and was delivered at the Masonic Temple, Boston, on December 18, 1839. The manuscript was dismembered and partially combined with the first lecture on "Literature" for two later readings, and the combined lecture was largely printed in "Thoughts on Modern Literature," *The Dial,* I (October 1840), 137–158 (see headnote to "Literature [first lecture]").

The present text restores the Boston reading by adding the remnant leaves to those now sewn in the combined lecture though not belonging to "Literature [first lecture]." The reconstructed text was all once sewn together and is paginated consecutively in ink except for four missing leaves. Since all emendations are recorded in the textual notes to this and the previous lecture, a reconstruction of the combined lecture is possible.

There are with this lecture the three leaves and double sheet which form the conclusion to Lecture 1 of "The Philosophy of History," where they are now printed. An extra leaf never sewn with this lecture is printed in the textual notes.

IN MY last Lecture I described the Literature of the Period as subjective and that so it was the expression of a great change in the spirit of mankind. As far as it is truly subjective, it indicates the revolutionary character of the Age and points at the sublime cause. It points at the uprise of the Soul and the new demands it makes. Of the great perception now fast becoming a conscious fact — that there is One Mind and that all the powers and privileges that lie in any, lie in all; — that I as a man may claim and appropriate whatever of good or fair or true or strong has anywhere been exhibited, that Moses and Confucius, Montaigne and Voltaire are not so much individuals as they are parts of man and parts of me, and my intelligence of them proves them my own — literature is far the best expression.[1] The facts of history are but rough and rudimental statements, though they are statements, of the doctrine. Literature is an incomparably finer and truer picture of this truth than has yet emerged into deeds. I like artists better than generals. Goethe and Swedenborg are far more formidable agitators than Napoleon or O'Connell.[2] State is a great game which is fit for strong natures to play out, though not for the strongest. It must be done by those who have a good deal of earth to temper their fire and who can bear to handle a good deal of pitch. These persons can never compete with the artist. He draws out of the invisible his material. He takes his counters from heaven and plays his game by a skill not taught or quickened by his appetites. The Cromwells and Caesars are a mob beside him.[3] Why should we be cowed by the name of action? The ancestor of every action is a thought. And so is literature far in advance of history. I regard the American and French Revolutions in the last century, the South American states in this, and the general movement of reform throughout Christendom as only symptomatic of this interior movement. They are cutaneous appearances. Literature lies next the heart.

This spirit discovers itself in Literature in a most determined Realism throughout every department. See how ancient history has been dealt with by Niebuhr, Wolf, Müller, and Heeren. From Wolf's attack upon the authenticity of the Homeric poems, dates a new epoch in Criticism. Ancient History has been found not to be yet settled. It is to be subjected to Common Sense. It is to be cross examined. It is to be seen whether its traditions will consist not with universal belief but with universal experience. Niebuhr has attempted to sift Roman history by the like. Heeren has made admirable essays towards ascertaining the necessary facts in Greek, Persian, Assyrian, Egyptian, Æthiopic, Carthaginian nations. How thoroughly English history has been analysed let Hallam, Brodie, Lingard, Palgrave, Turner tell. Goethe has gone the circuit of human knowledge as Lord Bacon did before him, writing True or False on every article. Bentham has attempted

---

[1] "Of the great perception . . . best expression" ("Thoughts on Modern Literature," W, XII, 316–317).
[2] Daniel O'Connell (1775–1847), Irish political leader.
[3] "State is a great . . . beside him" (D, 363).

the same work in reference to Civil Law. Pestalozzi has attempted an analogous reform in Education. In philosophy the German school of French philosophers, Cousin, Jouffroy, Coleridge in England, attempted to find a foundation in thought for every thing that existed in fact.[4] Wordsworth has occupied himself in an attempt to reform poetry which had become meretricious and secondary.[5]

. . .

or a sufferer from the very affluence of the poetic diction accumulated by centuries of cultivation, so that good stock verse was written by hundreds and passed unchallenged for poetry which was nothing but a dextrous combination of the images and words in use without one primary glance at nature. Wordsworth relying on his direct observation of Nature has attempted to bring it back to truth.

It would be easy to show the same spirit at work quite near us, all around us in even more vivid and impressive energy, in the most recent works and attempts; in what is just printed; in what is written and not printed; in what is spoken and not written; in what is projected and not yet done. The popular doctrine with the youth of this generation is Being not Seeming, is the effort to cast off all that is foreign and false and to unfold the intrinsic. All the activity of man, — look where you will, is rebellious if you see it from the side of Custom: All is tender and obedient, if you see it from the side of spiritual Law.

But this statement is far from exhausting the fact. Literature not only carries out the imperfect revolutions of civil history but it goes a point farther. It betrays the nearer action of the cause. It is not only real; it is transcendental. It is not only true (as in the examples just quoted) to experience, to the appearances of nature; but it is true to the soul; to the most general and exalted nature of man.

It asks new questions. It ponders new problems. It explores the necessary in History. It studies the philosophy of history and

[4] "This spirit discovers . . . existed in fact" (cf. notes to "Thoughts on Modern Literature," W, XII, 470).
[5] One leaf missing at this point.

of life, the theory of society, of politics, of education; it disdains the abutments of authority and custom. It begins to appear how history should be written. The old Egyptians built vast temples and halls in some proportion to the globe on which they were erected and to the numbers of the nation who were to hold their solemnities within the walls. They built them not in a day nor in a single century. So let us with not less gigantic purpose write our history. Let us not, as now we do, write a history for display, and make it after our own image and likeness, — three or four crude notions of our own, and very many crude notions of old historians hunted out and patched together without coherence or proportion, and no thought of the necessity of proportion and unity dreamed of by the writer, — a great conglomerate, or at best an arabesque, a grotesque containing no necessary reason for its being nor inscribing itself in our memory like the name and life of a friend. But let us go to the facts of Chronology as Newton went to those of Physics knowing well that they are already bound together of old and perfectly, and he surveys them not that he may invent or imagine a theory but detect the bond already there. Let us learn with the patience and affection of a naturalist all the facts and looking all the time for the reason that *was,* for the law that prevailed, and made the facts such; — not for one that we can supply and make the facts plausibly sustain. We should then find abundant *aperçus* or lights self-kindled amid the antiquities we explored. Why should not history be godly written out of the highest faith and with a study of what really was? We should then have Ideas which would command and marshal the facts and show the history of a nation as accurately proportioned and necessary in every part as an animal. The connexion of Commerce and Religion explain the history of Africa from the beginning until now. Nomadism is a law of nature. And Asia, Africa, Europe present different pictures of it. The architecture of each nation had its root in nature. How ample the materials show when once we have the true Idea that explains all! The modern inhabitant, the geography, the ruins, the geology, the traditions as well as authentic history recite and confirm the tale. Out of histories written in so narrow a mind as most of our histories are, laborious indeed but without a pious and loving eye to

227

the universal contributions of nature to a people, nothing can come but incongruous, broken impressions, unsatisfactory to the mind. But the views obtained by patient wisdom studious of facts and open to the permanent as well as partial causes would give an analogous impression to the landscape.[6]

As it studies history, so it looks at the sciences in a higher connexion than heretofore. Meantime under higher instruction the genius of the time is learning to hold its facts cheap.

When it has ascertained by immense study the truth of the history and the truth of science, it then sets light by it all, turns on it as a fair legend which conceals a fine meaning worth all its chapters. It ponders analogies: Unity: Poetry: Music. It finds poetry everywhere, and music in sight no less than in sound. It has a kind side for mysticism. It sees the foundations of all things in thought. And large and small and time and space become of no account. It ponders the relation of man to the world. Ever he follows with his eye the sun and moon, the hill and the river, the plant and the animal. They mumble somewhat but what it is he understandeth not.

Our own country, I may remark, shares largely in whatsoever is new and aspiring in thought. Our young men travel in foreign countries and read at home with hungry eyes foreign books. Wishful eyes are cast on Germany which ten or twenty years ago was wont to yield this fruit of new thought to the nations. But here is Germany or nowhere. The spirit they seek is as native here as there.[7] Nay, I doubt not, at this moment, is more deeply active in this country, than in that.

I deceive myself greatly if there be not already awakened among the young a love for truth which no merely formal instruction can satisfy, a truth which is not literal or mathematical but human, and apt to content the affections as well as the intellect; to occupy the hands as well as the brain; an object to fill the whole of love, the whole of power, and the whole of reason.

But chiefly as that which includes all its faith the modern mind proclaims the Universal Nature of Man. It charges the church and the state, it charges the old literature with a certain

6 "The old Egyptians . . . landscape" (D, 129–130).
7 "Our young men . . . as there" (cf. D, 178).

treason and profanation. It charges them with a want of respect to the pupil soul. The question which the newborn man should ask of his pretended teachers is, "What is that thou sayest to me? What have I to do with thee? What with thy fact; with thy history; thy person; thine alleged inclinations and aversions? Because thou art old and soiled, think not me so. I am here. Come with thy persons and facts to judgment." And the Church and the State and the Book should deal in a corresponding reverence with the new heir of the world. They should say to him; "Hearken and say: Is not this that we have kept for thee, thine? Rings it not truly?" [8]

.   .   .

In the light of this immense faith the mind of the age revises all reputations. The greatness of all heroes is to be tested anew. Very few immutable men has History to show. We are to issue a Quo Warranto and revoke the charters of old fame. There are all degrees of greatness and this foolish praising so vague and superlative must be retrenched. We admire in Napoleon the obedience to animal instincts, the self command, the closeness to facts, the combination, the immense executive faculty and so cannot read his life without feeling that here was honor done to faculties of ours which have nowhere been so great. But so in a horse or in a dog we admire strength and valuable properties which we also possess in less degree. Yet as we turn from a crocodile or a leopard which we have admired in a menagerie if an illustrious man goes by in the street, so on the approach of spiritual greatness we turn away with pity from a man who was incapable of apprehending the loftier instincts of his nature. So it happens in a degree with many better reputations.[9]

It is true that a certain superior wisdom does seem to adjust sooner or later all the claims in the temple of Glory. Mankind are always right at last in their fames, and stars ascend to the zenith whose rising was not seen, whilst the atmospheric meteors which for a time put out the moon end in sulphur and darkness. For example, is it not passing strange that Jesus should stand as he

[8] One leaf missing at this point.
[9] "In the light . . . reputations" (E, 40).

does at the head of history, — the first character of the world, without doubt, but considering what world we live in the unlikeliest of all men, one would say, to take such a rank? Well then as if to indemnify ourselves for this vast concession to truth, we must put up the militia — Alexander, Charles V, Napoleon, and the rest into the next place of proclamation. Yet it is a pit to Mount Atlas — this fame by that, or even by the place of Homer, Pindar, and Plato.[10]

Always under the light of a new thought our old guides dwindle to the eye. And the deeper ambition of the modern mind has already obscured many names which glittered to the last generation. We are forgetting our Hume and Locke and Shaftesbury and Butler. The English Classics are a forgotten race and twenty English poets have gone silent for us.

Lastly in the same faith, Literature explores its own pretensions, and disparages all books. What are books? They can have no permanent value. How obviously initial they are to their authors. The books of the nations, the universal books, are long ago forgotten of him who wrote them. And one day we shall forget this primer literature. We must learn to judge books by absolute standards.[11] When we are aroused to a life in ourselves, these traditional splendors of letters grow very pale and cold. Literature is made up of a few ideas and a few fables. It is a heap of nouns and verbs enclosing an intuition or two.[12] It has this endemic vice, that it will not fit our case. Why should I quit the task however narrow and mean assigned to me by the Soul of Nature, to go gazing after the tasks of others or listening to the rumor of their performance? There is other peeping beside setting the eye to chinks and keyholes.[13] This everlasting reading, for example, of what others have done. Let us think more nobly. Let us, if we must have great actions, make our own so. Let us seek *one* peace by fidelity. Let us do our own duties. Why need I go gadding into the scenes and philosophy of Greek or Italian History, before I

[10] "Mankind are always . . . and Plato" (D, 367).
[11] "How obviously . . . standards" (E, 2).
[12] "Lastly in the same faith . . . intuition or two" ("Thoughts on Modern Literature," W, XII, 468); "Literature is . . . intuition or two" (D, 173; cf. "Experience," W, III, 47).
[13] D, 264.

have built my own house and justified myself to my own benefactors? How dare I read Washington's Campaigns or Xenophon's
before I have answered the questions of business or thought proposed to me? [14] Is not that a just objection to much of our reading? It is a pusillanimous desertion of our work to gaze after our
neighbors. It is peeping. Byron says of Jack Bunting,

> He knew not what to say and so he swore.[15]

I may say of our preposterous use of books,

> He knew not what to do and so he read.

I can think of nothing to fill my time with and so without any
constraint I find the Life of Jefferson. It is a very extravagant
compliment to pay to Jefferson or to General Schuyler or to General Washington. My time should be as good as their time, — my
world, my facts, all my net of relations, as good as theirs, or either of theirs. Rather let us do our work so well that other idlers
if they choose may compare our texture with the texture of these
and find it identical with the best.[16] St. Augustine complains in
such manner of the schools in which his youth was spent. "I was
constrained to lay up the follies of I know not what Æneas whilst
I forgot my own, and to bewail Dido dead because she killed herself for love; meanwhile I most miserable did endure with dry
eyes to depart and die from thee O my God and my life!" [17]

This overestimate of the possibilities of Paul and Pericles, this
underestimate of our own comes from a neglect of the fact of an
identical nature. The only difference between man and man is
larger or less reception of one spiritual influence. Bonaparte knew
but one Merit and rewarded in one and the same way, the good
soldier, the good astronomer, the good poet, the good player.
Thus he signified his sense of a great fact. The poet uses the
names of Caesar, of Tamerlane, of Bonduca, of Belisarius; the

---

[14] "Let us seek . . . to me" (D, 261, modified).

[15] *The Island,* III, v, 12, modified. The line refers to Jack Skyscrape rather
than to Ben Bunting, another character mentioned in the same stanza.

[16] "Let us, if we must . . . with the best" ("Spiritual Laws," W, II, 164–165);
"Byron says . . . with the best" (D, 259, modified).

[17] *Confessions,* I, xiii; D, 269.

painter uses the conventional legend of the Virgin Mary, of Paul, of Peter. He does not therefore defer to the nature of these accidental men, of these stock heroes. If the poet write a true drama, then he is Caesar and not the player of Caesar; then the selfsame strain of thought, emotion as pure, wit as subtle, motions as swift, mounting, extravagant, and a heart as great, self-sufficing, dauntless, which on the waves of its love and hope can uplift all that is reckoned solid and precious in the world — palaces, gardens, money, navies, kingdoms — marking its own incomparable worth by the slight it casts on these gawds of men — these all are his and by the power of these he rouses the nations. But the great names cannot stead him if he have not life in himself. Let a man believe in God and not in names and places and persons. Let the great soul incarnated in some woman's form, poor and sad and single, in some Dolly or Joan, go out to service and sweep chambers and scour floors, and its effulgent daybeams cannot be muffled or hid, but to sweep and scour will instantly appear supreme and beautiful actions, the top and radiance of human life, and all people will get mops and brooms until lo, suddenly the great soul has enshrined itself in some other form and done some other deed and that is now the flower and head of all living nature.[18]

Thus in the plenitude of its self-reliance the soul makes light of men and of books. It is the eternal instinct of the soul to turn its back upon its own past. The immortal bird leaves its egg in the wilderness to the incubation of the elements. The Future is so rich that it scorns to notch and calendar the poor trophies of its youth.

It may be well here to say a further word of explanation inasmuch this pretension gives great offence to those who do not look at letters from the same philosophical point of view. It is not that the new Man thinks he can write a better book or build a better temple than his father or his grandfather but it is true that he shares a higher and truer perception of the nature of man and a broader hope of what may yet be done than his father had.

It pleases the great soul that the present perception should arise in the universal heart of man of the soul's all-sufficiency and

[18] "This overestimate . . . living nature" ("Spiritual Laws," W, II, 165–166); "The poet uses . . . living nature" (D, 278–279, condensed).

so that literature, art, persons, space, time should be undervalued. Do not doubt that this mood is one sign in Heaven's eternal Circle or mistake the spirit of piety in which this old noblesse is assailed. It is not as old men fancy in a bragging spirit that philosophy now tends to disparage books and affirm that the reader of Shakspeare is also a Shakspeare or he could find no joy in the page. Nor does the young student persuade himself that he could bodily restore the Parthenon whilst he affirms the ultimate identity of the artist and the spectator but only in the spirit of a child who says, I am but a child but I am the heir.

Certainly we concede that the new time has no fixed works to boast but we will not therefore distrust its faith. The greatness of the Age is in its prayer. You say you see no Miltons or Dantes, and are disgusted when those who could not fasten their shoe-latchet dare to arraign and dispose of these grandeurs with complacency.

But if the objector would give himself the trouble of mastering this seeming pretention he would find that it had no such low origin as he fancies in conceit and presumption, but was merely a new point of view which the general mind is constrained to take in the present age and which in these slight alterations of our critical vocabulary which it has already effected implies the presence of a sublime cause.

The doctrine of One Mind to which all have a potential access and which is the Creator predominates in criticism as it does in religion and will subdue all the forms of language, civil, learned, or social, into expression. In the influence of that thought use your literature more impersonally. Strip it of this envious individuality. Take all that you call Dante, the whole mass of images, thoughts, emotions, facts, and believe what is certainly true, that it is not poorly confined to certain Florentine flesh and blood but that it is an eternal flower of the world, a state of thought indigenous in all souls because in the One Soul, a sign of your Zodiack, and so shall you in your progress learn that the deified Alighieri was only a type of the great class of [divine] shapes to which he led you, the book a brute harp string which vibrating on your ear causes you to see God and his angels, and that you have a right not derived but original to all the pomp [of] real nature to which the name of Dante was a frontispiece. Observe then that his humour which offended you as brag is not so but only a different manner of considering literature and leaves in the pupil as much veneration for Shakspeare and Homer as before; only they are made still alive, their power still accessible and crescive and not an ornamented tomb.[19]

.   .   .

It seems the one lesson which this miraculous world has to teach us to be sacred, to stand aloof, and suffer no man and no custom, no mode of thinking to intrude upon us and bereave us of our infinitude. We must come in doors very circumspectly. Safest is the open sky and the eternal stars. We have to fear that limiting tendency in our constitution which in the moment when the mind by one bold leap, an impulse from the Universal, has set itself free from the old church and a thousand years of dogma and seen the light of moral nature (say with Swedenborg), on the instant the defining lockjaw shuts down his fetter and cramp all around us, and we must needs think in the genius and speak in the phraseology of Swedenborg, and the last slavery is even worse than the first. Literature gives no exemption. The mind falls as readily into a mill-round in colleges and libraries as elsewhere. Perhaps the danger is greater because scholars converse with books instead of things and do not come into rough contact with the facts of all-healing nature. "Detestable," said Immanuel Kant, "is the company of mere literary men." [20]

And let me warn the youth, — if peradventure I speak to any generous and endeavoring soul, — let me warn thee O chosen youth — to hold himself dear and holy, to fear and hate whatever threatens to invade his royal solitude, his Home in Universal Being, whether it come in the shape of system of philosophy, of a literary clique, of a thought destroying Caucus, of a worship of Fashion, and keep ever the door wide to the Chapel of the great God as ever thou wouldst be no slave but the warmer of the

[19] "It pleases the great soul . . . tomb" (E, 14–16). Two leaves missing at this point.

[20] Emerson apparently read this saying on May 24, 1838 (L, II, 135; J, IV, 456); H, 106. Also used in cancelled passage of "The Present Age," Lecture 1 (p. 458, below).

heart, the enlightener of the mind, and an accepted brother of the Fraternity of Truth. It seems meritorious to read but do not lightly dismiss the conviction stamped there in thy breast that the slightest wood-thought, the least significant native emotion of thine own is more to thee than libraries. Believe always in the possibility of a circle to be drawn around your outmost thought and being and thus that your laws, your relations to society, your Christianity, your world may at any time be superseded and decease.[21]

The primary question that distinguishes like a Day of Judgment between men is: Are they still advancing? or are the seals set to their character and they now making a merchandise simply of that which they can do? In general men of genius who know no period are incapable of any perfect exhibition because however agreeable it may be to them to act on the public it is always a secondary matter. They are humble, self accusing, moody men whose worship is toward the Ideal Beauty which chooses to be courted in sylvan solitudes, in retired libraries, in nocturnal conversations with a few, with one companion, or in silent meditation. Their face is forward and their heart is in this heaven. By so much are they disqualified for a perfect success in any of the arenas of ambition to which they can give only a divided affection. But the man of talents who has attained and who has ceased to advance has every advantage in the controversy. He can give that cool and commanding attention to the thing to be done as shall secure its just performance.[22] Yet are the failures of genius better than the victories of talent.[23] Those only can sleep who do not care to sleep, and those only can act or write well who do not respect the writing or the act.[24]

In speaking thus of the value of Books when measured by an absolute standard I certainly do not wish to be superstitious or absurd. I also am a reader of books and always have been a debtor to them. I have no wish to rail at my benefactors who wrote them, the living or the dead. I wish only to state as strongly

[21] E, 28; cf. "Circles," W, II, 301.
[22] "The primary question . . . just performance" (E, 49).
[23] "In general men . . . of talent" ("New Poetry," *Uncollected Writings*, pp. 139–140).
[24] "Works and Days," W, VII, 182; D, 360.

as any feel it, the worthlessness of any Scripture in comparison with a man, a truth which I note it as a marked and an auspicious tendency of the modern mind to open and magnify. In this point of view, a book cannot be underrated, though it were the best. The letter is nothing, the spirit is everything. But the moment this is seen as it is, then the student is qualified both to read books and to write them. He only can read books well who values books not all beside a thought.

This is the thought (looking as I aim to do rather at creating tendency than at hardened fact) which the Literature of this Hour meditates and labors to say. This is that which tunes the tongue and fires the eye and sits in the silence of the youth. Verily it will not long want articulate and melodious expression. There is nothing in the heart but comes presently to the lips. The very depth of the sentiment which is the author of all the cutaneous life and movement we see is guarantee for the riches of science and of song in the age to come. He who doubts whether this age or this country can yield any contribution to the literature of the world only betrays his own blindness to the necessities of the human soul.

Do you imagine the power of poetry has ceased or the need? Have the eyes ceased to see that which they would have and which they have not? Have they ceased to see other eyes? Are there no lonely, anxious, wondering children who must tell their tale? Are we not evermore whipped by thoughts,

> In sorrow steeped and steeped in love
> Of thoughts not yet incarnated? [25]

The heart beats in this age as of old and the passions are busy as ever. Nature has not lost one ringlet of her beauty, one impulse of resistance and valor. From the necessity of loving none are exempt and he that loves must utter his desires.[26] A charm as radiant as any ever, a love that fainteth at the sight of its object is new today.

[25] Not located.
[26] E, 99.

The world does not run smoother than of old
There are sad haps that must be told.[27]

Man is not so far lost but that he bears ever the great Discontent which is the Elegy of his loss and the prediction of his recovery. In the gay saloon he laments that these figures are not what Raphael and Guercino painted. Withered though he stand and trifler as he is, the august spirit of the world looks out from his eyes. In his heart he knows the ache of spiritual pain and he can animate the sea and land. What then shall hinder the genius of the time from speaking its thought? It cannot be silent if it would. It will write in a higher spirit and a wider knowledge and with a grander practical aim than ever yet guided the pen of a poet. It will write deep into life and unite on its page the heaven and the earth. It will write the annals of a changed world and record the descent of principles into practice, of love into Government, of love into Trade. It will describe the new heroic life of man, the now unbelieved possibility of simple living, and of clean and noble relations with men. Religion will bind again these that were sometime frivolous, customary, enemies, skeptics, self seekers into a joyful reverence for the circumambient whole and that which was extacy shall become daily bread.[28]

[27] Not located.
[28] "This is the thought . . . daily bread" ("Thoughts on Modern Literature," *W*, XII, 333–336).

4

Politics

The fourth lecture in this course was read first at the Masonic Temple in Boston on January 1, 1840. It was probably the "Politics" read as the fourth lecture in Providence, Rhode Island, on March 27 in the mixed series called "Human Life," and it was read as the third lecture in the Concord, Massachusetts, "Present Age" series on April 15.

In addition to Emerson's notation on the first page, "Present Age Lect IV," there is also in his hand on the cover: "Read in NY before the Mercantile Liby. Socy March 7, 1843." That reading, for which Emerson received a substantial fee of $50, came after he had completed under other sponsorship in New York a financially unsuccessful course on "New England" (L, III, 150). It may well have been a revision of the 1840 lecture which approximated the essay "Politics" published in 1844 in *Essays, Second Series* (W, III, 197–221), which drew heavily on both the 1840 lecture and the lecture with the same title in "The Philosophy of History" (*Lectures*, II, 69–82).

The present manuscript is fragmentary, lacking fourteen leaves from the 1840 reading. Of what remains, those leaves once sewn with the first page, that is the 1840 version, are labelled "Politics" and numbered in ink. They have once been sewn together and also once sewn with the 1843 cover. In addition one leaf has been assigned to the 1843 version only and printed in its place in the textual notes, along with what is recoverable from a few scraps and a double sheet not belonging to either version of the lecture. In the 1843 reading Emerson probably omitted those few passages which had been printed in *Essays* (1841); all of them now are struck through with use marks which for the later reading would serve as cancellations.

THERE are some subjects which have a kind of prescriptive right to dull treatment. A sprightly book on the Civil Law or on Tithes or on Dogmatic Theology or on Liberty and Necessity would be presumptuous. The State and the Church guard their purlieus with a jealous decorum and the etiquette of these august courts as of palaces requires of all comers sleepy manners, half-shut or whole-shut eyes, and the rigorous exclusion of all wit. The ignorant reader in these profane days when all men take all books in hand with such impatient haste to get at their value and conclusion, may sometimes wonder where such massive volumes found writers and where they found readers among mere mortals who must sometimes laugh and are liable to the infirmity of sleep.

But in the face of our libraries it must still be affirmed that every subject of human thought down to the most trivial crafts and chares ought to be located poetically, — religion, war, law, politics, money, housekeeping. It would be easy to show that they must all be handled poetically in action in order to any success. A judge and a banker must drive their craft poetically as well as a dancer or a scribe. That is they must not suffer the facts to stand superior to them but they must master the facts, exert that higher vision of their own mind which constrains the facts to take a new and better order from the man instead of imposing their mere mechanical order of time and place on him. Then they are inventive; they detect the capabilities of their affair.

No one will doubt who reads Livy, Plutarch, or Las Cases that battles must be fought poetically.[1] Let us hear one who had a right to speak to this point. "The fate of a battle," said Napoleon, "is the result of a moment of thought. The hostile forces advance with various combinations; they attack each other, and fight for a certain time; the critical moment arrives, a mental flash decides, and the least reserve accomplishes the object." [2] Will any lawyer question the advantage however he may name the tactics of a bold, original treatment of a case over the most patient and fault-less drudgery? In the management of an estate, in household expenses one man, one woman treats the details of prudence poetically or exercises an economy which is poetical, inventive, alive and therein distinguished from mere parsimony which is a poor, dead, base thing. Economy inspires respect, is clean, and accomplishes much. In every art this discriminates the master and the

---

[1] "But in the face . . . fought poetically" (E, 101, modified).
[2] Las Cases, *Journal*, I, ii, 10; C, 299; "Napoleon," W, IV, 237.

apprentice. All human affairs need the perpetual intervention of new thought to raise the facts to keep them sweet and supple as the earth needs the presence of caloric through its pores to resist the tendency to consolidation. If you would write logarithms or a code or a cookbook you cannot spare the poetic impulse. We must not only have hydrogen in balloons and springs to coaches but we must have fire under the Andes at the core of the World.[3]

We must treat the state poetically with the more need. Especially is it necessary to be on our guard in treating such a subject as the state against the encroachment of mere size and quantity which are apt to disguise political questions and hide the truth. Let us treat the state wisely, — with sight, that is, and not with closed eyes. Surrender to the fear of it nothing. If sensually seen, it daunts and overpowers by the immense extent of the particulars and personal interests involved.

Let us not politely forget the fact that its institutions are not aboriginal though they existed before we were born: that they are not superior to the citizen: that every one of its institutions was once a man: that every one of its laws and usages was a man's expedient to meet a particular fact: that they all are alterable; all imitable; we may make as good; we may make better. All society is an optical illusion to the young adventurer. It looks to him massive and monumental in its repose with certain names, men, institutions rooted like oak trees to the centre round which all arrange themselves the best they can and must arrange themselves. But the fact is Society is fluid; there are no such roots and centres but any monad there may instantly become the centre of the whole movement and compel the whole to gyrate around him[4] as every man of strong will, like Cromwell or Pitt, does for a time and every man of truth, like Plato or Paul, does forever:[5] Christ, Christianity; Aristotle, Scholastic logic; Linnaeus, Natural History; Justinian, Roman Law; Alfred, Trial by Jury.

But let us not understand this duty of treating the subject of Politics wisely and with resolution as giving us any right to be

---

[3] "economy which is . . . of the World" (E, 101, rearranged).
[4] "All society . . . around him" (D, 257–258).
[5] "Let us not politely . . . does forever" ("Politics," W, III, 199).

wilful or ingenious in the matter. Politics are real and must be treated really. The vice of young politicians in which republics always abound is the belief that the laws make the city and the people: that the gravest modifications of the policy, the modes of living, and the character of the population may be accomplished by voting them: that commerce, education, religion, may be voted in or out and that any measure, though it were absurd, may be imposed on a people if only you get sufficient numbers to make it a law. But the wise know that all foolish legislation however strong in numbers and noxious for the time in the people, is a rope [of] sand that perishes in twisting, that the state must follow the character and progress of man and does not lead it, that the state goes not by will but by fate, that the strongest usurper is presently swept away and they only who build on Ideas build for eternity, that the form of government that prevails is always the expression of what cultivation exists in the population which permits it, that the Law is therefore always only a memorandum. We are too superstitious. We think the statute somewhat. So much life as it has in the character of living men is all its force. The statute is a memorandum only. It stands there to say, "Yesterday we agreed so and so, — but how feel ye this article today?" Our statute is always an approximate statement of our aggregate character, and through it our character governs or works. Nature is despotic and will not be fooled or oppressed by the pertest of her sons and as fast as more of man is unfolded the Code is seen to be brute and stammering. It speaks not articulately and must be made to. Meantime it is always learning. The reveries of the true and simple are prophetic. What you dream and pray and paint today, but shun the ridicule of saying aloud, shall presently be the resolutions of large bodies, then shall be carried as Grievance and Bill of Rights through conflict and war, and then shall be triumphant law, usage, establishment for a hundred years until it gives place in turn before new prayers and pictures.

The history of the state simply records in a coarse external way the progress of thought and follows like a spaniel the culture of man, his faith, his aspiration.[6] The state and the aspiration:

[6] "Politics are real . . . his aspiration" ("Politics," W, III, 199–201).

and no matter how powerful this looks and how faint that, the state always follows close on the track of the hope and sentiment of the people.[7]

.   .   .

Still considering this subject theoretically (as it respects men as they should be, not men as they are) we proceed to say that the less government we have, the better; the fewer laws, the less confided power. We say next that the great antidote and corrective in nature to this abuse of Formal Government is the Influence of Private Character, the growth of the Individual, the appearance of the principal to supersede the proxy, the appearance of the Wise Man of whom the existing government is, it must be confessed, a very shabby imitation.[8]

The world has never been aware and is not yet of the extent of one man: of the possible influence of character. The Wise Man is a man without bounds. He sits at home with might and main, and does not suffer himself to be bullied by kings or empires, for he knows that he is greater than all the geography and all the government of the world; he feels that there is a great responsible Thinker and Actor moving wherever moves a man;[9] that a true man belongs to no other time or place but is the centre of things. Where he is, there is Nature. He measures you and all men and all events. You are constrained to accept his standard.[10] Every body in society reminds us of somewhat else, of some other person. Character, reality, reminds you of nothing else. It takes place of the whole creation. The man must be so much that he makes all circumstances indifferent, — puts all means into the shade. This all great men are and do. Every great man is a cause, a country, and an age; requires infinite spaces and numbers and time fully to accomplish his thought — and posterity appear to follow his steps as a procession. A man Caesar was born and for ages after we have a Roman Empire. Christ is born and millions of minds so grow and cleave to his genius that he is confounded

---

[7] Six leaves are missing at this point.

[8] "Still considering this subject . . . shabby imitation" ("Politics," *W*, III, 215–216).

[9] Cf. "Self-Reliance," *W*, II, 60, and above, pp. 7 and 188.

[10] "a true man . . . his standard" (C, 143).

with virtue and the possible of man.[11] Men see the institution and worship it. It is only the lengthened shadow of one man. Scipio, Milton well called "the height of Rome." [12] The Reformation is the shadow of Luther: Quakerism of Fox: Methodism of Wesley: Abolition of Clarkson.[13]

That which all things tend to educe, which all cultivation, all freedom, all intercourse, all revolution go to form and deliver, is character, to educate the human will, to balance the soul on itself so that its natural perception and decision shall appear — that is the end of nature, her secret, to reach unto this coronation of her king. To educate the wise man the state exists and with the appearance of the wise man the state expires.[14] Every step toward this is sacred and great. All events are steps towards it. A single new thought, a new elevation of character is worth all the eaters on earth. It is of very little importance what the foolish do, or what the wise do when they are foolish. A single man avails more to the world than whole kingdoms of China and Japan. The mind of one Paul outweighs a whole island of Crete or kingdom of Bohemia. In taking account of the age we take no account of the sleeping nations. When they emerge from their chrysalis, it will be time enough to describe their fortunes.

The appearance of character rebukes the state. It makes the state unnecessary. It leaves the ambitious statesmen far below. The wise man is the state. Louis XIV, if he knew what he said, was right. The wise man needs no army fort or navy. He loves men too well. Even if they turn upon him he is invulnerable. He needs no bribe or feast or palace to draw friends to him. He angles with himself and with no other bait. He asks no vantage ground, no favorable circumstance. He needs no library, for he has not done thinking — he gets thought where the bookmaker got it; no church, for he is himself a prophet; no statute book, for he hath the Lawgiver; no money, for he is value itself; no road, for he is at home where he is; no experience, for the life of the Creator shoots through him and looks from his eyes. He has no personal

[11] "A man Caesar . . . of man" (D, 143).
[12] *Paradise Lost,* IX, 510; D, 143, 271; see above, pp. 12–13.
[13] "that there is a great responsible Thinker . . . of Clarkson" ("Self-Reliance," W, II, 60–61).
[14] "That which all things . . . state expires" ("Politics," W, III, 216).

friends, for he does not need to husband and educate a few to share with him a select and poetic life, who has the spell to draw the select prayer and piety of all men unto him. His relation to all men is angelic. His memory is myrrh to them, his presence frankincense and flowers.[15]

The power of character is the simplest of all known powers. We are used to avail ourselves [of such a cumbrous apparatus of means that we do not believe in immediate action on others; we do not believe in a power that works without means.] [16]

．　　　．　　　．

It is plain that where a good man is set to do a public act he should occupy himself only with the measure, not with the opinion of the people. By directing all his understanding and affection on the fact and not allowing the people or their enemies to arrest it he is able to make his hands meet to come at his end. But when the eye of the political agent veers too frequently from the measure to the opinion, and in course of time fastens on opinion mainly, — he must lose just so much steadiness of conduct and therewith so much success. In this country there is no measure attempted for itself by legislatures but the opinion of the people is courted in the first place and the measures are perfunctorily carried through as secondary. Instead of character there is a studious exclusion of character. We see that Mr. A will deliver an oration on the Fourth of July and Mr. B before the Merchants or the Farmers and we do not go because we know that these gentlemen will not communicate their own character and being to the audience. A speech ought to be a man: — the heart and soul of the speaker made manifest: — but our speeches are screens and escapades, and not communications.[17] The people are feared and flattered. They are not reprimanded. The country is governed in bar-rooms and in the mind of bar-rooms.[18] The low

[15] "The wise man . . . flowers" ("Politics," W, III, 216; E, 105).

[16] At this point five leaves are missing from the 1840 manuscript, and there is a fragment only of another. See textual notes for continuation of 1843 version.

[17] "We see that Mr. A . . . not communications" ("Spiritual Laws," W, II, 152, modified; D, 247).

[18] Cf. E, 78.

can best win the low and each aspirant vies with the other which can stoop lowest, depart widest from himself.

Under our wooden or brick houses lies the living magical earth, yet lies not still a moment but whirls forever on in its orbit true to the orbs and its system, and its system just to the vast balance of nature. In like manner if we have seen that under our ridiculous routine of selfish trade and government bloomed unhurt the life of God and found ever and anon vent in our consciousness and in our action, that we have not set ourselves systematically and invariably to stifle it and so kill ourselves but in sane moments have opened it a passage into the laws and institutions, have let our private bark follow the course of the river and be blown in the path of the monsoon, have not selected for honor the mean and the dead in whom no virtue lived and such therefore as honor could not cleanse or great aims enliven, but have let our votes follow Ideas and our elections express our character and aspiration, so that the highest sentiment cheered us in the assembly of the people, and the ballot was a voice of truth and veneration, — then, the state will stand; then the laws will be memorable and beautiful for long thousands of years; will shine by intrinsic light as easily through many as through few ages.[19]

It is the privilege of this Idea of the all-sufficiency of private character that it is never absent, that it is never reduced to wait for means. Its kingdom begins with the perception of it. It needs no crusade against the state but the simple abstinence from participating its wrong deed. A new epoch is dawning on us. Let us accept its grand instructions. Let us abjure the use of all unjust and unworthy strength which the state has put in our power. Let us make again the form of man great and venerable. Let us treat all men as gods. Let us drop violence. The prompt objector says, that is to bare your bosom to the knife. Men do not see that the disuse of force is itself the education of men to do without. Leave force to those who like it and try the magnetism of truth. Only charity admitteth of no excess.

We have a vicious way of esteeming the defects in men organic.[20] We distrust men's capacity for self government. We

---

[19] "Under our wooden . . . few ages" (E, 99–100).
[20] Cf. "New England Reformers," W, III, 268.

esteem them incapable now of self direction nor think they can be in a lifetime. This is a falsehood of our own heart. The only distinction which the good acknowledge is that of the old and the young. Trust men and they will be true to you.[21] Love them and do what you will. Where was ever a kindness which flew from the heart that did not bring back the same?

Luther tells us that "at the Imperial Diet of Augsburg certain princes discoursed one day in praise of the riches and regalities of their several countries. The Elector of Saxony said he had in his countries store of silver mines which brought him great revenues. The Prince Elector Palatine extolled the wine of his vineyards that grew on the river Rhine. Others, etc. Now when the turn of Eberhard Prince of Wirtemberg came to speak he said, 'I am but a poor prince, and noway to be compared to you; yet I have also in my country a rich and precious jewel, namely that when although unawares I should ride astray in my country and were left all alone in the fields yet I could in safety sleep in the bosom of every one of my subjects. They all are ready for my service to set up and venture body, goods, and blood.' And indeed his people esteemed him the country's Father. When the other princes heard this they confessed that it was an unrivalled jewel." [22]

. . .

Of course it follows since the real government is ever this Theocracy whose seat is not in the heart of only one man or one set of men, but in the heart of every man, that all forms of government are in themselves imperfect and evil. They are a surrender of that which the man ought not to surrender: he does by delegate that which he should do himself. They are temporary: — as much as he has delegated, he must some day resume: — they are unnecessary, being a complex way of doing somewhat he can accomplish directly. The very idea of Government in the world is Interference.

That all governments are defective instantly appears in the

[21] "Prudence," W, II, 237.
[22] *Colloquia Mensalia: or, Dr. Martin Luther's Divine Discourses at his Table* . . . , trans. H. Bell (London, 1652), p. 459; Σ, 13–14. Three leaves are missing at this point.

loss of truth and power that befals one who leaves working for himself to work for another. Absolutely speaking I can only work for myself. When moved by love a man teaches his child or join[s] with his neighbor in any act of common benefit or spends himself for his friend, or does at an immense personal sacrifice that touches limb and life somewhat public and self-immolating like the fight of Leonidas or the hemlock of Socrates or the cross of Christ it is not done for others but to fulfil a high necessity of this proper character; the benefit to others is merely contingent, is not contemplated by the doer. Men of that stamp do not cant. Others may cant after them and even strive to put cant in their mouths; but they know well that it was the sublime idea of a most private and beautiful Right, the way to which led through this valley of death, that drove them to their act and not any calculation of good to be done to individuals or to multitudes.

5

Private Life

The fifth lecture in this series was delivered in the Masonic Temple, Boston, on January 8, 1840, and was the fourth lecture in the Concord, Massachusetts, series on April 17. It is possible that it was the fifth or sixth in the Providence, Rhode Island, series on March 30 or April 1, but there is no evidence. Only fragments remain of the lecture manuscript; it probably was bodily incorporated into the essays Emerson was writing in the late spring and summer of 1840. He wrote to Samuel Gray Ward on June 22, 1840, that he was "just now finishing a Chapter on Friendship (of which one of my lectures last winter contained a first sketch) . . ." (*Letters . . . to a Friend*, p. 21). The reasonable supposition that the lecture was "Private Life" is supported by passages in these extant fragments which were used in the essay. Similarly, there is a passage still remaining which finally was used in the essay "Domestic Life" (*W*, VII, 128) but which may have got there by way of whatever Emerson began "to scribble & copy" on the subject of "Domestic Life" in August 1840 (*L*, II, 322). If so, some leaves of the manuscript may have gone the likely route of "Home" (see headnote above, p. 23). It should be noted that in the last lecture of this course Emerson refers to the subject of this lecture as "Domestic Life" (see below, p. 302; also *L*, II, 246).

There is no certainty that the four fragments printed here as text belong to the lecture, though the last two offer greater certainty than the others. Three other fragments filed with these have been rejected on internal evidence. For these and for information on the fragments printed in the text, see the textual notes.

I T IS a fact full of meaning, the infinite self-trust of men. Nothing delights us more, nothing gives us the austere joy of the sublime, like the spectacle of an invincible faith. Men wholly uncultivated, who have as yet given no allowance to the soul in themselves, yet betray their instinct, by the awe they feel when it is exhibited in another. For this reason, it is, too, that the charge of pride, which is a spurious self-trust, is always pleasant to men.

Never was a saint who was not pleased to be accused of pride.[1] But there is a deeper implication of this self-trust in another fact, namely in the severity with which we judge other men's derelictions and pardon our own. No man likes any body's intemperance or defilement or cruelty but his own.[2] We admit the universal obligation of the law and prefer only a single private good to it, namely our own. No other exception whatever. Now what is the reason that we admit this one exception, but that our perfect consciousness of the universal law even in the hour of our transgression warrants *us*, we think, from a total dereliction? We cannot believe that we shall ever in the whole, and at last, be false to the spiritual law.

The spontaneous sentiment is the remedy. Utter the great sentiment of the world against your own private one. The universal tide rises in our cistern, in every man's, heart-high; but the little private puddle of the blood trickles to the tongue, to the finger ends. We are in thought wise and sublime, in word and deed silly and foolish.[3]

.   .   .

This immense preponderance of the senses, it is the end of Culture to balance and overcome. I do not think much of any man that he cows and silences me in conversation. Any fool can do that; but if his conversation enriches and rejoices me, I must reckon him wise. I thank those that teach me not to be easily depressed. A respect for principles always teaches a lesson and whenever a man writes or speaks or acts in an entire forgetfulness of other people and from his own heart we catch from him a sublime admonition.

I say to the noble soul that has not lost its first faith, the world is like a birth of this hour to a pure and heroic mind. Every day is new, every glance you throw on nature ought to bring you new information; the gains of each day ought to bestow a new vision on tomorrow's eyes, a new melody on tomorrow's ears. I entreat him to go near the transcendant energy of spiritual laws and see how coarse and clumsy is the finest architecture of chemistry, of

---

[1] "For this reason . . . accused of pride" (C, 121).
[2] D, 187.
[3] "The spontaneous sentiment . . . and foolish" (C, 313).

vegetation, of animal organization when compared with the creations of the Soul.

I would show to the student the great things done for him in time and nature, the vast preparations made for the Culture of the spirit in this world; that nothing has been left undone; that nothing grand, nothing high, nothing infinite has spared to work for the education of the single soul; that the ages of time and the spaces of nature and all the resources of Being play into his private tutelage.

Before it, Time — which usually we think the strongest of powers, — is weak. We think in idle hours that the ancients have perished, are dead and inoperative. Then we awake and see that through the force of soul nothing alive dies. In the present moment all the past is ever represented. The strong roots of ancient trees still bind the soil. Nothing dies. A learned critic praises to me the old remnants of Provence and the troubadours. But the Provençal literature is not obsolete for me for I have Spenser to read and all that faded splendor revives again in him for some centuries yet. Nor will Homer or Sophocles that have been bards to seventy or eighty generations let me go, though I read them not, for they have formed those whom I read. Nor will the Egyptian designer even die to me; my chair and tables forget him not — but their graceful ornament has come down from his cunning hand.[4] The traveller who explores the ruins of Memphis and Thebes detects on the Egyptian tombs and temples the identical scroll ornaments and designs of every kind which are faithfully copied on the Cashmere shawl, the upholstery and furniture of rich men's houses in this town.[5] Every beautiful line that was ever drawn was an expression of a deep thought and according to the depth whence it came, so long will it last. A musical tone is heard farther than a noise. A bell or the march of a band in the streets of a city, is heard for miles beyond the uproar of trades and cartwheels. In like manner, a word of truth, a devout sentiment, an act of honor — a thought so harmonious that it took in utterance a form all melody — these float yet by their own aerial nature in the air of Eternity and come unbroken to us.

[4] "In the present moment . . . cunning hand" (C, 179, expanded).
[5] Cf. C, 168.

There where you stand, Time yields to you its soul. To your increasing insight old sages live again. The old revolutions find some correspondence in the experiences of your mind. All the wonderful spiritual natures like so many princedoms and potentates of heaven stand bending around you. Give yourself to Virtue and to truth, — and Virtue and truth shall give themselves to you. Pierce the shows of things and see them as they really affect you. Do not think the ray of light less divine because it falls on stones and fools than if it glided alone from its native star a private messenger to your proper eye. So look at the wondrous associates with whom you accompany. Every one of the twenty individuals we best know represents to us a vast multitude of men, a class so that always you walk as a king amidst a choir of ambassadors, each bringing the claims of one department or empire of nature to his eyes. One man represents to me Learning and one Comedy, one Finance, and one Politics, one the Fine Arts, and one the Useful. One the Church. One the Actual and one the Ideal. Every change in your relation to these persons indicates change and if so be progress in the verities of which these persons are the merely vanishing symbols. Your altered relation to persons is the mercury of your changed relation to the ideas they represent.

What is our art, what is our literature, what is our religion but endless reproduction of what was immortal in the past, that is, of what was truly alive before? Indeed what is our own being but a reproduction, a representation of all the past? When I remember the manifold cord — the thousand or the million stranded cord which my being and every man's being is, — that I am an aggregate of infinitesimal parts and that every minutest streamlet that has flowed to me is represented in that man which I am so that if every one should claim his part in me I should be instantaneously diffused through the creation and individually decease, then I say I am an alms of all and live but by the charity of others. What is a man but a congress of nations? Let him evoke out of time the host of his ancestry. All have vanished. He — the insulated result of all that character, activity, sympathy, antagonism working for ages in all corners of the earth — alone remains. Such is his origin. Is his nurture less compound? Who has not, —

what has not contributed something to make him that he is? Art, science, institutions, black men, white men, vices, virtues, of all people; the church; the prison; the shop; poets; nature; joy; and fear; all help, all teach him. Every fairy, and every imp have brought a gift.[6]

Indeed it seems to me that the true culture of the soul has no better measure than the confidence of the man in the compensations of Being. Men doubt a divine power and because the divine nature to our best meditation refuses to impersonate itself, they think God is not. When behold! all around them the great Cause is alive, is life itself, and all matter seems but the soft wax in his hand, is a picture book illustrative of moral sentiment. The world looks like a multiplication table or a mathematical equation which turn it how you will — balances itself, take what figure you will, — its exact value — nor more, nor less — still returns to you.[7]

Sow what seed you will — the sure hours will bring you the harvest of that seed. We are planters of various grains in the acre of Time. We try the experiment every day; it is so pretty to scatter this poisoned dust, — we don't believe we shall hear of it again; in frolic we throw it broad-cast on the summer wind, and watch the alluring cloud as it rolls off. It vanishes, and long years elapse, and it has rooted and grown and ripened and we eat sickness and infamy and curses like bread. Peace is extracted from the pillow, convenience is extracted from our property, and society is a place of fear and suspicion.

With a fidelity not less admirable, with a fidelity that is dear and comes in the semblance of angels and friends, Time receives into its faithful bosom the brave and just deed — the humble prayer scarce uttered — (so that the hand prayed also) — and it turns out that the Universe was all Ear, that the solitude saw as if every leaf was an eye, and choirs of witnesses shall certify the Eternal approbation. I say that I think a man's conviction of the perfectness of the Divine Justice the best measure of his culture: because, in the degree in which the soul cleanses itself of sensual pollutions and assumes its state, and makes the body serve, it ceases to judge from appearance; itself enlarges; its dams and

[6] "When I remember . . . brought a gift" (A, 116–117).
[7] "Compensation," W, II, 102.

jealous floodgates disappear, and the inundation of truth comes in. A man's progress seems to be the continual transference of his *me*, of his egoism, back from his person, his body, his name, his circumstances, to the great soul which animates him and all, the justice, love, and beauty which are the eternal mind. In them let him aspire to live that the visits of the soul shall not be rare and interrupted but that he draw fuller inspirations of the common soul continually; then he will surmount also the fear of death, seeing that his heart is the Eternal Life.

.   .   .

[The ornament of a house is the friends who frequent it. There is no event greater in life than the appearance of new persons about our hearth, except it be the progress of the character which draws them. It has been finely added by Landor to his definition of the *great man*, "It is he who can call together the most select company] when it pleases him." [8] And a beautiful verse of the old Greek Menander remains which runs in translation:

> Not on the store of sprightly wine,
> Nor plenty of delicious meats,
> Though generous Nature did design
> To court us with perpetual treats,
> 'T is not on these we for content depend
> So much as on the shadow of a friend.[9]

But this topic is too large to open at the close of a lecture and I only name it in honor of its importance. Friendship is indeed the asylum in which we find honorable shelter from the injuries of time and fate. "What is given to a friend," said Scaliger, "is redeemed out of the power of Fortune." [10] And I will add, that, fine, subtle, and dainty as is that web we call Friendship, it is the solidest thing we know. For now, after so many ages of experi-

---

[8] Walter Savage Landor, "Diogenes and Plato," *Imaginary Conversations, Second Series,* 2 vols. (London, 1829), I, 465; Blotting Book IV [A], 6; Encyclopedia, 131.
[9] Inaccurately quoted from Plutarch, "Of Brotherly Love," *Morals,* III, 69; C, 131. "The ornament . . . of a friend" ("Domestic Life," *W,* VII, 128, which supplies bracketed material).
[10] Given in Latin and ascribed to J. C. Scaliger in E, 66, and Index Major, 127. An earlier source is Martial, *Epigrams,* V, 42.

ence, — what do we know of Nature or of ourselves? Not one step has man taken toward the solution of the problem of his destiny. In one condemnation of folly stand the whole universe of men. But the sweet sincerity of joy and peace which I draw from this alliance with my brother's soul, is the nut itself — whereof all nature and all thought is but the husk and shell.[11]

.   .

Respect so far the holy laws of this fellowship as not to prejudice its perfect flower by your impatience for its opening. We must be our own, before we can be another's. There is at least this satisfaction in crime, according to the Latin proverb, *You can speak to your accomplice on even terms:* Crimen quos inquinat aequat.[12] To those whom we admire and love, at first we cannot. Yet the least defect of self-possession vitiates, in my judgment, the entire relation. There can never be deep peace between two spirits, never mutual respect until in their dialogue each stands for the whole world.[13] "I will not dine in the house of a man who does not head his own table," said the Duke of Clarence to the hospitable but too modest mulatto.[14]

Nor are they yet ripe for the noblest relations who are not each free in the other's presence.

We walk alone in the world. Friends such as we desire are dreams and fables: but a sublime hope cheers ever the faithful heart that elsewhere in other regions of the universal power souls are now acting, enduring, and daring which can love us and which we can love. We may congratulate ourselves that the period of nonage, of follies, of blunders, and of shame is passed in solitude, and when we are finished men, we shall grasp heroic hands in heroic hands. Only be admonished by what you already see, not to strike leagues of friendship with cheap persons, where no friendship can be.

Our impatience betrays us into rash and foolish alliances

---

[11] "And I will add . . . husk and shell" ("Friendship," W, II, 201; E, 95–96). Three leaves are missing at this point.

[12] Cf. Lucan, *Pharsalia,* V, 290; Jeremy Taylor, *Twenty-Seven Sermons,* Sermon XVI, in *The Whole Works,* VI, 40; Blotting Book I, 47.

[13] "Respect so far . . . the whole world" ("Friendship," W, II, 211).

[14] "There is at least . . . mulatto" (E, 83).

which no god attends. What has been said of Glory is true of Friendship. "If thou love Glory, thou must trust her truth: She follows those who do not turn and look after her." [15] By persisting in your path, by holding your peace, though you forfeit the little you gain the great. You become pronounced. You demonstrate yourself so as to put yourself out of the reach of false relations and do draw to you the firstborn of the world, those rare pilgrims whereof only one or two wander in nature at once and before whom the vulgar great show as spectres and shadows merely.[16] Nothing is more deeply punished than the neglect of the great affinities by which alone society should be formed and the foolish levity of choosing associates by others' eyes.

[15] Landor, "William Penn and Lord Peterborough," *Imaginary Conversations, Second Series,* II, 258; Q, 69; Encyclopedia, 159.
[16] "We walk alone . . . shadows merely" ("Friendship," W, II, 213, with quotation and second to last sentence omitted).

6

Reforms

The sixth lecture in the series was read in Boston at the Masonic
Temple on January 15, 1840, and at Concord, Massachusetts, as the
fifth lecture in the course on April 22. It may have been read at Providence, Rhode Island, on March 30 or April 1 or elsewhere, but evidence is lacking. The subject was of great current interest to Emerson, and he apparently turned to it again in August 1840 (*L*, II, 322).
"Man the Reformer" was read to the Mechanics' Apprentices' Library
Association in Boston on January 25, 1841, and printed the following
April in *The Dial*. It was probably that lecture rather than a repeat
of the 1840 lecture which he read to the Concord Lyceum on March
10, 1841, as "Reform." The present lecture was used extensively in at
least the printed version of "Lecture on the Times," and a substantial
passage from it went into "Spiritual Laws" and one into "Self-Reliance."

The manuscript is nearly complete; the leaves are labelled and
paginated in ink and, except for inserts, were once sewn together.
However, at one point duplicate page numbering and revision of text
indicate alternate readings; the version containing an April 1840 journal passage, perhaps indicating revision for the Concord reading, has
been printed in the textual notes along with a large double sheet which
recasts a passage of the lecture and two larger leaves which were
once sewn together but not with this lecture.

NOTHING has more remarkably distinguished the Present
Age than the great harvest of projects it has yielded for the reform of domestic, social, civil, literary, and ecclesiastical institutions.

They have moreover a high historical value from the fact that
in a coarse, external way the several conspicuous movements of
Reform are the discipline and education of the public mind. How
can such a question as the slavetrade be agitated for forty years

by the most enlightened nations of the world without throwing great light on ethics into the general mind? The fury with which the slavetrader defends every inch of his bloody deck and howling auction only serves as a trump of doom to alarum the ear of mankind to wake the dull sleepers and drag all neutrals to take sides and listen to the argument and verdict which justice shall finally pronounce. The Temperance question which rides the conversation of ten thousand circles, which divides the community as accurately as if one party wore blue coats and the other red, which is tacitly recalled at every public and at every private table, drawing with it all the curious ethics of the Pledge, of the Wine question, of the equity of the manufacture and of the Trade, is a gymnastic training to the casuistry and conscience of the time. The question of antimasonry had a deep right and wrong which gradually emerged to sight out of the turbid controversy.

The political questions, of Banks; of the limits of Executive power; of the right of the people to instruct their representative; of the tariff; of the treatment of Indians; of the Boundary Wars; the Congress of Nations; are all pregnant with ethical conclusions.[1] The student of the history of this Age will hereafter compute the singular value of our active discussion to the Mind of the Period.[2]

The Age cannot be described without taking some account of these its aspirations and laborious efforts for the Better. Perhaps they are not all wise. Perhaps they are all of a mixed character; but it would be neither generous nor just in essays which make any pretention to sketch the features of the time, to omit facts so creditable, and which, beyond their present value are pregnant with purer results. The number and variety of these enterprizes indicates the depth and universality of the movement which betrays itself by such variety of symptoms at the surface. And, so far, what can be better? What fairer renown can an epoch ask with all following ages, than that it did not sleep on the errors it inherited, but put every usage on trial, and exploded every abuse?

[1] "How can such . . . ethical conclusions" (C, 245–246, condensed).
[2] "How can such . . . Mind of the Period" ("Lecture on the Times," W, I, 269–270).

The cause of this impatience is deep, and its expression does honor to men. Our modes of living are not agreeable to our imagination; we suspect they are unworthy. We accuse our daily employments; they appear to us unfit, unworthy of the faculties we spend upon them. In conversation with a man whom we highly esteem we apologize for our employments, we speak of them with shame.[3] The fancy flies from the work that is due today to its various fairylands, to some agreeable hope, some object of affection, some foreign residence, some passage of poetry. The farther off the thought from the matter in hand, the more wishfully we entertain it; as children at school prefer a history of wars and battles to the daily lesson; Robinson to the history; and Sinbad the Sailor to Robinson Crusoe. When we are on the way to do a disagreeable affair, every far off hill, every road or woodpath that opens in opposite direction looks seductive to us.

In what decided contrast with the tameness of our business stand ever the objects of nature. When we are galled and disgusted with our bondage, if by chance we go into the forest the stems of pine and hemlock and oak trees almost gleam like steel on the excited eye. How old, how aboriginal these trees appear though not many years older than the spectator. They seem parts of the eternal chain of destiny whereof this sundered will of man is the victim. Is he not touched even with a sense of inferiority in the presence of these natures which preserve their beauty in growth, in strength, in age, in decay? The invitation which these fine savages give as you stand in the hollows of the forest works strangely on the imagination. Little say they in recommendation of towns or a civil Christian life. Live with us, they say, and forsake these wearinesses of yesterday. Here no history or church or state is interpolated on the divine sky and the immortal year.[4]

Life should not be prosaic. The reason why it is, is because it is false and violates the laws of the mind. Life tends ever to be picturesque. This beauty the fancy finds in everything else certainly accuses that manner of life we lead. Why should it be hateful? Why should it contrast thus with all natural beauty? Why

[3] "Our modes of living . . . with shame" ("Lecture on the Times," W, I, 271).
[4] "When we are galled . . . immortal year" (E, 77); cf. "Nature," W, III, 170.

should it be shameful? Why should it not be poetic and invite and raise us? Is there a necessity that the works of man should be sordid? Perhaps not.[5] Certainly there is little difference between the tasks of one and another workman, — take the crafts and professions as they rise. We are all restless and each at first supposes that only his manner of living is superficial, — that all other men's is solid. On inspection he finds all are alike shallow.[6] Out of this fair Idea then in the mind springs forever the effort at the Perfect.

It is the eternal testimony of the soul in man to a fairer possibility of life and manners than he has attained that agitates society every day with the offer of some new amendment.[7]

But whilst [reforms] have this high origin it must be confessed they do not retain the purity of an idea. They are presently organized in some low inadequate form and present no more poetic image to man than the tradition which they reprobated. They mix the fire of the moral sentiment with personal and party heats, with measureless exaggerations, and the blindness that prefers some darling measure to justice and truth.[8]

But let us not be guilty of the vulgarity of joining in the cry that defames the innovator. Let us honor his perception and his courage to proclaim it. Let us not lose our temper the moment his project is named because we think by some possibility of implication it may accuse us, or threaten our repose. We owe much to these beneficent reformers of all stripes and qualities. Each one shows me that there is somewhat I can spare; shows me thus how rich I am. Within my trench, there is a wall; if the town be taken there is yet a citadel; if the tower be stormed, there is still the invincible me.[9] Is not his reproach better than silence? Children like the story that makes them weep better than that which makes them laugh. Men love the play or the fight or the news that scares and agitates them. And the great man loves the conversation or the book that convicts him, not that which soothes and flatters

[5] "This beauty . . . Perhaps not" ("Lecture on the Times," W, I, 271–272).
[6] "We are all . . . shallow" (D, 289).
[7] For editorial emendation see textual notes.
[8] "But whilst [reforms] have . . . justice and truth" ("Lecture on the Times," W, I, 277).
[9] "We owe much . . . invincible me" (D, 337).

him.[10] For this opens to him a new and great career; fills him with hope; whilst compliments bereave him of hope.[11]

Certainly it seems better to use than to flout them. Shall it be said of the hero that he opposed all the cotemporary good because it was not grand? Is it not better to get their humble good and to catch a golden boon of purity and temperance and mercy from these faithful men of one idea?[12] Indeed if we can by thought put ourselves at a sufficient distance from the persons and details of the various philanthropies what can be more than this outburst of humanity and love in so many forms, this youthful hope in its aged heart that is indicated by the great connexion of reformation that is now on foot?

What then is our true part in relation to these philanthropies? Let us be true to our principle that the soul dwells with us and so accept them. The one doctrine we urge under many forms is the sacred. Accept the reforms but accept not the person of the reformer nor his law. Accept the reform but be thou thyself sacred, intact, inviolable, one whom leaders, one whom multitudes cannot drag from thy central seat. If you take the reform as the reformer brings it to you he transforms you into an instrument. It behoves you to receive into a willing mind, every trait, every bold stroke which is drawn. Let the Age be a showman demonstrating in picture the needs and wishes of the soul: take them into your private mind; eat the book and make it your flesh. Let each of these causes take in you a new form, the form of your character and genius. Then the Age has spoken to you, and you have answered it: you have prevailed over it.

I have said that each of the popular reforms is an accusation of some lapse from the fair Ideal life. This departure from nature is felt of our diet and the consciousness of that fact appears in the movement on the subject of Temperance for many years back. I conceive that the whole movement in England and America which has made so loud a din in all ears proceeds from the simple fact that the diet of men in these countries is not agreeable to

[10] "Greatness," *W*, VIII, 312.
[11] "Children like . . . with hope" (*D*, 357).
[12] "Certainly it seems . . . idea" (*D*, 287, where "these faithful men of one idea" are identified as "these poor Grahams & Garrisons & Palmers").

the imagination. Other creatures eat without shame. We paint the bird pecking at fruit, the browsing ox, the lion leaping on his prey, but no painter ever ventured to draw a man eating. The subject is burlesque. Partly the difference seems to consist in the presence or absence of the world at the feast.[13] The caterpillar and robin and squirrel mix the sun and blue sky with their diet. We hide our bread in cellars, in caves, and houses and there it is sodden and eaten. It matters not how plain is the fare which is spiced by the sun and moon. This gives dignity to the hunter, the mountaineer, and the Indian. If you have eat your bread on the top of a mountain or drunk water, if you have camped out with lumbermen or travellers on the prairie, if a child have eat the poorest rye or oatcake with children in the wilderness, did not the mixture of the sky with your food give it a certain mundane savor and comeliness?[14]

Plainly our artificial modes of life, our sequestration from the simpler, cleanlier life of nature deform our diet to the imagination. We have polluted our water with decoctions from all substances in nature, with alcohol, with cider, with wine, malt. We have made eating a science and an end not a means. For the hasty fruit plucked from the apple tree or the palm by the traveller intent on his high errand, we have a most elaborate and stimulating diet which many climates, many mills, many stills, and many laborers prepare.

The question forever recurs to the young man, the young woman in their hopeful religious hour. Cannot this blood which in all men rolls with such a burden of disease roll pure? Might not a simpler and shorter dinner leave me a clearer head and a kindlier heart and an unclouded afternoon? Hence the effort to introduce water as drink, and the many experiments to find a vegetable diet. The experiments are not new. They come to men in such shape as to annoy them and bereft of their own loveliness but the same impulse has visited the wise in every age and will visit the good heart every where until by many compunctions, by many efforts the right way appears and the vicious usages of

[13] "the diet . . . the feast" (E, 84).
[14] "The caterpillar . . . and comeliness" (E, 80, 84).

society are seen for what they are and forever discredited. Temperance is an universal sign by which we communicate with the pure of every sect and tongue.[15] Is it agreeable to you to see the diet overpower the character? to know that the liveliness or wit of your companion is the effect of strong waters? Is it becoming or agreeable to your imagination that the bursts of divine poetry, that the new delineations of God and his world should be the inspirations of opium or coffee? [16]

Certainly the facts are far from settled, the evidence is by no means yet complete before the world on which a verdict can stand. But it is to be considered that our practices if wrong tend to keep us wrong.

Who argues so sourly for the slaughterhouse against the man of herbs and grains? The fat and ruddy eater who hath just wiped his lips from feeding on an ox whose blood is spouting in his veins and whose strength kindles that evil fire in his eye. It is not then the voice of man that I heard but it is beef and brandy that roar and rail for beef and brandy. But shall these sit judges in their own cause? [17]

The common reply to the physician is — "see how many healthy men use the foods and liquors and practices which you reprehend." And men see in this fact a treachery in nature herself instead of esteeming it the bending goodness of the god — the resistance of the soul, the moral purchase, the interceding of the spirit, the elasticity straining still against this noxious wrong and giving the poor victim still another and yet another chance of self-recovery and escape.[18]

Meantime it makes this reform almost odious to man the foolish detachment which it makes of this consideration of diet. Temperance when it is only the sign of intrinsic virtue is graceful as the bloom on the cheek that betokens health, but temperance that is nothing else than temperance is phlegm or conceit. Temperance that knows itself is not temperance, when it peaks and pines, and knows all it renounces.[19]

[15] E, 53.
[16] E, 34.
[17] "Who argues . . . own cause" (E, 70).
[18] "The common reply . . . escape" (E, 34).
[19] "Meantime it makes . . . renounces" (E, 22, condensed).

But if the connexion of this asceticism with the highest prudence is considered and its connexion with that health and that beauty which is now rather the exception than the rule of human nature, if its connexion with that higher instinctive life which will give us to know the properties of plants, of animals, and the laws of nature by our coincidence and sympathy with the same which is now the dream of poets, it becomes at once an object of interest to the philosopher and from its elegance worth the thought of every pure and refined spirit.[20]

.   .   .

Religion does not seem to me to tend now to a cultus as heretofore but to a heroic life. We find extreme difficulty in conceiving any church, any liturgy, any rite that would be quite genuine. But all things point at the house and the hearth. Let us learn to lead a man's life. Write your poem, brave man, first in the earth with a plough and eat the bread of your own spade. I have no hope of any good in this piece of reform from such as only wish to reform one thing which is the misfortune of almost all projectors. A partial reform in diet or property or war or the praises of the country life is always an extravaganza. A farm is a poor place to get a living by in the common expectation.

A city doll who comes out into the country and takes the hoe with such ends as the city loves, namely that he may have a good table and a fashionable drawingroom, may easily be disappointed. But who goes thither in a generous spirit with the intent to lead a man's life will find the farm a proper place. He must join with it simple diet and the annihilation by one stroke of his will of the whole nonsense of living for show; he must take Ideas instead of Customs. He must make the life more than meat[21] and see to it, as it has been greatly said by one of my friends, that, "the intellectual world meets men everywhere," in his dwelling, in his mode of living. He must take his life in his hand too. I do not think this peaceful reform is to be effected by cowards. He is to front a corrupt society and speak rude truth,

[20] One leaf missing at this point. See textual notes for alternate reading.
[21] Cf. Matthew 6:25.

and emergences may easily arise where collision and suffering must ensue. But all objections to the great projects of philanthropy are met and answered by a deep and universal reform. Thus it is said if money were given up and a system of universal confidence and largess adopted the indolent will prey on the good. But our doctrine is that the labor of society ought to be shared by all and in a community where labor was the point of honor the vain and the idle would labor. What a mountain of chagrins, inconveniences, diseases, and sins would sink into the sea with the uprise of this one doctrine of labor. Domestic hired service would go over the dam. Slavery would fall into the pit. Shoals of maladies would be exterminated, and the Saturnian Age revive.[22]

It is very evident that the subject Anti-Slavery is a subordinate branch of this Reform. Whenever idleness becomes ignoble the ambitious will toil. When the best hands shall work with love and honor there will be no slave.

I think that every sober mind will be conciliated in a degree to the introduction of an education so austere and unsparing, so Roman and manly as this if he consider the present aspects of what is called by distinction *Society* among us. There seems to me no excess of fortitude in the character of the most cultivated portion of the people. The sinew and heart of man seem to be drawn out and we are become timorous, desponding whimperers. We are afraid of reality, afraid of truth, afraid of fortune, afraid of death, afraid of each other. We are parlour soldiers. The ragged battle of fate where strength is born we shun. If our young men fail in their first enterprizes they lose all heart. If the young merchant fails men say he is ruined. If the finest genius studies at one of our colleges and is not installed in an office within a year or two afterwards in the cities or suburbs of Boston or New York it seems to his friends and to himself that he is justified in being disheartened and in bemoaning himself the remainder of his life. A sturdy lad from New Hampshire or Vermont who in turn tries all the professions, who *teams it,* — *farms*

---

[22] "Religion does not . . . Age revive" (D, 328–329, modified). The last clause is a translation of Virgil, *Eclogues,* IV, 6, as the Latin of the journal shows.

it, — peddles, keeps a school, preaches, edits a newspaper, goes to Congress, and so forth, in successive years, and always, like a cat, falls on his feet, is worth a hundred of these city minions. He is content to live now and feels no shame in not studying any profession for he does not postpone his life but lives already and pours contempt on these puppets of routine. He has not one chance but a hundred chances. Let a stern preacher arise who shall reveal the resources of man and tell men they are not leaning willows but can and must detach themselves, that with the exercise of self-trust new powers shall appear, that a man, a woman is a sovereign mind born to shed healing to the nations, that he should be ashamed of our compassion, should not ask of our eyes leave to be, but listening steadfastly for his own law, should act it out to our wonder and esteem, and that the moment he acts from himself, tossing the laws, the books, the idolatries, the customs out of the window — we pity him, we pity her no more but thank and revere them, and he shall have the benedictions of America from age to age.[23]

The same spirit which has spoken for the health, the equality of man has also urged the doctrine of non-resistance to injury and to force, and carried out that doctrine to its extremes. This too has gone hand in hand with the denial of the right of ecclesiastical and of civil power over the individual. All these are obviously parts of one thought all in their origin, man's vindication of himself; protests that he has been wronged; pledges that he will find the truth and will obtain justice.

In regard then to all these projects of reform it appears that the individual should use them and not be used by them. To the young man diffident of his own ability and full of compunction at his unprofitable existence the temptation is always great to lend himself to these movements and as one of a party accomplish what he cannot hope to effect alone. But he must resist this degradation of a man to a measure.[24] "Will you not come to this convention and nominate a Temperance, an Abolition, a

[23] "I think that every . . . age to age" ("Self-Reliance," W, II, 75–76, modified); "If our young . . . age to age" (D, 299–300, where Thoreau is named as the one who "lives already").

[24] "To the young man . . . to a measure" ("Lecture on the Times," W, I, 278).

Peace, a Church ticket? Let me show you the immense importance of the step." — Nay, my friend, I do not work with these
tools. The principles on which your church and state are built
are false and a portion of this virus vitiates the smallest detail
even of your charity and religion. Though I sympathize with
your sentiment and abhor the crime you assail yet I shall persist
in wearing this robe, all loose and unbecoming as it is, of inaction, this wise passiveness until my hour comes when I can see
how to act with truth as well as to refuse.[25] A patience which is
grand, a brave and cold neglect of the offices which prudence
exacts so it be done in a deep, upper piety, a consent to solitude
and inaction which proceeds out of an unwillingness to violate
character, is the century which makes the gem.[26] Whilst therefore I desire to express to the full the sincere respect and joy I
feel before this sublime connexion of reforms now in their infancy around us, I desire to urge still more earnestly the paramount duties of the Individual. I cannot find language of sufficient energy to convey my sense of the sacredness of private
Integrity. All men, all things, the state, the church, yea the
friends of the heart are phantasms and unreal beside the sanctuary of the heart. With so much awe, with so much fear let it be
respected.[27]

We must learn to respect inaction more than prodigious activity without. We are full of these superstitions of sense, the worship of magnitude. God loveth not size: whale and minnow are
of like dimension. But we call the poet inactive because he is not
a president, a merchant, or a porter and we adore an institution
and do not see that it is founded on a thought which we have.
But real action is in silent moments. The epochs of our life are
not in the visible facts of our choice of a calling, our marriage,
our acquisition of an office and the like, but in a silent thought
by the wayside as we walk, in a thought which revises our entire
manner of life and says, "Thus hast thou done but it were better
thus." And all our after years like menials do serve and wait on

[25] "Will you not come . . . to refuse" (E, 14).
[26] "A patience . . . the gem" (E, 36).
[27] "A patience . . . let it be respected" ("Lecture on the Times," W, I, 278–
279).

this and according to their ability do execute its will. This revisal or correction is a constant force which as a tendency reaches through our lifetime.[28]

Why should we make it a point with our false modesty to disparage that man we are and that form of being assigned to us? A good man is contented. I love and honor Epaminondas, but I do not wish to be even Epaminondas.[29] I hold it more just to love the world of this hour than the world of his hour. Nor can you if I am true excite me to the least uneasiness by saying he acted and thou sittest still. I see action to be good when the need is and sitting still to be also good. Epaminondas if he was the man I take him for would have sat still with joy and peace in another age, in other circumstances. Heaven is large and affords space for all modes of love and fortitude. Why should we be busybodies and superserviceable? Action and inaction are alike to the true. One piece of the tree is cut for a weathercock and one for the sleeper of a bridge; the virtue of the wood is apparent in both.

I desire not to disgrace the soul. The fact that I am here certainly shows me that the soul had need of an organ here. Shall I not assume the post? Shall I skulk and dodge and duck with my unseasonable apologies and vain modesty and imagine my being here impertinent, less pertinent than Epaminondas or Homer being there? and that the soul did not know its own needs? Besides when I am faithful to myself, I have no discontent. The good soul nourishes me alway, unlocks new magazines of power and enjoyment to me every day. I will not meanly decline the immensity of good because I have heard it has come to others in another shape.[30]

Besides, why should we be cowed by the name of action? 'T is a trick of the senses, no more. We know that the ancestor of every action is a thought. The poor mind does not seem to itself to be anything unless it have an outside badge, some Gentoo diet or Quaker coat, or Abolition Effort or a great donation or

---

[28] "God loveth . . . our lifetime" (D, 289–290).
[29] Epaminondas (c. 420–362 B.C.), military commander who through a series of victories against Sparta raised Thebes to primary importance in Greece.
[30] "A good man . . . another shape" (D, 266–267, modified).

a high office or, anyhow, some wild contrasting action to testify that it is somewhat. The rich mind lies in the sun and sleeps and is Nature.[31] To think is to act.[32]

But whilst the man keeps himself thus sacred and aloof from the common vices of the partisan let him only bide his time and not hold himself excused from any sacrifice when he finds a clear case on which he is called to stand his trial. Let him not like our eleven thousand martyrs expend himself in petulance when no need is. Let him reserve his fire. Let him keep his temper, render soft answers, bear and forbear. Do not let him dream of suffering for ten years yet. Do not let that word *martyrdom* ever escape out of the white fence of his teeth. Be sweet and courtly and merry these many long summers and autumns yet and husband your strength so that when an authentic, inevitable crisis comes and you are driven to the wall, cornered up in your Utica, you may then at last turn fairly round on the baying dogs all steel with all Heaven in your eye and die for love with all heroes and angels to friend.[33]

The wise man is always cheerful. It is for those who have not yet raised their eyes to the radiant law which prevails through all things and assures me of my welfare in assuring me of the welfare of all — it is for such to despond. He will not set so high a value on your frivolous municipal accommodations which you call life as to look grave when their security is threatened. Life is a May game to him; no more. He defies your strait-laced, weary, social, ways and modes. He will play his game out his own way. And if any shall say him nay, shall come out with swords and staves against him to prick him to death for their evil laws, he bids them strike and welcome. He will not even look grave for such a matter. His life shall be a May game still.[34]

Still the wise man in that which he calls action must and will be found faithful. His scale of duty is different from yours but he has one, and it leads to action. It makes all things practical.

---

[31] "The poor mind . . . and is Nature" (D, 298).

[32] "We are full of these superstitions . . . To think is to act" ("Spiritual Laws," W, II, 161–163).

[33] "Let him not . . . angels to friend" (C, 347).

[34] "Life is a May game . . . May game still" (D, 309, condensed and changed from first person singular).

People hold to you as long as you please yourself with the ideal life only as a pretty dream, and concede a resistless force to the limitations of the same, — to structure or organization, and to society. But, as quickly as you profess your unlimited allegiance to the first, so far as to be no longer contented with doing the best you can in the circumstances, but demand that these mountain circumstances should skip and disappear before the presence of the Soul,[35] then they distrust your wisdom and defy your resolutions. And yet Nature is in earnest. That aspiration which they like that you should paint, or carve, or chant, — anything but enact — is not a castle in the air. They moreover admit it in the moral world; they concede that a perfect justice should be sought and done; but an intellectual equality, an intellectual society, a mode of domestic life in which trifles should at last descend to their place, confectionary should come down and character, art, and joy ascend, this is an incredible proposition. But what they concede destroys the force of their denial. Nature is unique throughout. The prayer of the soul predicts its own answer in facts. The moral nature is not a patch of light here whilst the social world is a lump of darkness there but tends incessantly to rectify and ennoble the whole circumference of facts. Never was anything gained by admitting the omnipotence of limitations but all immortal action is an overstepping of these busy rules. In Rome a consul was thanked by the senate because he had not despaired of the republic.[36]

Let us then neither be ungrateful nor unwise. There is a new possibility in every man that is born. Indeed nothing strikes us so forcibly in each new biography that commands our notice as the circumstance that it is a new combination of elements which men would have pronounced incompatible. Then against your private belief that you can effect somewhat, the experience of all mankind is worth nothing; for this belief of yours is a new fact which appears to you first, but which in your action shall shine to them. Let every aspiring mind feel the deep congratulation of this consent of thousands of our contemporaries to a cooperation in works so just and arduous nor heed too much the auk-

---

[35] Cf. Psalms 114:4–7, and textual notes.
[36] "People hold . . . republic" (E, 41–42).

wardness and half apprehension of the first attempts. That which is separate in their eyes do thou blend in thine: that which is finite in their plan, do thou exalt to an infinite aim — what they limit to the attainment of a measure do thou expand into the treasures of the character.

7

Religion

Read at the Masonic Temple in Boston on January 22, 1840, as the seventh in the series on "The Present Age" and again at Concord, Massachusetts, on April 24, this lecture may have been read at Providence, Rhode Island, or elsewhere, but it is more likely that it, too, quickly became material for *Essays* (1841). Nine days before the Concord delivery Emerson wrote that "for a fortnight nearly I have been redacting a chapter . . . out of many papers of various date to get a *Doctrine of the Soul*; and this task I have nearly ended." Five days later it apparently was finished and hesitantly entitled "The Over-soul" (*L*, II, 282, 284). Extensive and numerous passages from this lecture went into the essay. Other passages were used in "Self-Reliance" and "Spiritual Laws," and two passages found their way into "The Preacher," which was prepared for Emerson by Cabot and published in *The Unitarian Review*, XIII (January 1880), 1–13, and collected in 1883 in *Lectures and Biographical Sketches*.

The lecture is complete and in good condition, retaining both its front and back covers. It was once sewn together and the leaves are labelled and paginated in ink. In the textual notes is a larger leaf, formerly sewn, but not with this lecture, which is a version of the first paragraph.

The last paragraph of this lecture announces the eighth lecture of the course as "Ethics," the title Emerson listed both before and after the lecture (Notebook Ψ, 166; E, 118), and it was the title announced in the *Boston Daily Advertiser* for the reading on January 29, 1840 (*L*, II, 244). The two succeeding lectures suggest that the subject was a natural extension of the topic treated in "Religion" (see below, pp. 286, 304). The manuscript of the eighth lecture is missing. In its place is now filed a manuscript belonging with the course on "The Times," but which Cabot listed and summarized as the eighth lecture in "The Present Age" and which he called "Prospects. Duties" (Cabot, II, 745–746; see headnote below, pp. 366–367). The missing manuscript may have been used in the preparation of *Essays* (1841), since it appears not to have been read again except as the seventh lecture in the series at the Concord, Massachusetts, Lyceum on April 29, 1840, under the title of "Ethics."

FEW propositions are oftener stated in the ear of the present generation than that the annals of the world are to be found first in the mind. A few thoughts made all this great history which fills the heads of scholars and statesmen. A few thoughts, an impulse of sentiment in the heart of some oriental shepherd explodes once for all the considerations of prudence, the ties of custom, the old forms of thought and instals him as the interpreter of nature and the organ of the moral sentiment to his country and to half mankind. There seems no proportion between the cause and the effect. But who can tell from what profound crater that spark of sentiment shot up, which set his heart on fire? It is the fatality attending these realizations of a thought that they always entomb at last the spirit which built them.

Look at it how we will, the most wonderful fact in history, is Christianity: the fact that ten or twenty persons or, if you please, twice so many did receive consciously or unconsciously the revelations of the moral sentiment with such depth and tenacity as to live and die in and for them and to propagate their statement, each one to so wide a circle of contemporaries and then to the next age, that the enthusiasm got a footing in the world, and throve and grew into this great Christendom we know so well. Their statement too is very impure, very unequal to the fact. They were instructed by their heart, not by their head. As pieces of argument, their sermons and letters would never be read: they are all local and limitary, — narrow, provincial, levitical; but they had this sentiment of humility and of trust in the eternal. They could not state it to the understanding but they carried it in their heart and it gave them dominion over nations and ages. It quickly got embodied, and, as the rapture was presently lost in the wider diffusion of the doctrine, it came soon as all such things do, to be supposed inherent in certain times and persons.

A knot of young, ardent, impassioned men probably of ingenuous and bashful complexion — their simple devotion has resounded farther than they dreamed. Could they be incarnated again in the nineteenth century — they would never recognize their own work: the formal church has overlaid the real, and the creeds of the nations traverse and caricature the spiritual perceptions which those peasants announced in the joy of their hearts.

The radical vice of the popular thought is that with the Christian era a new state of things took place. It supposes the divine government to be a thing of time, and in it are changes of administration, changes of measures, law for gentiles, law for Jews, and law for Christians. The hour presently comes to each mind when it perceives that this chronology and biography so much insisted on, is only an optical illusion for different states of perception, just as the sunrise is an optical illusion, whilst the real fact is the rotation of the globe. It is curious to see in religious literature that men have been hunting for some statement in Christianity that was new, and those who look for such, can easily persuade themselves that they have found it, whilst the fact is that always a soul at the same elevation saw the same facts. The facts being not new but immutable, as soon as any soul sees them, it instantly recognizes the perception of them in others, catches in proverbs and poesies that are current in all men's mouths the implication of the same, and thereafter is pained by this poor, cramp, degrading picture of the heavenly law as if it were a history of England or of Judea.

Their religious movement has had the usual fate of revolutions based on a thought, though it be on the most enlarged and splendid scale of any the world has seen. Their detached utterances and actions fell first into a cyclus of narrations of which presently the letter and the circumstance became superstitiously sacred; then, by being viewed in this detachment and exaggeration, gave false impressions. Then, as it became more and more false through usage and convention, the virtuous, the living, were revolted and withdrew in silence, and the wit and cultivation of society preserved a cold silence on the subject of these revelations which, in their first state, to them more than to any should have been dear. Then, the devout everywhere sought to treat the history as a mythus, so as still to fit it to the spiritual wants of a reasoning and instructed society. But now, in every country, the spiritual nature of man refuses any longer to be holden in the wooden stocks of what was called the Gospel Scheme, and the famous Articles of the Roman, English, and Genevan Churches, and insists that what is called Christianity shall take rank not formal or peculiar, but strictly on its universal merits as one act, one out of many acts of the human mind.

At the present day, the tradition, — the relation of the sentiment, that is, — to persons and times, is fast losing and with the youthful mind of the period has quite lost all force. With Judaea, what has the genuine life of Paris and New York to do? with Moses or with Paul? It is seen and felt by all the young that the entire catechism and creed in which they were bred, may be forgotten with impunity. It stands now on the poor footing of a respect to the establishment — if such mere remaining can be called standing. This then is our position: we have found out the mythical character of Christianity, and are every where adopting a new manner of speech in regard to it. Philosophical expressions are supplanting the technical ones of the last century and men adopt everyday forms of speech which a few years ago they would have repudiated with heat. We are in a transition state from this Jewish idea before which ages were driven like sifted snow and which all the literatures of the world, Latin, Spanish, Italian, French, English, have tingled with, which has so cleaved to men's brains, to a more human and universal and heavenly country, namely to a perception of the universal presence of the law in all action and passion which we were wont to suppose had its special resorts and its darling men.

In consequence of this revolution in opinion it is or it appears for the time as the misfortune of this period, that the cultivated mind has not the happiness and dignity of the religious sentiment. We are born too late for the old and too early for the new faith. I see in those classes and those persons in whom I am accustomed to look for tendency and progress, for what is most positive and most rich in human nature, and who contain the activity of today and the assurance of tomorrow — I see in them both skepticism and character; a clear enough perception of the inadequacy of the popular religious statement to the wants of their heart and intellect, and explicit declarations of this fact. They have insight and truthfulness; they will not mask their convictions; they hate cant; but more than this I do not readily find.

The gracious motions of the soul, piety, adoration, I do not find.

Scorn of hypocrisy, pride of personal character, elegance of taste and of manners and pursuit, a boundless ambition of the intellect, willingness to sacrifice personal interests for the integrity of the character, all these they have, but that religious submission and abandonment which give man a new element and being and make him sublime — it is not in churches, it is not in houses.[1] In the denominations which have had a good repute among us for more sanctity and love, the same coldness creeps in which congeals the rest. One certainly finds in the Methodist, — sometimes in the Calvinistic Churches, — the old ardor of faith among those individuals whose intellectual inactivity permits them to receive the tradition just as their parents did. To such it is still capable of being made alive by their affections. For a time, I have seen the doctrine of the New Jerusalem Church expand the receiver with the joy and peace of believing; and that Church, I believe, does at this moment furnish a singular exception to the increasing torpidity of the rest. But it is too easy to see that the place given to the text of Swedenborg and so to the limitations of his individual mind are untenable for any long period and must as soon as the disciple has come up with the thoughts and perceptions of the Master become a prison.

Where then has the religion of society found its lodging? It lurks in the philanthropic assemblies and in the private efforts which urge those Reforms which I enumerated in my last lecture; in the chapels and committees which preach Peace, Temperance, the freedom of the servant and the slave. The same class of spirits which in Switzerland, in France, and in England contended of old against the papal power and which in the seventeenth century sought religious liberty in this country now contend in these obscure connexions for principles and sentiments not less precious to man.

But religion has an *object*. It is — does not grow thin or robust with the health of the votary. The object of adoration remains forever unhurt and identical. We are in transition from the worship of the fathers which enshrined the law in a private

[1] "In consequence of this revolution . . . not in houses" ("The Preacher," W, X, 217–218).

and personal history to a worship which recognizes the true eternity of the law; its presence to you and me, its equal energy in what is called brute nature as in what is called sacred history. The next age will behold God in the ethical laws, and will regard natural history, private fortunes, and politics not for themselves, as we have done, but as illustration of those laws — of that beatitude, — and love. Nature is too thin a screen, — the glory of the One breaks in everywhere.[2]

But mainly is there a growing homage to the influence of Character. Character is the true Theocracy. It will one day suffice for the government of the world.[3] This may seem to many now an abstraction; as if never we could embody in a church a faith so intellectual, so inaccessible to the eyes and hands and speech as this is. But there is no thought so delicate and interior but it can and will get a realization. One would have said the same of the lowliness of the blessed soul that walked in Judaea and hallowed that land forever. Yet see at Rome the functionary who still wears at this hour the name of Pontiff once every year in the presence of representatives of all the Christian states, washes and wipes with a towel the feet of beggars and pilgrims.

So will this new perception which came by no man but into which all souls at this era are born indue its own body and form and shine in institutions, — that the world will say: The Men of that Age found Christianity to be a painting on time and saw that it was not proper to any time or any person but the inheritance of men; they found that it was not large enough to hold the moral sentiment which is too vast to be contained in any form and merely traverses for moments successive persons and events and books but refuses to abide in any, and they dropped the hereditary reverence which the world had for these passages of its history and worshipped the sentiment itself.

Certainly men will not always be contented with accepting such parodies of truth as the understanding gives when it seeks to answer the questions which are beyond its sphere. The idea of a revelation — see how degraded it is! The idea of a revela-

---

[2] "But religion has . . . in everywhere" ("The Preacher," W, X, 222–223); last sentence is in C, 86, and G, 60.

[3] "Character is . . . the world" (textual notes to "Politics," below, p. 479).

tion which obtains in modern Christendom is, that, it is a telling of fortunes. The Deity is supposed to inform men how long they shall exist; and what they shall do; and who shall be their company. Men even dream that they find in the inspired Scriptures and men, answers to these questions; that Jesus has left replies to precisely these interrogatories. Never a moment did that sublime spirit speak in such patois. In fact these questions are the speech and confession of sin and there is no answer to them.

When shall we exercise a higher nature and see that the soul has its own solution for its own questions? An answer in words would be really no answer to the questions you ask. In the nature of man a veil shuts down always on the facts of tomorrow; for the soul will not have us read any other cipher than that of cause and effect. By this eternal veil which curtains events, it instructs the children of men to live in today. The only mode of obtaining an answer to these questions, is, to forego all low curiosity, and accepting the tide of being which floats us onward, work and live, work and live, and unawares we are already renewed and raised and the question and answer are one.[4]

To truth, justice, love, the attributes of the soul, the idea of immutableness is essentially associated. Jesus living in these moral sentiments, knowing nothing of sensual fortunes, heeding only the manifestations of these, never made the separation of the idea of duration from the essence of these attributes; never uttered a syllable about the simple duration of the soul. It was left for his disciples to separate duration from the moral elements, and to teach the immortality of the soul as a doctrine and maintain it by evidences.[5] The moment the doctrine of the Immortality is separately taught, Man is already fallen. But no loving heart, no heart absorbed in the sentiment of duty, no man inspired by the soul ever asks this question or condescends to these evidences. For the soul is true to itself, and the man in whom it is shed abroad, cannot wander from the present which is infinite to a future which would be finite.[6]

The mind of this Age discovers every where in unexpected

---

[4] "The Deity . . . answer are one" (D, 384, modified).

[5] "To truth . . . by evidences" (C, 40, modified; cf. also D, 345).

[6] "Certainly men will not . . . be finite" ("The Over-Soul," W, II, 282–285, rearranged).

sallies of argument and of speculation its impatience of the popular doctrine of miracles. The mind of this Age will endure no miracle and this not because of unbelief but because of belief. It begins to see that the sun and the moon and the man who walks under them are miracles that puzzle all analysis; and to quit these and go gazing for I know not what parish circumstances, or Jewish prodigies, is to quit the eternal signs scrawled by God along the dizzy spaces of the zodiack for a show of puppets and wax lights.[7] It is wonderful how slow men have been to see the dishonor which is done to the Divine Nature by the apology that venerable men have for ages set up for miracles. It is to call attention to truths. It is to make men stare that they may so accept the spiritual fact which in other circumstances they would refuse. I own when I hear that argument under its most polished forms I instantly think of the Capuchins.[8] They who say it do not and will not perceive that it is to distrust the deity of truth, its invincible beauty, — and to aim a high calumny at the supreme Soul, so to paint him. Truth scorns any aid but its own. This is violence and not love; and violence is always weakness, and always fails of its end. Our adventurers who give a political turn to each new reform, and who cover the land with buildings, with agencies, with tracts and missionaries in behalf of temperance or peace and wish to convert the people by main force, by votes and majorities to a sentiment, certainly do endeavor to vamp and abut principles, to give a mechanical strength to the laws of the soul. But in one case and in the other all these pains are lost. I think, my friend, the laws will explain themselves. They were before you were born and will be when you are rotten. Go paint the sky blue with a bluebag. Do.[9]

A material miracle to abut a spiritual law! The thing is intrinsically absurd and impossible. And in every particular example the absurdity appears, putting every fact as it were upside down. I am enlarged by the access of a great sentiment, of a virtuous impulse. It is the direct income of God. I am not enlarged by a prodigy, a raising of Lazarus, a turning water into wine. Open my eyes by new virtue and I shall see miracles

[7] "The mind . . . wax lights" (E, 93).
[8] Cf. D, 105.
[9] "endeavor to vamp . . . bluebag. Do" (E, 25, expanded).

enough in this current moment of time. You prefer to see a dove descending visibly on Jesus: I, to acknowledge his baptism by a divine thought in his mind which raises him once for all above himself and above nations of men. And which is greater and more affecting, to see some wonderful bird descending out of the sky or to see the rays of an inward majesty emitted from the countenance and port of a man? [10] How far nobler was the lofty word of Pythagoras directed to this very topic, *"Thou shalt not plant the palm tree,"* intimating that as that tree comes up best out of the ground self-sown so virtue and wisdom are the direct proceeding of God and are not to be overlaid and distorted by indiscreet and mechanical education, neither by miracle, neither by creed.[11]

In truth, the miracle is always spiritual; always within the man who beholds it, — affecting his senses from the soul. The lover walks in miracles, and the man beside him sees none.[12] Love is thaumaturgic. It converts a chair, a box, a scrap of paper, or a line carelessly drawn on it, a lock of hair, a faded weed, into amulets worth the world's fee. If we see out of what straws and nothings he builds his Elysium we shall read nothing miraculous in the New Testament.[13] The believer like the lover, — and the receiver of a new sentiment is a more noble lover, — sees nothing as ever he saw it before; the unbeliever looks at the same facts and reads the old dull story. The true disciple therefore never magnifies the sensible miracle. Like Paul he ignores it, and says, "I knew a man once, — whether in the body or out of the body I cannot tell, — God knoweth." [14]

There is no miracle to the believing soul. When I ascend to the spiritual state of a holy soul, enter into the rapture of a Christ, the wonderful anecdotes of his works seem fit drapery enough of such a man and such a thought. When I do not so ascend I cannot be said to believe the miracle. There it lies a lump. Any annotator may show the text to be spurious and I shall thank

[10] "I am enlarged . . . of a man" (D, 349).
[11] "How far nobler . . . by creed" (cf. E, 3; T, 185; Plutarch, "Of Isis and Osiris," *Morals,* IV, 69).
[12] "In truth . . . sees none" (D, 339).
[13] "Love is . . . Testament" (D, 309).
[14] "The believer . . . God knoweth" (D, 339); cf. II Corinthians 12:2–3.

him. Any caviller may suggest the profusion of testimony to this sort of marvel and I shall not care to refute him. Any philosopher may have my ear who offers me other truth in her own native lineament and proportion.[15]

But the Supreme Critic on all the errors of the Past and the Present and the only Prophet of that which must be is that great Nature in which we lie as the Earth lies in the soft arms of the atmosphere, that Unity, that Oversoul within which every man's particular being is contained and made one with all other; that common heart of which all sincere conversation is the worship, to which all right action is submission; that overpowering reality which confutes all our tricks and talents and constrains every one to pass for what he is, and to speak from his character and not from his tongue; and which evermore tends and aims to pass into our thought and hand and become wisdom and virtue and power and beauty. We live in succession, in division, in parts, in particles. Meantime within man is the soul of the whole, the wise silence, the Universal Beauty, to which every part and particle is equally related, the eternal One.[16] It is only by the vision of that living light that the horoscope of the ages can be read and it is only by falling back on our better thoughts, by yielding us up to the spirit of prophecy which is innate in every man, that we can know what it saith. Every man's words who speaks from that life must sound vain to those who do not dwell in the same thought on their own part. I certainly dare not speak for it. My words do not carry its august sense; they fall short and cold. Only itself can inspire whom it will, and behold, their speech shall be lyrical and sweet and universal as the rising of the wind. Yet I desire even by profane words, if sacred I may not use, to indicate the domain of this great light,[17] to remind you — how near — what a household guest it is, to recall to you the face of this visitant, and to fortify with the hope that always proceeds from this Power, our own expectations of the Religion of the coming Era.

A little study of what takes place around us every day would

---

[15] "There is no miracle . . . and proportion" (C, 303–304).

[16] "We live in . . . eternal One" (D, 152, condensed).

[17] "But the Supreme Critic . . . great light" ("The Over-Soul," W, II, 268–270).

show us that a higher law than that of our will regulates events, that our painful labors are very unnecessary and altogether fruit-less, that only in our easy, simple, spontaneous action are we strong and by contenting ourselves with obedience we become divine. Belief and love, a believing love will relieve us of a vast load of care. O my brothers, God exists. There is a soul at the cen-tre of nature and over the will of every man so that none of us can wrong the Universe. It has so infused its strong enchantment into nature that we prosper when we accept its advice and when we struggle to wound its creatures our hands are either glued to our sides or they beat our own breasts. The whole course of things goes to teach us faith. We need only obey. There is guidance for each of us and by lowly listening we shall hear the right word. Why need you choose so painfully your place and occupation and associates and modes of action and entertainment? Certainly there is a possible right for you which precludes the need of balance and wilful election.[18] If we will not be marplots with our miserable interferences, the work, the society, letters, arts, science, religion of the whole world would go on far better than now and the heaven predicted from the beginning of the world and still predicted from the bottom of the heart would organize itself as do now the rose and the air and the sun.[19]

The greatness of man is always in Trust. He is sure that his welfare is dear to the heart of Being. The things that are really for thee gravitate to thee. You are running to seek your friend. Let your feet run but your mind need not. If you do not find him will you not acquiesce that it is best you should not find him? for there is a power which, as it is in you, is in him also and could therefore very well bring you together if it were for the best.[20] You are pre-paring with eagerness to go and render a service to which your talent and your taste invite you and the love of men and the hope of fame. Has it occurred to you that you have no right to go unless you are equally willing to be prevented from going?[21]

[18] "Why need you . . . wilful election" (D, 128, expanded; above, p. 139).

[19] "A little study . . . and the sun" ("Spiritual Laws," W, II, 139–140).

[20] "You are running . . . the best" (D, 196).

[21] "He is sure that . . . from going" ("The Over-Soul," W, II, 293); for last sentence, cf. D, 59, where Emerson uses first person in reference to his going to deliver the Address at Divinity School.

To this power, the most intimate of all energies, there is no age, there is no country, there is no personal limit. In my dealing with my child my Latin and Greek, my accomplishments, my personal forces stead me nothing. They are all lost on him; but as much soul as I have avails. If I am merely wilful he gives me a Rowland for an Oliver, sets his will against mine, one for one. But if I renounce my will and act for the soul, setting that up as umpire between us two, out of his young eyes looks the same spirit also; he reveres and loves with me.[22]

It is by virtue of this inevitable nature that private will is every where overpowered, and maugre all our efforts or all our imperfections your genius will speak from you and mine from me. That which we are we shall certainly teach, not voluntarily but involuntarily. Thoughts come into our minds by avenues which we never left open and thoughts go out of our minds through avenues which we never voluntarily opened. Character teaches over our head.[23]

As this power manifests itself in you, it acquaints you in all particulars with its sufficiency. Calm, majestic, it makes no appeal from itself. Our religion vulgarly stands on number of believers. Whenever the appeal is made, no matter how indirectly, to numbers, proclamation is then and there made that religion is not. He that finds God a sweet enveloping thought to him never counts his company.[24] It makes no difference whether the appeal is to numbers or to *one*.[25] A religion that stands on *authority*, — what degradation in the word! What a gulf between that supple soul and its well-being! Man is timid and apologetic. He is no longer upright: he dares not say, *I think; I am;* but quotes some saint or sage.[26] The reliance on authority measures the decline of religion, — the withdrawal of the Soul. Yet the position men have given Jesus now for many centuries of history is a position of authority. It characterizes themselves. It cannot alter the eternal facts.

Great is the soul and plain. It is no flatterer; it is no follower;

[22] "In my dealing . . . loves with me" ("The Over-Soul," W, II, 279; D, 245).
[23] "It is by virtue . . . over our head" ("The Over-Soul," W, II, 286; cf. "Self-Reliance," W, II, 58).
[24] "Our religion . . . company" (D, 195).
[25] "Our religion . . . or to *one*" ("The Over-Soul," W, II, 294–295).
[26] "Man is timid . . . saint or sage" ("Self-Reliance," W, II, 67; cf. D, 331).

it never appeals from itself. The soul always believes in itself.[27] Before the immense possibilities of man all mere experience, all past biography however spotless and sainted shrinks away. Before that holy heaven which our presentiments foreshow us we cannot easily praise any form of life we have seen or read of. We not only affirm that we have few great men but absolutely speaking that we have none; that we have no history, no record of any character or mode of living that entirely contents us. The saints and demigods whom history worships we are constrained to accept with a grain of allowance. Though in our lonely hours we draw a new strength out of their memory, yet pressed on our attention as they are by the thoughtless and customary they fatigue and invade.[28] The soul gives itself alone, original, and pure to the Lonely, Original, and Pure who on that condition gladly inhabits, leads, and speaks through it. Then is it glad, young, and nimble. It is not wise but it sees through all things. It is not called religious but it is innocent. It calls the Light its own and feels that the grass grows and the stone falls by a law inferior and dependent on its nature.[29]

Nature through all her kingdoms admonishes us of our fall, of a broken analogy. Our life of consciousness should be obedient and great and equal as is the existence of her vegetable and animal tribes. Now, man is ashamed before the blade of grass and the blowing rose. These roses that open in July under my window make no reference to former roses or to better ones: they are for what they are: they exist with God today.[30] There is no time to them. There is simply the rose; it is perfect in every moment of its existence. Before a leafbud has burst its whole life acts; in the full-blown flower there is no more; in the leafless root there is no less. Its nature is satisfied and it satisfies nature in all moments alike. There is no time to it. So is it with the soul. So should it be with the life of man. But man as we know him is always anticipating or remembering. Man does not live in the great present but with reverted eye laments the past or wasting his riches stands a

[27] D, 374.
[28] "We not only . . . fatigue and invade" (E, 50).
[29] "The reliance on authority . . . on its nature" ("The Over-Soul," W, II, 295–296); "The soul gives . . . on its nature" (D, 374).
[30] D, 331.

tiptoe to foresee the future. He cannot be happy and strong until he too lives with living nature in the deep present above time.[31]

And this deep power in which we lie and whose beatitude is all accessible to us is not only self-sufficing and perfect in every hour but the act of seeing and the thing seen, the seer and the spectacle, the subject and the object are one.[32] An ignorant man thinks the divine wisdom is conspicuously shown in some fact or creature: a wise man sees that every fact contains the same. I should think water the best invention if I were not acquainted with fire and earth and air.[33] But as we advance, every proposition, every action, every feeling runs out into the infinite.[34] If we go to affirm anything we are checked in our speech by the need of recognizing all other things until speech presently becomes rambling, general, indefinite, and merely tautology. The only speech will at last be action.[35] We see the world piece by piece, as the sun, the moon, the animal, the tree; but the Whole of which these are the shining parts is the Soul.[36]

This energy does not descend into individual life on any other condition than entire possession. It comes to the lowly and simple, it comes to whomsoever will put off what is foreign and proud — it comes as insight, it comes as serenity and grandeur. When we see those whom it inhabits we are apprized of new degrees of greatness. Before their elevation, the reputations of the great decline. It requires of us to be plain and true. The low Englishman begins to idealize his life by quoting my Lord, and Sir John, and the Countess, who thus said, or thus did, to *me*. The ambitious vulgar show you their spoons and brooches and rings; and preserve their cards and compliments. The more cultivated in their account of their own experience cull out the pleasing poetic circumstance; the visit to Rome; the man of genius they saw; the brilliant friend they know; still further on perhaps the gorgeous landscape, the mountain lights, the mountain thoughts they enjoyed yesterday — and so seek to throw a romantic color over

[31] "These roses . . . above time" ("Self-Reliance," W, II, 67); "There is no time to them . . . above time" (D, 338, modified).
[32] "The Over-Soul," W, II, 269; D, 370.
[33] Cf. C, 101.
[34] "I should think . . . the infinite" (cf. "Art," W, II, 355–356).
[35] "An ignorant . . . action" (D, 152; see also D, 265).
[36] "The Over-Soul," W, II, 269.

their life. But the soul that ascendeth to worship the great God is plain and true, has no rose color, no fine friends, no chivalry, no adventures; does not want admiration; dwells in the hour that now is, in the earnest experience of the common day; by reason of the present moment and the mere trifle having become porous to thought and bibulous of the sea of light.[37]

Men like these treat you as gods would, walk as gods amongst us; accepting without any admiration your wit, your bounty, your virtue even — say rather your act of duty — for your virtuous sentiment they too own as their proper blood, royal as themselves and over-royal, the father of the gods. But what rebuke their plain fraternal bearing casts upon the mutual flattery which passes current in the best society. These flatter not.[38] They make us feel that sincerity is more excellent than flattery. They deal so plainly with man and woman as to constrain the uttermost sincerity and destroy all hope of trifling with you. "Their highest praising," said Milton, "is not flattery, and their plainest advice is a kind of praising." [39]

How can it be that this eternal nature, this Oversoul, the supreme fact, should never in the circling ages find an adequate expression in the world? that the Godhead who does not dwell neither in multitudes neither in chosen men but in every man — who is made apparent never in personal attributes but ever in sublime universal laws should not be worshipped purely in them? If this age is called skeptical it is because it loves this truth. If the heart beats with this immense private hope will not another age find modes to embody the faith?

I shall adventure in my next Lecture under the head of Ethics to offer a sketch of some of those great facts by which the genius of the Divine Providence is known and which really constitute in every sound mind the facts on which faith rests and to which the progress of the human mind does every day more and more determine its attention.

[37] "This energy does not . . . sea of light" ("The Over-Soul," W, II, 289-290); "The low Englishman . . . sea of light" (D, 37).
[38] "Men like these treat . . . flatter not" (D, 172).
[39] "Areopagitica," A Selection from the English Prose Works, II, 19; "Men like these . . . a kind of praising" ("The Over-Soul," W, II, 291-292).

9

Education

This lecture was ninth in the course at the Masonic Temple, Boston, and was read there on February 5, 1840, and as eighth at Concord, Massachusetts, on May 1. The manuscript is intact. There is in the manuscript considerable emendation of pagination, indicating not that the lecture was restructured, but that pages were used elsewhere. All of the leaves are now filed together except a single leaf which is with "The Present Age," Lecture 1, where it does not belong. It has been placed in the present lecture on the basis of sewing marks, pagination, and context. There are with this lecture an unnumbered double sheet, never sewn with the rest of the manuscript and having no context, and an inserted leaf on later paper; these have been printed in the textual notes. A double sheet of quotations on education drawn from Montaigne and Fénelon are also now filed with the manuscript.

Some leaves from the lecture were once sewn elsewhere, and in certain instances emendations resulting from such bodily transference have been rejected in the text, though recorded in the textual notes. Emerson used passages from the lecture in "New England Reformers," "Spiritual Laws," "Character," "Self-Reliance," and "Culture," and Cabot used large parts of it for the lecture on "Education" which he prepared in December 1877 for Emerson to read; the version of this synthetic lecture, published in 1883 as "Education" in *Lectures and Biographical Sketches* (W, X, 123–159), draws extensively from the 1840 lecture.

WE HAVE considered in the foregoing discourses the literature, the politics, the domestic life, the philanthropic projects of the present day, and lastly at some length the aspect of the religious institutions and the relation which the institution holds to the eternal Conscience. In the last lecture I endeavored to give a sketch of that natural theology which conversation, fiction, proverbs, and the very thoughts of men at the present day, seem to strive to embody. I pass by natural connexion of topics this evening to the subject of Education.

But I have still one more remark to make upon the Church which will sum up all I have had to say upon the institutions and formularies which represent to the nations at the present epoch the deepest Idea in Man. Namely, it is poor. The instructions of the Church have no adequate breadth. It speaks in a dialect. It refers to a narrow circle of experiences, persons, and a literature of its own. What I hear of there, I never meet elsewhere. I cannot make it sufficient to me but by contracting myself, — and lovers of rest do this. It does not explain to me my fortune, nor my form, my affections, my talent, my disease, my trade; I see it not in the sunset; I hear it not in music; if I glance from the catechism to natural history the connexion of the two things is not quite obvious. The thermometer and microscope have a very unbelieving look. The very vane on the church steeple is little better.

Now it is plain to me that the very mark of a truth is, that it is rich, all related, all explaining. How impoverished is our popular statement of belief will appear by seeing the attraction that the doctrine of Swedenborg has for men. It classifies the world for the receiver. It explains his marriage, his fever, his dreams, his vocation, life and death, his presentiments, his insanity. See the attraction which phrenology has for the people. That instantly offers to give them an insight of the true order of temperament of taste, of talent, of fortune, of success. And thus, although nothing can be more rude or premature than the present state of this so-called *science,* yet the eagerness with which it is embraced by thousands and the contentment this shadowy classification gives them, shows plainly enough what they demand of a religion — what they are looking for.

The Church is not broad enough for man. What difference do we make in our view if we alter the word and say Education? The same remark is still to be made. Education should be as broad as man. Whatever elements are in him, *that* should foster and demonstrate. Is not the Vast an element of his being? Yet what teaching or book of today appeals to the Vast? [1] If he be dexterous his tuition should make it appear. If he be capable of dividing

[1] "Is not the Vast . . . to the Vast" (D, 105).

men by the trenchant sword of his Thought, Education should unsheath it. If he is one to cement society by his all-reconciling affinities, o hasten their action. If he is jovial, if he is mercurial, if he is greathearted, if he is a cunning artificer, if he is a strong commander, if he is a good ally, if he be ingenious or useful or elegant or witty, a prophet or a diviner, society has need of all. The vanity of Education is felt in our surveys of its result. Society is its result. Yet what a variety of misfortune, disaster, incapacity, ruin it offers us. What gloomy wrecks we daily meet drifting along this sea of life. What parrots of routine, what men of pasteboard, what triflers, what madmen whose culture is only a paint or enamel that never ennobles the lump. Now and then the mask is lifted and we see the clown still. Where is the wisdom that ought to look out on us from every eye; the religion that should hallow us perforce as we approached its atmosphere; the cheerfulness that should make us glad; the salient vivacity that should take possession of society? Should not every man we meet affect us as a magazine of unexhausted resources? Should not every one new paint the landscape and exalt our interest in the world because he had shown us of it a new side? But we do not care for those whose opinions we can predict.

But do those on whom society has concentrated its choicest means and lights, whom it has installed in its seminaries and there recited to it all its learning, repay its care by their expanding and productive genius? Or have we not seen many times the sad spectacle when a youth after ten years of public education comes out ready for his voyage of life — that the entire ship is made of rotten timber, of rotten, honeycombed, traditional timber without so much as an inch of new plank in the hull.[2]

It is wonderful and ominous — a presumption of crime — that this word Education has so cold, so hopeless a sound. A treatise on Education, a convention for Education, a lecture, a system, affects us with slight paralysis and a certain yawning of the jaws. We are not encouraged when the Law touches it with its fingers.[3] It is not broad enough for man.[4] If the vast and the spiritual are

[2] D, 353.
[3] See D, 350, for a comment similar to this written after attending the convention of the Middlesex County Education Association on September 13, 1839.
[4] "It is wonderful . . . enough for man" ("Education," W, X, 133–134).

beyond it and omitted, so are the practical and the needful. An education in things is not. We are all involved in the condemnation of words, an age of words. We are shut up in schools and college recitation rooms for ten or fifteen years and come out at last with a bag of wind, a memory of words, and do not know a thing. We cannot use our hands or our legs or our eyes or our arms. We do not know an edible root in the woods. We cannot tell our course by the stars nor the hour of the day by the sun. It is well if we can swim and skate. We are afraid of a horse, of a cow, of a dog, of a cat, of a spider. The Roman rule was to teach a boy nothing that he could not learn standing.[5] It seems as if a man should learn to plant, to fish, or to hunt that he might secure his subsistence at all events and not be painful to his friends and fellowmen.[6] It seems at least that pains should be taken to make the lessons of science as experimental as they can be. The sight of the star through a telescope is worth all the course on astronomy. The shock of the electric fluid in the elbow outvalues all the theories; the taste of the nitrous oxide, the making of an artificial volcano better than volumes of chemistry.[7]

One man seems often as much enervated by words as another by luxury. It makes little difference in what manner a man loses truth and reality. How many men can measure themselves with a ton of coals and not lose by the comparison? Over a thing power and awe hang inseparably. In every moment and change it represents Nature, a fresh, genuine, aboriginal force, but men transformed by books become impotent praters.

Our modes of Education are avowedly profane. That is they aim to expedite; to save labor; to do for masses what can never be done for masses; what must be done reverently, — one by one; — say rather, the whole world is needed for the tuition of each pupil. What else is this system of emulation and display? The advantages of it are so prompt and obvious; it is such a time-saver; it is so energetic on slow and on bad natures; and is of so

---

[5] Attributed to Seneca in Montaigne, "Against Idleness," *Essays*, II, 561; C, 19; *Lectures*, II, 135; "An education in things . . . learn standing" (D, 350–351).

[6] D, 137.

[7] "We are shut up in schools . . . volumes of chemistry" ("New England Reformers," W, III, 257–258).

easy application, — needing no sage or poet, but any tutor or schoolmaster in his first term can apply it, — that it is not strange that this *calomel* of culture should be a popular medicine. On the other hand, total abstinence from this drug, and the adoption of simple discipline and the following of Nature involves at once immense claims on the time, the thoughts, on the life of the teacher. It requires principles instead of expedients; character instead of rules. It requires time, use, insight, event, — all the great lessons and assistances of God, and only to think of using it implies piety and profoundness; and to enter on this course of discipline, is to be good and great. It is precisely analogous to the difference between the use of corporal punishment and the methods of love. It is so easy to bestow on a bad boy a blow, overpower him, and get obedience without words, that, in this world of hurry and distraction, — who can wait for the returns of reason and the conquest of self in the uncertainty, too, whether that will ever come? And yet the familiar observation of the universal compensations might suggest the fear that so summary a stop of a bad humour was more jeopardous than its continuance,[8] it is driven into the constitution, and has infected the brain and the heart.[9]

Our system is a system of despair. We do not believe in a power of Education. We do not think we can call out God in man and we do not try. We renounce all high aims.[10] We sacrifice the genius of the pupil, the unknown possibilities of his nature to a neat and safe uniformity, as the Turks whitewash the costly mosaics of ancient art which the Greeks left on their temple-walls.[11]

Well, language of this spirit is heard in the street, in the senate, in the household, and in the College. It has infected and paralysed the theory of Education.

Certainly this despondency is not in the plan of things. Not for this, not to be thus deserted and betrayed was he created and endowed the heir of Nature.

[8] "Our modes of Education . . . its continuance" ("Education," W, X, 153–155).
[9] "Our modes . . . the heart" (E, 47–48).
[10] "Our system . . . all high aims" ("New England Reformers," W, III, 267–268).
[11] "We sacrifice . . . temple-walls" ("Education," W, X, 138).

I call then our system a system of despair and I find all the correction, all the revolution that is needed and that the best spirits of this age promise, in one word, — in Hope.[12]

Let me say before all other considerations that I think it the main guard to a correct judgment, I may say the bulwark of all that is sacred in man — not to accept degrading views. It is a primal instinct and duty of the human mind to look with a sovereign eye of hope on all things. Let us apply to this subject the same torch under whose light we have looked at all the phenomena of the Time; the infinitude, namely, of every man. Everything teaches that. One fact constitutes all my satisfaction, inspires all my trust, viz. this perpetual youth, which as long as there is any good in us we cannot get rid of.[13] Is it not strange how long our noviciate lasts; that the period of our mastership still loiters, that, as long as we continue growing, and do not inveterate we are always subject to circumstances and do not control them? Many and many a time, we have said, how long will this false shame, how long this excess of sympathy, how long this malign sorcery of ungenial and antagonistic natures endure? Shall we not presently learn to surmount the irritations, the apathy, the gloom with which events and politics and company still torment us? But we do not mend or rise. All the circumstances, like chemical agents, act with energy on us, and we come greenhorns to every conversation. The young, the knowing, the fashionable, the practical, the political, the belle, the Pharisee, the Sadducee put us out; all overact on us and make us dumb.[14]

Who does not see in this temporary unhappiness a deeper good? As long as we are working up to things, we are young, we are safe. As long as things change and invite our energies, we grow and advance. We learn evermore. In smooth water we discover the motion of our boat by the motion of trees and houses on shore; so the progress of the mind is proved by the perpetual change in the persons and things we daily behold.[15] A wonderful perception of the simplicity and identity of all things is united in us with a profound ignorance and inexpectancy of all particular

[12] "Education," W, X, 136.
[13] "Let us apply . . . get rid of" ("Education," W, X, 136).
[14] "Is it not . . . dumb" (D, 376, expanded).
[15] "We learn . . . daily behold" (C, 34).

facts. In saying that man is always a youth, what say we but that the Universe will never let him exhaust it and know it to the end.

The simplicity of the Universe is very different from the simplicity of a machine. He who sees moral nature out and out and thoroughly knows how knowledge is acquired and character formed is a pedant. The simplicity of nature is not that which may easily be read, but is inexhaustible. The last analysis can in no wise be made. We judge of a man's wisdom by his hope, knowing that the perception of the inexhaustibleness of nature is an immortal youth. The wild fertility of nature is felt in comparing our rigid names and reputations with our fluid consciousness. We pass in the world for sects and schools, for erudition and piety, and we are all the time jejune babes. One sees very well how Pyrrhonism grew up. Every man sees that he is the middle point, that everything may be affirmed and denied of him with equal reason. He is old, he is young, he is very wise, he is altogether ignorant. He hears and feels what you say of the seraphim and of the tin pedlar. There is no permanent wise man except in the figment of the stoics. We side with the hero as we read or paint against the coward and the robber. But we have been ourselves that coward and robber, and shall be again, not in the low circumstance but in comparison with the grandeurs possible to the soul.[16]

This fact that always we are astonished by the events of the new day, that all the accumulations of our past experience will never bring us quite even with the new fact, — what is it but a mode in which the immense wealth of nature is made known to us? Why is it that we are always green? why that we are always abashed by new emergences? Only that a sense of the Perfect accompanies, overhangs us alway.

For this reason I greet the complaints of the young and aspiring. I congratulate them on their despondency and skepticism when they ask, What shall I do? How shall I live? They are not to be pacified by pointing them to the uncultivated and pious. No: they ask, Could these bear the ordeal of cultivation and leisure? If not we do not wish to be whipped by toil all day and

[16] "The simplicity of the Universe . . . to the soul" ("Spiritual Laws," W, II, 137–138).

whipped to bed at night. These mourners shall have their reward. Let them learn this fact that their sorrows are the ebbs of a happiness as delicate and spiritual and if they are proportionate to the preceding flux so are they also the preparation of a new tide.[17]

Let us be unhappy, let us be unquiet, ashamed, and always tormented by riddles we cannot expound, if this is all the price we pay for docility and intimacy with an Excellence which abashes us by its splendors.

I speak with diffidence on this subject because it really seems to me more embarrassing than others and I would rather offer my thoughts as conjectures than as opinions.

It seems to me that our experience does not justify the separation of education into distinct institutions, the separating education as an act or system of acts. In a wise society the education of the youth would be accomplished by the ordinary activity of the seniors. All men delight to teach what they know and to do what they can do well. The curiosity of youth meets the communicativeness of the mature and both find their account.

If we rigorously render account to ourselves of what we have owed to instruction, — deliberate, premeditated, organized instruction, — I think it is a very evanescent quantity. Like the poor man in the Arabian nights, day by day we received a bright new sequin and going at last to the drawer where we laid them, there is nothing but a bunch of dry leaves.[18] We owe a few arts, a few rules, reading and writing the Latin grammar and the rule of three, which to me seem undeniable conveniences though very low ones in a scale where into all humanity enters. A few of our attainments, these few I speak of, we keep alive by use and affection but far the greater part of our acquisitions, bought by so much time and labor, and labor too of those at home who pinched themselves that we might want for nothing, have died in the waste of the memory. My academical hours have yielded thus much.

But my life, my work and play, my pleasure and pain, my

[17] "For this reason . . . new tide" (D, 376). The third from last sentence is a paraphrase of a sentence attributed in the journal to "E. H.," i.e., Elizabeth Hoar.
[18] Emerson refers to "The Story of the Barber's Fourth Brother" in *Arabian Nights' Entertainments* as it was commonly derived from the French version.

loves and quarrels, my own reading, my business, my friend, the stranger, the observation of people pursuing their own affairs, their coldness from which I suffered, their cordiality which warmed me, the winter's frost, the summer's fruit — it is these which have taught me that lore which I cannot spare. Or rather it is these daily showers of facts under the light of that omnipresence which makes all these — illustrations of itself; — and what share has a college, a school, or an apprenticeship in this? One sees these organizations recede very fast in a true scale. Indeed always they seem to be nugatory. The college does not have more fine wits than the same population without a college, and it does not have less. It neither helps nor hinders. It is attended by this harm, that it causes those to be sent to study who ought not to go to study and those to be employed to teach who have no vocation to teach. The real advantage of the college is often the simple, mechanical one, I may call it, of a chamber and a fire which the parents will allow the boy without hesitation at Cambridge or at Andover, but do not think needful at home.[19] Undoubtedly they give us leisure and books and the separation from secular pursuits. This is of the highest importance as preparation but it is only that. But this good is to a degree neutralized by rigorous and inflexible courses of instruction not adapted to individuals but to large numbers.

The sum of my criticism on the institutions and systems of education is that education is not there, that it quite transcends all the methods on which they most rely, that it may be procured equally well near them or far from them, but must descend from higher sources than any routine of classbooks or academical exercises can ever supply.

I believe that our own experience instructs us that the secret of education lies in respecting the pupil. It is not for you to choose what he shall know, what he shall do. It is chosen and foreordained and he only holds the key to his own secret. By your tampering and thwarting and too much governing, he may be hindered from his end and kept out of his own.[20] But being born for himself alone, he can never be coaxed or chided or drilled into your

<hr />

[19] "Culture," W, VI, 156.
[20] "I believe that our own . . . out of his own" ("Education," W, X, 143).

place, form, and faculty. You have deprived him of himself and the world of a man to add another to the army of drones and blunderers and artisans which fill the towns and postpone the hope and faith of all beholders.

Respect the child. Be not too much his parent. Trespass not on his solitude. Fathers would be the fathers of the mind as well as the body of their children. Wait and see the new product of nature. Nature never rhymes her children; never makes two men precisely alike.[21] She loves analogies but not repetitions.[22] But a low self-love in the parent desires that his child should repeat his character and fortune; an expectation which the child, if justice is done him, will nobly disappoint. By working on the theory that this resemblance exists, we shall do what in us lies to defeat his proper promise and produce the ordinary and mediocre.

Let us wait and see what is this new creation, of what new organ the great Spirit had need when it incarnated this new Will. A new Adam in the garden, he is to name all the beasts in the field, all the gods in the sky. And jealous provision seems to have been made in his constitution that you shall not invade and contaminate him with the worn weeds of your language and opinions.[23] It is very certain that the coming age and the departing age seldom understand each other. The old man thinks the young man has no distinct purpose for he could never get anything intelligible and earnest out of him. Perhaps the young man does not think it worth his while to explain himself to so hard and inapprehensive a confessor.[24] Do not think that the youth has no force because he cannot speak to you seniors. For months perhaps you have got from him no reasonable word. Hark in the next room who spoke so clear and emphatic? It was he. It seems he knows how to speak to his cotemporaries. Bashful or bold then, he will know how to make us seniors very unnecessary.[25]

Let us respect the child and the youth. Let him be led up with a longsighted forbearance, and let not the sallies of his petulance

---

[21] "Character," W, III, 108; E, 62.

[22] "Respect the child . . . repetitions" ("Education," W, X, 143, rearranged); last sentence in E, 63.

[23] "Let us wait . . . language and opinions" ("Education," W, X, 137).

[24] "It is very certain . . . a confessor" ("Education," W, X, 136).

[25] "Do not think that the youth . . . seniors very unnecessary" ("Self-Reliance," W, II, 48; D, 114).

or folly be checked with too much disgust or indignation or despair.

So to regard the young child, the young man, requires, no doubt, rare patience: — a patience that nothing but faith in the remedial forces of the soul can give. You see his sensualism; you see his want of those tastes and perceptions which make the power and safety of your character. Very likely. But he has something else. If he has his own vice, he has its correlative virtue. Every mind should be allowed to make its own statement in action, and its balance will appear. In these judgments, one needs that foresight which was attributed to an eminent reformer, of whom it was said, "his patience could see in the bud of the aloe the blossom at the end of a hundred years." [26]

But I hear the outcry which replies to this suggestion — Would you verily throw up the reins of private and public discipline; would you leave the young child to the mad career of his own passions and whimsies, and call this anarchy a respect of the child's nature? I answer, Respect the child, respect him unto the end, *but also respect yourself*. Be the companion of his thought, the friend of his friendship, the lover of his virtue, — but no kinsman of his sin. Let him find you so true to yourself that you are the irreconcileable hater of his vice, and the imperturbable slighter of his trifling.[27]

It is plain that the right education of youth requires a wise society as well as wise individuals. If all men were self-respecting, the miscreant would find his vice bruised and repelled everywhere by the walls of character. That man has not read his own biography who underestimates the tacit energy of the true and self-relying in us. The costliest influence is that of character, that plant of slowest growth, the mutual veneration which grows up between men who have seen each other in every variety of event and never knew a tie of civility or of sanctity but the faith of boyhood still sacred and fragrant.

[26] Cf. William Hazlitt, "Mr. Jeffrey," *The Spirit of the Age* (London, 1825), p. 315; Blotting Book II, 19. Emerson's paraphrase misses the irony of Hazlitt's comment on the Whiggish moderation and complacency of Francis Jeffrey (1773–1850) as editor of *The Edinburgh Review,* but Hazlitt wrote before Jeffrey, entering politics in 1830, made something of a name for himself as a reformer. "So to regard . . . hundred years" ("Education," W, X, 151–152).
[27] "But I hear . . . his trifling" ("Education," W, X, 143–144).

So perfect is my confidence in that uplifting energy that I think the reason why Education is false and poor, is because there are few men, — there are no men. Let us be men, and the youth will learn of us to measure

> the ideal track of right
> More fair than heaven's broad pathway paved with stars
> Which Dion learned to measure with delight.[28]

We are faithless. We believe the defects of all these limitary people who make up society are organic; and so society is but a hospital of incurables. We do not believe that any education, any system of philosophy, any influence of genius, will lead a mind not profound to become profound.[29] Having settled ourselves into this infidelity our utmost skill is expended to procure alleviations, diversion, opiates. We adorn the doomed victim with manual skill, his tongue with languages, his eye with agreeable forms, his body with inoffensive and comely manners. So have we cunningly hid the tragedy of limitation and inner death which we cannot cure. Is it wonderful that society should be devoured by a secret melancholy which breaks through all the smiles, and all the gaiety and games? [30]

But if we made less account of special skills and talents, and more of that great inner force by which a man is distinguished from the more cunning animals it is possible that we might even come to think that a mind not profound could become profound. That which is best in nature, the highest prize of life, is the perception in the private heart of access to the Universal. How is a man a man? How can he weave relations of joy and good with his brother, but because he is inviolable, alone, perfect? I stand here glad at heart of all the sympathies I can awaken and share, clothing myself with them as with a garment of shelter and beauty and yet knowing that it is not in the power of all who surround me to take from me the smallest thread I call mine. If all things are taken away I have still all things in my relation to the Eternal. But the very worth and essence of this faith consists in its imper-

[28] Wordsworth, "Dion," lines 50–52 (misquoted).
[29] Cf. E, 113.
[30] "We believe the defects . . . gaiety and games" ("New England Reformers," W, III, 268–269, condensed).

sonality. It is not mine; it is not thine. It knows not names or person or sex or accident. If I have any vantage of my brother I can lead him to feel that I do not wish to excel him but to suffice to myself. If I have any inferiority to him it becomes null, I know it not, it pains me not when I adore this Perfect which solicits me.

Is not the whole mission of genius always to reveal this gospel to men? What else do they teach — those great bards that in all ages have raised the hope and history of man and whose memory we associate with flowers and stars, with laurel and palm — what teach they but the insulation and selfsubsistency of a man; by the heart, by the soul and not by what roof he lives under, what stem he sprung from, man is great; and that what is of the heart and mind eludes all laws of property; and the child who understands Plato is already Plato so far. The costliest benefit of books is that they set us free of themselves also. The best picture makes us say, I am a painter also; the poem, I also am a poet. And is not that the charm, the highest charm of all works of art, that we feel this marble or canvas to be no prison of beauty but that it gleams with something essentially radiant and unconfinable, apprising us that the artist had risen into a region from which lustre played on all forms and objects and that whatever thing he did he had adorned? And conveying too by implication his own deep sense that no walls less broad than nature, no privilege, no preference could set limit or bound to this overflowing of God through every willing heart of man.

All social influences do daily labor to teach me the same thing. The office of conversation is to give me selfpossession. I lie torpid as a clod. Virtue, wisdom sound to me fabulous, all cant. I am an unbeliever. Then comes by a sage and gentle spirit who spreads out in order before me his own life and aims not as experience but as the good and desireable. Straightway I feel the presence of a new and yet old, a genial, a native element. I am like a southerner who having spent the winter in a polar climate feels at last the south wind blow, the rigid fibres relax, and his whole frame expand to the welcome heats. In this bland, flowing atmosphere I regain one by one my faculties, my organs: life returns to a finger, a hand, a foot. A new nimbleness, almost wings unfold at my side, and I see my right to the heaven as well as the farthest fields of the earth. The effect of the conversation resembles the effect of a beautiful voice in a church choir which insinuates itself as water into all chinks and cracks and presently floats the whole discordant choir and holds it in solution in its melody. Well, I am a ship aground; and the bard directs a river to my shoals, relieves me of these perilous rubs and strains, and at last fairly uplifts me on the waters and I put forth my sails and turn my head to the sea.[31]

There is an upper influence in external nature too which always addresses man with the like admonition, an influence which detaches him, which does not speak to masses nor to select companies nor to a pair of friends but which speaks alone to the alone. It cannot be interpreted in human language. Nature will not have us fret and fume. She does not like our benevolence or our learning much better than she likes our frauds and wars. When we come out of the Caucus or the Bank or the Abolition Convention or the Temperance Meeting or the Literary Club into the fields and woods she says to us, "So hot? my little Sir." [32] There is an intimation breathed by the sea and land more intelligible when our ear is open: that our life is not obedient and concordant with theirs and that when it shall be we shall understand their speech.

I say that what is called Education in the world fails because of its low aim. It aims to make amends for the Fall of Man by teaching him feats and games. It aims not to retrieve but to conceal; to save appearances; at best to solace him. It offers a jest to the sick. It rouges the cheek which is pale with death. Worst of all, it tends to insanity by amusing the man with this show of accomplishments instead of exposing to him his fatal want. Now to what end have good and great men walked in the world, — sane souls from time to time, — Moses, and Jesus, Zoroaster, and Zeno, to what end philosophy, poetry, Christianity; to what end these affecting experiences, never omitted in any private life, the influence of conversation, the relation of absolute truth which love, which terror, which need, do not fail to establish between each of

---

[31] "The office of conversation . . . the sea" (D, 262).
[32] "Nature will not . . . my little Sir" ("Spiritual Laws," W, II, 135; D, 303, expanded).

us, and some of his mates, to what end this instruction of genius, of society, of external nature, if the truth is not [in] some manner to be incorporated into our schools, — that a man is not a man who does not yet draw on the eternal and universal Soul? It lies within, — it lies behind us all, — the dullest drone, the shallowest fop. Those unhappy who come into every one's thought when the question is proposed — Can a mind not profound, — by education become profound? — those unhappy persons are capable of this sentiment. They can be ennobled and made to know their relation to the All. They are capable of humility, of justice, of love, of aspiration. The clay can be tempered with this fire. If of these, then are they already on a platform that commands the sciences and arts, speech and poetry, action and grace. For whoso dwells in this perception does already anticipate those special powers which you prize so highly, just as love does justice to all the gifts of the object beloved. The lover has no talent, no skill which passes for quite nothing with his enamoured maiden, however little she may possess of related faculty. And the heart which abandons itself to the Supreme Mind finds itself related to all his works and will find a royal road to particular knowledges and powers.

I confess myself utterly at a loss in suggesting particular reforms proposed in our modes of teaching. No discretion that can be lodged with a school committee, — with the Overseers or Visiters of an Academy, a College, can at all avail to reach a wrong as deepseated and intrinsic as this. A vicious society cannot have virtuous schools. A society which wishes its youth bred to certain dexterities cannot have schools which condemn that aim. But all difficulties and perplexities solve themselves when we leave institutions and address individuals.[33] To whatsoever upright mind, — to whatsoever beating heart I speak, — to you it is committed to educate men. By simple living, — by true speech, — by just action, — by an illimitable soul, you inspire, you correct, you instruct, you raise, you embellish all.

By your own act you teach the beholder how to do the practicable. According to the depth from which you draw your life such is the depth not only of your strenuous effort, but of your

[33] "I confess myself . . . address individuals" ("Education," W, X, 156–157, condensed).

last act, of your manners, and presence. The beautiful nature of the world has here blended your happiness with your power. Work straight on in absolute duty, and you lend an arm and an encouragement to all the youth of the Universe. Consent yourself to be an organ of your highest thought, and lo! suddenly you put all men in your debt and are the fountain of an energy that goes pulsing on with waves of benefit to the borders of society, to the circumference of things.[34]

[34] "To whatsoever upright . . . circumferences of things" ("Education," W, X, 158–159).

10

Tendencies

The final lecture in the series on "The Present Age" was read at the Masonic Temple in Boston on February 12, 1840, and repeated on May 6 as the ninth and concluding lecture in the series for the Lyceum at Concord, Massachusetts. Emerson drew upon this lecture for "The Over-Soul," "Spiritual Laws," and "Circles" and for central passages of "Self-Reliance." One leaf was printed by Cabot in 1883 in the posthumous essay "Aristocracy," *Lectures and Biographical Sketches*, apparently after it had also done service in a lecture in the series on "New England" in 1843.

The manuscript was once sewn together and its leaves are labelled and paginated in ink. One extra double sheet now with the manuscript is printed in "Human Life," Lecture 9 where it belongs (see textual notes, p. 438), and another double sheet not labelled and never sewn with the rest of the manuscript is printed in the textual notes; its removal from the text leaves a lacuna of two leaves in the otherwise complete lecture.

IN THE views we have taken in the preceding discourses of the Commerce, Letters, Government, Domestic Life, Philanthropic Efforts, Religion, and Education of the Present Age, it will be easily perceived we have arrived always at one and the same result, namely, that whatsoever abuses mark the existing forms, flow from a want of simplicity, a want of religious trust in the Soul itself, and the attempts of men to interfere with that living order which always tends to establish itself in all the parts of humanity. And the remedial forces traceable in each part work in that direction, grow out of secret persuasions in the breast of men that by a reliance not on combinations, not on tricks, not on magnitude and numbers, not on any invariable or dead *means* but

302

on the vital, alert Soul ever equal to the emergency — reform and regeneration appear.

In all parts of action, society is divided between two opinions and courses of conduct, in the one part the assiduous endeavor to govern, to manage, to repair, crutch and bolster, to supply straps and buckles by which the world may be made to last our day. On the other part, the young, the philosophic, the unambitious complain of the usages and conventions and combinations by which every thing is achieved on earth as excessive, and they forfeit their connexion and vantages, disuse and throw away first one, then another habitude, aiming still at a simpler and simpler life, until the world fears the loss of all regulated energy in the dreams of idealism.

That bifold fact may be called the philosophy, the genius of this time. It pervades the whole network of our works and fortunes. In Politics universally we have taken the step of Force which we must take back and choose the way of Love. In Literature men have thought they could choose what to say and that the value of a book was in proportion to its labor and ingenuity until in a wiser mind they perceive that every thing so said is false, harsh, and unheard; whereas, what they speak because it will be said is true, musical, and welcome to all ears. In Domestic Life again all indicates that the genius of man instead of a stupid and wilful Imitation should prevail. We wish it to be remembered that the house stands there to the end of Culture, the house for the children and not for the furniture as many housekeepers believe; that the genius of the man should be suffered to flow sovereign, ordaining throughout his dwelling and not tyrannized over by his house and its foolish customs; that he should know and honor himself again in his friends, and accept of the great God the Angels he sendeth in a religious acquiescence not in presuming, intriguing election of them.

In like manner in regard to those enterprises that are from time to time presented for the amelioration of society, the movement of Temperance, of Freedom, of Peace, of an exchange of goods on the fraternal instead of the mercenary principle, and the like; these all are right, inasmuch as they involve a return to simpler modes and a faithful trust of the Soul that it has and can show its own royal road through the obvious hardships and difficulties of the evil custom.

In Religion he has imagined that by some fidelity in preserving the facts of yesterday he may escape the trouble of living today, that having found a good man a thousand years ago he can embalm the corpse with amomum and spices, he can dress it with such costly attire that it will be almost as good as the man alive. He does not believe the miracle which he is. He does not see that the dead is made alive in him, that dead matter in him starts from the dust and doth the will of thought and affection. A statue of flesh, he grows, he breathes, he walks, he sees, he thinks, he loves, he speaks, he creates. But while he tugs in vain at this impossibility his health and reason return in the conviction of the eternity of the Soul. Out of the darkness that great light shineth.[1] That which he thought was, is — young, entire, almighty, entrancing as of yore. I too am, he saith, I live forever.

The same error has marked our systems of education, the reliance on a given means — the numbering of pages, the counting of hours, the performance of themes, of recitations, of work by rule and with the same result that we have timid, unable martinets — operatives, machines instead of self-helping, self-directing, vivacious men. The grand, the poetic, the daring Soul does not shine through them with its all enlivening ray.

In all the activities of the present day the same fact may be still observed. They rely on new circumstances, on new means for the extermination of all those evils under which they suffer, and for the regeneration of society. The old French Revolution attracted to its first movements all the liberality, the virtue, the hope, the poetry in Europe. By the abolition of kingship and aristocracy, — tyranny, inequality, poverty would end. Alas! no; — tyranny, inequality, poverty stood as fast and fierce as ever. We likewise put our faith in Democracy, in the Republican principle carried out to the extremes of practice in universal suffrage, in the will of majorities.

The young adventurer finds that the relations of society, the position of classes irk and sting him and he lends himself to each

[1] Cf. John 1:5; II Corinthians 4:6; Matthew 4:16; Isaiah 9:2.

malignant party that assails what is eminent. He will one day know that this is not removeable but a distinction in the nature of things, that neither the caucus nor the newspaper nor the Congress nor the mob nor the guillotine nor halter nor fire nor all together can avail to outlaw, cut out, burn, or destroy the offence of superiority in persons. The manners, the pretension which annoy me so much are not superficial but built on a real distinction in the nature of my companion. The superiority in him is an inferiority in me, and if he were wiped by a sponge out of nature, this my inferiority would still be made evident to me by other persons, every where and every day.[2]

To this point a fable has come down to us from an old poet. Hephaestion the Corcyraean wished all his friends dead on very slight occasion. Whoever was privy to one of his follies had the honor of this Stygian optation. Had Jove heard all his prayers Corcyra would soon have been unpeopled. At last it occurred to Hephaestion that instead of wringing this hecatomb of friends' necks every morning he would dine better if he gave as much life as he now took. He found to his astonishment the embryos of a thousand friends lying hid under his own heart and that for every offence he forgave and for every just vote he made, suddenly from afar a noble stranger knocked at his street gate.[3]

Society has dreamed that a new era opened in the wonderful invention of our system of credit in trade, the facilities it afforded for setting in activity all the slumbering energies of the community; it seemed to breathe new life over stagnant, melancholy, pastoral nations; it not only gave new vigor to the maritime population but to the agricultural. Instantly the value of the farm rose, and all its real, all its possible products, it insinuated its attraction into mountain gorges and declivities, into sandy deserts, into cold and forgotten islands. What power, what beneficence, what civilization in a means so simple. It was compared to a road through the air by which every one went whither soever he would and was no longer constrained to consult the intrusion of mountain chains, of unseasonable rivers, bogs, or lakes. But the despised

[2] "The old French . . . every day" ("Aristocracy," *W*, X, 34–35); "The young adventurer . . . every day" (D, 142–143).
[3] "Hephaestion the Corcyraean . . . his street gate" (E, 109, where "Guy" is used instead of Hephaestion).

mountain and sea had their revenge. The road in the air was only good for the magnetised. It was found that the wings would melt and Icarus would fall. An advantage shared by all was followed by crises and ruin which involved all. Loud cracks were suddenly heard in this palace built by magic in which we dwelt so pleasantly and it threatened [to] bury in its ruins all who had quit their own cabins to lie under its magnificent roof. And the gravest evils, political, domestic, moral, were found to grow out the fluctuations incident to this metaphysical currency of Credit.

Now men think just as wisely that the system is noxious and that redemption is to be found in the disuse of credit, in bullion and in barter. As if these were not also means, dead means, to which their own proper harm is also incident. There is never salvation but in life.

Observe the confidence of all the sanguine patriots, the public spirited citizen, the editor, the subscriber. It reposes on the new arts which have been invented; on new machinery, on steam, on the glimpses of mechanical power to be derived from electricity or galvanism, on photogenic drawing, on lamps that shine without shadow, on stoves that burn without fuel and clocks to be wound by the tide, on iron boats and cast steel tools, on steam batteries, life preservers, and diving bells. And the actual familiarization of railways and of india-rubber shoes seems to such the payment of the first dividend, the solid certainty of the new era.

It is wonderful how hard it is to disabuse our ingenious, repairing, prudent race of this continual hankering to add to the simplicity of Nature. Is there not an incident related of the successors of Copernicus and cotemporaries of Galileo somewhat in this wise?

As soon as the philosopher had made known the falsehood of the Ptolemaic vortices it was proposed to form a very large society to devise and execute means for propping in some secure and permanent manner this planet. It had filled the minds of the benevolent and anxious part of the community with lively emotion the consideration of the exposed state of the globe; the danger of its falling and being swamped in absolute space; the danger of its being drawn too near the sun and roasting the race of mankind and the daily danger of its being overturned; and if a stage coach overset costs valuable bones, what will not ensue on the upset of this Omnibus? It was thought that by a strenuous and very extensive concert aided by a committee of master-builders and engineers, a system of booms and chains might be set round the exterior surface and that it might be underpinned in such a manner as to enable the aged and the women and children to sleep and eat with greater tranquillity henceforward. It is true there was not a perfect unanimity on this subject and it is much to be regretted that some pert and flippant youths did not hesitate to say that the world could stand without linchpins and that even if you should cut away all the ropes and knock away the whole underpinning of the society, it would swing and poise perfectly for the poise was in the globe itself.[4]

But such an hypothesis, it was argued, tended directly to Pyrrhonism.

And this is the doctrine which all the events, all the new and best movements, and all the youngest and truest spirits of our era unconsciously or consciously preach: that all reliance on this or that means, all reliance on means, on methods is vain. If each has its good so it has its tax. Nature is not to be cheated. We shall be born to no inheritance. We must buy it with ourselves. Man must rely on Man, on himself, on principles, on his thought, on his soul.

The sad Pestalozzi, who shared with all ardent spirits the hope of Europe on the outbreak of the French Revolution, after witnessing its savage steps recorded his deep conviction, "That the amelioration of outward circumstances will be the effect but can never be the means of mental and moral improvement." [5]

These doctrines, these movements, all operate with a steady force, as I stated in my first lecture, to detach the individual man from his mates, to teach him his separate value. It is remarkable that not only the action of the age but the poetry and philosophy of the age tend at last to the same conclusion. The poetry is con-

---

[4] "it was proposed . . . globe itself" (cf. D, 331–332, where the passage occurs in present tense and is followed by: "But this is Transcendentalism," referring presumably to the counterstatement expressed by a "pert & flippant orator . . . last Sunday").
[5] Edward Biber, *Henry Pestalozzi and His Plan of Education* (London, 1831), p. 23; Blotting Book III, 37; "Lecture on the Times," W, I, 281.

templative and opens the world within; the philosophy recedes to grounds more and more purely ideal and at last entrenches man in the sentiment of Duty as the only reality. Will they not cause the question of his moral and metaphysical energies to be explored with a new and personal interest; and will not men set themselves to learn by experiment how much a man avails? Have not the events of the age already given a new value to Self-reliance? This indeed seems to me the moral of nature. This is that which the ages, this is that which the hours and moments show. Personal merit is that which men and events past, present, and future inexorably require and with that they give all things in giving the worthiness of all.

It is of no importance as far as I am concerned on what times, in what company, I fall; it boots not, how good works are projected, or what brave men I follow; they heal me not, they protect me not, I cannot gain aught by moving in the wake of a saint or a benefactor or commander of men, only that energy, only that love and sight which I attain, can tell in my behalf, can go to remove or abate the ills which encompass a human being.

If then the genius of this age is such a divider and judge, a Discerner, a Critic, a Separator tending steadily by the continual onward course of revolution in church and state, in schools and domestic institutions to retrench every kind of expedient and makeshift; to hate and abolish all privilege, usage, and countenance and set every man on his merit alone, it behoves all good hearts to take counsel with themselves and prove their own reality. In an age of truth let us not be danglers; in an age of men let us not be frivolous and timid.

The foes to Self-reliance are the sympathies which incline us to defer to the opinion of society without inquiry into the grounds of that opinion. Hence vice itself fronts the day as virtue and we allow it and embrace it. Conformity is the Diana and Jove, the Bel and Nebo whose shrines have encroached on the worship of the true God.

It needs a great heart fortified by wise and habitual study of the world to win that high and firm carriage which shall never accept what others call virtue which is not virtue, which is not hindered by the name of goodness but explores if it be goodness, and to which nothing is sacred but the integrity of its own nature.[6]

The objection to conforming to usages that have become dead to you is that it scatters your force. It loses your time and blurs the impression of your character. If you maintain a dead church, contribute to a dead Bible society, vote with a foolish Whig party, or with a profligate government, spend your time, arrange your house, or drive your traffic with the multitude, under all these screens I have difficulty to detect the precise man you are. And of course so much force is withdrawn from your proper life. But do your work and I shall know you.[7] Do your work and you shall reinforce yourself. Moreover conformity destroys all. A man must consider what a rich realm he abdicates when he becomes a conformist. I hear a speaker announce for his text or topic a known article of his church or party with a coldness that approaches contempt. For do I not know beforehand that not possibly can he say a new or spontaneous word? Do I not know that with all this affectation of examining the grounds of the institution, — of the creed, of the law, he will do no such thing — that the establishment is to him sacred? Do I not know that he is pledged to himself beforehand not to look but at one side; the permitted side, not as a man but as a parish minister, a sworn partisan, a paid vote? What folly then to say *let us examine* and purse up the mouth with the wrinkles of a judge. He is a retained attorney, and these airs of the Bench are the emptiest affectation. It is so with all partisans and all men are partisans. This conformity makes them not false in a few particulars, authors of a few lies, but false in all particulars. Their every truth is not quite true. Their two is not the real two, their four not the real four. So that every word they say chagrins me and I protest against the entire creature.[8] Nature punishes conformity by stamping on its features an asinine expression. There are few experiences in common life more mortifying than "the foolish face of praise," [9] the forced smile which we put on in company where we do not feel at ease

[6] Cf. "Self-Reliance," W, II, 50; *Lectures*, II, 151.
[7] "The objection . . . know you" (D, 337, modified).
[8] "A man must consider . . . entire creature" (D, 265–266, modified).
[9] Pope, "Epistle to Dr. Arbuthnot," line 212; Wide World XIII, 38; XVIII [A], 4.

in answer to conversation which does not interest us. The muscles, not spontaneously moved but moved by a low usurping wilfulness, grow tight about the outline of the face and make the most disagreeable sensation, a sensation of rebuke and warning which no brave young man will suffer twice.[10]

For nonconformity the world whips you with its displeasure. It is pleased to turn from you its ugly face. And therefore a man must know how to estimate a sour face. The bystanders look sourly on him in the public street or the friend's parlor. If this aversation had its origin in contempt and resistance like his own he might well go home with a sad countenance, but the sour faces of the multitude like their sweet faces have no deep cause — disguise no god — but are put off and on as the wind blows and a newspaper directs. And yet I esteem the discontent of the multitude more formidable than that of the Senate and the Academy. It is easy enough for a firm man who knows the world to brook the rage of the cultivated classes. Their rage is decorous and limitary for they are weak and their rage never very deep. They are timid as being very vulnerable themselves; but when to their feminine rage the indignation of the people is added, when the ignorant and the poor are aroused, when the unintelligent brute force that lies at the bottom of society is made to growl and mow, then it needs more than nerve, it needs the heights of magnanimity and religion to treat it godlike, as a trifle of no concernment.[11]

The other terror that scares us from self-trust is the bugbear of *consistency,* a reverence for our past act or word because the eyes of others have no other data for computing our orbit than our past acts and we are loth to disappoint them.

A foolish consistency is the hobgoblin of little minds, adored by little statesmen and philosophers and divines. With consistency a great soul has simply nothing to do. He may as well concern himself about his shadow on the wall. Out upon your guarded lips. Sew them up with packthread; do. Else if you would be a man speak what you think today in words as hard as cannonballs and tomorrow speak what tomorrow thinks in hard words again though it should contradict everything you spoke today.[12]

[10] "There are few . . . suffer twice" (C, 138).
[11] "It is easy . . . concernment" (D, 97).
[12] D, 334.

Ah! then exclaims the aged prudence, You shall be sure to be misunderstood. Misunderstood! It is a right fool's word. Is it so bad then to be the misunderstood? Pythagoras was misunderstood and Socrates and Jesus and Luther and Copernicus and Galileo and every pure and wise spirit that ever took flesh. To be great is to be misunderstood.

But truly no man can violate his nature.[13] Let him record in speech or action day by day his honest thought without prospect or retrospect and it will be found symmetrical though he mean it not and see it not. Fear never but you shall be consistent in whatever variety of actions so they be each honest and natural in their hour. For of one will the actions will be harmonious, however unlike they seem. These varieties are lost sight of when seen at a little distance, at a little height of thought. One tendency unites them all. The voyage of the best ship is a zigzag line of a hundred tacks. This is only microscopic criticism. See the line from a sufficient distance and it straightens itself to the average tendency.[14] Your genuine action will explain itself and will explain your other genuine actions. Your conformity explains nothing. Act singly and what you have already done singly will justify you now. Greatness always appeals to the future. If I can be great enough now to do right and scorn eyes, I must have done so much right before as to defend me now. Be it how it may, do right now. Always scorn appearances and you always may.[15] The force of character is always cumulative. All the foregone days of virtue work their health into this. What makes the majesty of the heroes of the senate and the field which so impresses the imagination? The consciousness of a train of great days and victories behind. There they all stand and shed an united light on the advancing actor. He is attended as by a visible escort of angels to every man's presence. This it is which throws thunder into Chatham's voice and dignity into Washington's port and America into Adams's eye.[16]

It is by no means the highest yet it is a ready illustration of

[13] Cf. *Lectures*, II, 171.
[14] "The voyage . . . tendency" (D, 324).
[15] "Act singly . . . always may" (D, 269).
[16] "The objection to conforming . . . Adams's eye" ("Self-Reliance," W, II, 54–60, modified); "The force of character . . . Adams's eye" (Q, 25).

the invincible forces of man which every knot of talkers, which every business in which men are associated will furnish,[17]

.   .   .

Yet a strong will is a feeble force. It is a surrender of the man to the visible facts of his desire, the habit of proceeding directly to them without any reckoning of other wills, of opposition or of favor. It is a low species of self-reliance and inspires among the trustless fear and respect. But it has no power over the good. It is strong beside custom, imitation, and indulgence. It is weakness beside the renunciation of Will. Beside love and wisdom, the self-abandonment of goodness and of truth, this which seeks merely low and conventional gratifications, power and fame, self-aggrandizement, is unholy and profane. The moment we enter into the higher thoughts fame is no more affecting to the ear than the faint tinkle of the passing sleighbell.[18] Power is a toy for which we have lost our taste. Will is strong but Trust is stronger. Will is strong but it works to finite ends but Trust is stronger for it is the adoration of infinite power as it enters into the affairs of man. Trust gains by faster and surer increments than study or Will. He that trusts conforms himself to the constitution of Nature and receives wisdom at every organ. The growths of genius are of a certain voluminous, total unfolding that does not advance the elect individual first over Adam, then Guy, then Richard and give to each the pain of discovered inferiority, but by every pulsation he expands there where he works passing at each pulsation classes, populations of men[19] as the plumule of the oak passes the proportions of the plumule of the strawberry.[20]

The lesson is forcibly taught that our life might be much easier and simpler than we make it; that the world might be a happier place than it is; that perchance there is really no need of struggles, convulsions, and despairs, of the wringing of the hands and the gnashing of the teeth; that we miscreate our own evils. We interfere with the optimism of nature, for whenever we get this

---

[17] Two leaves missing at this point; see textual notes.
[18] B, 149; cf. also B, 182.
[19] "The growths of genius . . . populations of men" ("The Over-Soul," W, II, 274–275).
[20] "The growths of genius . . . strawberry" (C, 296).

vantage ground of the past or of a wiser mind in the present we are able to discern that we are begirt with spiritual laws which execute themselves.[21] To put off the foreign is the condition of insight, to put off the foreign the condition of growth.

We owe to ourselves a greater faith in that which is possible to man, a stronger faith in the faintest of our presentiments than in the testimony of all history, which contradicts it. A great man is always a contradiction to his age and to all foregoing history. If Plato had not been you would say no Plato could be. If Jesus had not been would not all mankind deny the possibility of so just a life? And yet steadily in the heart of every man the possibility of a greater than Plato, of a greater than Jesus, was always affirmed and still is affirmed, for every man carries with him alway the vision of the perfect, and the highest actual that fulfils any part of this promise instantly exalts the Ideal just so much higher and it can no more be attained than he can set his foot on the horizon which flies before him. The wildest poetry has yet to become familiar fact and every tune and pleasing fiction and romantic verse which haunts our imagination, — we know not why, — will yet show us why it was so agreeable to our constitution, when it has embodied itself under the common day.

Let us not sit down contented with a small satisfaction. Let us be of a religious greatness. Hope is great. Let us not be easily pleased. In proportion to the health of a nature, will its assurance of future good be. I shrink from those who urge an easy submission to the destiny which has made our lot low, our portion of good small, and who urge a squalid contentment therewith. I refuse the patience they preach as treacherous and sneaking. And why now for the first time should the elastic soul of man relax its tension and renounce its endeavor? Are all the experiments made and ended? Have the race of mankind dared and done the best, and produced its last saint and sweetest singer and we now fallen on the world's infirmity and age? Is not the circle still round? Have the laws of angles and of solids failed? The atmosphere — is the art of its manufacture lost? Does not the light still pierce it? Is it not respirable still to the lungs? The sense of justice and

---

[21] "The lesson is forcibly . . . execute themselves" ("Spiritual Laws," W, II, 135); cf. C, 97.

of truth — does not the child still exercise it untaught and live in it as his element? And the deep of Peace — is it withdrawn from under the innocent and confiding heart? Then still reaches this wonderful humanity through all the three vast kingdoms of nature obvious here under the sun and in matter a dweller in the region of effects; by the activity of his understanding, his mathematics, his prudence, a dweller in the region of causes; and higher and deeper there by his Faith and Joy a dweller in the region of unchangeable reality, of primary life. It has lost nothing of power which it ever possessed.

Who does not see the grandeur of this human destiny which in proportion to the cultivation and light of a period, in proportion to the gay invitation of society and of circumstance sends man home on his own heart; by means of things, raises him above things; through society and interaction raises him out of society; and in lieu of the whole world yields him the value of the world in his own nature. All that we know, all that is written on the page of history is the perishing means of the soul's education. Arts and sciences, states and churches, books and persons, power and property are means of education exhausted or exhaustible. Long time he refuses to believe them means; he accounts them ends; he asks for nothing better: he gives them his heart and his life. But they will not yield him the peace he craves.

He goes up and down, he changes his place, he visits distant countries, he wishes to lose himself in his employments, but there beside him is the stern Fact, the sad Self, unrelenting, identical that he fled from. His giant goes with him wherever he goes.[22] But when he resists this Spirit no longer, when he disposes himself to obey it, this great Presence assumes a benign and beatific face. Then he unrols these riches of the Universe as pleasing toys which the pupil of Nature can come to regard as momentary vehicles of the true life but all inadequate to contain it. He learns that silence is wiser than speech. Love acquaints him with the superfluousness of words. The length of the discourse indicates the distance of thought between the speaker and the hearer. When they are at one in any part no words are necessary. When

---

[22] "but there beside him . . . wherever he goes" ("Self-Reliance," W, II, 81–82, where Emerson uses first person).

at one in all no words are suffered.[23] He overlooks the work of art and wonders at the pains that so tediously produce a single work when every thought which he receives from the Fountain of beauty implies the existence of perfect and unfading forms. He wonders at your over admiration of the firstborn of mankind, at that Foreworld fading almost into the precincts of Fable which produced simple and colossal designs whilst he feels that deep in his own heart is the Foreworld again.[24] He thinks even your search after friendship superstitious for with all the joy those relations yield him he has learned to look at friends as only the reflections of every man's worth, reflections in persons, and that everywhere in all the regions of the Universal love, the same virtue will environ itself with equal companions. All progress in every sort tends in the same direction to a quiet yet sublime Religion the hem of whose vesture we dare not touch whilst from afar we predict its coming whose temple shall be the household hearth and under whose light each man shall work that which his genius delights, shall possess that which he can enjoy; shall draw to him those companions that belong to him, and shall have a property in entire nature by the renouncement of all selfish and sensual aim.

[23] "The length of the discourse . . . suffered" ("Circles," W, II, 311; D, 69).
[24] Cf. D, 274.

III

ADDRESS TO THE PEOPLE
OF EAST LEXINGTON

WHEN Emerson was invited to speak to the people of East Lexington on the occasion of the dedication of their new church on January 15, 1840, he was returning to a congregation which he had served frequently as supply preacher between 1835 and 1839 in the absence of a regular minister in charge. Charles Follen, who issued the invitation, had returned to his former charge from New York as regular pastor less than a year previously, but he had stabilized the small, relatively new congregation, had successfully introduced a few liberal innovations in its worship, and had brought its modest and beautiful church building near completion when on November 7, 1839, he wrote to Emerson asking him to participate in the dedication of the new meetinghouse. That Emerson, whose welcome in many Unitarian churches a year and a half after his Divinity School address was doubtful, was asked to be an especially honored participant is clear from Follen's letter: "No one has as yet been invited except Dr Channing who will preach the Sermon if his health permit, but requires me to be prepared to preach in case he should not be able to come. I hope you will comply with the cordial wish of the Society whose esteem and love you possess; and I beg you to choose among the parts that are usual on such occasions, that which you prefer. There are three Prayers, besides selections from Scripture, and several Hymns to be read. But if you prefer an Address to the People I feel assured it would be gratifying to them" (manuscript letter in Houghton Library). The suggestion that he might prefer a special part in the dedication, the part which Emerson finally chose, was made out of deference not only to Emerson's difficult relation to Unitarianism generally at this time, but also to his particular relation with this parish.

Even after he had resigned from the ministry of the Second Church of Boston in 1832, Emerson still maintained cordial relations with the churches, at least until his address on July 15, 1838, to the students at the Divinity School. After his return from Europe in 1833, it was natural that he should preach, though he wrote only five new regular sermons.[1] He preached as a supply minister in many places: at the Second Church and elsewhere in the Boston area, in Bangor, Maine, and in New York. There was apparently serious consideration of a permanent settlement at the New Bedford, Massachusetts, Church, but difficulties about not only the Lord's Supper but also public prayers prevented a call (*Life*, p. 199).

Emerson received payment for preaching at East Lexington two Sundays in May 1835 and once in the following July from Charles Follen, presumably as a supply minister (*L*, II, 6). After his second marriage and permanent settlement in Concord he took the nearby pulpit on a regular basis in November 1835 (Cabot, I, 237; *J*, III, 568), though under an agreement lasting only until May 1 of the following year when Emerson supplied his friend Frederic Henry Hedge, visiting from Bangor. At the same time Emerson extended the arrangement whereby he was responsible to supply others when he did not preach (*L*, II, 6, 8). Further flexibility was possible through the practice of exchanges (see *L*, II, 28, 37, 38). A suggestion of improvisation as well as testimony to Emerson's genuine sense of responsibility is implied in a reminiscence written to Emerson more than forty years later by Samuel A. Devens, who remembers that as a young unsettled minister he was requested as supply at East Lexington one Sunday and came to find Emerson already there, "who had come from Concord, fearing the Society would be without a Supply on that Sunday." Devens continues: "Margaret Fuller was there also, having come *with you*, if I am not mistaken. I surely did not like the idea of preaching before two such cultured & critical persons, but agreed to preach half a day if you would preach the other half, which you very kindly did. We all dined at the same house and I remember well the interesting conversation you & Miss Fuller had on Poetry" (*L*, VI, 310). This was probably in late July or early August 1836, during Margaret Fuller's first visit with the Emersons, for later that year Devens received payment from Emerson for preaching at East Lexington (*L*, II, 37).

[1] A. C. McGiffert, *Young Emerson Speaks* (Boston, 1938), pp. 255–256.

Emerson was a celebrity and a minister who had given up a far more prestigious church; the East Lexington congregation, liberal and open to new ideas, was only too pleased to have him. In October 1836 he was told that money had been raised to continue services with the stipulation that he would remain in charge (*L*, II, 79n). The following May, Hedge was again in the pulpit on Emerson's behalf, though writing to be relieved again by Emerson (*L*, II, 73). When Emerson was preparing to go to Providence, Rhode Island, for the dedication of Hiram Fuller's new school in Greene Street in June 1837, he wrote to John Sullivan Dwight, as yet not settled, asking him to "oblige the people of East Lexington & me" (*L*, II, 79). He did so, apparently more than once during the year.[2] But Emerson remained in charge, and the nature of that responsibility is made clear by his letter to William Silsbee, a young graduate of the Divinity School, on November 16, 1837, when Emerson was doubtless concerned with freeing himself for the forthcoming series of Boston lectures on "Human Culture": "Can you oblige the people of East Lexington & me by taking charge of their pulpit for eight or ten Sabbaths from the first Sunday of December — inclusive . . . The only condition of the supply is that when you do not go yourself, you must give them the very best preacher you can. I hate that they should be ill served, which has happened, as sometimes it must. I am accountable for the remuneration of the clergyman" (*L*, II, 103).

Although his solicitude for the congregation is evident here, Emerson seems already to have determined to give up preaching at last. His substantial second installment from the Tucker estate the previous summer may have been a liberating consideration, but the letter to Carlyle on November 2, 1837, doubtless gives the primary motive: "I find myself so much more and freer on the platform of the lecture-room than in the pulpit, that I shall not much more use the last; and do now only in a little country chapel at the request of simple men to whom I sustain no other relation than that of preacher. But I preach in the Lecture-Room and then it tells, for there is no prescription. You may laugh, weep, reason, sing, sneer, or pray, according to your genius. It is the

[2] George Willis Cooke, *John Sullivan Dwight* (Boston, 1898), p. 17.

new pulpit, and very much in vogue with my northern country-men" (*CEC*, p. 171).

The "new pulpit" engaged his attention, and while Emerson was apparently allowed great freedom by the liberal people of East Lexington — he was "not hampered in his manner of conducting the service," according to Edward Emerson (*J*, III, 568) — there was the restraint of the occasion itself. In 1834 he had designed "not to utter any speech, poem, or book that is not entirely & peculiarly my work. I will say at Public Lectures & the like, those things which I have meditated for their own sake & not for the first time with a view to that occasion" (*A*, 100). An irony may have emerged as Emerson repeatedly read to the East Lexington Church old sermons, written before his resignation from the Second Church. On one such reading, according to family remembrances, he stopped and commented, "The passage which I have just read *I do not believe*, but it was wrongly placed."[3] He did not, apparently, write new sermons, but McGiffert says that at East Lexington Emerson often read in the afternoon services lectures from his Boston courses and supplemented at least two old sermons with passages from lectures.[4] Certainly the occasion of Sunday sermons, mitigated by whatever improvisation, violates the spirit if not the letter of Emerson's resolve.

Within two weeks of the conclusion of his highly successful Boston course on "Human Culture," Emerson freed himself from the preaching obligation at East Lexington — or nearly so. On February 18, 1838, he told the committee of the Church that he wanted "to put off my charge & if possible commit it to Mr Dwight" (*L*, II, 113), but, as he wrote to Dwight, who still had no church, the committee was pleased that he was "disposed to come, the committee for themselves, — and they think it agreeable to all. But they are so systematically prudent that they think it will for the present be better if I engage to supply the desk, and then send you, than if they agree with you at first hand." He goes on to explain that he will go once or twice in person before May 1, when his current obligation was to expire, and then "re-

[3] Edward Waldo Emerson, *Emerson in Concord* (Boston, 1889), p. 68.
[4] McGiffert, *Young Emerson Speaks*, pp. xxxvii–xxxviii.

new the engagement, but with the understanding that you are to take the entire charge, only calling me in if any particular contingency should make it desireable." [5] The letter he wrote to Lidian Emerson the same day makes it clear that the committee felt this arrangement would "give the people more satisfaction" than an outright call to Dwight.

In both letters Emerson mitigates the residual charge and declares his amused astonishment "to arrive at the dignity of patronage"; but that the step was important to him and to his wife is only partially concealed behind his levity: "But does not the eastern Lidian my Palestine mourn to see the froward man cutting the last threads that bind him to that prized gown & band the symbols black & white of old & distant Judah?" (*L*, II, 113–114). The announcement to William Emerson is incidental to money matters, but again suggests a significance in relation to vocation: "But henceforth perhaps I shall live by lecturing which promises to be good bread. I have relinquished my ecclesiastical charge at E Lexington & shall not preach more except from the Lyceum" (*L*, II, 120). Emerson made himself generally unacceptable as a preacher the following July with the Divinity School address.

Dwight did not prosper at East Lexington, "being absent more than half of the time," according to his biographer, and finally was not called to settle there permanently. During the year he was, however, productive as a reviewer, critic, and translator of the minor poems of Goethe and Schiller. By May 1839 he was at last ordained in a church of his own in Northampton, Massachusetts. From the beginning he was looked upon with suspicion for his transcendental Unitarianism, and in a brief but happily engaged year of liberal innovation in the Church and of literary activity outside, he ended his ministry and went on to Brook Farm and to a distinguished career as a music critic. [6]

Charles Follen was called back from a church in New York and settled as regular minister at East Lexington in 1839, relieving Emerson at last from his nominal obligation. Without even the "mere bubble responsibility" which the East Lexington com-

[5] Cooke, *John Sullivan Dwight*, p. 18.
[6] Cooke, *John Sullivan Dwight*, pp. 18–47.

mittee had been "pleased to blow" (*L*, II, 121) when he placed Dwight in the pulpit, Emerson could not but be pleased with the development of the church under Follen, a promising representative of the newness. Born in Germany in 1796, he was graduated from Giessen as Doctor of Civil Law, where he became a lecturer, but for political reasons was forced to flee to Paris and again to Switzerland, finally settling at Basel. In 1824 he again fled, by this time having considerable reputation as a dangerous republican, and came to Boston where he studied theology with William Ellery Channing. He was considered for the associate pastorate at the Second Church in 1829, when instead Emerson was called (*L*, I, 260; Cabot, I, 145). After a lectureship in ecclesiastical history (1825) at the Divinity School, he became in 1830 the first professor of German literature at Harvard College. His strong abolitionism cost him his professorship at Harvard in 1834, and his liberal religious views as defined in *Religion and the Church* (1836) aligned him with the transcendental ministers.[7] Well known as a lecturer on various controversial and liberal causes, Follen also made a number of innovations in the relations of the congregations, even as Dwight was doing in Northampton; the conversational meetings which he introduced and the placement of the pulpit near the center of his new church were both directed against the formality of the priesthood.[8] The new church building was symbolic of the successful and promising installation of the liberal spirit of Follen.

Though the controversy which followed on the Divinity School address must have been painful to all of Emerson's friends, the people of East Lexington could not have been shocked by its content. Regardless of the threat to whatever some Unitarians wished to call orthodox theology, there is no attack upon those forms of religion, those institutions, which may yet have spirit breathed into them: in his call to "do what we can to rekindle the smouldering, nigh quenched fire on the altar" Emerson had said to the young candidates: "I confess, all attempts to project and establish a Cultus with new rites and forms, seem to

[7] William R. Hutchison, *The Transcendental Ministers* (New Haven, 1959), pp. 32, 48–50.
[8] Cooke, *John Sullivan Dwight*, pp. 39–40.

me vain . . . Rather let the breath of new life be breathed by you through the forms already existing." And he found in the existing churches "Two inestimable advantages": the Sabbath and "the institution of preaching" (W, I, 149–150). There is no quarrel in this with his own years at East Lexington nor with the promise of the new church under Follen.

A year and a half later there was still no reason for estrangement. The lectures on "The Present Age," only half delivered when Emerson came to the dedication, provide, not unexpectedly, the context for his brief address. In the lectures Emerson asserted that the coming era is the era of the Soul. The great fact of the present age, as of all ages, is the uprise of the Soul, even though not a conscious fact to many. Most consciously, the present age is an age of analysis, which makes it wholly compatible with tradition, but signs of fidelity and abdication of will give joyous auguries. For all Emerson's generalization about the formalism of the Church, the decay of religion, the congregation in East Lexington was of the Movement Party, the Party of the Future. When in the lectures he asked where religion has found its lodging, his answer was: "It lurks in the philanthropic assemblies and in the private efforts which urge these Reforms . . . in the chapels and committees which preach Peace, Temperance, the freedom of the servant and the slave." The East Lexington Church under Follen promised this in distinction to the "corpse-cold Unitarianism" of Brattle Street and State Street. There was other hope in January 1840. If Emerson had chosen to preach in the lecture-hall, other transcendental ministers were in the pulpit: aside from the promising ministries of Dwight, Hedge, and Follen, Orestes Brownson had his Society for Christian Union and Progress; the following year James Freeman Clarke would gather his Church of the Disciples; and George Ripley and John Pierpont, who finally preached the dedicatory sermon at East Lexington, were both headed toward immediate reformatory crises in their conservative Boston churches.

In Follen's first invitation to Emerson and in his urgent reminder eight days later, the dedication was to have been in December. Emerson apparently wrote a letter saying he could not come (see L, II, 236), but another exchange must have fixed the date at January 15, 1840. Channing finally could not preach and Follen planned to, but the change in plans meant that Follen, who was lecturing in New York in January, was to return by steamer for the occasion. Follen lost his life in the burning of the *Lexington* in New York Sound on January 13, 1840, and the dedication proceeded without knowledge of the disaster, as Emerson wrote a few days later: "I was on Wednesday at the dedication of the new Church at East Lexington, & took a part in it. All the morning the people expected the arrival of Dr Follen, & a sleigh was waiting in Boston until afternoon to bring him to L. As he did not come, Mr Pierpont preached. And the next day they learned these dire explanations . . . But of this nothing can be said" (*L*, II, 251). Emerson may have learned about the disaster on the evening of the dedication, when he lectured in Boston on "Reforms."

Memorial services for Follen were to be held by Channing at his Federal Street Church in Boston, but Follen was controversial enough to cause the Church to cancel Channing's plans. However, the modest structure in East Lexington, "Pleasing to the eye of the passing traveller," still stands as a memorial to Follen. In alluding to "the graceful circumference of these walls" which in turn may be "circumscribed by a higher truth," Emerson anticipates the central image of "Circles." But he alludes also to the design of the building which, unconventionally octagonal, approximates a circle: the physical church is but a "narrow circuit" out of which a great light and a great heat may go. The antithesis of physical and spiritual; past and future; tradition and hope are characteristic of Emerson's lectures on "The Present Age."

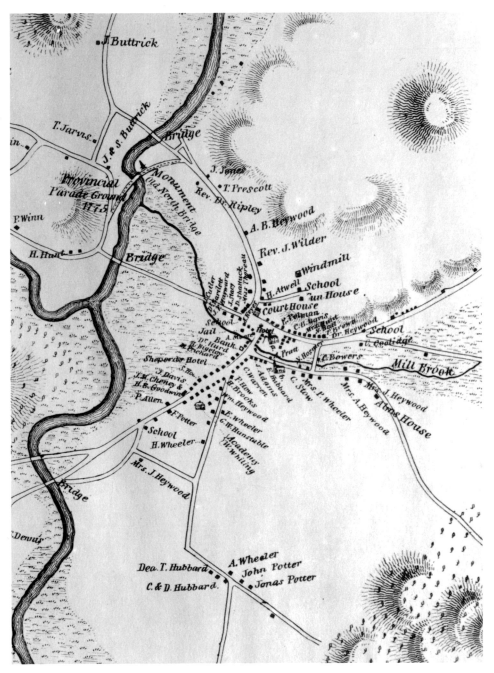

Central detail from "Plan of the Town Concord, Mass. in the County of Middlesex. Surveyed by John G. Hales. Published by Lemuel Shattuck— Boston, 1830."

II.137

I believe that those facts words & persons which dwell in a man's memory without his being able to say why, remain because they have a relation to him not less real for being as yet unapprehended. They are symbols of value to him as they can interpret parts of his consciousness which he would vainly seek words for in the conventional images of books & other minds. What therefore attracts my attention shall have it, as I will go to the man who knocks at my door, whilst a thousand persons as worthy, go by it to whom I give no regard. It is sufficient that these particulars speak to me. A few anecdotes, a few traits of character, manners, face, a few incidents, have an emphasis in your memory out of all proportion to their apparent significance, if you

II.137

From "Human Life 3." See pp. 37–38.

tion to go with it & to say what it is in the act of doing. It is always represented in a transition from that which is representable to the senses, to that which is not. Then first it ceases to be a stone. And the same remark holds of painting. And of poetry, Landor finely asks, "Whether it is not to be referred to some purer state of sensation & existence?" So must it be with Beauty. Then first is it charming & itself, when it dissatisfies us with any end; when it becomes a story without an end; when it suggests gleams & visions, & not earthly satisfactions; when it seems "too bright & good for humane nature's daily food." When it makes the beholder feel ~~his~~ unworthiness; when he cannot feel ~~all his right~~ ~~altered in theon~~ his right to it though he were Caesar; he cannot feel more right than to the firmament and the splendors of a sunset.

From "Human Life 4." See p. 60.

(This old age; this inveteration; this ossification of the heart; this petrification of the brain; this degeneracy — is the Fall of Man. The Redemption from this ruin is lodged in the heart of Youth.] [By resistance to this strong Custom & strong Sense, — by obedience to the soul, is the world to be saved.] The Saviour is as eternal as the harm. The heart of Youth is the regenerator of society; the perpetual hope; the incessant effort of recovery. To every young man & young woman, the world puts the same question, "Wilt thou be come one of us?" And to this question the soul in each one of them says, heartily, NO. Well for it if it can abide by its Protest. It is the voice of virtue It is the breath of Hope it is the pledge of God. The world has no interest so deep as to cherish that resistance No matter though this young heart do not yet understand itself; do not know well what it wants; knows nothing

From "Human Life 6." See p. 90.

risks he may no longer run. He is oppressed
by the melancholy discovery not that he incurs
misfortunes here & there but that his Genius whose invisible benevolence was tower
& shield to him is not longer present or
active.

It will be perceived at once that this
supernatural favoritism
personal aid & favor is allied with
a large class of superstitious facts; with the
revelations of ghosts which are a selecting tribe
speaking to one & avoiding millions;
with the traditions respecting fairies, angels, of saints,
scarcely less partial; the whole agents & the
                                 as
means of magic, magicians & amulets.
                                          faith in a
It will also be perceived that this power
partial
supposed power, so easily sliding into the
popular belief every where in its grosser
forms, & in the particular of lucky
days & fortunate persons as common
in Boston today as the faith in mean

From "Human Life 10." See p. 162.

[In looking around for some topic sufficiently general to include the various thoughts which from time to time occur present themselves to the mind of a retired scholar & which seemed to him fit to be imparted, & sufficiently definite to promise some convenient method, I found none so proper as the Character [Resources & Tendencies] of the Present Age. I hope it will not appear that I have selected a subject too little or too great. In the first place, I would not cripple myself by directing my attention on the interests of the Day, excluding myself from those treasures of past literature & history nor from those questions of philosophy, to which each man ought to guard his access as the high privilege of a rational being. And why need I need not.] For what is the Age? It is what the being is who beholds it. It is transparent to every man

From "The Present Age 1." See p. 186.

II.58 Tendencies

The other terror that scares us from self-trust is the bug bear of consistency — a reverence for our past act or word because the eyes of others have no other data for computing our orbit than our past acts & we are loth to disappoint them.

A foolish consistency is the hobgoblin of little minds adored by little statesmen & philosophers & divines. With consistency a great soul has simply nothing to do. He may as well concern himself about his shadow on the wall. Put your guarded lips. Sew them up with packthread; do. Else if you would be a man speak what you think today in words as hard as cannonballs & tomorrow speak what tomorrow

From "The Present Age 10." See p. 310.

15

We have suffered ourselves to live so
casually that we have defiled our own
houses to that degree that they suggest
to us places of indulgence & mere com
fort or outward convenience, & not
the residence of sacred & awful pleasures,
So that when Poetry & the joys of the
imagination are spoken of, we instantly
run from home to seek for it; ~~into~~
we run into memory, we run into
futurity, into early youth, into cottages,
into mines, into feudal keeps, or Arab
tents, or Iceland huts underground. And
yet the Genius of Poetry is here. He
worships in this land also, not by immi
gration but he is Yankee born. He is
in the forest walks, in paths carpeted
with leaves of the chestnut, the oak, & pine;
he sits on the mosses of the mountain;
he listens by the echoes of the wood; he
paddles his canoe in the rivers & ponds.
He visits without fear the factory

From "The Times 3." See pp. 361–362.

Address to the People of East Lexington

The manuscript of Emerson's brief address to the congregation he had preached to for nearly three years is sewn, complete, and in excellent condition; its leaves are numbered in ink and some headed "Lexington." On the cover, in Emerson's hand, is "Address to the people of East Lexington on the Dedication of their Church 15 Jan. 1840."

Emerson used one passage of the address in "The Over-Soul," and Cabot took two passages for "The Sovereignty of Ethics," printed in the *North American Review*, CXXVI (May–June 1878), 404–420, and reprinted in 1883 in *Lectures and Biographical Sketches*. This essay was a version of a lecture Cabot prepared for Emerson to read in 1877. Since there are small differences between the passages as printed in the essay and the 1840 manuscript version, it is possible either that Emerson authorized minor revisions in 1877 or that Cabot drew from an intermediate source. This address is not listed among the numerous lecture sources which Edward Emerson lists for "The Sovereignty of Ethics," which he calls "the best mosaic" Cabot could make of the materials (*W*, X, 549).

I REJOICE with you, my friends, in the grateful occasion which convenes us today. Pleasing to the eye of the passing traveller is this new edifice with which you have adorned the side of the publc road. More lively content it gives to those passengers who know you and partake of your zeal in this enterprize. A deeper satisfaction will the graceful circumference of these walls yield to you who have planned and constructed them and to you who see with serenity a house now secured to great and worthy associations. But in naming these gradations of joy in your new work I do not exhaust the degrees of interest which this house will awaken. Life is a song of degrees, and every action and work of man. Round every thought of ours is already dwelling a greater thought into which after some time we enter, and find it in turn circumscribed by a higher truth. And this because we hold not of the finite but of the infinite and our highest success is only comparative success, — is success seen beside the past, but failure and poverty contrasted with the future to which it invites us. Let me then pursue so natural a thought and invite you to no easy and cheap contentment with your present achievement but to that pious on-look of the Soul which counts gain loss beside the splendors of its hope.

It needs no ghost to tell that[1] the building of a church is often as profane a business as the building of a hotel; not more, not less. It betrays on the part of the builders prudence and some knowledge of the dependence of public order on private good habits. It may proceed from a love of liturgy, and of psalmody; from pleasure in partaking in a quiet social ceremony, and the circumstance of a tasteful and intellectual entertainment, from a desire of the contagion of good thoughts and influences. But, o my brothers, when we have carried it up to the best designs on which churches are ordinarily built, there yet remains a whole paradise beyond unattained. The Holy still soars above us, let us mount as high as we will, and is as far above the heights of thought as from the chaffering of the market.[2] Have you meditated ever upon the meaning and nature of Trust? Have you said to yourself ever, I abdicate all choice? I see it is not for me to interfere. I see that I have been one of the crowd, that I have been a pitiful person because I have wished to be my own master and to dress and order my whole way and system of living. I thought I managed it very well — I see that my neighbors think so. I have heard prayers, I have prayed even, but I have never up to this moment dreamed that this undertaking the entire management of my own affair was not commendable. I have never seen until now that it was small and made me small. I have never seen until this blessed ray flashed just now through my soul from side to side that there dwelt any power in Nature that loved me, that cared for me, that would relieve me of my load — but now I see.[3] I see that there is guidance for the childlike — I have been

---

[1] Shakespeare, *Hamlet,* I, 5:124–125.

[2] E, 46.

[3] "Have you said . . . now I see" ("The Sovereignty of Ethics," W, X, 196–197).

too soon a man — I see that all the great and generous have been so by their docility to the supernatural — I see, I hear the gracious condescensions of eternal goodness unto me. Resign thyself, o my son, it saith to me: suffer thyself to be led and thou shalt put off thy dwarfish proportions, thine early decrepitude and for that poor load of fagots which thou callest prosperity and wealth, I will give thee Peace and Love, I will give thee myself, and thou shalt be divine. Over thee, over me, over each of these wondrous pilgrims of time, broods alway this everlasting Love soliciting us in silent moments to surrender our officious activity to it. In doing thus, the heart is made wise and the tongue inspired. And instead of our former contemptible relations to a plot of ground, or a stock of merchandise, to a few men and a few women to whom we were holden by some tie of interest or of ease, lo! suddenly we belong to the world. We love all men. We have ceased to be strangers in Nature; the sun and the moon beam friendly on us. We feel that they exist from the same deep cause that is instilling waves of balm in our heart. To good men, as we call good men, this doctrine of Trust is an unsounded secret. They use the word: they have accepted a notion of a mechanical supervision of human affairs by which that certain wonderful King whom they call God, does take up their affairs where their intelligence leaves them, and somehow knits and coordinates the issues of them in all that is beyond the reach of private faculty. They do not see that He, that It is there, next, and within, is the thought of the thought, the affair of affairs; that he is existence; and take him from them and they would not be. They do not see that all particulars are sacred and beautiful and dear to him as well as the scope and outline of all: that these passages of daily life are his magical work: that the moment they recede from the belittling interference of a sensual will these particulars take sweetness and grandeur and become the language of mighty principles.[4] Men have yet to learn the depth and beauty of the doctrine of trust. O believe as thou livest, that every sound that is spoken over the round world which thou oughtest to hear will vibrate on thine ear. Every proverb, every book, every byword,

[4] "To good men . . . mighty principles" ("The Sovereignty of Ethics," W, X, 193–194).

that belongs to thee for aid or comfort shall surely come home through open or winding passages. Every friend whom not thy fantastic will but the great and tender heart in thee craveth, shall lock thee in his embrace; and this because the heart in thee is the Heart of all: not a valve, not a wall, not an intersection is there anywhere in nature, but one blood rolls uninterruptedly an endless circulation through all men as the water of the globe is all one sea and truly seen its tide is one.[5]

O friends, it was in commemoration of these glad tidings that from time to time in all countries men have erected temples. This enthusiasm, this great ardor that catches them up for a moment into its heights they fall out of, they forget, and blaspheme: but it returns, it bursts out afresh, and is never long absent from the nations. They may well build it churches to refresh their own memory and affection, to certify to their sons that such a thing can be and that the Most High has dwelled with men. But this fatal lapse, this Adam's fall cometh anew to the builder. He builds the church with common and profane purposes quite absent from this celestial estate. Then the church becomes base wood and stone; it is a bed to sleep in; it is a street, a shop, an infirmary merely. And the affirmation in it, if any should be so bold, that God still is in Man will be heard with wrath, with contradiction, with fear and the hands shall be holden to the ears.

Know then that your church is not builded when the last stone, the last rafter and clapboard is laid, not when we have assembled, not when we have adhered to the customary rite, but then first is it a church when the consciousness of his union with the Supreme Soul dawns on the lowly heart of the worshipper — when the church becomes nothing and the priest nothing for all places are sacred and all persons: when he sees that virtue goes out from him and hallows the ground whereon he stands — then instantly the humble church is made alive: its deadwood and stone are warmed and lighted by thought and love. It is alive and maketh alive — it ennobles and binds in one the inmates. It is a point of civilization, of culture, of poetry, of knowledge by which a whole community is educated. It propagates influences to re-

[5] "Men have yet . . . is one" (E, 4); "O believe . . . is one" ("The Over-Soul," W, II, 293–294).

mote countries and to all history. These fair and modest walls may the influx and benediction of God thus hallow and establish! Out of this narrow circuit may a great light and a great heat go that shall enkindle all men. Your hands which have wrought with such energy and visible success may they find that they knew not what they did, that the effect has vastly transcended the cause and the builders gladly disclaim the praise when they see another and a higher spirit which is more themselves than their hands or their purposes taking up their deed and making it divine.

IV

THE TIMES

☞ **R. W. Emerson** proposes to deliver at the Masonic Temple, a Course of Lectures ON THE TIMES. The Course will consist of Eight Lectures, to be delivered once a week, on *Thursday Evenings,* beginning on the 2d December.

Tickets to the course and to the single lecture, for sale at E. P. Peabody's, at Little & Brown's, and at James Munroe & Co's book stores.   nov 6

[Newspaper announcement in the *Boston Daily Advertiser and Patriot,* November 30, 1841]

IN AN analysis of his dissatisfaction at the end of the Boston reading of "The Present Age" Emerson had remembered that the 1839–40 series was begun with the intention to "try this thing once more" (*L*, II, 256; *E*, 119). Perhaps because he was cheered by the attentive young people in his audiences (*CEC*, p. 261), Emerson made no decision, however, to give up lecturing. The fact that he did not give a regular private series at the Masonic Temple in Boston in the winter of 1840–41 seems to have resulted at least in part from the push to complete *Essays* (1841). This effort, already once interrupted by the necessity to lecture in the winter 1839–40, was complicated further by work for *The Dial*, which at last began under Margaret Fuller's editorship with a July 1840 number, by much involvement in the complexities of publishing Carlyle in America, and by Emerson's well established and hospitable way of life in Concord. By the end of August 1840 he wrote to Carlyle: "I can brag little of my diligence or achievement this summer. I dot evermore in my endless journal . . . but the arrangement loiters long . . . Consider, however, that all summer I see a good deal of company, — so near as my fields are to the city. But next winter I think to omit lectures, & write more faithfully. Hope for me that I shall get a book ready to send you by New Years Day." A month later there is a sense of semi-penitent urgency: "I am ashamed to tell you, though it seems most due, anything of my own studies they seem so desultory idle & unproductive. I still hope to print a book of Essays this winter, but it cannot be very large. I write myself into letters, the last few months, to three or four dear & beautiful persons my country-men & women here. I lit my candle at both ends, but will now be colder & scholastic. I mean to write no lectures this winter" (*CEC*, pp. 277–278, 284).

The book was sent to the press on January 1, 1841, though apparently with some work yet to be done, and Emerson turned to preparation of "Man the Reformer," which was read to the Mechanics' Apprentices' Library Association at the Masonic Temple in Boston on January 25. In addition, he is known only to have lectured this winter twice at Concord, once each at Waltham and Worcester, and probably once or twice at Billerica, Massachusetts. The December 9 lecture before the Concord Lyceum may have been the manuscript of "Thoughts on Art," which he was about to send to Margaret Fuller for the January number of *The Dial*, and the lecture there on March 10 may have been the manuscript of "Man the Reformer" revised for publication in the April number of *The Dial* (*L*, II, 365–366, 372, 384). One should not take too seriously Emerson's answer to his brother's query in late December 1840: "No I don't lecture any where. No body asks me, Sir" (*L*, II, 372); he was too busy with his book and too much distracted by other concerns in the winter of 1840–41 to write a new lecture series of his own, and the backlash from the controversy which followed the Divinity School address no doubt continued to discourage invitations from others.

The publication of *Essays* on March 20, 1841, left Emerson with diminished manuscript resources. Even more than in the fall of 1839, when he had had to write extensively for the preparation of "The Present Age," he now had drawn heavily from his journals to date and had used up the best parts of his lecture series, less from "The Present Age" than from those before. *The Dial* was a further drain on his resources. Beginning with his new journal G in the early summer of 1841 and continuing through journal H and that part of journal J which was written before January 20, 1842, Emerson developed almost all of the material that went into his new lecture course, "The Times."

Despite the work in the journals there seems to be little concern on Emerson's part with a new series of lectures until early autumn. Though he had accepted the invitation in April (*L*, II, 390, 392), Emerson did not begin concentrated work on "The Method of Nature," his oration at Waterville College, Maine, until his retreat alone to Nantasket Beach in July. But even there he was unable to bring it to focus as his "outline grew larger & larger," and he rushed home at the end of the month to finish it in time for delivery on August 11 (*L*, II, 413, 421, 427, 434, 439–

440). Only after his return from Maine, apparently, did he first consider, in early September, another lecture course, and in writing to William Emerson he juxtaposed lecturing and the *Essays*: "I begin to recover my pen which has lain on the shelf. Perhaps I shall write more lectures. I hope I shall one day write something better than those poor cramp arid 'Essays' which I almost hate the sight of" (*L*, II, 444). However, after writing "Walter Savage Landor" for the October number of *The Dial*, Emerson found a familiar and compelling reason to turn to lecturing. On October 7 he wrote William: "I must tell you my sad plight again — the City Bank — that rueful institution pays no dividend, so that I go six months more with half a loaf." He continued, explaining that he had lived during the "summer by means of the payments made by Carlyle's booksellers here of monies advanced by me in former months or years," and projected winter plans for recouping his finances: "This winter I must hang out my bush again & try to sell good wine of Castaly at the Masonic Temple. Failing there, I will try the West End of New York or of Philadelphia, or, as I have lately been challenged to do, of Baltimore" (*L*, II, 454).

Ten days later, even before he had fixed on a topic for the lectures, he wrote his brother at length with an awakening enthusiasm for lectures *as a form:* "I believe I shall lecture in Boston this season: But on what topics? Shall it be The Times; or Books; or Ethics; or Manners; or Philosophy? I have a dream sometimes of an eloquence that is still possible that drawing its resources from neither politics nor commerce but from thought, from the moral & intellectual life and duties of each man, shall startle and melt & exalt the ear that heareth, as never the orators of the caucus or the parliament or the forum can. I think these 'lectures' capable of a variety of style & matter which no other form of composition admits. We can laugh & cry, curse & pray, tell stories & crack jokes, spin a web of transcendentalism a thousand times finer than spiderthread or insist on the beauties & utilities of banks, railroads, india rubber shoes & the Cunard line, nay, do all this in one discourse" (*L*, II, 460). More pointedly and perhaps more seriously Emerson wrote to Carlyle at the end of the month in direct reference to the newly arrived English edition of *Essays*: "But no more printing for me at present. I have just decided to go to Boston once more, with a course of lectures, which I will perhaps baptise 'On the Times,' by way of making once again the experiment whether I cannot — not only speak the truth, but speak it truly, or *in proportion*. I fancy, I need more than another to *speak*, with such a formidable tendency to the lapidary style. I build my house of boulders . . . Besides I am always haunted with brave dreams of what might be accomplished in the lecture room — so free & so unpretending a platform, — a Delos not yet made fast — I imagine an eloquence of infinite variety — rich as conversation can be, with anecdote, joke, tragedy, epics & pindarics, argument & confession" (*CEC*, p. 308).

Aside from a renewed excitement about the potential rhetorical variety of the lecture as opposed to other forms of expression, Emerson reveals in these letters a consciousness of stylistic differences between his essays and his lectures. In December 1840, referring to a "poor obsolete essay" in proof for *The Dial*, doubtless "Thoughts on Art," which he had worked up from old lecture material, he noted "that disconnectedness which they say constitutes so eminent a beauty in my style" (*L*, II, 372). This characteristic must have been obvious to him in the last stages of piecing together his book; but if he found the "poor cramp arid 'Essays'" "lapidary" in style, the looseness of *speaking* would be a corrective. Ideally the freest form would be the spontaneous lecture, perhaps a "conversation" such as Margaret Fuller gave. Emerson continued in the letter to Carlyle, who regularly spoke from notes without a prepared text: "I should love myself wonderfully better if I could arm myself to go, as you go, with the word in the heart & not in a paper" (*CEC*, p. 308). But the seasoned lecturer and old sermon writer did not work that way and instead set himself to a freer written expression for the lecture hall.

With this renewed hope for eloquence he had begun to plan his new course sometime in the middle of October, though little can be inferred from the undated lists he jotted down in Notebook Ψ (pp. 166 ff.). There is in a list of available topics a possible suggestion by brackets that "Expression" and "Poet" fall together as one subject and that "Fashion," "Riches & Poverty," and "Screens" are similarly connected. Topics which apparently did not finally come into the course are "Beauty," "Marriage," "Love," "Power of Circumstances," "Apology for Hermits," and "Philosophy." The genesis of the course is difficult to trace, though journals G, H, and J show a great concentration of material for it throughout the fall and early winter of 1841.

He was, for example, much taken with the idea of the early photographic process discovered in 1839 by Louis Daguerre; it suggested to him the creation of accurate portraits, objective in detail, and not filtered through the medium of an artist. On October 21, a little more than a week before he announced his topic to Carlyle, Emerson wrote in a journal: "And why not draw for these times a portrait gallery? The genius of this day does not seem to incline to a deed but rather to a beholding . . . A camera! a camera! cries the century, that is the only toy. Come let us paint the agitator and the dillettante and the member of Congress and the College professor the Unitarian minister the editor of the newspaper the fair contemplative girl, the aspirant for fashion & opportunities the woman of the world who has tried & knows better, — let us examine how well she knows . . . So should we have at last if it were done well a series of sketches which would report to the next ages the color & quality of ours" (H, 98–99, see also H, 76–77, 130, 136).

Emerson did not, of course, take portraits of all those he suggested here, but at least two characteristic types had occupied his thought recently. His views on reformers had already been stated more than once — in "Reforms" two years earlier and more recently in "Man the Reformer," which had followed closely upon something of a personal crisis in his decision in December 1840 not to join George Ripley and other friends at Brook Farm. Emerson, who never clearly and comfortably identified himself as a transcendentalist, was yet attracted and involved with them. "The Protest," in the "Human Life" series, and perhaps whatever he projected in the topic "Apology for Hermits" were related to his concern for one aspect of transcendentalism, the side represented better by Thoreau than by his other young friend Charles King Newcomb. In September 1841 Emerson copied into his journal a provocative passage from a letter lent to him by Mary Moody Emerson: "'The Transcendentalists do not err in excess but in defect . . . They do not hold wild dreams for realities: the vision is deeper broader more spiritual than they have seen. They do not believe with too strong faith: their faith is too dim of sight, too feeble of grasp, too wanting in certainty'" (G, 116–117; cf. L, II, 451). If Emerson did not wholly agree with his Aunt Mary's correspondent, he found an important idea which he would develop in his own way.

If the reformer and the transcendentalist were important representative facts of the times, yet partial and thus defective, why not others? A few characters would do: "I own that all my universal pictures are nothing but private sketches; that I live in a small village, and am obliged to guess at the composition of society from very few & very obscure specimens . . . yet I supposed myself borne out in my confidence that each individual stands for a class by my own experience. Few as I have seen I could do with fewer and I shrink from seeing thousands when in fifteen or twenty I have already many duplicates" (H, 128). The tendency to find universal significance by means of his reportorial method is revealed in his observation "that whatever human trait has been shown in any times is shown in our times," but it is Emerson's wit that saves this thesis from the more ponderous uses to which it might be put: "If you know anything that was in Ctesiphon or Rome, I can find its counterpart in Boston. Was there religion in Jerusalem there is at least criticism in Massachusetts — criticism which appeals to a high, the highest standard" (H, 75–76). Clearly the emphasis, as in "The Present Age," would remain on the actualities of the 1840's.

The middle of November found him "in the rage of preparation for my lectures 'on the Times,'" though he could not "yet accurately divide the topics" (CEC, p. 310). Nearly three weeks later, two days after he had read the first lecture at the Masonic Temple in Boston, he wrote William Emerson his plans for the course: "I read my first Lecture night before last at the Temple. The Audience was much the same in numbers & in character as in former years at the first lecture. I always begin with fewer hearers & our snowball grows a little as it rolls. I am to read but eight lectures instead of ten this winter. I think to take Universal Whiggery for my text next week & perhaps call the lecture 'The Conservative' and perhaps the next following 'The Transcendentalist.' One I have written called 'The Poet' and another in prospect called 'The Fashionist' & so we will go on with our portrait gallery. They told me in town this time that I was grown more direct & intelligible than in former years" (*L*, II, 469).

The idea of drawing characters, a portrait gallery, may not have sustained itself through the remaining weeks of the course. He did not mention in these plans "Character" or "Relation of Man to Nature." These may have been in their original lecture form an obvious continuation of the ideas suggested in the initial lectures, or they may have been fillers. "The Poet," which contains no passages to suggest composition after the beginning of November, may have been on hand because it had been written for the Concord Lyceum and read there as "Nature and Powers of the Poet" on November 3, 1841. It is difficult, however, to comment on the course as a whole since it survives in lecture form so fragmentarily.

The eight lectures were read at the Masonic Temple in Boston, beginning on December 2, 1841, and continuing on successive Thursday nights through January 20, 1842. Their order in Boston was "Introduction," "The Conservative," "The Poet," "The Transcendentalist," "Manners," "Character," "Relation of Man to Nature," "Prospects" (Charvat, p. 19). A week before the conclusion of the Boston course Emerson seemed not to have definite plans for carrying the lectures elsewhere; he wrote to his brother in New York: "I think I will not cast my hook in your great bay, but if I find on reckoning my estate that I need pence I will go into the provinces, say Providence" (*L*, III, 4). Ten days later he had cast his accounts and found he must certainly go to Providence — "possibly to Plymouth also — so far will the love of *paying debts* draw me. In Boston my course has paid me about $320.00 or about $40. for each lecture. One year I received $57.00. And I find by my best ciphering that I stand in need of about $200.00 more" (*L*, III, 5).

On January 27 Waldo Emerson died of scarlatina; but two weeks later, on February 10, the grieving father had to begin his lectures in Providence. His plans to come home for the weekend, after two lectures, to comfort the sad remnant of his family were frustrated by difficulties in scheduling, and he remained away a little more than a week, giving a combined lecture of "Introduction" and "The Conservative" the first night, followed by "The Poet," "The Transcendentalist," an unnamed lecture from the course, and "Prospects." The audience was "a very friendly & faithful one, but is small," and Emerson could see "no help" but to "go to New York" (*L*, III, 10–13). There he read six lectures at the Society Library from March 3 through March 14 in the following order, which differs slightly from the earlier readings: "Introduction," "The Poet," "The Conservative," "The Transcendentalist," "Manners," "Prospects." The course was reviewed favorably by *The Evening Post*, with some complaint of incoherence, and William Emerson reported that the course had "produced a marked sensation in the best part of our community, & has created for him many lovers & admirers here." On his return home Emerson recorded that his lectures, attended by three or four hundred people and yielding a net profit of about two hundred dollars, "had about the same reception there as elsewhere: very fine and poetical, but a little puzzling. One thought it 'as good as a kaleidoscope.' Another, a good Staten Islander, would go hear, 'for he had heard I was a rattler' " (*L*, III, 14, 21; K, 11).

Only two of the eight lectures in this series, "The Poet" and "Prospects," survive in manuscript and are therefore included in this volume; three were published in *The Dial* and the manuscripts no longer exist; the remaining three were probably absorbed into essays with the result that these manuscripts have also been lost or destroyed.

Partly because the lectures read in New York were reported in the "penny papers" (*CEC*, p. 321) and partly because *The Dial* needed good prose, Emerson published in three successive numbers of that journal "Introductory Lecture on the Times" (July 1842), "Lectures on the Times. II. The Conservative" (October 1842), and "Lectures on the Times. III. The Transcendentalist" (January 1843). Edward Emerson indicated that the essay "Manners," published in *Essays, Second Series*, was the lecture by that name from "The Times" (*W*, III, 315n). Certainly there is internal evidence to support this assertion, but it is equally certain that there were additions after the lecture was read. Similarly, his statement that part of the essay "Character" in *Essays, Second Series* was in the 1842 lecture of the same name seems sound (*W*, III, 310n). Only a few rejected leaves from the lecture manuscript survive and are printed here in the textual notes. The "certain stray leaves" from what Edward Emerson called "Relation to Nature" (presumably the lecture from "The Times," though he errs in dating it) have not been identified. Yet his suggestion that the lecture was revised for publication as "Nature" in *Essays, Second Series* (*W*, III, 328n) is again supported by the internal evidence of many journal passages from the date of composition of the lectures and again qualified by the evidence of journal passages from later dates. A sizeable section of this essay, including parts which may well have been in the 1842 lecture, Emerson published as "Tantalus" in *The Dial* for January 1844. Ralph L. Rusk identified the second essay "Nature" with the chapter by that name which Emerson said he "could not finish to my mind" for inclusion in the 1841 volume (*Life*, p. 300; *L*, II, 387). If this is true, Emerson may well have used the leftover essay as the basis for his lecture "Relation of Man to Nature," but again there were further revisions after the winter of 1841–42.

In March 1842 Emerson wrote to Carlyle that during the coming summer he "must try to set in order a few more chapters from these rambling lectures [on "The Times"], one on 'the Poet' & one on 'Character' at least" (*CEC*, p. 321). Aside from the three lectures printed and identified in *The Dial*, then, it is reasonable to suppose that three others were revised in such a way that the lecture manuscripts were consumed in the process, perhaps even serving partially as printer's copy. That the manuscript of the lecture "The Poet" was not so consumed is owing to extensive rewriting on the subject for the essay, which contains only a few passages from the lecture. "Prospects" was partially mined for *Essays, Second Series* in about the same way earlier lectures had been and thus survives in manuscript.

The fact that only two of the original eight lectures survive in manuscript indicates an important shift both in Emerson's method of composition and in the relationship between the spoken and published forms of his work. The series on "The Times" indicates that he was becoming aware of a new kind of speaking eloquence which he juxtaposed to the "lapidary style" of *Essays* (1841). The stylistic development from the hortatory pulpit eloquence of "The Philosophy of History" to a new style which he now thought of as based on truthful observation, with a stronger implication of detachment than before, can at least in part be attributed to his finding on the lecture platform an opportunity for the variety of tone, the play of wit, and the subtlety of indirection which he had lost in the first *Essays*, but which he now found could, in lecture form, be carried over directly into print. The process of reworking his lectures for the 1841 collection had doubtless taught him much about his own writing.

Taken separately, the three lectures which he published in *The Dial* have great merit as examples of Emerson's strongest writing, but they lose much of their context without "The Poet" and "Prospects." The reformer, the conservative, and the transcendentalist are dealt with sympathetically, but Emerson's sympathy for them falls short of his deeper emotional involvement in the poet, the expresser. They fail to live up to the basic theme of the series, as defined in "Prospects": they lack "an exuberance of nature requiring a correspondent receptiveness and ardor of obedience in man to carry out her great tendencies." They are defective as full representatives even of these times, for, Emerson adds: "Of this richness and prodigality the Present Age seems to me to partake." "Everything is good but this pursing of the lips and the pretension to have already learned." It is this lack of expectant, joyous receptiveness that lies behind the early choosing of sides between "the party of Conservatism and that of Innovation" and creates the partialism, the cloud that hangs on the American brow, "the tone of sorrow and anxiety which characterizes so much of the speculation of the present times."

These two previously unpublished lectures are therefore an important addition to the Emerson canon at a critical point in his intellectual development. They do not easily support the common assumption of Emerson's growing acquiescence to circumstance at this time, nor do they simply signify a literal shift in his concerns from pure thought to actualities. Yet it is difficult to avoid finding in what we have of this series of lectures a new departure for his thought, not yet wholly articulated, but suggestive of future expansion.

The decision to extend the range of his lecturing outside New England — first to New York, Philadelphia, and Baltimore; then to England; and later to the West — is also important as marking a major step in his career. It of course attests his growing reputation, and if not immediately, at least potentially, it opened the way to far greater financial success. More important, it was the means of escape from the restricting confines of the Unitarian controversy, which had provided his first opportunity to attract public attention and then, with the public reaction to the challenge of the Divinity School address, had closed in around him in spite of his efforts to remain detached. The expansion out of eastern New England represents a professional maturity, a cutting loose from his first statement and a movement on to other, less provincial subjects and to new and less limited audiences. The series on "New England" in 1843 opened this new phase of his career.

3

The Poet

On November 3, 1841, Emerson lectured at the Concord, Massachusetts, Lyceum on "Nature and the Powers of the Poet" (Charvat, p. 19). The manuscript of this lecture has not been identified, and Cabot does not mention it in his list of lectures in the *Memoir*. The title is third in a list of seven, lacking "Prospects," which Emerson jotted down just below a draft of the announcement for the Boston course on "The Times" (Notebook Ψ, 166). Two days after the course began the subjects were not all settled, according to a letter he wrote his brother William, but "One I have written called 'The Poet'" (*L*, II, 469). Since the lecture does not fit well into what we know of Emerson's plan for the course, it is possible that it was written earlier for another purpose, read at Concord on November 3, and then incorporated into "The Times" and read at the Masonic Temple in Boston on December 16. It was repeated as the second lecture in the series at Providence, Rhode Island, on February 12, 1842, and as second in the series in New York on March 5.

Edward Emerson noted that little of this lecture had been printed. There are surprisingly few and insignificant passages used in "The Poet," *Essays, Second Series* (1844). A few sentences were printed in "Poetry and Imagination" and a long passage in "Eloquence," both published in 1875 in *Letters and Social Aims*, which was edited by Cabot after Emerson's breakdown, though according to Cabot, Emerson had got "Poetry and Imagination" to one unsatisfactory stage of proofs (*W*, X, x) and "Eloquence" was basically, at least, a lecture Emerson had read in 1867. Though Edward Emerson wrote, "My own feeling is to publish it among other early papers," he did not do so, and it is here published for the first time as a significant statement quite different from the famous essay with the same title.

The manuscript is complete. On the first page it is identified as "Lecture III. *The Poet*" in ink in Emerson's hand. It is incompletely paginated in ink in the upper right, and the sequence is also indicated on the rectos of leaves (or on the recto of the first page of double sheets) by pencil numbers. There are three leaves printed in the textual notes which are identified in Emerson's hand as "Poet" but which have never been sewn with the other leaves and do not seem to belong to the lecture as first read. The first paragraph has been cancelled in pencil but has been retained in the text as the introduction to the lecture.

I INVITE the attention of the audience to a consideration of the nature and offices of the Poet: to the power he exerts and the means and materials he employs; to the part he plays in these times, and is likely to play. I hope I shall not terrify any dear lover of poetry who regards it with a species of religion, and hears with alarm as a sort of sacrilege, that criticism so busy in these days threatens now at last to seize this mountain flower, and pick it to pieces with unhallowed fingers. Let me appease at once such apprehensions by declaring my persuasion, that the thing is impossible. If I were not, as I am, a devout lover of the Muse, I must still feel that its nature is not in danger from critics, that it is something not to be reached by criticism.

As one relates eagerly anecdotes of the youth or private life of an eminent person and collects minute particulars of his behavior, how he stood, how he looked, how he dressed, and does not thereby slake but inflame the curiosity of the hearer, so is it with the best analysis of poetry which we can make. You can tell me anecdotes of the Muse, — but there is no fear that you will exhaust or dispose finally of a subject so subtle and evasive.

I think of poetry as of that angel which sits on the highest and most inaccessible cliff of all the mountain round which the hierarchies are ranged. It is a presence you cannot profane. On its person hands were never laid, — never can be laid. It bids defiance to the pursuer. If you come where it was, lo! it has departed and glitters in the distance like a planet; for its essence is inviolable, it is ever wild and new.

If then we proceed to inquire what we know of that element which is called Poetry, we shall find it to be no solitary fact, but one so intertwined with the nature of all things, that it is by no means easy to separate it, and say what is Poetry, and what is not. Your definition is sure to be too large, or too small. Poetry finds its origin in that *need of expression* which is a primary impulse of nature. Every thought in man requires to be uttered, and his whole life is an endeavor to embody in facts the states of the mind. When he lays out a garden, or builds a house or a ship, when he frames a law, or plans a colony, or a war, or when he seeks to inform an individual or an assembly of his views, you see the need he stands in and the joy he finds in unbosoming himself, and contemplating his thought in a new form, on the face of the world, or in the minds of other men. When my thought has passed into a thing, I am one step farther on my way. To be unfolded, explained, expressed, that is the boon we crave of the Universe. The man is only half himself; the other half is his Expression,[1] or the aggregate of his saying and doing. That man is serene who does not feel himself pinched and wronged by his condition but whose condition in general and in particular allows the utterance of his mind; and that man who cannot utter himself goes moaning all the day. Does happiness depend on "uninterrupted prosperity," as it is called? Oh no, but on Expression. Expression is prosperity. I must say what is burning here: I must do what I shall perish if I cannot do, I must appear again in my house, in my fortune, in my marriage, in my speech, or else I must disappear, and the brute form must crowd the soul out of nature.[2] All possessions must obey and paint my thought, and, failing this, all the aids and advantages you can add to me are mountains of aggravation and impediment. That makes, and that only, the value of Old Age, — that it gives ample vent to all the parts and needs of the individual character.[3] That is the value of wealth, that it is external freedom, and allows the man to conform the general outline of his condition to his thought and to signify his bent and tendency in his house and lands, in his possessions, and the disposition of his time. That is the esteem of Eloquence, that it is a wondrous power to report the inner man adequately to multitudes of men, and bring one man's character to bear on others.

All the facts of the animal and organic economy, — Sex, Nutriment, Gestation, Birth, Growth, are emphatic symbols of this

[1] "The Poet," W, III, 5.
[2] "That man is serene . . . out of nature" (H, 57).
[3] H, 57.

eternal fact of the passage of the world into the soul of man to suffer there a change, and reappear a new and higher fact, another yet the same.[4]

Expression; — all we do, all we say, all we see, is that, or for that. The reason for doing or avoiding anything is, that, in one fact I am represented, — in the other not. The love of nature, what is it, but that I find with wonder in the landscape certain high portraiture of my thoughts and emotions? For the same reason I follow particular persons: they do justice to my opinions and wishes. I love Guy, because he expresses my thought: I hate Jeffrey, because he does not. Am I warlike? Am I smitten with a rage for prodigious energy of action? I follow some Napoleon or Nelson as his shadow. Am I bound to certain local or political objects? It is easy to see how the head of a party can draw my regard. Every artist draws me so. Taglioni must dance,[5] and Paganini play.

In every feat of genius the beholder feels his latent and slumbering powers vindicated. If Paganini "with three or four whips of his bow elicited points of sound as bright as the stars"; if it appeared to the audience that "he drew from the strings tones more than human which seemed to be wrung from the anguish of a broken heart, and in his hands the violin appeared to be some wild animal which he was endeavoring to quiet in his bosom, and which he occasionally lashes with his bow, — tearing from the creature the most alarming, fearful, horrid, as well as the most delightful tones," [6] — what is the origin of our enjoyment but an apprisal of our own power, — that the range of human articulation reaches higher and lower than we had yet found, and every hearer goes away to copy or appropriate to himself as far as he can the new art?

The world runs to see some perfect dancer, some incomparable Taglioni or Bayadere,[7] to admire the wisdom of the feet, —

---

[4] "The Poet," W, III, 21.

[5] Maria Taglioni (1804–1884) was the best known of a celebrated family of European ballet dancers.

[6] "If Paganini . . . delightful tones" (condensed from T, 51; William Gardiner, *Music of Nature* [London, 1832], p. 220).

[7] Bayaderes, female Hindu temple dancers, were widely known after a troupe of them came to Paris in 1839.

not certainly to see the leaps of the rope dancer, the impossible in attitude performed, but to rejoice in the grace of movement in wavelike form and action, in the fun of the coquetries, in the beautiful erectness of the body and the freedom and determination of her carriage, and in the perfect sympathy with the house, the mixture of deference with conscious superiority which puts her in perfect spirits and equality to her part. When the fair creature curtsies, her sweet and slow and prolonged Salam which descends and still descends until she seems to have found new depths of grace and condescension, earns well the profusion of bouquets and flowers which are hurled on the stage. But what is her charm for the spectators other than this, that she dances for them, or they dance in her feet, not being, — fault of some defect in their forms or education, — able to dance themselves? We must be expressed. In our wooden and prosaic ways of life, we seem to have lost our muscular vigor and alacrity, and still more we are bound up and pinioned in woolen and leather, in steel and india-rubber, so that we seem to walk with our feet alone and not with our whole person; — and to see the body in some graceful specimen as God made it, free for motion and delighting in the infinite variety of movement, is some indemnity and refreshment. Hence the cheer and exhilaration which the spectacle imparts.[8]

If one considers the hunger with which men seek spectacles of every sort where anything rare and extreme in its kind is done, whether theatres, galleries, angry debates, the circus, the ring, land or naval battles; foreign cities, countries, savage tribes, men will seem to him a race of children running up and down for that end only, — to be gratified with the exhibition of a good deliverance of every fancy of the brain.

This need of expression is thus the cause of our action and of the love of spectacles or witnessing what is extraordinary in the action of others. But besides the need which every man has of doing something, and making his mark somewhere, which is the first result of the eternal impulse at the heart of things, it needs

---

[8] "The world runs . . . spectacle imparts" (H, 64–65, modified, Emerson's account of seeing the Austrian ballerina Fanny Elssler).

that not only his will, or the direction of his practical faculties should have this justice done it, but that his science or his perception of things in the intellect, should have an expression also.

To this need and desire the world or the face of nature very readily lends itself — so expressive, so changeable, so fruitful in names and methods and metres that it appears to be a sympathetic cipher or alphabet, and to exist that it may serve man with a language.

All things are symbols. We say of man that he is grass, that he is a stream, a house, a star, a lion, fire, a day; and if we wish to accuse him at any time, we call him a snake, a baboon, a goat, a gull, a bat, an owl, a toad, and an infinity of names beside. These names are comparatively unaffecting in our ears, hearing them as we do merely caught by the ear from others and spoken without thought, but the man who first called another man Puppy or Ass was a poet, and saw at the moment the identity of nature through the great difference of aspect. His eye so reached to the thought and will of the wretch he beheld, that he could hear him bark or bray, with a bestial necessity under this false clothing of man.

We still feel this strong poetry whenever a powerful mind which disregards appearances signifies its sense in metaphors. As when Napoleon says of the Bourbons, "They were a hereditary race of asses, whilst I made my generals of mud." [9] But every one of these images and every other image may be applied to the world and the universe. There is no word in our language that can not become to us typical of nature by giving it emphasis. The world is an animal; it is a bird; it is a boat; it is a shadow; it is a torrent, a mist, a spider's snare; it is what you will, and the metaphor will hold, and it will give the imagination keen pleasure. Swifter than light the world converts itself into that thing you name, and all things find their right place under this new and capricious classification.[10]

Small and mean things serve just as well as great symbols. The meaner the type by which a spiritual law is expressed, the

[9] Cf. C, 296, 297; "Napoleon," W, IV, 239; Barry Edward O'Meara, *Napoleon in Exile*, 2 vols. (Boston, 1823), I, 88, 164.
[10] "There is no word . . . classification" (G, 43–44).

more pungent it is, and the more lasting in the memories of men, just as we value most the smallest box or case in which any needful utensil can be carried.[11] The soul derives as grand a joy from symbolizing the Godhead and his Universe under the form of a moth or gnat as of a Lord of Hosts. Shall I call the heaven and the earth a maypole, a country fair with booths, an anthill, or an old coat, to give you the shock of pleasure which the imagination loves, and the sense of spiritual greatness. Call it a blossom, a rod, a wreath of parsley, a tamarisk crown, a cock, a sparrow, the ear instantly hears and the spirit leaps to the trope.[12] A man must not, to be sure, go seeking for trivial or fantastic tropes, but every one is legitimate which occurs to any mind without effort or study. It is related of Lord Chatham that he was accustomed to read in Bailey's Dictionary when he was preparing to speak in Parliament. A similar fact has been related of other eloquent men. I think we may easily see how mere lists of words should be suggestive to a highly imaginative and excited mind.[13]

It were a curious inquiry which one sees would lead at once into the heart of nature to ask what it is that so charms us in a symbol or trope. The fact I suppose is manifest enough of the extreme delight which all men take in symbols. See how fond of symbols the people are! See the great ball which they roll from Baltimore to Bunker Hill. See in the political processions Lowell in a loom, and Lynn in a shoe, and Salem in a ship. They fancy they hate poetry and they are all poets and mystics.[14] Witness the striped pig, the cider barrel, the old Hickory, the log-cabin, and all the cognizances of party. See the national emblems, the star, the cross, the crescent, the lion, the eagle, or some similar figure on an old rag of bunting blowing in the wind on a fort in the ends of the earth makes the heart beat and the blood tingle

[11] "Small and mean . . . be carried" ("The Poet," W, III, 17).
[12] "The soul derives . . . to the trope" (G, 44).
[13] "It is related . . . excited mind" ("The Poet," W, III, 17–18); cf. G, 44; Encyclopedia, 78.
[14] "See how fond . . . and mystics" (E, 206); E, 180, describes the great ball which was part of the spectacle in the presidential campaign of William Henry Harrison. According to JMN, VII, 379, 394, footnotes 302, 349, the ball was an attraction in the Whig celebration in Concord on July 4, 1840, and represented Concord in the parade, described in this passage, for the Whigs' national Bunker-Hill Convention on September 10.

under the most civil and cultivated exterior.[15] Hear our speech, see our dramatic exhibitions, see our dress, our furniture, our figure-heads, the ciphers on our seals and carriages, on the sleds of the children, the names of fire engines, of locomotives, and of ships. Hear the language of anger, of poetry, of love, and of religion.

What does all this love for signs denote, if not that the relation of man to these forms in nature is more intimate than the understanding yet suspects; and that perhaps the metamorphoses which we read in Latin or in Indian literature are not quite so fabulous as they are accounted?

Who knows but more is meant than yet appears? Every gardener can change his flowers and leaves into fruit, and so perhaps is this man who astonishes the senate or the parlor by the splendor of his conversation, who seems to stride over all limits, — this genius who today can upheave and balance and toss every object in nature for his metaphor, capable in his next appearance in human nature of playing such a game with his hands instead of his brain. An instinctive suspicion that this may befall, seems to have crept into the mind of men. Genius may be dangerous. What would happen to us who live on the surface, if this fellow in some new transmigration should have acquired power to do what he now delights to say? He must be watched. Who shall set limits to the soul? Caius Gracchus dies imprecating slavery on the Romans, a prayer granted in no long time.[16] The soul goes forth to do what it prayed might be done.

Meantime with this passion and fury to be explained and expressed, and this plastic world of things yielding itself as a dictionary, adequate intellectual expression is very rare. Sufficient vent is got to prevent suffocation, we wriggle into some sort of nest or hole that will fit the body, into some mode of action that will employ our talent, get some grist between the stones to save the mill from grinding itself, but we do not get beyond serving the present distress, we do not attain to an example or universal picture and demonstration of the talent that is born with us to this time, to all time. Go into a senate or other assembly of public

[15] "See the great . . . cultivated exterior" ("The Poet," W, III, 16–17).
[16] See Plutarch, "The Lives of Tiberius and Caius Gracchus," *Lives*, trans. John Langhorne and William Langhorne, 8 vols. (New York, 1822), VI, 227.

debate and listen to the speakers. It is easy to see that every man represents a new and perfect style of oratory, and each, if he speak long enough, and the matter is important enough to show his genius, will actually come to the verge of good deliverance; — comes so near that the professional poet or orator begins to feel himself quite superfluous: — What need of the deputy, when here the principal can state his own case? But neither of the speakers quite hits it, and none does, of thousands and thousands; and in a nation the one or two who do best, are separated by a whole length from all the rest.[17] And this in the expression of right and wrong respecting their own affairs. An obscure old instinct revives in the beholder, that this man who does what the beholder had panted in vain to do, or said what he was bursting to speak, is himself, himself with some advantages, — and he begins to love him as himself. We love, we worship the expressors of that which we have at heart. We forgive every crime to them. The head of a party can do no wrong. This is true of excellence in every department, of the genius in mechanics, in military command, in music, in dancing, in eloquence, in the fine arts, but most of all in intellect.

For whilst we are able to do some justice to our private thought upon those facts which concern private and particular duties, we find much more difficulty in giving any expression to their great and universal relations. I know not how it is that we all should need an interpreter but so it happens that the great majority of men seem to be minors who have not yet come into possession of their own, cannot quite report the conversation we have had with nature. To no man is his position in the world, to no man are the sun and stars, the hills and waters quite indifferent objects yet there seems a little too much phlegm in our constitution to allow them to make their due effect. Too feeble fall the impressions of our sense upon us to make us artists. Every touch should thrill. Now it is made with sufficient vivacity for knowledge but not for poetry or an adequate report. It would seem as if every man should be so much an artist that he could report in conversation what had befallen him.[18]

---

[17] "It is easy to see . . . all the rest" (H, 69).
[18] "I know not how . . . befallen him" ("The Poet," W, III, 5–6).

Now the Poet is the person in whom these demands are answered, the person without impediment, who by the favor of God is sent into the world to see clearly what others have glimpses of, to feel richly what they suspect, to gaze with sound senses and responding heart at full leisure, and in a trance of delight, at the heavens and the earth; a soul through which the universe is poured, — into his eyes, and it comes forth not a blur, but a fair picture; into his ears, and it comes forth not a squeak nor a scream, but a song of rich and overflowing beauty: the complete man, who traverses the whole scale, who is at home in gaiety and in tears; in rich men's palaces and in poor men's huts; in the desarts of nature and the galleries of art; — the hospitable soul, which entertains in its spirit all travellers, tongues, kindreds, all employments, all eccentricities, all crimes even, in its vast charity and overcoming hope. Man knowing and man speaking is he. This is he whose speech is music; who gives name to whatever he beholds, and the name clings thenceforward: who announces news — the only teller of news,[19] of news that never get old or not in a thousand years. It is he who atones for all calamities and short comings, who gives a reason for the beauty of nature and revives hope in the heart. He adores the adorable: "He is the guardian of admiration in the hearts of the people," [20] he is not free, but freedom; he is not tasteful, but he is taste: he is not the beneficiary but the benefactor of the world, and is the representative of man, in virtue of being the largest power to give and to receive. He is the man whose being soars higher and sinks deeper than another's, to a softer tenderness, a holier ardor, a grander daring. This is the man who makes all other men seem less, the very naming of whose name is ornamental and like good news, and the sound of his words for ages makes the heart beat quicker, and the eye glisten, and fills the air with golden dreams.

And Nature who gave to poets this high representative office and wished them to stand for the Intellect and not for the Will, did not make them blackhaired, hotheaded, and violent men, but of fair complexion and gentle manners: for she meant that they should not need any physical force or weapons to defend them,

---

[19] "Poetry and Imagination," *W*, VIII, 30.
[20] C, 99; D, 230; cf. *Memorials of Mrs. Hemans*, ed. Chorley, II, 225.

but that the love and pride of all mankind should shield and cherish them.[21]

The universal knower and singer, he must have an universal experience. Nothing exists unrelated to him: he is covetous of sweet and of bitter things, of simple and of artificial experiences. He cannot spare any grief or pain or terror: he wants every rude stroke that has been dealt on his irritable texture: he hangs out his life like an Aeolian harp in a tree, where every wind from the northern tempest to the softest breath of southwestern air may play on it. He needs his fear and his superstition as much as his purity and courage, as notes for the anthem which he is to compose. Pain has a new aspect for such a man. This wonderful gift of expression is a charmed life and turns bane to antidote. "Some god gave me the power to tell what I suffer," said a poet. This made the curse a benediction. Do not judge the poet's life to be sad, because of his plaintive verses and confessions of despair. Because he was able to cast off his sorrows into these writings, therefore went he onward free and serene to new experiences. You must be a poet also to draw a just inference as to what he was, from all the records, be they never so rich, which he has left. Did you hear him speak? His speech did great injustice to his thought. It was either better or worse. He gave you the treasures of his memory, or he availed himself of a topic rich in allusions to express hopes gayer than his life entertains, or sorrows lamented with an energy and religion which was an intellectual play, and not the habit of his character. You shall not know his love or his hatred from his speech and behavior. Cold and silent he shall be in the circle of those friends whom, when absent, his heart walks with and talks with evermore. Face to face with that friend who for the time is unto him the essence of night and morning, of the sea and land, the only equal and worthy incarnation of thought and faith, silence and gloom shall overtake him, his talk shall be arid and trivial. There is no deeper dissembler than the sincerest man. Do not trust his blushes, for he blushes not at his affection but at your suspicion. Do not trust his actions, for they are expiations and fines often, with which he has amerced himself and not the indications of his desire. Do not conclude his igno-

---

[21] "And Nature who gave . . . cherish them" (E, 296).

rance or his indifference from his silence. Do not think you have all his thought when you have heard his speech to the end. Do not judge him worldly and vulgar, because he respects the rich and well bred, for to him the glittering symbol has a beauty it has not to other eyes, and his heart dances with delight in which no envy and no meanness are mixed. Him the circumstance of life dazzles and overpowers whilst it passes, because he is so delicate a meter of every influence. You shall find him noble at last, noble in his privacy, noble in his dealing.[22]

And what is the weapon which the poet wields? What the materials and means of his power? Verse or metrical language. Language, the half god, language, the most spiritual of all the works of man, yet language subdued by music — an organ or engine, it must be owned, scarcely less beautiful than the world itself, a fine translation into the speech of man of breezes and waves and ripples, the form and lights of the sky, the color of clouds and leaves. As the world is round, and not square, — as bodies have shadows; and sounds, echoes; and meeting balls a rebound; as there is beauty in a row of balls, or pillars, or buildings, or trees, or statues, beyond their beauty as individuals, so is there a beauty in rhythm or metre (whereof rhyme is one instance) which has its origin in the pulse and constitution of man, and will never be quite absent from sane speech. Rhyme is one of its primary or rudest forms. The child sings or chaunts its first words, sings or chaunts before it talks, as we say. Poetry, in like manner, is found in the literature of all nations to precede prose. But the ear soon finds that there are finer measures than the coarse psalmody which tinkled in the nursery, and wondering, it listens after that sweet beauty, as the eye pines over the colors of a gem, or the transparency of water or of glass. By and by it learns the secret, that love and thought always speak in measure or music, — that with the elevation of the soul, the asperities and incoherence of speech disappear, and the language of truth is always pure music. We are very far from having reached the term of our knowledge on this subject. How can we, unless we had reached the boundaries of thought and feeling? The finer poet, the finer ear. Each new poet will as certainly invent new metres

[22] "Do not judge the poet's . . . noble in his dealing" (E, 266–267).

as he will have new images to clothe. In true poetry, the thought and the metre are not painfully adjusted afterward, but are born together, as the soul and the body of a child. The difference between poetry and what is called "stock poetry," I take to be this, that in *stock poetry* the metre is given and the verses are made to it, and in poetry the sense dictates the tune or march of the words.[23]

I think a person of poetical temperament cannot indulge his veins of sentiment without perceiving that the finest rhythms and cadences of poetry are yet unfound, and that in that purer state which his thoughts prophesy, rhythms of a faery and dreamlike music shall enchant us, compared with which the happiest measures of English poetry are psalm-tunes. I think even now, that the very finest and sweetest closes and falls are not in our metres, but in the measures of prose eloquence which have greater variety and richness than verse.[24]

In the history of civilization, Rhyme may pass away, yet it will always be remembered as a consecrated and privileged invention possessing what I may call *certain rights of sanctuary.* Herein it resembles music, viz. in the privilege of speaking the truth, — not apparent but spiritual truth, which is not allowed to prose. Music is the uncultivated man's Parnassus. With the very first note of the flute or horn, with the first strain of a song we quit the world of common sense and launch at once into the sea of ideas and emotions. Every note is an insult to all the common sense that has been droning in our ears all day. It gives it the lie. I seem to hear nothing but mocks and laughter in those tripping, lilting, faery sounds, which speak of love and moonlight, of wildness and dreams, and all audacious, extravagant, religious, and tender themes. The sturdiest proser sits by and is silent. Say one half so much treason in articulate speech, and he would open his logic upon you by the hour. But the tune makes wild holiday. Well, the like allowance is the prescriptive right of poetry. You shall not speak truth in prose: You *may* in verse.[25] In verse, you may treat the good uncles and aunts of this world and all the

[23] "Poetry and Imagination," W, VIII, 54; H, 38.
[24] "I think a person . . . than verse" (H, 37–38).
[25] "Herein it resembles . . . in verse" ("Poetry and Imagination," W, VIII, 51–52; D, 326, expanded).

solemn matters that pass for so great in the street as peppercorns, and make them dance and sing again, and because it is poetry, no man shall forbid you.

This fact is by no means unimportant, as in this way poetry serves a great office to mankind in keeping before the mind of the most critical and unbelieving age those cardinal truths and ideas which make the religion of man, and which would be rejected and insulted, if stated in the newspaper, but when spoken in verse disarm criticism, and for the music's sake are allowed currency in the circles most committed to an opposite creed, — where they serve to mitigate and modify manners and laws, and keep the door open to a better knowledge. So that it has been well said by those who hope highest of the present time, that "the poetry of the Old Church is the philosophy of the New." [26]

But the poet, as we intimated at the outset, is not to be painted in parts. When we have told all our anecdotes of detail, there yet remains the total wonder. We must add then the fact that no enumeration of particulars brings us nearer to an explanation; for poetry is always a miracle not to be explained or disposed of, a miracle to the hearer; a miracle to the poet; he admires his verses as much as you do, when they are the right inspiration: he cannot tell where or how he had them. The sign of genius is originality: its word cannot be guessed: it is new, yet tallies with all we know: it has an expected unexpectedness, a new oldness. The bee flies among the flowers and gets mint and marjoram and makes a new product which is not mint or marjoram but honey; and the chemist mixes hydrogen and oxygen to yield a new product which is not hydrogen or oxygen but water: and the poet listens to all conversations, and receives all objects of nature, to give back, not them, but a new and radiant whole.[27] Whence the new proceeded, is the secret of nature. Only what is new delights us, for it is the last communication from God. I must know that the scholar who wrote, *only* wrote, and did not alter it: as I know a poet who had the honesty to say that he valued his poems not because they were his, but because they were not.[28]

[26] This clause also appears in quotation marks in F No. 2, 122.
[27] "The bee flies . . . radiant whole" ("Poetry and Imagination," W, VIII, 16–17; G, 141).
[28] G, 116.

We are a little afraid of poetry, — afraid to write and afraid to read it; are we not? We do not very willingly trust ourselves on the back of that wild winged horse of the Muses, ignorant whither he will carry us and where we shall alight. Surprise and wonder always fly beside him. There is no poetry where they are not. Poetry ever descends like a foreign conqueror from an unexpected quarter of the horizon, carries us away with our wives and children, our flocks and herds, into captivity, to make us, at a later period, adopted children of the new land, and, in the end, to disclose to us, that this is really our native country.[29]

And yet, as nothing so much concerns us as the question, if it can be a question, whether Poetry is possible in the present time, Why not? What is poetry but the truest expression? and if the *thing* exists, so will its expression follow. It may not appear in quarters or in forms where we look for it; in such, namely, as it availed itself of in the last, or in earlier generations: for Nature does not repeat herself, but invents. How unlike is each to the last preceding! After Dante, and Shakspeare, and Milton, there came no grand poet until Swedenborg in a corner of Europe, hitherto uncelebrated, sung the wonders of man's heart in strange prose poems which he called "Heaven and Hell," the "Apocalypse Revealed," the "Doctrine of Marriage," Celestial Secrets and so on, and which rivalled in depth and sublimity, and in their power to agitate this human heart — this lover of the wild and wonderful, — any song of these tuneful predecessors. Slowly but surely the eye and ear of men are turning to feed on that wonderful intellect, and severing the wheat from the chaff.

But nature never pauses. Whilst we admire and exaggerate one genius, and, perhaps, after a century or two, have learned to appreciate it, she throws into our neighborhood another and another to be the study and astonishment of other times and distant eyes.

We have suffered ourselves to live so sensually that we have defiled our own houses to that degree that they suggest to us places of indulgence and mere comfort or outward convenience, and not the residence of sacred and awful pleasures, so that when poetry and the joys of the imagination are spoken of, we instantly

[29] Cf. H, 38–39.

run *from home* to seek for it; we run into memory, we run into futurity, into early youth, into cottages, into mines, into feudal keeps, or Arab tents, or Iceland huts underground. And yet the genius of Poetry is here. He worships in this land also, not by immigration but he is Yankee born. He is in the forest walks, in paths carpeted with leaves of the chestnut, oak, and pine; he sits on the mosses of the mountain; he listens by the echoes of the wood; he paddles his canoe in the rivers and ponds. He visits without fear the factory, the railroad, and the wharf. When he lifts his great voice, men gather to him and forget all that is past, and then his words are to the hearers, pictures of all history; and immediately the tools of their bench, and the riches of their useful arts, and the laws they live under, seem to them weapons of romance. As he proceeds, I see their eyes sparkle, and they are filled with cheer and new faith. Every achievement looks possible to them, and the evils of life are ebbing away. In strange, improbable places, — perhaps, as we said, not so much in metrical forms, as in eloquence, we may detect the poetic genius.

You may find it, though rarely, in Senates, when the forest has cast out some wild, black-browed bantling, some great boy, to show the same energy in the crowd of officials, which he had learned in driving cattle to the hills, or in scrambling through thickets in a winter forest, or through the swamp and river for his game. In the folds of his brow, in the majesty of his mien, nature shall vindicate her son; and even in that strange and perhaps unworthy place and company, remind you of the lessons taught him in earlier days by the torrent, in the gloom of the pine woods, when he was the companion of crows and jays and foxes, and a hunter of the bear.

Perhaps you may find it in some lowly Bethel by the seaside where a hard-featured, scarred, and wrinkled methodist whose face is a network of cordage becomes the poet of the sailor and the fisherman, whilst he pours out the abundant streams of his thought through a language all glittering and fiery with imagination. A man who never knew the looking-glass or the critic; a man whom patronage never made, and whom praise cannot spoil; a man who conquers his audience by infusing his soul into them, and speaks by the right of being the person in the assembly who has the most to say, and so makes all other speakers seem puny and cowardly before his face. For the time his exceeding life throws all other gifts into deep shade, "philosophy speculating on its own breath," taste, learning, and all; and yet how willingly every man consents to be nothing in this presence, to share this surprising emanation, and be steeped and ennobled in the new wine of this eloquence. It instructs in the power of man over men! We feel that a man is a Mover, — to the extent of his being a Power, and in contrast with the efficiency thus suggested, our actual life and society appears a dormitory.[30] We are taught that earnest, impassioned action is most our own, and invited to try the deeps of love and wisdom, — we who have been players and paraders so long.[31]

But in purer forms than these will it rise — the poetic genius of the time, — in forms not unworthy of nature which it is to represent; in forms which shall not need, like these, to be praised with a grain of allowance, but which shall speak in tones that enrich and elevate those who hear. The Poet shall yet arrive — the fortunate, the adapted, the timely man, whose heart domesticated in Ideas sees them proclaimed in the face of the world of this Hour, in the men and women of today, and their institutions and covenants, their houses and shops; — who coupling what we do with what we are, the last effect with the first cause, shall search the heart and soul with every word he speaks, and in his lightest and gayest mood, — painting as if for idleness the creaking wagon or the poultry stepping round the farmhouse door, — adds with every picture insights and presentiments, hopes and fears, and gives to the old dull track of daily life more than the blush and wonder of a lover's dream.

To doubt that the poet will yet appear is to doubt of day and night. Wherever there is a fact there must follow the expression of the same. Shall the grass grow with its wonted rankness; shall the water flow as silver-clear; and the light stream up the morning sky with no dimness in its ray, — and the higher life, which

[30] "You may find it . . . a dormitory" ("Eloquence," W, VIII, 113–115).
[31] "Perhaps you may . . . paraders so long" (expanded from E, 148–149, where Emerson records his admiration for Edward Taylor, of the Seamen's Bethel in the North End of Boston); last sentence printed in notes to "Eloquence," W, VIII, 385.

these things tend upward unto and predict, fail of its ripeness and advent? These are fears of the drowsy and the blind. New topics, new powers, a new spirit arise, which threaten to abolish all that was called poetry, in the melodious thunder of the new.

There is a great destiny which comes in with this as with every age, colossal in its traits, terrible in its strength, which cannot be tamed, or criticised or subdued. It is shared by every man and every woman of the time, for they are as leaves on this tree which bears them. In solid phalanx the generation comes on; the pattern of their features is new in the world: all wear the same expression, but it is that which they do not detect in each other. The Genius of the time is one spirit but of many operations. One and the same it ponders in the philosophers, drudges in the craftsmen, dreams in the poets, dilates in the love of woman. It inspires every exertion that is made. It makes life sweet to all who breathe it. It is this which the ambitious seek power that they may controul: this they wish to be rich that they may buy; when they marry, it is out of love of this; when they study it is this which they pore after; this which they aim to read and write and carve and paint and build. It is new in the Universe: it is the attraction of time: it is the last work of the Creator: calm and perfect it lies on the brow of the enormous eternity: and if in the superior recesses of nature there be any abode for permanent spectators, what is there they would hang upon but this, the cumulative result, the new morning with all its dews, rich with the spoils of foregoing time? Is there not a strange folly to fear whilst the world stands here and we in it, that the day of poetry and creation is past? Is there not something droll to see the darlings of this age, those for whom a happy birth and circumstance and the rarest influences of Culture have done the most, — timid and querulous, ignorant of this mighty support which upbears them — ignorant of this resistless onward Fate, which makes the Individual nothing, — to hear them interrupt the awe and gladness of the time with their officious lamentations that they are critical and know too much? If ever anybody had found out how so much as a ryestraw was made! They seem to me torn up in a whirlwind, borne by its force they know not whence, they know not whither, yet settling their faces and their robes in the moment when they fly by me with this self crimination of impertinent melancholy. But the grandeur of our life exists in spite of us — all over and under and within us, — in what of us is inevitable and above our control. Men are facts as well as persons, and the involuntary part of their life is so much, as to fill all their wonder, and leave them no countenance to say anything of what is so trivial as their private thinking and doing.[32]

We are all poets at last, and the life of each has high and solemn moments which remind him of that fact in a manner he cannot choose but understand. Each of us is a part of eternity and immensity, a god walking in flesh, and the wildest fable that was ever invented, is less strange than this reality. Let us thank the poets as men who saw and celebrated this marvel whilst we slept.

[32] "There is a great . . . thinking and doing" (H, 7–9); "But the grandeur . . . thinking and doing" ("Poetry and Imagination," W, VIII, 75).

8

Prospects

The eighth lecture in the series on "The Times" was first read in the Masonic Temple in Boston on January 20, 1842, and repeated as the fifth lecture in the Providence, Rhode Island, series on February 17 and as the sixth in the New York series on March 14; in each instance it was the concluding lecture. It may have been read elsewhere in 1842. Emerson may also have referred to this lecture when he wrote to Margaret Fuller at the end of 1842 that he was taking to Baltimore and Philadelphia, along with his new course on "New England," "an ethical discourse, a sort of *result* of 1842. which, if all Pennsylvania should rise and demand its delivery at a mass meeting, I might comply; otherwise, I may force it on the unwilling ears of nine or ten." If this is the lecture referred to, it was duly demanded of him after the regular series, and he read it to the Mercantile Library Association on February 3, 1843 (*L*, III, 108, 139–140).

The lecture manuscript is nearly complete, though there are difficulties with it as a result of revision after the first reading. The Boston version was once sewn and the sequence of leaves established by pencilled numbers on the rectos of single leaves and the first rectos of double sheets. After a few leaves of a different kind were inserted (including a passage from "Lecture VII," which lecture, if the allusion refers to this series, was read in Boston but not in Providence or New York) ink pagination was added throughout. Certain small emendations resulting from the revision have been rejected in restoring the first reading; these have been preserved in the textual notes along with the added leaves in their proper position. From the first version three to five leaves are missing; from the later version six leaves are missing. A report of the lecture as delivered in New York was printed in the New York *Tribune* on March 17, 1842, and reprinted by Jeanne Kronman in "Three Unpublished Lectures of Ralph Waldo Emerson," *The New England Quarterly*, XIX (March 1946), 99–105. It conforms closely to the revised version of the lecture, including material now lost from the manuscript.

The manuscript of the present lecture has been filed in the place of the missing manuscript of "The Present Age," Lecture 8. Cabot summarized it as that lecture, which he called "Prospects. Duties" and gave no summary for the eighth lecture of "The Times," which he correctly called "Prospects" (Cabot, II, 745–746, 748). Against what may be Cabot's arrangement and the concurrence of Edward Emerson, who did not change it, there is compelling evidence: Lecture 8 of "The Present Age" was announced only as "Ethics," and this is Emerson's own listing of it (see headnote above, p. 271); unlike the lectures from the earlier course, none of this lecture was used for *Essays* (1841); the journal sources for this lecture are almost exclusively from a later date than 1840, and indeed an outline exists in H, 96, written apparently in the fall of 1841; finally, there is the detailed newspaper report of this as the final lecture in "The Times." It is not likely that Emerson would read to a Boston audience within two years the same lecture, even in a revised form; it is more plausible that the earlier manuscript is now missing because it was used in *Essays* (1841).

Emerson had apparently not written this lecture when he wrote to William Emerson on December 4, 1841 (*L*, II, 469), and in an undated list in Notebook Ψ, 166, immediately following a draft announcement for eight Boston lectures in this course, only the first seven titles are given. On the first page of the lecture manuscript, a page belonging to the revised version, Emerson wrote in ink, "Lecture VIII Prospects"; on page 3, "Lect 8 Prospects Duties"; on page 7 and subsequently throughout the lecture, he uses "Lect 8 Duties." This accounts for Cabot's title. However, since the lecture was announced in the *Boston Daily Advertiser*, as well as in Providence and New York, as "Prospects" (*L*, II, 468n, III, 11n, 21n), it is reasonable to suppose that Emerson may have written the lecture as "Duties" but changed his mind about the title before delivering it.

The missing leaves may have gone into "Nominalist and Realist" and "New England Reformers" in *Essays, Second Series* since passages of the extant manuscript were used there. Two paragraphs found their way into the printed version of "The Sovereignty of Ethics," *North American Review*, CXXVI (May-June 1878), 404–420 (collected in *Lectures and Biographical Sketches*), which was based on a lecture Cabot prepared for Emerson in 1877.

At the end of the textual notes for this lecture are printed three leaves supposedly belonging to other lectures from "The Times."

THERE is something very low and impertinent in the tone of sorrow and anxiety which characterizes so much of the speculation of the present times. I am sorry also to read the observation of M. De Tocqueville that a cloud always hangs on an American's brow.[1] Least of all is it to be pardoned in the literary and speculative class. I hate the builders of dungeons in the air. "Ascending souls sing Paean," said the Magian. Ascending souls congratulate each other on the admirable harmonies of the world.[2] We read another commission in the cipher of nature: we were made for another office, professors of the Joyous Science, detectors and delineators of occult symmetries and unpublished beauties, heralds of civility, nobility, learning, and wisdom, affirmers of the One Law, yet as those who should affirm it in music or dancing. Cannot the great laws of the Universe be celebrated without sighing and groans, by the beauty of health, by musical harmonies?[3] We never learned it of Nature. A firm and cheerful temper infinitely removed from sadness reigns through all the kingdoms of chemistry, of vegetation and animal life. The expression of storm and night is not sad. What absence of all sadness in the flakes of snow, in the fall of drops from eaves of the house or the leaves of trees.[4] They rather express vigor, proportion. The effect of every fine natural gift is to exhilarate.[5] Can you sing well, dance well, speak, write, blow the flute, or horn, jump, dive, swim, fell a tree, build a house, paint a picture, whistle, mimic, ventriloquize, or whatsoever? With mastery, you cheer and not sadden the spectator, and yourself also. A true talent always delights the possessor first. Nicias the painter took such pleasure in the work of his hands that he often so far forgot himself as that he was fain to ask his servants whether he had washed or dined. Archimedes was so intent on the table on which he drew his geometrical figures that his attendants were obliged by force to pluck him from it and strip him of his clothes that they might anoint him whilst he in the meantime drew new schemes on his anointed body. Canas the piper was wont to say that men knew not how much more he delighted himself with his playing than he did

[1] Alexis de Tocqueville, *Democracy in America, Part II,* trans. Henry Reeve (New York, 1840), p. 144; E, 297.

[2] "Ascending souls sing . . . of the world" (see G, 37, indexed in H, 96). In E, 195, Emerson ascribes the quotation, an oracle, to Zoroaster, but in "Ethnical Scriptures," *Uncollected Writings,* p. 131, he ascribes it to the Theurgists. Either ascription is authorized by his probable source, "The Oracles of Zoroaster, the Founder of the Persian Magi," *The Phenix; A Collection of Old and Rare Fragments* (New York, 1835), p. 158.

[3] "I hate the builders . . . musical harmonies" (see G, 10, indexed in H, 96).

[4] Cf. H, 96.

[5] Cf. H, 96.

others, for that then his hearers would rather demand of him than give him a reward.[6]

All beauty is a cordial and a heartwarmer, a sign of health, prosperity, and the favor of God. Everything sound, lasting, and fit for men the Divine Power has marked with this stamp. What delights, what emancipates, not what scares and pains us is wise and good in speech or writing or the arts.

Beauty is the only sure sign, so that if your word threatens me, I know it is a bully, I know it is weak, I know there is a better discoverable and returnable. That word only which is fair and fragrant, which blooms and rejoices, which runs before me like verdure and a flowering vine sowing an Eden in the path, is truth. Nay, Beauty is strong and we understand why the ancient built altars to Beauty the Defender; for when we seek it for itself in the arts, in song, or in character we suddenly find it to be sword and shield; for it is the asylum of man and has a great privilege of sanctuary. For whilst we contemplate it we find ourselves above the region of fear and unassailable like a god at the Olympian tables.[7] To it is duration given. Redeemer also and Saviour it is. A pure ray of beauty in thought or deed shining out from what society stigmatizes as sin, forgives the sin, and puts society in the wrong.

With all our necessary actions, therefore, some degree of pleasure is connected and a certain plenitude of beauty poured in thinner or deeper flood over entire nature. The rise and the fall of the day, the spring and fall of the year, the air and water and flame and earth, the plants, animals, the muscular movements of our own bodies, respiration and the circulations are not devoid of pleasure which in each particular admits of indefinite increase. Who can take up the Farmer's Almanack and scan so much as the well known figures of the signs of the Zodiack with the rude metres under them without some degree of enjoyment?[8]

.　　.　　.

[6] These three anecdotes, also in Σ, 23, Emerson found in Plutarch, "Whether an aged Man ought to meddle in State Affairs," *Morals*, V, 63–64.
[7] "for when we seek . . . Olympian tables" (D, 324; cf. D, 6; indexed in H, 96).
[8] At this point two leaves are missing from the later version and one or two leaves from the earlier version. For continuation of the reading in New York, see Kronman, pp. 100–101, and H, 26, indexed in H, 96.

We are saturated with good as in mid summer the heavens and the earth are inundated with the fine deluges of heat. Our very blunders lead us into success how often and our famous countryman styled Lord Timothy Dexter who sent warming-pans to the West Indies and made his fortune so, is a type of much of our success.[9] Soldiers say that most generals who get victories are not entitled to them; only Napoleon won it in his head before he won it in the field and so had it honestly, as honestly as that kind of ware is ever got. Well, I fancy that if men were honest about it, they would confess to blundering into most of our private victories.[10] We are helped by our very foibles and sins, like the water in the riddle,

And the more falls we get, move faster on.[11]

Our disasters befriend us, our false associations even have some good in them for all our solitudes yield a precious fruit and this is the most remarkable of all our solitudes.[12]

To push these documents of the cheerful riches, the redundant spirits of Nature to a little extreme, does it not sometimes appear as if Nature was inclined to droll a little with us when we see how speedily every error and misdeed of man reacts on Nature so that every perversity of ours presently incarnates itself in a man? Sickness gets organized as well as health, vice as well as virtue, and when war or trade has existed so long it stereotypes itself in the human generation and men are born warriors or traders. So instead of great universal men fit for all the offices of war and peace she seems to take a pleasure in forming men fit for wheels and pins in all the chinks of the social machine. She will make a scholar inapt for every thing but his office of scholar — a lens that has no power but at the focus; at any other distance it gives all blur and dislocation; or like cannon which destroy at a distance but bring the battle hand to hand the weapon is cumbrous and use-

---

[9] Timothy Dexter (1747–1806) was a wealthy merchant of Newburyport, Massachusetts, noted for his extravagant and eccentric life.

[10] "Our very blunders . . . private victories" (see H, 96, 129, where "Lieut. Greene" is given credit for what is here more generally ascribed to "Soldiers").

[11] Adapted from Anna Letitia Barbauld, "[The Brook]," a riddle; cf. Blotting Book III, 56; A, 78.

[12] For insertion from Lecture VII into later version of this lecture, see textual notes and Kronman, p. 101.

less and no match for a knife. She makes for our holidays public persons born not for privacy but for publicity, who are dull in a tête-à-tête, but summon them to preside, the eye brightens and dilates, a certain majesty sits on the shoulders, they have wit and a happy deliverance you should never have found in the closet. She makes Doctors of Divinity and captains and presidents and sheriffs to order. Marshals she delights to make. At one of our country colleges you may commonly find a natural sheriff with a loud voice, a pompous air, and a fine coat whose aid the college shall thankfully ask to order its annual procession. He is in his element; he commands the whole with that despotic condescension in that dignified assembly which puts all dignities and talents but his own quite aside. The college follows him like a tame dog.[13]

And so she delights in manufacturing antiquaries, genealogists, rattle-brains, crotchets, and bores of all sorts for the sake it would seem of using up all her chips.[14]

. . .

Nature pours her energy into human beings as she does into particular regions of the world, feeding this from a thousand springs and elements and starving that other. The travellers in some parts of the southwestern country of the United States say that the planter or the factor of the planter becomes little better than a cottongin; he has no conversation, no thoughts but cotton, — qualities of cotton, long staple and short staple, and its advance or fall a penny or a farthing. They say therefore that the negro is more a man in some districts than the white; alive to more human interests, much the best companion of the two; and how should he not be, since, though low in his organization he is yet no wooden machine but a wild cedar swamp rich with all vegetation of grass and moss and ferns and flags whither come in turn rains and sunshine, mist and moonlight, birds and insects, filling its wilderness with life and promise?[15]

[13] "At one of our country . . . a tame dog" (see D, 310, indexed in H, 96). That Emerson recalls his own observation at Dartmouth College, which he visited in July 1838, is apparent from the journal entries.
[14] One leaf missing at this point. For continuation of lecture in New York, see Kronman, p. 102, and "Nominalist and Realist," W, III, 237–238.
[15] "They say therefore . . . life and promise" (H, 22, modified).

Nature delights in breaking all bounds in her creation of men. She indulges herself in every extravagance and disappoints every expectation. The men who evince the force of the moral sentiment and of genuis are not normal, canonical people but wild and Ishmaelitish: Cromwells, Mahomets, Shakspeares, and the like.[16] Whilst she likes well to sow squadrons of discreet citizen-like, secret-keeping men, good providers for their households, whom you know where to find, so she pleases herself well with now and then bestowing a rare and wild power, that shall lie enormous, indefinite, hastening out of all limitation and to be treated like oxygen and hydrogen, of a diffusive, universal, irrevocable elasticity that can keep no secret, can keep no money, can keep no law but his own.[17]

The opulence of nature in every district of her immeasureable domain we all feel in the allurement of every study and occupation to which we chance to come very near. For example, I opened the other day the Poems of Robert Herrick, an author, as those who are conversant with English Poetry know, not of the first rank, and defaced by certain blemishes which discredit his books to almost every eye; but still a poet; perhaps England has no example of a lyric poet to equal him. And with this virtue, that I feel in reading him how rich is nature.[18] How much more I find there than I can tell. What possibilities in the poetic art! What the man has done is a very small part of what he has shown me may be done. In the careful carelessness of these little pieces, in the accidental elegance, and the charm with which every trifle is embellished, every fly put in amber, I am won to the art of poetry. I see that here is work and beauty enough to justify a man for quitting all else, and sitting down with the muses.[19] The paucity and triviality of these odes and elegies is nothing to the purpose. The door has been opened wide enough for me to

> Look in and see each blissful deity
> How he upon his thunderous throne doth lie.[20]

[16] G, 107.
[17] "Whilst she likes well . . . but his own" (H, 108).
[18] J, 45, indexed in H, 96.
[19] J, 45.
[20] Milton, "Anno Aetatis XIX, At a Vacation Exercise, etc.," lines 35–36. Also in "Milton," W, XII, 260, and *Lectures*, I, 152.

But whilst I am taught the extent of the kingdom of the Muse by this one book to which a chance leads me, I know that I have derived the like pleasure and seen that frontier pushed out into a new, unknown direction a hundred times before by other books. So I infer the wealth of the region. Caesar talked with the Egyptian priests and Achorens, and said, "Come, I will quit empire, army, Cleopatra, and all, if you will surely show me the fountains of the Nile":[21] and in our gratitude to the Poets, who has not — would not abandon all other goods for the power to enrich the world with one flask from their spring? But if I go into a laboratory and watch the chemist in his analysis and see how the world is made and changed — why speedily this becomes the "Fountains of the Nile" for which my world is well lost. The telescope of Galileo, of Sir William Herschel, and now of Sir John Herschel can easily degrade all other pursuits to my imagination. And yet a botanist can draw me back again from that dazzling dance of orbs and constellations by the description of the lowliest flower that blooms in an inch of meadow in the lowliest of planets.[22]

Well, what is the lesson of all this wild and waste fertility, this opulence bursting its garners on every side; what but joy, what but congratulation, wonder, and trust? Come let us sit down and learn the lesson. The lesson is long and the time is Eternity to learn it in.

Everything is good but this pursing of the lips and the pretension to have already learned. We finish our education a great deal too quick. We have scarce left our mother's breasts before we assume the professor's chair and begin to consider our reputation. Is anything more contemptible than this precocious pedantry? It seems as if the foolscap and the dame's birch would be a good application to many and many of us children of thirty, forty, and fifty years, when we consider how baleful is this influence of those Doctors who sit at the entrance of every road which freeborn, ardent youth would travel, and before the early pilgrim has yet paced a furlong of the Eternal Road, he encounters this false guide, who assures him there is nothing beyond; — that he with

---

[21] Cf. Lucan, *Pharsalia*, X, 191–192; "New England Reformers," W, III, 274, 276; J, 45.
[22] For variation in later version see textual notes.

his bat-eyes has explored and mapped the whole; and that any interest which men hereafter may wish to take in nature, they will be good enough to transfer to himself.

Do not let us be too early old, or in too much haste to mount the rostrum. I wonder any body who has ever seen children, should not have learned that our ignorance is as handsome and admirable as our knowledge, *whilst we are advancing,* — and that, if a man is real and selfrelying, his declaration that he does not know something which everybody knows, or has not read a book which all suppose him to have read, is just as agreeable to us or even better, than if he knew or had read it.

Let us be satisfied to see prosperity, calamity, virtue, crime, or whatever spectacle the great Spirit proposes to us — to see it, and hold our tongues. Who asked you for an opinion? Who entitled you to decide? You cannot see for this preposterous haste to say somewhat. Your wits are preoccupied with the opinion you should give. Like the poor magnetised people who read with the back of their head, you see with your memory and not with eyes.

I find a particular illustration of this general tendency in the impatience of our people to rush into the lists without enduring the training. The Americans are too easily pleased: and remind us of what was said of the Empire of Russia, that "it was a fine fruit spoiled before it had ripened." [23]

We get our education ended a little too quick in this country. As soon as we have learned to read and write and cipher, we are dismissed from school, and we set up for ourselves. We are writers, and leaders of opinion, and we write away without check of any kind, — play what prank, indulge what spleen or oddity or obstinacy comes into our dear head, and even feed our complacency thereon, and thus fine wits come to nothing, as good horses are spoiled by running away and straining themselves.

I cannot help seeing that our best authors had been better had they found a strict tribunal of writers, a graduated intellectual empire established in the land, and knew that bad logic would not pass and that a severe examination awaited all who enter these lists. Now if a man can write a paragraph for a newspaper,

---

[23] First half of sentence is in H, 91; the source of the quotation has not been located.

next year he writes what he calls a history, and reckons himself a classic incontinently, nor will his contemporaries in Critical Journal or Review question his claims. How can they? They have no high standard; they do not know but a book of such a size, with such topics, and such quotations and sent forth from the best publishers, is a good book. It is very easy always to reach the degree of culture that prevails around us, very hard to pass it. And had this writer found Scaliger, Milton, Addison, or Hume around him, he would as easily have been severe with himself and risen a degree higher as he has stood where he is. I mean of course a genuine intellectual tribunal, not a literary junto of Edinburgh wits or dull conventional Reviews. I wish the writers of this country would begin where they now end their culture. We are wits of the provinces, — Caesars in Arden, who easily fill all measures and lie on our oars with the fame of the villages. We see none who calls us to account, and so consult our ease; no Douglas cast of the bar, no pale Cassius reminds us of inferiority.[24]

I speak of the men of talent. True and high genius will make its own law, and will not write down to the low permitted standard. Milton wrote his verse to his own ear, well knowing that England did not hold, and might not for a century, another ear sufficiently fine to hear their rhythm. That is the magnanimity of the poet that he writes for the gods, as the works of Phidias which Lord Elgin brought to London, are found to be carved with the utmost precision and minute finish on the upper surface and on those toward the walls, which man was never to see.[25] But they were for the gods and were finished for the gods.[26]

We take sides with the same unnecessary speed. Church and State are in danger and we must set our shoulders to those heavy loads now in our tender youth when all the Muses, all the demigods are sporting in the fields and long ere yet we have measured what are called Church and State by the golden measuring wand of Justice. God forgive this rapid conservatism of ours! His world, we think, needs many a patch and cleet to make it hold together for our short day, which we hasten to put on.

[24] "We get our education . . . us of inferiority" (H, 89–91).
[25] "Milton wrote his verse . . . never to see" (H, 21, modified).
[26] For variation here and after next paragraph in later version see textual notes and Kronman, pp. 103–104.

Those who defend the establishment are always less than it; those who speak from a thought must always be greater than any actual fact. I see behind the Conservative no mighty matter. Through his eyes sparkles nothing better than the small and well known fact of that good order and convenience of living we know. But through the eyes of the theorist stares at me a formidable gigantic spirit, who will not down, if I bid him; who has much more to say than he has yet told, and who can do great things with the same facility as little.[27] Of course I have the same objection to dogmatism in Reform as to dogmatism in Conservatism. The impatience of discipline; the haste to rule before we have served; to prescribe laws for nations and humanity, before we have said our own prayers, or yet heard the benediction which Love and Peace sing in our own bosom; then all dwarfs and degrades; the great names are profaned; our virtue is a fuss, and sometimes a fit. The upward eye, the forward foot, a life with living nature is that which we require.[28]

This exuberance of nature requiring a correspondent receptiveness and ardor of obedience in man to carry out her great tendencies meets on the contrary in him a dulness and inertia, a disposition to stop and recede. I look upon a moment of nature as representative of all time. Of this richness and prodigality the Present Age seems to me to partake. I see it capacious, undefinable, far-retreating, still renewing, as the depths of the horizon appear when seen from the hills.

For that culture then which every noble mind in these times needs and should seek, let me say, that it should be built on the broadest base of experience, and open to every influence of pain and pleasure, of science, and of speculation.

Shall we rear houseplants only; or the robust tree which the frost and the whirlwind shall nourish, as well as summer sun and rain? Shall the Ages have revolved and pour their concentrated light on this moment of time and yield no generosity, no new element to the fortunate youth who now begins his career? Shall the youth born and bred in this hour which witnesses the dissolution of so many antique plausibilities before the dangerous inter-

---

[27] "Those who defend . . . facility as little" (J, 19).
[28] For variation in later version see textual notes and Kronman, p. 104.

rogation of Conscience and the love of Reality be trained only in the old Catechism with answers of words that he may be sure to be a coward and a fugitive when these tremendous inquisitors arrive? It is impossible. The very Spirit of the Time, this Conscience and love of Reality are inspiring already their own method. "O friends," say they with the first Quaker, "lie low in the Lord's power!" [29] Although it is very hard to play well the game of life for a single day or hour, and the most dexterous may easily be at fault, it is very easy to submit oneself and let the game be played through us.

Patience and truth, — patience with our own frosts and negations, and few words must serve. Let us not use convulsion and a fantastic theism and philosophy in default of the saliency of health. If our sleeps are long, if our flights are short, if we are not plumed like orioles and birds of paradise, but like sparrows and plebeian birds, if our taste and training are earthen, let that fact be humbly and happily borne with. The wise God beholds that also with complacency. Wine and honey are good, but so also are rice and meal. Perhaps all that is not performance is preparation or performance that shall be.[30] We play but a part. The piece must have shades too. When the musicians are learning their first scores every one wishes to scream, and country orchestras usually have a reasonable volume of voice. Afterwards they learn to be still and to sing underparts. Perhaps we may trust the Composer of our great Music to give us voice when our aid is needed and to apply the bellows to other stops when we should mar the harmony.

The man of this age who will embrace with a great heart his lot as it leaps from the Urn of Time should be matriculated in this University of sciences and tendencies flowing from all past periods. He should not be [one] to be surprised and shipwrecked with every bold or subtle word which malignant or acute men may utter in his hearing but should be taught all skepticisms, all unbeliefs and made the destroyer of all card-houses and paper walls

[29] C, 225, 309. A paraphrase of a constant theme in George Fox's exhortations; available to Emerson in Sewel, *The History of the . . . Quakers,* which he owned, or in Fox, *A Journal,* upon which Sewel's work depended. *Lectures,* II, 293, 351.
[30] "Patience and truth . . . that shall be" (H, 51–52).

and the sifter of all opinions, by being put face to face from his infancy with Reality.[31]

He must know that all men's life is superficial; that as our warm, commodious houses and spacious towns are built on a planet swimming unpiloted in the frightful hollows of space so all our talents and our life is enveloped and undermined by wonder. The last fact is still astonishment, mute, bottomless, boundless Wonder. When we meet an intelligent soul, all that we wish to ask him — phrase it how we will, — is, "Brother! have you wondered? Have you seen the Fact?"[32] Over the deep facts we all weave a cunning web often of many colors, of many thicknesses and in that web live, shunning the interior recesses which it conceals.

We deceive each other with these films and masks. Life often looks like a masquerade ball. Bring together after twenty or thirty years the old members of a youthful club or those who formed a class at an academy or a college or a military school and see what pleasure mere unmasking can give. Each has been thoroughly measured and known to the other as a boy and they are not to be imposed upon by later circumstances and acquisitions. One, may be, is a governor, and one a senator, and one a judge, they are professors, and military men of high rank, and eminent in law, in trade, or in politics. They have removed from New England to the South; or from the East to the West. Well, all these are imposing facts in the new neighborhood, or in the imaginations of the young men among whom they come, but not for us. When they come into the presence of either of their old mates, off goes every disguise, and the boy meets the boy as of old.[33]

Well, this is but a symbol of what is always taking place. We have closer garments which must be taken off. A man has more coats than an onion. How much of our experience is superficial. They say that the mathematics leave the mind where they found it. What if Life or Experience should do the same?[34] What if

---

[31] "The man of this age . . . with Reality" ("The Sovereignty of Ethics," W, X, 213).

[32] "so all our talents . . . seen the Fact" (G, 147).

[33] "Each has been . . . as of old" (G, 94, where Emerson writes of his own class reunion).

[34] "They say that . . . the same" (J, 43).

friendship should? Sometimes it seems as if we used friends as expedients much as we do stoves. We are very cold, miserably cold; we build a fire and get warm; but the heat leaves us where it found us. It has not forwarded our affair a single step; and so the friend when he has come and gone. Most of life seems to be mere advertisement of faculty: information is given us not to sell ourselves cheap; that we are very great.[35] But this secret is communicated in a moment of time, and years and years are spent on trifles.

A man who has accustomed himself to look at all his circumstance as very mutable; to carry his possessions, his relation to persons, and even his opinions in his hand as a bird that flieth, and in all these to pierce to the principle and moral law and every where to find that, has put himself out of the reach of skepticism. All its arrows fall far short of the eternal towers of his faith. And it seems as if whatever is most affecting and sublime in our intercourse, in our happiness, and in our losses, tended steadily to uplift us to a life so extraordinary and, as one might say, superhuman.[36]

As he is prepared for all skepticism by his own philosophy, so let him meet wisely this great fellowship in which Nature has placed him with his race. Has she drawn him to many individuals by inexplicable attractions, has she made his personal ties the crises of his history and signalized every thought and new state of his mind by some new friendship, has she made all his larger and more general sentiments and aims real and precise by directing them on particular societies of persons, not only on classes that surround him as politicians or scholars, his townsmen or his countrymen, but sometimes on men of former times, the poets and sages of the past or by a sympathy equally natural on the class of those who are born and to be born into the same thought in which he lives, and who are to walk in the light of the great day whose aurora he beholds;[37] let him accept with equal mind this great ordination and felicity of society and know how to use it highly and well. He will know that society is his outward con-

---

[35] "Experience," W, III, 73; below, p. 482.
[36] "A man who has accustomed . . . superhuman" ("The Sovereignty of Ethics," W, X, 213–214).
[37] Cf. "New England Reformers," W, III, 274–276.

science, that more truly and frankly than it knows or intends, it advertises him punctually of his rise and fall. And thus it does: All that a man hath will he give for right relations with his mates. All that he hath will he give for an [erect demeanor in every company and on each occasion.] [38]

.   .   .

And this is the way that man the pilgrim travels in this world.

Hills peep o'er hills, and Alps on Alps arise. [39]

Society when it has done all, when it has exhausted its ministrations, when it has agitated his bosom with honor and shame, with hope and rapture, introduces him to Solitude, and leaves him on the vestibule of a grander temple than its own. Life has its moments of awe and majesty when perchance in speeding away from some trifle to chase some other trifle we meet ourselves and know instantly that we had eaten lotos and been strangers from our home all this time. Again days pass and we are again startled with the perception that whilst that word and thought were in our minds another wave took us and washed away our remembrance and only now we regain our reason and turn a little in our sleep. [40]

Society has shown me this and that hero, this and that company, but that which I seek is not in this, is not in that. I see that while each figure stood for some part, none represented the whole; that it takes them all to make a mind; they are hints and segments, no more. Each hero was like a gem or bit of crystal that reflected a particular ray but when too nearly seen, the illusion of this diamond brightness ends. A personal influence is an *ignis fatuus;* if they say it is great, it is great; if they say it is small, it is small. You see it, and you see it not, by turns; and it seems to have no fixed value, just as Will of the Wisp vanishes if you go

[38] "All that a man . . . each occasion" ("New England Reformers," W, III, 275; J, 44). At this point three leaves are missing from the later version and one or two leaves from the earlier version. For continuation of the reading in New York, see Kronman, p. 104, and "New England Reformers," W, III, 275–276.

[39] Alexander Pope, *An Essay on Criticism,* line 232.

[40] "Life has its moments . . . in our sleep" (F No. 2, 27, where it is in first person singular).

too near, vanishes if you go too far, and only blazes at one angle. Who can tell if any man is great man or no? It depends on who asks, and at what stage of his progress. The time shall come when his great men shall have strangely dwarfed to his eye.[41]

Why should we quarrel with this irresistible law of Being, which ever and anon stands revealed before us, this namely; that whilst every thing is permitted to love, whilst man cannot serve man too far, whilst he may well and nobly die for his friend, yet are there higher experiences in his soul than any of friendship or love, — the revelations of impersonal truth, the broodings of the spirit, there is nothing at last but God only. Let me do as I will, the truth will not be hidden from me; the vast fact will return and be met, that all perishes except the Creator, the Creator who needs no companion, who fills the Universe with his own fulness, and instantly and forevermore reproduces Nature and what we call the world of men, as the sea its waves. The times, the men, what are we all but the instant manifestation of his energy? but each of us is constrained by the necessity of thought as soon as we leave the external fact, and come to the soul, to behold something which refuses to be disparted. When I think of Reason, of Truth, of Virtue, I cannot conceive them as lodged in your soul and lodged in my soul, but that you and I and all souls are lodged in that. And I may easily speak of that adorable Nature — there where only I behold it — in my own heart, in such terms as shall seem to the frivolous who dare not fathom their consciousness, as profane. When we go home, home to the Eternal Miracle which dwells in man, we feel that all the debts we could accumulate to other men by conversation, by book, by their actions or arts could never disturb our consciousness of originality.

That which is best in nature, the highest prize of life is the perception in the private heart of access to the Universal. How is a man a man? How can he exist to weave relations of joy and good with his brother but because he is inviolable, alone, perfect? I stand here glad at heart of all the sympathies I can awaken and share, clothing myself with them as with a garment of shelter and beauty, and yet knowing that it is not in the power of all who

[41] "A personal influence . . . dwarfed to his eye" ("Nominalist and Realist," W, III, 229, modified; E, 155, modified).

surround me to take from me the smallest thread I call mine. If all things are taken away, I have still all things in my relation to the Eternal. But the very worth and essence of this faith consists in its impersonality. It is not mine; it is not thine: it knows not persons or names or sex or accident. The ministrations of books and of the minds to which we are most indebted are but a whiff of smoke to that reality, most private reality, with which we have conversed. Our self-reliance it is reliance on this. Our sin it is the condemnation of this majesty: our hope, our Future, — it is the irresistible asseveration of this Prophetic Heart.

Bibliography
Textual Notes
Index

Bibliography of Principal Sources

Bacon, Sir Francis, *Works*, London, 1824. 10 vols.

Bell, Sir Charles, *The Hand, Its Mechanism and Vital Endowments, as Evincing Design*, Philadelphia, 1833.

Belzoni, Giovanni, *Narrative of the Operations and Recent Discoveries within the Pyramids, Temples, Tombs, and Excavations, in Egypt and Nubia*, Third Edition, London, 1822. 2 vols.

Biber, Edward, *Henry Pestalozzi and His Plan of Education*, London, 1831.

Briefe an Johann Heinrich Merck von Göthe, Herder, Wieland und andern bedeutenden Zeitgenossen. Mit Merck's biographischer Skizze, ed. Karl Wagner, Darmstadt, 1835.

Browne, Sir Thomas, *Works, Including His Life and Correspondence*, ed. Simon Wilkin, London, 1835–36. 4 vols.

Burton, Robert, *The Anatomy of Melancholy*, London, 1804. 2 vols.

Chorley, Henry F., ed. *Memorials of Mrs. Hemans*, New York, 1836. 2 vols.

Clarendon, Edward Hyde, Earl of, *The History of the Rebellion and Civil Wars in England*, Boston, 1827. 6 vols.

Coleridge, Samuel Taylor, *Biographia Literaria*, New York, 1834. 2 vols. in 1.

—— *The Literary Remains*, ed. Henry Nelson Coleridge, London, 1836–39. 4 vols.

—— *Specimens of the Table Talk*, New York, 1835. 2 vols. in 1.

Duppa, Richard, *The Life of Michael Angelo Buonarroti*, Second Edition, London, 1807.

Gardiner, William, *Music of Nature*, London, 1832.

Goethe, Johann Wolfgang von, *Werke*, Stuttgart and Tübingen, 1828–33. 55 vols.

Jahn, Johann, *History of the Hebrew Commonwealth*, trans. Calvin E. Stowe, Andover, 1828.

Johnson, Samuel, *Works*, New Edition, London, 1806. 12 vols.

Landor, Walter Savage, *Imaginary Conversations* [First Series], vols. I, II, Second Edition, London, 1826; vol. III, London, 1828.

—— *Imaginary Conversations, Second Series*, London, 1829, 2 vols.

Las Cases, Emmanuel, Comte de, *Mémorial de Sainte Hélène. Journal of the Private Life and Conversations of the Emperor Napoleon . . .* , Boston, 1823. 4 vols.

Lives of Eminent Persons, London: Society for the Diffusion of Useful Knowledge, 1833.

Marshman, Joshua, trans. *The Works of Confucius* . . . , Serampore, 1809.

Milton, John, *A Selection from the English Prose Works,* Boston, 1826. 2 vols.

———— *The Prose Works of John Milton,* ed. Charles Symmons, London, 1806. 7 vols.

Montaigne, Michel de, *Essays,* trans. Charles Cotton, vols. I, III, Second Edition, London, 1693; vol. II, Third Edition, London, 1700.

O'Meara, Barry Edward, *Napoleon in Exile,* Boston, 1823. 2 vols.

Plutarch, *Lives,* trans. John Langhorne and William Langhorne, New Edition, New York, 1822. 8 vols.

———— *Morals,* trans. "several hands," Fifth Edition, London, 1718. 5 vols.

Reed, Caleb, "The Nature and Character of True Wisdom and Intelligence," *The New Jerusalem Magazine,* III (Jan. 1830), 147–151.

Review of A. C. Thibaudeau's *Mémoirs sur le consulat* . . . and *Le Consulat et l'empire* . . . in *The Foreign Quarterly Review,* American Edition, XVII (July 1836), 173–197.

Review of Mlle. Cochelet's *Mémoirs sur la Reine Hortense et la Famille Impériale* in *The Foreign Quarterly Review,* American Edition, XXI (July 1838), 157–175.

Schlegel, August Wilhelm von, *A Course of Lectures on Dramatic Art and Literature,* trans. John Black, Philadelphia, 1833.

Sewel, William, *The History of the Rise, Increase, and Progress of the Christian People Called Quakers,* Third Edition, Philadelphia, 1823. 2 vols.

Staël-Holstein, Anne Louise Germaine, Baronne de ("Mme. de Staël"), *Germany,* New York, 1814. 3 vols. in 2.

Stewart, Dugald, *Works,* Cambridge, Mass., 1829. 7 vols.

Taylor, Jeremy, *The Whole Works,* ed. Reginald Heber, London, 1822. 15 vols.

Turner, Sharon, *The History of the Anglo-Saxons,* Second Edition, London, 1807. 2 vols.

———— *The Sacred History of the World* . . . , New York, 1832–38. 3 vols.

Textual Notes and Variant Passages

These notes, keyed to the text by page and line, are intended to record all of Emerson's manuscript cancellations and insertions, as well as any editorial changes not covered by the general editorial principles set forth on pages xviii–xxiv of the introduction. A number of changes that are so covered are included here also, as well as some variant passages and some supplementary material from Emerson's working notes. The text printed here is a literal transcription of the manuscript and thus differs in some respects from the edited version above. Minor eccentricities and slips of the pen, a few doodlings and other ephemera, and merely mechanical material (such as pointing hands) are usually omitted.

The symbols used in these notes are explained on pages xxii–xxiii. The symbol [E] here applies to what immediately precedes it, when that might otherwise be mistaken for an editorial insertion. When matter in these notes immediately follows a cancellation, without space, as in "The⟨se⟩y," "⟨was⟩proved," and so forth, it is partly or wholly written over the cancellation in the manuscript; a space is left when the new matter follows the cancellation in the manuscript. A small superior number represents a number inserted by Emerson, usually subscript, to indicate a reversal in the order of words or longer units.

I. HUMAN LIFE

1. DOCTRINE OF THE SOUL

Lines	Page 5
2	this ⟨place⟩ hall
3–4	topics ⟨as are familiar to me⟩ in the ⟨great⟩ problem of Human Life, ↑as are familiar to me.↓ ⟨I have⟩ In approaching
5–6	great ⟨ethical⟩ question of primary philosophy ⟨And⟩ who lives? What is the Life? ⟨If⟩ I
7–8	historical ⟨phenomena⟩ appearances
8–9	recent ⟨growth⟩ ↑activity and what that Doctrine is.↓
11–12	domains ⟨now strong⟩ ↑of of youth↓, ↑of↓ now ga⟨y⟩iety now tender[end line]ness
12–13	↑with divine omens & guidance↓
18–(6)1	A ⟨different⟩ ↑new↓ . . . age. ⟨from any that has appeared before. The⟩ It

Lines	Page 6
7–8	freedom /
	⟨Yet⟩ I see with joy a certain ⟨deeper thought⟩ ↑⟨better intelligence⟩↓ shared
9–10	consequence which ⟨literature philoso⟩ religion, literature, & philosophy, ⟨have⟩ enjoy
10–11	↑The indications of it are not always agreeable facts↓
17	apt to ⟨distrust⟩ overlook
18–19	deeper ⟨thought⟩ ↑truth↓ whereof they were a ⟨mistaken and⟩ very modified ↑& imperfect↓
20–23	announce. /
	The ⟨spirit of th⟨e⟩ is new time is dyed⟩ ↑movement of which . . . is marked↓ as is all modern history ⟨in texture⟩ with a deep religious tinge. And at ⟨some⟩ times
26–27	religious history. /
	⟨↑This is ↑dyed↓ marked as is all modern history ⟨so strongly⟩ ↑in texture↓ with a deep religious tinge↓
	A religious history which is only religious does not satisfy the whole mind of man ⟨but only⟩ ↑It only meets↓ one sentiment. ⟨It is the unbalanced sentiment⟩. True history will be religious but it will not be a religious history.⟩ Yet
29–30	whilst the ⟨appearance of⟩ ↑perfection of the arts of war,↓
31–(7)2	appetites. ↑A↓ [on previous page, marked "A":] ↑That I may illustrate a little in particular the ⟨forward⟩ ↑apparent↓ . . . And first f some notices . . . into more ⟨conspicuous⟩ ↑consequence↓ . . . history of mankind.↓ [end of "A"] ⟨↑A passage like the one I am about to quote is only to be found↓ In modern history. ⟨first appear such passages as the following⟩. ↑It is from the worthy Dutchman Sewel who wrote the annals of the Quakers. describes England in 1648.↓⟩ "About this

	Page 7
5	souls. And th⟨e⟩ese now
6–8	thereunto." ↑About the same time . . . following testimony↓
	⟨Hear the testimony of another piece of history, the testimony of Milton⟩ to the interior character of the ⟨same⟩ period. ⟨h⟩He describes
18–19	convincement." — Then see further the reason ⟨[?]e⟩with which
26	↑reading,↓
28	written of, ⟨argues first a singular good will, contentedness & confidence in your prudent foresight & safe government lords & commons.⟩ x x x x x it betokens
29–30	ages."
	⟨In such⟩ This is
31	names ⟨&⟩ which s⟨r⟩o many
32–33	fact for . . . ↑not only an Assyrian Empire & Roman Empire but a↓ a human

Lines   *Page 8*
1–3   So in the ⟨fact⟩ pause . . . makes in ⟨his chronicle⟩ ↑the
       thread of his narrative↓
4   event ⟨occurs⟩ ↑transpires↓
12–13 Falkland."
                                    History of the Rebellion
                                         Vol III p 1518.
15–18 unfolding of the ⟨same idea, a growth of humanity. Their his-
       tory⟩ ↑higher elements of the human nature   Its value is↓ is
       in the↑ir↓ literature & their laws. ↑Much of↓ The ↑external↓
       activity of the people ↑their trades . . . life↓
21   ↑masters↓
23   certain ⟨deeper⟩ ↑higher↓
26–27 last 150 years
28   called ⟨a⟩out the
33–(9)3 living ⟨whilst⟩ ↑between whom & us↓ the broad Atlantic roars,
       ⟨betwixt us & our poet⟩, I will say that the fame of ⟨Mr⟩
       Wordsworth . . . modern litera⟨r⟩ture when

                                Page 9
7   that of the ⟨Cause or⟩ Idea ↑or principle↓
8–9   expressing. ⟨It is the He is the poet of humanity⟩ ↑His ⟨g⟩
       inspiring genius . . . of humanity↓
15–17 same ⟨agitation⟩ ↑perception↓ . . . revelation is is ⟨the revela-
       tion of itself.⟩ ↑of course . . . It craves realities.↓
20–23 than ever, ⟨summoning us we know not whither, but ⟨by⟩ ↑in↓
       going, it shall guide⟩ ↑& follow whithersoever it may lead↓
       us. / ↑⟨Men have become introversive & speculative. even
       to tediousness. At ball rooms & d⟨inn⟩ancing parties we meet
       the scowl of metaphysics⟩↓
            ⟨Its⟩
       Every part of life shows ⟨new⟩ the . . . spirit. ⟨As the man
       has become introversive & speculative, so⟩ ↑Men have become
       introversive & speculative even to embarrassment. & fear.↓
       ⟨t⟩The
24–28 ↑A wild striving . . . those understand . . . vast conceptions
       & aspirations⟨.⟩than . . . attempted before.↓
30–33 histories b⟨y⟩ut opens the crust of the earth ⟨itself⟩, to study
       organic remains, & strata ⟨that it⟩ ↑that the core . . . con-
       science↓ may tell its own ↑tale.↓ ⟨Every⟩ This

                                Page 10
1   reflection. ⟨t⟩The
2–3   suffrage the ⟨attack upon⟩ ↑denunciation of↓ Oaths, ⟨upon⟩
       ↑of↓ Capital punishment ⟨upon⟩ ↑of↓
4   good ⟨old fashioned⟩ public

Lines
5   let it ⟨put on its night cap⟩ ↑sleep↓
6–8   is ⟨the⟩ based . . . movements ⟨give the same⟩ ↑are↓ disagree-
          able as is the ⟨litter & scaffolding of new⟩ felling . . . noise &
          ⟨materials⟩ piles
9–10   seen as ⟨signs⟩ ↑signs↓ of that which shall be, they ⟨are heav-
          enly signs & cheer the heart with light⟩ may
11   uneasiness ⟨to refl the⟩ too conscious
17   side. ⟨A ne⟩ New thoughts
19   begins. ↑M p. 116↓ [in pencil; pencil scribble possibly cancels
          the passage: "Undoubtedly this . . . begins." However, this
          passage and nothing else is on a single leaf, properly num-
          bered and once sewn with the rest.]
28–29   degree. ↑Insert M p.↓ [in pencil]
30   whole ⟨secret of & mystery⟩ ↑tendency↓
33–34   today the ⟨p⟩ old problem

Page 11

1–2   whose ↑memory↓ names when dead
4   Man beautiful
9   Labor; ↑Laughter;↓ Society [caret] Religion
10   Death. ⟨Here in the same old walls of Nature & Circum⟩ And
12   Here in the ⟨same⟩ old
19   powers ↑& merits↓
21–22   history ⟨pleasing not⟩ unpleasing. ⟨⟨The new⟩ Saturn or Time,
          according to the most ancient fable, devours his children. The
          new thought, the new age swallows up the memory of the
          old, ⟨and⟩ comes because the old was imperfect. Man carries
          ever before him a lofty Ideal which refuses to unite with the
          actual appeals from the best history to a better not less than
          from the worst. Yet is the history of man full of noble traits
          which the soul will not refuse to entertain. Beautiful his na-
          ture the ornament of the world encumbered ⟨as⟩ ↑tho'↓ it is
          with the great institutions which have almost buried him alive
          Scarce now can the nature be seen for the cumbrous ⟨gar-
          ments of law⟩ usages & ceremonies of law property Church
          Customs Books⟩ In all the madness & sorrow of history the
          appearance of noble traits in private souls makes it / dear &
          admirable. Man has
24–25   institutions ⟨s⟩Yet
29–30   race. /
               ⟨And⟩ something
35   feel that ⟨fortu⟩ he is not the ⟨p⟩ ball

Page 12

1   Homer ⟨ar⟩is
6   Troy & ⟨shows⟩ ↑points out to↓

Lines

7–34   Ulysses. /
Tell . . . Ulysses here. [quotation marks supplied through-out]

9–10   who is that? ⟨less⟩ ↑shorter↓ by a head than Agamenon ⟨Atrides⟩ ↑son of Atreus↓, but ⟨to⟩ he seems ⟨straighter⟩ ↑broader↓

11–13   on the ⟨fruitful⟩ earth . . . leader ⟨rules⟩ ↑walks about↓ the bands of men ⟨I liken him to⟩ ↑He seems to me like↓ a ⟨fleecy⟩ ↑stately↓ ram ↑the↓ ⟨who goes⟩ ↑as a master↓ thro the ⟨great⟩ flock. ⟨of white sheep.⟩

15–16   the ↑state↓ demos of ⟨barren⟩ ↑mor↓ [below cancelled word] craggy Ithaca, knowing all ⟨st⟩ wiles & ⟨prudent⟩ ↑wise↓ coun-sels. ⟨T⟩

18   For ⟨formerly⟩ ↑once↓

19–21   on an em⟨[?]⟩bassy with ⟨Mars⟩ ↑Menelaus be↓loved by ⟨Menelaus⟩ ↑Mars↓. ⟨Them⟩ I received ↑them↓ & entertained ⟨in⟩ ↑them at↓ my house. Of both I ⟨knew⟩ ↑learned to know↓ the ⟨n[?]⟩ genius & the prudent ⟨counsels⟩ ↑judgments↓. ⟨But⟩ when

22–23   ↑the broad shoulder⟨ed⟩s of Menelaus rose above ⟨him⟩ the other↓ ⟨Menelaus s[?] was taller in his broad shoulders⟩ but

24–26   majestic. ⟨But⟩ when they ⟨wove⟩ ↑conversed & interweaved↓ stories & ⟨counsels for⟩ ↑opinions with↓ all, Menelaus ⟨⟨s⟩ ha-rangued⟩ ↑spoke↓ succinctly, few ⟨words⟩ but very ⟨sonor↑o↓us⟩ ↑sharp words↓

26–27   nor ⟨sinning⟩ ↑exceeding↓ in speech, & was {the ⟨last in his race⟩.} ↑younger↓

28   ground ⟨nor⟩ ↑and↓

29–30   neither ⟨behind nor before⟩ ↑backward nor forward↓ but held it ⟨unmoveable⟩ ↑still↓ like an awkward ⟨man⟩ ↑person↓

30   fool & ⟨unwise⟩ ↑simple man↓

31   voice ⟨from⟩ ↑forth out of↓

32–36   mortal ↑compare↓ contend with Ulysses; and we ⟨all⟩ rejoice⟨d⟩ not in beholding ⟨his⟩ the countenance of Ulysses here. /
    a system grinder hates the truth
    Beethovens music
    feeble influence of thot /
↑And what is there . . . another man.↓

37–(*13*)1   ↑Milton calls Scipio "the height of Rome."↓

Page 13

2   ↑one of his↓
10–11   haunted by ⟨a⟩ hope & ⟨a⟩ faith
13   justified in ⟨expressing⟩ ↑indulging.↓
19   grand ↑design↓ plan ten
21   Sir ⟨Horace⟩ ↑Robert↓
22   dinner. And ⟨the worthy President⟩ Fontanes

26–(*14*)1   ↑Be it so. With all the godlike . . . in history, we can spare it all.↓
    ⟨And⟩ frankly

Page 14

3   mans ⟨nature⟩ ↑intellect↓
4–6   better ⟨before⟩ ↑within↓ him ↑unrealized↓ . . . points, there is ⟨something before him⟩ ↑that in hope↓
11–13   worthless? ⟨When the⟩ Six thousand . . . chambers & & magazines of the soul. /
    ⟨We are haunted by Hope & by Faith⟩. Philosophy
14   experiments ⟨in the⟩ there
16   is on that somewhat /
    ⟨The argument for hope rests always⟩ on that somewhat miraculous
19–20   forgive ⟨your⟩ ↑the man of calculation his↓ want of faith if ↑he↓ you had
28   Not foreknown not fore-⟨estimable⟩ ↑measureable↓
29–30   new unknown most subtle powers no boxes, but ↑a↓live
32–33   ↑More therefore than . . . calculator↓
    ⟨Therefore⟩ we always welcome the ↑inexact↓ rare extravagant

Page 15

1   profound ⟨spirit⟩ [erased] thought [over erasure]
2   repelled & ⟨reproa⟩ discredited
5–6   ↑without adequate results↓ & ending ill perhaps do ↑us↓ yet ⟨bring⟩ a high ⟨message to us.⟩ ↑service↓
7   heaven. ⟨⟨Be as⟩ If you Show hospitality to their souls⟩; ↑If you↓ Give
10–11   action of ⟨his⟩ ↑such a↓
12   ↑single↓
14–15   evil suggest↑s↓
16   condition ⟨& for whose final consummation we have the pledge of nature. word of the soul.⟩ and so
19   in it, ⟨ev⟩ as
21   Soul. Who
23   ↑in remorse,↓
26–29   masquerade in wild . . . ourselves the droll . . . notice we shall
30–(*16*)20   knowledge ⟨that there is an immense background to our being, an ⟨unpossessed⟩ Immensity not possessed & that can not be possessed; but which is the Soul; that the Intellect & the Will must obey the Soul which is not a faculty but a Light. ↑From within or from behind I may say a light shines thro him on things & makes him aware that he is nothing but the light is

all. A man is the least part of himself↓ A man is but the facade
of a temple wherein all wisdom & all good abide. The whole
evil of the Intellect is when the Intellect would be something
of itself & not simply the organ of the Soul. The whole evil
of the Will is when the Individual would be something of
himself & not simply the child of the Soul. All Reform is to
break down this busy Interference & to let the great soul have
its way through us; in other words, to live simply & obey.⟩ /
[The two leaves following, enclosed within a double sheet, are
different paper from the rest, but are paginated in ink to fit
between "38" and "39" thus: "38 1/2," "38 3/4," "38 7/8,"
verso. They have been sewn with the others once, but not at
one other time.]

↑All goes . . . Light; ⟨which is the immense background
of our being⟩ which . . . through us / upon things . . .
drinking, ⟨digging⟩ ↑planting↓, counting, speaking man ⟨is⟩
does . . . action — would ⟨cause⟩ ↑make↓ our knee↑s↓ ⟨to⟩
b⟨ow⟩end. It is yet th⟨is⟩e life . . . something of itself / &
not . . . All ⟨r⟩Reform . . . simply & obey. / [blank] / ↓

⟨It perceives truth. We are wiser than we know. If we will
not interfere with our thought but will act entirely or see how
the thing stands in God we know the particular thing & every
thing & every man. For the Maker of all things & all persons
stands behind us & casts his dread omniscience through us over
things.⟩ It shines

Page 16

30   see it ⟨from⟩ [erased] let [over erasure]

Page 17

1   greatness of his ⟨mind⟩ perception
13–14   was a↑n↓ ⟨m⟩ important
15   among ⟨our⟩ the existing generation the poet ⟨w⟩Wordsworth
17–18   higher than ⟨conscious⟩ thought.
20   ↑the partisan↓
25–26   Shelleys, & ⟨Hemanses⟩ ↑Hugoes↓
30   worth. ⟨i⟩It includes

Page 18

6   works which which he
13   same ⟨Light⟩ ↑Soul↓
19   him, he ⟨had a perfec⟩ ↑put↓ no ⟨confidence⟩ ↑trust↓
21–22   might be ⟨trusted⟩ ↑confided in↓ as one who had ⟨more⟩ interest
          in his ⟨soul. than any⟩ ↑character↓. There is a ↑natural↓
30   smiles, in ⟨the grasp of⟩ salutations

Lines

31–32 well ⟨whether we we have⟩ which of us has been ⟨faithful⟩
↑just↓ to ⟨to⟩ himself ⟨w⟩& so

33 aspiration or ⟨an⟩ ↑our honest↓ effort also. ⟨No man here doubts
my conviction of the things I now say though it may easily be
apparent to him that I do not speak from above down to him
but standing on the same platform urge him to ascend in a
tone which indicates my own sense that I have yet to ascend
also.⟩ /

Page 19

2–3 society, its ⟨business⟩ ↑trade↓ its religion, its ⟨feasts⟩ ↑friend-
ships↓ . . . one ⟨grand⟩ ↑wide↓

4 committee, ⟨examinations⟩ or ⟨w⟩ confronted

12 And as ⟨in truth⟩ it perceives truth & ⟨per⟩ discerns

13 shame has any man

14 when ⟨h⟨is⟩e brings his⟩ in the

18–21 higher ⟨Judge is also⟩ Judgment seat is also ours. /
⟨Now why is this that⟩ we know ⟨so much⟩ better than we
do ⟨that⟩ we . . . much more? I

27 all their ⟨interior wealth⟩ display

Page 20

5 faith in the ⟨unlimited improvement⟩ ↑possib↑l↓i↑l↓ties↓ of man

6 moment he ⟨s[?]⟩ is

9 infinite ⟨possibility to man⟩ ↑scope to his spirit↓

11 time, ⟨the riches of⟩ ↑entire↓ existence ⟨are⟩ ↑is↓

12 does not ⟨c[?]⟩ talk

13 infallible i⟨mage⟩ndex of

19 sentences, the / the ⟨rig⟩ ↑build↓

20 brave it ⟨h⟩out how

29 hoped that ⟨I could suggest⟩ ↑by naming↓

31 once. ⟨Grant⟩ ↑Own↓ this

Page 21

1–2 law /
⟨We read ourselves in all history. In enacting a law we
indicate a fact in human nature.⟩ Human life ↑as containing
this↓

6–7 ↑Because of this . . . superior beings↓

17 because there ⟨a[?]⟩law was enacted the ⟨land was⟩ sea

20–21 have ⟨the fr⟩ externally

33 character. yea further

Lines   *Page 22*

2   meet ⟨a sneer or two, or two million or⟩ vexations

[A leaf, now filed with this lecture but never sewn with it:]

Our society is very rich, has many ornaments of cloudier or purer light. Some of these are often long out of sight and are like stars which, ⟨only⟩ shining all the time, are only seen when the nearer sun and moon are withdrawn. How noble in spirit are the men who have never stooped nor betrayed their faith! The two or three, perchance, wearisome souls, who could never bring themselves to the smallest composition with society, rise with grandeur in the background, like statues of the gods, whilst we listen to the adroit flattery & literary politics of those who stoop a little. If these also had stooped a little, then had we no examples; our ideas had been all unexecuted; we had been alone with the mind. / The solitary hours; — who are their favorites? Who cares for the summer fruit the sopsavines that are early ripe by help of the worm at the core? Give us rather the winter apple the russetin & pippin cured & sweetened by all the heat & all the frost of the year. [G, 62 (Aug. 27, 1841).] /

[Another leaf, now filed with this lecture but never sewn with it:]

I may even say that not only in idea of the race but in actual history the emerging of each rare individual of a finished man always speaks to us a language of admonition & hope. That wonderful sympathy & attraction which we find in each great man by which we prefer one eminent individual to nations of Chinese & Indians what does it say but this that we have an inextinguishable conviction that the powers which he was permitted to unfold he folded in us. Man everywhere man alone possesses real attraction for us / [blank] /

2. HOME

Page 24

1   sketch of the ⟨recent⟩ spirit
4   indication⟨s⟩ of
5   Doctrine of the ⟨S⟩ True
7   made ⟨with a view to⟩ of
8   mind ⟨or⟩ respecting
9   life. / [five manuscript leaves missing at this point]
10–11   angels & mus⟨se⟩es resort
11   ↑elves &↓
14–15   Apollo ⟨s⟩ So Ceres ⟨Latona⟩ ↑Mercury↓
15–16   What ⟨radiant⟩ relations . . . land. Who . . . opens ⟨a shop⟩ ↑an office↓
22–24   iron 31 inches by 33. ↑Now if it happen . . . on that head↓ [in pencil] But that want

Lines   *Page 25*

1–2   blower. ↑and all the beautiful rules . . . in iron.↓

4–8   medicines. the naturalist . . . jury box. [no punctuation ex-
             cept as indicated] /
                   ↑I find that I am announced in the newspaper as prepared
             to read a course of Lectures on Human Life. Since my arrival
             in the city this morning the Directors of the Lyceum have re-
             quested me to select from two courses of Lectures delivered
             by me in another place a series of ⟨discussions⟩ ↑Discourses↓
             of topics of general interest ⟨in which⟩ ↑such as↓ I might hope
             ↑will↓ to interest the ↑audience↓ Lyceum & to begin this even-
             ing with a Discourse on the Genius of the Present Age.↓ [in
             pencil] /

11   ↑and where better than↓

12   cousins? ⟨In the childrens books⟩ Louis

16   then see ⟨buckr⟩ men

17   substance, ⟨who never⟩ whose

18   stilted & ⟨booted⟩ harnessed

22–23   garden, the ⟨family, wife, mother, son, & brother⟩ ↑house & the
             old & new familiar faces therein contained↓

26   attraction to ⟨o⟩life &

28–30   Man: ⟨B⟩↑And the most sublime consequences . . . & earth-
             born attachments.↓

32   benefits / [one manuscript leaf, possibly blank, missing at this
             point]

33   fact every

34   Home? What ⟨fact &⟩ principle

                                           Page 26

2   Home ↑which↓

7   same. ⟨In⟩To the

8   walls, ⟨d[?]⟩ supply

9   as a ⟨permanency⟩ ↑fixture↓. If a table or chair ⟨which it has
             [?]⟩ falls

12   & he ⟨passes⟩ ↑enters↓ into new ⟨rooms⟩ ↑apartments↓

13   goes in his ⟨wagon⟩ ↑basket coach↓

18   walls! ⟨Th⟩He & they

24   being! ⟨The brothers are scat⟩ He

29–30   before, — not in ↑house↓ walls, not in ↑a fenced↓ garden, not
             in ↑a↓ ⟨e⟩town

30–31   image of ⟨their⟩ ↑his↓

32   places & ⟨a⟩old

33   these ⟨But⟩ ↑Yet↓

35–36   connexion ⟨of⟩ ↑[erased letter]↓ in society; to his political
             ⟨party⟩ religious literary part⟨y⟩ies. The ⟨highly⟩ cultivated

                              396

Lines	*Page 27*
6	regard. ⟨When the soul comes to see that nature⟩ To very many persons ⟨the⟩ in
7	phlegmatic, ⟨the⟩ places
15	anomaly so ⟨common⟩ ↑frequent↓
17	to the ⟨passion⟩ ↑change↓
18	ever ⟨correspond⟩ ↑coincide↓
20–21	↑his own instincts would advertise him↓ his own connexion ⟨with⟩ &
22	perfect ⟨coincidence⟩ ↑consent↓
23	had ⟨dwelled⟩ ↑worked↓
26–27	Nature ⟨is⟩ which
28–29	flux & the ⟨gravitating spirit refuse⟩ ↑spirit fluttering like a bird ⟨for⟩ to find somewhere a resting place↓
29–31	ticklish & unste⟨e[?]⟩ady plank. ⟨for⟩ ↑Whither shall it go for a foothold? ⟨Slowly⟩↓ ⟨It learns to see stability at the heart of agitation regulating ⟨n⟩all motion & to find in Law the natural counterpart to its own spiritual fixedness and to be at home in Law. The sooner this lesson is practically learned, the better. The spiritual home is the natural home of the Soul. All places are alike to the good man for in all ↑appear↓ that Law & order which certify him of co-nature with his own constitution more than do the lineaments which resemble his own which he sees in his own house. ⟨appear.⟩ God is his home & ⟨n⟩all his knowledge & moral growth go to domesticate him in every fact & event ⟨in nat⟩ that transpire in Nature.⟩ / ↑It receives . . . stable causation.↓
33	resembling. as
33–(28)2	only ⟨metamorphoses⟩ ↑transformations↓ of a leaf. Every day ⟨differs from the last⟩ ↑resembles every other day↓ ↑tho'↓ [in left margin] the sky, ↑the light↓ the landscape, the temperature. ⟨Yet resembles it more than it differs⟩ ↑differ↓

	Page 28
6	agitation ⟨regulating all⟩ ↑& Law↓
11	men ⟨at last the⟩ in
18–19	eternity, and ⟨seeks⟩ therefore ↑when he comes . . . seeks↓
20–21	↑intelligent man, . . . wear out↓ ⟨an assembly of men⟩ seem
25	town ↑were↓
29–30	consciousness that ⟨ove⟩ within
31–33	Universal that . . . nearest that . . . infancy that . . . answers that
37	alike to him⟨. He is⟩ for

	Page 29
1	resemble his own ⟨h[?]⟩ which
2	house. ⟨All proceeding from The⟩ Having

Lines	
3	Cause of all all
10–11	As the ⟨mou⟩ ↑house the village↓
12	↑dwindle &↓
15–16	↑Now first he can go . . . with him↓
20–22	↑This ready domestication . . . in every degree↓
	⟨This easy domestication⟩ is always
22	that whi↑l↓st ordinary
25	↑their fireside corner↓
28–29	↑in conflagration;↓
30–31	↑It is the secret of perfect Heroism.↓
32	infuses a⟨n astonishing⟩ confidence
34–36	↑Not less is . . . intellectual research.↓
	⟨And truly⟩ if it be seen a little deeper ⟨a constant ef⟨o⟩fort⟩ all growth all progress is a constant ⟨eff⟩ endeavor
37	is a ⟨q⟩Question, and Nature is the ⟨a⟩Answer. ⟨So that⟩ to produce

Page 30

2–3	↑I wish to see my own nature in every fact.↓
5	Rome, ⟨Babylon⟩ ↑Memphis↓
10–11	gropes in the ⟨catacombs⟩ ↑mummy pits↓
22–23	uninhabited ⟨mas⟩ members
25–26	One Mind. ⟨I do not wish to know that my shell is a strombus or my moth a Vanessa but I wish to unite the shell & the moth to my being.⟩ To what . . . classification ⟨we call science⟩ ↑of botany of natural history↓

Page 31

5–6	↑is yet to be felt in public & private Education.↓ will give a gravity
8	lands with ⟨purpose w⟩light
9	idol / [four manuscript leaves missing at this point]
10–11	↑I have said that a true Culture goes to make ⟨a⟩man ⟨at home alike in⟩ a citizen of the world, at home in Nature.↓
17–19	out of it immediately . . . haunts once . . . of himself under
28	feasts ent⟨s⟩ers at
31–⟨32⟩1	from us." /
	⟨It is the effect of this domestication in the All to estrange the man in the particular. He that has learned by happy inspiration or by slow experience, that is, by gradual inspiration that his home & country are so wide that not possibly can he go forth out of it, immediately comes back to view his old haunts once so familiar as to seem like his own body, ⟨with⟩ under an altered aspect. They look strange & foreign. Now that he has learned to range & associate himself by affinities & not by custom, he finds himself a painful stranger ⟨at his⟩

under his own roof   And thus the saint in all ages has come
by progress to say We are strangers & pilgrims ⟨[?]s⟩in the
earth. It was a highly philosophic & poetic mind which under
the rude form of the Saxon Witan ↑said to the king Edwin↓
when ⟨Gregory⟩ the Christian missionaries arrived in Britain
from Rome to preach the gospel "Man's Life is like a sparrow
that enters at a window flutters a while round the warm house,
& flies out at another & none knoweth whence he came or
whither he goes."⟩
 The advancing

Page 32

2	such ⟨vile⟩ ↑poor↓
7	& with ⟨mo⟩ new curiosity
8	family, to his ⟨daily⟩ household
12–14	↑A nearer intimacy . . . not near us.↓
22–23	each others acts. ⟨He supposed that husbands & wives have no present time that their relation was retrospective that they had long already established their mutual connexion have nothing to learn of each other. Now he discerns the fact namely that they are often chance joined little acquainted & do observe each others carriage to the stranger as curiously as he doth.⟩ / Let him
28–29	opportunity no more ↑All men are . . . those nearest us↓

Page 33

9–10	↑the rich wisdom↓ that its hated necessities can teach↑.↓ ⟨him. They shall make him wise.⟩ [emendations in pencil] Here
12–14	↑the sublime compensations . . . every debt↓ [in ink] ↑keep exact balance in all the actions of man↓ [in pencil] the opium
17–18	There is ⟨Time⟩ Glee & ↑Hospitality↓ Ceremony &
20	Laws. if
22	reconcile the⟨m⟩se with
23–25	↑Nor has he seen its secret until until he . . . sanctities of nature↓ [in pencil]

[A leaf now filed with this lecture but never sewn with it:]

⟨As this Heart is the acknowledgment of the common nature the means &
occasions for its culture are universal. Yet it is observed that the habit of
privation and of giving & receiving mutual aid such as for instance the life
of the sailor & other dangerous vocations imperiously require is favorable
to it. And in general it is more likely to appear in the poor than in the rich.
And here let me say that this as every Culture has no better school than
that with which we are all familiar as what may be found in every village
all over New England the poor but educated family. Who has not seen

Lines

with pleasure & hope the eager blushing boys discharging as they can their household chores & hastening into the sittingroom to the study of tomorrow's merciless lesson yet stealing time to read a novel hardly smuggled into the tolerance of father & mother; atoning for the same by some pages of Plutarch or Goldsmith;) the warm sympathy with which they kindle each other in yard & woodshed with scraps of the last oration or mimicry of the orator; ⟨the youthful criticism⟩ the youthful criticism on Sunday of the sermons; the school declamation faithfully rehearsed at home, to the vexation more frequently than to the admiration of sisters; the first solitary joys of literary / vanity, when the translation or the theme has been completed, sitting alone near the top of the house; the cautious comparison of the attractive advertisement of the arrival of Kean or Kemble, or of the Discourse of a well known ↑speaker↓ orator with the expense of attending the same; the warm affectionate delight with which they behold & greet the return of each, after the early separations ⟨of⟩ ↑which↓ school or business require; the foresight with which, during such absences, they hive the honey which opportunity offers, for the ear ⟨of [?]⟩ [erased] ↑&↓ [over erasure] imagination of the others; and the unrestrained glee with which they ⟨profusely⟩ disburden themselves of their early mental treasures, when the holidays bring them together again. What is the hoop that holds them staunch? It is the iron band of poverty, of necessity, of austerity, which excluding them from the sensual enjoyments that make other boys too early old, has directed their activity into safe & right channels & made them, spite of themselves, reverers of the grand, the beautiful & the good. Ah shortsighted students of books, of nature, & of man! too happy could they know their advantages they pine for freedom from that mild parental yoke; they sigh for fine clothes; for rides; for the theatre; & premature freedom, & dissipation, which others possess. Wo to them, if their wishes were crowned! The angels that dwell with them, & are weaving laurels of life for their youthful brows, are Toil, & Want, & Truth, & Mutual Faith. [C, 242–243; "Domestic Life," W, VII, 119–121] /

[Notes, apparently for this lecture, from Emerson's working journal Φ, pp. 152–153:]

Home

The same care which covers the seed warm under husks provides for man the Mothers breast & the fathers house. warm, careless, cheerful, with good appetite, he runs in & out with boys & girls.
Welcome to the parents the little straggler comes with his comic lamentations which soften all to pity & good humor.

Domestic education   Shadows.
Natural affection [?]
Boy, child & snow
Poverty
Domestics
Housekeeping
    Mystics or [?] do not travel
    Stay at home like an axis

Lines

Yet let your eye see
Travelling is objectiveness
Homekeeping is subjectiveness
Travelling for the young it leans depends begs
Home for the strong it lives radiates commands
Let him learn the tragicomedy of his house; of woman; of [?]; of near relations; /

Philosophy of Home
sub-object   In Out
progressive transference   to Law to God
Easy domestication a trait of great men D 111
All growth the endeavor to realize thot
Philosophy is Homesickness
Belzoni   Science wd make Then Now
Effect of univ. domestication to make partic. estrangmt and so man comes to live a stranger and guest at home
Advantages of home to disengaged observer
Not a duty less
Home a school of human life
a school human power
a playground /

3. THE SCHOOL

Page 34

2–3   life, & the ⟨condition of⟩ Home & domestic relations in⟨to⟩ which
4   I ⟨proceed⟩ now to enumerate [perhaps an accidental cancellation]
8–9   experience, and ⟨to u⟩some . . . necessary to ⟨take a⟩ ↑examine↓ nearer. ⟨view⟩ But ⟨it seemed fit to examine⟩ the
12   relation ⟨so⟩so [cancelled and then rewritten over cancellation]
14   countenance, ↑(for his eye habitually asks or inquires,)↓
16   under that ⟨view.⟩ aspect
19   1. {Instincts.}
20   word ⟨as⟩ in

Page 35

8   ↑of essential life, the sense of being↓
13   reverence for
15   the one ⟨teacher⟩ ↑Soul↓
16   belief in the ⟨possib⟩ unlimited possibilities
18   fop ⟨nor ruffian⟩ /nor ruffian
20–21 ↑The co presence . . . to all teaching↓
22   ↑in amount↓
26–27 infusions of ⟨soul⟩ ↑itself↓. It ⟨make⟩ cares

Lines
27–28   docile⟨s⟩ ⟨soul⟩ ↑man↓ an apparatus, ↑out ⟨of⟩↓ of
31–34   quality   For ⟨as⟩ this ⟨is that which makes character, this
determines a man's use of all the means all the influences to
which he is open⟩ ↑contains in itself . . . primary ⟨life by⟩
wisdom as . . . *tuitions.*

Page 36

4   Here ↑we↓ lie ⟨we⟩ in
10–11   ↑speaking of the intuitive knowledge↓ "to inquire whence ⟨the
intuitive knowledge⟩ ↑it↓
14–20   ↑Every man discerns . . . He may err in ⟨e[x]⟩ his expression
. . . to be disputed.↓ ⟨Every man in his moment of reflection
sees & records this vision⟩ & therefore ↑when he affirms . . .
perception, he↓
21–22   caprice, ⟨& not made himself⟩ ↑when in truth he was the while↓
23   flow through. ↑D. 141↓ [in pencil]
25–26   Individual ⟨determines the⟩ makes ↑what we call distinctively↓
31–32   a progressi⟨n⟩ve

Page 37

4–6   drift wood, &c ↑or like the loadstone amongst splinters of
steel↓. In ⟨every place where is⟩ ↑the midst of↓ action &
thought God sets down ⟨a thousand of⟩ these
11–12   ↑affections & so on his↓
16   ↑the best of↓
18–19   fate." ⟨My⟩ ↑Our↓ . . . images in ↑the↓ my mind
21   yielded ⟨me⟩ ↑the man↓
22   bench at ⟨Latin⟩ School. ⟨Our indirect⟩ ↑What we do not call↓
27–28   its own /
⟨⟨[?]⟩ I believe that⟩ those

Page 38

3   door, ⟨&⟩ ↑whilst↓
4   sufficient that ⟨they⟩ ↑these particulars↓
8   standards. ⟨of history⟩. Do
11–15   usual in ⟨English⟩ Literature. Respect . . . nature ↑What
your heart thinks great is great↓ [in pencil above line "in
⟨English⟩ Literature. Respect"] ↑The souls emphasis is the
true one↓ [in pencil above line "them, for they . . . nature"]
⟨Who does not see⟩ ↑⟨Every day will show you⟩↓ [Insert cancelled in pencil] that time & space ↑are always↓ yield↑ing↓ to
↑the abiding instincts of the soul.↓ ⟨the spiritual nature⟩ ↑In our
real education↓ Magnitude
18   Jussieu. Let ⟨the⟩ ↑every↓
21   milleniums ⟨&⟩ makes

Lines
25   Time. ⟨[?]⟩And so always the⟨re⟩ soul's
31–(39)1   that the Millenium aproaches, & the like. when

Page 39

8   society & ⟨so is⟩ the
13–14   are the ⟨love⟩ ↑perception↓ of truth in thought; & the ⟨love⟩ of
                  [emendations in pencil]
16–17   far ⟨higher & tr⟩ ↑nobler↓ & ⟨more ⟨radi⟩ central⟩ profounder
                  ↑than Hope↓, ⟨the sentiment of⟩ an absolute
18   from the ⟨participation⟩ ↑beholding↓ of ⟨those counsels which
                  are⟩ [cancelled in pencil] everlasting. ↑elements↓ [in pencil]
20   pupil. ⟨They never sound⟩ They lie
22   ↑in nature.↓
24–25   that these ⟨heavenly orbs approach⟩ ↑celestial lights shine more
                  & more inward↓
27   And so as the weapons of this lordly intelligence are
31   satisfaction ⟨teach & teach⟩& teach
33–34   irritable & ⟨mor⟩ all-related

Page 40

1   II. His condition is
3   conditioned; ↑Space & Time↓ ⟨The frame of nature⟩, the sun
4–7   runs through ⟨nature⟩ things, Growth & Death. There ↑revolve
                  to . . . all sides,↓ ⟨hang the sun & moon, the great forma⟩lists,
                  in the sky
8   will not ⟨budge fr⟩ ↑swerve↓ a hairs [end line] breadth . . .
                  Here ↑spite of all we can do every↓ [faint pencil above the
                  line "is a planted . . . & belted with"]
10   ↑civil↓
11   young ⟨soul⟩ ↑inhabitant↓. He ⟨m⟩too must
14   ↑external↓
18   He ⟨plants his⟩ tills
20   ↑By this act of ownership↓
24–26   ↑or as ⟨if by⟩ one . . . for him.↓
31   What ⟨to⟩ activity

Page 41

1   The ⟨adm⟩ education
4   condition ⟨is⟩ ↑are↓
5   communication. & ⟨we never exhaust⟩ these
7   seen nearer; ⟨of being⟩ is
14–16   temperament, from our ⟨or[?]⟩ personal . . . defects & ⟨the
                  yoke of⟩ ↑all that we call↓
17   But this ⟨also⟩ is sub⟨ordin⟩sidiary [written continuously]
20   of condition; ⟨which⟩ for

Lines

25–26   differences of ⟨external⟩ Nature & Fortune. / [blank] / [pas-
         sage marked "A," below] /
         Persons
         III. Another

29   express to me ⟨the⟩ a . . . great ⟨soul⟩ instincts

33   admiration, ↑pity;↓

Page 42

2–17   war. ↑{Insert A}↓ [on previous page, marked "A":]
         ↑What influences . . . castles in the air. ⟨In⟩By tones
         . . . perpetually upon us.↓ [This insert is in ink over the
         following pencil passage:]
         ⟨These are the pungent instructors who ⟨speak in⟩ thrill-
         ⟨ing⟩ the ⟨b⟩ heart of each of us & make all other teaching for-
         mal & cold. In tones of triumph ⟨in⟩ of dear love in threats
         in cold pride that freezes these have the skill to make the
         world look bleak & inhospitable or the nest of tenderness &
         joy I do not wonder at the miracles which poetry attributes
         to the Music of Orpheus when I remember what I have ex-
         perienced from the varied notes of the human voice.⟩

21   cannot f⟨[?]⟩orego his ⟨instruction.⟩ tuition.

22   face in ⟨turn⟩ ↑rotation↓

23   turns, evince this

25–26   perforce his ⟨kinsman & his brother⟩ ↑follower & suitor. He
         is my brother↓

28   I think ⟨I⟩ ↑we↓

29   sound, from the ⟨insane⟩ ↑morbid↓

31–32   science & every man has a science [at bottom of page these
         pencil inserts:] ↑Conversation D 147↓ ↑Uninteresting Person
         D 118↓ ↑Persons & thoughts C 300↓

Page 43

13   It ⟨is⟩ ↑arches over them like↓

14   every ⟨one⟩ ↑heart↓

17   elevation. ⟨The⟩ From

30–31   world. / [blank] /
         Books.
         IV. Another

34   thought, I have ⟨the⟩ ↑my↓

Page 44

1–2   Organization; In persons, I have ⟨a th⟩ myself ↑repeated &
         modified↓

3–4   man. ⟨I⟩in Books I have ⟨the p⟩history; or, the ⟨p⟩ energy

6   With them ⟨I⟩ ↑many of us↓ spend the most of ⟨my⟩ ↑our↓

404

Lines

10–11	↑"Reading," ⟨m⟩Montaigne complained . . . Be it so, yet↓ ⟨T⟩the
12	perfect ⟨pliancy⟩ ↑tameness↓
12–13	bidding, ⟨make stand in⟩ ↑compensate the quietness &↓
14	sternness of the ⟨inf⟩ lessons
16	infusions of the ⟨Divine Spirit⟩ ↑high *Instinct*↓
16–17	great ⟨institution⟩ Magazine
19	books the best. ⟨And take men as they rise & see their debt to books. We are impotent creatures. Stung by this desire for thought we run up & down into booksellers⟩
20	History they
24	though ⟨compensated⟩ robbed
28	The book ⟨mak⟩ whilst
32	into athen↑a↓eums

Page 45

1–5	enriched. ↑{Insert A}↓ [on previous page, marked "A":] ↑Give me said . . . another ↑accomplished↓ person . . . shining ⟨in his sky⟩ ↑before him↓.↓ ⟨But⟩ ↑And↓ when
9–16	Light. ↑{Insert B}↓ [on previous page, marked "B":] ↑How comes it then . . . thinking of today.↓
17	↑Aristotle, ⟨Cicero⟩ Tully,↓
18	↑And Why? Because↓ So
19	↑*perception* & *creation;* between↓
26	poet th⟨i⟩ese million repeating↑s↓ of his name, ⟨ar⟩like
28	↑states &↓

Page 46

13	soul, ⟨that⟩, "what
16	And ⟨yet⟩ ↑therefore↓
17	consider ↑them↓ [in pencil]
18	must be ⟨reso⟩ esteemed
20	need less. ⟨{A few kernels of corn will support life as well as tables groaning meats & sauces from every zone of the globe. In the profusion of our books we slightly turn over the leaves of a journal & pass to a new one but in the barroom of a country tavern we find information & suggestion in every shipping list & auctioneers advertisement a few coals to kindle the fire are as good as a ton, & one book as good ⟨as⟩ to a wise man as the Bodleian Library.}⟩ ↑And in the multitude of books we ⟨are⟩ do not rate them at their true value.↓ [in pencil between the lines, above "from every zone . . . slightly turn"; presumably intended to be cancelled]
26	deep therefore
31	↑it may be said in abridgment of the value of books,↓

Lines	*Page 47*
7	alive when
8	write i⟨n⟩t in
9	↑iron↓ stereotype↑s↓
10–11	weapon he ⟨loses somewh⟩ abates somewhat of his ↑natural↓ energy if
14–15	forth. / [blank] / ⟨IV⟩ V. But beside
17–18	↑Nature which is One . . . in Facts.↓
26–30	existence.
	↑⟨But whilst these facts absorb our attention⟩↓ [in pencil] /
	↑With all the extreme . . . do not scrutinize↓ [in pencil]
	⟨O⟩Day creeps . . . desart. [no punctuation]
36	joy, that
36–(48)1	friend or t⟨[?]⟩hwart an

Page 48

5	wheeled & cha↑i↓ned in
6–7	sublimity.

⟨The truth is the Will cannot use facts   We can only by our total growth come to the di right administration of them The facts are like numerical ciphers or like letters of the alphabet they have no⟨v⟩ [erased] value until they take their order from conscious intelligence   Not the fact avails but the use you make of it. People would stare to know on what slight single observations ⟨Newton⟩ Kepler & Newton & Bradley had inferred those laws which they promulgated & which society receives with respect & writes down as Canons. A single flute heard out of a village window a single prevailing strain of a village maid will⟩ /

8	but ⟨a pro⟩ an
14	↑passing of a↓
34	sentiments & ⟨insists on⟩ refus⟨ing⟩↑es↓ the

Page 49

2	glorifies him. Or shall I say, the ⟨events of each hour ⟨fall⟩ descend on ⟨him⟩ man in continual & blinding succession like the flakes of snow falling on the traveller in winter. they cover & encumber him his true form is no longer seen: they have given him theirs; — but the spiritual perception is like a ray of heat which dissolves the shapeless ⟨drift⟩ ↑fleece↓ & suspends it again a bright transparent vapor in the air around him.⟩ /
4	come to ⟨a right administration⟩ a
6	them. The ⟨law⟩ soul
21–22	nature. A ⟨single⟩ flute heard out of a village window, a ⟨single⟩ prevailing

Lines

28–(50)4 see & do. [Insert from bottom of page indicated here:]
     ↑In what is small . . . & ↑scorns not to↓ [in margins]
     sympathise⟨s⟩ with . . . weight.↓

Page 50

5–8 A renouncement . . . to learn. [no punctuation]

4. LOVE

Page 51

2 nature o[page mutilated] the
5–(52)1 the ↑En↓umeration & inspection, accord-↑in↓g to [letters at left
    torn away and supplied in pencil on backing glued to leaf]

Page 52

7–8 carries him ⟨{inward}⟩ ↑with new sympathy↓
10 old; ⟨establishes marriage⟩ awakens
10–11 music, ⟨religion⟩ art
15 power ⟨[?]⟩of Love
16 brute ⟨nature⟩ ↑matter↓
18 inorganic ⟨nature⟩ ↑matter↓ strives & works ⟨in elective affini-
    ties⟩ in
20 In ↑the↓ vegetable ⟨nature⟩ ↑kingdom↓
22 ↑sons &↓
23–29 ↑At the same season . . . swell with↓ In spring ⟨⟨[?]⟩new life
    awakens the⟩ melody ⟨of the woods⟩. In spring new life appears
    brisk & jo⟨yful⟩cund in the animal tribes /
     ⟨Sacred to this influence since man was on the planet was⟩
    ↑In the temperate zones, . . . changes on↓ the
30 May day.

Page 53

5 lessons ⟨t⟩reach
11–12 poet ⟨3⟩ three centuries
16–17 mood. {Richard Edwards} /
    This seems ⟨to be poetic⟩ ↑pardonable↓
19 cold & ⟨equal⟩ ↑even↓
20 affections, ⟨d⟩but whose
22 glow as ⟨readily⟩ ↑genially↓
25–26 light, & ⟨make⟩ ↑warm↓ the ↑alpine↓ cabins of ⟨Switzerland⟩
    ↑New Hampshire↓ {⟨& the snowhuts of the Esquimaux⟩} & the
    cellars of ⟨⟨l⟩Lapland⟩ ↑the Fins & Laps↓
27 truth as ⟨well⟩ ↑readily↓ as the mansions of England & the
    ⟨warm⟩ ↑sunny↓

Lines
29–30 ↑And yet the natural association . . . the blood↓
⟨And this⟩ leads
31 ↑it↓ in vivid tints which ⟨sho⟩ every
33–34 philosophy, as ⟨impairing⟩ ↑chilling↓

Page 54

1–2 ↑of being unnecessarily hard & ⟨of being⟩ stoical↓
3–4 affections,. ⟨of being too hard & philosophic⟩ ↑But from these
. . . to my seniors.↓ ↑For↓ ⟨But i⟩⟨↑I↓⟩it is
6–7 rather ⟨lets⟩ ↑suffers↓ no one who is truly its servant ⟨to⟩ grow
old, but ⟨fires⟩ ↑makes↓
9–10 sort. / ⟨I[?]⟩For th it is
11 caught from ⟨the love⟩ ↑a wandering spark out↓
13 upon ⟨all⟩ ↑multitudes of↓
15–16 therefore ⟨how of⟩ whether we attempt to ⟨paint it in youth
or in⟩ ↑describe the passion↓ . . . eighty ⟨[?]⟩ years. he
24–25 this ⟨noble⟩ sentiment
25–26 For ⟨such⟩ ↑it↓ is the nature of man to ↑that each man always↓
see↑s↓
27–29 imagination. ⟨The slime of error we⟩ ↑If ⟨I⟩you will forgive the
expression every man↓ sees ⟨in our⟩ ↑over all his↓ own experience ↑a certain slime of error↓
33 embitter ⟨all⟩ in
35–36 point of the ⟨soul⟩ ↑intellect↓, or, as truth. But all is ⟨foul⟩
↑sour↓ if seen ↑as experience↓

Page 55

3–4 persons & ⟨today's⟩ ↑the partial↓ interests ↑of today & yester-
day↓
5–7 fall ↑forget the *you* & *me*↓ ⟨& you may⟩ ↑converse . . . and
you may↓ deal with all Creation — ⟨with bone & marrow, corn-
barn, flourbarrel⟩, things
8 naming nam⟨ing⟩es never
10–11 star.
⟨And so let us ponder these universal experiences of the
heart. They address all persons of all conditions with⟩ / equal
nearness.
The strong
16 circulate? What tales fill the outside column of all ⟨newspapers
except the ⟨political⟩ metropolitan where politics & trade have
taken the heart out? What sort of stories fill the journals &
magazines of London, Paris, New York, & Boston. And who lets
a tale of Leonora & Orville & Ludovico go by him without dip-
ping into the midst & ⟨then⟩ skipping ↑along↓ to the catastro-
phe?⟩ How
20 saw the⟨n⟩m ↑before,↓

Lines	
25	nature. ↑{Insert "Village love"D2}56 D256↓
28	go into ↑the↓ a shop↑s↓
33	girls ⟨are⟩ have

Page 56

2	Edgar & ⟨Harry⟩ ↑Jonas↓ & Almira & who was
7–16	great men. / ↑In strict philosophy . . . that of persons. ↑In Logic↓ The position of the Idealist . . . appearances & ⟨spectres⟩ ↑phantoms↓ merely . . . things as they appear↓ [in pencil] /
17	part ⟨that⟩ Persons
20–21	influence of Persons. ⟨But⟩ ↑For↓ Persons are love's world; and ⟨no one can⟩ the
26–27	↑although↓ a beauty
30	is a ⟨cro⟩ wreath
30–(57)5	brows. ↑Insert X↓ [on next page, marked "X":] ↑What I am going to say may sound strange, ↑yet I shall say it.↓. . . tender memory."↓

Page 57

7	things new which
12	memory. when
13	gone. when
15	carriage / [passage "X," used above] / [blank] / when
17	sweeter ⟨thoughts⟩ conversation
18	for the figure⟨s⟩ [erased] the
22	gone whe⟨[?]⟩reer
27–28	his pains" and
29–(58)1	recollections. ⟨when the moonlight was a fever and the stars were letters & the air was coined into song, when all business seemed an impertinence & all the men & women running to & fro in the streets mere pictures.⟩ when the head ↑throbs↓ [in very faint pencil; not Emerson's handwriting] boil⟨s⟩ed all night on the pillow with the generous deed it resolve⟨s⟩d upon [cf. W, II, 176]

Page 58

7–8	↑Nature grows conscious.↓ The ⟨s⟩bird who sung unheeded ↑yesterday↓
9	↑as the boy . . . as the bird,↓
10–11	articulate. ⟨t⟩The clouds . . . on them. ⟨t⟩The
12	grass be⟨low⟩↑neath↓, &
17–27	↑Fountain head↑s↓ [in pencil] & pathless . . . feed upon.↓ ↑{Insert B}↓ [on previous page, marked "B":] ↑Lo now there

409

in the wood ↑is the fine madman↓ he is . . . man; He walks . . . soliloquizes. he . . . veins. and . . . that wets his foot.↓

29–31   verse. ↑D↓ [at bottom of page, marked "D":] ↑It is a fact often observed that men ⟨who⟩ have . . . circumstances.↓

Page 59

4–5   which are ⟨peculiar to⟩ ↑the property & creation of↓

6   in the ⟨corners of⟩ newspapers & magazines ↑in corners↓

9   attain ⟨w⟩ a classic . . . ages, {⟨I am thinking⟩ now ⟨of a few lines written by Mrs Hemans & of others by anonymous hands⟩.} / The like

10   man; It ⟨m⟩expands

14   object. I⟨t⟩n giving

21–26   admire ⟨that⟩ Beauty . . . celebrate. Beauty welcome . . . shine which . . . themselves. (Brandt . . . ever so long.) / ⟨Then comes the fuller revelation of Beauty to the youth; of love & support to the maiden.⟩ Beauty . . . the ancient esteemed

31   gleam point

Page 60

8   Paul. "Away

12   criticism & can⟨no⟩ no longer

23–24   beholder feel ⟨its⟩ his unworthiness: when he cannot feel ⟨more right to them than⟩ his

Page 61

1   present ↑to↓

2–3   so the ⟨d⟩Divine ⟨l⟩Love

11   sorrow, ⟨but if accepting th⟩ body

15   ↑and the lovers↓

18–19   love of ⟨the⟩it &

22–23   of them so he

36   thought ⟨of⟩ have

37   This ⟨view⟩ ↑doctrine↓

Page 62

5   Base⟨st⟩ when

10   libertine. ⟨He dreams that⟩ There

16–21   joins ⟨the⟩ characters which are complements to each other. ⟨In woman is somewhat sacred & nearer to the divinity⟩ ↑{Insert B}↓ [on previous page, marked "B":] ↑Man represents Intellect . . . Truth Woman . . . goodness. Man loves

Lines

Reality woman order man power ↑woman↓ [in pencil]
grace   Man . . . acquires Woman . . . house beautiful↓
[no punctuation that is not shown here]

22 ↑whilst man excels in understanding↓ [in pencil]
24–29 Divinity. ↑A↓ [on previous page, marked "A":] ↑Woman in
very unfriendly ⟨circum⟩ condition very . . . surprise ⟨wom⟩
he finds . . . her natural home.↓
31–32 resources ⟨tries⟩ impelled

Page 63

3 her love ⟨of⟩ into
9 skirt of ⟨a⟩its
10 Nor ⟨in⟩let the
10–11 wife & b⟨e⟩lind ↑him↓ [in right margin] ⟨blind⟩ to
15 charms for ↑their↓ kindly
23 Neither ⟨m⟩ will
28 ↑But not to expand ↑at present↓ these trite ethics of society↓
[in pencil]

Page 64

1–2 ever group⟨ed⟩ing themselves according to higher or more interior ⟨relations⟩ laws
9–10 who ⟨v⟩are glancing at each other ⟨in the assem⟩ across
13–14 leafbuds. ⟨f⟩From exchanging glances they ⟨procee⟩ advance
18–20 ↑Her pure & eloquent . . . her body tho't↓
22 fine ⟨Then l⟩Life ⟨has⟩ with
25 all form.
  ↑("The person Love does to us fit
  Like manna has the taste of all in it.")↓ The lovers
29–30 alone to ⟨search narrowly their⟩ try

Page 65

2 pain ↑impend↓ arrive to them
12–13 defects ⟨in th⟩ disproportion in the behaviour of the o⟨f⟩ther
hence arises surprise & ⟨regret⟩ expostulation
21–28 other. ↑{A}↓ [on previous page, marked "A":] ↑For it is the
nature . . . taste of all in it."↓ All the ↑angels↓ virtues that

Page 66

1 breast losing in ⟨ardor⟩ ↑violence↓ . . . in extent it
15 society ⟨t⟩forty or
16 emphasis which
21–23 ↑a grain of Being . . . Yes & No↓ ⟨a grain⟩ of truth, above
26 Without it. to

411

Lines

26–27   Fate; ⟨and⟩ ↑& to prize . . . fading charms.↓ a justice
29   forgets, ⟨over all partialities & all fading charms.⟩ Present
31–33   ↑What perturbations & questionings . . . dismissed!↓ They
    . . . other ⟨the whole⟩ by
34   deed. to

Page 67

1   ↑the cheerful &↓
2   ↑love &↓
4   hours of ⟨extreme⟩ calamity
5   front un⟨h⟩terrified
9–10   ↑By strictest dependence . . . to independence↓
13   John & of ⟨Mary⟩ ↑Joan↓ [in pencil]
14–15   & meet ⟨as meet⟩ [in pencil] as ⟨worlds⟩ ↑nations should↓
    meet, perfect spiritual ↑self↓suffici⟨ent⟩ng eternal. [in ink]
21–22   soul. ↑Tho' slowly & with pain↓ [pencil, rewritten in ink] The
28–32   ↑But we need not fear . . . & that forever.↓ [in ink, written
    over the following pencil version:] But we need not fear that
    we can lose any thing by the progress of ⟨our⟩ the soul   The
    soul may be trusted   That which is so beautiful & attractive
    as these relations must be succeeded & supplanted only by
    what is more beautiful & that forever

5. GENIUS

Page 68

1   ⟨From the⟩ In my last lecture
3   healthy ⟨souls⟩ ↑minds↓
4   heat which ⟨en⟩ are
8   ↑What is Genius? ⟨What is that⟩ Genius — which↓
    ⟨The essence of Genius is spontaneity. That which⟩ in its
10–12   good which constrains us ⟨all⟩ to attribute to the possessor a
    ⟨certain miraculous & divine⟩ ↑rare & splendid↓
13–14   god & ⟨that⟩ a fragrance as of flowers ⟨exuded⟩ exhaled from
    ⟨all⟩ his ⟨person⟩ ↑skin↓
14   every ⟨person⟩ ↑one↓
17   freedom of ⟨all⟩ institutions, ⟨r⟩houses
18   the stage-coach, ⟨itself⟩, & begs

Page 69

4   men. ⟨The⟩ All
5   proverb in ⟨all⟩ fair
6   thus ↑or thus↓
7   against ⟨all opinion to⟩ the contrary ↑opinion↓
9   goes a ⟨deeper⟩ ↑finer↓

Lines
11   they cannot ⟨stand⟩ sleep & cannot ↑sit↓. ⟨stand⟩.
12   ear, ⟨& heart⟩ every
13   stranger ⟨brings⟩ ↑reports to↓
14   memories. ⟨By⟩ These
16   ↑cardinal↓
29   ↑The Venetian Florentine & Roman masters↓ ⟨Angelo Raphael & Titian in Italy⟩ do still ⟨th⟩ as
30–33   ↑through the hands ↑& on the easels↓ of other men . . . never saw↓ ⟨in England & America at this hour⟩. And why name ⟨our English household Gods⟩ ↑the gods of our English Parnassus↓ ⟨I will not name an English name for they⟩ ↑which↓ outshine in our memory all ⟨other⟩ foreign images⟨,⟩? the⟨y⟩se are th⟨cn⟩c synonyms
38   then for Shakspeare ⟨I see on the booksellers counters a fair book entitled "Insects mentioned by Shakspeare."⟩ we have ⟨not only⟩ libraries

Page 70

2–3   parish re⟨cor⟩gisters of
4–5   "Insects mentioned
8   goes ⟨everywhere⟩ ↑about↓ the willing adorer of one ⟨a⟩or another
14–18   Spontaneity {It is . . . inmost self}
20   us of ⟨the [?]⟩ trivial
21–22   easy to ⟨exhaust⟩ enter the dim infinity, ⟨to⟩ which all spontaneous action ⟨leads us⟩ ↑implies↓
24–25   worketh. — The
31–33   before ⟨I⟩ [erased] we [over erasure] . . . observe that this fact of Spontaneity . . . Genius in our tongue. / And this fact of Spontaneity . . . Genius in our tongue.
35   consult the ⟨childs⟩ ↑boy's↓

Page 71

1   things. ↑and relates to practice.↓
3   literature as ⟨[?]⟩history
5   ↑by↓ which ⟨each⟩ quite
6   class mak[page torn] a
8–11   ↑Its subject is truth its object a creation of tru↑t↓h without, — whether . . . astronomy.↓
      ⟨The sculptor instructed by the Soul sees hovering over all particular ↑human↓ forms ⟨of⟩ a fairer ⟨form⟩ & so a truer form than any actual beautiful person & copies it with ⟨enthusiasm⟩ ↑desire↓ in marble, & so we have the Theseus the Apollo, which with wonder all men allow is truer than nature. ↑D88 Dreams & Drawing↓ [in pencil]
      Then see how this is evinced in the arts of design. Not by

413

any conscious imitation of particular forms are the grand strokes of the painter executed but by repairing to the fountainhead of all forms in the mind. And it is very well worth considering as one of the facts that go to show us how much Unconscious knowledge we possess⟩ /

13   Its ↑s↓ object is . . . think Genius ⟨a⟩ converses

15–16   soul. the most articulate precise ⟨undeceivable Mind⟩ ↑of speakers↓. hating

16   things. ⟨In⟩ common

18   because it ha⟨th⟩s something

21–22   ↑poor↓ girl who having ↑over↓ heard an ⟨explanation⟩ ↑account↓

23   orbit ⟨relat⟩ ↑repeating the information in her own way↓

27   realism ⟨&⟩ ↑or↓

31   saith ⟨makes good⟩ therefore always ⟨makes fit⟩ ↑justifies↓

32–33   falsehood, ⟨wit⟩ playing

Page 72

2–3   perceiving ⟨the link to others invisible that joins the fact in question to every other fact &⟩ ↑the fact to be a mere appearance a mask & detecting↓

5   them it ⟨worships⟩ ↑seeks↓

9   things   At⟨he⟩the centre

11–13   ↑Let me illustrate . . . respect to the↓ ⟨↑of↓ The⟩ Greek genius. ⟨how perfect is our history⟩ Thus

15–16   us. ↑a very sufficient account . . . they did.↓

23–24   scale ⟨for⟩ of conditions from god⟨head⟩ to beast

26   we have ⟨to confirm the facts of the history of⟩ ↑for↓ one remarkable people, a ⟨three⟩ ↑four↓-fold

27–28   in ↑History, in↓ Literature, ↑in↓ Architecture, & ↑in↓

29   give back ⟨exactly⟩ the

Page 73

1–3   not ⟨remarked⟩ ↑found↓ that a ↑particular↓ picture ↑or copy of verses↓ a ⟨poem a landscape or conversation⟩ will awaken in your mind ⟨n⟩if not the same train of images yet th superinduce the

8   from th⟨is⟩ese ⟨but⟩facts ↑but↓ [in left margin] this

9–10   far ⟨inward⟩ down

10–11   ↑primarily↓ by a painful acquisition of many ⟨external⟩ ↑manual↓

17–18   pictures ⟨a⟩enkindle in me.
     Truth is the ⟨object⟩ ↑subject↓

21   thing. ⟨Hence That is what⟩ Therein

21–22   dart that ⟨infixes itself in his heart & incessantly⟩ ↑rankles↓ goads him ⟨on⟩ with

Lines
23–24   not ⟨the⟩ a mere copy
32   know. ⟨h⟩He ⟨crowds⟩ ↑collects↓
33–34   coexist in ⟨nature⟩ [erased] any [over erasure]

Page 74

6   knows the ⟨v⟩resources . . . bosom of the soul? ⟨That indeed
             beggars all description⟩. [cancellation in pencil]
13–14   comes. / ⟨that it requires no⟩ ↑Whence had you those primary↓
             lessons in drawing, — ⟨to give us⟩ the
22   sets ⟨a hundred⟩ ↑twenty↓
27–34   We entertain . . . with grief. [no punctuation]
35   repairs ⟨&c &c⟩ [in pencil] the [ink over the pencil] decays

Page 75

28   The few memorable hours [There follows an insert "A" for the
             next page and, inverted, at the bottom of the page:]
             ⟨Genius we say is the spontaneous perception & exhibition
             of truth. Hover with me a little over the deep to which that
             word points us⟩ /
             ⟨The origin of genius is very high as we may know from
             its deep effect.⟩ The few memorable hours of life
30   struck ⟨with thunder⟩ the thunder
31–32   coach ⟨rolling o⟩to roll on a ⟨rod⟩ ↑bar↓
33–36   walk has ⟨thought of God⟩ ↑mused on the Supreme Cause↓ &,
             ⟨written out⟩ *that* . . . next age. ↑A↓ [on previous page,
             marked "A":] ↑Some chemist has detected . . . through Na-
             ture↓

Page 76

10–11   exist ↑in short that it is allied to God↓
12   why they ⟨exist⟩ ↑are↓
16   prerogative of the ⟨work of genius⟩ ↑a⟨s⟩ masterpiece↓
22–23   in the ↑perfect↓ strict analogy that is between / ⟨genius² & vir-
             tue¹⟩ ↑virtue & genius.↓
25–26   nearer communion &, in
34   We ta↑l↓k⟨e⟩ of old
37   much of. / ⟨Will you⟩ ↑To this purpose↓

Page 77

10–11   every man. /
             Genius selfrelying
             1. To analyze
13–15   are ⟨om⟩ entire — ↑and to enumerate . . . first, Genius↓ ⟨it
             charms us⟩ captivates us by its ⟨e⟩self reliance

Lines

19   than to be ⟨an actor⟩ the

22–23   ↑We are admonished . . . another time↓

26–(78)22 his joys. ⟨{for example Wordsworth's picture of skating⟩ ↑Insert A↓ [ink] ↑Works, Vol. 1 p. 29.↓ [pencil; next page, marked "A":] ↑Let me adorn . . . an inferior ⟨poet⟩ writer . . . picture of skating . . . summer sea.↓

Page 78

23–24   trust is inde⟨d⟩ed very deep for the soul is sight, & ⟨knoweth well what⟩ all

25–26   what facts ⟨to choose⟩ ↑speak to the imagination & the soul.↓

28   fact ⟨less⟩ ↑no more↓ . . . violet. ⟨The⟩ To

30   yardsticks, ↑& sidereal years↓

35   itself, & i⟨s⟩t ⟨the voice of⟩ ↑leans on↓

37–38   ↑It raises . . . fertility↓ ⟨When thought is best then is ⟨it⟩there most.⟩ When [cancellation in pencil]

Page 79

2–5   ↑In our purest hours . . . both is ⟨resem⟩ alike.↓ ⟨Such is the genius of God⟩ in nature a leaf in the forest or ⟨the flower we call blue eyed grass⟩ ↑⟨an iris⟩ a field lily↓

6   ↑two↓ [in left margin]

9–10   But what an / profusion

13–14   wisdom. ⟨The very naming of a subject by a man of genius is the beginning of insight. W⟩ ↑Let a man of lively parts . . . his point of view↓

17–18   shining ether. /
Genius not predictable
2. And being spontaneous, ⟨it⟩the work

25–26   literal p↑r↓ose his ↑mystic↓ song.)
       "I know not if it ⟨is⟩be the ↑reflected↓ [pencil, re-written in ink] light of its ⟨⟨first⟩ maker ⟨impressed on the imagination⟩⟩ [pencilled cancellations under ink] ↑author↓

29   glows ⟨the⟩ ↑a↓ bright ray of ⟨its primitive state⟩ [cancelled in both pencil and ink] ↑⟨a pre-existence⟩ [in pencil under:] its preexistence [in ink]↓,

30   burning, ⟨which⟩ [cancelled in pencil] ⟨is perhaps⟩ [cancelled in pencil and ink] ⟨that⟩ [cancelled in ink] ⟨which⟩ [cancelled in pencil and ink] leads

Page 80

2   ↑at the same time↓

4   works of genius. ⟨↑⟨Talent draws & experiments & the soul says that is brave but not right⟩ Genius grasps the pencil & with sure ⟨& daring⟩ audacity goes daring daring on new &

Lines	
	incalculable ever.↓ ⟨Every line & stroke of genius is new & incalculable⟩ and yet the soul greets each ↑stroke↓ with entire welcome & says That is it. It is true. But how knew it that it was true?⟩ / Talent
9	Soul ⟨[?]⟩ ↑attentive↓
10–11	It is true; It is true. ⟨But o my friends! how knew the Soul that it was true?⟩ [cancelled in pencil] ↑Its tone its deed . . . genius itself↓ ⟨I see no clue to guide me to their origin⟩ Shakspeare
14–15	many; {⟨so as to know how I should / write the same things.⟩ Inferior
23	great ⟨g⟩Greeks who ⟨b⟩cut the
26–28	↑3. As one more ⟨document⟩ ↑sign↓ of . . . elements of spirit↓ Another trait ⟨of this brave spontaneous life we call Genius⟩, is, its *love*. Genius is always ⟨sportful⟩ humane
29–32	↑It has been observed . . . entrusted with political ⟨power⟩ or ecclesiastical power.↓ ⟨It never smells of fagots⟩! There

Page 81

7	bigots & ⟨traitors.⟩ juntoes
8	devout persons to be the
10	↑More,↓ Fuller, Herbert, ⟨More⟩ Milton
12–13	also. We ⟨have a⟩ trust Genius; we trust its integrity Its ⟨adherence to⟩ praise
14	sentiment ⟨of⟩ which
16	find ⟨our⟩ a
19	appearance. ⟨And he will know how to prize⟩ And
21	arrive ⟨in respect⟩ concerning
22	Science. or
25–26	it lack. / [blank] / *Genius Representative* 4. To add
29	Do not ⟨represent⟩ ↑describe↓
33	common-[end line]wealth And so I think [last two words lightly cancelled, probably by a slip of the pen]

Page 82

1	brotherhood to the ⟨more⟩ seers
2	Burns, if our ⟨own⟩ ↑American↓
8	reason why ⟨we are sl⟩ he
14	later. ⟨h⟩However
16	day, ⟨will⟩ recal his
17	verse ⟨of⟩ I
24–25	Whose was ⟨Shakspear⟩ ↑Bunyan's, Defoe's↓ & Cervantes & Newton whose

27   masters belong? ⟨And therefore the instant fruit of their several revelations always is to inspire a boundless confidence in
the resources of the human mind. But for them we should be
cowards & sleepers⟩ /

Page 83

1   he who ⟨sa⟩ [erased] can [over erasure]
2   bosom of ↑all↓
4–8   time & again. /
       ⟨I know no more striking instance of the representative
character of genius than we have in the familiar fact of popular eloquence. The orator triumphs by ⟨speaking for us⟩ ↑being
our tongue↓ As it was happily said of Sir James Scarlett, that
the reason of his extraordinary success with juries was that
"there were twelve Scarletts in the jury-box." Go into Faneuil
Hall & ⟨see⟩learn the lesson that is taught you there⟩ Join the
⟨black⟩ ↑dark↓ irregular thickening groups that ⟨hasten⟩ gather
in the old house when fate ⟨is⟩ ↑hangs↓ on ⟨a⟩ ↑the↓ vote ↑of
the morrow↓. As the crowd grows & the hall fills ⟨the old &
feeble withdraw & here is a⟩ ↑behold that↓ solid block of life
↑few old men[blot] mostly↓ young & middle aged, ⟨men⟩ with
shining heads & swoln ⟨full⟩ [erased] veins [over erasure]
12–13   sweltering ⟨multitude⟩ ↑assembly↓
18   They ⟨push⟩ back, push, ⟨scold⟩ ↑resist↓
19–23   stops the moderator ⟨co⟩persuades commands entreats ⟨Order⟩
The speaker ⟨gives way gets breath & a new hint & resumes⟩
↑gives way. At last . . . common heart. ⟨he⟩ [erased] With
[over erasure] his first words . . . know his word↓ goes to
the right place; ↑as he catches the light spirit of the occasion↓
25–27   magnetized, — & the h⟨all⟩ouse hangs suspended on the lips
of one man. ⟨for he is the voice of all. Whilst he hears e⟩Each
man ↑whilst he hears↓
28–30   voice of 4 or 5000 men in full cry, the ⟨finest⟩ ↑grandest↓ sound
in nature. If ⟨the⟩ ↑a dull↓ speaker ⟨be⟩come ⟨dull⟩ again

Page 84

8–11   ↑Its own idea genius never executed.↓ The Iliad ⟨of Homer⟩
the Hamlet ⟨of Shakspeare⟩ ↑the Doric . . . anthem↓ when
they are ended, the ⟨the poet⟩master ↑master↓
13   soul! ⟨H [partially formed]⟩Before
17   ↑Let those admire who will↓

6. THE PROTEST

Page 85

1–(86)22   Dr Johnson . . . members is another [This double sheet, a
different paper, may be a revision, though added to the lecture before it was sewn. It is enclosed in another double sheet
which consists of the cover, the blank verso of the cover, and

Lines

the material, partially cancelled, between lines (86)22 and
32 (see below).]

6–7 planet a⟨n⟩ [erased] new experiment, ↑to be & exhibit the full
& perfect soul.↓ and

8–9 ↑contemporary↓ experiments. ⟨to be & exhibit the full & perfect soul⟩. For ⟨every thing testifies⟩, notwithstanding . . .
who ⟨satisfy⟩ ↑meet↓

10 aspirations, — ⟨that⟩ ↑every thing testifies↓

12 individual; / that . . . soul, & ⟨seek⟩ that

13–14 will.
⟨In actual life, the⟩ We

17 after them, ⟨from us all⟩ indicates

Page 86

2 love ↑of genius↓

4–5 every ⟨soul⟩ ear & arouses mankind with its ⟨music⟩ ↑creative
teaching↓. All men ⟨greet it all⟩ hearken . . . greet it / it
↑creates &↓

10–12 finer organization, [caret] yield . . . soul. ↑those who have
succeeded who have ↑not only↓ sought but found↓

13–14 majority; of [caret at this point, at beginning of new line;
insert between lines] ↑who have not yet made their mark;↓

15 men & women in disease, or se⟨lf⟩nsual indulgence ⟨have⟩ ↑⟨do
now⟩↓ blocke⟨d⟩ up

17 itself ⟨to⟩ in . . . These ⟨boil⟩ ↑are fired↓

18–19 a flame. / Then arise

22 is another /
⟨In my last lecture I ⟨considered⟩ ↑attempted some analysis
of↓ the nature & attributes of genius. The obvious course was
followed of depicting it as it appears in those rare individuals
who are emphatically separated & as it were consecrated by
the suffrage of the great body of mankind as Men of Genius.
At the same time it was enumerated as a conspicuous trait of
this ↑Spiritual↓ Energy that it is Representative. It is loved
by all. But ⟨this⟩ what is this love but genius imperfect?
Genius is of man of every man. It sleeps potentially in every
breast. For ↑when pure↓ it is nothing but the unobstructed
expression of the one Soul that animates all men. When it
finds a clear & full voice its shrill song is heard ↑for↓ [in left
margin] a thousand years musical to all mankind, / ↑All the
exhibitions of pure genius are consonant with Goodness Truth
& Beauty & consequently are all agreeable↓ [in pencil]
But ↑there is another fact↓ sometimes it is obstructed. in
far the greater number of men. Then arise new & painful
appearances. ↑It prompts them also to create. But the world
resists them at every step↓ The law of the mind is one   The
law of the members is another.⟩ God the Soul

Lines
25   Yet How
27–28   life. There is ⟨melancholy⟩ heaviness
29–30   theory of life between ⟨the old & the young⟩ ↑every newly arrived soul & & the existing population of the planet↓ [cancellation in ink, insertion in pencil]
32–33   expose. /
         ⟨This is painful to society painful to the Protestant & what a waste of energy & how much peace & wellbeing it costs him how disagreeable & unamiable always is the attitude they assume. ⟨with all⟩ morose, sinister, with the aspect of Saturn digesting his children, porcupine all over; hated; hating; with all their might⟩ saying No.
         ↑The dissonance↓ [in pencil]
         ⟨But consider that this⟩ ↑The dissonance of which I speak↓

Page 87

1   dark ⟨f[?]⟩ legend is told of ⟨a⟩ the
4   reasonings ⟨ab⟩ respecting
7   of this ⟨deep⟩ persuasion
9   always in ⟨the⟩ ↑this↓ actual, ↑life↓
12–16   Eve." ↑Insert A↓ [on attached half sheet, marked "A":] ↑There is somewhat infirm . . . second thought ⟨W⟩He ha⟨ve⟩s done . . . his own past.↓ His past hour mort⟨a⟩gages the present hour. ↑yesterday is the enemy of Today.↓ [in pencil]
17–18   doing His . . . thinking; his ↑former↓ virtue ⟨of⟩ ↑⟨yesterday⟩↓ is apt to become an impediment to ⟨the⟩ ↑new↓ virtue. ⟨of today⟩. The
20   life of the s⟨[?]⟩enses is
22–23   born ⟨pure⟩ ↑sane↓. ⟨His sent⟩ instincts . . . affections ⟨pure⟩pure ↑⟨clean⟩↓. His senses are keen; ⟨&⟩his intellect
25–28   bribed His virtue ⟨ungreeted⟩ ↑sad & unsaluted in society↓ His virtue ⟨reproaches⟩ ↑accuses↓ their ⟨ways⟩ ↑customs↓ ⟨It⟩ ↑The fact↓ . . . perhaps too ⟨subtle⟩ deep
29   know why ⟨Cu⟩ we
31   speech; & ⟨had rather⟩ even
32   find a ⟨quotation⟩ ↑proverb↓
35–36   ↑the back side of↓ cities & common sewers, ↑rather↓ than incur the toil of cutting ↑choosing↓

Page 88

1–2   cataract & the ⟨lake⟩. seashore
7–8   again into ⟨the sea of life⟩ ↑new action↓. You must not ↑invite↓ ask the ⟨old⟩ ↑veteran↓
11–12   propose ⟨reform⟩ ↑strenuous↓
12–13   society to the ⟨famed⟩ saint of ⟨fifty⟩ ↑sixty↓ years; He ⟨is⟩ cannot

Lines

20–21   ↑It is just the same in letters.↓

23   forsooth; as if ⟨every man was not a new world &⟩ there

26–27   ↑this deliquium, of this falling back, this epilepsy. this↓ old age?that ⟨[?]⟩virtue

30–31   by young men. ⟨It is a fond error to⟩ ↑We ⟨cheat o⟩mislead ourselves by↓ talk↑ing↓ of the ancients ↑till we almost think they were bearded Methusalems↓

34–35   ↑are all that occur . . . a longer list.↓

35–36   condition ⟨th⟩which before the soul did over [end line] flow — asks

Page 89

5   world is ⟨endl⟩ incessant

16   desponds; ↑sneers;↓ serves; sits; it⟨s children⟩ talk↑s↓ from

17–20   It is ⟨low &⟩ poorspirited ↑it cannot bear freedom it craves ⟨to follow⟩ a rider for its neck↓ & says like the ↑old↓ French noblesse in the service of ⟨Napoleon⟩ ↑the new imperial court↓

20   somebody." ⟨It sneers⟩. It

21–22   ↑Its tediousness . . . advancing temper.↓

23   ↑fierce↓

24–25   ennui ⟨of so much pomp & nothing & gaped all day.⟩ ↑& insipidity . . . but ⟨[?]⟩gape all day.↓

30   halt ⟨paralytic⟩ ↑numb↓

35–(90)3   condemn. /

⟨This old age; this inveteration; this ossification of the heart; this ⟨petrification of man⟩ ↑⟨pinguifaction⟩ fat in the brain↓; this degeneracy — is the Fall of Man   And⟩ [2]{⟨t⟩The Redemption . . . heart of Youth.}   [1]{By resistance to th⟨e⟩is strong . . . is the world to be saved.}   The Saviour

Page 90

6–7   woman, ⟨society put⟩ the world puts the same question, "⟨w⟩Wilt thou be ⟨like us⟩ ↑come↓ one

9   virtue ⟨i⟩It is

15   saying No; ↑No; No;↓

20   To one ⟨it⟩ ↑the crisis↓

25   has ↑so↓

29–30   arms /

⟨But the second aspect in which genius appears in the world ⟨as⟩ is in antagonism to the world. Genius protests. Genius is always protestant.⟩   Look around society ⟨now look around⟩ at

Page 91

2   degree — more or less. you

9–10   war. / ↑One assails Alcohol, one [2]{Domestic Hired service [1]{Animal food↓ Each

11   point ⟨One fe⟩ according

15–16   grudge.

⟨Every reformer is partial & exaggerates some one grievance. ↑C↓ For men are not units but poor mixtures They
defend for a long time doctrines wholly foreign from their
nature & ⟨opinions⟩ connexion of opinions & which whilst for
moments & externally they espouse — from year to year & in
life & soul they reject & abominate. They accept how weary
a load of tradition from their elders & more forcible neighbors
↑D↓ By & by as the divine effort of creation of growth begins
in them, new loves,⟩ /

           Every

28   in single weak & single

31–32   new aversions / new aversions take

33–34   outbursts of ⟨the central life⟩ ↑light which make the epochs of
growth↓

35–(92)1   idols ↑and by an Idol I mean↓ ↑A↓ [passage marked "A" at
end of paragraph:] ↑an Idol any thing which . . . him to
honor.↓ But ⟨the⟩ ↑each↓ new ⟨expansion & upthrusting⟩ ↑in-
flux↓

Page 92

2   classify ⟨bur⟩ ↑more↓ facts ⟨by new radiation⟩ & will

6   growing Spirit. ⟨I call⟩ ↑A↓ [then follows passage marked for
insertion above: "an Idol any thing which . . . him to
honor."]

7   exercises of the ⟨a⟩unfolding

8   facts ⟨that⟩ which

11–14   excuse ⟨its absence⟩ ↑another spirit↓? this . . . power. What

17   dominion; & the ⟨y⟩ir ↑claims↓

24   study. ⟨He is of no party but is the patron of every just cause
of every liberal opinion⟩ He represents

27   ↑an image↓

28   beautiful to a ⟨so⟩ community

34–35   man. ⟨And hence as they poets say in the first age the sons of
God printed no epics carved no stone⟩ /

           ↑And is he not just in his view?↓

           ⟨And⟩ all

Page 93

1–4   ↑Nothing that is done . . . perfect the illimitable He finds
⟨somewhat⟩ in it . . . Finite. ↑What you . . . likes his
⟨thought⟩ ↑imagin⟨s⟩ation↓ better↓ [proper placement of inter-
lined sentence uncertain]

8   that there ⟨were⟩ ↑are↓

20–21   build St Peters . . . seeing eye which which beheld

Lines

22	grass & ↑the↓
23	years ⟨on the⟩ ↑in↓
28–31	↑These & such as these . . . art ⟨with⟩ or your best action with the wild & unconfinable excellence↓

Page 94

1–2	↑Alas too that friends, . . . aspirations↓
8–9	↑Besides; this impatient youth impatient . . . him will . . . a dreamer.↓
	⟨And yet t⟩This
13	suffers in in his
15	Actual. / [blank] / ⟨↑A↓ Alas that this graceful & dignified self trust & trust in others should be doomed to so prompt a downfall. that this free & noble creature son of God though he be should stoop presently to be a hack of society the mean fellow of mean men; ⟨to⟩ ↑should↓ forget the dreams of his youth ⟨in the practice⟩ first in the succumbing to the sins of others, & then in practising the same⟩ [The whole cancelled passage was once marked as an insertion to be used elsewhere.] How galled
16	presently the ⟨d⟩ claims
18–19	walk in ⟨th⟩ a
23–25	↑He will not listen . . . what he can earn↓ [in pencil]
29	walks & ⟨com⟩ young company is to end & John is to ⟨set⟩ choose
33	↑How will you earn that↓ [in pencil]

Page 95

7–8	at once ⟨fav⟩ tasks which taxed ⟨his⟩ ↑their↓ powers without violating ⟨his⟩their
10	new & un⟨ex⟩precedented
13–15	finds it↑self one too many, . . . that is↓ not easy to ⟨suit itself⟩ ↑put itself in harmony↓ with men & things & ⟨perform⟩ ↑find↓
16	congenial, ⟨& m⟩ for
17–18	day-labor ⟨fo⟩ to other works for its solace. / ⟨And therefore observe the longing glances which each ingenious soul is casting to some dear asylum when this tedious conflict is past.⟩ /
22	true, ⟨we should feel that all persons were infinitely deep natures⟩. We should
32–34	parties ⟨a conversation of the lips⟩ ↑a conversation of the lips. If people would live . . . their impulses.↓

Page 96

4–5	↑They are less together, than they are apart↓
7	negligent of ⟨c⟩the charities

Lines
13–14   same ⟨relation⟩ ↑capacity of attention↓
15   please to, ⟨[?]o⟩and magnify
27–(97)9   ↑Behold↓ In the . . . houses & lands. [leaf of different paper
             sewn into manuscript; possibly an insert]
29   trenchant ⟨world⟩ man

Page 97

1   he has. and
2   establishing ⟨relations⟩ with
25   book's book.   ⟨It is worth only⟩ Its
26   myself & ⟨leave⟩ there
27   he ⟨con⟩ slights
29–30   to the all the parts . . . society to the ⟨laws⟩ ↑forms of law↓
             ⟨to the⟩ ↑⟨forms⟩ of↓ religion⟨s⟩ ⟨to the⟩ charit⟨a⟩y⟨ble⟩ of educa-
             tion
34   society ⟨conf⟩ the
36–(98)2   ↑What is the passionate love . . . accusation of Society?↓

Page 98

4–6   village. ⟨Poor society what hast thou done to be the aversion
             of us all⟩ ↑The statesman, . . . towns hi⟨s⟩des himself in the
             country.↓ ⟨Consider that i⟩It is
6–7   yard. ↑⟨The ⟨retired⟩ poet⟩ He↓ hear↑s↓ the hen cluck &
             see↑s↓
8–9   ↑mark him↓ if a man goes by ⟨I have a⟩ ↑his countenance
             changes; there seems a shade of↓
10   passes, then ⟨I⟩ ↑he↓ rejoice↑s↓
24–30   John Thelwall says Coleridge ⟨in⟩at table had . . . to him
             Citizen John this . . . treason in. Nay Citizen Samuel replied
             he it . . . necessity for treason.
                   ⟨Observe the⟩ In the actual ⟨c⟩business

Page 99

4–5   music; one to ⟨literature⟩ & libraries
7   as thcsc. and
12–13   very un⟨happy c⟩desireable companions
15–16   ↑If it continue . . . morose men.↓
20   daunts the ⟨protes soul⟩ youth
21   his soul ⟨suggests⟩ ↑points↓
26–29   senses / ↑He compromises   He gets weary . . . or pleasure↓
             he makes
31   ancestors. and
32–33   death.
                   ⟨⟨But⟩ Or if the warlike ⟨instinct⟩ defence is made good by
             new impulses from within, if he give place to the Soul & wor-

Lines

ship it then it is presently revealed to him how he should live
& work   Quite naturally his own path opens before him; his
object appears; his aim ⟨gains⟩ becomes simple & ⟨turn⟩ losing
his dread of society which kept him dumb & paralytic he
begins to work according to his faculty. He has done protesting: now he begins to affirm: all art affirms: & with every new
stroke, with greater serenity & joy. Such has been the uniform
history of genius / There is no man to whom in some form this⟩
On the other hand

36   inquiry if ⟨compliments⟩ ↑praise from the young↓

Page 100

3–4   rebukes the babbl⟨ing⟩ers of puny taste & of false religion;
         ⟨Nothing⟩ If ⟨his⟩ he
14–15   before him. his
24   mortar.) but
26–27   all out & ↑tore down↓ [in pencil] scratched out all
29–30   relent ↑Neither afterwards cd. they get admission to his
         house.↓ [in pencil] & they

Page 101

1–2   and the↑n↓ the stout monk ↑in↓ [in left margin]
2   Yes, ⟨[?]⟩ and
5–6   furrows of the ⟨W⟩Ocean ↑with the keel of his galley↓
14   no ⟨grain⟩ kernel of ↑nourishing↓
20   enlarge ⟨& ex⟩ its
21   extent to ⟨charm⟩ ↑deck↓
22–23   adheres to his ⟨th⟩guiding thought which
24   true ⟨th⟩& discovers
28   acquiesce. ⟨Society Set your own rate Socie⟩ The world
29–30   man with ⟨utter indifference⟩ ↑profound unconcern↓
30–31   driveller it ⟨looks on with profound unconcern⟩ ↑meddles not
         in the matter.↓
31   measure of ↑your↓

Page 102

3   which ⟨r⟩looked so
5   ↑when analyzed↓
7–21   ↑On the whole, then, we think that the this crisis in the life of
         each ⟨yo s ma⟩ earnest man, . . . It puts to the ⟨sou⟩ man
         . . . soul or will you ⟨conform to⟩ yield yourself . . . soul,
         obey it ⟨and [?]⟩ Do your own work, . . . you have ⟨en-
         deavored to⟩ accepted . . . order & beauty.↓ [in pencil]

7. TRAGEDY

Lines	Page 103

4   world. formidable
7   considered the ⟨dark side of⟩ shades
11   so ⟨Tragedy⟩ Sorrow
12–(104)3   Felicity. ⟨See the⟩ care ⟨that⟩ sits close on every ↑mature↓ face; ⟨that has reached maturity⟩ ↑& ⟨hearken to⟩ the conversation of men, ⟨it⟩ is a mixture of regrets & apprehensions.↓ ↑Insert A↓ [in pencil; on opposite page, marked "A," and in pencil:]
    ↑And who the fool that doth not know

Unto the merriest of us all↓

Page 104

10   ↑in both hemispheres↓
16   less ⟨susceptible of pain⟩ vulnerable
17   slight the ⟨moanings⟩ audible moanings
18–19   any ⟨value⟩ ↑solidity↓ which ⟨omits⟩ leaves
20   Insecurity, Dis⟨appointed⟩ ↑union↓ Affection
22   encroaching ⟨a⟩All
28–29   There is a ⟨cotemporaneous⟩ ↑simultaneous↓

Page 105

3–5   resources ⟨of⟩ for the calamity that may arrive tomorrow.
    ⟨I propose to⟩ ↑Let us then↓ enumerate the ↑tragic↓ elements ⟨of⟩ in
8–9   nature ⟨is⟩ & events
13   idea ⟨of⟩ that
24–(106)2   Turk. ↑{Insert A}↓ [on next page, marked "A":] ↑The Arabians tell us . . . horror, "⟨w⟩What hideous . . . find him there."↓

Page 106

2–3   discover in ⟨c⟩uneducated
4–9   superstition.
    ⟨But this⟩ ↑as all the nursery fables . . . if you↑r↓ f⟨a[?]⟩ [erased] ork [over erasure] sticks upright . . . arbitrary will↓ / But this ⟨element⟩ terror
14–15   Necessity, ⟨it is important to observe⟩ ⟨by⟩ herein
18–19   Destiny, ↑it↓ is not ⟨the Best Will enacted or⟩ the good of the Whole or the Best Will ↑that is↓
20   ↑at all↓
21   ground of ⟨tragedy⟩ Terror
22   Hence ⟨only⟩ the
24   next ⟨a⟩tragic element

426

27–31   this by in the particulars of Disease ⟨Poverty⟩ ↑Want↓ ⟨i⟩In-
security Disunion /
     ⟨How⟩ ↑Sickness is↓ mean & dispiriting. ⟨is sickness⟩!
that . . . aching. And

33–34   sympathy wit⟨o⟩h external being. We prize in ⟨the great spirits⟩
↑our great contemporaries↓

Page 107

2–3   ↑Proportionally↓ ⟨Is it not on the other hand⟩ annoying ↑is it↓
that man may not ↑in this climate↓ sit down in the grass ⟨to⟩
nor

5   side ⟨sciatica⟩ ↑rheumatism↓

6   torture ⟨s[?]⟩ acute

8–9   world. / [blank] / [loose leaf of blue paper, never sewn with
lecture:]
⟨Want. ⟨is⟩ The radical tragedy of nature ⟨is⟩ [erased] appears
[over erasure] in the distinction of more & less. ⟨Want is a
growing giant whom the coat of Have was never⟩⟩ large
enough to cover. It makes little difference what the unit of
possession is the ⟨craving⟩ the hunger is transferred but not
satisfied ⟨Want is a⟩ [erased] We have [over erasure] the
fable of a farmer who thought he should be contented when
he had all the land which joined his own. ⟨Want is a growing
giant whom the coat of Have was never large enough to cover.
It⟩The suffering ma⟨n⟩y arise from a supposed poverty of
nature or from poverty of estate. Reason has her reliefs for
both. If another is *better* than I, I find therein a plain token
that my term of silence is not yet complete. Why should I
intrude into the guild of workmen before I receive a sign
Besides, each man can do somewhat which he was made for.
A true man can never feel rivalry All men are ministers ⟨to
him servants⟩ [in pencil] to bring him materials but none nor
all can do what he must do: he alone is privy if even he is
yet privy to his secret. / Much less reasonable is the grief at
wanting external goods. The advantage of riches seems to re-
side in the skin or not much deeper. The poor man suffers
from subserviency to those who hold the land & bread. But if
he have more will, less skin he can go without. Let him have
a little more resolution & he is the rich man. The effeminate
capitalist in gloves & surtout on the cold spring day, says by
his shrug that he fears the earth will not yield man bread this
year. The hardfaced farmer looks on contented & fearless. He
has fronted years more cold & grim. He knows the virtue
that resides in ⟨the⟩ oxen & plough ⟨in the⟩ harrow & ⟨the⟩
hoe, and knows that the hardest year that ever blew, afforded
to such straining & sweating as his, milk, rye, potatoes, maize,
⟨beef⟩ & mutton, & he does not think of famine any more than

a sailor rowing to a ship thinks of sinking. he rows & goes:
landsmen may do the doubting if they will. The brave man
will always be rich in the best sense, he will do the best of
his character & genius, will do substantially the same things
whether rich or poor; will make the same impression / Want.
The

15   ↑men↓
16–17   love. ⟨This⟩ I can still receive. ↑Beside, my turn will come.↓
25   know ⟨t⟩ [erased] until [over erasure]
28   goods. The ↑Insert B↓ [not with manuscript] The advantage
30   ↑dreadful↓
34   goes ⟨ab⟩ up & down

Page 108

2   this ↑and so he will↓ If he
13   ship ↑mistrusts↓ doubts at all
21   guillotine ⟨are the fit symbol⟩ aptly
25–26   efflux ⟨from⟩ ↑of↓
34–(109)1 Death. as it ⟨take⟩ breaks ⟨union takes⟩ up all the ⟨highest⟩
        fittest partnerships of life, & ⟨breaks up⟩ the

Page 109

5   concerned me ⟨to⟩ the
8   providing ⟨a coffin & [?]i[?]g for my funeral⟩ ↑myself with
        coffin & sexton↓.
11   indolence, ⟨&⟩ the
14–15   felicity by ⟨the⟩ vice. ⟨of others⟩.
20   inn?" ⟨Then⟩ ↑So↓ [in left margin] are we ⟨pagans⟩ ↑devils↓
23   is ↑godlike↓ divine. Other
26–27   circumstance. ⟨o⟩Obedience & disobedience / ⟨& d⟩make the
30–32   laborer or ⟨grocer⟩ or farmer ↑or debtor↓ as a thing; ↑women;
        children; the poor;↓ & so we do hold slaves. ⟨We⟩ In
33–(110)1 think of persons as things.
        ↑1 The belief in Fate
        2 the hindrance of my satisfaction by laws of ye world
        3 the hindrance of my satisfaction by vice↓ / [loose leaf of
        blue paper, never sewn with lecture:]
        The next tragic element in life is the hindrance of private
        felicity by vice. The senses would make things of all persons
        ⟨for our behoof⟩. Our enjoyments are cruel   Our enjoyments
        do rob kidnap & kill. We separate ourselves from the happy
        human family & from remembrance of debt to aught above us,
        & say, shall I not take my ease in mine inn? So are we devils.
        Only that good which we taste with all doors open, not sepa-
        rate but in the chain of beings, so that the spark freely passes,
        makes all happy as well as us, only that is divine. ⟨Other⟩

Enjoyments sought for enjoyment are false, & degrade the partakers & ministers. The act makes no difference, that depends
on fortune. Obedience & disobedience make the difference in
man. We read Lear & hate the unkind daughters, but our fathers & mothers / find us hard & forgetful as the civility of the
times will allow. We swell the cry of horror at the slaveholder
& we treat our labourer or farmer or debtor women children
the poor as a thing. and so do we hold slaves   In the base
hour we become slaveholders. We use persons as things & we
think of persons as things. /
       But

Page 110

6	indefinite; a↑n↓ ⟨dark⟩ ominous
7–8	low ⟨hung⟩ haggard ⟨cloud, it⟩ ↑sprite↓
8–10	evils; ⟨a dread ↑in↓security⟩; a ⟨dark⟩ ↑sinister↓ presentiment; ⟨a⟩ gloom on the brow; ⟨a dead⟩ weight ⟨in⟩at the h↑e↓art; — ⟨and therefore⟩ a certain ⟨uneasy⟩ looking
12–13	wind the . . . house see
14	riot; ⟨that suspicious look⟩ ↑⟨detected⟩↓ ↑the whisper over-heard; the detected glance↑
17	quick & ⟨regular minds⟩ steady
19–20	causes. / And ⟨And if you⟩ look
25–26	↑They mishear; & misbehold; they suspect; & dread;↓ They
36	Itself oer

Page 111

3	element. that
4–5	illusions. ⟨It⟩ ↑Tragedy↓ is in the ↑eye of the↓ observer, & not in the ↑heart of the↓
7	analyse it; It is
8–9	tormented. ⟨And that which would rend you falls on tougher textures & is easily borne⟩ ↑If a man says . . . for ⟨g⟩Grief is dumb.↓ It is so distributed as ↑not↓ [in left margin] to
12–13	sleep. ⟨Few are capabl⟩ Some
20–21	moors; — ↑⟨[?] terror⟩ ↑a fright↓ at uncertain sounds heard by a family at ⟨mid⟩night in the cellar on the stairs↓ these
22–23	withering that ⟨may & do paralyse the intellect & the will⟩ ↑make the knees knock & the teeth chatter↓
28–30	↑in any condition; . . . felicity↓ as ⟨a⟩the frailest
34–(112)1	power & benef⟨-icence⟩ ↑it.↓. The

Page 112

2–3	make ⟨us⟩ wise
3	vice, ⟨they⟩ are

Lines

8   but for the ⟨ho⟩terrors of

13–14   grief   ⟨How true was the antique idea of Beauty⟩
                 ↑It is observed that the first ↑works of the art of↓ sculpture
are countenances of sublime rtanquillity↓ [insertions in pencil]

15–16   Greek came & viewed them & ⟨pa⟩ departed

17   ↑and as they will still sit when↓ as the Turk

18–19   Englishman, ⟨& American fixed⟩ ↑who visit them now shall
have passed by,↓

21–22   health. ⟨thus⟩ ↑deserving their permanency &↓

24   To this ⟨perm⟩ architectural ⟨permanency⟩ ↑stability↓

26   ↑permitting↓

28   ↑even↓

29   soul. ⟨few⟩   All

34   irregular Catalinarian

Page 113

7–8   education↑;↓ ⟨but⟩ not [emendations in pencil]

8–9   time. ⟨The expression⟩ His face

11   nature on ⟨its⟩ & fortune on their

15   life. that

17   clings ⟨to what is best⟩ by tendrils of affection to society mayhap to

23–25   again {& his despair takes at first the form of rage & hatred
against the act or actor which has broken the seeming peace of
nature}   But

30   If any ⟨on⟩man ↑neighbor or stranger↓

Page 114

5   which ⟨the⟩ fit

6–7   evils.
                1 Time [no other numerals following]

11–12   As the ⟨drying⟩ ↑west↓ wind lifts up again the heads of the
⟨grass⟩ ↑wheat↓

16   bent. ⟨Quickly he⟩ ↑Time↓

17   life. ⟨new hopes are born⟩ Nature

21   Our ⟨natu⟩ human

22–23   plastic: If . . . satisfaction. ⟨it⟩here it

Page 115

2–4   slave trade /
⟨Temperament.
              To the evil to be borne the remedial force of nature sup-
plies sufficient resistance.⟩ Especially

8–9   not the ⟨less⟩ least

15   I should ⟨e[?]⟩have to

Lines	
19–20	on my ⟨ph⟩ moral or physical nature." / [loose leaf of different paper; drawn from journal passage later than lecture:]

    I can be wise very well for myself but not for another nor among others. I smile & ignore wo & if that which they call wo shall come to me I hope & doubt not to smile still   They smile never & think joy amiss   All their facts are tinged with gloom & all ⟨th⟩my pains are edged with pleasure. But if I intermeddle, if I quit my divine island, & seek to right them in particulars, and treat them as corrigible, & their fortunes as curable, I grow skeptical presently.

    Age is to be parried & annihilated to thee, o Son of God, by wrapping thyself in God's eternal youth   Generously sleep in thy sentiment in thine act the arms of the wise God being around thee & thou shalt take thy being again from him / presently refreshed & exalted. Seest thou not that in nature every set sun rises, every loss has a gain and the bark grows over the wound on a tree. [whole passage modified from D, 367–368 (Sept. 28, 1839)] / [blank] / [blank] / ↑philosophy↓ [in pencil at top of page]

    Another relief

21	facts so
28	thought of
32	daily ⟨goo⟩ benefit

Page 116

1	suffer ⟨f⟩some
15–16	See ⟨Napoleon⟩ ↑Alexander↓
22–23	↑The wisest men have owed their wisdom to the common day↓ [in pencil]
26	spirits. ⟨s⟩Sobs
28–29	tragedy of ⟨these⟩ ↑these↓ same. [emendations in ink] ↑Teachers D32↓ [in pencil] / ⟨Reason⟩ Reflection

Page 117

13	is ↑excellent↓ [in pencil] beautiful though
19–20	ajar and my [blank] age
27–28	to me ⟨the very highest⟩ a simple in the highest pharmacopia the ⟨v⟩anodyne

Page 118

2–3	to the worst. ⟨A⟩so another
4	treasuries of the ⟨poe⟩ reading
5	Tam O Shanter & Lilis Park
7	us up into ⟨s⟩ brief
14	after walking & ⟨again⟩ by walking

20–21   wonder & ⟨joy of⟩ [erased] inquisition [over erasure]
27   ↑again↓
33   asked ⟨of⟩ ↑concerning↓

Page 119

3–5   ↑The one resource . . . apprehensions or ⟨with⟩ crippled by calamities↓ [in pencil]
9–10   ↑of labor↓ [in pencil]
12   seclusion   What
13   other peoples
16   must ⟨warm⟩ clothe
19–20   rich you are literary ↑have taste, your . . . detaches you↓ [insert in pencil] you
25–26   children beside
34   poor rates

Page 120

3   ↑and behold who & what he is.↓

8. COMEDY

Page 121

2   elements in life
14–16   mind. ⟨Go into⟩ ↑In↓ any collection of men in⟨to⟩ the . . . See ⟨how truly the⟩ ↑the wistfull↓ human history ⟨is⟩ written out in the faces. ⟨around you⟩. The
17–20   ↑The sailor . . . rough weather↓ [in pencil, between lines; no place of insertion indicated] ↑The merchants face . . . thrift & calculation↓ [in pencil, at bottom of previous page; no place of insertion indicated] The old farmer carries ⟨as it were⟩ palpable

Page 122

2   ↑of virtues↓
4–5   ↑And if↓ Beauty, softness, & faith ↑in female form↓ have their own ⟨expression⟩ ↑influence↓. Vices even in slight degree ⟨it is said⟩ ↑are thought to↓
8   invariable ⟨expression⟩ ↑character↓ [emendations in pencil]
9–14   tire. ⟨I prefer⟩ ↑Compared with↓ universal faces countenances of a general humane type, ↑they look less safe.↓ which pique less ⟨but to which we can always safely return home.⟩ ↑A↓ [marked "A":] ↑In such a study . . . ↑figures & other↓ modes of being than heroes & sages↓ [end insert A] ↑In the silentest & motionless meeting the eye↓ ⟨I⟩ reads↑s↓

432

Lines	
15–16	↑ignorance↓
18	December. [Then follows passage marked "A" for insertion above: "In such a study . . . & sages"]
20	comic & ⟨to make⟩, though
21–22	nature) to ⟨make⟩ inquire
22	life. /

⟨There remains the perception of the ridiculous the phenomenon of laughter & the various relations in ordinary life which give occasion to that activity of the risible muscles.⟩

23	Man ⟨seems to be⟩ ↑is↓
24	grave. The ⟨plants the⟩ rocks [cancellation in pencil]
27	other. ⟨Neither the horse nor the hyena laughs, nor does the field or the hen smile; however by ↑our↓ proverbs calumniated as so doing.⟩ [cancellation in pencil] ⟨And while⟩ [cancellation in ink] Nor are
28	↑As thus the lower nature never jests neither does the highest↓ [in pencil]
30	ludicrous. ⟨It is the most violent of hyperboles the oriental speech "God laughs at their calamities"⟩ The . . . with ↑an↓ [cancellation in pencil]
32–33	laughter ⟨originates⟩ ↑begins↓

Page 123

| 2–4 | only ⟨r⟩jest. / |

↑Mr Coleridge in his excellent Essay on Wit has cited↓ [in pencil]

We owe to Aristotle the definition of the ridiculous

6–7	if not, ⟨absurd &⟩ comic. [cancellation in ink] ⟨To me⟩ ↑I confess . . . all we know↓ [emendations in pencil]
8	Halfness; ⟨a pledge to perform⟩ a
10–11	performance. The ⟨disappointment⟩ ↑baulking↓ of the intellect the ⟨false step⟩ the frustrated expectation ⟨breaks⟩ the
13	pleasant {convulsions or} spasms [brackets in pencil]
19	with the other ⟨end⟩ ↑function↓
20	attained. ⟨But⟩ The
21	observes, 'that
25	appears ⟨in nature⟩ the ⟨conscious⟩ [cancellations in pencil] ⟨r⟩Reason:
27	disunited, or ⟨divided⟩ ↑halved↓

Page 124

1	itself, & ⟨instantly⟩ the
7	↑particular bodily↓
9	↑standing↓
11–12	ludicrous. /

⟨In fact, if it be truly considered I think it will appear that⟩ in virtue of of man's [cancellation in pencil]

Lines	
13	man is ⟨always⟩ a pledge of a Whole: ⟨instantly⟩ suggests [cancellations in pencil]
14	goodness; & ⟨therefore instantly⟩ shows [cancellation in pencil]
15	appearance of ⟨man,⟩ the [cancellation in pencil]
22	does not ⟨laugh⟩ joke
33–35	↑His perception . . . thieving fact↓ ⟨It⟩ makes
37	literature. ⟨t⟩The

Page 125

2–7	the intellect. ↑Insert B↓ [partial leaf marked "B," once with this lecture but now filed with Lecture 3 of the course on "The Present Age," where it does not belong (see p. 473, below):] ↑The activity . . . moral⟨[?]⟩ sympathies do not interfere↑,↓ [comma in pencil] become ludicrous.↓ ⟨t⟩The
9	ideal ⟨makes⟩ exposes
12	Understanding ⟨Prince Hal in Shakspeare stands for the Reason Falstaff for the Senses⟩ [cancellation in pencil] /
17–19	we the ⟨utter⟩ inconsistency betwixt reason & ↑& the ⟨utter⟩ negation of reason, in other words,↓ [emendations in pencil]
26	contrast ⟨between⟩ in
28–29	appears ⟨instantly⟩ why we should be so ⟨s⟩deeply affected by the exposure. We ⟨a⟩ have ⟨obviously⟩ no
30	aware ⟨in⟩ by joke & by stroke of ⟨the⟩ ↑any↓
32–33	truth. ↑{Insert A}↓ [in pencil; on previous page, marked "A," also in pencil:] ↑Besides a perception . . . structure of man.↓

Page 126

11	for ↑as↓ it is ⟨not only, ⟨as Plato says,⟩⟩ the
12	seem so, ⟨but⟩ ↑so it is↓
22	or a ⟨very⟩ mystic
23–24	welcome. ⟨It says with Sir Toby: "Dost thou think because thou art virtuous, there shall be no more cakes & ale?"⟩ Wit [cancellation in pencil]
27	exemption, they
29–31	all. ↑It says to them with Sir Toby Dost thou think because thou↓ [in pencil; see cancelled passage above]
33	Wit & ⟨the⟩ Comedy

Page 127

1–3	cognisance. / ⟨And yet⟩ so painfully susceptible are some men to the↑se↓ ⟨assaults on these muscles⟩ ↑⟨perceptions⟩ impressions↓
4	take them⟨se⟩ [erased] out [over erasure]
6	when ⟨I have seen⟩ ↑such↓
7	ear of ⟨my⟩ ↑a↓ man of wit, ⟨I have thought that the peace of

society seemed to require that next to so notable a wit should always be posted a phlegmatic bolt upright man able to stand without movement of muscle whole broadsides of this Greek fire. And yet) the person who has just ⟨d[?]⟩ [erased] received [over erasure]

16	In all ⟨we⟩cases we
18	↑& eye↓ whilst it is broken to the ⟨sense⟩ soul
21	it ⟨touches⟩ ↑approaches↓, communicating glory ⟨[?]⟩ as ⟨in⟩by the
26	intellect; the ⟨disproportion as detected by it⟩ lack
27	pain merely
29–30	↑the↓ perception of the disproportion is ⟨the⟩ comedy
32	lie or ⟨impos⟩ or an
35	fling at ⟨false⟩ hypocrisy
36	↑religious↓

Page 128

2	them, ⟨to⟩ when
4	mistake of the ⟨c⟩ wig
7	fun of the ⟨cel⟩ step taken by ⟨the celebrated⟩ Captain
10–11	Blackhawks, ⟨&⟩ Roaring Thunders & Walk the Water↑s↓
12–13	↑in letters out of England↓
16	home in ⟨a⟩the
17	convert ⟨him⟩ ↑one↓
18	satire ⟨is⟩ [erased] reaches its climax when the ⟨formal⟩ ↑actual↓
19–20	↑religious↓ sentiment, as in the famous ⟨charge⟩ ↑account↓
25	As lately it happe⟨d⟩ned. In

Page 129

5	Of league he↑l↓d forth
21–22	where the ⟨popular⟩ persons & acts ⟨of⟩ reverenced . . . are ⟨degraded by being⟩ actualised
26–27	↑by sheets,↓ by volumes; & every ⟨profane sailor⟩ boatswain & ⟨wanton⟩ ↑street↓
28	pedantry ⟨& ignorance⟩ is
31	or a ⟨mere⟩ ↑bare↓ illustration ⟨& e⟩of his
32	memorandum ⟨merely⟩ ↑only↓
33	face of it, ⟨implying⟩ merely
34–37	staircase, a ⟨tent wherein to lodge⟩ ↑bivouac↓ for a night, ⟨but⟩ ↑and↓ implying a march, ⟨tomorrow⟩ a . . . becomes, ⟨as we know in all e⟩ [end line] perience, ⟨a⟩ through . . . barrack, a ⟨castle⟩ ↑stronghold,↓

Page 130

2	wit of ⟨one of the finest jokes in history⟩ the remark
5	by which ⟨according to the⟩ they

TEXTUAL NOTES AND VARIANT PASSAGES

Lines
8could have ⟨suggested⟩ ↑given↓
13↑ordinary↓
16↑now↓
17porpoise, or marsou↑i↓n
18–19they ⟨are⟩ ↑look↓ all ↑⟨now⟩ either↓ narwhales or marsounes [a dot above the "n," as if over an "i"]
20–22↑a good while ago . . . as ye laws of health ⟨As⟩ [erased]↓ ⟨when⟩ ↑As↓ I
23friend, ⟨wh⟩ [erased] an [over erasure]
24condition, ⟨to meet⟩ ↑I met↓
25–26how is ⟨the Doctor⟩ ↑my friend↓
29–(131)2delight. ↑for it would seem . . . diagnosis of the books.↓ [in pencil]

Page 131

10Deuce! ↑cries the boy↓ is
14–15cypraea ↑maculata↓ the nerita ↑formosa↓ and the trochus ↑nodosus↓ [insertions in pencil in spaces left for them]
17↑&↓ but could not help ⟨thinking some⟩ ↑querying whether any↓
27↑not↓ made good, ⟨arms⟩ points
28–30poverty is the ⟨subject⟩ ↑occasion↓. ↑According to↓ The famous ⟨Latin⟩ verse of the Latin moralist ↑which↓ has been rendered into English doggrel

Page 132

4–8condition. ↑If↓ [in left margin; vertically in left margin:] ↑If ye man is not . . . no joke↓ [between lines:] ↑The poorest man . . . philosopher, of the ⟨In⟩ [erased] naked [over erasure] Indian . . . the pretender↓ ⟨H⟩ [incomplete and written over by the insertion] Here
11upside / or to see
12–14always ⟨slightly⟩ droll; ↑The relation of the parties . . . master.↓
14multiplication of ⟨wants⟩ artificial wants
15of all ⟨the⟩ trifling
20that they ⟨all⟩ came
26party ⟨into the⟩ for
29remark, ⟨the party⟩ ↑his comrades↓
30behold ⟨a gay cascade⟩ on
31↑with foam & rainbows↓
32–33piece his ⟨own⟩ ↑vest↓. ⟨waistcoat⟩.

Page 133

2↑truth & virtue, that is,↓
4Beau Brummel

436

Lines	
6	art ⟨of all Religion⟩ of
18	↑Alike In all these cases . . . paltry end.↓
28	So in ⟨women studious of the arts of dress⟩ ↑the street among the fair promenaders↓

Page 134

4	makes ⟨m⟩the meat
5–6	appearance ⟨not only⟩ of face & form & ⟨but of⟩ manners ⟨& dress⟩, with
12	tremendous. of
13–14	↑in the Memoirs o↓ of Queen Hortense, that when ⟨Madam⟩ a
17	opinions, ⟨Madam⟩ the
18	Pere la Chaise." a
19	fail to ⟨p⟩ circulate. ⟨in whatever company she entered⟩.
21	particulars. / Timur
23	since the ⟨time⟩ ↑hour↓
28–29	hours. ⟨Hereon⟩ ↑On this,↓ some co⟨m⟩urtiers began
31–32	began ⟨to⟩ now first ↑to↓ weep ↑a↓ [in left margin] ⟨more⟩ ↑amain↓
32–33	to Chodscha, "Hearken!
34	because ↑although↓ I ⟨not only⟩ am Caliph, ⟨but⟩ ↑& have↓

Page 135

2–5	wept. ⟨And⟩ ↑But thou — ↓ . . . ceasing?" C⟨ch⟩hodscha answered, If thou ↑hast↓ only see⟨ing⟩n thy . . . seeing it has not . . . but has we⟨e⟩pt, what
6–7	Timour ⟨could scarce contain⟩ almost
14–23	half man. ↑{Insert A}↓ [on previous page, marked "A":] ↑Or when ⟨in the effort to execute its will⟩ ↑patriotism merges itself in↓ parties. We . . . understanding are ⟨lost sight of⟩ ↑postponed↓ ⟨in⟩to [written over] growing . . . which ↑alone↓ they . . . I like best.↓ In ⟨the⟩ ↑every ward-room & barroom↓ shop ⟨I saw⟩ the dictators of our {rural} jacobins teach⟨ing⟩ th⟨is⟩eir little circle of ↑gapers↓ villagers their political lessons. And here, ⟨thought I⟩ ↑says the philosopher↓
29–32	↑Fair shines the sun . . . shadows of night↓ ⟨All of North or South⟩ all

Page 136

1	this to ⟨feed [?]⟩have no
3–4	towns & ⟨w⟩voters. / But But I will
10	↑houses↓

Lines

16–17   terrors. those of us who can, ⟨even⟩ to get fat thereby, & al⟨w⟩l
          of
20   house to ⟨hear what buffoons⟩ see
21   ↑to listen to↓ [in pencil]
24–25   brains ⟨but⟩ [cancellation in ink] for wise reasons, ↑but when
          we have no more to say be content to lie by↓ ⟨but⟩ to [emenda-
          tions in pencil]
33   snow. ⟨Do not laugh too much for then you show all your
          faults⟩ [cancellation in pencil; cf. D, 166 (ascribed to "Mine
          Asia"); cf. "Behavior," W, VI, 182] ⟨How⟩ We [cancellation in
          ink]

Page 137

2   mirth It ↑then↓
9–13   ↑On the whole ⟨Like Tragedy⟩, then, it will be seen, Comedy
          ↑like Tragedy↓ . . . its even ⟨tone⟩ articulate tone.↓ / ↑Sim-
          plicity↓ ⟨One thing⟩ disarms ⟨laughter⟩ wit & makes laughter
          die in ⟨its own⟩ ↑the↓ throat which formed it. ⟨& that is sim-
          plicity⟩. Truth

9. DUTY

Page 138

1–(139)23 We foolishly think . . . Chaos and the Dark [double sheet
           paginated 23–26 now filed with Lecture 10 of the course on
           "The Present Age," where it does not belong; placed here on
           the basis of paper, pagination, sewing marks, and an ink trans-
           fer]
4   some ⟨d[?]⟩ [erased] places [over erasure]

Page 139

1   ↑enviable &↓
3   echo, ⟨as,⟩ If
3–4   think whether it is or is not, before he ducks / to
9   which ⟨are⟩ may
31   stream of ⟨almighty⟩ power

Page 140

2–3   beauty. /
          ⟨And i⟩In this
6   before. ⟨th⟩To sign
9–10   ↑& declaration↓
12–13   dangerous to be very [end of line] ↑transfer our respect . . .
          or acts↓ [in pencil; no mark of insertion] good indeed. The

Lines	
19–20	that watches the ⟨beef [?],⟩ ↑food you eat↓ & watches the ⟨cider in the ↑⟨s⟩↓ pitcher⟩ ↑orbit of the pitcher↓
29–30	always to the ↑depth↓ value of the thought ↑& o to↓ & the number
32	pupil. ⟨The pupil takes the same delight in subordinating⟩ But

Page 141

2	Highest. It s Such is
4–5	Botany in . . . thereby which
6	happen ⟨th⟩for a time
11	means so ⟨)⟩ that
24	statement. ⟨& so provoke if I can the moral sympathies of my audience.⟩ I
30	create the ⟨world⟩ whole
34	past. {It ⟨has God & wants not man. It has truth spirit life & cares not for names or stories for man or miracle.}⟩ The

Page 142

4	Cause, & ⟨therefore⟩ in
10–13	world ⟨believe him not⟩ ↑believe him not. The stricken soul . . . that now spoken.↓
15	do ⟨fail in⟩ ↑lack↓ faith ⟨to see God face to face to see Time pass away & be no more &⟩ to utter directly from ⟨him⟩ ↑God↓
16–17	rather ⟨imprison it in⟩ ↑wrench to their present wants↓ the old Hebrew language, ⟨mimic⟩ ↑borrow of↓
24	↑of the men of talents & character we met:↓
29	good, ⟨as⟩ ↑when↓
32–33	disburthen ⟨of⟩our ⟨o⟩memory
35	brook ⟨or⟩& the

Page 143

11	being. ⟨There shall be no fear in it. You shall tread on fear⟩. You
12	to man. ⟨That state asks nothing. Fe[?]⟩ All
13	ministers. ⟨That state asks nothing⟩ ↑There shall be no fear in it↓
14	↑It asks nothing.↓
15–16	Hope. ⟨Trust, the conviction that all is well that Good & God is at the centre will always rest as basis to the intellectual & outward activity of a great man. In the highest moments w⟩We are ↑then↓
33	meet; (As

Page 144

11	It is the ⟨conforming⟩ endeavor
13	never ⟨who⟩ ↑quite↓

439

Lines

14–20   particular.

↑⟨This is that standing obligation⟩ Duty is the application ⟨that⟩ of the sentiment . . . sense. & Character is the ⟨education⟩ ↑cumulative force↓ of the Will ↑acquired↓ by the uniform . . . sovereign instinct.↓ [whole insertion in pencil]

26–27   Socrates↑,↓ of Confucius↑,↓ Menu↑,↓ Zoroaster↑,↓ . . . Paul↑,↓ [commas in pencil]

31   mere r⟨a⟩hapsodies to

Page 145

10   inexhaustible ⟨interest⟩ ↑affection↓

15   say it as ↑men,↓ [in pencil] heathens would; they

26   made by it. / [blank] /

⟨It is in the world & the world was made by it.⟩ ⟨The⟩ All

28   perfect ⟨justice⟩ ↑equity↓

30   ↑every wrong redressed↓

31–(146)3   season. ²{Punishment is a fruit . . . that conceals it.} ¹{The wild murder . . . an exact revenge.} ⟨The house praises the carpenter. The reward of a thing well done is to have done it.⟩ ↑Cause & effect; . . . illustrations of this truth.↓

Page 146

6   ↑Every opinion reacts on him who utters it.↓

13   measureable by ⟨their⟩ its

17   men; if ⟨it⟩ ↑the pages↓ instruct⟨s⟩ you

19–21   ↑Not less certain . . . first or tenth.↓

23   think that to⟨o⟩ be

27   he light he

29   covets he

Page 147

3   chest. swells

9   ↑What has made him civil↓

12–13   contrives to ⟨in⟩ [line break] ↑in↓ [in left margin] tenerate . . . felspar, — Takes

15–(148)23   This view of the Genius . . . extirpated from Sparta." [double sheet paginated 53–56 now loosely laid in journal Σ; placed here on the basis of paper, pagination, and sewing marks. In pencil at top of first page, centered:] ↑Story of Glaucus.↓

18   son of Ep⟨i⟩yc⟨y⟩ides

22   by the ⟨haz[partial letter]⟩ chances

Page 148

17   ⟨The God⟩ Jove never fails

23   Sparta."

Herodotus
Book VI

DUTY

Lines

27   escapes ⟨from⟩ them
28   vital part. if
34–(*149*)1 contumacy—You

Page 149

4   nature; ⟨B⟩but
11–15   ↑The house praises . . . her own applause"↓
16   world ⟨are⟩ know
24   are wise ⟨w⟩you will

Page 150

2–3   ↑cent for cent↓
4   ↑It will fast corrupt & worm worms↓
11   ↑By a force as perfect . . . pervaded↓ [in pencil]

[The following is a small double sheet, never sewn with this lecture, but now filed with it:]

One thing is certain that whatever may be the cry in books of philosophy or in the ↑rising↓ popular politics against {the vices of intellect &} [brackets joined to form enclosure] the dangers of egotism, the energy & ⟨the⟩ wisdom of the universe do express themselves through individual integrity. It is a power now in its beginning, and its power is not demonstrated As every house that would be most solid stable, must be built of square stones; so, every society that can be depended on, must be composed of men that are themselves complete. It is vain to attempt anything without them. The communities that are quo-/tcd as successful, were nothing but the presence & influence of some noted man; and he owed nothing to the rules of his order. In the judgment of Socrates, in Gorgias, "one wise man is better than 10 000 who are unwise." [Plato, *Works*, trans. Floyer Sydenham and Thomas Taylor, 5 vols. (London, 1804), IV, 406.] And it is idle to attempt any balance of rogues, to educe honesty, or, by combining follies, to make wisdom. ⟨It is the one only thing wanted, — the one man:⟩ the ⟨state⟩ good town, the good state, quite naturally crystallizes round the one healthy heart. Give us one, & the state seems to be redeemed. The majority ⟨have⟩ carry the day, because there / is no real minority of one. If Lycurgus were here, the majority would not laugh any longer. There is something in him which he cannot be laughed out of, nor argued out of, nor can he be terrified or bought off. I am afraid that in the formal arrangements of the socialists the spontaneous sentiment of any thoughtful man will find that poetry & sublimity still cleave to the solitary house. / [blank] /

[The following is a small single leaf, once sewn with the previous sheet, but not with the rest of this lecture, with which it is filed:]

↑The members will be the same men we know.↓ To put them in or out of a phalanx, will not ↑so↓ much mend matters.

People here expect a revolution. There will be no revolution, none that deserves to be called so. There may be a scramble for money. But, as all people we see want the things we now have, & not better things, it is very certain that they will, under whatever change of forms keep the old system. Whoever is skilful in heaping money now, will be skilful in heaping money again. When I see changed men, I shall look for a changed world. [LM, 50 (1848)] /

When men say, "These men occupy my place," the revolution is near. But I never feel that any men occupy my place, but that the reason why I do not have what I ⟨want⟩ ↑wish↓ is, that I want the faculty which entitles. All spiritual or real power makes its own place Revolutions of violence then are scrambles merely [LM, 66 (1848); "Aristocracy," W, X, 47] /

10. DEMONOLOGY

Lines	Page 151
6	↑Sortilege↓
7	↑the presence of↓
10	Demonology; ⟨& it is to that subject⟩ and

	Page 152
2	↑for this↓ & for ⟨their⟩ the
4–5	1. Let us consider ⟨a little the necromancy⟩ ↑first that↓ with which we are familiar, ↑the necromancy of sleep↓ [there are no further numbers]
5–9	divides with ⟨truth⟩ ↑solid fact↓ . . . lives; ⟨sleep. & Dreams.⟩ ↑How strange this alien despotism . . . the lot of all.↓
19	remains ⟨w⟩ that
20–21	become the ⟨chamber⟩ ↑theatre↓ [emendations in ink] of ↑delirious shows↓ [in pencil] all wild & grotesque puppets; and
23	be told; ↑⟨the visions the most serene & sweet amore⟩↓ sometimes
24–30	recalled;
	↑"They come in dim procession led.
	. . .
	As if they parted yesterday."↓ /
	↑⟨visions the most serene & sweet⟩, [cancellation in pencil] a delicate creation outdoing the prime & flower of ⟨waking life⟩ daily life↓ that antic
30–31	pictures; ⟨with gloom & terror⟩ transcending [cancellation in pencil]
31–32	record. ⟨s⟩that we should be so earnestly busied ⟨in wh⟩ as
32–33	days in ⟨weary⟩ peregrinations [cancellation in pencil]
33	lands, ↑in↓ ⟨long &⟩ earnest [cancellation in pencil]

Lines

Page 153

2–3   our ⟨uncontrollable &⟩ [cancellation in pencil] ghastly laughter ⟨at the most ghostly nonsense⟩ ↑to be rebuked by the↓ [emendations in ink]

4   memory the ⟨most⟩ [cancellation in pencil and ink] ⟨ghostly⟩ [cancellation in ink] gibbering

5–6   that this ⟨wild⟩ [cancellation in pencil and ink] spawn & ⟨tadpole⟩ [cancellation in ink] limbo ↑& dusthole↓ [in pencil] ↑of thought↓ [in ink]

10   foremost ⟨characteristic⟩ [cancellation in pencil and ink] ↑⟨trait⟩ [pencil and erased] trait [in ink]↓ of ⟨D⟩the Dream. ⟨Strange is this alien despotism that visits two children lying locked in each others arms & carries them asunder by wide spaces of land & sea & wide intervals of time⟩   A

11–13   ↑The fairest forms & ⟨landscapes⟩ The most noble . . . circumstance↓

14   cloak or ⟨or⟩coat

24   he shall ⟨also⟩ travel

26   ↑shall↓ walk

28   This ⟨tr⟩fcature

32–33   waking,—⟨an obscure reminiscence⟩ ↑a suspicion↓ that they ⟨t⟩have

Page 154

1   this ⟨discourse⟩ dialogue

3–4   dreams, is, ⟨their animal creation⟩ ↑that they have their own Fauna.↓

4–5   nature." ⟨I think⟩ ↑Perhaps↓

9   Our ⟨contemplations of⟩ ↑thoughts↓ in a barn ⟨stable⟩ or

11   awaken ⟨in us⟩. You

12   which ⟨seems to suggest something like consciousness which⟩ seems to ⟨ask⟩ lay

13–14   brotherhood. ⟨He too is related to you.⟩ What! . . . Does ⟨he⟩ ↑the dog↓

15   relations. ⟨In us arises a kind of compassionate⟩ ↑We↓

16–17   calamity ⟨would be one moments endowment of reason to know⟩ ↑if they should see for one moment↓

18–20   them! ↑See Middlebury↓ [pencil insertion not in Emerson's hand]
    The ⟨single⟩ glance that suggests this ⟨strange speculation &⟩ strange . . . explains ⟨to us⟩ those

22   see ⟨at once⟩ that this ↑is↓

24–25   wild ⟨thought⟩ fact itself ↑to↓ [in left margin]

25–26   theory ⟨& explanation⟩   Nor is the fact quite ⟨singular &⟩ solitary

27   predominate ⟨⟨& in a d⟨g⟩egree tyrannize⟩⟩ over

30   awakens ⟨the same feeling⟩ ↑it↓

Lines

32–33   suicide. / [blank] /
          ⟨The fact is⟩ our

Page 155

4   startled ⟨sometimes⟩ two

6   phantasmagoria. ⟨Sometimes⟩ Once

9   of us. ⟨They are not me⟩   My

12–13   like ↑mutineers↓ [in pencil] volunteers, — & ⟨thwart my incli-
nation⟩. ↑fire on their commander.↓ ⟨They make⟩ ↑Showing↓
[insertion in pencil] me feel that

15–18   the counter↑-↓act↑ion↓ . . . struck; If . . . pursued⟨;⟩. ⟨If I
give, I receive But most remarkable in them is that augury
that⟩ ↑A↓ prophetic character ⟨which⟩ in all ages has ⟨had⟩
haunted them, ⟨& strongly or faintly in all individuals. It seems
to be true that⟩ our dreams ⟨are⟩ ↑show like↓

19   night ⟨will always⟩ bear some ⟨proportion⟩ ↑kindred↓

20   we ⟨really⟩ possessed

21   out to ⟨such extreme⟩ statements

22   character of ⟨Julius⟩ ↑Rupert↓

24   seem ⟨extraordinary⟩, preposterous

26–27   character, & the ⟨loose⟩ Sibyl [cancellation in pencil]

27–28   fact. ⟨In like manner the soul contains in itself the event that
shall presently befal it; for the event is only the actualizing of
its thoughts. Why then should not symptoms auguries forebodings also be, &, as one said, the moanings of the spirit? We
are let by this experience into the high region of Cause & the
identity of of very unlike seeming effects.⟩ ↑We learn . . .
own character.↓

30   ↑own↓ evil

Page 156

1–2   to his ⟨family⟩ ↑boys↓ scared by a ⟨no[?]⟩ figure

5–9   effects. [inverted caret indicating insertion of passage at bottom of page and top of next:] ↑He learns that . . . differ-
ent↑ly↓ ⟨in the eye of the law⟩ ↑reputed↓ . . . will / rushes to
a deed↓ A man ⟨indulged⟩ ↑amused↓

11   murderers

12–15   intelligence. [followed by insert used above] /
⟨This then seems to be the whole value of⟩ Dreams, ⟨that⟩
however monstrous & grotesque ⟨in⟩ their apparitions, ⟨they
do yet⟩ have a substantial truth. ⟨to our own character & reality.⟩ The same remark ⟨acquires some new importance when
we see how far it⟩ may be extended: ⟨namely⟩ to ⟨all⟩ the
omens

16   person ⟨in the⟩ [erased] once

17   ↑Of all it is true↓

Lines

17–18 appearance is ⟨always⟩ latent

20 contains ↑in↓

21–22 thoughts. ⟨W⟩ "A man's

23 dreams, ⟨just now⟩ so

24–25 colossal, ⟨in⟩ without

30 south. or

30–(157)1 ↑And why not?↓ ⟨The way of this correspondence is seen by considering that⟩ his

Page 157

2 neglect ⟨that of⟩ another

3–4 in his ⟨fellowmen⟩ ↑associates↓

7 Therefore ⟨the wonder⟩ it

13–15 ↑hints↓ when all . . . sense /
⟨Of dreams prophecies omens coincidences one general remark may be made that they all are prophetic because all things are prophetic.⟩. Every man

19 tree, ⟨the⟩ in

20 notices that ⟨every⟩ every

21 hour the ⟨shad⟩ moon

23 changed ⟨image⟩ ↑figure↓

24 knows. but

25 man↑'s↓ ⟨can be read from⟩ ↑fortune ⟨is written in⟩ may be read in↓

26 palmistry, — ⟨from⟩ ↑in↓

27 physiognomy, ⟨by⟩ ↑in↓

29–30 ↑instructed↓ mariner ⟨with certainty⟩ that there is no ↑near↓ land ⟨in the neighborhood⟩ in

31 describes ⟨with care⟩ the

Page 158

2 who ⟨h⟩ [erased] & [over erasure] what

4 himself ⟨involuntarily⟩ in

5–7 whole. ⟨Every⟩ "Head with foot
Hath private amity, & both with moons & tides."

8–9 The ⟨merest⟩ jest & byword to an intelligent ⟨eye⟩ ↑ear↓

10 Indeed ⟨it seems as if⟩ all productions of man ⟨were inevitably⟩ ↑are↓

11–12 shall ⟨not immediately be discovered to⟩ ↑not↓ have . . . moral, & ⟨to⟩ be

13 intended ⟨or dreamed⟩ by . . . all the ↑idlest↓ wild fables

14 ↑can↓

16–17 Lucian has ⟨a foolish⟩ ↑an idle↓ tale ⟨of no meaning⟩ that . . . Memphis to Coppus

25 pervaded with ⟨myriads of⟩ secret

445

Lines

29–30   ↑And in those times . . . most ⟨extreme⟩ faith to↓
⟨In⟩ these fancies & whimsies, ⟨of the human mind it is ⟨agr⟩ pleasing to observe that⟩ they

Page 159

1–2   grave ⟨& grand⟩ spirit of Reason & humanity. ⟨When Hector is told ⟨i⟩In the Iliad⟩ When Hector

6–8   guesses well ⟨but⟩ ↑and↓ he is ↑not↓ the wisest man ⟨not⟩ whose . . . but ↑the↓

10–11   divine ⟨inte⟩ foresight

12   Heaven." ⟨And so⟩ the

17   sense. in

21   all the ⟨g⟩Greeks

24–27   The augur ⟨inquired⟩ showed . . . told him, "if that bird remained where ⟨it did⟩ he . . . return." The

Page 160

2   replied, "Wherefore

6–8   here to ⟨s⟩be killed . . . Jew."
Hecateus of Abdera
apud *Jahn, Heb. Com.* p. 215
It is

8–9   importance to the⟨se⟩ whimsical pictures of sleep or to ⟨signs⟩ omens

18   guided. ⟨i⟩If of

22–23   eyes of ⟨the⟩ man, they ⟨preferred⟩ ↑rather waited↓

24   commanding ⟨even⟩ to

25–26   ↑the single ear of↓

32   perceived by ⟨c[?]m[?]⟩ men

Page 161

2–3   awake." Plutarch. /
⟨It is easy to see how⟩ this doctrine ⟨which⟩ is ⟨but⟩ a

7   *Ant.* Whose

8   *Sooth.* Caesar's

22   fulness. the belief ⟨in⟩ that ⟨certain⟩ ↑particular↓

Page 162

1   this fai⟨r⟩th in different degrees. Especially ↑it is familiar↓

3   is ⟨ne⟩ an

10   seem ⟨to have exerted him⟩ as he

17–19   active.
⟨It will be perceived at once that⟩ [cancellation in pencil]
this ⟨strictly⟩ ↑supernatural favoritism↓ [emendations in ink]

Lines

<personal aid & favor⟩ is ⟨strictly⟩ allied with a large class of superstitious ⟨facts⟩; with the revelations [cancellations in pencil; "superstitious," without further emendation, can easily be read "superstitions" after the cancellation of "facts"]

21–23   partial; the ⟨whole⟩ agents & the means of magic, ↑as↓ [emendations in ink] magicians & amulets. ⟨It will also be perceived that⟩ [cancellation in pencil] this ⟨power⟩ ↑faith in a↓ ⟨supposed⟩ ↑partial↓ [emendations in ink]

24   every where ⟨in its grosser forms⟩, & [cancellation in pencil]

26   ancient ↑Rome↓ [in ink], or in the ⟨consecrating & exorcising⟩ ↑beneficent↓ [emendations in pencil]

27   this ⟨all⟩ supposed

28–29   powers ⟨of nature⟩ ↑natural↓ & ⟨of⟩ moral ⟨to⟩ which

30–33   ↑This power heeded in many actions & partnerships, is not the power ↑to↓ which . . . nature. Accordingly↓

35–(163)1   'who . . . she is?'
       —"That

Page 163

5–6   men spy
             ⟨In⟩With the half shut eye

8   insight ⟨whose least notice of any fact is sufficient to rivet attention to it, has⟩ Goethe

9   recorded ⟨his⟩ speculations

10–11   citing /
           ⟨Goethe nachgelassene werke vol. 8 p 178⟩
           ⟨He⟩ ↑I↓ believed that ⟨he⟩ ↑I↓

15   unreasonable; not ⟨devilish⟩ human

20   ↑our↓

22   possible ⟨with⟩ to

26–27   similar. {I sought to redeem . . . behind an image.}

28–29   itself in ⟨all⟩ ↑the↓ corporeal & ↑the↓

31   forms ⟨one of the m element of⟩ ↑in↓ the moral world, though not ↑an↓ antagonist yet ↑a↓

32   warp; [blank] ⟨;⟩ the

Page 164

4   life ²have ¹I been [numerals in pencil]

6–7   men ⟨n⟩either in genius ⟨n⟩or in talents ⟨&⟩ seldom [cancellations in pencil]

7   heart. but

11–12   that the ⟨clearer⟩ ↑more intelligent↓ [emendations in ink] part of men will ⟨make⟩ ↑discredit↓ them ⟨suspicious⟩ as ↑deceived↓ betrayed or [emendations in pencil]

13–14   find they ⟨co⟩ the⟨y⟩ir match

16–18   observations ⟨may well that strange⟩ ↑doubtless arose↓ but

Lines

monstrous proverb, ⟨arise,⟩ [emendations in pencil] 'Nobody against God but God' "

Goethe; Nachgelassene
Werke; Vol. 8 p. 178–

It

19–20 We certa⟨n⟩inly may find ⟨me [?]⟩among

24 favor. The ⟨ex⟩ crimes

26 strangely t⟨o⟩urn to

29 relate ⟨all⟩ these [cancellation in pencil]

30 poetic ⟨these obscure phenomena⟩ these [cancellation in pencil]

33 demonological. The insi⟨[?]⟩n↑u↓ation ⟨that⟩ [emendations in ink] ⟨undoubtedly⟩ is that the ⟨great⟩ known [cancellations in pencil]

34–35 by this ⟨obscure⟩ ↑lurking↓ ⟨wild partial⟩ ↑gypsy↓ [emendations in pencil]

Page 165

5 Individual, of the ⟨particular⟩ personal [cancellation in pencil]

9–10 renouncing ⟨father mother⟩ ↑family↓, town, clan, ↑country,↓

12–13 chief, ⟨and⟩ an Indian sachem, ↑or a feudal baron↓

16 & the ↑one↓

20 universal. he

21 angel; that he ⟨ha⟩ is

22 Destiny; ⟨when he is to die ghosts will announce the fact⟩ when he acts, ⟨subtle agents &⟩ unheard

26 this ⟨mighty⟩ exuberant

27 generic ↑&↓ [in pencil] cosmic↑al↓ [in pencil, re-written in ink] ⟨& universal⟩ laws [cancellation in pencil]

31 will is / is an

Page 166

1 beholding ⟨wh⟩ one

2–4 but ⟨we know very well in our saner hours, that⟩ the law of the Universe is ⟨one; —⟩ one for each, & one for all; — & ⟨that⟩ [cancellations in pencil] there is as precise & as ⟨assignable⟩ ↑describable↓ [emendations in ink]

7 sugar. ⟨A⟩ [cancellation in ink] ⟨The wonder is explained as soon as we see the man close at hand & the men with whom he has to do.⟩ [cancellation in pencil] Lord Bacon

12–13 ↑in actions of a low & common pitch↓

17–18 Whereas the ⟨greater part⟩ ↑fault of most↓ men is that they are busy bodies, that they ⟨interfere⟩ do

26 been ⟨used⟩ ↑employed on the facts,↓

27 has ⟨been⟩ learned

Lines

29   senses, the man of ⟨u⟩calculation

31   find that ⟨it⟩ he

32–34   instinct.

               ⟨So it may be said⟩ [cancellation in pencil] of those ⟨wh⟩ [cancellation in ink] bodily [first cancellation rejected for minimal sense]

Page 167

1   ↑habitually↓

10–11   semi-medical questions, ⟨merely⟩ respecting

11–12   doubtless, ⟨in⟩ ↑&↓ ranging themselves with ⟨all⟩ the

14   is the ⟨very⟩ [cancellation in pencil] curious

15   ↑from sleep↓

19   belong ⟨also⟩ [cancellation in pencil] the

20–21   Magnetism. The ⟨whole⟩ [cancellation in pencil] interest

24   are ⟨of so fuliginous⟩ the phenomena

29   natural ⟨&⟩thing

31–33   disclosures of the so⟨n⟩mnambulist. The peculiarity of ⟨these facts⟩ ↑the history of Animal Magnetism↓ is that ⟨they⟩ ↑it↓

34   known ⟨to⟩ ↑as↓ stud⟨y⟩ents & ⟨ac⟩↑in↓quire↑rs↓. Of course

36   It ⟨is⟩ ↑becomes in such hands↓

Page 168

8   known to get⟨t[?]⟩ [erased] a

9   this prod⟨ug⟩igious promiser

15   book & ↑to↓ the

18   cry with ⟨s⟩ to

25–26   exhaust his ⟨wonder⟩ ↑astonishment↓

27   causal ⟨wonder⟩ ↑miracle↓

30   ↑They savor of nothing great or noble↓

Page 169

11   It is ⟨wholly⟩ [cancellation in pencil] a

12   sentiments & a ⟨most⟩ [cancellation in pencil] dangerous

15   Meantime far be from me ⟨the lust of explaining away⟩ the

16   vast: ⟨and⟩ ↑Far be from me↓

24   betrays his ⟨per⟩ conviction

26   ↑inexhaustible & sublime↓

Page 170

3   until ⟨you⟩ ↑the↓

4–5   Shadow of ⟨t⟩Theology

10–11   cattle. / [The following conclusion, a double sheet, is numbered continuously with the rest of the lecture and was once

sewn with it; at top of first page it is marked in pencil: "Human Life 1838–9".]
It is with

15	↑series↓ course by ⟨a⟩ ↑two↓ discourses ↑more↓ {on the
17	given m scope
18–19	wall us in, ⟨than could be allowed⟩ ↑and ⟨to⟩ which I had only named↓
20	Lecture. I
24–25	↑to read a line of the Doctrine of the Soul,↓
26	betray ⟨an infinite⟩ a power
29	soul. *then;* to
30–31	Instincts, ⟨th[?]⟩ Condition, Persons, Books, Facts. *then;* in
32–33	Intellect. *then;* to describe the position ↑of antagonism↓
34	imposes. *then;* to

Page 171

1–4	element *then;* the nature of the Comic *then;* the grand element of Virtue And, *tonight;* the alleged exception to the law ⟨But⟩ The
5–6	Two ⟨or twenty⟩ or two hundred of our sketches of nature ⟨are⟩ would
12	↑one man's belief that his words↓ ⟨that these words of mine⟩ &
13–15	ignorance in the ⟨conviction that⟩ ↑presence of↓ Truth ⟨is⟩ & Goodness & Beauty ↑that overhang & ⟨s[?]⟩ environ us all↓ I shall hope that ⟨I have made it felt in⟩ ↑you have heard through↓
16–17	teaching." ⟨I would bow ⟨w⟩ inspire the love of that grandeur of character which knows naked simplicity to be the perfectness of man⟩ And to this
18	high as ⟨you⟩ ↑the↓
20–22	↑Plain dealing the summit of benevolence & wisdom.↓ . . . any ⟨soul⟩ mind until he has no ↑self-↓will
23	which ⟨r⟩creates &

[The following is a small folded sheet, never sewn, but now filed with this lecture. It is numbered "6" in green pencil and is headed on the first side *"Demonology."*]

The history of man is a series of conspiracies to win from nature some advantage without paying for it. Tis curious to see what grand powers we have a hint of, & are mad to grasp, & yet how slow Heaven is to trust us with such edge-tools! "All that frees talent without increasing self command is noxious." Thus the fabled ring of Gyges making the wearer invisible, which is represented in modern fable by the telescope as used by Schlemel, [acute accent over last "e" cancelled in pencil] is only mischievous. A new or / private language used to serve only low or political purposes; the desired discovery of ⟨the⟩ [erased] a [over erasure] guided balloon; the steam-battery, so fatal as to put an end ⟨by⟩ [erased] to [over erasure] war by the threat of universal murder, are of this kind. By the time we have acquired great power, we shall have acquired sufficient wisdom to use it well. Animal magnetism inspires the prudent & moral with a certain terror. Men ↑are not↓ [in left margin] good enough to be trusted with such power. ["All that frees . . . such power" (B, 164)] So with the tran⟨[?]⟩sfusion of ⟨the⟩ blood; the / divination of contingent events; the alleged second sight of the pseudo-spiritualists; and the navigation of the air. Tramps are troublesome enough in the city & the highways, but tramps flying through the air & descending on the lonely traveller, or the lonely farmers house, or the bank-messenger in the country, can well be spared. / [blank] / [whole passage in "Demonology," W, X, 20]

[The following is a single leaf, never sewn with this lecture, but now filed with it. It is numbered "35" in pencil and "51" in red pencil. The heading, "Dreams", is circled and cancelled in pencil; written vertically in left margin in blue pencil: "Demonology".]

The text of life is accompanied ⟨all along⟩ [cancellation circled in pencil] by th⟨is⟩e gloss or commentary of dreams. I owe to the Genius of my life many a special friendly hint dropped in a dream. The⟨y⟩ ↑nights↓ serve as explanation of the days. A ↑seer will↓ skilful man [last two words circled in pencil] read⟨s⟩ not their details, but their quality. Their extravagance from nature is yet within a higher nature. / Sometimes there is a certain ⟨fun⟩ ↑malice↓ & humor in them; sometimes a poetic bliss; Ford says,
"I have found
More sweets in one unprofitable dream
Than in my life's whole pilgrimage.
⟨Ford. "Sun's Darling."⟩ [I, 1]
Sometimes they make dreadful revelations, and leave the stern preachers, Pythagoras, St Paul, Behmen, & Swedenborg, little to tell you. /

II. THE PRESENT AGE

1. INTRODUCTORY

Page 186

[In pencil, inside front cover:]
↑I offer to the candour of the Lyceum some considerations on the character of the Present Age. A topic, I suppose it will be admitted of universal pertinence needing no preface & requiring no postscript For what is the life of each one of us but itself his own ↑summary↓ speculation o⟨n⟩f the resources & tendencies of this Epoch of time

Nor need I fear that the subject will be ⟨too g[illegible]⟩ too little nor too great for the ⟨grasp of an individual⟩ profitable employment of our thoughts Not too little in ye first place as confining our thoughts to the present hour to the exclusion of past & future↓ / [On a half leaf with the lecture

451

	is an ink transcription of the passage, not in Emerson's hand. At top of first page of lecture:]

Read at the Masonic Temple 4 Dec. 1839

P. A. Lect. 1

1–12	{In looking around . . . need not.} [brackets in pencil]
2	time to time ⟨present themselves⟩ ↑occur↓
5–6	{Resources and Tendencies}
8–9	would not ⟨cripple myself⟩ ↑⟨exclude⟩↓ by directing my attention on the interests of the Day ↑exclude myself↓
11–12	And ⟨why need⟩ I need not
16	Eternal. {I [bracket in pencil]
20	hand, ⟨if⟩ ↑neither will↓ this topic ↑if properly handled↓
22	inquiry of ⟨those⟩ the
23	enumeration ⟨b[?]⟩of all

Page 187

3	immoveable ⟨state⟩ ↑polity↓
4	civility into ⟨[?]⟩Australasia
7–13	{No foregoing . . . elder world.}
9	society no ⟨single⟩ ↑peculiar↓
13	mountains of ⟨[?]⟩the elder
23	↑many activities↓
24	parties ⟨which divide⟩ to

Page 188

1–2	East. ⟨Th⟩ Constantinople
5	If ⟨I⟩ ↑we↓
7–27	illustrative of this. ↑Insert X↓ / [on inserted leaf, marked "X":] ↑The key to the period is ⟨in⟩ the . . . The former ⟨men⟩ ↑generations↓ acted under the belief that a shining social prosperity was the aim of men: & ⟨compromised ever⟩ ↑sacrificed uniformly↓ . . . ↑public↓ movements. In the mind of the philosopher has far more precision, & ⟨energy⟩is attaining a depth & splendor /
	In the eye . . . {has ceased . . . He} . . . union with Nature.↓ /
	⟨The key to the period is the knowledge of the fact that the Soul has ⟨acquired⟩ [cancellation in ink] become in recent times ⟨conscious⟩ ↑aware↓ [emendations in pencil] of itself The Individual man learns his access to the Universal mind, is inspired by the sentiment of a deep & total union with Nature.⟩ [all cancelled in pencil] This perception
28	detaches ⟨the⟩ bone & marrow ⟨the⟩ soul
31	steadily ⟨[?]⟩sunders
32	holdings. ⟨It is All Souls⟩ ↑Every man for himself↓ [cancellation in ink, insertion in pencil]
34	Souls

Lines	Page 189
2	civil society, the ⟨neck of the⟩ new race is stiff ↑heady &↓ & rebellious
4	neck of ⟨the⟩ unspeakable
6	↑It tends to solitude↓ [in pencil]
7	accidental & ⟨[erasure]⟩momentary [over erasure]
9	merely, for [comma in pencil]
10–11	things: there [colon in pencil]
13	wine, but [comma in pencil]
14–27	girth. /⟨b⟩But two parties . . . Future. ↑{Insert R}↓ [on half leaf, marked "R":] ↑But whilst [blotted word] great fact I have mentioned . . . Understanding. ⟨We may name⟩ the ⟨age⟩ still reigning school . . . destruction rather than of creation. / The old leaf . . . by a new leaf bud below. This ⟨Ana⟩ [erased]

> ⟨sweeter is the law
> Than all the grace Love ever saw
> Brother there is [blank indicated]
> We are its servants. we
> Draw the breath [incomplete letters]
> We are its [blank indicated] by it we
> Draw the breath
> Serve thou it not for daily bread
> Serve it for fear
> Love if the
> By love⟩↓ /

But whilst the great fact I have mentioned, the uprise of the soul, remains underneath as the master spring of all the activity we witness, [comma in pencil] it appears superficially in comparison with foregoing periods as the Age of Analysis. And here

28–29	advert ⟨o[?] moment⟩ to ⟨our mysterious nature as men, & to⟩ the ⟨great⟩ metaphysical distinction which ⟨remains always an ultimate fact. Man ↑recognizes in↓ is capable of apprehending the Absolute & also capable of apprehending the finite.⟩ The power
30	absolute truth ⟨seems to have⟩ stand↑s↓
31	apprehends ⟨th[?]⟩ particular
32–34	ends. The former ⟨contemns⟩ ↑holds↓ the latter ↑in contempt,↓ ⟨& cannot tarry for its tardy creepings. T⟩When . . . former is ↑most↓ withdrawn

	Page 190
11	{It is aimless bluster.}
19	fruits of ⟨his⟩ [erased] its [over erasure]

Lines

22–23   check of the sentiments. / [one leaf missing at this point] ⟨calculable. It is full of varieties, of successions, of contrivances. The country, on the contrary, offers an unbroken horizon, the monotony of an endless road, of vast uniform plains, ⟨&⟩of distant mountains, the melancholy of uniform & infinite vegetation; the objects on the road are few & unimportant; the eye is ever invited to the horizon, & the clouds; ⟨to the⟩ types of the Absolute & Eternal.⟩ [E, 38]

Commerce is

23–24   thought. ⟨Commerce is the analysis of labor. or production⟩. Yet such ↑is the↓ [insertion in ink over pencil] predominance ↑that↓ [in left margin]

25   viewed ⟨externally⟩ ↑superficially↓

27   nature ⟨all⟩ that

29   enlightened /

⟨The present age may be fitly called the Age of Analysis. Viewed externally, it might as fitly be called the Age of Commerce, such predominance belongs to Trade & its consequences. But Commerce is only a single fruit of the new habit of thought. Commerce is a mechanical analysis. It is the analysis of labor or production.

It is not the tactics of nature to give power faster than we learn how to use it Rules & bounds every creature provides itself with. In the infancy of society, where the Reason or the Soul is not active in the religious sentiment, it has a sort of passive presence as Dread. A salutary dread guards the savage from profanation. Every thing runs speedily for him into mystery & he is defended in his nonage from crimes & degradations / by superstition. He is kept in bounds all his life by fear as he is kept in his house at night by darkness. Analysis the activity of the Understanding destroys step by step this check Especially Commerce dissipates this infinity that overhangs all things, by confining the attention on the economical alone. Analysis brings every thing close to his eye. Commerce touches every thing.⟩ — At this day

34–35   Soul claims. /

⟨Commerce realizes this autocracy to the senses.⟩ [cancelled with ink line; the red pencil lines which cancel the following passage also extend through it] ⟨Analysis like the Devil promised the world to the man if he would sell his soul & Commerce is the fulfilment of the bargain. Commerce which looks at every fact only in one aspect its gainfulness. which turns its penny amidst sublime scenery & on the worst calamities on a revolution a famine a fire a war a plague sees everything partially. {These that I see are not the sacred ships of Will but the dire ships of necessity}⟩ [brackets in pencil] Commerce has no

454

Lines	Page 191
2	byword. ⟨And all for what? For the senses, not for the mind.⟩ Th⟨is⟩e end
5	↑virtual↓
14–15	which it works [followed by horizontal pencil line and passage marked with pencil brackets:] {We have no religion. We are up to everything diabolic or divine. But we are divided & so undone. The Universe must still be propitiated let the members gain what they may. Being divided the man's aims are steadily baulked. Commerce has subdued the world holds all nature / in fee & yet the merchant is not more a man than the farmer or soldier he has supplanted. Meantime Analysis has its extremes, and then its great reaction. Things part to reunite. Forever springs in the soul of man the gracious effort to unite Nature, to see one Cause. And this of course is strongest when things have wandered farthest from their natural bent When the novelty of Commerce charming men by the magnitude & number of transactions is a little worn off, Men see that the heart is no gainer, that man is a drudge, & they come back lowly & selfabandoning to the Eternal Sentiments of Love & Truth. It is to be considered that this activity of the Understand} / [blank] /
	⟨It is not the tactics of nature to give power faster than we learn how to use it. Rules & bounds every creature provides itself with. In the infancy of Society a salutary dread guards the Savage from profanation. Every thing runs speedily for him into mystery & he is defended in his nonage from the last crimes & degradations by superstition He is kept in bounds all his life by fear as he is kept in his house all night by darkness. Analysis the activity of the Understanding destroys step by step this check Especially Commerce dissipates this infinity that overhangs all things by confining the attention on the economical alone. Analysis brings everything close to his eye. Commerce touches everything.⟩ See what structures
16	sufficed / ⟨resolve &⟩ destroy
17	are ⟨gone⟩ ↑⟨laid⟩↓. [emendations in pencil] ⟨Demonology⟩ [cancelled in ink] The very last ghost is ⟨gone⟩ ↑laid↓ [emendations in pencil]
20	rosy ⟨a⟩Analyst
22–23	Sunday, if ⟨you tell a lie,⟩ ↑baulk water↓
31	as usual. / [The leaf following, "in the streets . . . generous impulse. ⟨In like manner . . . apparent to me. / Nature is always . . . somewhat to say.⟩," belongs, according to ink pagination, below and is printed in the text at its proper place. See textual note for page 195, lines 8–13.]

Lines	Page 192
1	sight as ⟨any⟩ almost
10	Browne ⟨writes⟩ in
25	resurrection." *Works.* Vol IV. p 420.
27	influences. as
33–(193)3	hours."" *Works* Vol IX p. 522 /

↑I am less familiar with the history of opinion here, but in New England, I can attest from the recollections of my childhood↓

How richly this old stream of antique faith descended {⟨into New England⟩ {the ⟨childish⟩ remembrances . . . witness.} Th⟨is⟩at country

Page 193

7	↑comparatively cold↓
12–13	Education. ⟨I heard⟩ ↑It raised . . . I heard↓
16–17	but the ⟨timid⟩ family ⟨did not;⟩ ↑were timed↓; ⟨& i⟩Immediately
21–22	died. ⟨Who has not heard⟩ ↑In every town in Maine you may ⟨hear⟩ still hear↓
23	Moody of ⟨York?⟩ ↑Agamenticus↓
24–25	wounded by ⟨the⟩ ↑his↓ pointed preaching, ⟨of⟩ would
28	went ⟨boldly⟩ in ↑after them↓
32	line ↑the minister of Malden, Mass↓ ⟨sto[?]⟩ [erased] whilst [over erasure]

Page 194

2	language ↑of devotion in the American Churches.↓ /

20 & 30 miles to ⟨church⟩ Lectur

turn the hourglass

cold chh [entire page in pencil] / [passage marked "B" for insertion below] /

of devotion in the American Churches.

3–4	faith ⟨see what⟩ a vast body of religious writings ↑which↓
8–23	unbelieving {honey combed} & hollow. ⟨but when it tingles & trembles with earnest will beauty be born.⟩ ↑Insert B↓ [on previous page, marked "B":] ↑By our processes of thought . . . awaken no ⟨wonder⟩ ↑astonishment↓ . . . supernatural ⟨hi⟩ ties. ↑I was much struck one night last winter with the spirit in which↓ Here came the other night an Aurora so wonderful . . . arithmetical eyes; we ⟨knew how many⟩ ↑counted the↓ colors; . . . Dutchman, ⟨St⟩ [cancellation in pencil] Erics cap, St Elmo's light, the lucky & unlucky days, & the terrors of the day of doom?↓
23–24	decay of learning. {⟨The spirit of this age says to the scholar "Leave your old books "Come forth into the light of things

456

Let Nature be your teacher" Away with your pedantic cart-
loads of grammars & dictionaries & archaeologies. The Now is
all. Instantly the indolence & self indulgence of the scholar
is armed⟩ / with an apology. Be it as you say: — I will have
a good time.} [D, 96; Wordsworth, "The Tables Turned,"
lines 15–16] [brackets and cancellation in pencil; following
cancellation in ink]

⟨It is not to be doubted that the true reason why we have
so few scholars is that⟩ the Genius of the Age does not tend to
⟨Learning⟩ Erudition

26 ↑fruit↓

29 into their ⟨keeping⟩ ↑judgment↓

Page 195

3 state, th⟨s⟩is whim

4 disposition ⟨in America to apologize for Scholarship &⟩ ostentatiously disclaim

5–6 ↑as the newspapers call them,↓

8–13 Latin Schools.

⟨The practical effect of this Criticism or Analysis running
through all the parts of society has its inconveniences Every
where Privelege, Prerogative, Authority is trenched upon. The
attorney questions the discretion & the award of the ⟨Court⟩
Bench; & the ⟨people⟩ ↑mechanics & tradesmen↓ in their turn
are jealous of the attorney & of ⟨all⟩ the ↑learned↓ professions.
The want of faith of which I have spoken in the Church is
alleged with equal vehemence against the practitioners of
Medicine. Our Boston School of Medicine like our Boston
School of Divinity it seems lacks due faith in its own skill &
are less acceptable in the Country than the / the graduate of
remoter colleges who still believe in the power of medicine.⟩
[C, 191] / [The leaf following, "That which is best in nature
. . . sex / or accident . . . Perfect which solicits me," belongs in Lecture 9 in the course on "The Present Age" and is
printed there. See textual note for page 297, line 25, to page
298, line 6. According to ink pagination, there is a lacuna of
three leaves at this point as the manuscript is now filed, but
the third leaf is here supplied by the misplaced leaf noted
above in textual note for page 191, line 31: "in the streets
. . . generous impulse. ⟨In like manner . . . apparent to
me. / Nature is always . . . somewhat to say.⟩." This reduces
the lacuna to two leaves according to ink pagination. The material bracketed in the text is supplied from C, 314.]

10 faubourgs. and ⟨it is worthy to remark⟩ ↑⟨observed⟩↓ ↑insisted↓

11–12 Antoine {in which . . . found,} the

13–14 generous impulse. ⟨In like manner we are perpetually advertised that our way as men lies out into nature & not as a ⟨[?]⟩ conscious purpose inward into mind {The beauty that piques us in in every object in a straw a chip of steel a stone in the wall is an announcement that always our road lies out into nature} The ray of light passes invisible through space & only when it falls on an object is it seen. So your spiritual energy is barren & useless until it is directed to something outward: then is it a thought   The relation between you & it first makes *you*, the value of you, apparent to me. ["The ray . . . to me" ("Intellert," W, II, 335; D, 174)] /

Nature is always honest & ⟨the weariness of⟩ Scholars who have allowed themselves to become mere readers of books at the loss of all habit of manly activity & earthly interest & prowess become unmanned & appear to the eye like old grammars & decayed catalogues. They fall out of the world into the bookcase   The sun & air the stars love & hope know them not & they may be said to have no part in all that is done under the sun. "Detestable," said Kant, "is the company of mere literary men." [see p. 234, above] In this humour we are relieved by the rude & strong. The mob are always interesting   We hate Editors, preachers, & all manner of scholars & praters fashionists   A ⟨blac[partial letter]⟩ smith a truckman a drover we follow into the ↑market or↓ [in pencil] bar-room & watch with eagerness what they shall say, for such as they do not speak because they are expected to, but because they have somewhat to say.) ["The mob . . . to say" (D, 353)] / [blank] /

Let not

17–18	matter, ⟨on thought⟩ on
20	were ⟨s[?]t⟩ [erased] legitimate [over erasure]

Page 196

1–6	centuries. ⟨See what wonderful results it effects.⟩ ↑Let us be just to this wonderworker & see its results↓ the prodigious expansion of trade. ↑It was Commerce that settled . . . occasions therewith.↓
9	↑steamboat trade↓ the army of ⟨its⟩ ↑our↓
11	so that ⟨we⟩ ↑the rail cars↓ shall skate ⟨as it were⟩ over
13	freedom, ⟨the disclaimer which every ⟨man⟩ speaker makes in his harangue disowning responsibility⟩. Now
14	Wealth [could be read as "Health"]
17	all, ↑it↓
18–19	↑who work in these reforms↓ [in pencil]
24–25	Meantime ⟨under⟩ ↑along with the↓ this activity of ⟨destruction⟩ ↑mere commodity of which I have spoken↓
26	reforms ⟨the movements⟩ are

Lines	
3	joy. ⟨Let⟩ Wait a little & ↑it↓ will
5–6	remains the ⟨T⟩surviving Tradition
7	forms. numbering in its train a ⟨vast⟩ ↑⟨great⟩↓ [insertion cancelled in pencil] multitude↑s↓ [insertion in pencil] ⟨of defenders⟩. composed of those ⟨men⟩ in
9	talent predominates over ⟨genius⟩ ↑character↓
11	lastly of ⟨the merely sensual who lie wherever they fall⟩ ↑those↓ [emendations in pencil]
12	institutions & ⟨so⟩ ↑therefore↓ [emendations in pencil] hate any change. The ⟨entire⟩ [cancelled in ink] *inertia*
13–14	Usages, the ⟨whole force of the ⟨old⟩ ↑aged↓⟩ ↑the aged↓
15	all this ⟨immense force⟩ ↑numerous vote↓
20	dynamical means, ⟨as Classes⟩ for
23	such institutions ⟨are⟩ always
25–26	to the institutions. /

⟨The actual struggle between these two great interests ⟨does generally ⟨do⟩no great credit to either party⟩ ↑goes on with various fortune but to a predestined result↓. Some Burke arises on the side of the ⟨old⟩ ↑state↓, endeavoring by the single force of Genius to stay the movement & rally all ⟨goodness⟩ ↑the virtue of the land↓ around the good old cause. ⟨It is remarkable that w⟩What Burke in the French Revolution essayed to do for the English Constitution Coleridge has essayed to do in our riper agitation for the English Church, — to reconcile it, that is, with Reason. ↑A man of genius arises like Scott who dedicates prodigious powers to the reproduction of the Past & consecrates it to the Imagination & the affections↓ On the other hand

36–37	educates the man. ⟨It⟩ Each
38	himself {greater than he was, ⟨greater than ⟨ten⟩ ↑⟨many⟩↓ men⟩,} [brackets in pencil] greater than all

1	receive ↑it.↓ / ⟨like him the omnipotence of a principle.⟩ Never
2	shows its ⟨truth &⟩ nearness
7	↑Whilst the tradition is every day assailed↓
	In their
8–10	back ⟨with new affection⟩ to the old books, reprint ⟨the old literature,⟩ ↑them↓ . . . celebrate ⟨the⟩ ↑ancient↓ anniversaries ²⟨{of ⟨[?]⟩ [erasure] things [over erasure] fallen into decay or} ¹{of the foundation of towns,}⟩ praise
11	copy the ⟨ancient⟩ ↑elder↓
12–16	↑Roxburgh Clubs are founded Shakspeare Societies. Camden Societies Cheetham Societies↓ ⟨Such books⟩ as the Retrospective Review↑s↓, Percys Reliques ↑Ellis's Letters Froissart & Joinville are reprinted↓ and the entire effort of Walter Scott's

genius designate our time, then [places for interlinear insertions uncertain]

17–18   body of ⟨c⟩archives . . . history of of the

19–20   ↑This dilettantism↓

⟨All this flatters the fancy & ↑the↓ affections laps us in a pretty dream, but⟩ is . . . foot. ⟨Heroes are in the field & we are at play⟩. This ⟨very⟩ holding

21   forward. ⟨In actual experience I think it will be found that this⟩ ↑The↓

24   ↑friends mixed with foes↓

29–30   the Past. / [blank] /

⟨{Meantime the warfare does no great credit to either party. The foremost ⟨defenders of⟩ conservatives cast a certain shame over their cause by their ill management & their low motives. The virtue of the party is silent   Its fear & wrath & worldliness come loudly forward. The⟨y⟩ champions defend their altars & hearths but not in the faith of the altar or the love of the hearth but for the end of property only. — Then the defence of forms has the worst effect upon the intellect. Deprived of real objects it loses its sinews, its alacrity its equality to Nature and becomes dwarfish trifling & talkative /

The assailants meantime degenerate also. They merge their spirit presently in personal considerations. They form angry parties & wreck their unity very soon on the old rock of transferring the sacredness of the end to some accidental means. They lose the sentiment which was their guiding star & learn to apply their weapons of logic & philosophy only to destroy & so become malignant & odious. Every sentiment builds, creates. Analysis without sentiment destroys. They aim to reform dynamically or by votes laws ⟨pub⟩ associations public opinion & not spiritually by the omnipotence of private thought. Evil men men of talent without heart / gain power in their counsels & deprave the cause. They destroy for wages as their opponents build for wages hirelings on both sides.}⟩ [brackets in pencil]

⟨Meantime⟩ ↑But↓, whilst

34–35   itself — The

Page 199

2–3   refuses to ⟨be⟩ give its glory to a man. /

⟨Meantime under this activity of destruction appears ever & anon & now more steadily, as I have intimated, a new agent. These Reforms these movements are ethical religious humane. Men ask for better doctrine. Men ask for pure truth & in practice for simple equity. The age is characterised by a ⟨new love of the Vast. which is⟩ certain yearning & aspiration which has given a strong colour to poetry & is called the feeling of the Infinite. This new love of the Vast which is native in Germany which was imported into France by ⟨M⟩De Stael, which appeared in England in Coleridge, Wordsworth, Byron, Shelley, Felicia Hemans, — which may now be noted in every copy of verses or college exercise, what is it but the very breathing & sobbing of the long imprisoned but now ascending Soul? Pardon it, if it is impatient of our schools & books. Do not turn from it if it propose strange & incredible changes. ↑{⟨What if it be sub-⟩jective↓ [insertion in pencil] / ↑D↓ [in pencil]

What if it be subjective? and prone to act on thought? Must we therefore bewail the Dark Ages. Can we not rather see the immense promise of such a period? What education is this. It is to induce on mankind a habit of piercing appearances & seizing things. The ages have been sensual. That has been admired which was not great & that has been sought which was not good And now slowly & painfully the well kept secret of his divine nature is transpiring. He learns that the modes & fashions good & ill fortunes, circumstances, the persons who so bewitch & oppress him, are ⟨the⟩ emanations of himself The coat, the cloak which he wears, — when it hampers his motion he throws aside, for his body is nobler. Will he not learn that calamity is also a costume which only marks some crisis in the progress ⟨&⟩or retrocession of his mind? ↑E↓ [insertion in pencil]⟩ /

The whole hope

3	centres, ⟨in my judgment⟩, in
6	↑no church,↓
9–10	itself. representing in his person ↑in virtue of his possible perfection↓
12	course; the ⟨cont⟩ attack
13–19	systems of Education⟨s⟩ & the religious Traditions ↑the inferior estimate . . . resources of the soul.↓ [insertion in pencil]
28–29	mechanisms {⟨breathes on them & they become shadows⟩} & calls us to the Holy & the Eternal ⟨not by the past but by the present,⟩ not
29–30	thought & ⟨lowliest submission of the heart.⟩ ↑lowliness↓

Page 200

2	Dark Ages? ↑{go back to D}↓ [in pencil; what follows is written over it] ⟨↑⟨What if it be subjective & prone to act on thought? Must we therefore bewail⟩ Can we not rather see the immense promise of such a period? ⟨What education is this? It is to induce on mankind a habit of piercing appearances & seizing things.⟩ The age↑s↓ ha⟨s⟩ve been sensual. That has been admired which was not great & that has been sought which was not good. And now slowly & ⟨painfully⟩ ↑circuitously↓ the well-kept secret of his ⟨divine nature⟩ ↑royal birth↓

is transpiring. He learns that the modes & fashions good & ill fortunes, circumstances the persons who so bewitch & oppress him are emanations of himself. The coat the cloak which he wears when it hampers his motion he throws aside for his body is nobler   Will he not learn that calamity is also a costume which only marks some crisis in the progress or retrocession of his mind↓⟩ /

Trust

7   waves ⟨before⟩ behind, & ⟨for⟩↑on↓ward to

17   stand ⟨face to face⟩ ↑front to front↓

21   any. ⟨And, doubt not, the moment & the opportunity are divine⟩. Wondering

22   office of espi⟨onage⟩al. We

30–33 acknowledge.

⟨{We act in the presence of an agent who destroys ages & the petty distinctions on which in weak hours we so mightily insist. I have adverted to the impulses of pure Reason which renew themselves in many places & many men. Before / all movement of that nature on literature or on conversation, all differences, all disadvantages become null. Genius which alway beholds this soul, therefore, knows no eras. Genius belongs to the past & to the future. The Eternal Soul will still overpower the men who are its organs, & enchant the ears that hear them by the same right & energy by which long ago & now it enchants the mountains & the sea the air & the globes in their musical dance.}⟩

↑{And what is the daily work & noblest aspiration of each of us but his study of this problem}↓ [insertion and brackets in pencil] /

Besides

Page 201

4   ↑I look not at the work of its hand↓

7–10 ↑Far wider in the noble . . . sure of themselves.↓ ⟨It knows its own⟩. [cancellation in pencil] The source of information on which I ⟨most⟩ rely

11–12 ↑is my love of it,↓ is the acceptance of ⟨ne⟩the

18   God! ⟨Hither⟩ ↑Right onward↓

19   stand ⟨here⟩ waiting

23   lined with ⟨wonderful⟩ ↑beautiful↓

27   disappointed; ⟨and⟩ thou

2. LITERATURE [FIRST LECTURE]

Page 202

2   Literature. ⟨And yet men imagine that⟩ There

3   Fate. ⟨The Every composition proceeds out of All⟩ ↑Every↓

5   that depth ⟨is it permanent.⟩ is

Lines	Page 203
1	element the next ⟨those which⟩ works
2–3	realities what ought to be, what ⟨we wish⟩ ↑really is↓, & what ⟨is⟩ ↑appears↓
6	mind. {Those [bracket in pencil]
7–8	without / a beautiful [bracketted word supplied from E, 1]
11	soul is the ⟨par[?]t⟩ [heavy cancellation] ⟨source⟩ [light cancellation] of thought
13	↑some fierce antagonism↓
15–24	{As good . . . the facts.} [brackets in pencil]
21	thought to ⟨evoke⟩ ↑yield↓
23	never ↑in↓
27	natures & ⟨had the⟩ shared
30	fortune that ⟨a⟩the Trade ⟨can crack up one into [?]⟩ and
31	circulation & ⟨hind⟩ defeat

	Page 204
10	words of ↑the↓
12–15	{But we . . . a hack.} [brackets in pencil]
19–20	rhetoric ⟨a⟩knowledge
29	nations. And
31–32	degradations of this. ⟨It⟩ The
34	speech of th⟨ese⟩at book. ⟨Whatever is⟩ I

	Page 205
10–19	secondary. ⟨On the othe⟩ {One of . . . muse.} [brackets in pencil]
11–12	↑and one to whom the learning of antiquity lay all open↓
13–14	dwell in a solit⟨ary⟩ude, ⟨island⟩ with one ⟨book⟩ ↑volume↓
15	soon ⟨despatch⟩ drop
26	fancied that ⟨c[?]⟩ it
27–28	place in ⟨literature⟩ history
28–(206)19	balance an ounce ↑Insert F↓ [in pencil] / [at top of next page and continuing overleaf, marked "F":]
	↑The same necessity . . . appears. but . . . understand Plato, never enough⟨t⟩ [erased] to pay . . . come duly / down . . . ourselves valuable.↓ /
	{I⟨t⟩n looking at [bracket in pencil]

	Page 206
22	writ to ⟨these⟩ them
28–29	Caillaud, Burkhardt

Lines

6–7   sentiment. ⟨What⟩ the lessons of the good the alway desireable ⟨These the soul wrote & these the soul reads⟩. But ⟨nothing⟩ ↑no circumstance↓

8   ↑who is↓

10–11   ↑& writes a poem↓ which when at last it is published is ↑at↓

18   jokes, ↑wh.↓

20   See ⟨this⟩ what

21   purpose ⟨was⟩ inspired

23   fact of ⟨its⟩ ↑so↓ immense a miscellany. ⟨In the first place it has all books the wisdom of the world it has not let die.⟩ It

24   book for ⟨it⟩every

25   whim & ↑folly↓ humbug has [insertion in pencil]

29   breathe ⟨the breath⟩ of ⟨life⟩ ↑new morning↓

1–2   ↑which leave no man . . . better or worse↓

6–15   include
    1 What it quotes
    2 What it writes
    3. What it wishes to write.
    ↑I. In the first place . . . not let die↓
    ⟨I.⟩ {And here . . . riches.} [brackets in pencil]

10   nature to ⟨which⟩ whose

14–15   ↑Donne & Sir T. Browne↓

18   ↑epics, lyrics,↓ [in pencil]

19–31   them. [insertion indicated from bottom of page:] ↑{In literature whilst many masters . . . or to cease.} The prodigious . . . last 150 years . . . England & America
    Lecture on the Doctrine of ye Soul↓
    {And here [last bracket in pencil]

9   stars ⟨are⟩ [lighter cancellation] ⟨but⟩ [heavier cancellation] white points, the roses ⟨but⟩ brick

12   read ⟨a page or two⟩ ↑some sentences↓

24–(210)3   {Once more . . . twenty years.} [brackets in pencil]

1–2   Yet ⟨almost⟩ we ⟨[?]⟩can count

6–8   reprints, ↑one or two influences are conspicuous. 1. Shakspeare↓ ⟨our age has sought out with avidity⟩ ↑2.↓ [revisions rejected] the history of civil liberty ↑explored↓ every monument of Anglo Saxon history & law↓

13   Hans Sach

Lines	
15	ballads & of Scotland ⟨& E[?]⟩ & Robinhood
16–17	*writes* — Not
22–24	in ↑civil eccles. & lit history↓ quiet imitation of the old conventional ⟨[?]⟩histories ↑of these we ⟨take⟩ need take no account.↓ They [no point indicated for interlinear insertions]
26–27	passable & ⟨prai⟩ laudable
31–32	be written. /
	⟨⟨II⟩. And now to consider what the Age writes. Not many great names have been added to the procession of the Wise since the present century came in. Chiefly the time is marked by the multitude of writers; soldiers sailors nobles princes women write books.⟩ All facts are clearly exposed. the
33–(*211*)1	↑Let there be no ghost stories more.↓

Page 211

3–4	↑Puckler Muskau will go . . . of Nassau↓
6	stood & ⟨know⟩ ↑settle↓
11–18	clubs. {This . . . as if ⟨the Petrarch⟩ [lighter cancellation] the ⟨Jesus⟩ [heavier cancellation] could . . . Petrarchs . . . *himself*.} [brackets in pencil] /
	⟨The character of⟩ our books
19–21	propriety the conseque↑n↓ce of th⟨is⟩e immense multitude of writers & readers & the ⟨diffusion⟩ ↑flight↓ . . . information {by . . . travelling} The [brackets in pencil]
22–24	distinguished from ⟨⟨the⟩ Elizabeth⟨an⟩ & Charles II's wits⟩ ↑⟨Q⟩ learned ages that preceded ours↓. ⟨In reading⟩ ↑There's no fool . . . illustrated in↓
27–(*212*)1	↑The best heads of their time↓ They accept such ⟨flimsy⟩ ↑cardhouse↓

Page 212

2–3	that a ⟨child would⟩ clever boy would ⟨now ridicule⟩ ↑blow away↓.. ⟨exhibiting at the same time on other matters strong common sense.⟩ What stuff in Kepler, in ↑Cardan↓ Lord Bacon, ⟨what a baby house he builds of diet & domestic rules.⟩ Montaigne
7–9	↑They remind us . . . Eastern romance↓
25	nonsense ⟨of this kind,⟩ concerning
28	↑wearing↓
29–30	↑rings . . . worn for cramp.↓ to find all this ⟨precious⟩ ↑masses of↓
32	Browne (Vol 4 p. 398) recommends
36	spiders

Page 213

17	away 130 children
20–22	Humboldt & ⟨Niebuhr⟩ Herschel. ↑have arrived.↓ ↑If I were

Lines

called upon to name a writer as a representative of the last↓
Horace

28–29   nature. ↑G↓ [in pencil] / ↑G↓ [in pencil] ↑cf. Lect III, 3–7↓
[pencil annotation, perhaps not by Emerson, indicating that
this inserted leaf, rejected in the present text, is copied for the
combined lecture from Lecture 3 of "The Present Age"; see
above, pp. 225–226:]

↑There is a most determined realism throughout every department of literature   See how ancient history has been
dealt with by Niebuhr Wolf Muller Heeren   From Wolf's attack upon the authenticity of the Homeric Poems dates a new
epoch in criticism. Ancient History has been found to be not
yet settled. It is to be subjected to Common Sense. It is to be
cross examined. It is to be seen whether its traditions will consist not with universal belief but with universal experience.
Niebuhr has attempted to sift Roman history by the like methods   Heeren has made admirable essays towards ascertaining
the necessary facts in Grecian Persian Assyrian Egyptian Ethi-
opic Carthaginian nations. ⟨How⟩ [erased] How [begins new
line] thoroughly English history has been analyzed let Hallam,
Brodie, Lingard, Palgrave, Turner tell. Goethe has gone the
circuit of human knowledge as Lord Bacon did before him
writing True or False on every article / Bentham has attempted the same work in reference to Civil Law. Pestalozzi
has attempted an analogous reform in Education. In philosophy the German School of French philosophers Cousin Jouffroy Coleridge in England attempted to find a foundation in
thought for every thing that existed in fact.↓

↑It would be easy to show the same spirit at work quite
near us all around us in even more vivid & impressive Energy.
in the most recent works & attempts; in what is just printed in
what is written & not printed in what is spoken & not written
in what is projected & not yet done. The popular doctrine with
the youth of this generation is Being not Seeming — is the
effort to cast off all that is foreign & false & to unfold the
intrinsic↓ /

2. The poetry

29   are ⟨indeed⟩ marked
30–31   from the ⟨p⟩ works

Page 214

1   ↑of Hardiknute↓ "how stately stepped ⟨Hardiknute⟩ ↑he↓
4   ↑and what am I?↓
10   Creator.) which
19   already, ⟨[partial "w"]⟩and what
25   parties to ⟨refer⟩ ↑stand↓
26   the ↑mind↓ [in pencil] Age is

Lines
31   ↑to prolong ⟨life⟩ or sweeten life↓ [in pencil]
32–33   else. ⟨w⟩Whatever subject is referred to them they ⟨weigh it⟩ behold

Page 215

9   But the ⟨question⟩ criterion is ↑the tendency;↓
11–12   us ↑alway↓ to themselves. The great even whilst he
31–32   coalmine. Nay they are far more Nature ↑but its↓ [insertion in pencil] ↑heart & soul↓ [insertion in ink]

Page 216

7   all the ⟨odes⟩ poems
9–13   *London.* ↑A↓ [in pencil; at bottom of page, marked "A":] ↑The water we wash with . . . universal good.↓
16–17   gossipping ⟨account of himself⟩ ↑confession↓ [emendations in pencil]
18–19   you drink?" [then follows passage marked "A" for insertion above] / [passage marked "R" for insertion below] /
          ⟨3. Akin to this subjective tendency is another to which I alluded in my last Lecture as having furnished a new element to the Poetry of the era the Feeling of the Infinite. {Insert R}⟩ [on previous page, marked "R":]
          ↑Of the great perception, — now fast becoming a conscious fact, — that there is One Mind, & that all the powers & privileges that lie in any lie in all; that I as a man may claim & appropriate whatever of true or fair or good or strong, has anywhere been exhibited; that Moses & Confucius Montaigne & Leibnitz are not so much individuals as they are parts of man & parts of me, and my intelligence of them proves them my own — literature is far the best expression↓ [insertion rejected in present text as copied for the combined lecture from Lecture 3 of "The Present Age"; see above, pp. 224–225]
          It is not
21–22   senses ⟨dictate⟩ ↑write↓

Page 217

5   exclamations. sentiments
6   themselves ⟨in⟩ on
12   impatience ⟨of⟩ by
17–18   wishes. ⟨This feeling of the Infinite has deeply coloured the Poetry of the period.⟩ The
24–26   period. /
          ⟨Akin to this subjective tendency is another to which I have alluded in my last lecture as a new element in Poetry of the era the Feeling of the Infinite.⟩ This new love of the vast

Lines

⟨which⟩ was native in Germany; ⟨which⟩ was imported into France by De Stael; ⟨which⟩ appeared . . . Hemans, and ⟨which⟩ finds

27–(218) 11   mind. ↑{Insert B}↓ [on previous page, marked "B":]
↑The fame of Wordsworth . . . itself {through . . . literature.} More [brackets in pencil] . . . wiser than any of its works.↓

Page 218

13   objective   The ⟨character⟩ ↑effect↓
19   establishes the ⟨genuineness⟩ ↑prevalence↓
22–23   Its ⟨is⟩ only unity is in ⟨its⟩ ↑the↓ subjectiveness & ⟨its yearning⟩. ↑aspiration common to the three writers.↓
25   composite. All [rest of line blank] A fine
27   he has ⟨never⟩ ↑not.↓
27–28   ↑Richter, Chateaubriand Manzoni &↓ Wordsworth ⟨&⟩ the
30   lines / arbitrary

Page 219

1   well; ⟨[?]⟩or, is
5–6   things. & so he describes ⟨one⟩ ↑each↓
9–10   Goethe. ⟨& hence his e[partial letter] wonderful influen⟩ce. ↑All that we . . . find in him.↓ He has
11–12   wealth. ⟨The⟩ ↑such was his capacity that the↓
16–17   ↑A thousand eyes looked through his.↓
18   breathe. ⟨And in him this Encyclopaedi⟩. Of all
20   effect   ⟨He had the air of one⟩ He
23   It did more
⟨The Age infected him with its subjectiveness also and that in both the senses I have discriminated.⟩ It ⟨gave him⟩ made
32   period because of his analysis always

Page 220

3–4   this. ⟨This h⟩He does not ⟨express in words⟩ ↑say so in syllables↓
9–10   medals, ⟨and⟩ persons, & manners, he ⟨was⟩ never
12   good, w⟨a⟩hat he
16   beheld to ⟨k⟩find
23   Venetian music⟨,⟩ of [comma erased]
29–30   Italy; /
But
31   time ⟨he⟩ infect⟨s⟩ed him

Page 221

1   There is ⟨an⟩ ↑a↓ good letter from Wieland ⟨written⟩ to
2   reading ↑of↓

Lines

3–4   duke & t⟨[?]⟩heir passage through Valois

9–10   concealed ⟨as⟩ ↑is↓ the art ⟨is⟩ also

27   syllable. ⟨But ⟨he is a pledge that the antique force of men is not spent & tis gay to think what men shall be.⟩ [written over this is:] ↑For e I t f s you canot gess the antiquity of the golden time of ⟨?⟩Haroun Alraschid in[?]↓⟩ But I

Page 222

15–16   our own. ⟨⟨He is a pledge that the antique force of men is not spent & tis gay to think what men shall be.⟩ [written over this is:] ↑I [?] sarcasm fell on sarcasm nor could the man present think↓⟩

                     It is

29–30   what the age quotes & [words set off by pencil marks]

Page 223

1   ↑often↓ [in pencil]

2–3   ↑Still Nature is never poor.↓ Of th⟨e⟩ose ⟨many instructors who have appeared⟩ ↑who already belong to the irreversible Past↓

6   eternal men. who

8–12   genius & as ⟨will doubtless appear⟩ ↑the ages have yet to show↓ [emendations in pencil] with the most unequal result. /

                 ↑⟨It is These are the⟩ With the memory . . . the third ⟨division⟩ consideration What the Age wishes to write.↓ [in pencil] / [This ends Lecture 2 as originally sewn. Emerson's page number is 70. The present sewing of the combined lecture manuscript continues with a transitional leaf, printed below, and then Emerson's pages 25–54 from Lecture 3 of "The Present Age," now printed in their original sequence, above, page 230, line 15, to page 237, line 21. Transitional leaf, paginated "71" on recto in pencil in another hand, now sewn with the combined lecture, but not sewn with the rest of the manuscript at an earlier time:]

III We have considered very hastily what the Age quotes & what it writes. But the ⟨habits of thought⟩ ↑advancing opinions↓ which in the present era predict the future require that we add to th⟨i⟩es↑e↓ sketches some remarks on ⟨what⟩ the new habit of thought, on the new view ⟨in⟩ under which Literature itself is regarded

The modern mind charges the literature of the past with a certain treason & profanation; with a want of respect to the pupil soul. [above, pp. 228–229] ⟨T⟩Man does not stand in awe of man, nor is the soul provoked & admonished to stay at home in God, to stand by itself & accept the whole of nature, the whole of history, the whole of thought, but it leaves its natural rest & goes ⟨gadding⟩ abroad a secondary & fugitive.

Lines

We are catechised & tutored & drilled; our admiration be-
spoken for what is not admirable, & our spontaneous senti-
ment⟨s⟩ superseded by this officious & superserviceable tuition,
⟨until we cannot call our soul our own⟩ until we are ceasing to
know that a man is / is an oracle & when lowly true an inlet
of Omniscience. In the light of this immense faith, the mind
of the age revises all reputations. We are to issue a Quo Warranto & revoke the charters of old fame. Always under the light
of a new thought, our old guides dwindle to the eye, & the
deeper ambition of the modern mind has already obscured
many names which glittered to the last generation. We are forgetting our Hume, & Locke, & Shaftesbury, & Butler, & Paley;
The English classics are a dwindling race & twenty of the
poets have gone silent for us. Lastly in the same faith, ["In the
light . . . same faith" (above, pp. 229–230)] /

3. LITERATURE [SECOND LECTURE]

Page 224

10–(225)1   exhibited, ↑that Moses . . . proves them my own↓ literature

Page 225

6   Oconnel
14–15   ↑Why should we be cowed . . . is a thought↓
16   ↑I regard↓ The
17   South American ↑states↓ establishments in
18–19   Christendom ⟨were⟩ ↑as↓ only sym⟨[?]⟩ptomatic of
23   Muller, & Heeren, From
24   upon the ⟨popular doctrine of Homer⟩ ↑authenticity of the
         Homeric poems↓ [emendations in pencil]
28   ↑not↓
29   attempted to ⟨verify or to discredit⟩ ↑sift↓ Roman history by
         the like ⟨sifting⟩ / Heeren
32–33   ↑How thoroughly English history . . . Turner tell.↓

Page 226

3   German ⟨French⟩ school
7   secondary. / [one leaf missing, according to ink pagination]
9   cultivation. ⟨so that⟩ [cancellation erased] good stock ⟨poetry⟩
         ↑verse↓
17   attempts; in what is ⟨writt⟩ just
21–22   foreign & ⟨sham⟩ ↑false↓ & to unfold the intrinsic. ⟨[partial
         letter]⟩ All
23–24   tender & ⟨docile⟩ obedient, if you see it from the side of ⟨the⟩
         spiritual

470

Lines	Page 227
1	life. the
7	So let us with ⟨inveterate⟩ ↑not less gigantic↓
14–15	↑containing no necessary reason for its being↓
17	those of ⟨[?]⟩Physics

Page 228

1	universal ⟨working⟩ ↑contributions↓ of nature ⟨on⟩ ↑to↓
7–9	↑Meantime under higher instruction the ⟨[?]⟩genius . . . facts cheap.↓
	⟨Meantime w⟩When it
12	analogies. Unity Poetry Music [punctuation supplied from cancelled passage below]
15–19	become of ⟨[?]⟩no account. ↑It ponders the relation . . . understandeth not↓ [in pencil]
25–26	here as ⟨here as⟩ there
31–32	intellect; ⟨the whole of love⟩ to
33	whole of reason. /

⟨But this statement is far from exhausting the fact. Literature not only carries out the imperfect revolutions of civil history but it goes a point farther. It betrays the nearer action of the cause. It is transcendental. It is not only true as in these examples just quoted to experience to the appearances of nature but it is true to the soul. to the most general & exalted nature of man.

It asks new questions   It ponders new problems. It explores the Necessary in History. It studies the philosophy of history & of life; the theory of society; of politics; of Education; it disdains the abutments of authority & custom. It ponders analogies: Unity: Poetry: Music. It finds poetry every where: & music in sight no less than in sound. Its passion is for the abstruse the central. It scorns the superficial & material.⟩ /

34–35	faith ⟨it⟩ ↑the modern mind↓
36	↑a certain↓

Page 229

6	old & ⟨fallen⟩ ↑soiled↓
8	deal ⟨with⟩ ↑in↓
9–11	↑They should say to him;↓ "Hearken & say Is not . . . thine? Rings it not truly / [one leaf missing, according to ink pagination]
14–15	issue a ⟨[?]⟩Quo Warranto
18–19	self command, the ⟨objectiveness or⟩ closeness to ⟨external nature⟩ ↑facts↓
21	great. ⟨And yet as we turn from a⟩ But
30–31	Mankind ⟨al⟩ are always right at last in their fames, and ⟨they⟩ ↑stars↓

Lines	*Page 230*
5	militia Alexander, ⟨Caesar⟩ ↑Charles V,↓
9–14	↑Always under the light . . . guides ⟨diminish⟩ dwindle . . . names which ⟨flourish shone⟩ glittered / ⟨[?]⟩to the last . . . race and ⟨the⟩ ↑twenty↓ English poets have gone silent for us.↓ [in pencil] /
15–(237)21	Lastly in the same faith Literature . . . become daily bread. [These pages, numbered 25–54 in ink, are now sewn with Lecture 2 of "The Present Age" to form the combined lecture on literature (see textual note for page 223, line 12, above).]
16	They ⟨h⟩can have
22–23	Literature ⟨seems to be⟩ ↑is made up of↓ . . . fables. ⟨[?] i⟩It is
32	↑Let us do our own duties↓

	Page 231
11–12	Life of ↑↑Jefferson↓ [in pencil] Luther or↓ Brant It is . . . pay to ⟨Brant⟩ ↑Jefferson↓ [emendations in pencil] or to General Sch↑u↓yler
17–22	best {St Augustine . . . my life!"} [brackets in pencil]
18	↑which↓
25–26	nature. ↑A↓ [in pencil; on previous page, in pencil, marked "A":] ↑The only difference . . . spiritual influence.↓
27	rewarded in ⟨the⟩ one

	Page 232
1	conventional ⟨stor⟩ legend
7	love & ⟨pride⟩ hope
21	living nature.} [bracket in pencil]
27–29	youth. / ⟨T⟩It may be well here to say a ⟨w⟩further word of explanation ⟨[?]⟩inasmuch this

	Page 233
2–3	eternal ⟨Zodiack⟩ ↑⟨Year⟩↓ ↑Circle↓
12–13	greatness of the ⟨time⟩ ↑Age↓
22–23	implies ⟨a⟩ ↑the presence of a↓
24	Mind which to which
35	class of d. shapes [cf. E, 15]
38	pomp real [cf. E, 15]

	Page 234
2	brag ⟨was⟩ ↑is↓
6–24	tomb. / [two leaves missing, according to ink pagination]

LITERATURE [SECOND LECTURE]

	{It seems the . . . mere literary men."} [brackets in pencil]
9	thinking to ⟨close⟩ intrude
10	infinitude. ⟨Liter⟩ We must ⟨keep⟩ come
14	itself frree from
19	Literature ⟨is⟩ ↑gives↓
21	because ⟨they⟩ ↑scholars↓
26–29	soul, — let me warn the⟨e⟩ O chosen youth to ⟨keep the door wide⟩ ↑hold himself dear and holy↓. to fear & hate ⟨the paltry bondage⟩ ↑whatever threatens . . . system of philosophy↓
30	Caucus of a ⟨fear⟩ ↑worship↓ of Fashion, and keep ever the door ⟨open⟩ ↑wide↓

Page 235

2	Truth. ⟨Believe always in the pos-⟩ It seems
10–29	{The primary question . . . or the act.} [brackets in pencil]

Page 236

2	man. a truth which I ⟨enumerate⟩ ↑note i⟨s⟩t↓ as
3	magnify. ⟨T⟩In this
7	only ⟨w⟩can read
20–(237)11	human soul. / [insert A, used below] / [continuation of insert] /

⟨This then [caret] ⟨seems to me the spirit which Literature meditates to say⟩ {looking, as I have promised to do, rather at creating tendency than at hardened fact.} This it is which seems to me to tune the tongue & fire the eye & sit in the silence of the young.⟩ ↑A↓ [two pages previous, marked "A":] ↑Do you imagine the power . . .
↑The world does not run smoother than of old
There are sad haps that must be told↓
. . . figures are / not what . . . ↑What then shall hinder
. . . if it would↓[in pencil]↓ [end insert A] It will write in a higher spirit and a ⟨more universal information⟩ ↑wider knowledge↓ [last emendations in pencil]

Page 237

19	↑self seekers↓ [in pencil]

[There is now filed with this lecture a partial leaf marked "B." It was formerly with Lecture 8 of "Human Life," where it belongs, and is printed as insertion B in that lecture, above, page 125, lines 3–7 ("The activity . . . become ludicrous."). There are also with this lecture the three leaves and double sheet which form the conclusion to Lecture 1 of "The Philosophy of History," where they are now printed (see *Lectures*, II, 374, textual note for page 17, lines 35 ff.).]

[The following is a leaf, never sewn, now filed with this lecture. It is a redaction of the early pages of Lecture 1 of "The Philosophy of History" (cf. *Lectures,* II, 7–11).]

It is remarkable that most men read little history. Even scholars & philosophers find it uninteresting; a fact which ↑naturally↓ suggests the suspicion that it is not rightly written. History is for the most part a vague account in geographical & chronological divisions of the predominance of certain families & tribes around the shores of the Mediterranean Sea of the founding of cities the peopling of a territory the wars & colonies of each tribe & its final defeats by another race. The unity of the story is secured by fastening ⟨[?]⟩the attention on the man or woman on the throne the incidents are little varied one period is like another. Nothing is recorded but what addresses itself to the eye. Number is the only preference; war the only association & battle the only crisis   Pharaoh Ptolemy Philip Caesar & Justinian are the proxies of the rational mind and a few ignorant & burly gentlemen monopolize to the foolish lists of their armies & gallies / every sympathy & remembrance which I can spare to the countless millions of rational men.

The modern mind feels the outrage of this pretension & demands that History should become humane & related to the reader. It makes the defects of actual history felt by comparing it with the ideal i. e. with the nature of man. Let me to this end solicit the attention of my audience to a consideration of man's nature under two points of view. Before offering them, however, let me say before all other considerations that I think it the main guard to a correct judgment not to accept degrading views. It is a primal instinct & duty of the human mind to look with a sovereign eye of hope on all things. If you look without awe or wonder into the attributes of the soul it is all idle to discourse of History. It can teach you nothing until you feel your interest in it your right over it. Let us not be an appanage to Caesar & Alexander to London or to Rome. Let us see the world that God made for us with eyes of love & resolution /

4. POLITICS

Lines	Page 239
1–2	these ⟨solemn places⟩ ↑august courts as of palaces↓
3	wit. ⟨To t⟩The
5–7	conclusion, ⟨it⟩ may sometimes ⟨stir no small⟩ wonder ⟨that⟩ ↑where↓ such massive volumes ⟨were writ by mere men like himself & have been read by mere men where s⟩found writers . . . readers. among
8	laugh & ⟨mus⟩ are
10	down to the ⟨lowest⟩ most
19	place on ⟨the man.⟩ him.
22–23	↑Let us hear . . . this point↓ [in pencil]

Lines

28   ↑however he may name the tactics↓

35–(240)1   ↑In every art . . . the apprentice↓

Page 240

8   ↑We must treat ye state . . . more need↓ [in pencil]

10   against the ⟨influence⟩ encroachment

13   ↑the fear of↓ it nothing. I⟨t⟩f sensually

16   forget the ⟨great⟩ fact

18   to ↑the citizen↓ men: that

26   fluid. there

30–34   Paul does forever.

Christ⟨ianity⟩	Xy
Aristotle	Scholastic logic
Linnaeus	Natural History
Justinian	Roman Law
Alfred	⟨J⟩Trial by Jury /

But let us not understand ↑this duty↓ of treating the sub-
ect of Politic↑s wisely↓ & with resolution as giving us ↑any↓
[insertions supply words torn away]

Page 241

6   ↑Commerce,↓

9–11   ↑But↓ the wise know that all foolish ⟨[torn away]on⟩ ↑legisla-
tion↓ however strong in numbers & ↑noxious↓ ⟨[torn away]us⟩
for the time in the people, is a rope [torn away] sand [inser-
tions supply words torn away]

13   goes ⟨by⟩ [erased] not [over erasure]

15   eternity. that

16–17   population ⟨that⟩ ↑which↓ permit↑s↓ it

19   has in the ⟨will⟩ ↑character↓

20–22   ↑It stands there to say↓ 'Yesterday we agreed so & so, — But
. . . today?' ⟨Is it not clear that o⟩Our statute is always
⟨merely⟩ an

27   ↑Meantime it is always ⟨advancing⟩ learning.↓

28   What you ⟨wish⟩ ↑dream↓

30–31   ↑as Grievance & Bill of Rights↓

32–34   ↑triumphant↓ law usage establishment ↑for a hundred years↓
until it gives place in turn ⟨to⟩ ↑before↓ new prayers & pictures /
⟨Let this then be distinctly considered that t⟩The history

36–(242)4   ↑The state & the aspiration:↓ & no matter how powerful th⟨e⟩is
⟨Empire⟩ ↑looks↓ & how faint ⟨& weak the⟩ that, ⟨that must
increase & this decrease⟩ the state always ⟨obeys treads on the
heels⟩ ↑follows close ⟨[erasure]⟩ on the track↓ . . . people /
[pages 11–22 missing]
Still ⟨loo[partial letter]⟩ [erased] considering [over
erasure]

Lines

Page 242

8   is the ⟨[?]f⟩ [erased] Influence [over erasure]

9   Individual. the

18   world he

21–22   men & all e⟨[?]⟩vents

23   us of some↑w↓⟨one⟩hat else

Page 243

5–6   Clarkson.

             ⟨Numbers go for nothing.⟩ [There follows passage marked "X}" for insertion below.] /

             ⟨Now t⟩That which

9–10   so that its ⟨divine power⟩ ↑natural↓ . . . appear — That

10–11   reach ↑unto↓ at this coronation of ⟨the sovereign of the state⟩ ↑her king↓

12   expires. {Every step

13–21   steps towards it. ↑{Insert X}↓ [on previous page, marked "X}":] ↑⟨a⟩A single new thought . . . describe their fortunes.}↓ /

24   Louis XIV, if ⟨[?]⟩he ⟨spoke in⟩ knew

27   to him. {⟨He is supremely fair⟩}   He

29–30   circumstance   {⟨Obedient nature bends around him & all stars lend their ray to the hour & the man. The field the trees speak extempore to him & light up a sudden festival whithersoever he bends his steps⟩}   He needs no library, for he has / not done thinking; ↑he g⟨o⟩ets ⟨his⟩ thought where the bookmaker got it,↓ no

Page 244

4   myrrh ⟨his⟩to them

5–10   flowers.} [pencil bracket; single pencil use mark continues to bottom of this page and through the next page]

       The power of character is the simplest of all known powers ⟨men are [?] the⟩ We are used to avail ourselves / [The following leaf is a different paper, has been sewn with the 1843 lecture but not with the other leaves, and contains journal passages later than the 1840 version. Though the leaf has been rejected in the present text, it supplies the remainder of the sentence begun on the previous leaf.] ↑of such a⟨n⟩ cumbrous apparatus of means that we do not believe i⟨m⟩n immediate action on others; we do not believe in a power that works without means.↓

       What means did you employ? was the question asked on a celebrated occasion; and the answer was, "Only that influence which every strong mind has over a weak one." You believe in magnetism, in new & preternatural powers, powers contrary to the experience of a thousand years, & do you not think

that Caesar in irons can shuffle off the irons & transfer them
to the person of Hippo or Thraso the turnkey. Is an iron hand-
cuff so ⟨im⟩unmanageable & immutable a fact? ["Only that influence . . . immutable a fact" (G, 142)] Suppose that a
Guinea slaver should take on bo⟨rd⟩ard a gang of negroes who
should all be such persons as Toussaint L'Ouverture has been
described to be: or let us fancy that under these swarthy masks
/ he has a company of George Washingtons in chains. When
they arrive at Cuba, will the relative order of the ship's company be the same? Is there nothing but rope & iron in the
world. Is there no such element as love none such a Reverence
Is there never a force in a poor slave captain's mind that is
called Conscience & can none of these be supposed available
to break or elude or in any manner overmatch the tension of an
inch or two of iron ring? ["What means did . . . iron ring"
("Character," W, III, 94–95); "Is there no such . . . iron
ring" (G. 142–143)] / [Of the 1840 manuscript pages 31–40
are missing; pages 41–42 are torn vertically in half, and only
the following can be recovered:] In the actual st . . . certainly a great . . . Trade is a grea . . . as a means of . . .
man   The Pop . . . ments on th . . . and the ↑civil↓ fr . . .
or New York . . . enviable . . . ↑the subject of↓ position of
. . . with ⟨the⟩ . . . ⟨great⟩ ↑natur↓ . . . ⟨our politics⟩ . . .
The Spirit . . . low & degr . . . not quite . . . Man exis
. . . add a la . . . The Spirit . . . most p[?] . . . the sacred . . . man to th . . . as dru . . / . . . l questions even
. . . Temperance on . . . a proven rogue . . . ⟨party⟩ test
question, . . . nate able . . . ing to be a . . . a sectarian
. . . an abolitionist . . . are a sort . . . le.} [pencil bracket]
they . . . real in⟨a⟩en . . . mere forms . . . integrity . . .
weight . . . the authority . . . govern- . . . eat men /
          It is plain
16   fastens ↑on↓
22   exclusion of character. ↑Insert L↓ [missing]
30   in bar-rooms . . . of bar rooms, ⟨t⟩The

Page 245

2–4   widest from hi⟨s⟩mself. /
          ⟨⟨If⟩ we have seen ⟨that⟩⟩ under our wooden or brick houses
          ↑lies↓ the living magical earth, ⟨lay⟩ yet ⟨lay⟩ ↑lies↓ not still a
          moment but whirl⟨s⟩⟨ed⟩s forever
6   ↑In like manner↓
13   be blow⟨m⟩n in⟨to⟩ the [erasures]
23   absent. that
24–26   ↑It needs no . . . participating its wrong deed.↓ . . . on us.
          let

Lines

27   instructions   Let us ⟨renew abhor⟩ ↑⟨refuse⟩ abjure↓ the
30–31   {The prompt . . . knife.} [brackets in pencil]

Page 246

4–5   ↑Trust men . . . do what you will.↓
6   back ⟨kindness⟩ ↑the same?↓
7   that at the Imperial
12   Rhine. Others &c.
13–14   he said I . . . ↑and noway to be compared to you↓
16   ↑although↓
19   goods & bloods. And
22–(247)15 jewel." / [Pages 49–54 are missing. Page 55 ("Of course it
            . . . for myself. When") is marked "A"; overleaf ("moved by
            love . . . or to multitudes") is marked "B" and has two pen-
            cil lines drawn through it. The leaf, probably once an insertion
            laid into the manuscript, has never been sewn and is not
            labelled "Politics" as are the other leaves belonging with the
            1840 manuscript. It is printed here on the basis of its pagina-
            tion; there is no certainty that it is the conclusion to the lec-
            ture.]
26   evil. they
29   he has ⟨surrende⟩ delegated
31–32   ↑The very idea of Government in the world is Interference.↓

Page 247

2   another. [a mark which may indicate an insertion] Absolutely
3–5   When / moved by love ⟨I⟩ ↑a man↓ teach↑es↓ ⟨my⟩ ↑this↓ child
            or join with ⟨my⟩his . . . ↑or spends himself for his friend,↓
            or do↑es↓ at
6–7   like the f⟨ea⟩ight of Leonidas or the ⟨crucifixion⟩ hemlock
10   contemplated by the ⟨man⟩ ↑doer↓
11   them & ⟨for them⟩ ↑even strive to put cant in their mouths↓
15   done to ⟨few or to many⟩. individuals

[The following are the recoverable fragments from a double sheet and a
single leaf once sewn with the 1843 lecture only. They have been torn
vertically and only the formerly sewn edges remain. See "Politics," *Lectures*,
II, 70–72, 77, and "Politics," *W*, III, 201–203, 206.]

It is very e . . . Politics which has . . . of men and wh . . . pressed
⟨more or⟩ ↑the best th↓ . . . laws & in th . . . ⟨I should say⟩ it . . . the
two objects . . . Government ex . . . property; 1. that, of . . . ⟨[?]⟩ equal
rights . . . are innocent; . . . of being all ident . . . of ⟨being all⟩ ↑exist-
ing as↓ ra . . . of course with . . . demands a . . .
        2. Whi . . . rights of all . . . virtue of the . . . their rights . . . One
man . . . owns a c . . . pending . . . virtue of . . . is every . . . pat-
rimony . . . of course . . . rights . . . / . . . a democratic . . . ty does

not . . . nment framed on . . . census, but on the . . . & ↑of↓ owning.
Laban . . . & wishes them looked . . . on the frontiers, . . . shall drive
them . . . to that end. Jacob . . . no herds, & no . . . ianites, & pays
. . . ficier. It seemed . . . Jacob should . . . t to elect the . . . of their
per . . . n, & not . . . officer who . . . s & herds. . . . ether additional
. . . should be . . . Isaac, & . . . their herds / to buy protection . . .
better of this & . . . Jacob, who, bec . . . and a traveller . . . & not his
own.

It will be . . . earliest society, . . . wealth, have a . . . product of
their . . . a man found . . . the woods: (w . . . sauntered in [?] . . .
spring, & water . . . he has a . . . Another wh . . . for walking . . .
whole, m . . . Another . . . mats; . . . had w . . . / . . . me out of
frolic . . . would not make . . . but hindered . . . ⟨[?]ere⟩ ↑In this use
of nature↓ was the . . . , and so long as . . . the owners in this . . . other
opinion . . . y equitabl . . . property should . . . property, & . . . persons. . . . s by donation . . . ose who . . . Gift in the . . . as really
. . . labor made . . . much / [end fragmentary double sheet; lower left
recto of fragmentary single leaf:] I . . . say . . . but . . . have . . . law
of . . . year . . . that . . . proprie . . . the prop . . . wish to . . . of
prope . . . the law, . . . / [verso of fragment blank] /

[A double sheet of different paper, numbered "59," and never sewn with this
lecture:]

But I must draw to a close these few sketches of a power which is now
in its infancy, but of which it is to be hoped the coming ages will write the
history. If the dream of good men be true that there is progress in the intellect of men, not only as individuals, but as societies, & as a race, then the
Religion of the next centuries will be this pure white holy influence. For
character is the true Theocracy. It will one day suffice for the government
of the world ["For character . . . the world" ("Religion," above, p. 276)]
when each aims at no connexions or conversation or offices or property which
he has not served up to, offers at nothing in which his faculties will not
play him true, attempts nothing he cannot as easily do as forbear & reaches /
forth at nothing which does not gravitate to him. ↑Insert S↓ [on next page,
marked "S":]

↑Before the greatness in the private mind, the ensigns of ancient command the coin, the census, the geographical extent lose their importance.
⟨He makes them appear shortlived makeshifts.⟩ And what⟨so⟩ever may be
the date in these short years of our epoch of our political fabrics, the true &
faithful soul is always leaving them behind him, as the go carts & hobbies
of his early youth.↓

Herein is the consolation of life the private man's heart is the sanctuary
& citadel of freedom & goodness   Society is as men of the world have always
found it tumultuous insecure unprincipled. Society is cajoled & cowed &
betrayed   They who in any country wish to make a private advantage of its
credulity have only to blind the public with a new lie for each emergency as
we put a headboard on an ox to hinder the animal from breaking fence.
Society must come again under the yoke of the base & selfish, but / the indi-

vidual heart, faithful to itself is fenced with a sacred palisado, not to be traversed or approached unto & is free forevermore. [insert S, used above] / [blank] /

5. PRIVATE LIFE

Lines	*Page 248*
1–(249)18	It is a fact . . . silly & foolish [This leaf, paginated "9" and "10," has once been sewn but not with the extant cover.]
2–3	us the ⟨stern⟩ ↑austere↓ joy of the sublime, like ↑the spectacle of↓

Page 249

1	pleased to be ⟨charged⟩ accused
4	man ⟨forgives⟩ ↑likes↓
8	reason ⟨of⟩ ↑that we admit↓ this one exception, ⟨[?]⟩ [erased] but [over erasure]
13–18	{The spontaneous sentiment . . . silly & foolish.} /
19–(253)9	This immense preponderance . . . Eternal Life [This sequence of leaves consists of three double sheets and one enclosed leaf. There is no pagination. Except for the enclosed leaf, which is an insert, they have been sewn together but not with the cover or with other leaves in this folder.]
19–28	⟨⟨To t⟩This immense preponderance . . . ↑in conversation↓ Any fool can do ⟨so⟩ that; but . . . always teaches a ⟨noble⟩ lesson . . . forgetfulness ⟨that⟩ of . . . sublime admonition⟩ [Because there is no context, this paragraph has been retained in the text although it has a diagonal ink line drawn through it.] / [inserted passage marked "S" for insertion below]
	I say to the ⟨young⟩ noble
28–29	world is ⟨new at⟩ ↑like a ⟨creation⟩ ↑birth↓ of↓
30	glance ⟨I⟩ ↑you↓ . . . bring ⟨me⟩ ↑you↓
33	to ↑go near↓ look steadily at the

Page 250

1–9	creation↑s↓ of the Soul. ↑⟨Let me show him for example the Soul's victory over Time⟩↓ ↑Insert ⟨S⟩↓ [at top of page, marked "S":] ↑{Let me show to the student what energies act & react ⟨fo⟩on his education nay how the ages of Time the spaces of Nature & all the resources of Being play into his private tutelage.}↓ ↑R↓ [a loose sheet, never sewn, marked "R":] ↑I would show to the student . . . vast prep⟨re⟩arations made . . . infinite has ⟨been⟩ spared . . . soul. That . . . private tutelage.↓
15–17	↑Nothing dies. . . . troubadours But↓ The Provencal

Lines

25	tombs & ⟨palaces⟩ ↑temples↓
27–28	furniture of ⟨a⟩ rich m⟨a⟩en's house↑s↓
28	was ↑ever↓
31–33	{A bell or the march of a band ⟨is heard mil⟩ in . . . cart-wheels.} ↑In like manner,↓
35	these ⟨sail⟩ ↑float↓
36	unbroken ⟨unfaded⟩ ↑⟨untarnished⟩↓ to us.

Page 251

4	wonderful ↑spiritual↓ [in pencil]
17	Church One
21–23	represent. / ⟨Indeed⟩ What
24	in the past ⟨of⟩ that
28–29	mans . . . I am an an aggregate
30	man ↑which↓
38	origin. ⟨i⟩Is his ⟨natu⟩ ↑nurture↓

Page 252

11	but the ⟨tame⟩ ↑soft↓
12	↑illustrative↓
14	how you will — ⟨forever⟩ balances
16–17	seed you will — ⟨in secret in public⟩ — the sure hours will bring you ⟨at last⟩ the ⟨precise⟩ harvest of that seed. We ⟨all⟩ are ⟨the⟩ planters
18	experiment ⟨once & again &⟩ every
19	dust, — We dont
19–20	again; ↑in frolic↓
20–21	watch the ⟨pretty⟩ ↑alluring↓ cloud⟨s⟩ as
22	rooted & ⟨ri⟩grown &
23	infamy & ⟨[?]⟩curses
27	angels & ⟨gods⟩ ↑friends↓
33–34	Justice ⟨a⟩the best measure of his culture: because, in the ⟨measure⟩ ↑degree↓
36–(253)1	appearance / ⟨&⟩itself enlarges; its dams & jealous floodgates ⟨op⟩ disappear

Page 253

5–9	mind. ⟨In them let him aspire . . . draw ⟨[?]⟩fuller inspirations of the common soul continually. then he . . . Eternal Life.⟩ [Because there is no context, this passage has been retained in the text although it has a single ink line drawn through it.] /
10–15	The ornament . . . select company [supplied from "Domestic Life," W, VII, 128]
15–(255)12	when it pleases him." . . . by others' eyes. [This grouping of leaves consists of one single leaf and one double sheet pagi-

Lines

nated in ink on rectos "47," "55," "57" and marked in pencil "PL." They have been sewn together and with the extant cover but not with other leaves now in this folder.]

23–28 ↑But this topic . . . its importance↓ ⟨Friendship is indeed the asylum in which we find honorable shelter from the injuries of time & fate. "What is given to a friend" said Scaliger, "is redeemed out of the power of Fortune." And I will add, that, fine, subtle,⟩ [Because there is no context, and for minimal sense, this passage has been retained in the text although it has a single ink line drawn through it.] / & dainty as is that web

Page 254

6 husk & shell. / [pages 49–54 missing]
8 flower by ↑y↓our impatience
11–12 ↑Crimen quos inquinat aequat.↓
20 Others

Page 255

1–10 ↑What has been said of Glory is true of Friendship. [asterisk at this point indicates further insertion from bottom of page:] ↑If thou love G⟨[?]⟩lory, . . . turn & ⟨[?]⟩look ⟨[?]⟩after her.↓↓ ⟨Follow not love but be great & love shall follow thee⟩. ↑{Insert A}↓ [on same page, marked "A":] ↑By persisting in your path . . . shadows merely. ↑Nothing is, &c.↓↓ Nothing is more

[A double sheet, never sewn, paper like that used in "The Times," numbered "2" and "4" in pencil at top center of rectos:]

to this exhibition of our faculty, but sincerity counts all the time lost or all but a little. There are other angels of a grander race Humility Patience Abstinence Mortification which can teach us pleasures of a higher strain. Most of life seems to be mere advertisement of faculty: information is given us not to sell ourselves cheap; that we are very great. ["Experience," W, III, 73; see above, p. 379] The hours of common life are very easily described & understood; the others have an experience which is incommunicable   Its ↑quality↓ can only be suggested to those who have known the like themselves. These two Experience & Idea divide between them unequally the life of man   Experience & Idea the wonderful twins the Castor & Pollux of our firmament which never ⟨c⟩appear at one time. One rises & the other instantaneously sets. Today & / for a hundred days experience has been in the ascendant   Idea has lurked about the life merely to enhance sensation the firework maker master of the revels & laureate poet of the powers that be; but in an instant a revolution; the dream displaces the workingday & working world, & they are now the dream & this the reality. All the old landmarks are swept away in a flood the laws & manners method & aim of society are as fugitive as the colors which chase each other when we close the eye

When I was in college one of my companions said to me one day that he had thoughts of becoming religious next week — but perhaps he should join the Porcellians. It was gaily said & yet is no joke but a grave question still for every man. I have often thought the same thing /

Which of these to choose is the question which every one must decide. There is a continual sacrifice of either to the other. One goes to make the artist, the other to make the man. The man of Talent is the victim of talent The ⟨artist⟩ man is sacrificed to the artist. Michel Angelo to paint Sistine frescoes must lose the power to read without holding the book over his head: [cf. "Michael Angelo," W, XII, 228; Lectures, I, 107] & Dr Herschel to keep his eyes for nocturnal observation must keep them covered all day: and these are but illustrations of deeper sacrifices made by men ⟨who⟩ to do some feat ⟨s⟩ of art or eclat before the world. / [blank] /

[A single leaf, same paper as above, never sewn, numbered at top of recto "2" in pencil and "61" in ink:]

An individual soul well constituted stands united with the Just & the True as the magnet arranges itself with the Pole so that he appears to all beholders to stand like a transparent object betwixt them & the sun, & whoso journeys towards the sun journeys towards that person. [cf. E, 37] He is thus the medium of the highest influence to all who are not on the same level. / [inverted at bottom of page:] ⟨In sketching the aspirations of the Transcendentalist we simply describe man as he ought to be man in his tendency & not in the fact⟩ /

[A single leaf, same paper as above, never sewn, numbered at top of recto "3" in pencil and "63" in ink:]

↑The↓ ⟨a⟩ great ⟨man⟩ ↑of character↓ [emendations in pencil; the last insert may be heading at top of page] conquers not because he hits on some new expedient but because his arrival alters the face of affairs   It is the presence of a new element. O Iole how did you know that Hercules was a god   Because, answered Iole I was content the moment my eyes fell on him. ⟨When I saw Theseus I desired that I might see him fight a battle or at least guide his horses in the chariot   But⟩ Hercules did not wait for a contest or for the aid of fortune: he conquered whether he stood or sat or whatsoever thing he did. ["The great . . . thing he did" ("Character," W, III, 90, modified); "O Iole . . . thing he did" (E, 117); cf. Sophocles, Trachiniae.] The confines of divine things are reverend   It is the property of suns to shine, no more can the nature of virtue be concealed / [blank] /

6. REFORMS

Lines	Page 256
1	⟨M[?]⟩Nothing has
5–6	↑They have moreover a high historical value from the fact that↓
	In a coarse

Lines	
	Page 257
3	which ⟨the slaveholder &⟩ the slavetrader defend↑s↓ every inch of their bloody
5	↑dull↓
6	↑argument &↓
8–10	circles, {which divides . . . red,} which is tacitly recalled ⟨in⟩at every
13–14	Trade. ⟨ — Is that of no use & of no result beyond the squabble on the law?⟩ ↑is a gymnastic . . . the time.↓
19–20	Wars; ⟨of⟩ the
22	value of of our
23–30	the Period. /
	⟨Nothing has ⟨nor⟩more remarkably distinguished the Present Age than the great harvest of projects it has yielded for the reform of domestic social civil ecclesiastical & literary institutions.⟩ ↑{Insert A}↓ [third page previous, marked "A":]
	↑The Age cannot be described ⟨certainly⟩ without taking . . . facts so creditable, ⟨as these⟩ & which, beyond . . . purer results.↓
33	epoch ⟨have⟩ ↑ask↓
35–⟨258⟩1	abuse. ⟨Our⟩ The ⟨foundation⟩ ↑cause↓

	Page 258
10–11	wishfully we ⟨embrace⟩ ↑entertain↓
11–13	↑a history of wars . . . to the history &↓ ⟨th⟩Sinbad the Sailor to Robinson Crusoe. ⟨& Robinson even to the best history of wars & battles⟩. When
15	opens in ⟨another⟩ ↑opposite↓ direction
17	stand⟨s⟩ ever the object↑s↓

	Page 259
4	another workm⟨[?]⟩an
7	other mens
8–9	↑Out of this fair Idea . . . the Perfect↓
12–24	↑the offer of↓ some new amendment. ↑{Insert S}↓ [The insert, which is missing, presumably replaced the cancelled passage which follows. Restoration of the passage is necessary for what follows, and further emendation, supplied from the printed version, has been necessary.]
	⟨But whilst they have this high origin . . . image to man than the ⟨evil⟩ ↑tradition↓ which they reprobated. They mix ⟨& debase⟩ the fire of the moral sentiment with ⟨the sulphurous flames of⟩ personal & party heats, with measureless exaggeration↑s↓, & the blindness . . . justice & truth.⟩ /
	{But let us . . . our repose.}
25	all ⟨colors⟩ ↑stripes↓
33	convicts him not that

Page 260

Lines	
7–12	these ⟨poor⟩ faithful men of one idea. ↑Indeed if we can . . . forms ⟨not one re⟩ this youthful hope in its aged heart ⟨not one rev[?]⟩ that . . . now on foot↓ /
15–16	↑The one doctrine we ⟨[?]⟩ [erased] urge [over erasure] under many forms is the sacred↓
18	inviolable one whom ⟨multitudes⟩ leaders
21	willing ↑mind↓
22	drawn. let
27–30	prevailed over it. ⟨It will be seen ⟨that⟩ I hope that under whatever form we urge in this place still but one doctrine the universal rights of the Individual I cannot find language of sufficient energy to express my sense of the sacredness of private integrity All men all things the state the church ye⟨s⟩a the friends of the heart are phantasms & unreal beside the simple man.⟩ / ↑I have said that . . . fair Ideal life.↓ This departure from nature is ⟨true⟩ ↑felt.↓ of
34	the Diet

Page 261

7	↑in caves & houses &↓
10	↑If you have↓ Eat your
12–15	if ↑a child↓ you have eat the poorest rye or oatcake with ⟨[?] beautiful maiden⟩ ↑children↓ in the wilderness y did not . . . with your food give it a certain mundane savor & comeliness.
18	have ⟨a⟩polluted
20	science and ⟨en⟩an end
24	laborers prepare⟨s⟩.
28	leave me ⟨more⟩ a
33	but ⟨they are⟩ the

Page 263

4	life ⟨which is now the dream of the poets⟩ which
7–(265)26	poets ↑{back D}↓ [second page back, marked "D":] ↑it becomes at once a↑n↓ object . . . refined spirit.↓ / [This is the end of Emerson's page 22. Duplicate page numbers, both sets of pages once sewn with the manuscript, now follow to page 33: "Religion does not . . . will obtain justice," the sequence printed in the text, is numbered "25"–"32" and leaves a lacuna of one leaf. The following pages, numbered "23"–"32," contain a journal passage probably dated April 1840 and may have been used in the Concord reading:]

Another great institution involving many abuses is undoubtedly our institution of Property, and the ⟨[?]⟩system of money ↑by↓ which it stands & moves. ↑We all know the arguments on which the existing system stands let us hear what may be urged in behalf of a change.↓ The child appropriates everything it sees so long as its need is, & then relinquishes the same things to all others. The man would readily do like-wise but the world with all its bread & stuffs is bought & sold & the ⟨m[?]⟩new man let him be as great hearted as laborious and as munificent as he ⟨[?]⟩may, cannot get his own bread, much less scatter bread to others without stooping himself to this petty system of monopoly force distrust & barter in which the fears & avarice of little men have locked up the gifts of nature & the energies of men. /

The system of money ⟨evidently⟩ is a system of pledges. You will not take my word that I have labored honestly today, have added to the amount of value & happiness in the world & so am entitled to what service you can render me as I most willingly would render to you whatever you need from my peculiar ability. You will not take my word for this fact but demand a certificate of so much labor in the shape of a piece of silver or paper. By this exchange we are both degraded — we have exchanged the broad brow of honor for the wrinkles of suspicion & the insinuation of a threat. The coin owes its value to a law which again stands on force. Our relations are altered & we meet without joy. Then the certificates of labor become / themselves a subject of ⟨a⟩trade whereof the pri-mary labor for which they stand was not susceptible. and the labor of many comes to be commanded by the undeserv-ing. ↑For they can deal well with these cards who could not work. There are other bad results of our currency.↓ The de-mand for your aid which I made before the introduction of coin was founded on my sense of desert & my faith in your virtue   But the demand I make by means of this piece of silver implies neither my desert nor yours; I learn to use it ill: to buy with it things I should never have had the front to ask, & which you would never have had the weakness to yield me.

It is remarkable that sore as society always is on this topic, [comma in pencil] confident as it is that the present system is equitable & perfect, [comma in pencil] it yet betrays on a few occasions a slight sense / of shame in relation to it ↑and these precisely the highest occasions.↓ for instance in all coun-tries in regard to the maintenance of the priesthood the priest being unwilling to receive & the people unwilling that he should receive an acknowledgment of sacred services in money If the money were still sacred if it represented character it would be fit to give & receive. The same hesitation is found to qualify this exchange for all literary labor and all works of art. It is submitted to, but it is submitted to as an abuse. Then ⟨betwee in⟩ ↑between the members of↓ a family; be-tween friends; & with the advance of the character in all its

Lines

intercourse; this trade is virtually abrogated, and a man's expenditure becomes plastic to such high laws that he uses money as though he used it not, and insensibly the law of Love prevails in his Economy. / [end of double sheet paginated "23"–"26"]

Here again one ⟨[?]⟩feels that however we may be misled ⟨by⟩ a moment by the fact that this topic has been presented by political parties with a malignant purpose, it is a doctrine of the highest nobleness & is as I have said virtually carried into practice by every magnanimous person in his own use of property. / [blank] / [end single leaf paginated "27"–"28"]

↑Another heresy [last word written over pencilled "W"] of like parentage & tendency with these is↓ {I think the ⟨[?]⟩doctrine of selfreliance ought to regulate the pursuits & business of men. I think it strongly preaches} the doctrine that every man ought to share in the manual labor of the world. I think it is the neglect of this which is punished ⟨with⟩ ↑in↓ the puny bodies of literary & contemplative men. Most of the great men of today if you put them in a potato field, or in a ship, or in a mob, would be contemptible; they would act like women. If a bankruptcy befals the commercial class or the dealers in paper money, they turn pale at their desks with terror lest they should not have bread to eat. ["Most of the great . . . to eat" (cf. D, 119)] If they do not fear it yet the least disturbance of the social order the failure of some ⟨booksellers ⟨or⟩ [cancellation in ink] firm⟩, [cancellation in pencil] ↑bank↓ [insertion in pencil] or of some college to pay their quarter's salary puts their family at once into beggary. And the lord of this world as the / poet is, is now surrounded with the ⟨ve⟩ chagrins & temptations of a city poverty. Nature ⟨teaches this⟩ ↑inculcates the doctrine of manual labor↓ by the rapid impoverishing which brings every man continually to the presence of the fact that bread is by the sweat of the face & ⟨why⟩ by this ⟨bod⟩ [erased] continual [over erasure] necessity in which we all stand of bodily labor by walking riding fencing pitching shooting or ⟨billiards⟩ ↑bowling↓ if not by ploughing ⟨or⟩& mowing. And by this indigenous sentiment of independence which cannot receive a pecuniary benefit, ↑except in the greatest natures↓ until the man has suffered a fatal slackness on his springs. I suppose his needs of labor are such to the health of his organization, his life, & his thought that these hints are so broad. Labor makes solitude & makes society It kills fo⟨lly⟩ppery, shattered nerves & all kinds of emptiness. It makes life solid. It puts Pericles & Jack on a firm ground of sweet & manly fellowship ["Nature inculcates . . . fellowship" (D, 304)] /

Why should not the philosopher realize in his daily labor his high doctrine of self trust Let him till the fruitful earth under the glad sun & write his thought on the face of the ground with hoe & spade. Let him put himself face to face with the facts of dire need & know how to triumph by his own warlike hands & head over the grim spectres ⟨of⟩ that haunt the great. Let him thus become the fellow of the poor & shew them by experiment that poverty need not be. Let him show that Labor ⟨& [?]⟩need not enslave a man more than Luxury; that Labor may dwell with thought; & that a man may cultivate his garden in the same spirit with which he woos a maiden or writes a poem. This is the heroic life possible in th⟨ese⟩is age of London⟨s⟩, Paris, & New York. It is not easy; if it were, it would not be heroic. But who can solve this problem for himself, has / solved the problem not of a clique or corporation ⟨of⟩but of entire humanity. He has shown every young man ⟨on [?]⟩for a thousand years to come, how life may be led independently gracefully justly.

I see with great pleasure the growing inclination in all persons who aim to speak the truth for manual labor & the farm. It is not that commerce law & state employments are intrinsically unfit for a man or less genial to his faculties, but that these are now in their general course so vitiated by derelictions & abuses at which all connive that it requires more vigor & resources than can be expected of every young man to right himself in them, he is lost in them he cannot move hand or foot in them. The more genius & virtue he has the less does he find them fit for him to grow in; and if he would thrive in them he must sacrifice all the brilliant dreams of his boyhood & youth as dreams & take on him the harness of routine & obsequiousness. If not so minded nothing is left him but to begin the world anew as he does who puts the spade into the ground for food. ["I see . . . for food" (E, 123, expanded)] ↑Insert L↓ [missing] / [end double sheet paginated "29"–"32"]

14–15   {Write your poem . . . own spade}. [brackets in pencil]

Page 264

12   exterminated. ⟨Morning calls would be no more⟩ and
14   subject ⟨of⟩ ↑Anti↓ Slavery is
17   no slave. / [end double sheet paginated "25"– [28]]
33–34   disheartened & in ⟨complaining⟩ bemoaning himself the r⟨[?]⟩emainder of

Page 265

3   city ⟨dolls⟩ ↑minions↓.
19–20   equality ⟨and⟩ of
26   he will ⟨strive⟩ find . . . justice. / [end double sheet paginated "29"–"32"; end duplicate page numbers]
27   it ⟨[?]⟩appears

Page 266

Lines	
13–24	↑Whilst therefore I desire . . . earnestly the ⟨high duties⟩ paramount duties of the ⟨single man⟩ Individual I cannot find language of sufficient ⟨force⟩ [erased] energy [over erasure] to to convey . . . be respected. /
	We must learn to respect ⟨its⟩ inaction more than prodigious activity without↓
33–34	says Thus hast . . . better thus."

Page 267

19	The fact tha I am
34	or quaker coat, or ⟨Calvinistic Prayermeeting⟩ or Abolition

Page 268

15	you are ⟨fairly⟩ driven [cancellation in pencil]
16	at last ⟨fairly⟩ turn fairly
18–(269)1	friend ↑Insert Y↓ / [inserted leaf, marked "Y":] ↑The wise man . . . despond. ⟨I⟩ ↑He↓ will not . . . threatened ⟨Let us understand ourselves distinctly. We do not think much of those⟩ Life . . . modes ⟨And if you⟩ He will play . . . to prick / him . . . things practical↓ /
	People hold

Page 269

3	structure ↑or↓
7	skip ⟨like rams & the little hills like lambs before⟩ ↑& disappear before↓
14	trifles should ⟨be trifles⟩ at
17	force of ⟨w⟩their denial
26–27	There ⟨are⟩ ↑is a↓ new possibilities in
30	incompatible. ⟨All experience⟩ then ⟨is good for nothing⟩ against
31	effect / some⟨thing all⟩ ↑what↓ the
33–34	shall ⟨appear⟩ ↑shine↓ to them. Let ⟨us with⟩ ↑every aspiring mind↓
35	consent of ⟨[?]⟩ [erased] thousands [over erasure]

Page 270

2	separate ⟨with⟩ in
3	exalt to ⟨the⟩ an infinite
4–5	thou ⟨absorb⟩ ↑expand↓ into the treasures of the character. [inverted at bottom of page:]
	⟨Indeed in the last analysis Friendship is only the reflection of the Soul in the forms of other men.⟩ /

[Two larger leaves numbered "37"–[40] which have been sewn together but not with this lecture:]

Great causes are never tried assaulted or defended on their merits. they need so long perspective & the habits of the race are marked with so strong a tendency to detach & exaggerate particulars. The stake is Europe & Asia; & the battle is for some contemptible village or doghutch. A man shares the new light that is breaking on the world & promises the establishment of the kingdom of heaven, & ends with champing unleavened bread, or ⟨devoting⟩ ↑dedicating↓ himself to the nourishment of a beard, ⟨or making a fool of himself about his hat or his shoes.⟩ A man is furnished with this superb case of instruments the senses & perceptive & executive faculties, & they betray him / every day: he transfers his allegiance from God to this adroit little committee. A man is an exaggerator. In every conversation, see how the main end is still lost sight of by all but the best, & with slight apology or none, a digression made to every creaking door or buzzing fly. What heavenly eloquence could hold the ear of an audience if a child cried? A man with a truth to communicate is caught by the beauty of his own words & end[s] by being a rhymester or a critic, & genius is sacrificed to talent every day. /

So has it been with every combat for human right — since the beginning of the world, that the best cause is not at first defended on its merits, but the contention is ever hottest on some minor & perhaps insignificant particulars. [Cf. "Nature," W, III, 187; "Tantalus," *Uncollected Writings*, p. 117; H, 88.] And this from necessity. For the majority of men holding fast not to truths not to things but to usages, are keenly sensible when usages are invaded. They who have no care for religion or philosophy can see the least deviation from custom in manners or dress & resent an omission of courtesy more than atheism   The Quakers, abused & tormented on the ground of plainness of speech & apparel, in defending themselves came naturally to exaggerate ⟨their⟩ ↑its↓ importance. It became the badge of their tribe, & was preserv[ed] / with great exactness when the spiritual distinctions of the sect were lost by diffusion in the surrounding society or through formalism in the Friends themselves.

A [The ink letter may indicate that the following paragraph, which is written in pencil, was used as an insertion on a subsequent page.]

↑The good self complacent Luther declares with an emphasis not to be mistaken that "God himself cannot do without wise men." Jacob Behmen & George Fox betray their selfesteem in the pertinacity of their controversial tracts & James Naylor suffered himself to be worshipped as Christ, though he recovered his reason before his death.↓ ["The good self complacent . . . death" ("Nature," W, III, 187–188; "Tantalus," *Uncollected Writings*, p. 117; cf. E, 126).]

[A double sheet never sewn, numbered "R1"–"R4"; headed "Reform" on each recto as are the other leaves of this lecture, and marked "R" as if used for an insert. It appears to be a revision of part of the lecture (pp. 258–259, above), but there is no evidence that it was a lecture sheet.]

R   And hence has arisen that discontent which so characterizes the Present Age yielding such an abundant harvest of projects of public & private Reform

⟨The cause of this impatience is deep & its expression does ⟨n⟩honor to men.⟩ Our modes of living are not agreeable to our imagination & we suspect they are unworthy. We accuse our daily employments They appear to us unfit, unworthy of the faculties we spend on them. In conversation with a man whom we highly esteem we apologise for our employments we speak of them with shame. The fancy flies from the work that is due today to its various fairy lands to some agreeable hope some object of affection some foreign residence some passage of poetry. The farther off the thought from the matter in hand the more wishfully we entertain it. When we are on the way to transact / a disagreeable affair every far off hill every road & path into the woods that opens in an opposite direction looks seductive to us.

In what decided contrast with the tameness of our business stand ever the objects of nature. When we are galled & disgusted with our bondage if by chance we go into the forest the stems of the pine hemlock & oak trees almost gleam like steel on the excited eye. They seem parts of the eternal chain of Destiny whereof this sundered will of man is the victim. Is he not touched even with a sense of inferiority in the presence of these natures which preserve their beauty in growth in strength, in age, in decay. The invitation which these fine savages give as you stand in the hollows of the forest works strangely on the imagination / Little say they in recommendation of towns or a civil Christian life Live with us, they say, & forsake these wearinesses of yesterday. Here no history no church or state is interpolated on the divine sky & the immortal year. ⟨⟨Life should not be prosaic. The reason why it is, is because it is false & violates the laws of the mind. Life tends ever to be picturesque.⟩⟩ [brackets and cancellation in pencil] This beauty the fancy finds in everything else certainly accuses that manner of life we lead. Why should it be hateful? Why should it contrast thus with all natural beauty? Why should it be shameful? Why should it not be poetic ⟨[?]⟩& invite & raise us? Is there a necessity that the works of man should be sordid? Perhaps not. Certainly Life tends to be picturesque The reason why it is not is because it is false & violates the laws of the mind. If the household the vocation the estate the mode of living of the man flowed from himself, obeyed to the utmost ⟨extent of⟩ the circumstance, the law of his genius & character, instead of obeying an insane & vicious Custom he would find beauty & poetry in his living as well as in books & amusements /

7. RELIGION

Lines	Page 272
1	stated ⟨at the [?]⟩ in
2	that the ⟨history⟩ ↑annals↓ of the world ⟨is⟩ ↑are↓
3–4	history ⟨whose renown⟩ which ⟨absorbs⟩ ↑fills↓ the heads of ⟨all⟩ scholars
4–5	thoughts, ⟨a single⟩ ↑an↓
6–7	explodes ⟨forever all⟩ ↑once for all the↓ considerations of prudence, ⟨all⟩ ↑the↓ ties of custom, ⟨all⟩ ↑the↓ old forms of thought & ⟨uplifts⟩ ↑instals↓

Lines

10–11   what ⟨creative abyss⟩ ↑profound crater↓ that ⟨impulse⟩ ↑spark↓
of sentiment ⟨blazed⟩ ↑shot↓

13–14   them. /
⟨In looking at the⟩
Look at it how ↑we↓

15–16   Christianity: ⟨⟨T⟩the⟩ ↑the↓ fact that ten or twenty persons ↑or,
if you please, twice so many↓

22   Their state↑ment↓

27   understanding ⟨they could not⟩ but

32   men ⟨[?]⟩probably

35   in the ⟨19th⟩ ↑nineteenth↓ century — they would ⟨scarce⟩
↑never↓

Page 273

3–5   peasants ⟨declared⟩ ↑announced↓ in the joy of their hearts /
⟨The preacher's⟩ ↑⟨popular⟩↓ ↑The radical vice of the popu-
lar↓ thought is that with which the ⟨advent of that Person⟩
↑Christian era↓

5–6   place. ⟨He⟩It supposes the divine government ↑to be↓

8   The ⟨time⟩ ↑hour↓

10   illusion ⟨s⟩for different

12   globe. ⟨The[?]⟩ It is

16   same facts⟨,⟩↑.↓ ⟨t⟩The facts

18   recognizes the⟨[erasure]⟩ perception

19   all mens

20–21   poor cramp⟨ing⟩ degrading

22–23   Judea. ⟨In our feeble endeavors to resist this low popular
statement we no doubt fall into objectionable statements but
it will be perceived that we contradict this popular notion of
time by representing all as in the Now; and this error of
another by saying It is in the *Me.* and this error of *sacred individuals* by denying the *personality.*⟩
Their religious

24   be ↑on↓

27–28   letter ⟨became⟩ ↑and the circumstance ↑became↓↓ superstitiously sacred; ⟨and Then⟩ ↑then↓

34   sought to ⟨expand &⟩ treat

35   still to ⟨a⟩fit it

Page 274

4–5   mind. /
⟨But at⟩ ↑At↓

7–8   ↑With↓ Judaea, what ⟨have we to do⟩? ↑has the genuine . . .
to do?↓ with

10   were ⟨educ⟩ [erased] bred [over erasure]

12   respect to the ⟨feelings & prejudices of the aged,⟩ ↑establish-
ment↓ — if

Lines

14   the mytho⟨logical⟩↑tical↓ character

15–16   expressions are ⟨trans⟩ ↑⟨sup⟩↓ ↑sup↓planting the

18   We are ↑Je[partial "w"]↓ [between lines as a false start for insertion below]

19–21   from this Judaea ↑Jewish idea . . . have tingled with↓ which has [interlinear insertion as indicated with no point of insertion marked]

22   to mens

23   country. namely

25–26   ↑special↓ resorts & its darling⟨s⟩ ↑men.↓ / ↑In consequence . . . opinion↓
             It is

30   I see ⟨among those⟩ ↑in those classes & those persons, ⟨both ⟨in⟩here & elsewhere⟩,↓ in

32–33   contain the ⟨ri⟩activity

33–34   them ⟨a cle⟩ both skepticism & character; ⟨I⟩ a clear

36   intellect, and ⟨a⟩ explicit declaration↑s↓

37   truthfulness, they

Page 275

1   soul ⟨the⟩ piety, adoration ⟨is⟩ I

3–4   ↑a boundless ambition of the intellect↓

5   these ⟨we⟩they

6   which ⟨soften⟩ give

7–8   churches, it is not in ⟨closets⟩ ↑houses↓. ↑} to here↓ [last insertion in pencil; possibly not Emerson's hand] ⟨Religion surely is an element of man & not of certain conjunctures of time & place; but where is it lodged in our society?⟩ ↑{↓ [bracket in pencil] In the denominations / which have had a ⟨r⟩good repute [ink line avoids cancelling "In the denominations"; diagonal pencil lines (accidentally?) cancel the phrase]

12–13   inactivity ⟨suffers⟩ ↑permits↓

14–15   affections. — For

22   become a ⟨noxious as a⟩ prison

25–26   urge th⟨e⟩ose Reforms {which . . . lecture;} in

27–32   slave. ⟨among men.⟩ [erased] ↑The same class . . . precious to man.↓ /

33   It is does not grow

Page 276

5   history, private fortunes, [commas in red pencil]

6   as we ⟨do⟩ have done

7–11   glory of the ↑one↓ One break⟨i⟩s in everywhere.
          {But mainly is there a growing ⟨disposition to the worship⟩ ↑homage to the influence↓ . . . of the world.} This ↑mav↓ seem⟨s⟩ to ⟨you⟩ ↑many↓

Lines

17–18   Rome the ⟨s⟩functionary who still wears ⟨in⟩ at this hour the
         name of Pontiff ⟨st⟩once
23   say; The Men
25–26   but the ⟨privilege⟩ inheritance of ⟨all souls⟩ ↑men↓
31   itself. / [page heading:] {Idea of Revelation}

Page 277

1   ↑which obtains in modern Christendom↓
11   ask ⟨The only mode of obtaining an answer is⟩ ⟨[?]⟩In the
20–21   idea of ⟨eternity⟩ immutableness
23   never ⟨uttered a syllable about the⟩ made
28–29   ↑The moment the doctrine . . . already fallen.↓
30   absorbed in ⟨[?]⟩the
33   abroad, ⟨is⟩ cannot
34   finite. / [page heading:] {Revelation supposed to rest on mira-
         cles.}

Page 278

13   may ⟨[?]⟩so accept
17   beauty, — & ↑to↓ aim⟨s⟩ a high
19–20   weakness. & always
25   principles. to
26   ↑in one case & in ye other↓
29   rotten. ⟨W⟩ [erased] Go

Page 279

4–5   And which is greater / [page and half of erased pencil fol-
         lows:]
                ⟨↑But the Critic forever on all the falsehoods of the past &
         present & the only prophet of that wh must be is ⟨to descend
         & take counsel of th⟩at Great Nature in which we lie which is
         Unity that Oversoul within which every mans particular be-
         ing is contained & made one with all other — of which all
         [?]tion is the worship to which all right action is submission
         that overpowering reality which confutes all our tricks &
         talents & constrains every one to pass for what he is & to teach
         by character not by his word but ⟨to⟩ in the soul which opposes
         no volition but gives him way it becomes wisdom & virtue &
         power & beauty.
                Soul in dealing with child D245
                S[?] 356
                By it things gravitate
                It can find your friend
                It counts never many nor one / [half page unrecovered]⟩↓
         [ink passage marked for insertion below] / and more affecting

7–13   port of a man? ↑{Insert A}↓ [on previous page, marked "A":]
↑How far nobler . . . *plant* ⟨a⟩ ↑the↓ *palm tree*." intimating
. . . by creed.↓
15–16   soul. ⟨so that⟩ the lover
29   rapture⟨s⟩ [erased] of

Page 280

8   every mans
13   speak ⟨thr[?]⟩from his
29   Yet ⟨[?]⟩I desire ⟨to⟩ even
31   is, ⟨and⟩ ↑to↓ recall to you ⟨your own⟩ the
33   Power, ⟨the⟩ our

Page 281

5   will ⟨rid⟩ ↑relieve↓
28   as it is in ⟨him⟩you is in ⟨you⟩him
31   talent & ↑your↓

Page 282

1   most ↑intimate↓ familiar of all
6   mine, ⟨cent for cent,⟩ ↑one for one↓
8–9   ↑out of↓ his young eyes looks ⟨with soul⟩ ↑the same spirit↓ also.
he
11   overpowered⟨. That which⟩ and
17–18   head. / [blank] /
⟨The things that are really for thee gravitate to thee. You
are running to seek your friend. Let your legs run but your
mind need not. If you do not find him will you not acquiesce
that it is best you should not find him? for there is a power
which as it is in you is in him also and could therefore very
well bring you together if it were for the best. ↑You are preparing with eagerness to go and render a service for which
your talent & your taste both invite you yes & the love of men.
Has it occurred to you that you have no right to go unless you
are equally willing to be prevented from going?↓⟩
As this
21–22   indirectly to numbers / ⟨no matter how indirectly⟩ proclamation
24–25   ↑It makes no difference . . . to *one*↓
29–33   sage. He is ⟨ashamed before the blade of grass or the blowing
rose. These roses that in July open under my window make no
reference to former roses or to better ones; they are for what
they are. they exist with God today. There is no time⟩ ↑The
reliance on authority measures the decline of religion, — the
withdrawal of the Soul. Yet the position men have given Jesus

Lines

now for many centuries of history is a position of authority. It characterizes themselves. It cannot alter the eternal facts.↓ [interlinear insertion between horizontally cancelled lines; two vertical lines, perhaps use marks, are drawn through the entire passage after "sage."]
Great is

Page 283

1–2   appeals from itself. ⟨Yet see the position ⟨of⟩ ↑men have given to↓ Jesus ↑in the mind of the world↓ to the souls of men is a position of authority.⟩ The soul always believes in itself. ⟨It gives itself alone original & pure to the Lonely Original & Pure who on that condition gladly inhabits ⟨it⟩ [erased] leads [over erasure] & speaks through it. T⟩Before

6   affirm that ⟨there⟩ we

12–13   fatigue. ↑& invade↓ The

19–20   on its nature.
       ⟨So it calls us to⟩
       Nature

22–23   ↑the existence of [partial letter]↓ her vegetable & animal ⟨existence.⟩ ↑tribes.↓

26–27   no time to them ⟨to them.⟩ / [blank] / to them   There is

31–32   ↑So is it . . . life of man↓ But man ⟨is⟩ ↑as we know him is↓

Page 284

6   are one. ⟨{We live in succession in division in parts in particles Meantime within man is the soul of the whole the wise silence of the Universal Beauty to which every part & particle is equally related the eternal one.} Speech⟩ An ignorant

10–11   advance every proposition every action every

18–(285)18   This energy . . . kind of praising." [This double sheet, noted in *Lectures*, II, 83n, as misplaced, has subsequently been restored to its proper manuscript.]

21   grandeur   ⟨It⟩ When

24   true. The ⟨ambitious⟩ ↑low↓

27–28   rings; ⟨& record⟩ ↑& preserve↓

31   know. Still

Page 285

7   gods would walk

9   virtue even ⟨y⟩say rather

21–22   dwell ↑neither↓ in multitudes ↑neither↓ nor in

25   If this ⟨heart⟩ age

[A larger leaf, once sewn, but not with this lecture. It is drawn from the first paragraph of the lecture.]

EDUCATION

It is a maxim getting to be sufficiently familiar in modern ears, that the annals of the world are to be found first in the mind. A few thoughts made all this history which fills the heads of scholars & statesmen   A few thoughts built these towns & cities & gave this or that direction to a man or a tribe of men that is prolonged in history over wide tracts of country & long thousands of years. A few thoughts, a religious sentiment in the heart of some eastern shepherd or peasant ⟨exploded⟩ ↑burned up↓ once for all the ties of prudence & custom, the old forms of thought, & installed him as the interpreter of nature & the organ of the moral sentiment to his country, & to half mankind. There seems no proportion between the cause & the effect. But who can tell from what profound crater that spark of sentiment / shot up which set his heart on fire? The wonderful power of that Jewish idea which has so written itself on the nations has had its full force in the Saxon race. /

9. EDUCATION

Lines	*Page 287*
5	nations ⟨today⟩ ↑at the present epoch↓
7	breadth. ⟨What⟩ It
12	form, ⟨my s[?]⟩ my affections,
13–16	music; / ↑If I glance . . . not quite obvious↓
	The thermometer & microscope ⟨are little deists⟩. ↑have a very unbelieving look↓
17–19	mark ⟨&⟩of a truth is, that it is ↑rich,↓ all related, all explaining; ↑How impoverished . . . by seeing↓ ⟨See then⟩ the
22–23	vocation, ⟨his bodily life⟩ ↑life & death↓, his presentiments, his insanity,
	See the attraction
24	offers to ⟨put them⟩ give
33	made. ⟨T⟩Education

	Page 288
3–6	↑If he is jovial . . . ally / if he be ingenious or usef⟨f⟩ul or . . . need of all↓
11–13	what mad! ↑Men whose culture . . . the clown still.↓ Where is the ⟨genius⟩ ↑wisdom↓
15–17	↑the cheerfulness . . . possession of society?↓
21–22	predict /
	⟨As soon as you once come up with a man's limitations, it is all over with him; has he talents, has he enterprizes, has he knowledge, it boots not. He has lost his charm for you Infinitely alluring piquant was he to you yesterday, a great hope, a sea to swim in. ⟨Y⟩ [erased] Now you have found his shores; found it a pond & you care not if you never see it again.⟩
	But do those ↑on↓
23	lights, ⟨to⟩ whom it has installed in its seminaries ⟨t[?]⟩& there

497

Lines
27   life — that ⟨his⟩the entire
33–35   jaws. {⟨⟨If⟩We are not . . . its fingers} It

Page 289

4   college⟨s⟩ recitation
10   rule ↑was↓
12   should learn ⟨to fish⟩ to
17   The ↑shock↓ [in pencil] twinge of
18–22   theories↑; the taste of . . . better than ⟨a⟩ volumes of chem-
            istry↓ [in pencil] /
            ↑⟨A⟩One man seems often . . . loses truth & reality.↓ [in
            ink]
25–26   but ⟨these⟩ ↑men↓ transformed ⟨men are⟩ ↑by books become↓
27–28   Education {are avowedly profane. That is they} aim [brackets
            in pencil]
28–29   masses what can⟨not so be done⟩ ↑never be done for masses↓

Page 290

9–10   God, & to ⟨dream⟩ ↑only to think↓ of using it ⟨only⟩ implies
11–12   analogous to the differe⟨[?]⟩nce
13–14   overpower him, / ⟨in a moment⟩ & get [Enclosed in the
            double sheet at this page break is an unnumbered single leaf,
            never sewn with the rest of the lecture, which may at some
            time have replaced lines 22–24 (see below):]
            ↑I pass then to ↑enumerate↓ consider some of the partic-
            ulars of that faith in men↓ [in pencil] /
            ↑In speaking just now of our system of Education I spoke
            of the deadness of its details but it is open to graver criticism
            than the deadness of ⟨its⟩ [erased] many [over erasure] of its
            details. It is a system of despair. All men are becoming sen-
            sible that the disease with which the human mind now labours
            is want of faith. Men do not believe in a Power of education
            Men do not think ⟨they⟩ we can call out God in man & they
            do not try↓ [in ink] / ["I pass then . . . do not try" ("New
            England Reformers," W, III, 267–268)]
15   return↑s↓
21–24   heart. [in pencil, centered between lines:] ↑Carnot↓
            ⟨Our system . . . God in man / and we do not try. ⟨Our
            a⟩ We renounce all high aims.⟩ We sacrifice [Pencil lines
            may be use marks or cancellation for subsequent revision (see
            lines 13–14, above). Possible emendation rejected in this
            text.]
26   uniformity. as the Turks
27–(291)1   temple-walls ↑{Insert S}↓ [in pencil; on next page, marked
            "S":]
            ↑Well, language . . . and in the ⟨A⟩College. It . . . the-
            ory of Education.↓

Lines

{Certainly this despondency . . . for this ↑Not↓ to be thus deserted & betrayed was ⟨the⟩ he . . . heir of ⟨this world⟩ Nature} [brackets in pencil] / [passage marked "S"; used above] / [passage marked "T"; used below] /
    I call

Page 291

3–8   Hope. ↑{Insert T}↓ [on previous page, marked "T":]
    ↑Let me say before all other . . . hope on all things.↓
9   same ⟨view⟩ ↑torch↓
10–11   ↑Everything teaches that.↓ ⟨The sense of want & sin is a fine inuendo by which the great soul makes its enormous claim.⟩ One fact
12–13   trust, viz. ⟨Our perpetual youth⟩. ↑this perpetual youth . . . cannot get rid of.↓
15   as we ⟨remain⟩ ↑continue↓
19   sorcery of ⟨the⟩ ungenial
21   gloom ↑with↓
22–23   mend. or rise. All ↑circumstances, like↓ chemical agents↑,↓ [insertions in pencil]
25–26   ↑put us out↓ [in pencil]
29–30   As long ↑as↓ things change & invite our energies, we ⟨are⟩ grow
30–31   discover the motion of ⟨the⟩ [erased] our [over erasure]
35   us with ⟨th⟩ a

Page 292

1   facts. ⟨It is the learning the⟩ In
7   can ↑in↓
26   new ⟨event⟩ ↑fact↓
27–28   known ↑to us?↓
35   ↑No: they ask↓

Page 293

1   night.. ↑These mourners shall have their reward.↓
6–8   unhappy. let us be unquiet. ashamed. and always tormented by ⟨o⟩riddles we cannot expound, if ⟨So we can but keep our⟩ ↑this is all the price we pay for↓ docility and ⟨our⟩ ↑⟨an⟩↓ intimacy
10   I ⟨write⟩ speak
21   ↑organized↓
24   ↑new↓
26   the latin
28   where ↑into↓
35   But ⟨it is⟩ my life, ⟨it is⟩ my ↑work &↓ play, ⟨& work⟩ my pleasure

Lines   *Page 294*

4   winter's ⟨cold⟩ ↑frost↓, the summer's fruit ↑it is these↓
11   without a college. / and
14   those to be ⟨called⟩ ↑employed↓
17–18   ↑without hesitation↓ at Cambridge or at Andover, but ⟨not⟩
        ↑do not think needful↓
19   leisure ↑&↓
21–23   {But this . . . large numbers.} [pencil brackets]
27   near them or ⟨a⟩far
30   believe that ⟨the secret of⟩ our
31   you to ⟨s[?]⟩choose
33–34   your ⟨interference⟩ tampering

Page 295

1–2   deprived him⟨self⟩ of himself & the world of a man to ⟨make⟩
        add
2–3   drones & ↑blunderers↓ tidewaiters &
4–7   beholders. /
        ⟨So to regard the young child the young man requires,
        no doubt, great patience: — a patience that only faith in the
        remedial forces of the soul can give. You see his sensualism,
        you see his want of those tastes & perceptions which make
        the safety of your character. But every mind should be al-
        lowed to make its own statement in action and its balances
        will appear.⟩ /
        Respect the child. (Be . . . their children.) [parentheses
        in pencil]
11   fortune; ⟨w⟩ an
12   theory ⟨of⟩ ↑that↓
14–15   mediocre. /
        ⟨{Let us respect the child and the youth. Let him be led
        up with a long sighted forbearance and not the sallies of his
        petulance or folly checked with too much disgust or indig-
        nation or despair.}⟩
        Let us wait & see what is this new creation. Of
18   sky. And ⟨in order great⟩ ↑jealous↓
25–26   worth his w⟨[?]⟩hile to . . . hard & ⟨pragmatical⟩ ↑inappre-
        hensive↓ . . . think that ↑t↓he ↑youth↓
27–28   ↑For months perhaps . . . reasonable word↓
29   was he. ⟨Well⟩ ↑It seems↓
33   forbearance, & ↑let↓ not

Page 296

1   much dis / disgust or
8   else. ⟨H⟩ If he
11–13   of whom ⟨it was said "h⟨e⟩is ⟨was very⟩ patien⟨t⟩ce ⟨and⟩
        could see in the bud of the aloe the blossom at the end of
        a / hundred years.⟩ ↑it was said "his patience could see in

the bud of the aloe the blossom at the end of a hundred years."↓ [insertion in a very late hand]

18–19   I ⟨reply⟩ ↑answer,↓ Respect ⟨your⟩ ↑the↓ [last word in pencil, written over in ink] child, ↑Respect him unto the end↓

27   character. ⟨I cannot⟩ That

32   knew a tie [possible reading: "lie"]

Page 297

4–6   ↑of us to measure↓ "the ⟨"⟩ ideal track of right
        "More fair

11   will ⟨make⟩ ↑lead↓

12–14   ↑Having settled ourselves into this infidelity↓ Our utmost skill ⟨then⟩ is ↑expended↓ to procure alleviations ⟨amusements⟩ ↑diversion↓

14–15   manual skill, ⟨with⟩ his

15–16   forms his ⟨hand⟩ ↑body↓

20–(298)6   games? /

⟨But if we made less . . . could become profound.⟩ [Two pencil lines through this passage perhaps indicate emendation for subsequent rearrangement of manuscript and are rejected as cancellation in the present text.] / [An unnumbered double sheet follows; once sewn, but never with this manuscript:]

Men must be impressed with the indispensableness of the office of a Teacher. Because they are not taught they think the office is a sinecure. Christs idea of a Teacher was the best blessing. As soon as they are taught they will know it. The Teacher when he comes will not have the cushioned chair nor the title of Reverend nor constrained attentions ↑these would be incumbrances↓ but the hard pursuit the intense attention the ⟨indefatigable⟩ ↑⟨incessant⟩↓ ↑unwearied↓ imitation the dear love of his disciples. They will not ⟨higgle⟩ cheapen his services they will give him themselves they will be a troop not of followers but of friends enlisting themselves as the lovers & servants of his thoughts not with an esprit de corps — not with a personal engagement to defend him for better or worse — faults & follies — but so bound as he is bound to the truth that they see quicker than others & condemn as much every flaw offence in him or themselves. They will feel a true gratitude to him The eye will sparkle at the sound of his name The inner soul will move. For he will lead them forth out of that house of bondage in which all men are born into the light of the new heavens He will deliver them from the yoke of fear into the peaceful family of love. He will so teach by being more a man than other men. /

He cannot work without his scholar works Now men would not give a segar for Socrates or Goethe. They will have to work before they will ⟨It is exercise⟩ Some peristaltic motions surely must be before the pupa will work off and the wings open. The true Teacher has not come. Why because his scholars have not. There is electricity enow in the room if the receiver were empty. The true Teacher will appear whenever the docile mind doth. But he cannot work without his scholar works. Solus docet qui dat & et discit qui recipit [Robert Leighton, *The Select Works,* 2 vols. (London, 1823), I, 444. Also in *Lectures,* II, 423; Encyclopedia, 31; C, 192; and, translated, "Spiritual Laws," W, II, 152.] You cannot have ⟨learning⟩ wisdom ⟨in⟩ ready made to fit like a coat. It is little that any man can do for his fellow. ⟨When I have the right view & you the wrong⟩ I can see that you are wrong without yet being able to show you where ⟨we⟩ your error begins. I cannot see clear enough for that. /

In some sort, teaching is the perpetual end & office of all things, it is carried on by all that is done The very man that despises a Teacher — that would not give a segar for all the stuff of Goethe, huddles close to the ring in the Insurance office, scrapes acquaintance with an eminent merchant who walks up the same street, catches with sharpened ear the chance word that drops from a lawyer ↑& retails it with evident respect at his own table — ↓ — persons whom Goethe dont care a button for, but who are the true teachers of this person He is in the confined element of Action & wants the aid of dexterous actors. Dont quarrel with him for not relishing speculation any more than with a horse for not relishing roast beef. They must eat that they have stomachs to digest.

There is no man — there is no state — but has its fit teacher and teaching. Once Montaigne was good for me, then Scougal, now Science — Shakspear — Goethe — myself — & God. /

⟨I say *to be taught* is the ⟨great⟩ ↑main↓ design hung out on the sky & earth. He that has no ambition to be taught let him creep into his grave. What is he doing among good people. The play is not worth the candle — the labourer is not worthy of his meat — the sun grudges hi⟨m⟩s light & the air ↑this↓ breath ↑to him↓ — who stands with his hands folded in this great school of God & does not perceive that all are students all are learning the art of life the discipline of virtue, how to act, how to suffer, how to be useful, & what their Maker designed them for. It is this persuasion only that can invest existence with any dignity or hope. and make the life of a man better than a brutes. And this will do it. If you believe that every step not only enables you to make another, but also brings you within reach of influences before inert acts like Day which not only brings more objects in view

Lines

every moment but brings out new properties in every particular object   You will then accept Instruction as the greatest gift of God & anxiously put yourself in the attitude of preparation   The University cannot make a Teacher⟩ /
[A leaf now filed with "The Present Age," Lecture 1, which does not belong there but which according to sewing marks and pagination belongs at this point in this lecture:] ⟨That which is best . . . or sex⟩ [Single pencil line through this page perhaps indicates emendation for subsequent rearrangement of manuscript and is rejected as cancellation in the present text.] / or . . . Perfect which solicits me. /

25–26 perception ⟨of⟩ in

Page 298

5 it not ⟨I suffer⟩ it
10–11 stars↑,↓ [comma in pencil] with laurel & palm — What ⟨say⟩ ↑teach↓ [emendations in ink] they but ↑the insulation & selfsubsistency of a man↓ [in pencil] by
12–13 what ↑roof he lives under, what stem he sprung from,↓ he eats & wears man
16 also. The ⟨painting⟩ ↑best picture↓ makes ⟨me⟩ ↑us↓

Page 299

1 side. &
11 admonition. an
25–26 but to ⟨solace⟩ ↑conceal;↓
27 death. ⟨It⟩Worst
28 man with this [final letter blotted]
34–(300)3 truth which love↑,↓ which terror↑,↓ which need↑,↓ . . . each of us↑,↓ & some of his mates↑,↓ . . . genius↑,↓ of society↑,↓ of external nature, if the truth is not is some manner . . . our schools↑, — ↓ [insertions in pencil]

Page 300

4–5 draw ⟨an⟩ ↑on the↓ eternal & universal Soul↑.↓ It lies within↑, — ↓ it lies behind us all↑, — ↓ the dullest drone↑,↓ [emendations in pencil]
6 Those ⟨whom⟩ unhappy who come into every one's ⟨mind⟩ ↑thought↓
7 not profound↑, — ↓ [in pencil]
11 ↑The clay can be tempered with this fire↓
16 beloved. ⟨The lo No talent⟩ The lover
17 his ↑enamoured↓ maiden [end line] ⟨or his wife⟩, however
19 all ⟨its⟩ ↑his↓ [emendations in pencil]
21 loss ⟨when⟩ [cancellation in pencil] ↑in suggesting↓ I ⟨hear⟩ [insertion and cancellation in ink] particular
23 committee↑, — ↓ [in pencil]
24–28 Academy↑,↓ a College↑,↓ [insertions in pencil] can at all

Lines

avail to reach⟨)⟩ [in pencil and erased] ↑them.↓ ↑(↓a wrong
. . . condemn that aim.↑)↓ But [insertions in pencil]

30   mind↑, — ↓ [in pencil]

32   soul↑,↓ [in pencil]

34–35   how ⟨to vanquish the vanquishable⟩ [cancellation in pencil]
to do the practicable. ⟨You⟩ [cancellation in ink] According

36–(*301*)1   is the depth ⟨of your⟩ not . . . but of your ↑⟨negligency⟩↓
last act

Page 301

3   Work ⟨[?]r⟩ [erased] straight [over erasure] on in absolute
duty, ⟨and you⟩ and

4–5   ↑Consent yourself to↓

10.   TENDENCIES

Page 302

1   taken ⟨o⟩in the

9   humanity. And the ⟨healing⟩ remedial force↑s↓

10   secret persu⟨s⟩asions in

12–(*303*)1   ↑or dead↓ *means* but on the vital alert ⟨alw⟩ Soul

Page 303

2–14   appear. ↑{Insert A}↓ [on next page, marked "A":] ↑In all
parts of action, . . . straps & ↑buckles↓ pins by . . . and
↑they forfeit their connexion & vantages↓ [point for interlinear insertion uncertain] ⟨th⟩ disuse & throw away first
. . . dreams of idealism.↓ Th⟨e⟩at ↑bifold↓ one fact

17   back & ⟨take⟩ ↑choose↓ the way of ⟨l⟩Love.

18–19   ↑and that the value . . . labor & ingenuity↓

22–23   ears. In ⟨d⟩Domestic Life again ↑all indicates that↓ ⟨we wish⟩
the

24   Imitation ⟨to⟩ ↑should↓

25   stands there ⟨for⟩ to

26   many house⟨s⟩keepers believe

27–28   sovereign ⟨creating⟩ ordaining

34–35   society the ⟨ref⟩ Movement

36   ↑the fraternal↓ ⟨principle⟩ instead of ⟨coin⟩ ↑the mercenary↓

Page 304

7   spices, he can ⟨attire⟩ dress

16   was, is. young

25–(*305*)11   In all the activities . . . & every day. [at top of recto of this
single leaf, in Emerson's hand:] ↑{Tendencies} Inserted in
Lect III New England at p 36↓

Lines
26–27   means ⟨to⟩for [a cancellation line has been erased] the ⟨regenera reform of⟩ extermination

28   society. ⟨Thus⟩ the ↑old↓

29–30   liberality the virtu⟨ous⟩e the hope⟨ful⟩ the

33   Democracy in ⟨R⟩the

37–(305)1   ↑& he lends himself . . . what is eminent↓

Page 305

2   not ⟨fluent or⟩ removeable

3–4   Congress ⟨nor the tax⟩ nor the mob nor the guillotine nor ⟨halter nor⟩ fire

13   Hephaestion ↑↑the↓ of Corcyra↑ean↓↓

15–16   prayers ⟨Athens⟩ ↑Corcyra↓ [cancellation in pencil, insertion in ink]

19   his aston⟨s⟩ishment the

21   & for every ⟨great choice⟩ ↑just vote↓ he made suddenly [cancellation in pencil, insertion in ink]

24   trade the

25–26   community it

28–29   rose, & all its ⟨poss⟩ [erased] real [over erasure] all its possible products it

32   simple. ⟨But they quickly learned that⟩ It

34   intrusion ⟨& impertinences⟩ of

35   ↑despised↓

Page 306

5   this ⟨magic⟩ palace

6   threatened bury

8   evils ⟨domestic⟩ political

14–23   in life.

      ⟨Observe the confidence of all the sanguine patriots the ⟨private⟩ public spirited . . . ↑on lamps that shine without shadow↓ . . . ↑steam batteries↓ life preservers & diving bells. ⟨on steam batteries⟩⟩ [Two pencil lines through the passage have been rejected as cancellation in the present text for the sense of the next sentence.] /

      And the actual

      And the actual familiarization

24–(307)15   new era. ↑{Insert X}↓ [beginning on next page, marked "X":]

      ↑It is wonderful . . . ↑successors of Copernicus &↓ cotemporaries of Galileo somewhat in this wise.

      As soon as . . . It was thought that / by . . . in the globe itself. /

      But such an ⟨idea⟩ hypothesis . . . Pyrrhonism.↓

Page 307

26   steps ⟨expressed⟩ recorded

29–(308)8 {These doctrines these movements . . . new value to} Self reliance [brackets in pencil]
31–(308)3 separate value ⟨to⟩ ↑{Insert B}↓ [on previous page, marked "B":] ↑It is remarkable . . . same conclusion. ⟨The poetry has become philosophical the philosophy poetical⟩ The poetry is . . . only reality.↓

Page 308

4 moral & ⟨intellectu⟩ metaphysical
6 avails. ⟨Will not⟩ Have
12–13 worthiness of all /
     {⟨Thyself must be great & good⟩ It i⟨[?]⟩s of . . . concerned ⟨how⟩ on [bracket in pencil]
16 aught by ⟨⟨[?]⟩sailing⟩ ↑moving↓ in the wake of ⟨of⟩ [erased] a [over erasure]
20 If ⟨as⟩ then
21 steadily ⟨to⟩ by
32 Conformity is ⟨D⟩the
36 carriage which ⟨is never endangered by⟩ shall
37 not virtue. which
38–(309)1 explores ⟨wheth⟩ if it be goodness. &

Page 309

7–8 government ⟨spread your table like base housekeepers⟩ ↑spend your time . . . multitude↓
20 sacred. Do I not know ⟨beforehan⟩ that he

Page 310

9 friends
14 esteem the ⟨newspa⟩ [erased] discontent [over erasure]
27 have no ↑other↓

Page 311

4–5 Galileo. & every
9 though he ⟨sees it⟩ [erased] mean [over erasure]
15 all. The voy⟨[?]⟩age of
22 have done ⟨right⟩ so
28 train of ⟨[?]⟩great
31 thunder into ⟨Mirabeau's⟩ ↑Chatham's↓

Page 312

2 furnish, / [Pages 37–40 of the original manuscript are missing. The lacuna is filled by the following double sheet, properly paginated, but not labelled and never sewn with the rest of the manuscript:]
     And what can be more desireable than these great re-

coveries of the Soul when it starts up into an infinite amplitude & mocks at your academies, at the libraries, & feels well assured it hath no need of your books, much less to be harnassed like a pedant into a system of criticism; for it is at home in Nature, it has yet no want of thought, and it has not yet lost that youth & innocency which give it to feel that there is progress for tomorrow also, & so on forever. It will not do itself the dishonor ⟨as⟩ to set any term to its own advances One thought is as good as another thought. One thought shuts out all others And whoever is faithful to his perception comes presently to see no superiors but all co-operators. It is the wonderful property of the world that whoever advances into its law anywhere is admitted *ad gradum,* as we say in / the colleges, (to the same rank) everywhere. By his own activity he has attained a wonderful exaltation. The great who affected him with despair he can now calmly measure. The Epics are majestic trifles He can well spare them. Shakspeare the unique genius of the world showed himself hitherto a central sun but now in his own movement Shakspeare instantly takes his true place as only another thinker. He sees the condition of that & of every greatness It is only by doing without Shakspeare that we can do without his book. Be Shakspeare & we shall value the particular works no longer. ["It is only . . . no longer" (D, 357)] And in seeing that, he has already the pledge that God has put all spiritual grandeurs within his own reach.

I own, for myself, that I see always with joy the impatience of youthful genius of these scales & boundaries which we so readily erect for them on the field of human wit. Admire this we say Reverence that and lastly Behold that other name with eternal despair. /
They erect none for themselves They feel the generous expanse of the kingdom of thought: they taste its infinite air
And we too have been aware of the same fact when we have beheld with love & wonder at any time a new & rich character. A great person refuses to be resolved Literature cannot classify him. He has no taste for Shakspeare. What can Shakspeare do There still stands the person and as long as he holds by nature we must hold our peace & wonder & wait. Literature looks unsatisfactory, by-play, neither here nor there while it cannot resolve him. Before a divine person a book is foolishness

The dreams of youth the passion of love the charm of external nature are the constant reproduction of the vision of the Ideal which God will not suffer a moment to remit its presence or to relax its energy as a coagent / history. [E, 30] It is the certificate Reverence this angry freedom even if it be disdainful & unmannerly. It is the certificate of being

507

in nature still & not sold to any of the merchants that bid for the soul. It is strange by how many doors we are always invited out into nature and the moment we go abroad thither by any one we are redeemed from limitations we are pedants no more. We may go by the love of plants, or by the love of woman, or by the love of solitude, or by the love of God. Any sentiment that is dearer than habit & inertia will redeem us from the danger of a parrot's life from being mere secondaries & things, that commodiously repeat what has been said a thousand times & endorsing with our foolish compliance. all the stereotypes of common fame. /

3	strong will is ⟨one of the⟩ ↑a↓ feeble⟨st⟩ force⟨s of man It is weakness by the side of renunciation of Will⟩. It
9	Will. ⟨It is⟩ Beside
10	truth, this ⟨is unholy & profane⟩ which
18	man. ⟨It⟩ Trust gains by ⟨s⟩faster
28	make it. that

Page 313

5	↑We owe to ourselves↓ A greater
6	man. A ⟨great⟩ stronger
7	history. which
10–11	↑of so just a life?↓ And yet steadily in ⟨every⟩ ↑the↓
16	higher & it can⟨no⟩ [erased] no more
17	before him. {The wildest [bracket in pencil]
31–32	done ⟨its utmost⟩ ↑the best,↓ & produced its last saint & ⟨highest poet⟩ ↑sweetest singer↓
33	worlds
34	laws of / of angles

Page 314

1	child still ⟨embrace⟩ exercise
2	deep ↑of↓
3	under the ⟨co⟩ innocent & confiding heart Then still ⟨extends⟩ ↑reaches↓
8	by his ⟨perception by his⟩ Faith
13	↑gay↓ invitation of society & of circumstance ⟨stea⟩ sends
18	history ⟨are⟩ ↑is↓ . . . souls
19–20	↑power & property↓
22	ends. he ⟨g⟩ asks
23	life. ⟨T⟩But they will not yield him the p⟨[?]⟩eace he
32	life ⟨[?]⟩but all
33–34	↑Love acquaints him with the ⟨unnecessariness &⟩ superfluousness of ⟨spe⟩ words↓

Page 315

1	He ⟨[?]⟩ overlooks
6	Foreworld ⟨in the⟩ fading

Lines
6–8   ↑which produced . . . designs↓ whilst he feels that deep in his ↑own↓
8   thinks ↑even↓
11   mans worth, reflections in persons. and
14   quiet ⟨serene⟩ ↑yet sublime↓
16   coming ⟨under⟩ whose
20   nature ⟨&⟩by the renouncement of ⟨his⟩ all

[There is now filed with this lecture a double sheet paginated 23–26 which belongs with "Human Life," Lecture 9, where it is printed, above, page 138, line 1, to page 139, line 23 ("We foolishly think . . . Chaos and the Dark").]

III. ADDRESS TO THE PEOPLE OF EAST LEXINGTON

Page 327

2–3   ↑passing↓ traveller is this new edifice ↑with↓ which ⟨graces⟩ ↑you have adorned the side of↓
4   ↑passengers↓
6   will the⟨se⟩ graceful
7–8   planned & ⟨exe⟩ constructed them and to you who ⟨a⟩see
9   But in ⟨co⟩ naming

Page 328

6–7   but ↑to↓
13–15   liturgy, ↑&↓ of psalmody; ↑from pleasure . . . & the circumstance↓
15–16   ↑from a desire . . . tho'ts & influences↓
17   best ⟨grounds⟩ ↑designs↓
25   been ↑a↓ pitiful
26–27   living. I ⟨think⟩ ↑thought↓ I manage↑d↓ it very well — ⟨my⟩ I
28–29   never u⟨nt⟩p to this moment dreamed that this undertaking ⟨my own⟩ the
34   load — But

Page 329

9   everlasting ↑Love↓
11   to it. ⟨The instant we do so, we are glorified,⟩ ↑In doing thus,↓
13   or a ⟨little parcel⟩ ↑stock↓
19   this ⟨is⟩doctrine
21–22   certain wond⟨[P]⟩erful King
25–26   within. ↑is↓
29   scope & ⟨end⟩ ↑result↓ ↑outline↓ of all. that

Lines   *Page 330*

5   wall, not a↑n↓

11   catches ⟨us⟩them up

24   is not builde⟨n⟩d when

27   consciousness of ⟨its⟩ ↑this↓

34   alive — It ennobles & binds ⟨together⟩ ↑in one↓

36   is ⟨fashioned⟩ educated

IV. THE TIMES

3. THE POET

Page 348

1–12   ⟨I invite the attention . . . reached by criticism⟩ / [entire page cancelled by three pencil lines but retained in text as introduction]

5   lover of ⟨the M⟩ [erased] poetry [over erasure], who ⟨con[?]⟩ [erased] regards [over erasure]

16   inflame ↑the↓

27   If ⟨now⟩ ↑then↓ we ⟨come to say⟩ ↑proceed to inquire↓

Page 349

1   nature. ⟨⟨In nature there is no rest. All things are in perpetual procession, flow, & change.⟩⟩ Every [cancellation in pencil]

2   endeavor to ⟨execute⟩ ↑embody↓ [emendations in pencil]

6   stands in & the ⟨delight⟩ [erased] joy he [over erasure]

7   his though⟨ts⟩t in

8   or in the ⟨c⟩mind↑s↓ [insertion in pencil]

15   of his mind; / [At this point, never sewn, but laid into the manuscript, is the following leaf. It has an ink heading *"Poet."* and pencil annotation "1841–2". It is numbered "4" in pencil and does not fit into the pagination of the lecture, but a pencilled "B" suggests the possibility that it was an insertion.]
All books of Imagination endure, all which ascend to that power of thought that the writer sees ⟨[partial "n"]⟩Nature as subordinate to the soul & uses it as his language. Every sentence every verse indicating this ⟨superiority {or health} {is memorable &}⟩ ↑virtue↓ [emendations and brackets in pencil] will take care of its own immortality. A man apparently foolish & helpless↑,↓ [comma in pencil] with nothing magnetic in him, — who is a churl in ⟨a saloon,⟩ ↑the drawing-room,↓ an id⟨e⟩iot in the legislature, — hides himself ↑in his garret↓ from the pride & pity of men, ⟨in his ⟨chamber⟩ ↑⟨garret⟩↓

Lines

[last insertion in pencil and erased]⟩, & writes a poem which,
(when at last it is published,) [parentheses in pencil] is at
first neglected, then hissed, & it pushes all potentates from
their thrones, changes the course of affairs in a few years, &
actually wipes out the memory of that triumphant state of
things under which he suffered when he existed. / [in pencil:]

Plato
Aristophanes
Syrtaeus
Rouge   Rogé de Lisle
Rousseau
Machiavel
Voltaire
Tom Paine
Swift
Luther
Rabelais
Mahomet
Mirabeau /

29   tendency⟨,⟩ in [comma erased]
29–30   possessions, & ⟨[?]⟩the

Page 350

1   world: ⟨of th⟩ [erased] into [over erasure]
5   anything is, ⟨this,⟩ that, [cancellation and commas in pencil]
7   what is ⟨that⟩ ↑it,↓ [emendations in pencil]
8   For ⟨that⟩ ↑the same↓ [emendations in pencil]
21–22   wrung from the ⟨⟨deepest⟩⟩ anguish of a broken heart↑,↓ [emendations in pencil]
23   bosom↑,↓ [comma in pencil]
24   his bow↑,↓ — tearing [comma in pencil]
25   most ↑alarming↓ ↑fearful↓ horrid↑,↓ as well [insertions in pencil]
26–27   tones↑,↓" — what is the origin of ⟨their⟩ ↑our↓ enjoyment but an apprisal of ⟨their⟩ ↑our↓ own ↑[partial "th" above next word]↓ power↑, — ↓ [emendations in pencil]
28   lower than ⟨they⟩ ↑we↓ [emendations in pencil]

Page 351

11   hurled on ⟨to⟩ the
12–13   this↑,↓ that she dances for them↑,↓ [commas in pencil] or they dance in her ↑feet↓, not being,↑ — ↓ [dash in pencil]
14   education, ↑ — ↓ [dash in pencil]
19   whole ⟨body⟩ person
22   Hence ⟨all⟩ the [cancellation in pencil]
22–24   spectacle imparts↑,↓ ⟨⟨and the intimate property which each

511

beholder feels in the dancer.⟩⟩ [brackets and emendations in pencil]
　　If one

25	anything ⟨strong⟩ ↑rare↓ [emendations in pencil]
26–27	Ring, ⟨the⟩ [erased] ↑land or naval↓ Battle↑s↓ ⟨fields⟩; foreign
29	only↑, — ↓ [punctuation in pencil]
31	expression is ⟨not only the cause of our love of all spectacles ⟨&⟩ but is⟩ ↑thus↓

Page 352

1	direction of his ⟨character⟩ ↑practical faculties↓
2–3	perception ⟨of things⟩ of things
5	expressive so / so changeable so ⟨swift⟩ fruitful
7	alphabet↑,↓ [comma in pencil]
10	↑a house↓
11–12	snake, a⟨n ass⟩ ↑baboon↓, a ⟨puppy⟩ ↑goat, a gull,↓
15–16	another man ⟨⟨Puppy or⟩ Thunderbolt⟩ or Puppy ↑or Ass↓
19	bark or ⟨neigh⟩ ↑bray,↓
22–23	signifies ⟨his⟩ ↑its↓ [emendations in ink] sense in ⟨these⟩ [cancellation in pencil] metaphors. As when Napoleon ⟨calls⟩ [cancellation in ink] says
24	asses, ⟨[?]⟩whilst
27	nature ⟨or⟩by giving
29	spiders snare, it

Page 353

12	↑is legitimate↓
14	Baileys
22	people are! ⟨See the great⟩ / See
23–24	Lowell in a ⟨L⟩loom

Page 354

1–2	exterior. ⟨all over the globe⟩. / Hear our speech, ↑see our dramatic exhibitions↓
3	figure-heads, the c⟨[?]⟩iphers on
4	↑of fire engines↓
7–8	love for ⟨these⟩ signs . . . man to ⟨all⟩ these [cancellations in pencil] forms in nature is ⟨deeper &⟩ more
9	perhaps the metamorphos⟨i⟩↑e↓s which [emendation in pencil]
10–12	literature ⟨is⟩ ↑are↓ not quite so fabulous as ⟨it is represented⟩ ↑they are accounted↓. [emendations in ink] ⟨⟨The soul passes through all forms, the same soul is at home in all, & ever seeks to rise from the lower to the next highest.⟩⟩ [cancellation in pencil, brackets added in ink]
Who knows

Lines

14   parlor ⟨today⟩ by

17   next ⟨[erasure]⟩ appearance [over erasure]

19   brain⟨s⟩. An [cancellation in pencil]

25   Romans ⟨which⟩ a

27   Meantime with ⟨all⟩ this [cancellation in pencil]

27–28   expressed, & ⟨all⟩ this plastic world of ⟨objects⟩ ↑things↓ [emendations in pencil]

Page 355

5   ↑professional↓ poet, ⟨the⟩ ↑or↓

10–11   ↑And this . . . wrong ⟨or⟩ [erased] respecting their own affairs.↓

12   does what ⟨he⟩ ↑⟨himself⟩ the beholder↓

14–15   ↑begins to↓ love⟨s⟩ him

21–24   ↑For whilst we are able . . . their great ⟨general⟩ [cancellation in pencil] & universal relations.↓

25–27   happens that ⟨we all⟩ ↑the great majority of men↓ seem to be ⟨kept out of ourselves⟩ ↑minors who have . . . their own↓

28–29   ↑To no man is his position in the world↓ To no man are the

34–35   seem ⟨th⟩as if

Page 356

11   poor mens

17   name ⟨stands⟩ ↑clings↓

22   people." he

25   power ⟨in⟩to give

Page 357

12   such a man. ⟨as this⟩. This

15   benediction. — Do

28   those friends who↑m,↓

Page 358

4–5   symbol has a ⟨[?]⟩beauty it has not to other eyes, ⟨& ⟨[?] he[?]⟩ [erased] fills his [over erasure] eye,⟩ & his

9   his dealing. / [At this point, never sewn, but laid into the manuscript, is the following double sheet. It is numbered on the rectos "35" and "36" but does not fit into either pencil or ink pagination of the lecture, though it follows a verso which should have been numbered "34" in the ink sequence. Both rectos are headed "Poet" in ink; at top of first recto, in ink: "(Transcribed in PY 263)".]
Swedenborg had this vice that he nailed one sense to each image; — one & no more. But in nature every word we speak is million faced or convertible to an indefinite number of ap-

513

plications If it were not so we could read no book. For, each sentence would only fit the single case which the author had in view. [in left margin adjacent to next sentence, in pencil and circled: "Fuller"] Dante who described his circumstance would be ⟨i⟩unintelligible now. But a thousand readers in a thousand different years & towns shall read his story, & find it a version of their story.

There is nothing which comes out of the human heart — the deep aboriginal region, — which is not mundane, thousandfaced, — so that if / perchance strong light falls on it, it will admit of being shown to be related to all things. The rose is a type of youth & mirth to one eye, of profound melancholy, of fever, of rushing fate↑,↓ [comma in red pencil] to another. There is nothing in nature which is not an exponent of ↑all↓ nature. /

The sense of nature is inexhaustible You think you know the meaning of these tropes of nature, & today you come into a new thought, & lo! all nature converts itself into a symbol of that; & you see it has been chanting that song like a cricket ever since the creation. Nature is a tablet in which any sense may be inscribed, only not anything cunning, & consciously vicious. Draw the moral of the river the rock & the ocean. The river the rock & the ocean say "Guess again." / [blank] /

16	ripples, the ⟨lights &⟩ form ↑& lights↓
19	balls, or ⟨posts,⟩ ↑pillars,↓ [emendations in pencil]
29–30	eye ⟨after⟩ ↑pines over the↓ colors of a gem, or ⟨of⟩ the

Page 359

8–9	indulge his ⟨finer⟩ veins
11	thoughts prophe⟨c⟩sy, rhythms
19	*certain rights of sanctuary* [underlining in red pencil]
20	music↑, viz.↓ in
22	is the ⟨poor⟩ ↑uncultivated↓
28	lilting [first "l" accidentally crossed]
30	themes. ⟨Yet⟩ the [cancellation in pencil]

Page 360

4	unimportant↑,↓ [comma in pencil]
5	serves a great & ⟨important⟩ office to mankind in keeping ⟨afloat⟩ before the ⟨people⟩ ↑mind↓
6–7	those ⟨great⟩ cardinal truths & ideas [last two words circled] which
9–10	↑for the music's sake↓ are allowed ⟨to⟩ currency in the ↑circles↓

Lines

10   opposite ⟨spirit⟩ ↑creed↓
15   poet ⟨is⟩, as we intimated at the outset, ↑is↓
21   you ↑do,↓
30   new ⟨&⟩ [cancellation in ink] ⟨perfect⟩ [cancellation in pencil] & radiant
32   for it is ⟨a fresh⟩ ↑the last↓

Page 361

4–5   Surprise and ⟨wonder⟩ [cancelled in red ink; retained in text for sense of what follows] always ⟨attend⟩ ↑fly beside↓ . . . they are
9   children of the ⟨great king⟩ ↑new land↓
10   us, that ⟨he was our real parent, &⟩ this ⟨realm & palace⟩ is
12–13   time, ⟨I proceed to say / that there are the highest grounds for for believing that poe⟨s[?]⟩try exists for us⟩. ↑Why not?↓ What
17   repeat ⟨its⟩herself
20   uncelebrated, s⟨a⟩ung the
22   Marriage," ⟨the⟩ Celestial
25   tuneful ⟨f⟩predecessors
26   eye ⟨of⟩ [erased] & [over erasure]
35   comfort or ⟨e⟩outward

Page 362

1   seek for it; ⟨into⟩ we
6   chestnut, ⟨the⟩ oak
11   ↑to the hearers,↓
15   Every ⟨thing⟩ ↑achievment looks↓ ⟨is⟩
27   taught him ⟨by⟩ [erased] in [over erasure] earlier days by the torrent, in ⟨[erasure]⟩ the [over erasure]
28–29   foxes, & ⟨the⟩ [erased] a [over erasure] hunter of the bear. [In addition to the ordinary cross reference to the Riverside Edition for the passage following, there is in pencil, in a hand probably not Emerson's, the following annotation: "Times lect. 6."]
36   patronage never ma⟨[?]d⟩de, & whom
38–(363)1   who has ⟨most⟩ [erased] the [over erasure] most

Page 363

5   nothing in ↑t↓his
7   eloquence. ⟨How he⟩ ↑It↓
22–23   coupling what ⟨I⟩ ↑we↓ do with what ⟨I⟩ ↑we↓ a⟨m⟩re
23–24   search ⟨my⟩ ↑the↓
26   door, — ⟨scatters⟩ ↑adds↓ [emendations in pencil]

Lines

28   life ⟨th⟩ [erased] more [over erasure]

30–31   is to doubt ⟨that day is day⟩ ↑of day & night↓

Page 364

9   them. ⟨As a⟩ ↑In↓

12–13   ↑The Genius . . . many operations.↓ ⟨It is this⟩ one & the same ⟨Spirit which⟩ ↑it↓

14   love of ⟨the⟩ wom⟨en⟩an. ⟨{It is full of romance: the roughest Scythian or Troglodyte of old is not more rude with aboriginal force than this Spirit is.}⟩ It

16   breathe ⟨at this time⟩ ↑it↓

20–21   Universe: {it is the attraction of time:}

25   morning ⟨rich with⟩ [erased] with all [over erasure]

26–(365)13 foregoing time. ⟨{Is there not . . . impertinent melancholy.} But the grandeur . . . than this reality. {Let us thank . . . whilst we slept.}⟩ [This passage has a single ink line drawn diagonally through it but has been retained as conclusion in the present text instead of the incomplete insertion which follows it (see below).]

32   ignorant of this ⟨overwhelming⟩ ↑resistless↓

36   much as a⟨s⟩ ryestraw

Page 365

5   life ↑is↓

9   him of th⟨e⟩at fact

11   walking in ⟨the⟩ flesh

13   whilst we slept.} [Followed by incomplete insertion in another ink:]

     ↑Weak & imperfect & petty as ↑are↓ the individuals, ⟨may be⟩ they are yet overpowered by a great social spirit which consolidates them all into one. To every member of this host has been confided some weapon of the armory of Heaven. They represent in flesh & blood the essences of Justice & Truth & Beauty. Here now they stand for their hour in this great / public square of rational & organized being, children of the pleasant day, or, if you will, Caryatides in the wall of the Temple of Destiny, & so they play their parts. ⟨What wages do these pay for their good lodging in this inn of Nature. What fee to these bounteous elements, these fair lights which hang round us in the deep? ⟨Have they no office to dis⟩⟩ Can we divine nothing brave, nothing mysterious, nothing ⟨o[?]⟩ [erased] noble [over erasure] or sweet in the bearing of this host? No method in their distribution, no purpose in their array? ⟨Let us study them well, let us listen with stillest heed for the signals of command. ⟨for e⟩Each of us ↑is↓ at moments invited to the privy chamber & council of the camp.⟩ Will no minstrel celebrate ⟨these⟩ ↑this↓ wondrous power and explore ↓/

516

8. PROSPECTS

Lines   *Page 367*

[A single leaf never sewn with the rest of the lecture; num-bered "1"–"2" in ink, not numbered in pencil. This intro-duction does not conform precisely to what is known of the order of titles in Boston, Providence, or New York. It does suggest a curtailed series, however, and is reported in Kron-man, pp. 99–100. It may have been written as Emerson planned his readings in Providence and New York.]

I have offered to the indulgent ear of this audience un-der the general head *of the Times* speculations on the sub-ject of Conservatism of Poetry of the new philosophical views that seem to rise with most energy; of ⟨the ch⟩ reverence for character which seems to be the Religion of the day; and on the form which our civilization takes in manners and behavior. I am well aware that many topics more must be included in any proportioned ⟨vie⟩ picture of the Present Age But as my present plan limits me to a few subjects I have selected those which seemed to me most prominent I propose to draw these speculations to some conclusion this evening by taking a general view of the ground on which we stand, the reasons of hope, and the duties, which at this mo-ment seem to occur with most force to intelligent men. / [Be-ginning of lecture as once sewn follows with a double sheet numbered "3"–"6" in ink and "1" in pencil:]

1   There is something

Page 368

1–2   brow. [in left margin and between lines, as if for insert:] ↑A↓ [immediately after, between lines:] ↑Least of all . . . speculative class↓

3   said ⟨Zo⟩ the
4   ↑of the world↓
7   occult ⟨harmonies⟩ ↑symmetries↓
7–8   beauties heral⟨s⟩ds of
13–14   all ⟨her⟩ ↑the↓ kingdoms of chemistry of vegetation ⟨of⟩& an-imal
17   ↑They rather express vigor proportion↓
20   swim, ⟨chop⟩ fell
21   whatsover, With
22–23   spectator, ⟨[?]n⟩ [erased] and [over erasure] yourself also. ↑A true talent . . . possessor first↓
29   whilst ↑the↓

Lines   *Page 369*

3   heartwarmer, a ⟨Does not threaten⟩ [in pencil] sign of health
             [in ink over pencil]
5–6   stamp. / ⟨Be⟩ [erased] What delights, . . . what scares [two
             lines begin over erasure]
8   {Beauty is . . . so that}
9   bully, I know it is ⟨a⟩ [erased] weak [over erasure]
13   strong and ⟨like the ancien⟩ we . . . the ancient
17   For ↑whilst we contemplate it↓ {dwelling there in its depths}
             ⟨I⟩ ↑we↓ find ⟨[partial "m"]⟩ourselves
27   earth the ↑plants↓ animals the
30   ↑so much as↓
32   degree of ⟨happiness⟩ ↑enjoyment↓ / [pages 11–14 missing
             from ink sequence; pencil "4" missing]

                                 Page 370

1   as in Mid [end of line] summer
3   and our ⟨good⟩ famous
7   them; ⟨but⟩ ↑only↓
10–12   victories. ↑We are he⟨[?]⟩lped by our very foibles ⟨& sins⟩
             ↑& sins,↓↓ Like the water in ⟨an⟩the riddle,
16–18   remarkable of ⟨them⟩ all our solitides
             ⟨Insert passage from Lect VII Nature p[?]⟩
             ↑To push these documents of the cheerful riches the redun-
             dant spirits of Nature to a little extreme, — does not Nature
             sometimes appear as if inclined a little to droll with us? Ex-
             aggeration is one of her laws. ⟨{Insert P. & Q.}⟩ [cancelled in
             pencil]↓ [insertion rejected as revision for later reading] /
             [pages 17–22 missing from ink sequence; no lacuna in pencil
             sequence] ↑To push th⟨i⟩ese documents of the cheerful riches
             the redundant spirits of Nature to a little extreme↓
                Does it not
20–21   so that ⟨it seems to stereotype⟩ every perversity of ours ⟨in
             the human generation⟩ ↑presently incarnates itself in a man↓
22–23   and ↑war or↓ when trade has ⟨organized itself⟩ existed
24   ↑warriors or↓
26–27   fit for ⟨holes⟩ ↑wheels↓ & pins in all the ⟨nooks⟩ ↑chinks↓
27–29   machine. / She ⟨makes scholars who⟩ ↑will a scholar inapt
             for every thing but his office of scholar↓ a⟨re⟩ lens⟨es⟩ that
             ha⟨ve⟩s no power but at the⟨ir⟩ focus;

                                 Page 371

1   our ⟨politics⟩ ↑holidays↓
3   tete a tete
3–4   ↑& dilates↓
7   ↑Marshals she delights to make.↓
10   ↑annual↓

PROSPECTS

Lines

12 ↑in that dignified assembly↓

14–15 delights in ⟨making⟩ ↑manufacturing↓ antiquaries genealogists ↑rattle brains↓

16 her chips / [blank] / [pages 27–28 missing from ink sequence; pencil "7" missing]

17 pours her ⟨riches⟩ ↑energy↓ into human ⟨nature⟩ [erased] beings [over erasure]

19–20 travellers in ⟨th⟩some parts

22–23 but cotton↑, — ↓qualities of cotton↑,↓ [punctuation in pencil] ↑long staple & short staple↓

25 man ⟨than⟩ in

25–27 ↑alive to more human interests, ⟨greatly⟩ ↑much↓ the best companion of the two;↓ ⟨than one of⟩ [erased] & how should he not be, ⟨[?]⟩since

29 flags wh⟨er⟩ither come

Page 372

12 elasticity ⟨w⟩that

13–14 his own. / How much more . . . may be done. [used as insertion below] / The opulence

15–16 every ⟨occupation⟩ study & occupation ↑to↓

17 day ⟨Herrick's⟩ ↑the↓ Poems ↑of R. Herrick↓

18 Poetry, know, not

22–25 nature. [insertion from previous page; no point of insertion indicated:] ↑How much more . . . has done is ⟨the⟩ a . . . may be done.↓

26 and the ⟨pow⟩ charm

32 each ⟨th[?]⟩ [erased] blissful [over erasure]

33–(373)5 doth lie. ↑S↓ [at bottom of page, marked "S":] ↑But whilst I am taught . . . leads me, ⟨what⟩ I know . . . the region.↓

Page 373

10 their ⟨fountains⟩ spring?

18–24 planets / ⟨And of this richness & extent the Age seems to me to partake. I see it capacious undefinable far retreating still renewing as the depths of the horizon appear when seen from the hills.⟩ [end double sheet numbered "9" in pencil and "33"–"36" in ink] / [leaf numbered "37"–[38] in ink; not numbered in pencil:]

I will not like the Indian ⟨Bramin⟩ ↑god↓ in the Bhagavad Gita, seek to impress you with the ⟨opulence⟩ ↑affluence↓ of the world by enumerating ↑by name↓ all the things in it; ⟨by name⟩, but Nature is rich, only our words are poor. We must stand silent if we would appreciate this wild & waste fer-

519

tility this opulence bursting its garners on every side. Well what [word once cancelled, but cancellation erased] ⟨must correspond to this in man⟩ is the lesson which this plenitude must teach? What but joy, what but congratulation, wonder, & trust? What ↑attitude in man↓ must correspond ⟨in man⟩ to this overrunning riches? Reception; Reception & transmission of the same, which in man is forwardness, the act of going forth, the forward foot, the forward hand, the religious upward eye, the indefatigable brain, the loving striving heart. /

⟨Come let us ⟨sit down⟩ ↑up↓ & learn the ample lesson. The lesson is long and the time is Eternity to learn it in.⟩ The whole difference between men is whether the foot is advancing or receding. An ample lesson we have to learn and the time is Eternity to learn it in. But whilst nature opens & grows & bestows & aspires man pauses, appropriates, fortifies the old, resists the new.

↑If Nature is so large Man should be as large. ⟨&c {s}⟩ If nature is so generous, man shd. not be timid, a drudge of custom & of rules. Yet here in this country where nature yields her riches with such an open hand; in these Times, when the slow yet advancing spirit of the race has thrown off so many external checks, & made, as it w⟨d⟩ould seem, a condition friendly to freedom each individual seems to contrive to load himself with a chain for every one he breaks, so that freedom & grandeur of spirit in a man, — heaven speaking out of a form of clay — is nowhere to be met with.↓ / [double sheet numbered "10" in pencil, "39"-"42" in ink:]

⟨Well what is the lesson of ⟨thi⟩ [erased] all [over erasure] this wild & waste fertility this opulence bursting ⟨out of⟩ its . . . to learn it in.⟩ [passage retained in present text because of rejection of later revision] Everything

28	Is any [end of line] thing
33	before ⟨they⟩ ↑the early pilgrim↓ ha⟨ve⟩s yet
34	Road, ⟨[erased]⟩ he [over erasure] encounters

Page 374

1	↑explored &↓
5	seen ⟨a child⟩ ↑children↓
9	which every [end of line] body
11	↑even↓
13	↑or whatever spectacle . . . to us↓
15–17	cannot see ⟨now Y⟩ for this preposterous haste to ⟨give an opinion⟩. ↑say somewhat.↓ Your wits are preoccupied with ⟨what⟩ ↑the opinion↓ you should ⟨say.⟩ ↑give↓ ⟨You see with your memory. & not with eyes. which God in this hour gives you.⟩ Like the poor magneti⟨c⟩sed
22	↑the Empire of↓

24–25 country. ⟨and in these times⟩   As
28   kind,↑ — ↓play what⟨soever mad⟩ prank, indulge what⟨ever⟩
      spleen
31   horses ⟨spoil themselves⟩ ↑are spoiled↓
32   best ⟨writers⟩ ↑authors↓

Page 375

3   can they? They ⟨are⟩ have
4–5   book ⟨will⟩ of such a size, with such topics, & such ⟨authe⟩
      quotations and ⟨put⟩ ↑sent↓
6   publishers, is a a good
8   And ⟨t[?]⟩had this
10   ↑higher↓
14   provinces, — ⟨village Crichtons⟩ ↑Caesars in Arden,↓
18   I speak ⟨of course⟩ of
21–22 another ear / ⟨that could⟩ ↑sufficiently fine to↓
27–28 for the gods.
      ↑But in speaking of their intellectual education ⟨it will⟩
↑we must ⟨not⟩ [erased]↓ not omit to mention the appetite
for eloquence which in common with all republics has
evinced itself here & made↓ [added in different ink; end
double sheet, also sewn elsewhere, numbered "11" in pencil
and "43"–"46" in ink] / [blank, numbered "47" in ink, not
numbered in pencil] / ["48" in ink, not numbered in pencil;
marked "R" for insertion below:] ↑It is to be regretted
⟨r⟩when Church & State must have the aid of a fine genius.
The loss is irreparable. Could they not manage to do with
less costly materials? He is a Church & a State himself &
should not desert the priesthood of ideas. Nature is rich,
but to a defender of the establishment, to a fixture, to one
who has halted & sat down, she gives nothing; only to the
Marchers, only to the Actors, only to the Innovators. ⟨As
you⟩ Which class interests us? The Forward class have this
good, that every thing they do & say, their mere presence
has great significance, gives rise to comic & picturesque sit-
uations, suggests tho'ts, & is worthy of record by the histor-
ian: whilst the life & actions of the wittiest defender of the
establishment, has nothing generative, but is tame   For the
last always rest on a fact, whilst the first always rest on a
thought.↓ ["The Forward class . . . on a thought" (J, 17)]
/ [double sheet numbered "12" in pencil and "49"–"52" in
ink:]
      We take sides with th⟨is⟩e same
29   our ⟨[?]⟩shoulders
32   golden ⟨scale⟩ measuring wand
35–(376)1 put on. ↑{Insert R}↓ [above, omitted as not belonging to
      the earlier pagination]
      ⟨But t⟩Those who

Lines	*Page 376*
4–6	small ⟨fact⟩ & well known fact of ↑that good order . . . we know.↓ ⟨{his ⟨land⟩ warranty deed & certificates of stock, bales of cotton & barrels of flour⟩. But
14	all ⟨is little⟩ ↑dwarfs & degrades;↓
15	fuss, ⟨and a friskiness⟩ and
17–26	require. / ↑Insert L↓ [see below; emendations rejected as not belonging to earlier reading version]

⟨This ⟨fact to which we have adverted of the⟩ exuberance of nature . . . representative of all ⟨its being⟩ ↑time↓. Of this richness & prodigality the Present Age ⟨the Times⟩ seem . . . from the hills. ⟨How shall man be put in harmony with his place & duties.⟩⟩ [end double sheet numbered "12" in pencil and "49"–"52" in ink] / [leaf, never sewn with others, numbered "53"–"54" in ink, not numbered in pencil; marked "L" for insert above:]

↑The exuberance of Nature is offered in turn to every individual man. The Eternity of Nature is represented to him in the short limits of a human life. The opportunities of the physical & metaphysical worlds come to ⟨him⟩ us ⟨in⟩ ↑under↓ the aspect of the Present Age. It opens itself before us↓ / [blank] / [leaf numbered "55"–"56" in ink, not numbered in pencil:] It opens itself before us ever larger & larger. An unit in the procession of Ages, heir of all the past, it is the mother of all that shall follow. Is it for us who at the present day find ourselves not expressed in the literature, the science, the religion of our fathers, to be ashamed of that fact? If we find new thoughts of a deeper origin, hopes of a bolder wing, thronging into the mind, shall we deny them;↑?↓ or shall we assume the new duties to which we are called with meekness, yet with courage? The inevitableness of the New Spirit is the grand fact, and *that* no man lays to heart, or sees how the hope & palladium / of mankind is there; but one blushes & timidly insinuates palliating circumstances — for a new thought, — & one ridicules the foible or absurdity of some of its advocates. But on comes the God to confirm & to destroy, to work through us if we be willing, to crush us if we resist. ["The inevitableness of the New Spirit . . . if we resist" (H, 2)] It may well become us then to consider a little how shall man be put in harmony with his place & duties. / [double sheet numbered "57"–"60" in ink and "13" in pencil:]
For that culture then which ⟨the⟩ every

Page 377

| 4–5 | impossible. ⟨t⟩The very Spirit of the Time, this ⟨Genius of⟩ Conscience |

PROSPECTS

Lines	
5	already ⟨a⟩their
6	with the ⟨old⟩ ↑first↓
7	hard to ⟨see⟩play well
14–27	{If our sleeps . . . mar the harmony.}
24	still & ↑to↓
31	should not be to be surprised
33–34	unbeliefs ⟨by being instructed himself to be the⟩ ↑& made the↓

Page 378

2	infancy ⟨& every day⟩ with
3	mens
4–5	built on ⟨this⟩ ↑a↓ planet swimming ⟨in⟩ [erased] unpiloted [over erasure] in ⟨a f⟩ [partially erased] the frightful [over erasure]
7–8	boundless⟨, endless⟩ Wonder
11	cunning ⟨superficial⟩ web
14	We ⟨all⟩ deceive
16	↑old↓
17–18	college ⟨and⟩ ↑or a military . . . can give.↓
24	West; Well
26	men ⟨wh⟩ [erased] among
30–31	{A man has more coats than an onion.}
31–32	superficial & [partial letter] They
33–(379) 1	↑What if friendship should?↓

Page 379

2	expedients ⟨just⟩ ↑much↓
11	mutable; to ⟨hold⟩ ↑carry↓
12–13	flieth, & ⟨only to ⟨[?]⟩converse with⟩ in
14	reach of ⟨all⟩ skepticism.[cancellation in pencil]
16	as if {⟨all our life,⟩} whatever
21	let him ⟨stand⟩ meet
22–33	individuals by ⟨[?]⟩inexplicable attraction↑s↓ {has she made his . . . scholars, ⟨the⟩ his . . . he beholds;} Let him accept with ⟨a great⟩ ↑equal↓

Page 380

1–2	intends ⟨h[?]⟩ [erased] it [over erasure] advertises
2–3	fall And thus it does; All
4	give for an / [pages 69–74 missing from ink sequence; pencil "14" missing; words supplied in text from W, III, 275]
7	peep oer
8	Society ⟨itself instructs⟩ when
21	not in that. ⟨Now⟩ I
23	make a ⟨man⟩ ↑mind↓. they
26–27	{A personal influence is an *ignis fatuus*;}

Lines	Page 381
5–6	Being, ⟨by⟩ which
7–8	every [end of line] thing is permitted to love, ⟨that⟩ ↑whilst↓ man cannot serve man too far, ⟨that⟩ ↑whilst↓
17	but the ⟨mome⟩ instant
18	{by the necessity of thought}
22	but that ⟨I⟩ [erased] you [over erasure]
29–(382)5	originality. ↑{Insert R}↓ [at bottom of opposite page, marked "R":] ↑{That which is best in nature, . . . sex or accident.}↓ [end insertion "R"] ⟨for t⟩The ministrations

Page 382

9	hope, ⟨it is⟩ our
10	asseveration⟨s⟩ of this Prophetic Heart. [two horizontal lines and passage marked "R" for insertion above]

FRAGMENTS FROM "THE TIMES"

[A few leaves from other lectures in the series on "The Times" are doubtless among the miscellaneous leaves printed in the textual notes of this volume. Those with Lectures 4, 5, and 6 of "The Present Age" merit particular attention. See also textual notes for page 362, lines 28–29, and page 370, lines 16–18. Below are printed three single leaves which are filed together and identified on an enclosing double sheet, in a hand not Emerson's, as "Fragments (supposed) of Lectures on the Times 1841?"]

[A single leaf of paper like that of other lectures in "The Times"; never sewn; numbered "17" in pencil at top and "16" in pencil at bottom of recto; labelled at top of recto "Character" and additionally headed "onward!" both in ink:]

It is not quite elegant to change the conversation of a circle & bring it to topics on which only two or three can converse; nor to divide the company too suddenly or too long into *tête* a têtes; nor to speak French in English society; — nor in any way unkindly to exclude the major part of a company from your discourse but one mode of securing a privacy is always elegant, to raise the tone of sentiment to that height as to leave all the degrees of vulgarity far below you — to carry off — where none can breathe but the great & good into the difficult air of truth & selfdenial   The privacy of true glory protects you. / [blank] /

[A single leaf of paper which was once second leaf of double sheet with above leaf; once sewn; numbered "8" in pencil at bottom of recto; labelled at top of recto "Character" in ink and "representative" in pencil:]

I see only two or three persons & allow them all their room; they spread themselves at large to the horizon. If I looked at many as you do, or compared these habitually with others, these would look less. Yet are they not entitled to this magnificence? Is it not their own? And is not munificence the only insight?

Our exaggeration of all fine characters arises from this, that we identify each in turn with the soul. Presently the individual warps & shrinks away, & we accuse him. Hard to find an ideal in history. By courtesy we call saints & heroes such, but they are very defective characters: I cannot easily find a man I would be. / [blank] /

[A single leaf of different paper; once sewn; recto numbered "85" and verso "86" both in ink:]

Every truth is thousandsided — universally applicable — Every drop of blood has ↑(shall I say?)↓ great talents. The original vesicle, the original cellule seems identical in all animals, & only varied in its progress by the varying circumstance which opens now this kind of cell, & now that, causing, in the remote effect, now horns, now wings, now scales, now hair; and the same numerical atom, it would seem, was equally ready to be a particle of the eye or brain of man, of the claw of a tiger, /

In the body of a man, all those terrific energies which belong to it, the capability of being developed into a saurus, or a mammoth, or a baboon that would twist off mens heads, or a grampus that tears a square foot of flesh from the ²whale or ¹grampus that swims by him, — are held in check & subordinated to the human genius & destiny. — But it is ready at any time to pass into other circles, & take its part in baser or in better forms; Nay, it seems that the animal & the vegetable texture are at last alike. Well, as thus the drop of blood has many talents lurking /

525

Index

This index is for the complete three-volume set of the *Early Lectures* and supersedes those in the first two volumes. Editorial references, whether in footnotes or elsewhere, are marked with an "n" to distinguish them from Emerson's references in footnotes and text. Only a few selected items are included from the textual notes. References to Emerson's writings are grouped under "Emerson, Ralph Waldo," by subheadings: "JOURNALS," "LECTURES," "LETTERS," "WORKS."

Abernethy, John, I, xx, 2n; II, 133n;
  Physiological Lectures, II, 247n, 367n
Abolition, *see* Slavery, Abolition of
Abolitionist, III, 477
Abraham, II, 178
Absolute, The, I, 226, 384; II, 354–355;
  III, 453, 454
Abstemiousness, I, 199
Abstinence, III, 482
Abstractions, I, 216, 219, 223; Meta-
  physical, II, 13; Moral, III, 215
Achilles, II, 154
Action(s), I, xix, 107, 119, 120, 142,
  181, 186, 187, 198, 219, 225, 226,
  273, 302, 315, 328, 364, 378; II,
  4, 42, 45, 55–56, 59, 106, 114, 132,
  145, 146, 150, 156, 158, 166, 218,
  224, 245, 299–300, 304, 314, 355;
  III, 11, 18, 19, 20, 37, 39, 62, 70,
  87–88, 112, 124, 138, 144, 150, 155,
  156, 158, 225, 245, 266, 267, 268,
  284, 300, 302, 311, 350, 363, 381;
  Accepted Modes of, III, 97; Counter-
  action, III, 155; Genuine, III, 311;
  Half, II, 240, 296; Immortal, III,
  269; Law of, I, 370; II, 144; Moral,
  III, 118, 119; Necessary, III, 369;
  Past, III, 310; Right, II, 86, 87; III,
  280; Spontaneous, II, 250; III, 137,
  281; Total, II, 296; Virtuous, III,
  149; Wrong, II, 87
Actor(s), III, 7, 188, 242, 521
Actual, The, I, 144; II, 4, 217–220,
  248, 280–281, 336, 343, 347; III,
  54, 94, 251
Adam, I, 138, 160, 161; II, 62; III,
  67, 295, 312, 330

Adams, John Quincy, II, 60; III, 311
Addison, Joseph, I, 148, 149, 213, 216,
  259, 276, 306, 310, 356n, 366, 384,
  483; II, 67, 141; III, 375; *Spectator*,
  I, 366, 483n; II, 141n
Adige River, I, 43
Admetus, II, 105
Admiration, III, 41
Adventitious, The, II, 47
Aeneas, III, 231
Aeolian Harp, II, 200; III, 104, 357
Aeschylus, II, 51, 455
Aesop, II, 126, 153n
Aesthetic Papers, III, xx
Affection(s), I, 79, 143, 157, 190, 191–
  192, 352, 353; II, 85, 102–103, 227,
  229, 245, 249, 278–295, 321; III, 32,
  43, 53, 56, 62, 67, 68, 82, 104, 111,
  114, 155, 156, 187, 188, 197, 228,
  275, 287, 459; Discipline of, I, 140;
  Divine, III, 52; First, II, 85; Law of,
  II, 318; Natural History of, III, 170;
  Progress of, III, 63; Social, I, 138
Africa, I, 31, 42, 256; III, 206, 227
African, II, 160, 253, 352; III, 154
Agamemnon, II, 134; III, 12
Agamenticus (York), Me., III, 193–
  194n, 456
Agassiz, Louis, I, xxi; II, 33
Age, The, *see* Present Age, The
Agesilaus, I, 140n, 167n; II, 70
Agis, I, 140; II, 170
Agnes, Saint, I, 121
Agrarianism, II, 73
Agrippa von Nettesheim, Henry Cor-
  nelius, I, 332; III, 169, 213; *De Oc-
  culta Philosophia*, I, 332n; III, 169n

Ahriman, I, 79
Ahura Mazda, *see* Ormazd
Aikin, John, I, 215; *Evenings at Home,* I, 18n
Ajax, II, 154
Alabama, III, 135
Aladdin, II, 361; III, 168
Alanus, I, 241
Alaric, II, 20
Albert, Archbishop of Mentz, I, 120
Alchemy, II, 68; III, 168
Alcibiades, II, 16, 91, 420; III, 97
Alcott, Amos Bronson, I, 208n, 337n; II, 192n, 455; III, xii, 1n; *Conversations with Children on the Gospels,* II, 192n, 210n; *Doctrine and Discipline of Human Culture,* II, 210n; *Psyche,* II, 210n
Alexander the Great, I, 254, 256, 330; II, 11, 15, 76, 241; III, 68, 69, 88, 116, 122, 230, 474
Alfieri, Vittorio, I, 117, 242
Alfonso X, King of Leon and Castile, III, 130
Alfred the Great, I, 138, 150, 244, 248, 250, 251, 252, 286; II, 60, 79, 132; III, 240; trans. Boethius, *De Consolatione Philosophiae,* I, 244–245
Algiers, II, 165n; III, 211
All, The, II, 32, 259, 266; III, 31, 124, 300; Encroaching, III, 104; Good of, III, 106; *see also* Whole, The
Allegheny Mountains, I, 54; III, 135
Allegory, I, 222, 253n, 257–261, 290; II, 47; *see also* Analogy; Symbol(s), Symbolism
Allen, William, *An American Biographical and Historical Dictionary,* II, 333n, 367n
All Souls' Day, III, 188
Allston, Washington, II, 48, 480
Almack's, London, I, 278
Alps, I, 44, 48, 52; II, 17, 118; III, 155, 380
Alternation, III, 170
Amadis of Gaul, I, 260
America, I, 31, 74–75, 201, 233, 277, 278, 381, 382; II, 12, 14, 54, 56, 80, 97, 116, 128, 138, 139, 165, 166, 167, 224, 237, 325, 337; III, 8, 10, 66, 75, 187, 195, 208, 261, 265, 311; Discovery of, I, 255, 385
American(s), I, 75, 195, 273; II, 77, 112, 174; III, 367–368, 374
American Character, I, 233

American Churches, III, 194
American Colonization Society, II, 82n
American Institute of Instruction, I, xxii, 205n, 209n, 210n, 217n
American Journal of Education, I, xx
American Language, I, 75
American Literature, I, 75, 212, 215–216; III, 82, 375
American Mind, I, 277; III, 217
American Peace Society, III, xi, xx
American Revolution, I, 75, 186; III, 225
American Scholar, I, xix, 381
American Society for the Diffusion of Useful Knowledge, *see* Society for the Diffusion of Useful Knowledge, Boston
Ames, Fisher, I, 472
Amici, Giovanni Battista, I, 2n
Ammon, Priests of, III, 122
Ampère, André Marie, II, 38
Amphitheatre, III, 220; Roman, II, 53
Anabasis, II, 134n
Analogy, I, 25, 220–221, 224, 289–291; II, 26, 29, 33–34, 37, 50–51, 60, 73, 180, 234, 253; III, 158, 204, 228, 283, 295; *see also* Allegory; Correspondence; Symbol(s), Symbolism
Analysis, III, 188–190, 195–197, 454, 455, 457, 460; Age of, III, 453, 454
Analyst(s), The, III, 191, 198
Anatomy, I, 71, 102–104, 108; II, 24, 27–28, 33, 265; III, 168; *see also* Physiology
Anaxagoras, II, 38, 175
Ancient(s), The, I, 348; II, 11, 136, 154, 168, 187, 264; III, 6, 88, 126, 160, 204, 250
Ancient Mariner, I, 214
Andes, I, 52, 73; II, 118n, 171; III, 28, 78, 240
Andover, Mass., III, 294
Andromache, II, 62
Aneurin, I, 239
Anglo-Saxon Chronicles, I, 134, 248
Anglo-Saxon Language, I, 238, 248–249, 253–254
Anglo-Saxon Literature, I, 243–248, 251–252, 253
Anglo-Saxons, I, 134, 138, 213, 237–238, 241–252, 253, 276, 360; II, 52, 131, 197
Angra Mainyu, *see* Ahriman
Animal(s), I, 61–62; II, 24, 26–27, 247; III, 154; Domestication of, I, 42–43;

Relation to Human Mind, I, 79–80; Relation to Man, I, 10, 27, 33, 34–35, 42–43; II, 253; Succession of, I, 30–31

Animal Magnetism, I, 10, 332; II, 167, 253; III, 167–168, 451

Anlaff, I, 243

Anne, Queen of England, I, 366

Antaeus, I, 11

Antenor, III, 12

Antigone, III, 105

Antimasonry, I, 216; III, 257; Idea of, I, 219

Antique, The, I, 348; II, 20, 134

Antiquity, I, 358; II, 38, 265; Spirit of, III, 6

Antislavery, see Slavery, Anti-

Antoninus, see Marcus Aurelius Antoninus

Anusherwan, II, 152n, 425

Apicius, II, 163

Apollo, I, 222; II, 105, 224; III, 24, 93, 126

Apollo, The Belvedere, I, 104 (?); II, 49, 270; III, 73 (?), 76 (?), 80 (?)

Apparent, The, II, 62, 217, 248, 297

Appearance(s), I, 154, 162, 168, 260, 381; II, 89, 245, 249, 302; III, 25, 56, 86, 111, 132, 225, 252, 311, 352

Apuleius, III, 61

Aquinas, Saint Thomas, I, 212

Arab(ians), II, 118, 179; III, 19, 105, 144

Arabia, I, 42

Arabian Nights' Entertainments, I, 8, 79; II, 59; III, 293

Arabius, Mt., I, 256

Ara Coeli, Stairs of, I, 106

Arago, Dominique François, I, 2n

Arbela, Persia, II, 241

Archidamus, II, 170

Archimedes, I, 21, 284; III, 368

Architecture, I, 100; 104; II, 4n, 36, 45–46, 52, 58–59, 63–64; III, 77, 84, 93, 220, 227; Gothic, II, 36, 52, 63; III, 220; Greek, II, 52; III, 72; Laws of, II, 64; Roman, II, 44, 53, 269–270

Arcola, Italy, III, 116

Arctic, The, I, 41, 59, 61

Ariadne, I, 283

Aristarchus of Samos, I, 284

Aristides, II, 131, 140

Aristocracy, I, 194; Natural, I, 276–277

Aristocrat, II, 70

Aristophanes, III, 511

Aristotle, I, xx, 114, 131, 162, 189, 215, 229, 285, 302, 342, 384; II, 43, 59, 66, 110, 184, 255; III, 45, 123, 125n, 240; *De Partibus Animalis*, II, 43n, 184n; *Physica*, II, 43n; *Poetics*, II, 59n, 110n

Arkwright, Sir Richard, II, 18

Armenia, II, 134

Arminius, I, 353

Art(s), I, 72–73, 78, 89–90, 99–117 *passim;* II, 4n, 14, 20, 36, 42–60, 73, 94, 96, 112, 132, 143, 181, 187, 200, 217, 263–270, 315, 352; III, 45–46, 57, 73–74, 79, 84, 92–93, 95, 100, 133, 233, 251–252, 298, 314–315; Fine, I, 104; II, 43–49, 55, 58; Greek, II, 14, 177; III, 95; History of, II, 19, 42–43; Law of, II, 44–45, 48, 51; Nature and, I, 72–73; Plastic, III, 60; Useful, I, 104; II, 43–45, 48–49, 55; see also Painting; Sculpture

Artemidorus Daldianus, *Oneirokritica* (trans.: *The Judgement, or Exposition of Dreames* and *The Interpretation of Dreames*), III, 169n

Arthur, King, I, 239, 241, 254, 256, 257, 265

Artist(s), I, 73, 100, 102, 114, 152; II, 46–51, 266; III, 92, 225, 233, 350, 355, 483; see also Painter(s)

Ascham, Roger, I, 355

Asia, I, 31, 238; II, 7, 76, 112, 335; III, 97, 227, 490

Asiatic Races, I, 238, 242

Aspiration, III, 200, 216–218, 241–242, 245, 269

Assyria, II, 178; III, 225

Assyrian Empire, III, 7, 78, 188

Assyrian Era, II, 225

Assyrian Monarchy, I, 250

Astley, John, III, 132

Astrology, III, 191

Astronomy, I, xvii, 18, 25, 28, 29, 46–48; II, 32, 38, 184, 354; III, 30, 49, 84, 117, 168; Copernican System of, III, 71; Ptolemaic System of, III, 130, 306

Asylum, III, 99, 117–118, 369

Atalanta, I, 259

Atheism, I, 180; II, 343; III, 36, 490

Athelstan, Ode on the Victory of, I, 233n, 243–244

Athenaeum, Boston, see Boston Athenaeum

Athenians, II, 133, 335

Athens, II, 12, 54, 131, 159
Atlantic Bank, Boston, III, 176n
Atlantic Ocean, I, 61; II, 31; III, 143
Atlas, Mt., III, 230
Atmosphere, Adapted to Man, I, 32–33
Attila, I, 141
Aubrey, John, I, 150, 151, 301, 325; *Letters . . . and Lives of Eminent Men*, I, 151n, 390n
Augsburg, Imperial Diet of, I, 122n; III, 246
Augsburg Confession, I, 127, 135
Auguries, III, 156, 201
Augustan Period, II, 157
Augustine, Saint, I, 380, 383; II, 16; III, 192, 208, 209, 231; *The City of God*, I, 383n; *Confessions*, III, 231n
Austin, Sarah, *Characteristics of Goethe*, I, 29n, 72n, 80n, 286n, 389n; II, 16n, 126n, 265n, 367n
Australasia, II, 214; III, 187
Australasians, II, 73
Austria, II, 14
Avesta, *see* Zend-Avesta

Baal, III, 100
Babylon, III, 211, 398
Bacon, Sir Francis, I, xx, 31, 114, 132, 149, 160–161, 162, 184, 187–189, 212–213, 214, 215, 222, 224, 230, 259, 285, 306, 315, 316, 318n, 320–336, 337n, 338, 353, 358, 361, 369; II, xiii–xiv, 60–61, 67, 78, 118n, 148–149, 226, 252, 260, 284n, 333n; III, 45, 46, 71, 90, 166, 212, 225; *The Advancement of Learning*, I, 162n, 328n, 329–330; II, 118n, 333n; "Apophthegms," II, 118n; *De Augmentis Scientiarum*, III, 166n; *De Sapientia Veterum*, I, 259n; *Essays*, I, 149, 321, 333–335; *Historia Densi et Rari*, III, 71n; *History of Henry the Seventh*, I, 322; "In felicem memoriae Elizabethae," I, 316n; *Instauratio Magna*, I, 329–333, 334; II, 61; "Letter to Earl of Devonshire," I, 324n; "Medical Remains," III, 212; *Natural History*, I, 335, 358; III, 71n; *Novum Organum*, I, 210, 317–318, 320n, 321, 326n, 327n, 330–333, 335–336, 338, 353; II, 60, 226n; III, 71n; "Of Building," I, 334; "Of Ceremonies and Respects," I, 334; "Of Deformity," I, 334n; "Of Friendship," I, 334n; "Of Gardens," I, 334; "Of Great Place," I, 334; "Of Masques

and Triumphs," I, 334; "Of Studies," I, 334; "Of Travel," I, 334; "Of Truth," I, 333n; *Works*, I, 391n; II, 367n; III, 385n
Baglioni, Malatesta, I, 106
Bailey, Nathan, *Dictionarium Britannicum*, III, 353
Baltimore, Md., I, 419; III, 353; Emerson lectures in, I, xxii; III, v, xv, 337n, 345n, 366n
Baptism, I, 181–182; III, 279
Baptistery, Florence, I, 117
Barbarossa (Khair-ed-Din?), I, 130
Barbauld, Anna Letitia: "The Brook," III, 370n; *Evenings at Home*, I, 18n
Barclay, Robert, I, 172–173; *Apology for the True Christian Divinity*, I, 173n
Bard(s), I, 243, 340, 356; III, 298–299; British and Welsh, I, 239; *see also* Poet(s)
Barker, Anna, III, xii
Baroni, Leonora, I, 151
Barrow, Isaac, I, 337n, 369; II, 60
Barry, James, I, 191, 192
Bartram, William, II, 22n
Battas, II, 57
Bayadere, III, 350
Bayard, Pierre Terrail de, II, 140, 335
Beaumont, Francis, I, 300, 306, 309, 316, 338; II, 327–329, 334; *see also* Beaumont, Francis, and John Fletcher
Beaumont, Francis, and John Fletcher: *Bonduca*, II, 327; *Four Plays, or Moral Representations, in One*, II, 327n, 329n; *The Triumph of Honor*, II, 327–329; *see also* Fletcher, John
Beauty, I, 6, 19, 49, 100–102, 104, 110–115, 154, 348, 382–385; II, 45, 54, 144–145, 171, 181, 215, 224, 245, 262–277, 282, 299, 311–312, 358, 359; III, 59–62, 79–80, 81, 94, 117, 140, 171, 203, 214, 222, 253, 358, 368–369, 419, 458, 516; Eternal, III, 96; Fountain of, III, 315; Ideal, III, 112, 235; Idea of, I, 100; Idea of Intellectual, I, 231; Laws of, I, 383; II, 51, 263, 318; Moral, II, 294; of Nature, I, 24, 73–74, 83; of the World, I, 6; of Use, II, 245; Sentiment of, III, 190; Universal, III, 280
Becket, *see* Thomas à Becket
Beethoven, Ludwig van, III, 9, 84, 217
Behmen, *see* Böhme, Jakob
Behring, *see* Bering, Vitus

Being, I, 219, 296–297, 328; II, 86, 171, 200, 224, 225, 339, 342, 343, 358; III, 30, 47–48, 66, 249–253, 281; and Seeming, II, 79, 95, 150–151, 295–309; III, 226; Chain of, II, 50; Law of, III, 381; Law of Man's, I, 382; II, 171, 200; III, 381; Universal, III, 234; *see also* Divine Being; Highest Being; Supreme Being

Bel, III, 308

Belgium, I, 237

Belief, II, 96–97; Ages of, II, 96; Periods of, III, 222

Belisarius, III, 231

Bell, Sir Charles, *The Hand*, I, 40; II, 182n–183, 367n; III, 115n, 385n

Bell, John, *Observations on Italy*, I, 89n

Bellarmine, Robert, I, 353

Bellingham, Richard, I, 179

Belus, II, 178

Belzoni, Giovanni, III, 30, 157, 206; *Narrative of the Operations and Recent Discoveries . . . in Egypt and Nubia*, III, 30n, 157n, 385n

Benares, Rajah of, I, 195

Benedict XIV, Pope, I, 109

Benefit, III, 149–150

Benevolence, II, 155, 188, 216; Sense of, II, 344; Universal, III, 63

Beni, Paul, I, 367

Bentham, Jeremy, II, 67, 97, 289; III, 140, 225

Bentley, Richard, I, 357, 377; II, 65, 164; III, 194, 206

Beowulf, I, 248

Béranger, Pierre-Jean de, I, 449; II, 62

Bering, Vitus, II, 175

Bering Strait, I, 31

Bernardin de Saint-Pierre, Jacques-Henri, II, 154n

Berni, Francesco, I, 115

Berserkers, I, 242, 243; II, 131

Bertinazzi, Carlo-Antonio, III, 137

Bertrand, Alexandre, I, 10n

Best, The, I, 72; II, 354–355

Bethel, Seamen's (Father Taylor's), III, 362–363n

Better, The, II, 217–218, 229; III, 107, 182n, 257

Beza, Theodore, I, 353

Bhagavadgita, III, 105, 519

Biagioli, Giambattista, ed., *Rime de Michelagnolo Buonarroti il Vecchio*, I, 99n, 115n, 390n; III, 79

Bias, II, 100, 181

Bias of Priene, I, 14, 358

Biber, Edward, *Henry Pestalozzi and His Plan of Education*, III, 307n, 385n

Bible, I, 125, 126, 128, 129, 132, 170, 172, 176, 273, 286, 307, 360; II, 59, 61, 95, 112, 126, 346; III, 84, 101, 199, 204–205, 277; Acts, II, 278n, 296n; Apocalypse, I, 292; I Chronicles, II, 333n; I Corinthians, I, 289n; II Corinthians, III, 279n, 304n; Decalogue, I, 135; English, I, 307; Epistle of John, I, 121; Ezekiel, I, 132; Galatians, I, 121, 136, 138; Genesis, II, 32, 71n, 197n; III, 144n; Isaiah, II, 277n; III, 304n; James, I, 121; Jeremiah, I, 135, 137; Job, I, 139, 302; II, 257n; John, II, 219n; III, 304n; I Kings, III, 193n; Lord's Prayer, I, 249; Luke, II, 62n, 152n; Mark, II, 62n, 258n; Matthew, II, 90n, 258n, 355n; III, 263n, 304n; New Testament, III, 279; Proverbs, I, 335; II, 152n, 202n; Psalms, I, 129, 175, 248; II, 51; III, 269; Revelation, I, 224n, 292, 293n; I Samuel, II, 115n; Sermon on the Mount, II, 90; Songs of David, II, 51; Ten Commandments, I, 135, 136

Bigelow, Charles C., II, 357n

Bigio, Nanni di Baccio, I, 106

Bigot, Emeric, I, 151

Billerica, Mass., III, xiv, 336n

Biography, I, 75–76, 79, 93–201; III, 283

Biot, Jean Baptiste, I, 2n

Birmingham, Eng., I, 236

Black, Joseph, I, 59

Black Hawk, III, 128

Black Hawk War, II, 227n

Blackmore, Sir Richard, I, 212; II, 65; III, 206

Blackstone, Sir William, *Commentaries on the Laws of England*, II, 59

Blair, Hugh, *Lectures on Rhetoric and Belles Lettres*, I, 215

Blank Verse, I, 308–309

Blessing of the Bay, The (ship), II, 128

Blosius, Caius, II, 290–291

Boar's Head, The, Eastcheap, London, 306

Boccaccio, Giovanni, I, 117, 270, 284

Bodenstein, *see* Carolstadt

Bodin(e), Jean, III, 213

Bodleian Library, Oxford University, III, 405

Body, I, 40, 79, 103, 115, 178, 289, 299–300, 334, 368; II, 88–89, 130, 133, 136, 183, 188, 199, 228–229, 263–264; III, 32, 39, 52, 61, 64–65, 106–107, 121, 160–161, 252–253, 525

Body Politic, II, 12

Boece, Stephen de, II, 290

Boethius, I, 244, 279, 286

Bohemia, Kingdom of, III, 243

Böhme, Jakob, I, 378; II, 92; III, 80–81n, 451, 490

Boileau, Nicolas, *L'Art poetique*, I, 102n

Bolingbroke, Henry St. John, Viscount, II, 75n

Bologna, Italy, I, 105

Bonaparte, *see* Napoleon

Bonduca, III, 21

Boniface VIII, Pope, III, 191

Books, I, xix–xx, 130–131, 186, 210–216, 262, 382; II, 59–60, 65–66, 112, 149, 165–166, 213, 260–261, 342, 360–361; III, 11, 34, 35, 37, 43–47, 51, 92, 97, 168, 170, 202–211, 229, 230–232, 234–236, 265, 289, 298, 314, 382, 405, 456–457; *see also* Literature

Borgia, Caesar, II, 15, 334

Born, Catharine of, *see* Luther, Katherina von Bora

Boscovich, Ruggiero Giuseppe, II, 29

Bossuet, Jacques Bénigne, II, 60

Boston, Mass., I, 70, 77, 87n, 88n, 179, 371n, 419; II, 130, 207n; III, 39, 162, 204, 209, 264, 320n, 326n, 340n, 408; Emerson lectures in, I, xiv, xv, xvi, xxi, xxii, 5, 27n, 50n, 88n, 93n–94n, 205n, 207n, 209n, 210n, 217n, 253n, 269n, 287n; II, xi, xxi, 7n, 22n, 41n, 55n, 69n, 83n, 98n, 113n, 129n, 143n, 157n, 173n, 205n, 207n, 210n, 212n, 213n, 230n, 246n, 262n, 278n, 295n, 310n, 327n, 340n, 357n; III, xi, xiii, xiv, xv, xvii–xviii, xx, xxv, 5n, 23n, 34n, 51n, 68n, 85n, 103n, 121n, 138n, 151n, 173n, 175n, 176n, 179n, 183n, 185n, 202n, 224n, 238n, 248n, 256n, 271n, 286n, 302n, 335n, 336n, 337n, 338n, 340n, 341n, 347n, 366n, 367n

Boston Athenaeum, I, 145n, 287n; II, 3n, 22n; Emerson lecture at, I, 50n

Boston Bay, II, 335

Boston Daily Advertiser and Patriot, I, 5n, 97n, 98n, 144n, 205n, 209n, 253n; II, xxi, 205n; III, xxv, 2n, 173n, 271n, 333n, 367n

Boston Daily Evening Transcript, I, 27n, 144n

Boston Library Society, I, 269n

Boston Mechanic's Institution, I, xxii, 50n

Boston Medical College, III, 457

Boston Society of Natural History, I, xv–xvi, xxi, 5, 10, 69, 70; III, 131 (?)

Boswell, James, *The Life of Samuel Johnson*, I, 213n, 366; II, 314n

Boswellism, II, 307

Botany, I, 11, 46, 74, 75–76; II, 23–28; III, 30, 38, 145, 373

Botany Bay, Australia, I, 243

Botherwell, Dr., III, 131

Boundary Wars, III, 257

Bourbon(s), II, 20; III, 352

Bourke, William, I, 192

Bowditch, Nathaniel, I, 12

Bower, Alexander, *The Life of Luther*, I, 118n–139n *passim*, 390n

Bowring, Sir John, II, 289n

Boy and the Mantle, The, I, 260

Boyle, Robert, I, 358

Boylston Hall, Harvard University, III, 151n

Bradford, George P., III, 131n

Bradley, James, III, 49

Brahmin(s), I, 79, 166, 224; II, 89, 177; III, 519; *see also* Hindoo(s)

Bramah, Joseph, I, 67

Bramante, Donato d'Angnolo, I, 106n, 111, 114

Brant, Joseph, III, 472

Brasidas, II, 329

Brattle Street, Boston, Unitarianism of, III, 325n

Brawner, J. P., "Emerson's Debt to Italian Art," I, 99n

Brayton, Deborah, I, 164n

Brewster, Sir David, I, 75

Bridgewater, Francis Egerton, Third Duke of, II, 125

Briefe an Johann Heinrich Merck von Göthe, Herder, Wieland und andern bedeutenden Zeitgenossen, II, 276n, 315n, 367n; III, 130n, 221n, 385n

Brindley, James, II, 125

Bristol, Eng., I, 195

Britain, I, 237–241; II, 17; III, 399; Kingdom of, III, 78

British Language, I, 238, 253

British Poetry, see Welsh Poetry

Britons, I, 238–241

Brittany, I, 241

Brittin, N. A., "Emerson and the Metaphysical Poets," I, 337n

Brodie, George, II, 81; III, 225

Brompton, Eng., I, 81n

Brook Farm, III, 323n, 339n

Brougham, Henry Peter, Baron Brougham and Vaux, I, xx

Brown, Thomas (1663–1704), III, 90n

Brown, Thomas (1778–1820), Lectures on the Philosophy of the Human Mind, I, 74n, 389n; II, 154n, 367n

Browne, Sir Thomas, I, 361, 369; III, 208; Religio Medici, I, 361; Works, Including His Life and Correspondence, III, 192, 212–213, 385n

Brownson, Orestes, III, 325n

Bruce, James, III, 206

Brummell, George Bryan ("Beau Brummell"), II, 307; III, 133

Brunelleschi, Filippo, I, 114

Bruno, Giordano, I, 380

Brutus, Marcus Junius, II, 333

Brutus the Trojan, I, 265

Bryant, Jacob, I, 357

Buccaneers, I, 42, 237

Buckingham, George Villiers, First Duke of, I, 323, 325, 365; II, 138

Buckland, William, I, 47

Buffon, Georges Louis Leclerc, Comte de, I, 18, 221, 289

Bugenhagen, see Pomeranus

Bukharia, II, 332

Bulwer-Lytton, Edward George Earle Lytton, First Baron Lytton, I, 212; II, 62, 65; III, 206

Bunker Hill, III, 353

Bunyan, John, I, 260, 302, 361; II, 59, 60, 65; III, 80, 82; The Pilgrim's Progress, I, 361; III, 49–50

Buonarroti, see Michelanglo Buonarroti

Burckhardt, John Lewis, III, 206–207n

Burke, Edmund, I, xx, 94n, 146, 158, 183–201, 213, 222, 223, 276, 369; II, 60, 67, 78, 140, 163, 241, 301; III, 459; Discourse concerning Taste, I, 191; Letter to the Sher-

iffs of Bristol, I, 197; Letters on a Regicide Peace, I, 369; "The Perfect Wife," I, 191; A Philosophical Inquiry into . . . the Sublime and Beautiful, I, 184; Reflections on the Revolution in France, I, 196n; Speech for Bill for Repealing the Marriage Act, I, 194; Thoughts on the Cause of the Present Discontents, I, 197; A Vindication of Natural Society, I, 184; Works, I, 183n, 197n, 198, 391n

Burkhardt, George, see Spalatin

Burleigh, see Cecil, William

Burns, Robert, II, 65, 101, 316, 329; III, 82; "Epistle to Davie: A Brother Poet," II, 101n; "Tam o'Shanter," III, 318

Burton, Robert, The Anatomy of Melancholy, III, 213, 385n

Busen Island, I, 237

Butler, Joseph, I, 213, 369; II, xiv, 358n; III, 230

Butler, Samuel, I, 275; "A Degenerate Noble," II, 163n; The Genuine Remains in Prose and Verse, II, 367n; Hudibras, I, 275; II, 343n; III, 37n, 128–129

Button's Coffeehouse, London, I, 216

Buttrick, David, II, 323n

Byron, George Noel Gordon, Lord, I, xvi, 272, 274, 277, 311n, 350, 371n, 372–374; II, 126, 287; III, 1n, 17, 104n, 196, 216, 217, 218, 222, 231; Childe Harold's Pilgrimage, I, xvi, 89n, 242n, 372–374, 422n; Don Juan, I, 350n, 373n; The Island, I, 374; III, 231n; Sardanapalus, I, 311n; II, 324n; "The Siege of Corinth," III, 104n; The Vision of Judgment, III, 129; Works, I, 391n

Cabinet of Natural History, I, 81–82; see also Jardin des Plantes

Cabot, James Elliot, I, xiii, xxiii, xxiv, 27n; II, xvi; III, xviii, xxiii, 34n, 51n, 271n, 286n, 302n, 327n, 347n, 367n; A Memoir of Ralph Waldo Emerson, I, xxiv, xxvi, 5n, 28n, 50n, 69n, 87n, 89n, 97n, 205n, 206n, 209n, 217n, 233n, 253n, 419n; II, xvii, xix, 41n, 173n, 194n, 327n, 357n; III, xx, xxi, 51n, 183n, 271n, 320n, 324n, 347n, 366n–367n

Cadmus, I, 218

Caedmon, I, 248
Caesar, Caius Julius, I, 107, 234, 330; II, 8, 11, 138, 241, 316; III, 37, 60, 69, 97, 225, 231, 232, 242, 373, 375, 472, 474, 477
Caesars, Age of, II, 17
Caesars in Arden, III, 375
Cailliaud, Frédéric, III, 206–207n
Cain, I, 170; II, 342
Calculation, II, 281–282; Man of, II, 281; III, 166; Power of, III, 15
Calcutta, India, II, 147
Caldani(a), Floriano, I, 2n
Calling, *see* Vocation
Calmuc, *see* Kalmuck
Calvin, John, I, 2n, 118n; II, 214, 346
Calvinism, I, xvi; II, 2n, 25; III, 141, 187
Calvinist, II, 346
Calvinistic Churches, II, 92, 214; III, 274, 275
Calvinistic Prayermeeting, III, 489
Cambridge, Mass., I, 77; II, 246n, 262n, 327n; III, 294; Emerson lectures in, I, xxii; II, xi, 207n, 230n (?), 278n, 295n, 310n (?), 340n; III, xi, xx, 1n, 151n
Camden, William, I, 338
Camden Society, III, 198
Cameron, Kenneth W.: *Emerson the Essayist,* I, 5n, 27n, 50n, 88n, 89n, 96n, 97n, 98n, 144n, 183n, 209n, 217n, 218n, 220n, 287n, 320n, 331n, 356n, 359n, 365n, 371n, 419n; II, 3n, 211n–212n; *Ralph Waldo Emerson's Reading,* I, 1n, 4n, 97n, 145n, 184n, 287n; II, 4n, 22n, 212n, 301n, 319n; III, 30n
Campbell, Thomas, I, 268
Campeche, I, 45
Camper, Pieter, II, 28; III, 130
Canas the Piper, III, 368
Candolle, Augustin Pyrame de, I, 3n, 8; II, 22n
Canning, George, II, 138
Canova, Antonio, I, 104; II, 46
Cant, III, 298
Canton, China, II, 116
Canute, I, 250
Cape Verde Islands, I, 37
Capitalist, The, III, 108
Capital Punishment, II, 68; III, 10
Capitol, The, Rome, I, 106
Capitol, The, Washington, D. C., II, 54

Capitoline Museum and Gallery, Rome, I, 98n
Caponigri, A. Robert, "Brownson and Emerson: Nature and History," II, 2n
Capresi, Italy, I, 100
Capuchins, III, 278
Cardan, Girolamo, III, 212, 213
Carey, Matthew, I, 216n
Cariban Indians, I, 39; II, 112
Carlini, *see* Bertinazzi, Carlo-Antonio
Carlstadt, *see* Carolstadt
Carlyle, Thomas, I, xviii, xix, 2n, 3n, 94n, 118n, 207n–208n, 371n, 381n; II, 3n, 113n, 207n, 209n, 211n, 321n, 329, 357n; III, xii–xiv, 175n, 321n, 335n, 338n, 339n, 343n; "Characteristics," II, 101n; *Chartism,* III, xii; *The French Revolution,* III, xii, xiii, 210n; *History of Frederick the Great,* III, 130n; "Jean Paul Friedrich Richter Again," I, 123n, 390n; *The Life of Friedrich Schiller,* I, 230n, 389n; "Luther's Psalm," I, 123n, 126n, 390n; *Miscellanies,* III, xii; *On Heroes, Hero-Worship, and the Heroic in History,* I, xviii; *Sartor Resartus,* I, xvi, 164n; *Wilhelm Meister's Apprenticeship,* I, 326n; *Wilhelm Meister's Travels,* I, 227n; *see also* Emerson, Ralph Waldo, LETTERS
Carnot, Lazare Hippolyte (?), III, 498
Carolstadt (Andreas Rudolph Bodenstein), I, 123, 129
Carthage, III, 225
Cary, Henry Francis, trans. *The Vision; or Hell, Purgatory, and Paradise, of Dante Alighieri,* II, 351n
Casaubon, Isaac, I, 353
Castelli, Benedetto, I, 18
Castor and Pollux (constellation), III, 482
Cathedral(s), Cologne, II, 59; English, II, 52; Florence, I, 114, 117; Gothic, II, 52, 54, 268; Lincoln, II, 272; Strasburg, II, 59; York, I, 235
Catholic Church, *see* Roman Catholic Church
Catiline (Lucius Sergius Catilina), II, 13, 16; Catilinarian walk, III, 112
Catlin, George, I, xxi
Cato, Marcus Porcius (Cato the Censor), I, 165n; II, 75, 136; *De Agri Cultura,* II, 136n

Caucasian, II, 352

Caucasus, Mt., I, 238, 258; II, 7–8

Caucus, II, 214; III, 234, 299

Causa Causans, I, 80

Causation, Stable, III, 27–28

Cause, II, 247–248; III, 26, 29–30, 72, 76, 144, 155, 156, 197–198, 226, 242, 329, 490; Aboriginal, III, 144; Absolute, II, 248, 297, 348; and Effect, II, 224, 248, 352; III, 30, 38, 46, 48, 64, 145–146, 203, 272, 331, 363; Final, II, 29, 37; First, II, 43, 140, 296, 298, 353; III, 363; Great, III, 252; of All, III, 29; of All Beings, I, 167; of Causes, II, 249, 352; of Me, III, 30; One, I, 75; III, 455; Our, III, 30; Permanent and Partial, III, 228; Region of, III, 314; Self-Existing, II, 248; Spiritual, III, 72; Sublime, III, 233; Supreme, III, 75; Ultimate, III, 14

Cavalieri, Tommaso di, I, 110

Cavendish, Henry, I, 52n

Caxton, William, I, 284

Cecil, Robert, Earl of Salisbury, I, 315, 316n, 323, 328

Cecil, William, Lord Burghley, I, 315, 316n, 323 (?)

Cellini, Benvenuto, Bust of Bindo Altoviti, I, 114

Celtic Poetry, I, 239–241

Celts, I, 234, 238–241

Central Soul, *see* Soul, Central

Cerdic, I, 241

Ceres, I, 154; II, 234; III, 24

Cervantes Saavedra, Miguel de, I, 212; III, 82; *Don Quixote*, II, 60, 63; III, 125

Chaldean(s), I, 12, 71

Champollion, Jean François, II, 178, 226

Channing, William Ellery (1780–1842), I, xvi; II, xiv, 280n; III, 319n, 324n, 326n

Channing, William Ellery (1818–1901), I, 208n; III, 209n

Chaos, II, 14; III, 113, 139

Chapman, George, I, 315, 337n, 338, 341, 355

Character, I, 18–23, 160–161, 291, 331, 364–365; II, 8, 129–132, 137, 141, 146, 148, 161, 179, 196, 216, 218, 220, 226–228, 229, 239–240, 263, 265, 269, 299, 304, 327–331, 337–338, 340; III, 11, 13, 18–19, 21–22, 32, 33, 35, 42, 52, 85, 108, 115, 117, 118, 125, 126, 144, 155–157, 166, 170, 171, 197, 223, 230, 235, 241, 242–245, 247, 251, 253, 260, 262, 269, 270, 275, 276, 280, 282, 290, 292, 309, 311, 349, 357, 369, 479, 483

Charity, I, 192–193; II, 155, 214, 297; III, 6, 63, 96, 118–120, 193, 266

Charlemagne, I, 250, 254

Charles I, King of England, I, 146n, 147, 159, 338, 361; II, 138n, 183

Charles II, King of England, I, 170, 176; III, 465

Charles IV, Emperor, II, 102

Charles V, Emperor, I, 105, 123–126 *passim*, 129, 213; II, 154; III, 230

Charles XII, King of Sweden, I, 107

Charles Augustus, Grand Duke of Saxe-Weimar-Eisenach, II, 315

Charleston, S. C., I, 70, 419

Charlestown, Mass., I, xxii

Charleval, Charles-Fauçon de Ris, Seigneur de, "Ballade," III, 57n

Charvat, William, *Emerson's American Lecture Engagements: A Chronological List*, II, 7n, 173n, 207n, 213n; III, xx, 1n, 176n, 341n, 347n

Chastity, I, 155, 161, 363

Chateaubriand, François René, Vicomte de, III, 218

Chatham, *see* Pitt, William, First Earl of

Chaucer, Geoffrey, I, 4n, 46, 213, 214, 221, 230, 233n, 251, 263, 265, 268, 269–286, 356, 357, 381; II, 62, 67; III, 17, 81, 214; *The Book of the Duchess*, I, 281; "The Canon's Yeoman's Prologue," I, 282n; *The Canterbury Tales*, I, 275–283; "The Clerk's Prologue," I, 283n; "The Clerk's Tale," I, 281; "The Franklin's Tale," I, 280; "General Prologue," I, 46n, 275, 283n; *The House of Fame*, I, 270, 273, 284; "The Knight's Tale," I, 282, 283n; "Lak of Stedfastnesse" (?), I, 274–275; "The Legend of Ariadne," I, 282; "The Man of Law's Tale," I, 283; "The Nun's Priest's Tale," I, 275–276, 284; "The Physician's Tale," I, 282; "The Prioress's Tale," I, 283; *The Romaunt of the Rose*, I, 284; "The Squire's Tale," I, 282–283; *Troilus and Criseyde*, I, 284;

"The Wife of Bath's Tale," I, 278–280; *The Works,* ed. F. N. Robinson, I, 270n

Chaucer, Philippa, I, 270

Chayma Indians, I, 45–46

Chee Koong, III, 118

Cheetham Societies, III, 198

Chemist, The, I, 48, 53; III, 25, 75, 77, 360, 373

Chemistry, I, 25, 32, 46, 52; II, 29, 30, 33, 314; III, 145, 289, 368; Laws of, I, 78; II, 30

Cherokee Indians, II, 130

Cherubim, II, 281, 284

Chesterfield, Philip Dormer Stanhope, Fourth Earl of, I, 150, 367; II, 307

Chickasaw Indian, I, 272

Chickering's Hall, Boston, I, 287n

Child(ren), Childhood, I, 20–21, 192, 201, 259; II, 42, 120–121, 177–178, 302, 306, 314; III, 9, 26, 32, 98, 168, 217, 233, 258, 259, 295–296, 358–359

Chilo, I, 358

China, III, 187, 243

Chinese, I, 212; II, 52, 130, 160, 178; III, 395

Chladni, Ernst Florens Friedrich, II, 29

Cholula, Mexico, II, 178

Chorley, Henry F., ed., *Memorials of Mrs. Hemans,* III, 60n, 357n, 385n

Christ, *see* Jesus

Christendom, II, 97, 128, 130, 165, 175, 214; III, 187, 225, 272, 277

Christian(s), I, 135, 170; II, 108, 175, 256, 258; III, 273

Christian Era, II, 133; III, 273

Christianity, I, 155, 156, 242, 262; II, 82, 106, 142, 152, 175, 224; III, 205, 235, 240, 272–276, 299

Church, The, I, 119–143 *passim,* 174, 176, 356; II, 90–94, 169, 310; III, 11, 91, 128, 179n–180n, 187, 197, 228–229, 234, 238, 251, 252, 258, 260, 263, 287, 314, 360, 375, 457, 521; *see also* Calvinistic Churches; Church of England; Independents; Lutherans; Methodists; Presbyterians; Protestants; Quakers; Roman Catholic Church; Swedenborgians

Church of England, I, 175, 176, 177; III, 274, 459

Church of the Disciples, Boston, III, 325n

Cicero, Marcus Tullius, I, 197, 273; II, 75; III, 46; *De Officiis,* I, 359; *Tusculanarum Disputationum,* III, 27n

Cid, The, III, 210

Cimmerians, I, 238

Cincinnati, Ohio, I, 419

Circumstance(s), I, 13, 14, 130–131, 184, 188, 227, 263, 337, 358; III, 11, 143, 144, 156, 157, 188, 203, 242, 253, 269, 291, 307, 314, 358, 379

Cities, I, 219; II, 271, 273, 275; III, 42; Compared with Country, I, 20–21, 76–77

City Bank, Boston, III, 337n

Civilization, I, 76, 280; II, 82, 102, 112, 118, 128, 136; III, 106, 330

Civilized Man, I, 76; II, 174–175

Civil Liberty, I, 147, 159

Civil War, English, III, 7

Clarence, Lionel of Antwerp, Duke of, I, 270

Clarence, William, Duke of (later William IV, King of England), III, 254

Clarendon, Edward Hyde, First Earl of, I, 213, 276, 280, 356n, 361, 363–365; II, 140; III, 8; "The Difference and Disparity between the Estates and Conditions of George Duke of Buckingham and Robert Earl of Essex," II, 138n, 367n; *The History of the Rebellion and Civil Wars in England,* I, 213n, 363–365, 391n; II, 169n, 367n; III, 8n, 385n

Clarke, Edward Daniel, *Travels in Various Countries of Europe, Asia, and Africa,* I, 374

Clarke, James Freeman, III, 325n

Clarkson, Thomas, III, 243

Classics, The, II, 187; III, 88; *see also* Literature

Classification, I, 47, 80; II, 4n, 22–25, 252; III, 38, 129, 131, 140–141, 352

Claverhouse, *see* Graham of Claverhouse, John

Clay, Henry, III, 135–136n

Cleobulus, I, 358

Cleopatra, II, 265; III, 97, 373

Climate, I, 34, 44; II, 122–123, 130, 237, 313–314, 316; III, 11, 40, 170

Coal, I, 16, 33–34; II, 26–27

Cobbett, William, II, 67

Cobham, Lord, *see* Oldcastle, Sir John

Cochelet, Mlle., *Mémoirs sur la Reine Hortense et la Famille Impériale,* III, 134, 386n

Cochran Rifle, II, 286

Coincidences, II, 359; III, 151, 156, 157
Coke, Sir Edward, I, 323–324
Coleridge, Samuel Taylor, I, xviii, xix, 3n, 4n, 69n, 97n, 118n, 192, 206n, 207n, 228, 276, 280, 287n, 310, 371n, 377–380; II, 3n, 48, 67, 97, 167, 209n, 211n, 258, 456; III, 80, 98, 196, 217, 218, 226, 459; *Aids to Reflection*, I, 379; *Biographia Literaria*, I, 177n, 192n, 310n, 350n, 378n, 379n, 389n; III, 36n, 385n; "The Destiny of Nations: a Vision," I, 25n; "Essay on Wit," III, 123; *The Friend*, I, 81n, 82n, 133n, 191n, 192n, 207n, 228n, 277n, 296n, 320n, 362n, 376n, 378, 379, 389n; II, 110n, 179n, 367n; *The Literary Remains*, III, 123n, 385n; *On the Constitution of the Church and State*, I, 134n, 379, 389n; *The Poetical Works of Coleridge, Shelley, and Keats*, III, 218; "The Rime of the Ancient Mariner," I, 214; *Specimens of the Table Talk*, I, 101n, 276n, 280n, 310n, 389n; II, 264n, 367n; III, 80n, 98n, 385n; *The Statesman's Manual*, I, 219n, 228n, 362n, 389n; II, 78n, 367n
Collections of the Massachusetts Historical Society, III, 128n
College(s), I, 210, 216; II, 202; III, 197, 234, 294, 371
Collins, William, III, 82
Cologne, Germany, I, 124; Cathedral, II, 59
Colonization, Society of, II, 106; *see also* American Colonization Society
Colonna, Vittoria, I, 115; III, 144
Colorado River (Venezuela?), I, 45
Colquhoun, John C., trans., *Report of the Experiments on Animal Magnetism, Made by a Committee of . . . the French Royal Academy*, I, 10, 332; III, 169
Columbus, Christopher, I, 119, 250, 385; II, 18, 51, 56, 175, 306, 335, 359; III, 101
Combe, George, I, xxi
Comedy, I, 343; II, 9; III, 121–137, 152, 251
Comic, The, I, 304; II, 359; III, 171; *see also* Comedy
Commerce, I, 27, 41, 196, 233, 403; II, 14, 108, 128, 130, 161; III, 177n, 190–191, 196, 219, 227, 302, 454, 455; Age of, III, 190, 454; Amer-

ican, III, 196; *see also* Trade; Trades and Professions
Commercial Bubbles, I, 216
Common Sense, I, 256, 300, 305; II, 34, 37, 62, 67, 90, 249, 259, 311, 316; III, 72, 225, 359; *see also* Good Sense
Commonwealth, The, II, 76; Ideal, II, 70; Inward, II, 68; Outward, II, 68
Communities, The, III, 441
Comparative Anatomy, *see* Anatomy; Physiology
Compensation(s), I, 383; II, 68, 79, 127, 152–156, 171, 174–175, 180, 184, 333; III, 33, 44, 114–115, 145–150, 252; *see also* Asylum; Relief(s)
Competition, III, 42
Composition, I, 73–74, 101, 229, 317–319; II, 63–66; III, 33, 146, 202; Law(s) of, I, 317; II, 64–66
Conception(s), I, 165; and Idea, I, 378
Conchology, I, 74
Concord, Mass., I, 87n, 93n, 183n, 205n, 208n, 209n; II, 207n, 262n, 340n; III, xi–xii, 1n, 335n; Emerson lectures at, I, xvi, xxii, 27n, 69n, 87n–88n, 97n–98n, 183n, 205n, 209n; II, xi, 7n, 83n, 113n, 129n, 143n, 207n, 213n, 230n, 246n, 278n, 295n, 310n, 327n; III, xiii, xiv, 1n, 23n, 51n, 68n, 85n, 103n, 121n, 151n, 176n, 185n, 202n, 238n, 248n, 256n, 271n, 286n, 302n, 336n, 341n, 347n
Concord Lyceum, I, xx; Emerson lectures at, *see* Concord, Mass.
Condition, II, 357n; III, 21, 34, 35, 40–41, 43–44, 47, 51, 72, 88, 116, 119, 138–139, 146, 148, 154, 170, 349
Condivi, Ascanio, I, 115
Conformity, III, 308–311
Confucius, I, 166, 212, 280n; II, 88, 94, 95, 104, 150, 282, 283n; III, 118, 144, 224; *The Works of Confucius*, trans. Joshua Marshman, II, 88n, 94n, 104n, 150n, 282n, 368n; III, 119n, 386n
Congdon, Charles T., *Reminiscences of a Journalist*, I, 87n
Congress of Nations, II, 82; III, 257
Connecticut River, II, 335
Conscience, I, 126, 129, 133, 154, 158, 166, 243, 266; II, 344; III, 190, 377, 477; Common, II, 73; Eternal, III,

286; Outward, III, 112, 379–380; Poet's Professional, I, 274; Power of, I, 231

Consciousness, II, 57, 68, 99, 260–261, 343, 352; III, 28, 37, 47, 245; Common, II, 352; Double, I, 161, 325; III, 155; Fluid, III, 292; Infinitude of, II, 201; Morbid, II, 170

Conservatism, I, 190–196; II, 197–198; III, 187, 344n, 375–376

Conservatives, II, 81; III, 460; *see also* Establishment(s); Past, Party of

Consistency, III, 310–311

Constance, Council of, I, 124n

Constantinople, II, 316; III, 188

Constitution, American, II, 43

Constitution, British, I, 194; III, 459

Constitution of Man, I, 40, 71; II, 76, 130, 136, 200–201; III, 87, 91–92, 105, 152, 234, 290, 313, 355, 358; Mental, II, 130, 201; III, 91; Moral, II, 201; Physical, I, 40; II, 130, 136

Continental Drift, I, 31

Convention(s), III, 82, 90, 102, 273, 303; in Art, II, 47; Social, I, 376; III, 91; *see also* Custom(s); Tradition(s); Usage(s)

Conversation, I, 151–152, 190–191; II, 100–101, 289–293; III, 15, 19, 42, 55, 95–96, 103, 249, 280, 286–287, 292, 298–300, 360, 381, 524; Laws of, II, 292

Conway, Moncure Daniel, III, 23n

Cooke, George Willis, *An Historical and Biographical Introduction to Accompany The Dial*, II, 357n; *John Sullivan Dwight*, III, 321n, 323n, 324n; *Ralph Waldo Emerson*, I, 87n, 88n

Coolidge House, Concord, I, xvi, 209n; III, xii

Copernicus, Nicolaus, I, 284; II, 184; III, 306, 311

Coptus, Egypt, I, 259; III, 158

Cordilleras, *see* Andes

Cornwall, II, 227

Correggio, Antonio Allegri da, I, 152

Correspondence, I, 23–26, 27, 44–49, 72, 101, 220–225, 289–292, 327, 404; II, 7, 25–26, 73, 155, 177, 233, 235, 266–267; III, 28; *see also* Analogy; Symbol(s), Symbolism

Cossacks, II, 159

Cotton, Charles, I, 362; *see also* Montaigne, Michel Eyquem de

Country, I, 44, 113; Compared with City, I, 20–21, 76–77; Love of, I, 6

Courage, II, 285–286, 322

Courtesy, II, 320; III, 490

Cousin, Victor, I, 2n, 96n, 97n, 459; II, 3n, 97, 258; III, 48, 226; *Cours de l'histoire de la philosophie du XVIIIᵉ siècle*, I, 97n; II, 3n; *Cours de philosophie . . . Introducton à l'histoire de la philosophie*, II, 3n; III, 105n; *Introduction to the History of Philosophy*, trans. H. G. Linberg, II, 3n; III, 105n

Coventry, Sir Thomas, I, 365

Cowley, Abraham, I, 213, 349, 353; "Of Greatness," I, 11n; "Resolve to be Beloved," III, 65n

Cowper, William, I, 308; II, 316

Coxe, William, *Memoirs of the Life of Walpole, Earl of Orford*, III, 13n

Crabbe, George, I, 192–193, 206n; III, 218; *The Library*, I, 193; *The Village*, I, 193

Crabbe, George (son), I, 193; *The Life of the Rev. George Crabbe*, I, 192n, 391n

Crashaw, Richard, I, 355

Creation, I, 71, 72, 80–82; II, 29, 34, 184, 247, 265, 276; III, 45, 55, 73, 87, 91, 195, 242; Laws of the, I, 82

Creator, The, I, 26, 68; II, 18, 352; III, 65, 214, 233, 243, 364, 381

Credit, II, 242; III, 305–306

Creek Indians, II, 8

Crete, III, 243

Crichton, James, III, 521

Crime(s), I, 318, 321, 385; II, 330; III, 89, 145, 148–149, 164, 254, 356, 374

Criticism, I, 215, 297, 315, 348–349, 353, 354, 375–376, 384; III, 214, 225–226, 233–234, 348; Laws of, III, 177n–178n, 200; *see also* Literature

Croesus, I, 250; II, 118

Cromwell, Oliver, I, 132, 151, 170, 365; II, 169; III, 225, 240, 372

Crucifixion, The, III, 247, 478

Crusades, The, I, 254, 262

Ctesiphon, Mesopotamia, III, 340n

Cuba, I, 237; III, 477

Cudworth, Ralph, I, 213, 332, 356n, 365; III, 194; *The True Intellectual System of the Universe*, I, 215n, 359n, 391n; II, 43n, 184n, 367n

Culture, II, 199, 208n–212n, 213–230, 233–234, 246–247, 276, 278, 281,

293–294, 297–298, 311–312, 330, 337, 358; III, 2n, 28, 31, 79, 94, 192, 290, 303, 330, 364, 376, 399–400; End of, III, 22, 249; Ideal, II, 362; Intellectual, III, 37; Higher, II, 310; Human, II, 266, 269, 310, 340, 346, 355; III, 24, 241; of Soul, III, 250, 252; of Spirit, III, 250; *see also* Education

Custom(s), I, 226–228, 229, 303, 346, 377, 384; II, 129, 143, 187, 304, 358, 364; III, 11, 33, 82, 87, 90, 94, 109, 189, 210, 226, 227, 234, 263, 265, 272, 304, 312, 490; Power of, I, 231; *see also* Convention(s); Tradition(s); Usage(s)

Cuvier, Baron Georges Léopold, I, 1n, 3n, 18, 25, 31, 47, 50n, 61, 80, 132; II, 33, 37, 39, 126; III, 168; *A Discourse on the Revolutions of the Surface of the Globe*, I, 1n, 43n, 47n, 48n, 389n; *Règne Animal*, I, 47–48n; *see also* Lee, Sarah

Cynddylan, I, 240

Cyneward, I, 247

Cyrus the Great, I, 330 (?)

Cyrus the Younger, I, 150, 330 (?); III, 140

Daemon, I, 134; II, 284; III, 160–161; of Socrates, I, 172; II, 284

Daguerre, Louis, III, 339n

Dampier, William, I, 28n, 37–38, 39, 45n; *Lives and Voyages of Drake, Cavendish and Dampier*, I, 37, 38n, 39n, 45n, 390n

Danes, I, 241–242

Dante Alighieri, I, 112, 115, 274, 293, 321; II, 62, 264; III, 233–234, 361, 514; *Paradise*, II, 351n

Dares Phrygius, I, 254, 284

Dark Ages, I, 134; III, 200

Dartmouth College, III, 371n; Emerson oration at, I, xxii; III, xx

Darwin, Erasmus, I, 274

David, I, 175, 248; II, 51, 61, 93, 333; III, 142

Davy, Sir Humphrey, I, 25, 32, 80, 333; II, 18, 29, 37; III, 168

Death, I, 115–116, 171, 173, 312; II, 144, 155, 298, 338–339, 357n, 359; III, 11, 27, 33, 40, 96, 99, 104, 108–109, 119, 143, 247, 287; Angel of, III, 106; Fear of, II, 354; III, 109, 253

Debi Sing, I, 198

de Candolle, *see* Candolle, Augustin Pyrame de

Decius, Caius Messius Quintus Trajanus, Emperor, I, 256

Declaration of Independence, I, 285; II, 60, 213–214

Decorum, I, 175; II, 142, 161–163, 169, 304, 325; III, 180, 211

Defoe, Daniel, II, 254; III, 82; Robinon Crusoe, III, 258

Degerando, *see* Gérando, Joseph Marie de

Deities or Demons, II, 357n; *see also* God(s)

Deity, I, 103, 134, 154, 360; II, 96, 346; III, 49, 277; Temple of, I, 378; *see also* God

Delos, III, 338n

Delphi, Oracle at, III, 148

Democracy, II, 71, 214; III, 304

Democrat, III, 187

Democratic Tendency, I, 190; II, 67, 160; III, 9–10

Demoniacal, The, III, 163–164

Demonology, I, 332; II, 68, 357n, 359; III, 151–171, 191, 213, 450–451; *see also* Magic; Superstition

Demosthenes, I, 184, 198, 199; II, 111, 163

Dempster, Thomas, II, 164

Dennie, Joseph, I, xix

de Prony, *see* Prony, Gaspard Clair François Marie Riche de

Design, I, 17, 27–49, 68; II, 25, 34–35, 51

Despair, Ground of, III, 106

Despondency, II, 97, 170–171; III, 104

de Staël, *see* Staël-Holstein, Anne Louise Germaine Necker, Baronne de

Destiny, II, 58, 359; III, 105–106, 139, 156, 165, 254, 258, 314, 364, 516, 525

De Thoyras, I, 378

De Tocqueville, *see* Tocqueville, Alexis Charles Henri Maurice Clérel de

Devens, Samuel A., III, 320n

Devil(s), I, 121, 132–133, 135–136, 175, 242; II, 68, 94, 360; III, 213, 454

Devonshire, Charles Blount, First Earl of, I, 324

De Wette, Wilhelm Martin Leberecht, II, 172

Dewey, Orville, I, 87n
Dexter, Timothy ("Lord"), III, 370
Dial, The, II, 41n, 55n; III, xiii, xiv, xx, 103n, 121n, 176n, 202n, 224n, 256n, 335n–344n *passim*
Dial, The (Cincinnati), III, 23n
Diana, I, 283; II, 296; III, 308
Diderot, Denis, II, 67; III, 133; *Le Neveu de Rameau,* III, 133n
Dido, I, 283; III, 231
Diet, I, 154; III, 91, 260–263; Gentoo, III, 267
Diodati, Charles, I, 154
Diogenes, I, 180, 250, 299, 359; II, 175, 196
Diomed, II, 134
Dion, II, 329; III, 297
Discipline, I, 116, 152, 304, 334, 340; Learned, I, 167; Moral, I, 155, 242; Natural, I, 300; Rule of, I, 174; Rules of Virtuous, I, 194
Discontent, III, 14, 237, 310; *see also* Protest, The
Disease, I, 368; II, 11, 176, 196, 215, 330; III, 86, 104, 106–107, 108, 115, 167, 264, 287; Laws of, II, 119; III, 49, 130
Disraeli, Benjamin, *Vivian Grey,* II, 325n; III, 156n
Dissension, III, 86; *see also* Protest, The
Dissenter, II, 345
Disunion, III, 104, 106, 108–109
Diversion, II, 322, 324; *see also* Recreation
Divine Being, I, 181; *see also* God
Divine Impulse, I, 376; II, 215
Divine in Man, II, 343; *see also* God within Man
Divine Mind, *see* Mind, Divine
Divine Power, III, 252, 369
Divine Presence, III, 20
Divine Soul, *see* Soul(s), Divine
Divinity, I, 303, 341; II, 105, 185, 276, 352; III, 61, 62; Supreme, II, 91; *see also* God
Divinity School, Harvard University, III, 321n, 457; Emerson address at, I, xxii; III, xx, 1n, 320n, 323n, 324n
Dolland, John, II, 44
Domestic Hired Service, *see* Servant(s)
Domestic Life, III, 8, 269, 286, 302, 303
Dominic, Saint, I, 121
Donald, III, 165
Donatello, I, 114

Donne, John, I, 338, 341, 349, 353, 355, 361, 362; II, xiv; III, 208; "Ecclogue. 1613. December 26," II, 179n; "Epithalamion," III, 57n; "Of the Progress of the Soul: The Second Anniversary," III, 64n; "Song" ("Sweetest love, I do not goe"), III, 110n
Dorians, II, 52
Doric Architecture, II, 51–52; III, 84, 220
Double Consciousness, I, 161, 325; III, 155
Downing, Jack, letters of, I, 222; *see also* Smith, Seba
Drake, Sir Francis, I, 35, 315
Drake, Nathan, I, 215
Drama, Elizabethan, I, 288–319 *passim,* 338–345, 355
Drawing, II, 264–265; III, 74
Dream Book, The, III, 169; *see also* Artemidorus Daldianus
Dreams, I, 219, 332–333; II, 359; III, 15, 42, 74, 151–171 *passim,* 287, 451
Dresden Gallery, II, 315
Druids, I, 238; II, 177
Drummond, James L., *Letters to a Young Naturalist,* I, 2n
Dryden, John, I, 148, 213, 216, 274, 283, 284, 306, 313, 356n, 357, 360, 372, 384; *Conquest of Granada, Part I,* II, 133n; Preface to *Troilus and Cressida,* I, 313n
Dualism, I, 161; II, 343; III, 52, 155, 170, 187–188; in Writers, I, 161; II, 61–62; Law of, III, 40; of Sex, III, 52, 62–63; *see also* Polarity
Duhamel, Jean-Pierre-François Guillot, I, 12
Duhamel du Monceau, Henri Louis, II, 44
Dulauloy, Countess, III, 134
Dumont, Pierre Étienne Louis, I, 285
Duppa, Richard, *The Life of Michael Angelo Buonarroti,* I, 102n–115n *passim,* 390n; III, 100n, 385n
Duty (ies), I, 157, 358; II, 83, 86, 168, 218, 228, 245, 299, 338; III, 25, 136, 138–150, 268, 285, 301, 522; Christian, III, 192; Public, I, 196; Sense of, II, 338, 361; III, 43; Sentiment of, II, 84, 86, 355; III, 277, 308
Dwight, John Sullivan, III, 321n–325n *passim*

INDEX

Ear, The Eye and, II, 262–277; III, 356
Earth, I, 6–68 *passim*, 71, 166, 289; II, 23, 31, 32, 184, 201, 228, 230, 247, 342, 358, 363; III, 27, 245; *see also* Globe; World
East, The, I, 236, 262, 280; II, 177; III, 112, 188; Institutions of, II, 128
East, The (U.S.), III, 378
East India Company, I, 195
East Indians, I, 195
East Lexington, Mass., I, xxii; III, xi, 319n–326n
Eberhard, Prince of Wirtemberg, III, 246
Eck, Johann Maier (Eckius), I, 122, 123
Eckermann, Johann Peter, *Gespräche mit Goethe*, II, 211n, 326n, 367n
Economy, III, 239–240, 487; of Time, I, 213; II, 146, 147; of World, II, 32; Political, II, 70, 230; Precepts of, III, 33
Ecstasy, I, 312; II, 42, 90; III, xvi, xvii, 11, 180n–181n, 237; *see also* Enthusiasm; Rapture(s); Trance
Eddystone Lighthouse, II, 43, 44
Eden, I, 160, 161; III, 87
Edgar, Song of the Death of, I, 247–248
Edinburgh Review, The, I, 264n; II, 59n, 101n, 367n; III, 296n
Education, I, 14, 150–151, 210–216, 276–277, 305, 328; II, 12, 38–39, 54, 68, 78, 101, 146, 192n, 195–204, 213–214, 228–229, 287, 305; III, 6, 16, 31, 32–33, 34–50, 56, 92, 113, 188, 191, 193, 196, 199, 226, 279, 286–301, 302, 304, 314–315, 373–374; Idea of Popular, I, 219; in Things, III, 40–41, 289; Laws of, I, 383; Moral, I, 280; II, 97; National, II, 14, 54; Natural History in, I, 70–71, 76; of Women, II, 302; Practical, III, 24–25; Roman Rule of, II, 135; III, 289; *see also* College(s); Culture
Edward ("The Elder"), King of Angles and Saxons, I, 243
Edward I, King of England, I, 254, 265–267, 276
Edward III, King of England, I, 254, 269
Edwards, Richard, "May," III, 53n
Edwin, King of Northumbria, I, 250, 251; III, 31
Effect(s), II, 247–249; III, 314; Cause and, II, 224, 248, 352; III, 30, 38, 46, 48, 64, 145–146, 203, 272, 331, 363
Egoism, II, 248; III, 253
Egotism, I, 272; II, 49; III, 215, 220–221, 441
Egypt, I, 28, 78; II, 53, 58, 266; III, 97, 211, 220, 225, 250, 373
Egyptian Era, II, 225
Egyptians, I, 224; II, 52, 353; III, 227
Eichhorn, Johann Gottfried, II, 172
Eisenach Castle (Wartburg), Germany, I, 126; III, 101
Eisleben, Germany, I, 137
Elbe River, I, 237
Electra, II, 60
Elgin, Thomas Bruce, Seventh Earl of, III, 375
Elgin Marbles, III, 80, 375
Eliot, Sir John, II, 389
Eliot, John (1604–1690), II, 333
Elizabeth I, Queen of England, I, 315, 316, 321, 324, 328, 338, 354, 355, 360, 361; III, 465
Elizabethan Age, I, 315–316, 338–339, 355; II, 213; III, 198
Ella, King of the Deirans, I, 250
Ella, King of the South Saxons, I, 241
Elliott, Ebenezer, "The Village Patriarch," III, 222n
Elliott, G. R., "Emerson's 'Grace' and 'Self-Reliance,'" I, 145n
Ellis, George, I, 257
Ellis, Sir Henry, *Original Letters Illustrative of English History*, III, 198
Ellwood, Thomas, I, 172
Eloquence, I, 153–154, 197–201, 336; II, xii, 45–49, 99, 102, 109–111, 163; III, xvii, 82–83, 146, 180n–181n, 337n–338n, 349, 354–355, 359, 362–363, 521; Law of, II, 111; Natural, I, 199; Philosophical, I, 200; *see also* Orator; Speech(es)
Elssler, Fanny, III, 351n
Elves, III, 24
Elysium, III, 42, 279
Emblem(s), I, 220–221, 224; National, III, 353–354; *see also* Allegory; Analogy; Symbol(s), Symbolism
Emerson, Charles Chauncy (brother), I, xv, xvi, xxi, xxiv, 2n, 5n, 27n, 87n, 88n, 93n, 98n, 206n, 209n; II, xvii, 207n; III, xii; lecture on Slavery, I, xxiv; II, xvii

Emerson, Edith (daughter), III, xii, 51n

Emerson, Edward Bliss (brother), I, xv, xvi, 27n; II, 154n

Emerson, Edward Waldo (son), I, xiii, xxiii, xxiv, 5n, 88n, 371n; II, xvi, xx, 55n, 69n, 76n, 173n, 194n, 276n, 327n, 337n; III, xviii, xix, xxiii, 51n, 322n, 343n, 347n, 367n; *Emerson in Concord*, III, 322n

Emerson, Ellen (daughter), I, xxiii; III, xii

Emerson, Ellen Tucker (first wife), I, xv, xix

Emerson, George Barrell (cousin), I, xx, xxi, 2n, 209n

Emerson, Joseph, of Malden (great-grandfather), III, 193–194n

Emerson, Lidian (Lydia) Jackson (second wife), I, xv, 3n, 98n, 183n, 209n; II, 207n; III, 1n, 114–115n, 151n, 323n, 438n

Emerson, Mary Moody (aunt), I, xvi; II, 2n, 337n; III, 194n, 340n

Emerson, Ralph (cousin), I, 2n

Emerson, Ralph Waldo, I, xiii, xxiv, 1n–4n, 87n–88n, 93n–96n, 205n–208n; II, xi–xvi, 1n–6n, 191n–193n, 207n–212n; III, xi–xviii, 1n–4n, 175n–184n, 319n–326n, 335n–345n

JOURNALS: Blotting Book I, III, 27n, 152n, 159n, 254n; Blotting Book II, II, 75n, 358n; III, 156n, 159n, 191n, 192n, 296n; Blotting Book III, I, 140n, 144n, 288n, 337n, 350n; II, 149n; III, 159n, 307n, 370n; Blotting Book IV[A], III, 115n, 253n; Blotting Book Ψ, I, xx, 50n, 144n, 171n, 183n, 211n, 261n; III, 57n, 158n; Blotting Book Y, I, 354n; Encyclopedia, I, 277n, 278n; II, 43n, 111n, 136n, 152n, 154n, 164n, 257n, 264n, 289n, 423n; III, 11n, 27n, 57n, 60n, 72n, 131n, 132n, 137n, 140n, 149n, 158n, 159n, 166n, 206n, 253n, 255n, 353n, 502n; Index Major, III, 253n; Italy, I, 419n, 420n, 421n; II, 270n; Italy and France, I, 10n, 98n, 108n, 117n, 374n, 420n, 421n, 422n, 423n; Journal 1826, I, 17n; Journal 1826–1828, I, 341n; Journal A, I, 5n, 28n, 35n, 69n, 74n, 77n, 93n, 94n, 95n, 97n, 98n, 104n, 118n, 131n, 144n, 183n, 186n, 221n, 256n, 288n, 290n, 311n, 313n, 317n, 320n, 352n, 375n,

417n, 425n, 450; II, xii, 26n, 31n, 44n, 56n, 85n, 106n, 133n, 142n, 151n, 152n, 153n, 175n, 199n, 209n, 210n–211n, 284n, 289n, 290n, 337n, 338n, 342n, 362n, 480n, 481n; III, 41n, 79n, 100n, 131n, 154n, 222n, 252n, 322n, 370n; Journal AZ, II, 29n, 222n; Journal B, I, 95n, 97n, 144n, 183n, 209n, 223n, 224n, 231n, 250n, 253n, 261n, 271n, 288n, 290n, 304n, 308n, 318n, 320n, 332n, 337n, 338n, 349n, 354n–355n, 365n, 378n, 385n; II, 4n, 5n, 11n, 14n, 15n, 16n, 17n, 18n, 19n, 20n, 22n, 23n, 24n, 31n, 45n, 49n, 51n, 52n, 53n, 61n, 62n, 68n, 85n, 94n, 95n, 96n, 99n, 100n, 101n, 103n, 105n, 108n, 109n, 111n, 114n, 127n, 134n, 135n, 137n, 144n, 145n, 146n, 148n, 155n, 161n, 163n, 168n, 169n, 170n, 175n, 178n, 179n, 185n, 187n, 199n, 251n, 256n, 258n, 287n, 300n, 316n, 317n, 319n, 345n, 363n, 408n, 453n, 480n; III, 13n, 31n, 32n, 37n, 40n, 57n, 60n, 71n, 72n, 77n, 79n, 82n, 104n, 116n, 140n, 152n, 156n, 157n, 162n, 168n, 169n, 205n, 212n, 219n, 220n, 221n, 222n, 312n, 451n; Journal C, II, 76n, 86n, 95n, 158n, 186n, 192n, 196n, 197n, 207n, 208n, 210n, 211n, 212n, 216n, 222n, 224n, 225n, 226n, 227n, 236n, 240n, 242n, 243n, 244n, 248n, 250n, 252n, 253n, 254n, 255n, 257n, 258n, 259n, 260n, 261n, 265n, 268n, 270n, 274n, 276n, 280n, 282n, 283n, 285n, 286n, 287n, 289n, 299n, 300n, 301n, 302n, 303n, 305n, 312n, 314n, 316n, 320n, 321n, 322n, 323n, 325n, 330n, 335n, 336n, 337n, 338n, 357n, 359n, 423n, 480n, 481n; III, 8n, 13n, 17n, 21n, 25n, 38n, 40n, 42n, 43n, 50n, 59n, 60n, 62n, 63n, 64n, 65n, 66n, 74n, 76n, 78n, 81n, 82n, 83n, 89n, 93n, 97n, 98n, 104n, 108n, 109n, 110n, 112n, 115n, 116n, 117n, 120n, 126n, 127n, 130n, 131n, 132n, 133n, 134n, 139n, 143n, 144n, 146n, 149n, 153n, 155n, 156n, 161n, 167n, 194n, 195n, 221n, 222n, 239n, 242n, 249n, 250n, 257n, 268n, 276n, 277n, 280n, 284n, 289n, 291n, 310n, 312n, 313n, 352n, 356n, 377n, 400n, 404, 457n, 502n; Journal D, II, 148, 423; III, xiii, xvi, 1n, 2n, 9n, 10n, 13n, 14n, 15n, 16n, 17n, 18n, 19n, 20n, 21n,

22n, 23n, 25n, 30n, 31n, 33n, 37n, 38n, 39n, 42n, 43n, 45n, 46n, 47n, 48n, 49n, 53n, 55n, 56n, 58n, 59n, 64n, 65n, 66n, 67n, 68n, 72n, 74n, 75n, 79n, 80n, 88n, 89n, 90n, 91n, 92n, 93n, 94n, 95n, 96n, 97n, 98n, 100n, 101n, 102n, 107n, 108n, 109n, 110n, 111n, 112n, 113n, 114n, 116n, 117n, 118n, 122n, 130n, 132n, 133n, 134n, 136n, 138n, 139n, 140n, 141n, 142n, 143n, 144n, 145n, 146n, 147n, 148n, 149n, 150n, 157n, 165n, 167n, 168n, 177n, 180n, 181n, 182n, 194n, 195n, 206n, 210n, 211n, 225n, 228n, 230n, 231n, 232n, 235n, 240n, 243n, 244n, 249n, 259n, 260n, 264n, 265n, 267n, 268n, 277n, 278n, 279n, 280n, 281n, 282n, 283n, 284n, 285n, 287n, 288n, 289n, 291n, 293n, 295n, 299n, 305n, 307n, 309n, 310n, 311n, 315n, 356n, 359n, 369n, 371n, 401n, 402, 404, 409, 413, 431, 438n, 458n, 487n, 494, 507n; Journal E, II, 328n, 329n; III, xvii, 177n, 178n, 179n, 180n, 181n, 185n, 186n, 187n, 189n, 195n, 196n, 199n, 200n, 201n, 203n, 204n, 205n, 206n, 209n, 210n, 213n, 214n, 215n, 216n, 217n, 218n, 219n, 229n, 230n, 234n, 235n, 236n, 239n, 240n, 244n, 245n, 253n, 254n, 258n, 261n, 262n, 266n, 269n, 271n, 278n, 279n, 283n, 290n, 295n, 297n, 305n, 328n, 330n, 335n, 353n, 357n, 358n, 363n, 368n, 381n, 483n, 488n, 490n, 507n; Journal F No. 2, III, 14n, 360n, 380n; Journal G, III, 276n, 336n, 339n, 340n, 352n, 353n, 360n, 368n, 372n, 378n, 395n, 477n; Journal H, III, 234n, 336n, 339n, 340n, 349n, 351n, 355n, 359n, 361n, 365n, 367n, 368n, 369n, 370n, 371n, 372n, 374n, 375n, 377n, 490n, 522n; Journal IO, I, 320n; Journal J, III, 336n, 339n, 372n, 373n, 376n, 378n, 380n, 521n; Journal K, III, 342n; Journal LM, III, 442n; Journal No. XV, II, 184n; Journal PY, III, 513; Journal Q, I, xvii, xix, xx, 2n, 3n, 14n, 21n, 24n, 25n, 26n, 94n, 95n, 144n, 154n, 164n, 167n, 171n, 174n, 211n, 221n, 230n, 288n, 290n, 320n, 354n, 419n, 421n, 423n; II, 150n, 154n, 247n, 345n, 351n; III, 159n, 255n, 311n; Journal RO Mind, I, xviii; II, 84n, 90n, 363n; *The Journals and Miscel-*

laneous Notebooks of Ralph Waldo Emerson, II, xvi–xvii, 184n; III, xix, 2n, 37n, 81n, 216n, 353n; *Journals of Ralph Waldo Emerson*, I, xiv, xxiii, 1n, 4n, 5n, 88n, 89n; II, xvii, 56n; III, xix, 234n, 320n, 322n; Notebook XVIII[A], I, 183n; III, 159n, 309n; Notebook Autobiography, II, 173n, 209n; Notebook CR, III, 104n; Notebook Δ, II, xv, 113n, 208n, 247n, 270n, 278n, 281n, 282n, 357n, 480n–482n; III, 183n; Notebook F No. 1, II, xv, 5n, 7n, 59n, 61n, 173n; Notebook France and England, I, 5n, 10n; Notebook Genealogy, III, 194n; Notebook L Literature, I, 205n, 217n, 218n, 233n, 253n, 269n, 287n, 337n, 356n, 371n; Notebook Morals, III, 41n; Notebook Naturalist, II, 26n, 27n; Notebook NQ, III, 41n; Notebook Φ, III, 2n, 23n, 24n, 31n, 132n, 149n, 170n, 400n–401n; Notebook Ψ, III, 183n, 185n, 271n, 338n, 347n, 367n; Notebook S, II, 480n; Notebook Σ, III, 100n, 138n, 160n, 246n, 369n, 440n; Notebook T, II, 249n; III, 6n, 30n, 41n, 77n, 81n, 119n, 279n, 350n; Notebook Z, III, 221n; Scotland and England, I, 14n; III, 156n; Sea 1833, I, 5n, 36n, 37n, 38n, 39n, 42n, 144n, 154n; Sermons and Journal, I, 355n; III, 59n; Sicily, I, 36n, 144n; Wide World No. XIII, II, 136n, 184n, 323n; III, 309n; Wide World No. 1, I, 320n, 337n; Wide World No. 2, I, 144n; Wide World No. 12, I, 183n

LECTURES: "Address on Education" (June 10, 1837), I, xxii; II, xiv, 189–204; "Address to the People of East Lexington" (Jan. 15, 1840), III, 317–331; "The Affections," II, 278n (*see also* "The Heart"); "The Age of Fable" (Nov. 19, 1835), I, 207n, 249n, 253–268, 269n; III, 158n; "The American Scholar" (Aug. 31, 1837), I, xxii, 69n, 95n; II, xii, xiv, xvii, 191n; III, xi (*see also under* WORKS); "Analysis, the Character of the Present Age," III, 185n (*see also* "Introductory" [Dec. 4, 1839]); "Art" (Dec. 29, 1836), II, v, xvii, 41–54, 386–391; "Being and Seeming" (Jan. 10, 1838), II, 295–309; III, 2n; "Ben Jonson, Herrick,

Herbert, Wotton" (Dec. 31, 1835), I, 337–355; II, 324n; III, 72n; "Biography" (series, 1835), I, xvi, xix, xx, 93–201, 205n, 206n, 209n; "Character" (Jan. 6, 1842), III, xx, 341n, 343n, 515n; "The Character of the Present Age," III, 185n (*see also* "Introductory" [Dec. 4, 1839]); "Chaucer" (Nov. 26, 1835), I, 205n, 207n, 249n, 269–286; II, 283n; "Comedy" (Jan. 30, 1839), III, 121–137; "The Conservative" (Dec. 9, 1841), III, xx, 341n, 342n, 344n; "Demonology" (Feb. 20, 1839), III, 151–171, 183n; "Demonology" (Mar. 21, 1871), III, 151n; "Discourse at Middlebury College" (July 22, 1845), I, xxii; II, 194n; Divinity School Address (July 15, 1838), I, xvii, xxii; III, xi, xiii, xx, 1n, 175n, 281n, 319n–320n, 323n, 324n–325n, 336n, 345n (*see also under* WORKS); "Doctrine of the Hands" (Dec. 13, 1837), II, 230–245; "Doctrine of the Soul" (Dec. 5, 1838), III, 2n, 5–22, 208n; "Domestic Life" Mar. 23, 1840), III, 23n (*see also* "Home"); "Domestic Life" (Feb. 28, 1843), III, 23n, 248n; "Duties," III, 367n (*see also* "Prospects"); "Duty" (Feb. 6, 1839), III, 138–150, 302n; "Edmund Burke" (Mar. 5, 1835), I, 183–201; "Education" (Feb. 5, 1840), II, 194n; III, 185n, 286–301; "Education" (1877–78), II, 194n; III, 286n; Education, lectures on, in the 1860's, II, 194n; "Eloquence" (Mar. 4, 1867), III, 347n; "English Literature: Introductory" (Nov. 5, 1835), I, 206n, 207n, 210n, 217–232, 233n, 269n, 287n, 290n, 293n; III, 36n; "English Literature" (series, 1835–36), I, xvi, xix, xx, 23n, 205n–209n, 217–385; II, 210n; "English Prose and Poetry" (readings, 1869), I, 207n, 287n; "Ethical Writers" (Jan. 7, 1836), I, 207n, 230n, 356–370; II, 184n; III, 11n; 'Ethics" (Feb. 16, 1837), II, 83n, 143–156; III, 309n; "Ethics" (Jan. 29, 1840), III, xx, xxi, 183n, 271n, 366n–367n; "The Eye and Ear" (Dec. 27, 1837), II, 262–277; III, 59n; "General Views" (Feb. 7, 1838), II, v, xvii, 357–364; III, 2n; "Genius" (Jan. 9, 1839), III, 68–84; "The Genius of the Present

Age" (Feb. 15, 1848), III, 186n; "George Fox" (Feb. 26, 1835), I, 97n, 164–182; II, 70n, 91n, 351n; III, 7n; "The Head" (Dec. 20, 1837), II, 246–261; "The Heart" (Jan. 3, 1838), II, 101n, 278–294; III, 65n, 377n; Heroism" (Jan. 24, 1838), II, v, xvii, 327–399; 340n; "Historical Discourse at Concord" (Sept. 12, 1835), xvi, xxii, xxiv, xxvi, 205n, 209n; "Holiness" (Jan. 31, 1838), II, 340–356; III, 37n, 377n; "Home" (Dec. 12, 1838), II, 194n; III, 23–33, 248n; "Human Culture" (series, 1837–38), I, 206n; II, v, xiii, xiv, xv, 191n, 205–364; III, xi, xiii, xv, 1n, 2n, 182n–183n, 321n, 322n; "The Humanity of Science" (Dec. 22, 1836), I, 3n; II, xv, 5n, 22–40; III, 123n; "Human Life" (series, 1838–39), I, 206n; II, 98n; III, xiii, xiv, xv, xxv–171, 175n, 176n, 181n, 182n, 183n, 185n, 238n; "The Individual" (Mar. 2, 1837), II, xiii, 173–188; III, 182n; "Individualism," II, 173n (*see also* "The Individual"); "Intellectual Integrity," II, 295n; III, xiii, xx (*see also* "Being and Seeming"); "[Introduction]" (Jan. 29, 1835), I, 97n; II, 357n; "Introduction" (Dec. 2, 1841), III, xx, 340n, 341n, 342n, 344n; "Introductory" (Dec. 8, 1836), II, 7–21; III, 474n; "Introductory" (Dec. 6, 1837), II, 213–229; "Introductory" (Dec. 4, 1839), III, 185–201, 234n, 286n, 396; "Italy" (two lectures, after Jan. 17, 1834), I, xxii, xxvi, 87–90, 374n; "John Milton" (Feb. 19, 1835), I, 144–163, 356n; III, 372n; "Laws of Life," II, 357n, 480–482 (*see also* "General Views"); "Literary Ethics" (July 25, 1838), I, xxii; III, xi, xx; "Literature" (Jan. 5, 1837), II, 5n, 41n, 55–68; III, 206n; "Literature [first lecture]" (Dec. 11, 1839), II, 55n; III, 176n, 202–223, 224n; "Literature [second lecture]" (Dec. 18, 1839), II, 55n; III, 176n, 202n, 224–237; "The Literature of the Present Age" (Mar. 17, 1840), I, 371n; II, 55n; III, 176n, 202n, 224n; "Lord Bacon" (Dec. 24, 1835), I, 118n, 207n, 320–336, 337n; II, 226n, 252n; III, 168n, 169n; "Love" (Dec. 26, 1838), III,

51–67; "Manners" (Feb. 9, 1837), II, 129–142; III, 289n; "Manners" (Dec. 30, 1841), II, 129n; III, xx, 341n, 342n–343n; "Man the Reformer" (Jan. 25, 1841), III, xiv, xx, 256n, 336n, 339n (*see also under* WORKS); "Martin Luther" (Feb. 12, 1835), I, 118–143, 207n, 320n; "The Method of Nature" (Aug. 11, 1841), I, xxii; III, xiv, xx, 336n–337n; "Michel Angelo Buonaroti" (Feb. 5, 1835), I, 98–117, 144n; II, 264n; "Mind and Manners of the Nineteenth Century" (series, 1848–50), III, xv, 184n; "Modern Aspects of Letters" (Jan. 14, 1836), I, 206n, 371–385; II, 110n, 273n; III, 205n; Natural History (lectures, 1833–34), I, xvi, xviii, xx, 1–83; II, 22n; "The Naturalist" (May 7, 1834), I, 69–83, 87n, 317n; "Nature and Powers of the Poet" (Nov. 3, 1841), III, 341n, 347n (*see also* "The Poet"); "New England" (series, 1843), III, 184n, 238n, 302n, 345n, 366n; "On the Best Mode of Inspiring a Correct Taste in English Literature" (Aug. 20, 1835), I, xxii, 205n, 209–216; II, 66n; III, 206n; "On the Relation of Man to the Globe" (Jan. 6, 1834), I, xxii, 15n, 27–49; II, 16n, 35n, 320n; "Permanent Traits of the English National Genius" (Nov. 12, 1835), I, 207n, 233–252, 253n, 263n, 269n, 276n, 356n, 359n, 360n; II, 132n, 141n; III, 31n; "The Philosophy of History" (series, 1836–37), I, xxvi, 206n, 208n; II, v, xiii, xiv, xv, xxi–188, 191n, 192n, 207n, 208n, 210n; III, xv, 2n, 181n, 343n; "The Poet" (Dec. 16, 1841), III, xv, xvi, 341n, 342n, 343n–345n, 347–365; "Politics" (Jan. 12, 1837), II, 69–82; III, 205n, 238n, 478n; "Politics" (Jan. 1, 1840), II, 69n; III, 183n, 238–247; "The Present Age" (Feb. 23, 1837), II, 157–172; III, 6n, 181n, 311n; "The Present Age" (series, 1839–40), II, 7n, 157n; III, xiv, xv, 173–315, 325n, 326n, 335n, 336n, 340n; "Private Life" (Jan. 8, 1840), III, 183n, 248–255; Prospects" (Jan. 20, 1842), III, xvi, xxi, 271n, 341n, 342n, 343n–345n, 347n, 366–382; "Prospects. Duties," III, 366n–367n

(*see also* "Ethics" [Jan. 29, 1840]; "Prospects"); "The Protest" (Jan. 16, 1839), III, 85–102, 339n; "Prudence" (Jan. 17, 1838), II, 310–326, 327n, 340n; "Reform" (Mar. 10, 1841), III, 256n; "Reforms" (Jan. 15, 1840), III, 256–270, 326n, 339n; "Relation of Man to Nature" (Jan. 13, 1842), III, xx, 341n, 343n, 366n, 370n, 518; "Relation to Nature," *see* "Relation of Man to Nature"; "Religion" (Jan. 19, 1837), II, 83–97, 143n, 426n; "Religion" (Jan. 22, 1840), II, 83n; III, 81n, 271–285; "The School" (Dec. 19, 1838), II, 194n; III, 34–50; Shakspear [first lecture]" (Dec. 10, 1835), I, 25n, 206n, 207n, 217n, 221n, 287–304; II, 332n; III, 158n; "Shakspear [second lecture]" (Dec. 17, 1835), I, 74n, 206n, 207n, 287n–288n, 303n, 305–319; III, 205n; "Slavery" (Nov. 1837), I, xxiv; II, xvii; "Society" (Jan. 26, 1837), II, 5n, 98–112, 287n; III, 62n; "The Spirit of the Age" (Mar. 30, 1850), III, 186n; "The Spirit of the Times" (Feb. 21, 1848), III, 186n; "The Spirit of the Times" (Jan. 10, 1850), III, 186n; "The Study and Uses of Biography," *see* "[Introduction]" (Jan. 29, 1835); "Tendencies" (Feb. 12, 1840), III, 138n, 183n, 302–315; "Tests of Great Men," *see* "[Introduction]" (Jan. 29, 1835); "The Times" (series, 1841–42), II, v; III, xi, xiv–xv, xvi, xx, xxi, 3n, 182n, 184n, 333–382, 482n, 483n, 524–525 (?); "Trades and Professions" (Feb. 2, 1837), II, 113–128; "Tragedy" (Jan. 23, 1839), III, 103–120; "The Transcendentalist" (Dec. 23, 1841), III, xx, 341n, 342n, 344n; "The Uses of Natural History" (Nov. 5, 1833), I, xiv, xxi, 5–26, 27n, 34n, 287n, 290n; II, 99n; III, 158n; "War" (Mar. 12, 1838), III, xi, xx; "Water" (Jan. 17, 1834), I, xxii, 50–68, 87n; "The Young American" (Feb. 7, 1844), III, xv

LETTERS: *The Correspondence of Emerson and Carlyle* (ed. Slater), III, 175n, 176n, 322n, 335n, 338n, 340n, 342n, 343n; *The Correspondence of Thomas Carlyle and Ralph Waldo Emerson* (ed. Norton), II,

207n; *Letters from Ralph Waldo Emerson to a Friend,* III, 248n; *The Letters of Ralph Waldo Emerson,* I, xxi, 1n, 4n, 5n, 27n, 50n, 88n, 94n, 97n, 98n, 118n, 144n, 183n, 205n, 209n, 253n, 341n; II, 2n, 5n, 22n, 191n, 192n, 193n, 207n, 210n, 211n, 289n; III, xi, xiii, xiv, xv, 1n, 2n, 3n, 5n, 23n, 105n, 151n, 175n, 176n, 177n, 178n, 180n, 181n, 183n, 185n, 202n, 234n, 238n, 248n, 256n, 271n, 320n, 321n, 322n, 323n, 324n, 325n, 326n, 335n, 336n–337n, 338n, 340n, 341n, 342n, 343n, 347n, 366n, 367n

works: "The American Scholar," I, 69n, 95n; II, xvii, 191n; III, xi (*see also under* LECTURES); "Aristocracy," II, 139n; III, 302n, 305n, 442n; "Art" (*W,* II), I, 73n, 421n; II, 41n, 262n, 271n; III, 68n, 74n, 284n; "Art" (*W,* VII), I, 28n; II, 41n; III, 220n; "Art and Criticism," III, 210n; "Beauty," II, 262n, 276n; III, 59n; "Behavior," III, 438n; "Books," I, 213n, 214n; III, 44n, 206n, 209n; "Boston," III, 186n, 192n; "Character" (*W,* III), III, 286n, 295n, 343n, 477n, 483n; "Character" (*W,* X), II, 84n, 86n, 87n; "Circles," II, 246n, 255n; III, 85n, 235n, 302n, 315n, 326n; "The Comic," III, 121n, 122n, 125n, 126n, 127n, 129n, 130n, 131n, 132n, 135n, 137n; "Compensation," II, 75n, 109n, 127n, 143n, 153n, 154n, 230n, 244n, 246n, 259n, 260n; III, xv, 44n, 103n, 107n, 138n, 145n, 146n, 147n, 148n, 149n, 150n, 252n; "The Conservative," III, xx, 342n, 344n; "Considerations by the Way," I, 341n; II, 196n, 292n; "Culture," III, 286n, 294n; "Days," II, 235n; "Demonology," I, 332n; III, 151n, 153n, 154n, 155n, 156n, 158n, 159n, 160n, 162n, 165n, 166n, 168n, 169n, 170n, 451n; Divinity School Address, I, xvii; II, 143n, 155n; III, xiii, xx, 1n, 175n, 323n, 324n–325n, 336n, 345n (*see also under* LECTURES); "Domestic Life," III, 23n, 24n, 248n, 253n, 400n, 481n; "Education," II, 194n, 199n, 200n, 201n, 202n, 203n, 204n; III, 24n, 33n, 34n, 35n, 39n, 40n, 41n, 47n, 48n, 286n, 288n, 290n, 291n, 294n, 295n, 296n, 300n, 301n; "Eloquence" (*W,* VII), II, xii; III,

12n; "Eloquence" (*W,* VIII), III, 347n, 363n; *English Traits,* I, 233n; *Essays, First Series,* II, v, xii, 1n; III, xiii–xiv, xv, xvi, 34n, 175n, 176n, 182n, 183n, 238n, 271n, 335n, 336n–337n, 338n, 343n, 344n, 367n; *Essays, Second Series,* III, 183n, 342n–343n; "Ethnical Scriptures," III, 368n; "Experience," II, 295n; III, 230n, 379n, 483n; "Fate," II, 222n; "The Fortune of the Republic," II, 244n; III, 103n; "Friendship," II, 101n, 278n, 282n, 287n, 289n, 290n; III, 248n, 254n, 255n; "Greatness," III, 260n; "Heroism," II, 327–339, 340n; "Historical Discourse at Concord," *see under* LECTURES; "Historic Notes of Life and Letters in Massachusetts," III, 186n, 187n, 189n, 191n; "History," I, 11n, 259n, 261n; II, 7n, 12n, 13n, 14n, 15n, 16n, 18n, 19n, 52n, 99n, 135n, 173n, 177n, 178n, 182n, 187n, 262n, 268n; III, xv, 5n, 22n, 30n, 49n, 68n, 73n, 93n; "Immortality" III, 31n; "Intellect," II, 58n, 246n, 247n, 250n, 252n, 254n, 256n, 258n, 260n, 261n, 453n; III, 10n, 45n, 68n, 74n, 210n, 458n; "Lecture on the Times," III, xx, 42n, 256n, 257n, 258n, 259n, 265n, 266n, 307n, 342n, 344n; *Lectures and Biographical Sketches,* II, 194n; "Literary Ethics," II, 62n; III, xi, xx (*see also under* LECTURES); "Love," III, 51n, 52n, 55n, 56n, 58n, 59n, 62n, 66n, 67n, 409n; "Manners," I, 313n; II, 129n, 310n, 325n; III, 342n–343n; "Man the Reformer," II, 210n; III, xx, 256n, 336n, 339n (*see also under* LECTURES); "Merlin's Song," I, 341n; "The Method of Nature," III, xx (*see also under* LECTURES); "Michael Angelo," I, 98n; III, 483n; "Milton," I, 98n, 144–163; III, 372n; "Napoleon," III, 13n, 239n, 352n; "Nature" (*W,* I), I, xv, xvii, 1n, 3n, 5n, 23n, 25n, 28n, 69n, 71n, 101n, 205n, 206n, 208n, 211n, 217n, 221n, 222n, 224n, 226n, 227n, 287n, 290n, 293n, 371n, 385n, 496n; II, xi, xii, 3n, 208n; III, 3n, 36n, 158n; "Nature" (*W,* III), III, 98n, 258n, 343n, 490n; "New England Reformers," III, 206n, 245n, 286n, 289n, 290n, 297n, 367n, 373n, 379n, 380n, 498n,

523n; "New Poetry," III, 235n; "Nominalist and Realist," III, 367n, 371n, 381n; Notes to Centenary Edition, I, 102n, 371n; II, 55n, 69n, 76n, 82n, 276n, 327n, 337n; III, 206n 210n, 211n, 213n, 226n, 327n, 342n–343n, 363n; "The Over-Soul," II, 83n, 84n, 85n, 88n, 90n, 92n, 340n, 343n, 346n, 355n, 356n; III, xv, 5n, 14n, 16n, 17n, 18n, 19n, 20n, 34n, 39n, 42n, 43n, 96n, 218n, 271n, 277n, 280n, 281n, 282n, 283n, 284n, 285n, 302n, 312n, 327n, 330n; *Parnassus*, II, 363n; III, xxiii, 104n; "The Poet," II, 213n, 262n, 263n, 264n; III, 68n, 75n, 81n, 343n, 347n, 349n, 350n, 353n, 354n, 355n; "Poetry and Imagination," III, 347n, 356n, 359n, 360n, 365n; "Politics," II, 69n, 70n, 71n, 72n, 73n, 75n, 77n; III, 238n, 240n, 241n, 242n, 243n, 244n, 478n; "The Preacher," II, 96n, 342n; III, 271n, 275n, 276n; Preface to *The Hundred Greatest Men*, I, 217n; II, 55n, 57n; "Prudence," II, 230n, 243n, 310n, 311n, 314n, 315n, 317n, 318n, 319n, 320n, 321n, 322n, 327n, 340n, 471n; III, 40n, 246n; "Self-Reliance," I, 76n; II, 140n, 143n, 151n, 152n, 171n, 173n, 175n, 213n, 223n; III, xv, 8n, 11n, 13n, 23n, 31n, 34n, 35n, 36n, 68n, 77n, 101n, 138n, 139n, 141n, 142n, 143n, 150n, 188n, 242n, 243n, 256n, 271n, 282n, 284n, 286n, 295n, 302n, 309n, 311n, 314n; "The Senses and the Soul," II, 357–364; "Shakspeare," I, 284n, 287n, 288n, 306n; "The Sovereignty of Ethics," II, 84n; III, 327n, 328n, 329n, 367n, 378n, 379n; "Spiritual Laws," I, 186n, 212n; II, 66n, 83n, 95n, 143n, 145n, 148n, 149n, 150n, 151n, 163n, 270n, 295n, 300n, 302n, 423n; III, xv, 18n, 34n, 36n, 37n, 38n, 49n, 102n, 130n, 138n, 139n, 140n, 155n, 156n, 157n, 162n, 206n, 211n, 231n, 232n, 244n, 256n, 268n, 271n, 281n, 286n, 292n, 299n, 302n, 313n, 502n; "Suum Cuique" ("The rain has spoiled the farmer's day"), III, 103n, 116; "Swedenborg," II, 92n; "Tantalus," II, 357n; III, 343n, 490n; "Thoreau," II, 232n; "Thoughts on Art," II, 41–54; III, 220n, 336n, 338n; "Thoughts on Modern Literature," I, 371n; II, 55n; III, 8n, 9n, 17n, 18n, 196n, 202n, 204n, 208n, 209n, 216n, 217n, 218n, 219n, 222n, 224n, 225n, 230n, 237n; "The Tragic," III, 103n, 104n, 105n, 106n, 111n, 115n; "The Transcendentalist," III, xx, 85n, 342n, 344n; "Uses of Great Men," I, 95n, 97n; "Walter Savage Landor," III, 337n; "Walter Scott," I, 371n; "War," III, xi, xx; "Works and Days," III, 235n; "Worship," III, 133n; "The Young American," *see under* LECTURES

Emerson, Robert Bulkeley (brother), III, xii

Emerson, Ruth Haskins (mother), I, 87n, 88n

Emerson, Waldo (son), II, 207n; III, xi, xv, 1n, 341n

Emerson, William (brother), I, xv, xxi, 1n, 5n, 88n, 98n, 206n; II, 5n; III, xi, xii, xiii, xiv, 176n, 180n, 181n, 323n, 336n, 337n, 340n, 342n, 347n, 367n

Empedocles, II, 38

Encyclopedia Americana, I, 58, 141n, 322n, 389n

Endicott, John, I, 179

Ends and Means, II, 107; III, 129–133, 145–146, 189, 302–304, 460

England, I, 13, 16, 33, 65, 105, 117, 134, 147, 149, 151, 157–158, 159, 177, 178, 179, 183n, 184, 189, 191, 196, 212, 233–237, 243, 248, 255, 278, 307, 360–361, 381, 382; II, 12, 14, 56, 74, 97, 118, 139, 157, 166, 172, 180, 197, 213, 224, 272, 335, 359; III, 6–8, 10, 53, 128, 132, 187, 191, 196, 208, 210, 217, 226, 260, 273, 275, 372, 375; Emerson lectures in, I, xxii; III, xv, 23n, 345n

English, The, I, 212, 235–237, 242, 252, 307; II, 14, 187, 318–319, 325; III, 112, 192, 284

English Cathedrals, I, 235; II, 52, 272

English Commonwealth, III, 6–8, 192, 198, 210

English Language, I, 153, 158, 212, 238, 248–249, 253–254, 273, 307; III, 59, 142; *see also* Language

English Laws, I, 175, 360

English Literature, I, 75, 205–385; III, 274, 372; *see also* Literature

English Period, II, 14, 157

English Revolution, II, 213

English Traits, I, 233–252, 254, 275–277, 360; III, 104

Enjoyment, III, 109

Enthusiasm, I, 21–23, 136–138, 141, 168, 179, 299; II, 33, 37, 54, 90–92, 97, 105, 266, 345; III, 11, 52, 70; *see also* Ecstasy; Rapture(s); Trance

Entomology, III, 30

Epaminondas, I, 140; II, 140, 284, 329, 335; III, 267

Epicles, I, 198

Epictetus, I, 359

Epimetheus, I, 258

Equivocal Generation, II, 253

Erasmus, Desiderius, I, 123, 129, 141; II, 178, 360

Erfurt, Germany, I, 125; Augustinian Monastery at, I, 120

Eric's Cap, III, 194

Erie Canal, II, 43

Error, I, 359, 385; II, 11, 74, 82; Slime of, III, 54

Erudition, *see* Learning

Eskimo(s), I, 35; II, 118, 179, 214, 318–319, 362; III, 407

Essex, Robert Devereux, Second Earl of, I, 306, 315, 324, 353; III, 97

Establishment(s), I, 190, 193, 201; III, 187, 241, 309, 376; Defenders of, III, 521; Religious, II, 14; *see also* Conservatism; Conservatives; Past, Party of

Eternal, The, II, 310; III, 139, 178n, 186, 199, 272, 297, 382, 454; Region of the Grand and, III, 204

Eternity, II, 185, 187; III, 28, 76, 93, 178n, 250, 364–365, 373; Lectures on, III, 178n–179n; of Nature, III, 522

Ethelburga, Queen of West Saxons, I, 250

Ethelfrith, King of Northumbria, I, 250

Ethical Laws, *see* Law(s), Ethical

Ethical Writers, I, 356–370

Ethics, II, 73–74, 79, 143–156, 181, 239, 243; III, 158, 257, 285; Christian, I, 156; Fairy, I, 260; Law(s) of, I, 25, 290, 370; II, 201, 344; III, 66, 177n–178n, 200; of Mind, II, 151; of Society, III, 63

Ethiopia, II, 225

Etna, Mt., I, 249

Eulenstein, Charles, III, 138

Eumenides, III, 118

Euripides, I, 273, 359; II, 333; III, 126, 159; *Alcestis,* II, 105n

Europe, I, 31, 43, 201, 236, 238; II, 7, 8, 74, 80, 112, 164, 165, 260; III, 66, 75, 210, 227, 307, 361, 490; Western, III, 8

European(s), II, 73, 112

Eve, II, 62; III, 67, 87

Evening Post, The (New York), III, 342n

Event(s), I, 225–226, 234, 296, 327, 341; II, 145, 185, 343; III, 47–50, 105, 110, 139, 144, 149–150, 156–157, 159, 203, 242, 243, 276, 277, 281, 290

Evenus, II, 324

Everett, Edward, I, 183n; II, 136n

Evil(s), I, 135, 173, 359; II, 11, 145, 155, 182, 330; III, 15, 16, 86, 110, 112, 156, 306, 312, 362

Evolution, Theories of, I, 3n

Examiner, The (London), III, 83n

Exchange Coffee House, Boston, I, xx

Experience, II, 19, 158–159; III, 28, 39, 43, 54, 76, 86–87, 243, 292, 378; and Idea, III, 482–483; Universal, III, 215, 225

Expression, I, 24, 219, 289–292, 350; II, 264–266; III, 224–225, 233, 348–364

Extravagance, III, 85, 90

Eye(s), I, 6, 9–10, 15, 17–18, 38, 40, 42, 45, 49, 73, 81, 99, 102, 107, 110, 116, 132, 167, 213, 224, 297, 326–327, 329, 385; II, 44, 55, 146, 149, 156, 168, 184, 216, 225, 269, 282–286, 319; III, 28, 32, 34, 49, 54, 57, 72, 75, 111, 124, 157, 162, 167, 186, 194, 201, 211, 214, 222, 230, 236–237, 249, 251, 252, 268, 283, 288, 297, 310, 356, 374, 376; and Ear, II, 262–277; III, 356; Mind's, I, 132, 285, 296; of Hope, III, 291

Ezekiel, I, 132

Fabii, The, II, 134

Fable(s), I, 11, 221, 230, 254–261, 274, 297; III, 48, 154, 158, 315, 365; Age of, I, 253–268; Nursery, III, 106

Fabricius, Georg, II, 164n

Fabricius, Johann Albert (?), II, 164

Face(s), III, 63, 72–73, 74, 80, 121–122, 133–135, 309–310

Fact(s), I, 23–25, 79, 190, 197, 199–200, 220–221, 289, 327; II, 13, 20,

37, 68, 98, 179, 249, 252–254, 261, 343; III, 6, 25–26, 34, 37–39, 47–50, 51, 54, 71–73, 78, 84, 95, 115, 157, 167–169, 170, 182n, 203, 215, 227–228, 229, 239–240, 244, 278, 284, 285, 292, 314, 349–350, 363, 365, 378, 381; Age of, II, 166–167

Faculty(ies), I, 116, 200, 297, 336, 359, 373; II, 17, 18, 113, 153, 181, 215, 228, 268; III, 11, 15, 39, 45, 62, 100, 107, 114, 482; Active, II, 201, 204; Creative, II, 10; III, 46; Emotive, II, 215; Executive, II, 83; Higher, I, 353; II, 162, 196, 202, 215, 240, 310, 359; Ideal, II, 197; Imaginative, I, 302–303, 305; Intellectual, I, 116; II, 215; Physical, I, 116; Practical, I, 303, 305; Reasoning, I, 330; Reflective, I, 302–303, 305; Retrograde, III, 122; Spiritual, I, 305

Fair, II, 54, 110; III, 97; Idea of, I, 162

Fairies, I, 178, 260–261; III, 162, 168, 252

Faith, I, 80, 81, 120, 121, 134, 157, 171, 172, 231, 250, 384; II, 96, 97, 216, 219, 228, 229, 346; III, 20, 39, 81, 108, 162, 188, 191–194, 199, 200, 201, 204, 229, 241, 248, 274, 281, 285, 295–297, 313–314, 340n, 362, 382, 400

Falk, Robert P., "Emerson and Shakespeare," I, 288n

Falkland, Lucius Cary, Second Viscount, I, 306, 364–365; II, 140; III, 8

Fall of Man, I, 362; III, 86–89, 98, 277, 283, 299, 330

Fame, I, 145, 175, 201, 212, 369; III, 89, 146, 205, 229–230, 281, 312; *see also* Reputation

Fanaticism, I, 138–140; II, 148; III, 80, 108; a Mohammedan, I, 138; of Freedom, III, 196

Fancy, I, 160, 257, 265, 327, 375–376, 379; II, 50, 54; III, 118, 155, 258

Faneuil Hall, Boston, II, 200, 222; III, 83, 180

Faraday, Michael, II, 38

Farmer, The, II, 115; III, 108, 121–122

Farmer's Almanack, III, 369

Farming, III, 263

Farnese, Alessandro (1520–1589), Cardinal, I, 102

Fashion, II, 139, 161; III, 134, 234

Fate, I, 172; II, 42, 50, 187, 343, 357n, 359; III, 11, 37, 66, 83, 105–106, 157, 202, 241, 253, 364

Fear, I, 154, 231; II, 95, 112, 156, 177, 182–184, 228, 270, 284, 285, 320, 359; III, 41, 55, 57, 67, 104, 106, 111, 133, 143, 210, 252, 357, 363, 369, 454, 455

Federal Street Church, Boston, III, 326n

Fell, Dr. John, III, 90

Fell, Margaret, I, 170

Fell, Thomas, I, 170

Fellatahs, I, 38; II, 244

Fénelon, François de Salignac de La Mothe-, I, 132, 150, 341; II, 94; III, 286n

Ferrara, Italy, I, 43, 105

Fichte, Johann Gottlieb, I, 173; II, 68

Fiction(s), I, 256, 260–261, 375–376; III, 201, 286, 313

Fielding, Henry, I, 275

Fields, James T., I, 216n

Fingal's Cave, I, 57

Finisterre, Cape, I, 31

Finns, III, 53

First Age, The, III, 93

First Church, Concord, Mass., III, 131n

First Man, I, 160, 165, 384; II, 14

First Thoughts, *see* Thought(s), First

Fish, I, 61–63

Fitness, II, 51, 264; Idea of, I, 17

Flanagan, John T., "Emerson as a Critic of Fiction," I, 371n

Flathead Indian, III, 154

Flattery, III, 285

Flemish Language, I, 238

Fletcher, John, I, 306, 309, 316; II, 327–329, 334; III, 208; *The Double Marriage*, II, 327; *The Mad Lover*, II, 327; *The Nice Valour*, III, 58n; *The Sea-Voyage*, II, 334; *see also* Beaumont, Francis, and John Fletcher

Florence, Italy, I, 104, 105–106, 107, 108, 112, 114, 116–117, 187; III, 100; Baptistery, I, 117; Cathedral, I, 114, 117; Laurentian Library, I, 117; Mausoleum of the Medici, I, 108; Piazza del Gran Duca, I, 108; Santa Croce, I, 117; Santa Maria Novella, I, 117

Florentine Academicians, I, 65

Florentine Painters, III, 69, 100

Florentines, I, 105
Flux in Nature, II, 27, 32; III, 27–28, 510; of All Things, I, 221, 289
Flying Dutchman, The, III, 194
Follen, Charles (Karl), III, 319n–325n *passim; Religion and the Church,* III, 324n
Fonblanque, Albany, III, 83n
Fontanes, Louis de, III, 13
Fontenelle, Bernard Le Bouvier De, I, 25, 74, 317, 399
Food, *see* Diet
Fool(s), III, 10, 11, 103, 167, 211
Forbes, Edith Emerson, III, 51n; *see also* Emerson, Edith
Force, III, 245, 303, 310; Aboriginal, III, 516; Man's Inner, III, 297; Man's Invisible, III, 312; Moral and Intellectual, III, 91, 267
Ford, John, I, 316; *The Sun's Darling,* III, 451
Foreign Quarterly Review, The, II, 37n, 368n; III, 13n, 134n, 386n
Foreign Review, The, I, 123n, 390n
Foreign Reviews, II, 137
Foreworld, III, 315
Form(s), I, 10, 17, 73–74, 81, 103, 154, 168, 224, 317, 381; II, 143, 217, 263–265, 275–276, 305, 310, 359; III, 41–42, 56, 64, 72–74, 94, 97, 182n, 276, 287, 297, 302, 315, 324n–325n, 349, 354, 361, 363, 460, 525; Human, I, 160; II, 275–276, 283; III, 11, 41, 72–74, 112, 113, 124; in Dreams, III, 153–154; Limitary, III, 154; Literary, II, 61–63; of Religion, I, 166; II, 305, 310; III, 97, 128, 324n–325n; of Things, II, 276; Perfect and Unfading, III, 315; Social, III, 89, 97, 197
Forster, John, "John Hampden," II, 324n, 389n
Fortune, II, 58, 89, 357n; III, 11–12, 41, 97, 109, 113, 149, 156, 157, 161–162, 166–167, 170, 201, 253, 276, 287
Forum, Roman, III, 211
Forward Class, The, III, 521; *see also* Movement Party
Fourier, Baron Jean Baptiste Joseph, *Éloge. Mémoires de l'institut,* I, 73
Fox, Charles James, I, 183n, 184, 186, 193, 195, 200, 201; II, 138
Fox, George, I, xx, 94n, 97n, 118n, 119n, 164–182, 211n, 378; II, 91,

292–293, 351; III, 243, 377, 490; *A Journal,* I, 164n, 172n, 176, 391n; II, 293n, 351n, 367n; III, 377n
Fox Indians, II, 227
Framingham, Mass., I, xxii; Emerson lectures in, II, xi, 207n, 213n, 230n, 246n, 262n (?), 278n, 295n, 310n, 327n; III, xi
France, I, 12–13, 47, 67, 105, 150, 201, 222, 255; II, 12, 14, 74, 97, 166, 172, 175–176; III, 191, 196, 217, 275
Francis, Saint, I, 121
Franklin, Benjamin, I, xix, 12, 150; II, xiv, 65, 67, 242; Wisdom of Poor Richard, II, 317
Franklin, Sir John, II 175, 363, 480
Franklin Lectures, Boston, I, xxii, 27n
Franklin Lyceum, Providence, III, xiv, 1n–2n, 5n, 23n, 175n–176n, 185n
Franks, I, 234–235, 255
Frazer's Magazine, I, 123n, 126n, 390n
Frederick III, Elector of Saxony, I, 123–131 *passim,* 136–137; III, 246 (?)
Freedom, I, 158–159, 162, 201, 233; II, 67, 70, 85, 145, 167, 177, 186, 299; III, 48, 156, 196, 243, 303, 325n, 356, 479, 520; External, II, 160; Idea of, 1, 218–219, 231; II, 77; Inward, II, 67; Political, II, 54, 67; Sentiment of, III, 6; *see also* Liberty
French, The, I, 196, 234–235, 249, 253, 285, 360; II, 77, 165n; III, 89, 112
French Language, I, 253–254
French Literature, III, 274
French Period, II, 67
French Revolution, I, 162, 183n, 184–185, 186, 195, 196, 201; II, 74, 175–176; III, 108, 133, 222, 225, 304, 307, 459; of July 1830, II, 80n
Friends, Society of, *see* Quakers
Friendship, I, 191–194, 334; II, 100–105, 288–292; III, 19, 26, 33, 63, 253–255, 315, 379, 381, 489; Laws of, II, 104, 290; III, 254
Froissart, Jean, I, 221, 270; III, 198
Fuller, Hiram, II, 189n, 192n–193n; III, 321n
Fuller, (Sarah) Margaret, I, 208n; II, 41n, 192n; III, xii, xiii, 1n, 178n,179n, 180n, 183n, 320n, 335n, 336n, 338n, 366n, 514 (?)
Fuller, Thomas, III, 81; *The History of the Worthies of England,* I, 301

Fulton, Robert, I, 13, 260; II, 18; III, 158

Furies, II, 154

Furka Pass, III, 221

Furness, William Henry, I, 209n

Furnier, Isaac, I, 180

Future, The, I, 13, 187, 200, 232, 380; II, 159, 224; III, 141, 177n, 181n–182n, 187, 200, 232, 277, 284, 311, 328, 382, 462; Age, III, 177n–178n, 295; Party of, III, 187–189, 325n; see also Movement Party

Galeazzo II, Duke of Milan, I, 270

Galen, I, xx

Galileo, I, xx, 18, 117, 152; II, 37, 175; III, 90, 306, 311, 373

Gall, Franz Joseph, II, 25n

Galvani, Luigi, II, 26n

Garden of Plants, see Jardin des Plantes

Gardiner, William, Music of Nature, III, 350n, 385n

Garrison, William Lloyd, III, 260n

Garth, Sir Samuel, I, 357

Gaul, I, 237; II, 76, 180

Gaunt, John of, Duke of Lancaster, I, 269–270

Gay, John, I, 274, 357

Gay-Lussac, Joseph Louis, I, 2n; II, 18

Genelas, I, 260

Genius, I, 99, 100, 119, 134, 141, 145, 156, 172, 190, 191–192, 200, 218, 224, 231, 232, 272, 275, 285–286, 289, 302, 304, 307, 315, 317, 322, 326, 336, 339, 346, 373, 374, 378, 380, 381; II, 36, 99, 102, 130, 141, 152, 168, 268, 284, 303, 306–308, 316, 361; III, 13, 16, 22, 36, 45–46, 68–84, 85–86, 88, 89, 95, 100, 108, 112, 139, 154, 160–161, 203, 211, 212, 214, 223, 235, 282, 297, 298, 300, 312, 315, 350, 354, 355, 360, 361, 375, 419, 459, 462, 488, 490, 521, 525; Doctrine of Guardian, III, 160–161; English National, I, 233–252, 254, 360; Ethical, I, 360; Laws of, II, 268; Literary, II, 60–64; Man of, I, 166–167, 191–192, 272, 381; II, 99, 161, 315–316; III, 80–83, 85–86, 235, 284, 454; of a Country, I, 210; of an Age, III, 139; of France, I, 150; of Institutions, I, 377; of Poetry, III, 362; of the Artist, II, 46–48; of the Divine Providence, III, 147; of the German Nation, III, 8, 208; of the Greeks, I, 200; III, 72, 112; of the Time, III, 237, 303, 362–364; of Women, III, 64; Poetic, II, 39; III, 362–363; Spontaneity of, III, 70–81

Gentilis, Albericus, I, 353

Gentle Behavior, Doctrine of, I, 276–280, 483

Gentleman, The, I, 276–280, 364, 483; II, 139–142, 216; III, 17, 96–97

Gentoo, see Hindoo(s)

Geoffrey of Monmouth, Historia Regum Britanniae, I, 256n

Geoffroy Saint-Hilaire, Étienne, I, 3n

Geology, I, 15–16, 29–32, 33–34, 47, 53–58; II, 32–33, 196; III, 9, 30, 168, 277

Geometry, III, 61; Axioms of, I, 25

George, Duke of Saxony, I, 123, 137, 139

George, Saint, I, 252

Georgia, III, 135

Gérando, Joseph Marie de, II, 97; Histoire comparée des systèmes de philosophie, I, 97n; Du perfectionnement moral, II, 210n

German Age, I, 138

German Language, I, 138, 238; II, 303

German Ocean (North Sea), I, 237

Germans, I, 235

Germany, I, 119, 123, 137, 138, 150, 242, 381; II, 14, 67–68, 76, 97, 166, 172, 180; III, 187, 191, 196, 210, 217, 228; Genius of, III, 8, 208

Ghiberti, Lorenzo, I, 114, 117

Ghosts, III, 162, 170

Giant's Causeway, I, 57

Gibbon, Edward, I, 2n, 213, 371n, 377, 384; II, 81; III, 205; The History of the Decline and Fall of the Roman Empire, I, 384n; II, 323n

Gilbert, William, I, 358

Giza, Pyramid of, III, 157

Glasgow, Scotland, III, 23n

Glaucus, Son of Epycides, III, 147–148

Globe, I, 51–53, 63, 83, 166, 224, 291, 297; II, 26, 31, 32, 184–185, 201, 214, 215, 358; III, 306–307; of Crystal, I, 327; II, 252; of Matter, I, 327; II, 252; Relation of Man to, I, 27–49; II, 201; see also Earth; World

Glory, II, 142, 157; III, 77, 127, 255; of the One, III, 276; of the World, III, 222; Supernatural, II, 92; Temple of, III, 229

Gnomes, III, 24, 65

Goad, Doctor, I, 139

Goat Island, I, 28

God, I, 15, 18, 21, 22, 32, 46, 51, 53, 72, 73, 75, 110, 112, 116, 119–143 *passim*, 148, 157, 165–182 *passim*, 210, 212, 219, 221, 274, 286, 300, 325, 326, 333, 351–352, 355, 373; II, 2n, 15, 17, 24, 49, 62, 70, 79, 85, 91, 95, 97, 100, 114, 152, 169, 176, 186, 218, 226, 232, 241, 247–250, 255–257, 264, 275, 278, 284, 294, 298, 301, 302, 303, 309, 311, 323, 332, 333, 340–356 *passim*; III, 7, 11, 17, 20, 29, 34, 35, 37, 43, 52, 67, 69, 72, 76, 78, 86, 89, 90, 93, 96, 107, 108, 114, 120, 127, 141–142, 164, 191, 192, 193, 202, 204, 206, 215, 231, 232, 233, 234, 245, 252, 262, 266, 276, 278, 279, 281, 282, 283, 285, 290, 298, 303, 308, 329, 330, 331, 351, 353, 360, 369, 375, 377, 381, 439, 474, 490, 502–503, 507–508, 522; City of, I, 383; III, 29, 98, 114; Daughter of, III, 201, 203; Epiphany of, III, 47; First, II, 91, 353; Government of, I, 120; Idea of, I, 218, 231; II, 232; Image of, I, 32; III, 170; Law of, I, 171; Power of, I, 175; II, 293, 351; III, 377; Son(s) of, III, 93; Will of, I, 124, 126, 226; Wisdom of, I, 171; *see also* Creator; Deity; Divinity; Godhead; Highest, Highest Being; Providence; Supreme Being

God(s), I, 273, 359; II, 58, 184, 186, 224, 257; III, 68, 245, 285, 357, 365, 375; Demi-, III, 285, 375; Half-, III, 95; Indian, III, 519

Godhead, The, I, 378; II, 90; III, 108, 285, 353

Godwin, William, *The Life of Chaucer*, I, 269n

God within Man, I, 172, 180–181; II, 343; III, 290, 330

Goethe, Johann Wolfgang von, I, xvi, 2n, 4n, 29, 69n, 72, 79, 80, 95n, 97n, 103, 104, 132, 208n, 227, 250, 285–286, 287n, 326, 359n; II, 3n, 4n, 5n, 16n, 23–24, 31n, 48, 53, 68, 119–123, 125–126, 184, 211n–212n, 265, 270n, 326; III, 1n, 80n, 106, 163–164, 219–223, 225, 323n, 501, 502; *Dichtung und Wahrheit*, II, 323n; III, 164n, 222n; *Einwirkung der*

neuern Philosophie, III, 221n; *Italienische Reise*, I, 101n, 103n, 104n; II, 53n, 123n, 265n; "Lili's Park," III, 118; *Noten und Abhandlungen zu besserem Verständniss des West-östlichen Divans*, III, 135n; "Principes de Philosophie Zoologique par Geoffroy de Saint-Hilaire," II, 30n, 153n; *Rameau's Neffe, ein Dialog von Diderot*, III, 133n; *Torquato Tasso*, II, 315–316; *Werke*, I, 389n; II, 24n, 211n–212n, 367n; III, 385n; *Wilhelm Meisters Lehrjahre*, I, 326n, 389n; *Wilhelm Meisters Wanderjahre*, I, 227n, 389n; *Winckelmann und sein Jahrhundert*, III, 6n

Goldsmith, Oliver, III, 400; *Retaliation*, I, 185

Good, The, I, 135, 154, 160, 261, 381; II, 19, 76, 110, 198, 311; III, 68, 86, 97, 106, 143, 150, 156, 182n, 189–190, 214, 215, 267, 312, 370, 439; Absolute, II, 84; Common, II, 99; Idea of, I, 162; II, 198–199; Infinite, II, 248; Moral, II, 344; of All, III, 106; of the Whole, III, 106; Private and Public, II, 86; Sentiment of, III, 190; Universal, 216

Goodies, III, 140

Goodness, I, 100, 110, 116, 201, 382; II, 50, 54, 94, 96, 102, 186, 264, 293–294, 354–355; III, 81, 139, 140, 143, 171, 308, 312, 419, 479; Absolute, II, 354; Eternal, III, 329; Perfect, I, 117

Good Sense, I, 340; II, 38, 96, 127, 168, 363; III, 13, 123; *see also* Common Sense

Goose Pond, Concord, II, 4n

Gospel, I, 121, 126, 129, 130; Scheme, III, 273

Gothic Age, II, 168

Gothic Architecture, II, 36, 52, 63; III, 220

Gothic Ballads and Sermons, I, 134

Gothic Cathedrals, II, 52, 54, 268; Minster, III, 84

Government, I, 184–201 *passim*; II, 68–82 *passim*, 305; III, 92, 191, 196, 199, 237, 238–247 *passim*, 276, 302, 309; Divine, III, 273; God's, I, 120; Self-, III, 245–246; *see also* State

Gower, John, I, 271, 274, 356; II, 150; *Confessio Amantis*, II, 150n

Gracchus, Caius Sempronius, III, 354

Gracchus, Tiberius Sempronius (163–133 B.C.), II, 290–291

Grace, I, 110, 116, 120, 168, 200; II, 267; III, 62, 192, 300

Graces, The, III, 63

Graevius, Johann Georg, II, 164

Graham, Sylvester, III, 260n

Graham of Claverhouse, John, II, 138

Granacci, Francisco, I, 102

Grand and Eternal, Region of the, III, 204

Gray, John Edward, I, 69n

Great Britain, *see* England

Great Men, I, xviii, xix, 94n–97n, 113, 119, 145, 148–150, 231–232, 235–236, 285, 320–321, 326; II, 37, 57, 75–76, 175, 258, 279; III, 11–13, 29, 56, 116, 139, 165, 215–216, 253, 259–260, 283, 313, 380–381, 395, 483; *see also* Hero(es)

Greatness, I, 165, 230, 320–321; II, 307, 332–334, 337, 340; III, 310–311, 507; *see also* Heroism

Greece, II, 8, 14, 54, 74, 131, 133, 180, 226, 309; III, 148

Greek(s), I, 280; II, 14, 15, 54, 73, 77, 131–136, 177, 186–187, 257, 269, 284; III, 69, 80, 112, 147, 204, 225, 290; Genius, of, I, 200; II, 135–136, 177; III, 72, 112

Greek Age, I, 138; II, 168, 186, 213

Greek Architecture, II, 52; III, 72

Greek Art, II, 14, 177; III, 95

Greek Language, III, 282

Greek Literature, II, 165, 177; III, 72

"Greek Philosophy of Taste," II, 59n, 367n

Greek Sculpture, II, 269–270; III, 72, 112

Greene, Lt. William Batchelder, III, 370n

Greene Street School, Providence R.I., I, xxii; II, 189n–194n, 211n; III, 321n

Greenough, Horatio, II, 48

Greenwich Royal Observatory, I, 235

Gregory I, Pope, III, 450 (?)

Gregory XVI, Pope, III, 276

Grenville, George, I, 201

Grief, III, 110–111, 116

Griscom, John, I, xxi

Grotius, Hugo, I, 152, 284; *De jure belli et pacis*, I, 152n; *De veritate religionis Christianae*, I, 284n

Growth, III, 29, 40, 91–92, 312–313, 349–350; Moral, III, 29; of Mind, II, 250

Guadaloupe, W. I., II, 253

Guercino, Giovanni Francesco Barbieri, III, 237

Guido da Colonna, *Historia Destructionis Troiae*, I, 254, 284

Guillaume de Lorris, I, 284

Guinea, Gulf of, I, 31

Gyges, Fabled Ring of, III, 450

Hadley Meadows, Mass., I, 80

Hafiz, Shams ud-din Mohammed, I, 212

Hague, William, I, 209n

Hales, John, I, 306, 353

Hall, Basil, III, 213

Hall, Sir James, I, 57

Hallam, Henry, I, 134, 147; II, 81; III, 225; *Constitutional History of England*, I, 147n; *The View of the State of Europe during the Middle Ages*, I, 134n, 389n

Haller, Albrecht von, I, 22

Hamilton, William, "The Braes of Yarrow," III, 214n

Hammel, Saxony, *see* Pied Piper of Hamelin

Hampden, John, I, 364; II, 324n, 335, 389

Hand(s), The, I, 40–41, 109–110, 152, 317–318, 330; II, 262; III, 196, 228, 280; Doctrine of, II, 230–245; Law of, II, 231, 246; *see also* Labor

Handel, George Frederick, II, 18, 51

Hardenberg, Baron Friedrich von, (Novalis), I, 173; II, 101

Hare, Julius Charles, and Augustus William Hare, *Guesses at Truth*, II, 64n, 142n, 307n, 367n

Harefield House, Eng., I, 161

Harleian Miscellany, II, 329

Harrington, James, I, 213, 361; *The Commonwealth of Oceana*, I, 213n

Harris, James, III, 106n

Harrison, William, and Raphael Holinshed, *The Chronicles of England, Scotland and Ireland*, I, 291, 316

Harrison, William Henry, III, 353n

Hartford, Conn., III, 23n

Hartley, David, I, 2n

Hartlib, Samuel, I, 150

Harun al-Rashid, III, 469

Harvard College and University, I, 287n; III, 324n; Emerson lectures at,

I, xxii; III, xx, 1n, 151n, 320n, 323n, 324n

Harvey, William, II, 183

Hastings, Warren, I, 184, 195, 198

Hatchett, Charles, I, 82

Haüy, René Just, *An Elementary Treatise on Natural Philosophy,* I, 2n

Havana, Cuba, II, 118

Havre, France, II, 116

Hawaiians, II, 43, 176

Hazlitt, William (1778–1830), I, 228, 287n; "Mr. Jeffrey," III, 296n; "My First Acquaintance with Poets," I, 228n

Head, Sir Francis, III, 211; *Bubbles from the Brunnens of Nassau,* III, 211n; *Rough Notes Taken during Some Rapid Journeys across the Pampas and among the Andes,* III, 211n

Head, The, II, 246–261, 262; III, 100; *see also* Intellect

Health, I, 155; II, 145, 177, 229, 311, 322–324, 326; III, 11, 25, 40, 67, 106–107, 112, 261–263, 265, 304, 311, 313, 368–369, 370, 377; Laws of, II, 119; III, 49, 130; of the Soul, II, 145, 271

Heart, I, 140, 141, 143, 162, 170, 172, 177, 192, 200, 259, 274, 303, 310, 375–376, 381–382; II, 150, 179, 278–294, 295, 335, 336, 355, 356; III, 6, 7, 38, 43, 53, 54, 79, 81, 89, 90, 100, 111, 196, 225, 236, 246, 249, 254, 272, 277, 285, 297, 298, 300, 308, 314, 329–330, 356, 381–382, 399, 479–480; Common, III, 280; of All, III, 54, 330; Prophetic, III, 382; Religion of the, III, 90; Sentiment of, II, 342; III, 272; Universal, III, 54, 232

Heat, I, 56–59; Laws of, I, 63

Heaven, I, 71, 77, 333; II, 32, 218, 228, 237, 342; III, 15, 39, 56, 118, 159, 196, 233, 251, 267, 268, 281, 283, 299, 490, 516; Will of, III, 41

Hebrew(s), I, 360–361; II, 14, 187, 224; III, 69; *see also* Jews

Hebrew Epoch, I, 138; II, 93

Hebrew Language, III, 142

Hebrew Law, I, 108

Hebrew Poetry, I, 248

Hecateus of Abdera, III, 159–160

Hector, I, 283; II, 62, 154; III, 159

Hedge, Frederic Henry, I, 144n, 205n, 209n; II, 210n, 211n; III, 156n, 177n, 320n, 321n, 325n

Hedge's Club, II, 208n; III, xii, 1n

Heeren, Arnold Hermann Ludwig, II, 68; III, 1n, 225

Heine, Heinrich, I, 287n

Helen of Troy, II, 276; III, 12

Heligoland, I, 237

Hemans, Felicia, III, 196, 217, 393, 410; "Corinne at the Capitol," II, 283n; *see also* Chorley, Henry F.

Hengist, I, 238, 241, 248

Henry IV, King of France (?), II, 140

Henry V, King of England, I, 284

Henry VII, King of England, I, 322

Henry VIII, King of England, I, 360, 361; II, 87n

Hephaestion the Corcyraean, III, 305

Heraclitus, I, 326, 359, 380; II, 184, 249

Herbert, George, I, 213, 263, 315, 337n, 338, 349–353; II, 93; III, 81; "Affliction" ("When first thou didst entice to thee my heart"), I, 352; "Confession," I, 351; "The Elixir," I, 351–352; "Man," III, 158n; "Providence," I, 352n; *The Temple,* I, 349, 353; "Vertue," I, 351

Hercules, I, 11, 285; II, 13; III, 136, 483

Hercules, Torso of (statue), II, 270

Herder, Johann Gottfried von, I, 287n; II, 68; III, 45

Hermes Trismegistus, I, 380

Hero(es), I, 22, 201, 260, 311; II, 139–140, 184, 228, 229, 240, 241, 327–341 *passim;* III, 96, 229, 292, 311, 380–381; *see also* Great Men

Herodotus, I, 316; III, 72, 147, 206; *Herodotus,* trans. William Beloe, III, 147–148n; *History,* I, 112n

Heroism, I, 141–142, 149–150, 155–156, 190, 313, 384–385; II, 318, 327–341, 345–346, 351; III, 29; *see also* Greatness

Herrick, Robert, I, 213, 263, 264, 306, 315, 337n, 338, 346–349; III, 372–373; "The Apparition of his Mistresse calling him to Elizium," I, 306 (?); "The Argument of his Book," I, 346; "Cloaths for Continuance," I, 348; "The Definition of Beauty," I, 348; "Not every day fit for Verse," I, 349; "An Ode for him" [Ben Jonson], I,

246, 306 (?); *Poetical Works,* I, 348n, 391n; III, 372–373; "The Star-Song," I, 347–348; "To Blossoms," I, 347; "To Silvia" ("I am holy, while I stand"), I, 348

Herschel, Sir John, I, 67; III, 213 (?), 373, 483 (?); *On the Study of Natural Philosophy,* I, 67n, 390n

Herschel, Sir William, III, 213 (?), 373, 483 (?)

Hesiod, I, 273; II, 62

Hickey, John, I, 192

Higher Law, *see* Law(s), Higher

Highest, The, II, 355; III, 141, 201

Highest Being, The, II, 255; *see also* God

Hiller, Johann Adam, III, 220

Himalayas, I, 41; II, 27, 171, 253

Hindoo(s), II, 130, 160; III, 204, 267; *see also* Brahmin(s)

History, I, 79, 90, 94n, 213, 218, 221, 225, 228, 234, 250, 255, 257, 289, 370, 377; II, 1n–6n, 7–21, 36, 38, 58–60, 66, 70, 81, 96, 98, 129, 132, 139–144, 152, 155–159, 173–174, 177–182, 186, 216, 326, 344, 356; III, 6–8, 13, 20, 21, 24, 37, 44, 55, 98, 158, 210, 225–228, 230–231, 241, 258, 272, 313, 474; Ancient, I, 255; III, 225; Laws of, III, 177n–178n, 200; Modern, I, 255; II, 213–214; III, 6, 188; Philosophy of, I, 225; II, 181; III, 226; Philosophy of Modern, II, 20; Religious, III, 6; Sacred, III, 276; Supernatural, I, 220; Universal, II, 254; III, 21; *see also* Natural History

Hoar, Elizabeth, I, xxiv, 208n; III, xii, 1n, 177n, 178n, 293n

Hoar, Samuel, II, 300n; III, 113n

Hobbes, Thomas, I, 365

Holbrook, Josiah, I, xx

Holiness, II, 318, 340–356; *see also* Piety

Holinshed, Raphael, and William Harrison, *The Chronicles of England, Scotland and Ireland,* I, 291, 316

Holland, Province of, I, 43

Holofernes, I, 248

Holy, The, II, 229; III, 199, 328

Home, Sir Everard, I, 70n

Home, John, *Douglas,* I, 223 (*probable error for* John Home, *Alonzo; A Tragedy*)

Home, III, 24–33, 34, 51, 136, 362, 400–401; Deeper, III, 31; Higher, III, 26; in God, III, 20; in Universal Being, III, 234; Law of, III, 170; Philosophy of, III, 25–26, 401; True, III, 34

Homer, I, 138, 154, 161, 172, 212, 221, 222, 229, 285, 316, 330, 359; II, 48, 51, 60, 61, 62, 65, 133, 134, 151, 226, 260; III, 12, 17, 45, 69, 80, 82, 158, 168, 205, 206, 210, 214, 221, 225, 230, 234, 250, 267, 418; *Iliad,* I, 73, 184; II, 51, 151; III, 12n, 84, 159n

Honduras, I, 39, 45

Honor, I, 243, 276–278, 328; II, 140–142, 241, 338; Man of, II, 139–141; *see also* Gentleman

Hooi, II, 88

Hooke, Robert, II, 29

Hooker, Richard, I, 213, 214, 271, 338, 355, 361; *Of the Laws of Ecclesiastical Polity,* I, 213, 355

Hope, I, 258, 320–321; II, 11, 95, 159, 170, 177, 198–199, 203, 204, 228, 229, 245, 270, 272, 277, 359; III, 20, 39, 84, 85, 90, 104, 114, 143, 199, 201, 216, 242, 254, 260, 291–292, 313, 328, 356, 363, 382, 474, 522; Sentiment of, III, 39

Hopkins, Vivian C., "Emerson and Bacon," I, 320n; "Emerson and Cudworth: Plastic Nature and Transcendental Art," I, 356n; *Spires of Form,* I, 99n

Horace (Quintus Horatius Flaccus), I, 359; III, 47; *Odes,* I, 11n; *Satires,* I, 442n

Horn, Cape, I, 31

Horsa, I, 238, 248

Hortense de Beauharnais, Queen of Holland, III, 134

Hottentots, I, 42

Howard, Charles, Earl of Nottingham, II, 228

Howard, Henry, Earl of Northampton, I, 323

Howard, John, I, 201

Howell, James, I, 323; *Epistolae Hoelianae,* I, 323n

Howgill, Francis, I, 180

Huber, François, I, 20

Hudson, Henry, II, 175

Hudson River, I, 54, 57

Hugo, Victor Marie, III, 17

Humanity, I, 158, 300; II, 10, 14, 33, 37, 63, 67, 81, 288; III, 33; Mind of, II, 50; Universal, II, 110

Human Nature, *see* Nature, Human

Humboldt, Baron Alexander von, I, 18, 28n, 39, 45, 78; II, 37, 68, 126, 172, 201; III, 106, 213; *Personal Narrative of Travels in Equinoctial Regions of the New Continent,* I, 39n, 46n, 390n

Hume, David, I, 149, 167, 189, 213, 251, 302, 307; II, 81, 260; III, 230, 375

Humility, I, 156; II, 320, 346–347, 351; III, 300, 482; Doctrine of, I, 177; Sentiment of, III, 272

Humor, I, 249, 275–276, 302; III, 124, 234; Bad, III, 290; Good, I, 139, 142; II, 334

Hundred Greatest Men, The, I, 217n; II, 55n, 57n

Hunter, John, I, 22, 81; II, 133n

Hunting, I, 6–7, 133

Hurd, Dr. Isaac, III, 131n

Huss, John, I, 124; II, 217

Hutchinson, Thomas, *The History of Massachusetts,* I, 164n, 179n, 391n

Hutchison, William R., *The Transcendental Ministers,* III, 324n

Hutton, James, I, 1n, 56; II, 32

Hutton, William, II, 242

Huttonian Theory, *see* Hutton, James; Playfair, John

Hydrostatic Paradox, I, 219

Hydrostatics, I, 66–67, 410

Hypocrisy, III, 127–129

Ibn Haukal, II, 332; *The Oriental Geography of Ebn Haukal,* trans. Sir William Ouseley, II, 332n–333n

Icarus, II, 13; III, 306

Iceland, III, 362

Idea(s), I, 81, 218–219, 220, 225, 231, 307, 378; II, 10, 98, 170, 176, 217, 269; III, 9, 94, 97, 101, 144, 198, 205, 217, 223, 227, 245, 259, 260, 263, 363; and Conception, I, 378; and Experience, III, 482–483; and Notions, I, 219; Cardinal, III, 360; Deepest, III, 287; Divine, II, 171; Great Idea within, II, 199; New, II, 214; of Antimasonry, I, 219; of Antislavery, I, 219; of Beauty, I, 100; of Fitness, I, 17; of Freedom, I, 218–219, 231; II, 77; of God, I, 218, 231; II, 232; of Good, II, 198–199; of

Good and Fair, I, 162; of Immutableness, III, 277; of Intellectual Beauty, I, 231; of Justice, I, 218, 231; of Love, I, 218–219; of Man, I, 149; II, 11, 196–197, 288; of Matter, I, 218; of Missions, I, 219; of Necessity, I, 231; of Order, I, 218; of Orthodoxy, I, 219; of Perfect, II, 198–199; of Popular Education, I, 219; of Possession, III, 40; of Power, II, 86; of Present Day, I, 219; of Right, III, 247; of Self, I, 218; of Skepticism, I, 219; of Space, I, 218; of State, I, 379; of Temperance, I, 219; of Time, I, 218; of Virtue, I, 219; III, 144; of War, I, 231; Premature, II, 149

Ideal, The, II, 217–220, 228–229, 242, 260, 266, 297; III, 55, 94, 125, 251, 313, 474, 507, 525; Moral, II, 218; of Human Form, III, 74; of Human Mind, II, 230; of Right, II, 219–220; of Right and Truth, III, 124–125

Ideal Commonwealth, II, 69–70

Idealism, I, 175, 226–228; Dreams of, III, 303

Idealist(s), I, 168, 175; III, 56, 79, 124

Ideal Man, II, 12, 268, 272

Ideal Standard, III, 20

Ideal Tendencies, II, 159

Ideal World, I, 162; II, 316, 362

Identity, II, 14, 34–36, 42; III, 143; of All Things, III, 291; of Men, II, 20, 283–285, 346; of Revelation, II, 180; of Soul in Every Age, II, 187

Idol(s), I, 120, 331, 376; II, 226, 324–325; III, 91–92, 199

Idolatry, I, 216; II, 96; III, 265; of Facts, II, 37

Image, Imagery, I, 149, 150, 153, 221, 222, 225, 229, 230, 262, 265, 290, 296, 303, 327, 329, 330, 382; II, 217, 231–232, 250, 254; III, 37–38, 40, 53, 73, 92, 259, 352; of God, I, 32; III, 170

Imagination, I, 138, 162, 188, 224–225, 257, 263, 289–297, 305, 307, 313, 315, 321, 350, 358, 375, 379; II, 13, 169, 234, 245, 265, 268; III, 54, 59, 78, 109, 168, 198, 206, 218, 261, 262, 353, 361, 459

Imitation, I, 74–75, 131, 262, 382; II, 46, 60–61, 151, 228, 266; III, 71, 74, 88, 210, 303, 312

Imitation of Christ, see Thomas à Kempis

Immortality, I, 330, 360, 369, 383–384; II, 354; III, 117, 203, 251; of the Soul, II, 188; III, 277

Immutableness, Idea of, III, 277

Impersonal, The, II, 278–279; III, 43

Impulse(s), III, 95; Divine, I, 376; II, 215; Eternal, III, 351; from within, III, 99; Man of, II, 281; Virtuous, III, 278; Wandering, II, 336

Ina, King of the West Saxons, I, 250–251, 360n, 526

Inca, II, 177

Independents, I, 174; II, 94

India, II, 106; III, 105

Indian(s), *see* Brahmin(s); Hindoo(s)

Indian(s), American, I, 45, 132; II, 128, 135–136, 161, 225, 333; III, 128, 165, 257; Carib(s), I, 39; II, 112; Chayma, I, 45–46; Chickasaw, I, 272; Creeks and Winnebagoes, II, 8; Flathead, III, 154; Mohawks and Cherokees, II, 130; Patagonian, II, 112; Sacs and Foxes, II, 227

Indian God, III, 519

Indian Literature, III, 204, 354

Indians, Nations of, III, 395

Indian Temples, II, 52

Individual(s), I, 79–81, 225, 331, 359; II, 8–9, 15, 44, 48–49, 73–74, 84, 99–100, 129, 151, 152, 155, 160, 167, 171–188, 213–215, 228, 246–249, 266, 285, 310, 340, 343, 355; III, 11–12, 27–28, 36, 87, 106, 165, 188–189, 242, 265–266, 300, 307–308, 364, 495, 516

Individuality, I, 161; II, 49; III, 165

Induction, I, 330

Infinite, The, II, 54, 145; III, 10, 94, 118, 284, 328; Feeling of, III, 196, 217, 218

Infinity, I, 383; III, 454, 455

Innovation, Party of, III, 344n; *see also* Movement Party

Innovators, III, 521; *see also* Movement Party

Inquisition, The, III, 81; at Malta, I, 170

Insanity, I, 138, 325; II, 161, 227, 330; III, 108, 126, 129, 287, 299

Insecurity, III, 104, 106, 108

Insight, II, 223; III, 251, 284, 290, 313, 363

Inspiration, I, 197; II, 99, 181, 292; III, 36, 73; Doctrine of Proper, III,

36; Philonic, I, 311; Prophetic, II, 90, 99

Instinct(s), I, 42, 79; II, 42–43, 55, 70, 114, 144–145, 168, 173–174, 227–229, 250–251, 293–300, 310, 322; III, 14, 27, 29, 34–39, 41, 44, 47, 51, 66, 77, 87, 136, 144, 166–167, 169–170, 229, 248; Animal, III, 229; High, II, 85; Higher, III, 48–49; Idealizing, III, 64; Man of, II, 300; of Adoration, II, 341; of Life, II, 58; of the Ideal, II, 219; Primary, III, 39; Secondary, III, 39; Social, III, 56

Institutes of Hindu Law; or, The Ordinances of Menu, trans. Sir William Jones, II, 89, 124n, 367n

Institution(s), I, 190, 193, 201, 233; II, 54, 75, 106–107, 129, 156, 213; III, 11, 90–91, 94, 124, 197, 240, 243, 245, 252, 266, 276, 293, 300, 309, 363; Feudal, I, 213; Genius of, I, 377; Monarchical and Aristocratical, III, 9–10; Religious, III, 286–287, 324n–325n; Social, II, 132; Theological, III, 193

Integrity, II, 242; III, 125, 266, 309, 441; Ideal, II, 218; Intellectual, II, 295, 341–342; of Mind, II, 151

Intellect, I, 19–20, 188, 242, 297, 321, 335, 344; II, 16, 58, 91, 102, 132, 162, 181, 229, 246–261, 272, 273, 292, 344; III, 15–16, 22, 43, 47, 54, 62, 66, 68, 71, 85–86, 87, 88, 115, 117, 123–128, 133, 135, 144, 170, 187, 197, 228, 356, 441; Law(s) of, II, 252, 311, 330

Intemperance, Evil of, II, 107; Suppression of, I, 182; *see also* Temperance

Introversion, II, 170–171; III, 9–10

Intuition, II, 168, 249, 252; III, 35–36, 46, 230

Iole, III, 483

Irish, The, I, 239; II, 160; III, 115

Irving, Washington, I, xix

Isaac, II, 71; III, 479

Isaiah, I, 132; II, 61, 162

Ishmael, I, 170; III, 372

Italian(s), I, 242, 360; II, 264, 266

Italian Era, II, 157, 213

Italian Literature, III, 274

Italy, I, 89–90, 242, 255, 381, 419–423; II, 269; III, 191, 220

Ithaca, Greece, III, 12

Ivimey, Joseph, *John Milton: His Life and Times*, I, 144n–145n, 158n, 390n

Jackson, Dr. Charles Thomas, I, xv, 3n; III, 130n
Jackson, Lydia, *see* Emerson, Lidian (Lydia) Jackson
Jacob, II, 71, 219; III, 479
Jahn, Johann, *History of the Hebrew Commonwealth*, III, 160n, 385n
James I, King of England, I, 321–325 *passim*, 338, 354, 355, 360, 361; II, 138
Jamestown, Va., III, 128n
Japan, III, 32, 187, 243
Jardin des Plantes, Paris, I, 2n, 3n, 7–10
Jarvis, Dr. Edward, I, 88n
Jean de Meun(g), I, 284
Jefferson, Thomas, I, 285; II, 60, 132; III, 231
Jenner, Edward, I, 82; "On the Migration of Birds," I, 82n
Jeremiah, I, 135, 137; III, 142
Jerseys, The, II, 335
Jerusalem, III, 340n
Jesus, I, 134, 135, 166, 169, 170, 171, 221, 229, 238, 240, 245, 254, 284, 301; II, 90, 258, 271, 298, 315, 355, 455; III, 38, 144, 145, 229, 240, 242–243, 247, 276, 277, 279, 282, 299, 311, 313, 465, 490, 501
Jews, III, 215, 273; *see also* Hebrew(s)
Job, I, 139; II, 316
John, Saint, I, 136n, 292; II, 187, 241
Johnson, Richard, *The Famous Historie of the Seven Champions of Christendom*, I, 257
Johnson, Samuel, I, 144n, 148, 149, 157, 191, 193, 197, 213, 356n, 366–369; II, 67, 314, 324; III, 85, 192, 194; *Diary and Prayers*, III, 192; *Irene*, I, 309; Letter to Lord Chesterfield, I, 367; "Life of Milton," I, 144n, 355n, 367, 390n; *The Lives of the English Poets*, I, 210; Preface to *A Dictionary of the English Language*, I, 367–368; *The Rambler*, I, 368–369; II, 144n; *Works*, I, 391n; III, 385n
Joinville, Jean de, III, 198
Jonas, Justus, I, 123–124n, 134–135n
Jones, Richard, First Earl of Ranelagh, I, 160n
Jones, Sir William, trans., *Institutes of*

Hindu Law; or, The Ordinances of Menu, II, 89, 124n, 367n
Jonson, Ben, I, 207n, 213, 263, 264, 274, 300–301, 306, 310, 316, 322–323, 325, 337n, 338–346, 354, 357, 376, 384; *Catiline, His Conspiracy*, I, 339; *Cynthia's Revels*, I, 341; "Dedicatory Epistle of *Volpone; or The Fox*," I, 340–341; *English Grammar*, I, 346; *The New Inn*, I, 341; "An Ode. To himselfe," I, 345–346; III, 149n; *The Poetaster*, I, 342–343; *Sejanus, His Fall*, I, 339; "Song. From *Pleasure reconciled to Vertue*," I, 344–345; "Song. From *The Gypsies Metamorphosed*," I, 345; "Song. From *The Vision of Delight*," I, 344; *Timber; or Discoveries Made upon Men and Matter*, I, 346; *Works*, I, 207n, 341n, 391n
Jorgenson, C. E., "Emerson's Paradise under the Shadow of Swords," I, 145n
Joseph of Exeter, *Antiocheis*, I, 241n
Jouffroy, Théodore Simon, I, 2n; III, 226
Jove, I, 107; II, 107; III, 19, 24, 148, 305, 308; *see also* Jupiter
Judaea, II, 213; III, 273, 274, 276
Judah, III, 323n
Judgment, Day of, II, 151, 301; III, 38, 194, 235
Judgment Seat, III, 19
Judith (Anglo-Saxon poem), I, 248
Juno (statue), I, 104
Jupiter, I, 258; II, 224, 298; *see also* Jove
Jupiter (planet), I, 18, 29; II, 39
Jupiter Capitolinus, Temple of, Rome, I, 106
Jussieu, Antoine Laurent de, I, 2n, 3n, 8; III, 38; *Genera plantarum secundum ordines naturales . . .* , III, 38n
Jussieu, Bernard de, III, 38n
Just, The, III, 483
Justice, I, 160, 249; II, 75, 78, 84–85, 99, 154–155, 177, 188, 197, 216, 217, 227, 229, 248–249, 259, 279, 333, 344; III, 6, 29, 36, 39, 149, 252–253, 269, 300, 313, 375, 516; Absolute, II, 355; Divine, III, 252; Ideal, I, 146; II, 217; Idea of, I, 218, 231; Sense of, II, 344; Sentiment of, III, 6, 277

Justinian, Emperor, II, 9, 323; III, 240, 474
Jutland, I, 237
Juvenal (Decimus Junius Juvenalis), I, 359; *Satires,* II, 144n; III, 131n

Kalmuck, III, 154
Kant, Immanuel, I, 173, 299, 302; II, 68, 126, 149, 185, 260–261, 455; III, 220–221, 223, 234, 458
Kean, Charles John (?), III, 400
Keate, George, *The History of Prince Lee Boo,* II, 56n, 367n
Keats, John, III, 218; *The Poetical Works of Coleridge, Shelley, and Keats,* III, 218
Keble, John, "Morning," I, 167n
Kemble, Charles (?), III, 400
Kempis, Thomas à, *see* Thomas à Kempis
Kenilworth, Eng., I, 235
Kepler, Johann, I, 22, 353; II, 37; III, 49, 212
Kett, Henry, I, 215
Khan(s), The Great, II, 57, 245
Kindness, II, 104, 281–283, 294, 320–321; III, 25
King's College, Cambridge, II, 63–64
Kinnard (?), II, 286
Kish, II, 115
Knowledge, I, 14, 16–17, 23, 68, 81, 160, 171, 228, 327, 330; II, 78, 124, 127, 164, 182, 231, 251, 269, 359; III, 17–20, 29, 69, 211, 218, 292, 330, 374; Accepted Means and Modes of, III, 97; Angels of, III, 112; Intuitive, III, 36; Liberal and Useful, III, 24–25; of Good and Evil, III, 87; of Human Nature, III, 18; Perfect, III, 15
Knox, John, II, 217
Koran, I, 130; II, 95
κόσμος, I, 83, 100; III, 222
Kronman, Jeanne, "Three Unpublished Lectures of Ralph Waldo Emerson," III, 186n, 366n, 369n, 370n, 371n, 375n, 380n, 517n

Laban, II, 71; III, 479
Labor, II, 71, 77–78, 114–128 *passim,* 181, 215, 218, 230–245, 278; III, 11, 33, 95, 119, 264, 400, 486–488; Division of, I, 6; II, 100–102; Doctrine of, III, 264, 487–488; Law of, II, 318; *see also* Trades and Professions; Vocation; Work
Labrador, II, 225
Lacedaemon, III, 147
Laelius, Caius (Sapiens), II, 290
Laertes, III, 12
Lafayette, Marie Joseph Paul du Motier, Marquis de, II, 37, 80, 172
Lagrange, Joseph Louis, I, 72
La Guayra, Venezuela, I, 34
Lamarck, Jean Baptiste, Chevalier de, II, 24
Lancaster, John of Gaunt, Duke of, I, 269–270
Lancelot du Lac, I, 254, 257
Lander, John, II, 167; III, 211 (?); *Journal of an Expedition to Explore . . . the Niger,* III, 211n
Lander, Richard L., II, 167; III, 211; *Journal of an Expedition to Explore . . . the Niger,* III, 211n
Landor, Walter Savage, I, xix, 277; III, 1n, 60, 253; "Diogenes and Plato," III, 253n; "Duke de Richelieu, Sir Fire Coats, and Lady Glengrin," III, 60n; "Epicurus, Leontion, and Ternissa," II, 104n; *Imaginary Conversations,* II, 368n; III, 385n; "Marcus Tullius Cicero and His Brother Quinctus," II, 142n; "William Penn and Lord Peterborough," I, 277n; III, 255n; "Xenophon and Cyrus the Younger," III, 140n
Landseer, Sir Edwin, III, 138
Langbaine, Gerard, *Account of the English Dramatick Poets,* I, 287n
Langland, William, *The Vision concerning Piers Plowman,* I, 166
Langlande, Robert, *see* Langland, William
Language, I, 24–26, 152–153, 219–224, 229–230, 290, 291, 310–311, 331, 350; II, 45, 85; III, 41, 195, 207, 233, 297, 358–359; American, I, 75; Anglo-Saxon, I, 238, 248–249, 253–254; British, I, 238, 253; English, I, 153, 158, 212, 238, 248–249, 253–254, 273, 307; III, 59, 142; French, I, 253–254; German, I, 138, 238; II, 303; Greek, III, 282; Hebrew, III, 142; Latin, I, 248–249, 253; II, 303; III, 282; Norman, I, 253–254; Pelews', II, 149; Provençal, I, 270; Welsh, I, 238
Laocoon, The (statue), II, 49, 270; III, 80

INDEX

Laplace, Pierre Simon, Marquis de, I, 12, 25, 31, 53, 72, 73, 132, 229, 333; II, 18, 36, 38, 39, 102–103
Lapland, III, 407
Lapps, III, 53
Lardner, Dionysius, I, 1n; ed., *Cabinet Cyclopaedia: History of England*, by Sir James Mackintosh, I, 277n, 377, 391n; II, 154n, 368n; ed., *Cabinet Cyclopaedia: Lives of Eminent British Statesmen*, II, 324n, 367n, 389n; ed., *Lives of the Most Eminent Literary and Scientific Men of Italy, Spain, and Portugal*, II, 293n, 368n; *Treatise on Hydrostatics and Pneumatics*, I, 66n, 390n
Las Cases, Emmanuel Augustin Dieudonné, Comte de, III, 239; *Mémorial de Sainte Hélène. Journal of . . . Napoleon at Saint Helena*, III, 13n, 115n, 134n, 161n, 195n, 239n, 385n
Latimer, Hugh, I, 288
Latin Language, I, 248–249, 253–254; II, 303; III, 282
Latin Literature, I, 262, 273; II, 1n, 165; III, 274, 354; *see also* Classics, The
Latins, II, 12
Latona, III, 395
Laughter, II, 359; III, 11, 121–137 *passim*, 438
Laurentian Library, Florence, I, 117
Laurin, King, I, 261
Lavater, Johann Kaspar, III, 222
Law(s), I, 25–26, 73, 81–82, 107, 121, 187, 218–219, 274; II, 4n, 20–26, 39–42, 76–78, 88–95, 112, 115, 127, 144–147, 151–153, 181, 187, 200, 215, 218, 220, 223, 236, 248–258, 279, 291, 300, 311, 317–318, 341–344, 352, 360; III, 28–29, 47–48, 54, 72, 84, 88, 89, 102, 105, 111–112, 145–146, 151, 158, 164–167, 170–171, 202, 227, 235, 249, 265, 268, 274, 275–276, 362, 375; Blue-, II, 334; Civil, III, 226, 238; Cosmical, III, 165; Elemental, I, 80; English, I, 360; Eternal, II, 5n; Ethical, I, 131; III, 276; External, III, 164; for Persons, II, 72–74; for Property, II, 72–74; from Things, II, 218; General, III, 47, 112; Generic, III, 155, 165; Heavenly, III, 273; Hebrew, I, 108; High, II, 243–244; Higher, I, 195; II, 239; III,

281; Higher and More Interior, III, 64; Household, III, 33; Inward, I, 81; Intellectual, II, 330; Moral, I, xvii–xviii, 361; II, 330; III, 158, 379; Natural, I, xviii; II, 119, 330; III, 40; of Action, I, 370; II, 144; of Affection, II, 318; of Angles and Solids, III, 313; of Animated Nature, I, 72, 81; of Architecture, II, 64; of Art(s), II, 44–45, 48, 51; of Beauty, I, 383; II, 51, 263, 318; of Being, III, 381; of Chemistry, I, 78; II, 30; of Circulation, I, 63; of Composition, I, 317; II, 64–66; of Conversation, II, 292; of Creation, I, 82; of Criticism, III, 177n–178n, 200; of Diffraction, I, 93n; of Disease and Health, II, 119; III, 49, 130; of Dualism or Polarity, III, 40; of Education, I, 383; of Éloquence, II, 111; of Equal Pressure of Fluids, I, 66; of Expansion and Contraction, I, 65; of Ethics, I, 25, 290, 370; II, 201, 344; III, 66, 177n–178n, 200; of Fluids and Gasses, I, 59; of Friendship, II, 104, 290; III, 254; of Genius, II, 268; of God, I, 171; of Hands, II, 231, 246; of Heat, I, 63; of History, III, 177n–178n, 200; of Home, III, 170; of Human Nature, I, 291; II, 124; of Ice, III, 126; of Inquiry, I, 327; of Intellect, II, 252, 311, 330; of Labor, II, 318; of Laws, II, 95; of Life, I, 48, 215; II, 92, 146, 181, 233; III, 2n; of Literature, I, 212, 218; III, 202–206; of Living, II, 318; of Love, I, 383; III, 487; of Manners, II, 132; of Man's Being, I, 382; II, 171, 200; III, 381; of Marriage, II, 111–112; of Matter, I, 24–26, 48, 290; II, 148, 201, 311; III, 164; of Members, III, 86; of Mind, I, 99, 319; II, 13, 22, 73, 94, 98–99, 147–148, 181, 201, 218, 273, 311, 362–363; of Mind's Growth, II, 250; of Moral Agents, II, 201; of Moral Nature, I, 24–26, 290, 297; II, 95; of Morals, III, 164; of Moral Sentiment, I, 149; II, 353; of Nature, I, 23, 25, 80–82, 242; II, 10, 23–26, 36, 44, 48, 77–78, 103, 117, 127, 203, 221, 252–253, 350; III, 29, 263; of Outward Convenience, II, 318; of Physiology, I, 383; of Polarization, I, 78; of Providence, I,

560

380; of Sculpture, II, 64; of Senses, II, 316; of Sentiment, I, 215; of Social Element, II, 111–112; of Society, II, 292; of Soul, I, 381; II, 102, 150–151, 221, 345; III, 278; of State, II, 69; of Thought, I, 224, 291, 307, 311, 383; II, 318; of Undulation, II, 252; of Universal Mind, II, 12; of Universe, III, 166, 368; of Virtue, II, 256–257; of Will, II, 181; of Wisdom, II, 256–257; of Wit, I, 214; of World, I, 214; II, 114, 301; III, 40, 106; of Writing, II, 361; One, I, 82; III, 368; Physical, II, 25–33, 200, 316; Primary, I, 80; Profession of, I, 170; Roman, III, 240; Saxon, I, 213; Spiritual, I, 72, 156, 160; II, 103, 112, 126; III, 111, 167, 226, 249, 278, 313, 352; Statute, I, 159, 236, 242, 250; II, 129, 132, 215; III, 8, 11, 20–21, 94, 191, 196, 197, 199, 216, 239, 240, 241, 242, 245, 288; Universal, II, 103; III, 249, 285

Lazarus, III, 278

Lazzaroni, II, 119–123, 227

League, The, II, 178

Learning, I, 329–330, 336; II, 14, 164–165; III, 46, 126, 194–195, 251; *see also* Pedantry

Lee, Sarah (Mrs. R.), *Memoirs of Baron Cuvier,* I, 1n, 13n, 63n, 390n

Lee Boo, Prince, II, 56n

Le Havre, France, II, 116

Leibnitz, Gottfried Wilhelm, Baron von, I, 132, 224; II, 199; III, 45

Leicester, Robert Dudley, Earl of, I, 315

Leighton, Robert, I, 361; II, 94; *The Select Works,* II, 423n; III, 502n

Leipzig, Germany, I, 123, 137

Leipzig (Book) Fair Catalogue, II, 166

Lentuli, The, II, 134

Leo X, Pope, I, 121–126 *passim*

Leonidas, I, 384; III, 247

Lepanto, Battle of, I, 130

Leslie, Sir John, *Elements of Natural Philosophy,* I, 2n

Letters, *see* Literature

Leuctra, Victory at, I, 140

Lexington (steamer), III, 326n

Liberia, II, 82

Liberty, I, 158–160, 182, 194, 383; II, 167; III, 90, 238; Civil, I, 147, 159; *see also* Freedom

Library of Useful Knowledge, I, xx

Lido, The, Venice, III, 220

Life, I, 116, 251; II, 29–31, 40, 58, 87, 146, 177, 183, 186, 220–222, 247–249, 261, 270, 273, 304–306, 321, 330; III, 5, 10, 13, 21, 31, 48, 53, 89, 104, 139, 143–144, 158, 206, 209, 258–261, 263, 268–269, 283, 288, 327, 363–365, 368, 376–382; Common, II, 57; III, 482; Doctrine of, II, 30–31; Domestic, III, 8, 269, 286, 302, 303; Eternal, III, 53, 115, 253; Ideal, III, 259–260, 269; Laws of, I, 48, 215; II, 92, 146, 181, 233, 318; III, 2n; Primary, III, 314; Private, I, 370; II, 144; III, 248–255

Light, I, 166, 172, 220; II, 34, 105, 142, 177, 232, 252, 257, 258, 345, 364; III, 15–16, 141, 143, 144, 146, 167, 251, 283, 314, 456; Divine, I, 174, 181; II, 91, 94; Dry, II, 249; Exchequer of Truth and, I, 383; God's, I, 177; III, 7; Great, II, 204; III, 280, 304, 331; Immortal, III, 141; Infinite, III, 45; Intellectual, I, 286; Inward, I, 168; Living, III, 280; Material, I, 166; New, III, 490; Ocean of, III, 18; Ocean of Love and, I, 171; of Ideas, I, 218; of the Mind, II, 249; of Things, III, 456; Sea of, III, 285; Temple of the True and Living, I, 331; Universe of Love and, I, 384; Vital, I, 166

Limitation(s), II, 170–171; III, 170, 269, 297, 497, 508

Linberg, Henning Gotfried, trans., *Introduction to the History of Philosophy,* II, 3n; III, 105n

Lincoln Cathedral, II, 272

Lincolnshire, II, 272

Lingard, John, II, 81; III, 225

Linnaeus, Carolus, I, 3n, 18, 80, 221, 289; II, 37; III, 38, 240

Literary Borrowing, I, 283–286

Literary Man, I, 211, 226, 327–328, 383; II, 60–62; III, 235, 458

Literature, I, 210–231, 381–385; II, 14, 19, 20, 55–68, 73, 81, 94, 97, 132, 143, 181, 197–198, 304, 310, 352, 358, 361; III, 6, 24, 38, 71, 92–93, 187, 202–210, 400, 507; American, I, 75, 212, 215–216; III, 82, 374–375; Anglo-Saxon, I, 243–248, 251–252, 253; British, I, 239–241, 253; Celtic, I, 239–241; English, I, 75,

205–385; III, 274, 372; French, III, 274; Greek, II, 165, 177; III, 72; Indian (Hindoo), III, 204, 354; Italian, III, 274; Latin, I, 262, 273; II, 165; III, 274, 354; Law(s) of, I, 212, 218; III, 202–206; of Present Age, III, 8–9, 202–237, 251, 281, 286, 302, 374–375; Provençal, III, 250; Roman, II, 165; Spanish, III, 274; Welsh, I, 239–241; *see also* Books
Little Garden of Roses, I, 261
Liverpool, Eng., I, 5n; III, 186
Liverpool and Manchester Railroad, I, 14
Lives and Voyages of Drake, Cavendish and Dampier, I, 35n, 37, 38n, 39n, 45, 390n
Lives of Eminent British Statesmen, II, 324n, 367n, 389n
Lives of Eminent Persons, I, 18n, 22n, 109n, 112n, 113n, 114n, 389n; II, 66n, 368n; III, 77n, 386n
Lives of the Most Eminent Literary and Scientific Men of Italy, Spain, and Portugal, II, 293n, 368n
Livy (Titus Livius), III, 239
Llywarch Hen, I, 239–241; "Elegy on Cynddallan ap Cyndrwyn," I, 240; "Elegy on Urien Reged," I, 241
Locke, John, I, 132, 149, 229, 356n, 365–366; III, 140, 230; *An Essay Concerning Human Understanding,* II, 60
Λογος, Divine, II, 353
Lollius of Urbino, I, 284
Lombards, II, 12
Lombardy, I, 43
London, Eng., I, 2n, 147, 151, 184, 186, 192, 216, 270; II, 11, 56, 80–81, 116, 130, 139, 166, 335, 360; III, 7, 28, 70, 187, 204, 216, 375, 408, 474, 488; Emerson lecture in, III, 23n
London Company (Virginia), III, 128
Lonely, The, III, 283
Longfellow, Henry Wadsworth, II, 278n
Longfellow, Samuel, *Life of Henry Wadsworth Longfellow,* II, 278n
Long Wharf, Boston, II, 225
Lord, The, *see* God
Lord's Prayer, The, I, 249
Lord's Supper, The, I, xvii, 132n, 181, 182; III, 320n
Louis, Saint, II, 140
Louis XIV, King of France, III, 25, 243

Louvain, Belgium, I, 124
Love, I, 80–81, 132, 147, 154, 157, 165, 171, 177, 231, 300, 384; II, 18, 100–104, 124, 155, 177, 197, 248, 270–272, 278–294, 306, 320–321, 333, 344, 346, 355, 357n, 359; III, 29, 32–33, 41, 51–67, 68, 80, 96, 108, 112, 119–120, 136, 194, 203, 236–237, 247, 253, 268, 276, 277, 278, 279, 281, 290, 299–300, 303, 308, 312, 314–315, 329, 358, 363, 381, 455, 477; Divine, III, 61; Idea of, I, 218–219; Law(s) of, I, 383; III, 487; Platonic, I, 115; III, 60–62; Universal, III, 315
Lovejoy, Elijah P., II, 338
Lowell, James Russell, III, xii
Lowell, Mass., I, xxii; III, 353; Emerson lectures in, I, 207n; II, 213n, 230n, 246n, 262n, 278n (?); III, xi
Lower, Dr. Thomas, I, 177
Lucan (Marcus Annaeus Lucanus), I, 366; III, 159; *Pharsalia,* III, 159n, 254n, 373n
Lucian, I, 259; III, 158; "The Lover of Lies, or the Doubter," I, 259n; III, 158n
Luck, III, 151
Lucretius (Titus Lucretius Carus), I, 359
Ludicrous, The, *see* Comedy
Luther, Katherina von Bora, I, 127, 138–139; II, 178
Luther, Martin, I, 79, 94n, 98n, 118–143, 147, 222, 230, 274, 286, 296, 355, 384, 432; II, 51, 60, 78, 87, 91, 111, 162, 178, 217, 304; III, 81, 100–101, 243, 246, 311, 472, 490, 511; Augsburg Confession, I, 127; *Colloquia Mensalia: or . . . Divine Discourses . . . [Table Talk],* I, 118n, 119, 120n, 121n, 129n–137n *passim,* 138, 139n, 141n, 147n, 390n; II, 111n; III, 246n; *A Commentary upon the Epistle to the Galatians,* I, 121, 136, 138, 390n; Ninety-five Theses, I, 119, 122–123; Translation of Bible, I, 126, 128, 129, 131, 139, 286; III, 101, 116
Lutherans, I, 127
Lutzen, Battle of, II, 329
Lyceum, I, xx–xxi, 1n, 93n–94n; II, 166, 210n; III, xi, xvii
Lycophron, II, 266

Lycurgus (of Athens), III, 69 (?), 441 (?)
Lycurgus (of Sparta), II, 60; III, 69 (?), 441 (?)
Lydgate, John, I, 233n, 271, 284, 356; *Troy-book*, I, 284
Lyell, Sir Charles, I, 209n; II, 22n
Lynn, Mass., III, 353
Lyon, George Francis, III, 206–207n
Lysis, II, 284
Lytton, Edward George Earle Lytton Bulwer-, *see* Bulwer-Lytton

McCaffery, Alexander, III, xii
McCormick, John O., "Emeron's Theory of Human Greatness," I, 95n
Macedonian Era, I, 250
McGiffert, Arthur C., Jr., *Young Emerson Speaks*, III, 320n, 322n
Machiavelli, Niccolò, I, 117, 187, 228; III, 511
Mackintosh, Sir James, I, 2n, 207n, 276, 371, 376–377; II, 59; *A General View of the Progress of Ethical Philosophy*, I, 234n, 376, 391n; *The History of England*, I, 207n (?), 377, 391n; II, 154n, 368n; *History of the Revolution in England*, I, 377; review of Partitions of Poland, I, 376; review of de Staël's *Germany*, I, 376; reviews of Stewart's *A General View of the Progress of Metaphysical, Ethical, and Political Philosophy*, I, 376
Maelgwyn of Gwynedd, I, 240
Magellanic Clouds, I, 41
Magian, II, 177; III, 368
Magic, I, 260, 262, 332; III, 151, 162, 191; *see also* Demonology; Superstition
Mahomet, I, 166, 256; II, 323; III, 372, 511
Maine, II, 227, 239; III, 193
Majano, Italy, II, 293
Malay, II, 179; III, 154
Malden, Mass., III, 193
Malebranche, Nicholas, I, 362
Malone, Edmond, "Prolegomena," *The Plays and Poems of William Shakespeare*, I, 287n, 301n, 306n, 391n
Malory, Sir Thomas, *Morte Darthur*, I, 257
Malthus, Thomas Robert, II, 67; III, 213
Mammoth Cave, Kentucky, II, 22n, 34–35

Man (Men), I, 6, 10, 11, 17, 23, 24, 27n, 28, 29, 32, 70–71, 81, 83, 103–104, 119, 141–142, 148–150, 160–163, 165, 166, 167, 182, 200, 201, 218–228 *passim*, 242, 251, 272, 274, 289–305 *passim*, 321, 326, 329–335 *passim*, 340, 341, 358, 359, 365, 367, 370, 378, 379, 382, 383–385; II, 1n–6n, 7–21, 24, 25, 44–45, 50, 56, 67, 69, 70, 79, 82, 83, 88–89, 95, 96, 97, 99–100, 102, 107, 109, 111, 112, 113–114, 143–156 *passim*, 160, 169, 170–171, 186–187, 191n, 195–204, 208n–211n, 213–223, 228–229, 230–245 *passim*, 246, 247–248, 251, 254–255, 259, 260, 262, 272, 276–277, 280, 281, 282, 284, 296, 297–298, 308, 309, 311–312, 314, 326, 330–331, 336, 338, 341, 343, 344, 358–359, 364; III, 5, 7, 10–14, 16, 19–20, 22, 24, 31, 33, 34, 36, 46, 47, 48, 49, 52, 62–63, 65, 70, 75, 85–87, 91, 92, 98–99, 102, 103, 106–107, 109, 112, 122–124, 133, 143, 165, 169–170, 171, 178n, 186, 188, 189–190, 199, 201, 206, 224–225, 228–229, 231–232, 235, 236, 237, 239–247 *passim*, 248–251, 277, 281–284, 287–288, 291, 297, 300, 307–308, 312–315, 329–330, 349, 352, 356, 363, 370–372, 378–381, 395, 483, 520, 522, 525; Actual, II, 272; Civilized, I, 76; II, 174–175; Constitution of, I, 40, 71; II, 76, 130, 136, 200–201; III, 87, 91, 92, 105, 152, 234, 290, 313, 355, 358; Doctrine of True Nature of, III, 24; Fall of, I, 362; III, 86–89, 98, 277, 283, 299, 330; First, I, 160, 165, 384; II, 14; God within, I, 172, 180–181; II, 343; III, 290, 330; Great, I, xviii–xix, 94n–97n, 113, 119, 145, 148–150, 165, 231–232, 235–236, 285, 320–321, 326; II, 37, 57, 75–76, 175, 258, 279; III, 11–13, 29, 56, 116, 139, 165, 215–216, 253, 259–260, 283, 313, 380–381, 395, 483 (*see also* Hero[es]); Ideal, II, 12, 268, 272; Ideal Nature of, II, 262; Idea of, I, 149; II, 11, 196–197, 288; Identity of, II, 20, 283–285, 346; Individual, II, 173–188 (*see also* Individual[s]); Infinitude of, I, 180; III, 177n, 201, 234, 291; Inner, III, 74, 349; Literary, I, 211, 226, 327–

328, 383; II, 60–62; III, 235, 458; Natural, III, 216; Nature of, *see* Nature, *esp.* Human *under* Nature; New, III, 232; of Character, III, 483; of Calculation, II, 281; III, 166; of Genius, I, 166–167, 191–192, 272, 381; II, 99, 161, 315–316; III, 80–83, 85–86, 235, 284, 459 (*see also* Genius); of Honor, II, 139–141 (*see also* Gentleman); of Instinct, II, 300; of One Idea, III, 260; of Reason, II, 141–142; of Routine, III, 48; of Sense(s), II, 141–142; III, 48, 166; of Strong Will, III, 240; of Talent(s), II, 62, 361; III, 235, 375, 460, 483; of this Age, III, 377–378; of Truth, III, 240; of Understanding, II, 141; III, 48; of Wit, III, 127; of World, II, 258; III, 96–98, 149, 217; Perfect, I, 326; II, 312; Practical, I, 302; Pragmatical, I, 328; Public, I, 196; Relation to Nature, I, 10, 24–49, 79–81; II, 17–21, 22–40 *passim*, 253; Self-Made, III, 195; Spiritual Nature of, III, 273–274; Survival of, I, 34–41; Universal, I, 226, 272; II, 12, 68, 74; III, 370; Universal Heart of, III, 232; Universal Nature of, III, 228; Wild, I, 45–46; II, 56, 306 (*see also* Noble Savage; Savage[s]); Wise, I, 159, 199, 214, 229, 272, 274, 307, 383; II, 251, 257, 259–260; III, 19–21, 33, 119, 149, 242–244, 268, 284, 292, 441, 490; Young, *see* Youth

Manco Capac, I, 166

Mandeville, Sir John, I, 254, 288; *Travels*, I, 254

Mann, Sir Horace, III, 13n

Mann, Horace, II, 210n

Manners, I, 20; II, 129–142, 181, 187, 299, 304, 324–325; III, 20, 24, 70, 134, 297, 305, 490; American, I, 75; Greek, II, 133–137; Roman, II, 133–135; Law of, II, 132

Mansfield, Mass., II, 275

Mantua, Italy, II, 102

Manu, *see* Menu

Manufacturers & Farmers Journal and Providence and Pawtucket Advertiser, II, 189n

Manzoni, Alessandro, II, 347–350; III, 218; *I Promessi Sposi*, II, 347–350, 368n

Marathon, Greece, II, 241

Marchers, III, 521; *see also* Movement Party

Marcus Aurelius Antoninus, I, 186, 188, 359

Marengo, Italy, III, 116

Marie de France, *Lais*, I, 284

Marlowe, Christopher, I, 306, 315, 338, 341, 355; III, 208

Marriage, II, 102–103, 288; III, 62–66, 91; Law of, II, 111–112

Mars, I, 238; III, 12

Marshman, Joshua, trans., *The Works of Confucius*, II, 88n, 94n, 104n, 150n, 282n, 368n; III, 119n, 386n

Martial (Marcus Valerius Martialis), *Epigrams*, I, 15n; III, 90n, 253n

Martineau, Harriet, *Society in America*, II, 319n

Martyrdom, III, 268

Marvell, Andrew, I, 213; "An Horatian Ode upon Cromwel's Return from Ireland," I, 99n

Mary, Virgin, II, 315, 351; III, 232

Mary I ("Bloody Mary"), Queen of England, III, 81

Masaccio (Tommaso Guidi), I, 114

Masollam the Jew, III, 159–160

Masonic Hall, Providence, III, 5n

Masonic Temple, Boston, I, xiv, xvi, 5, 93n–94n, 205n, 253n, 269n; II, xi, xxi, 7n, 22n, 41n, 55n, 69n, 83n, 98n, 113n, 129n, 143n, 157n, 173n, 205n, 212n, 213n, 230n, 246n, 262n, 278n, 295n, 310n, 327n, 340n, 357n; III, xi, xiii, xiv, xv, xvii–xviii, xxv, 5n, 23n, 34n, 51n, 68n, 85n, 103n, 121n, 138n, 151n, 173n, 175n, 185n, 202n, 224n, 238n, 248n, 256n, 271n, 286n, 302n, 333n, 335n, 336n, 337n, 340n, 347n, 366n

Masons, II, 126; *see also* Antimasonry

Massachusetts, I, 54, 128, 275, 335; III, 142, 193–194, 209, 340n

Massachusetts Historical Society, I, 371n; *Collections*, III, 128n

Massillon, Jean Baptiste, II, 60

Massinger, Philip, I, 309, 316, 355

Mathematics, III, 314, 378; Axiom of, III, 158

Matter, I, 24, 215, 224–225; II, 4n, 31, 185; III, 40, 52; Idea of, I, 218; Laws of, I, 24–26, 48, 290; II, 148, 201, 311; III, 164

Matthiessen, F. O., I, 337n

Mawe, John, *Linnean System of Conchology,* I, 2n
May Day, I, 46; III, 52–53; May Game(s), I, 175; III, 268
Mayne, Jasper, I, 306
Means and Ends, II, 107; III, 129–133, 145–146, 189, 302–304, 460
Mechanics, II, 14, 26; Axioms of, I, 25
Mechanics' Apprentices' Association, Boston, III, xiii, xx
Mechanics' Apprentices' Library Association, Boston, III, xiv, xx, 256n, 336n
Mechanics' Institutes, II, 38
Medford, Mass., II, 128n
Medici, Cosimo, *error for* Giuliano de' Medici, Duke of Nemours, I, 108
Medici, Cosimo de' ("The Great") (?), Grand Duke of Tuscany, I, 112
Medici, Lorenzo, Duke of Urbino, I, 108
Medici, Lorenzo de' ("The Magnificent"), I, 100
Medicine, III, 457
Mediterranean Sea, II, 8; III, 474
Medusa (statue), I, 104n
Melancholy, I, 116; III, 104, 113, 137, 154, 297; English, I, 249, 252
Melanchthon, Philipp, I, 123–124n, 141, 147; III, 81
Melrose Abbey, Inscription on, II, 363n
Memory, II, 142, 144, 270; III, 37–38, 40, 56–57, 61, 69, 79, 89, 95, 142, 153–154, 244, 362, 374; Loss of, III, 104; Power of, III, 15
Memphis, Egypt, I, 259; II, 226; III, 30, 158, 250
Menander, III, 253
Mendelssohn, Moses, I, 285; *Phädon,* I, 285n
Menelaus, III, 12
Menu, III, 144; *Institutes of Hindu Law; or, The Ordinances of Menu,* trans. Sir William Jones, II, 89, 124n, 367n
Mercantile Library (Society), New York, III, xiv, 175n–176n, 185n, 202n, 238n
Mercantile Library Association, Philadelphia, III, 366n
Merchant, The, II, 115–116, 238–239, 362–363; III, 121
Merck, Johann Heinrich, III, 221; see also *Briefe an Johann Heinrich Merck*

von Göthe, Herder, Wieland und andern bedeutenden Zeitgenossen
Mercury, III, 24
Meres, Francis, I, 310; *Palladis Tamia,* I, 310n
Merlin, I, 257
Mesmer, Friedrich (or Franz) Anton, I, 10n
Mesmerism, *see* Animal Magnetism
Metamorphosis, I, 210; II, 23–24; III, 154, 354
Metaphor, I, 24–25, 220–222; II, 12–13; III, 352–354; *see also* Allegory; Symbol(s), Symbolism
Metaphysical Style, I, 349–350
Metaphysics, II, 167, 215; III, 36, 167, 389; Kantean, II, 185; Practical, III, 18
Meteorology, I, 63
Methodist(s), I, 174; II, 92, 94, 345–346; III, 187, 243, 275
Methusalems, III, 88
Metre, I, 305, 308–310; III, 358–359
Meuse River, I, 43
Mexico, Gulf of, I, 31
Michelangelo Buonarroti, I, 94n, 98–117, 152; II, 61, 66, 264; III, 46, 61, 79, 100, 144, 413, 483; Ara Coeli Stairs, I, 106; "Aurora," I, 108; Bust of, I, 117; Cartoon of Messer Tommaso di Cavalieri, I, 110; Cartoon of the Bathers, I, 108–109; "Christ," I, 103, 108; "Creation," I, 108; "David," I, 108; "Day," I, 108; "Last Judgment," I, 108, 111; Laurentian Library, I, 117; Medici Monuments, I, 108; "Moses," I, 108; "Night," I, 108; "Pietà," I, 108; "Prophets and Sibyls," I, 108; *Rime de Michelagnolo Buonarroti . . . ,* ed. Giambattista Biagioli, I, 99n, 115, 390n; III, 79n; St. Peter's, I, 99, 109, 111, 112; Self-portrait, I, 98n; Sistine Chapel, I, 106–108, 111; III, 100, 483; Sonnet I, I, 99n; Sonnet III, I, 99n; Sonnet VI, I, 99n, 110n; II, 264n; Sonnet VII, III, 79; Sonnet XXI, I, 99n; Sonnet XXXIX, I, 99n; Sonnet LI, I, 99n, 110n; Sonnet LVI, I, 99n, 116n; Sonnets, I, 115; III, 144; "Twilight," I, 108
Michigan, II, 147, 239
Middle Ages, I, 255, 273; II, 8, 66, 179; Literature of, I, 253–286

Middle Atlantic States, Emerson lecturing in, III, xv
Middlebury College, Vt., I, xxii
Middle Passage, The, III, 112, 114
Middlesex, Lionel Cranfield, First Earl of, I, 322
Middlesex County (Mass.) Education Association, III, 288n
Midianites, II, 71
Milan, Italy, II, 347
Miletus, Greece, III, 147
Millennium, The, III, 38
Milner, Joseph and Isaac, *The History of the Church of Christ*, I, 120n, 121n, 124n, 127n, 390n
Miltiades, II, 241
Milton, John, I, xx, 2n, 94n, 98n, 118n, 132, 144–163, 212, 213, 215, 216, 222–223, 251, 274, 275, 276, 283, 285, 303, 306, 308, 321, 332, 334, 337n, 344, 353, 354, 356n, 361, 362–363, 366–367, 369, 376, 384; II, 61, 62, 66, 67, 78, 140, 152, 162, 228, 287, 335; III, 7, 12, 17, 26, 46, 56, 62, 81, 168, 192, 205, 218, 221, 233, 243, 285, 361, 375; *Accedence commenced Grammar*, I, 157; "Anno Aetatis XIX, At a Vacation Exercise," I, 152; III, 372n; *An Apology for Smectymnuus*, I, 150n, 153, 155n, 161, 162n, 363; *Areopagitica*, I, 147, 158n, 223n; III, 7n, 285n; *Artis logicae plenior institutio*, I, 157; *Comus*, I, 155, 161, 353, 362–363; *The Doctrine and Discipline of Divorce*, I, 161, 162–163; Elegia VI: "Ad Carolum Diodatum," I, 154n; [First] *Defence of the English People*, I, 146–147; *The History of Britain*, I, 158; "Il Penseroso," I, 161; III, 117n; Italian Sonnets, I, 151; "L'Allegro," I, 153n, 161, 265; Latin Dictionary, I, 157; Latin Epigrams, I, 151; Letter to Charles Diodati, I, 154n; Letter to Emeric Bigot, I, 151; Letter to Peter Heimbach, III, 27n; Letter to Richard Jones, I, 160n; *The Likeliest Way to Remove Hirelings out of the Church*, I, 156n; *Lycidas*, I, 94n, 144n; *Of Education*, I, 150n, 151; *Of Reformation*, I, 156n; *Of the Christian Doctrine*, I, 145; *Paradise Lost*, I, 148, 160n, 161, 163, 222n, 242n, 266, 307, 308n, 334 (?), 336n, 367; II, 63; III, 13n, 87n, 243n; *Paradise Regained*, I, 161, 162n; *The Prose Works*, ed. Charles Symmons, I, 145n, 390n; III, 386n; *The Reason of Church Government*, I, 156, 157, 158, 161, 363; *Samson Agonistes*, I, 161; II, 347n; *A Selection from the English Prose Works*, I, 390n; III, 386n; "Sonnet XIX" ("When I consider how my light is spent"), II, 303n; Sonnets, I, 161; *The Tenure of Kings and Magistrates*, I, 159n
Mimir's Spring, II, 35
Mind, I, 24–26, 27n, 132, 218–220, 225–226, 260, 262, 285, 288–291, 296–297, 303–304, 317–318, 321, 327, 331, 333, 334–336; II, 7–24, 33–34, 37, 39, 42, 50, 59, 62, 66, 69–70, 73, 83, 89, 98–106, 109, 130, 133–134, 145–152, 155–159, 179, 181, 185, 187, 200–201, 215, 224, 227–228, 246–261, 263, 271, 275, 280, 286, 294, 345–346, 352, 359, 361; III, 6, 35, 41, 72–73, 84, 137, 140–141, 206, 267–268, 272, 274, 285, 291, 296, 349, 380, 382, 458; Absolute, II, 50, 188; Adaption of Body to, I, 40–41; and Body, III, 121; and Natural History, I, 18–26; Catholic, I, 304; Central, II, 87–88; Common, I, 262, 307; Common to Universe, II, 151; Constitution of, III, 91–92; Divine, I, 365; II, 51, 87–88; Eternal, II, 49; III, 253; Ethics of, II, 151; General, II, 86, 251; III, 256–257; Grand, II, 199; Higher, II, 73; Ideal of Human, II, 230; Individual, II, 50, 178, 185, 249, 251; III, 35; Law(s) of, I, 99, 319; II, 13, 22, 73, 94, 98–99, 147–148, 181, 201, 218, 273, 311, 362–363; III, 86, 258; Law of Growth of, II, 250; Laws of Universal, II, 12; Living, III, 203; Modern, II, 213; III, 160, 228–229, 236; Nature of, I, 211; II, 250; of Humanity, II, 50; of Nature, II, 33–34, 266; of the Period, III, 257; of this Age, III, 277–278; One, II, 4n, 11–14, 20, 50, 52, 60, 70, 83, 98–99, 132, 147–148, 154, 167–168, 181; III, 30, 214, 224, 233; Power of, I, 330; Power over Body, I, 178; Progress of Human, II, 254–255; III, 285,

291; Pure, II, 62; Science of, II, 167; Sovereign, I, 297; III, 265; Supreme, III, 300; Unity of, II, 17, 25, 83; III, 39; Universal, I, 304, 321; II, 12, 14, 15, 38, 44, 49, 68, 83–86, 99, 115, 181, 220, 355; III, 188; Voluntary Acts of, III, 36

Minerva, I, 107

Mirabeau, Honoré Gabriel Victor Riqueti, Comte de, I, 22, 285; III, 506, 511

Miracle(s), II, 228, 274; III, 142, 278–280, 304; Eternal, III, 381; Perpetual, I, 360; Popular Doctrine of, III, 278; Universal, III, 142

Mirandola, see Pico della Mirandola, Giovanni

Missions, II, 214; Idea of, I, 219; Society of, II, 106

Mississippi River, I, 54; III, 135

Missouri River, I, 215

Mitford, William, II, 81

Mitscherlich, Eilhardt, I, 31

Mob(s), II, 102, 109; III, 225, 305, 458

Modern Times, see Present Age, The

Mogul, Great, II, 57

Mohammedan Fanaticism, I, 138

Mohawk Indians, II, 130

Monadnoc, Mt., II, 223

Money, II, 202, 243, 325–326; III, 91, 239, 243, 264, 442; System of, III, 485–487

Monster(s), I, 17; II, 30, 56, 269; III, 74

Monstrous, The, III, 154–155

Montaigne, Michel Eyquem de, I, xx, 165, 209n, 350, 362, 366; II, xiii–xiv, 149, 162, 211n, 215, 290–291, 326, 466; III, 1n, 44, 81, 212, 216, 224, 286n, 502; "Against Idleness," II, 135n; III, 289n; *Essays,* trans. Charles Cotton, I, 362, 389n; II, 368n; III, 216n, 386n; "Observations of the means to carry on a war according to Julius Caesar," II, 138n; "Of Books," III, 44n, 209n; "Of Conscience," II, 334n; "Of Experience," II, 215n, 326n; "Of Friendship," II, 288n, 291n, 466n; "Of Glory," III, 149n, 159n; "Of Physiognomy," I, 165n; "Of the Education of Children," I, 350n

Mont Blanc, II, 166

Montesquieu, Charles de Secondat, Baron de, I, 132

Montgomery, James, "Monti," II, 293n

Monti, Vincenzo, II, 293

Moody, Samuel, III, 193–194n

Moore, J., I, 176

Moore, Thomas, I, 268, 274, 310; II, 62; *Memoirs of the Life of Richard Brinsley Sheridan,* I, 184n, 195, 391n; II, 301

Moral(s), I, 166; II, 115, 126; III, 206; External Law of, III, 164; of Science, II, 39; Practical, I, 170

Moral Code, II, 311

Moral Discipline, I, 116, 155, 242; see also Discipline

Moral Faculties, I, 116; II, 215; see also Faculty(ies)

Moral Ideal, II, 218; see also Ideal, The

Morality, I, 286; III, 204–205; Rules of, I, 194

Moral Law, see under Law(s)

Moral Nature, see Nature, Moral

Moral Order, II, 364

Moral Perfection, I, 154; see also Perfection

Moral Powers, see Power(s), Moral

Moral Result, II, 243

Moral Science, I, 360

Moral Sense, see Sense(s), Moral

Moral Sentiment, see Sentiment(s), Moral

Moral Standard, II, 175

Moral Sublime, I, 214, 352

Moravian, II, 92, 346

More, Henry, I, 361, 365; III, 81 (?)

More, Sir Thomas, I, 288; II, 87, 334; III, 81 (?)

More and Less, III, 107–108

Moritz, Karl Philipp, I, 101

Mormon, II, 433

Morning Post, III, 178n

Morte d'Arthur, I, 257

Mortification, III, 482

Moses, I, 28, 137, 138, 166, 212; II, 60, 65, 152, 225; III, 69, 191, 206, 210, 224, 274, 299

Most High, The, III, 330; see also God

Movement Party, III, xv, 187–189, 197–198, 325n, 344n, 521

Müller, Johann Georg, III, 45n

Müller, Johannes von, II, 68, 226; III, 225; *Sämmtliche Werke,* III, 45n; *An Universal History,* II, 102n, 154n, 368n

Music, I, 151; II, 10, 12, 36, 45–47, 54, 359, 480; III, 57, 60, 93, 217, 228, 350, 358–359, 377
Mysticism, II, 167; III, 228
Mystick (Medford), Mass., II, 128n
Mythology, *see* Fable(s)

Nantasket Beach, Mass., III, 336n
Naples, Italy, I, 419–420; II, 50, 119–123; III, 137
Napoleon, I, 79, 95n, 114, 140, 141, 211, 424; II, 17, 36, 37, 138, 156, 172, 241, 304, 476; III, 13, 37, 75, 88, 89, 106, 115, 134, 161, 195, 225, 229, 230, 231, 239, 350, 352, 370, 431
Nash, Richard ("Beau Nash"), III, 133
Nassau, Germany, III, 210
Natural, The, II, 134
Natural History, I, 5–83, 220, 221, 289, 327, 331; II, 19, 26–28, 221, 274–275, 314, 354; III, 30, 145, 240, 276, 287; as Discipline to Mind and Character, I, 18–23, 75–76; as Healthful Occupation, I, 10–11, 23; as Knowledge, I, 11–14, 23–26, 46–48, 78–82; as Self-knowledge, I, 23–26, 78–82; as Useful Knowledge, I, 11–14, 23; Delight in, I, 14–18, 23, 46; in Education, I, 70–71, 76; Intellectual Influences of, I, 70–83; Uses of, I, 5–26, 46–48, 70–83; *see also* Science(s)
Natural History Society, *see* Boston Society of Natural History
Naturalist(s), I, 6, 10, 12, 15, 20, 69–83; II, 30, 33, 37, 219, 274–275; III, 49, 227
Natural Law(s), *see* Law(s), Natural
Natural Magic, I, 332–333; *see* Demonology; Magic
Natural Philosopher, *see* Naturalist(s)
Natural Philosophy, *see* Natural History; Science(s)
Natural Science, *see* Natural History; Science(s)
Nature, I, 5–83, 99, 101–102, 131, 132, 149, 151, 160, 166, 171, 174, 197, 200, 212, 215, 219–221, 225, 229–230, 243, 256, 265, 266, 272, 291, 292, 293, 296, 299, 300, 301, 317, 319, 326–327, 330–332, 340, 373, 376, 382, 384–385; II, 4n, 9–10, 17–20, 23–26, 36, 43–53, 59, 77–78, 88, 94, 102–103, 113–117, 122–

123, 127, 132, 136–137, 144–145, 152–159, 171–173, 181, 184–187, 203, 217–222, 227, 234–236, 245–248, 252–253, 255, 265–280, 283–286, 295, 298–303, 307, 312, 316–317, 322–323, 330, 337–339, 343–345, 354–355, 358–359; III, 11, 14, 22, 24, 27–33, 35–39, 40–41, 48, 52, 54, 55, 56, 57, 58, 63, 66–67, 73, 74–76, 79, 82, 84, 90, 92, 97–98, 104, 110, 113, 114–115, 117–118, 119, 121, 122–123, 127, 133, 136, 141, 145, 146, 147, 149, 151, 153, 154–155, 158, 165, 168, 169, 170, 171, 188, 190, 195, 199, 203, 204, 205, 206–207, 214, 215–216, 217, 222, 223, 226, 228, 233–234, 241, 242, 243, 250, 252, 254, 258, 260–261, 262, 268, 269, 276, 280–285, 289, 290, 292, 295, 297, 306–307, 308, 309, 312, 314, 315, 328, 329, 330, 348–357, 360, 361, 362, 368, 370–374, 376, 379, 381, 455, 457, 458, 507, 508, 519–520, 522; Absolute, II, 147, 171, 247; III, 124; Animated, I, 17; Balance of, III, 245; Bodily, II, 133; Brute, I, 220; II, 153; III, 276; Central, III, 101; Central Mundane, II, 297; Circle of, III, 49; Common, I, 359; II, 98–100, 111, 361; III, 20–21, 41, 43, 399; Constitution of, III, 312; Divine, I, 304; III, 252, 278; Eternal, III, 285; Everlasting Now in, I, 71; External, I, 7, 24, 39, 101; II, 200; III, 299, 300; Flux in, II, 27, 32; III, 27–28, 510; Great, III, 280–284; Harmony of, I, 188; Heir of, III, 290; Higher, II, 311, 343; III, 154, 277; Highest, II, 282; Human, I, 143, 149, 165, 174, 189, 212, 218, 221, 261, 284, 289, 304, 321, 326, 330, 331, 341, 358, 359, 362, 374; II, 4n, 9–13, 16, 35, 59, 69, 73, 79, 92, 95, 98–102, 108, 124, 126, 129, 137, 151, 155–156, 171, 180–182, 199, 215, 217, 220, 222, 229–230, 237–238, 257, 262, 269, 272–276, 293–294, 297, 309, 317–318, 324, 340, 344, 346; III, 8–14, 18, 24, 52, 54–56, 59, 62, 63, 82, 110–112, 114–115, 121, 127, 170, 204, 228–229, 232, 273–274, 277, 474; Ideal, II, 48, 53, 262, 347; Identical, II, 112, 346; Inanimate, I, 51; Individual,

II, 99–100, 181, 331, 341; Inferior, II, 343; Instinctive, III, 167; Intellectual, I, 384; Invisible, I, 219; Inward Law of, I, 81; Law(s) of, I, 23, 25, 80–82, 242; II, 10, 23–26, 36, 44, 48, 77–78, 103, 117, 127, 203, 221, 252–253, 330; III, 129, 263; Law(s) of Animated, I, 72, 81–82; Law(s) of Human, I, 291; II, 124; Law(s) of Moral, I, 24–26, 290, 297; II, 95; Love of, I, 44–46, 80, 151; III, 350; Material, I, 383; II, 9–10, 20, 25–27, 53, 66, 78, 95, 127, 144–145, 148, 313–314; Metaphysical, III, 14, 215; Mind of, II, 33–34, 266; Moral, I, 32, 290, 383; II, 50, 84, 95, 97, 127, 153, 203, 218, 270; III, 234, 269, 292; Moral of, III, 308; Nocturnal Side of, III, 103; of Mind, I, 211; of Things, I, 370; II, 95, 144, 145; III, 86, 205; of World, III, 301; One, III, 47, 214; Order of, III, 28, 105; Organic, I, 28–34; Perfection of, I, 71–73; III, 28; Permanence of, III, 41; Physical, III, 14; Power of, II, 225; Private, II, 299; Pure, II, 85; Relation of Man to, I, 10, 24–49, 79–81; II, 17–21, 22–40 *passim*, 253; Religious, I, 332; II, 20; Secret(s) of, I, 29, 48, 78, 299; II, 26, 31, 274; III, 299, 317, 360; Social, II, 293; Soul of, II, 247; III, 215, 230; Spiritual, I, 220, 226, 231, 383; II, 32, 85, 97, 133, 148, 351; III, 208, 209, 251, 273–274; Superior, II, 343–344; Superior Recesses of, III, 364; Symbolic Laws of, III, 29; Theory of Animated, I, 81–83; Unconscious, III, 20, 123, 167; Universal, I, 117; II, 287, 341, 343; III, 20–21, 228

Navigation, I, 35–38; III, 84; of the Air, III, 451

Nayler, James, I, 173; III, 490

Nebo, III, 308

Necessary, The, II, 51, 67, 264; III, 178n, 186, 189–190

Necessity, I, 370; II, 42, 44–45, 50–53, 60–65, 73, 94–95, 144, 221–222, 270, 295, 345, 354, 358; III, 86, 238, 400, 454; Great and Beautiful, I, 225; Idea of, I, 231; Philosophical, III, 106

Negro, II, 160; III, 371

Nelson, Horatio, First Viscount, III, 350

Nemesis, II, 154; III, 62, 146

Neptune, II, 234; III, 159

New Bedford, Mass., I, 94n, 164n; Emerson lectures at, I, xxii, 87n–88n; Unitarian Church, I, 164n; III, 320n; Whaleman, I, 35

Newcastle, Eng., II, 118

Newcomb, Charles King, III, xii, 339n

New England, I, 90, 179; II, 209n–211n, 237, 241–244; III, 128–129, 135, 193–194, 378, 399

New Hampshire, III, 53, 176n, 264–265

New Jerusalem, Church of the, *see* Swedenborgianism

New Jerusalem Magazine, The, I, 25n, 389n; III, 17n, 386n

Newman, Franklin B., "Emerson and Buonarroti," I, 99n

New Orleans, La., I, 419

Newton, Sir Isaac, I, xx, 21–22, 80, 99, 132, 229, 333, 384; II, 18, 23, 29, 37, 38, 39; III, 49, 82, 90, 227

Newton, Mass., I, 87n, 88n

New York, N.Y., I, 419; III, 151n, 176n, 186–187, 264, 274, 319n, 326n, 408, 477, 488; Emerson lectures at, I, xxii; III, xiv–xv, 23n, 175n–176n, 185n, 194n, 202n, 238n, 337n, 341n, 342n, 345n, 347n, 366n, 367n, 369n, 371n, 380n

New York Society Library, III, 342n

New York Sound, III, 326n

New-York Tribune, III, 366n

New Zealander, II, 174

Ney, Michel, Duc d'Elchingen, Prince de la Moscowa, III, 13

Niagara Falls, I, 41; II, 223

Nibelungenlied, III, 210

Nicholas, Saint, II, 298

Nicias the Painter, III, 368

Nicoloff, Philip L., *Emerson on Race and History,* II, 3n

Niebuhr, Barthold Georg, II, 68, 226; III, 225, 465

Niger River, III, 211

Nile River, III, 112, 373

Noble Savage, II, 133–136; *see* Savage(s); Wild Man

Nomadism, III, 227

Non-Resistance, Doctrine of, III, 265

Norman Language, I, 253–254

Normans, I, 249, 253–254

Norris, John, I, 365

Norsemen, II, 35
North, The (U.S.), I, 233
North American Review, The, I, 98n, 144n; III, 151n, 327n, 367n
Northampton, Mass., III, 324n
Northcote, James, III, 132; *The Life of Sir Joshua Reynolds,* III, 132n–133n
Northerner, The (U.S.), II, 313–314
Northmen, I, 241–243; II, 131
North Sea (German Ocean), I, 237
North Strandt Island, I, 237
Northumberland, Duke of, II, 239
Northwest Passage, III, 211
Norway, II, 123
Notions and Ideas, Distinction between, I, 219
Novalis (Baron Friedrich von Hardenberg), I, 173; II, 101
Now, The, III, 457, 492; Eternal, II, 158, 274; Everlasting, I, 71; II, 90; the Here and, III, 30
Numa Pompilius, I, 166; II, 60; III, 69
Nushirvan, *see* Anusherwan

Oaths, I, 176, 182; II, 297–298; III, 148
Obedience, III, 90, 109, 281, 344n, 376
Ockley, Simon, *History of the Saracens,* II, 329
O'Connell, Daniel, III, 225
Oedipus, III, 105
Oegger, G., I, 220; *The True Messiah . . . ,* I, 389n
Oersted, Hans Christian, II, 38
Ohio, II, 419
Ohio Circles, The, III, 30
Ohthere, I, 252
Old Age, II, 253; III, 88–89, 349
Oldcastle, Sir John, Baron Cobham, I, 360; II, 217
Oliver, III, 282
Olympiads, II, 9
Olympian Games, II, 131
Olympus, II, 224, 226, 335; III, 24, 63
O'Meara, Barry Edward, *Napoleon in Exile,* III, 352n, 386n
Omen(s), II, 359; III, 151–152, 156–160, 170
Omniscience, III, 470
One, The, II, 279; III, 276; Eternal, III, 280; Many in, I, 101; II, 264
Opie, Iona and Peter, ed., *The Oxford Dictionary of Nursery Rhymes,* II, 219n
Opinion, I, 358; II, 102, 107–109, 251, 304, 310, 337, 354; III, 18, 20, 36,

97, 146, 244, 288, 374; of Society, III, 308; Pride of, III, 50
Optimism, I, 72; II, 176; III, 106, 200, 312
Orator, I, 199, 221, 318; II, 46, 49, 57, 109–111, 163; III, xvii, 82–83, 180n, 355, 400; *see also* Eloquence; Speech(es)
Order, I, 190, 228; III, 62, 72; Idea of, I, 218; Moral, II, 364; of Nature, II, 34, 39; III, 28, 105; of the Universe, I, 74; of the World, III, 41; Social and Moral, II, 39; Universal, III, 27
Orestes, II, 60; III, 105
Organization, I, 81, 101; III, 35, 59, 86, 123, 154, 167, 269; Universal, III, 44
Oriental Nations, I, 280
Oriental Sculpture, II, 352
Original, The, III, 283
Originality, III, 205, 360, 381; *see also* Literary Borrowing
Orinoco River, I, 39
Orkney Islands, II, 118, 225
Ormazd, I, 79
Oromasdes, *see* Ormazd
Orpheus, I, 166, 259; III, 42
Orphic Verses, II, 95
Orthodoxy, Idea of, I, 219
Osborn, Francis, *Advice to a Son,* I, 320n, 322
Ossian, I, 302
Otaheitan, *see* Tahitian
Otway, Thomas, I, 309
Oude, Begums of, I, 195
Ouseley, Sir William, trans., *The Oriental Geography of Ebn Haukal,* II, 332n–333n
Oversoul, III, 280–285; *see also* Soul(s)
Ovid (Publius Ovidius Naso), I, 284, 310, 316
Owen, Robert, II, 97
Owen, William, trans., *The Heroic Elegies and Other Pieces of Llywarç-Hen,* I, 240n, 241n, 391n
Owhyhees, *see* Hawaiians
Oxford, Eng., I, 235; II, 52, 329

Pacific Islands, I, 238
Pacific Ocean, *see* South Sea
Paganini, Niccolò, III, 138, 350
Pain, II, 89, 144, 177; III, 65, 90, 103–104, 121, 123, 357; Appetite for, I,

174; House of, III, 103; Relish of, III, 57; Spiritual, III, 237
Paine, Thomas, II, 67; III, 511
Painter(s), III, 73–74, 232; American, III, 82; Florentine, III, 69, 100; German, II, 266; Italian, II, 266; Roman, II, 264; III, 69; Tuscan, II, 269; Venetian, II, 269; III, 69; Young, I, 286; see also Artist(s)
Painting, I, 99-117 passim; II, 45–46, 51, 58, 265; III, 60, 298; Speaking, II, 51
Palestine, III, 105, 211
Paley, William, III, 470
Palfrey, John Gorham, I, 144n, 442n–443n
Palgrave, Sir Francis, III, 225
Palmer, Edward, III, 260n
Palmistry, III, 191
Palmyra, II, 270
Pampas, III, 211
Pan, I, 259
Pancrates, I, 259–260; III, 158
Pandora, I, 258
Panic of 1837, II, 191n–192n
Parable(s), I, 221–222, 290; see also Allegory; Analogy; Symbol(s), Symbolism
Paracelsus, III, 213
Paraiba, Brazil, I, 31
Paris, France, I, 7, 8, 28, 47, 114, 124, 152; II, 74, 81, 130, 139, 179, 226; III, 89, 108, 274, 408, 488
Park, Mungo, I, 39; Travels in the Interior Districts of Africa, I, 39n
Parker Fraternity, Boston, III, 23n
Parnassus, III, 204, 359; English, III, 69
Parr, Samuel, I, 357
Parry, Sir William Edward, II, 175; III, 211; Journal of a Voyage to Discover a North-west Passage, III, 211n
Parthenon, III, 93, 233
Party, I, 158, 195–197; II, 81–82, 102, 108; III, 92, 135, 187–189, 265–266, 309, 353, 355, 460, 487; Movement, III, xv, 187, 197–198, 325n; of Conservatism, III, 344n; of Innovation, III, 344n; of the Future, III, 187–189, 325n; of the Past, III, 187–189, 197–198
Pascal, Blaise, I, 132, 150; II, 67
Passion(s), I, 290, 291, 381; II, 93, 111; III, 15, 41, 54, 58–59, 64, 66, 143

Passiveness, III, 178n–179n, 201, 266–268
Past, The, I, 232; II, 16, 19, 158–159, 224, 274; III, 14, 44, 87, 89, 99, 141, 177n–182n passim, 186–187, 198–200, 218, 223, 232, 250–251, 280, 283, 313, 328, 459, 462; Party of, III, 187–189, 197–198; see also Conservatism; Conservatives; Establishment(s)
Patagonian, II, 112
Patience, I, 139; II, 303–304; III, 296, 313, 377, 482
Patriotism, III, 135, 188
Patterson, Robert, Letters on the Natural History of the Insects Mentioned in Shakspeare's Plays, III, 70
Paul III, Pope, I, 106, 111, 112
Paul IV, Pope, I, 111
Paul, Father, see Sarpi, Paolo
Paul, Saint, I, 121, 136, 229, 289, 384; II, 60, 78, 87, 93–94, 156, 178, 298; III, 116, 142, 144, 208, 231–232, 240, 243, 274, 279, 451
Paul, Sherman, Emerson's Angle of Vision, I, 96n
Pauw, Cornelius de, Recherches philosophiques sur les Grecs, II, 122
Peabody, Elizabeth Palmer, III, 51n; ed., Aesthetic Papers, III, xx; Record of a School, II, 210n; trans., Self-Education, II, 210n
Peace, I, 168, 182, 190; II, 40, 76, 240, 299, 355; III, 10, 117, 200, 252, 266, 275, 303, 314, 325n, 329, 376; Society of, II, 106; see also American Peace Society
Peasants' War, The, I, 126
Pedantry, I, 262, 339–340; III, 129–131, 292
Pelew Islands, II, 56
Pelews' Language, II, 149
Pellico, Silvio, My Prisons, II, 350–351, 368n
Peloponnesus, III, 147
Penn, William, I, 164n, 172; II, 178, 241; Christian Quaker, I, 173
Pennington, Isaac, I, 172
Pennsylvania, II, 419; III, 135
Perceforest, I, 260
Perception(s), II, 204, 248–249; III, 28, 40, 45, 297, 352, 381; Involuntary, III, 36
Percy, Thomas, ed., Reliques of Ancient English Poetry, III, 198

Père Lachaise Cemetery, Paris, III, 134
Perfect, The, II, 198, 217, 268; III, 93, 259, 292, 298; Idea of, II, 198–199; Vision of, III, 313
Perfection, III, 13, 124, 199; Ideal, II, 198; Moral, 1, 154
Periander, I, 358
Pericles, II, 131, 140, 335; III, 69, 231, 487
Perkins, Jacob, I, 3n, 13–14
Perkins Steam Battery, II, 286; III, 306 (?), 450 (?)
Permanence, II, 32; III, 27–29, 41
Pernambuco, Brazil, I, 31
Persia, I, 42; II, 14, 17, 152; III, 211, 225
Persian(s), I, 79, 111, 212; III, 134, 204
Persian Era, II, 225
Person(s), II, 70–82, 94, 98, 105, 178, 278–279, 285, 305, 318, 353–354; III, 34, 37–38, 41–43, 44, 47, 50, 51, 56, 67, 135, 149, 170, 201, 232–233, 251, 253, 276, 305, 314–315, 350–351; Beautiful, I, 101, 115; Laws for, II, 72–74
Personal, The, II, 84
Personality, III, 165, 214, 492
Pescara, Fernando Francesco Davalos, Marquis of, I, 115
Pestalozzi, Johann Heinrich, II, 4n, 97, 125; III, 226, 307
Peter, Saint, II, 87; III, 232
Peter Schlemihl, III, 450
Petrarch (Francesco Petrarca), I, 115, 270, 284, 293, 384; II, 102, 264; III, 61, 211
Pettigrew, Richard C., "Emerson and Milton," I, 145n
Pharaoh, I, 170; II, 8; III, 474
Pharisee, III, 291
Phenix, The; A Collection of Old and Rare Fragments, III, 368n
Phi Beta Kappa Society, Harvard College, I, xxii; II, 191n, 211n
Phidias, I, 104; II, 51, 54, 61; III, 69, 76, 80, 375
Philadelphia, Pa., I, xxii, 419; III, xv, 337n, 345n, 366n
Philanthropist, The, II, 38, 196, 287; *see also* Reformer(s)
Philanthropy, II, 102, 106–107; III, 260, 264, 302; *see also* Reform(s)
Philibert, Prince of Orange, I, 105
Philip II, King of Macedon, I, 198, 199; II, 8; III, 474
Philip, King of Spain, I, 159
Philip (?), Elector Palatine, III, 246
Philippi, Battle of, II, 333
Philo Judaeus, I, 311n
Philonic Inspiration, I, 311
Philosopher(s), I, 15, 23–24, 186–187, 189, 221, 226, 299–302, 305, 328; II, 38, 76, 82, 179, 214–215, 226, 250, 292, 302, 307, 321–322; III, 8, 11, 31, 118, 124, 126, 135, 151, 158, 188, 196, 198, 263, 280, 310; Ethical, II, 233; Natural, I, 70; II, 219; *see also* Naturalist(s)
Philosophical Transactions of the Royal Society of London, I, 58n, 70n
Philosophy, I, 78, 167, 297, 302, 305, 331, 378–379; II, 12, 83, 98, 133, 144, 169, 176, 181, 209n, 311, 318, 358; III, 6, 14, 30, 36, 41, 48, 53, 56, 97, 126, 187–188, 226, 234, 297, 299–300, 377; and Politics, I, 186–190; First, I, xvii–xviii; II, 208n; Natural, *see* Natural History *and* Science; of Beauty, III, 60–61; of History, I, 377; II, 7–21, 181; of Modern History, II, 20; Primary, III, 5
Phocion, II, 131, 140, 175, 337; III, 72
Phoebus, I, 283
Photography, III, 339n
Phrenology, II, 25, 68, 167; III, 287
Physics, II, 28–29, 38; III, 227; Axioms of, I, 290
Physiology, I, 48, 82; II, 24, 27, 182–183; Laws of, I, 383; *see also* Anatomy
Pico della Mirandola, Giovanni, Count, II, 164n
Pied Piper of Hamelin, III, 213
Pierpont, John, III, 325n, 326n
Piety, I, 188, 313, 353, 360; II, 14, 33, 36, 93–94, 355; III, 108, 191–194; *see also* Holiness
Pindar, I, 179n, 273, 384; II, 51, 185; III, 41n, 72, 230; *Olympian Odes*, I, 50n
Pirates, I, 42, 237
Pisones, II, 134
Pitt, William, First Earl of Chatham, I, 201; II, 60, 111, 140, 163; III, 240 (?), 311, 353
Pitt, William (1759–1806), I, 183n, 186, 200; II, 138; III, 240 (?)

Pittacus, I, 358

Pitts, Captain, II, 259n

Place, III, 27; Time and, II, 159, 198, 224, 249, 335; III, 54–55, 123, 239; *see also* Space

Placita Philosophorum, II, 38

Plagiarism, *see* Literary Borrowing

Plain, The, II, 67

Plato, I, 115, 128, 187, 189, 212, 222, 224, 230, 259, 273, 285, 299, 306, 321, 341, 359, 361, 365, 378, 380, 384; II, 12, 43, 59, 60, 65, 66, 91, 149, 152, 187, 255, 261; III, 61, 69, 168, 206, 208, 230, 240, 298, 313, 511; *Apology*, I, 259n; *Gorgias*, III, 441; *Ion*, I, 259n; *Phaedrus*, I, 378n; *Republic*, I, 128n, 259n; II, 59n; *Sophist*, II, 43n; *Symposium*, I, 359; II, 91n; *Works*, trans. Floyer Sydenham and Thomas Taylor, III, 441n

Platonist(s), I, 361, 377–378; II, 91; Cambridge, I, 365

Playfair, John, I, 1n, 50n, 402; II, 26; *Illustrations of the Huttonian Theory of the Earth*, I, 1n, 54n, 58n, 390n; II, 26n, 32n, 368n

Pledge(s), III, 140; Ethics of the, III, 257

Pliny (Caius Plinius Secundus), I, 327

Plotinus, I, 299; II, 62, 91, 332; III, 36; *Enneads*, III, 36n; *Select Works*, II, 91n, 332n, 368n

Plutarch, I, xviii, xix, 4n, 94n, 95n, 154, 184, 209n, 273, 316, 320n, 359, 360, 366, 512, 526; II, 2n, 38, 149, 175, 211n, 254, 284, 329–330, 353, 432; III, 61, 72, 126, 159, 161, 208, 209, 239, 400; "Apothegms of Kings and Great Commanders," I, 140n, 167n; II, 70n; "Banquet of the Seven Wise Men," I, 14n, 358n–359; "Concerning such whom God is slow to punish," III, 146n; "A Discourse concerning Socrates's Daemon," II, 284; III, 159n, 161n; "How to Know a Flatterer from a Friend," III, 123n; "Laconic Apothegms," I, 140n, 167n; II, 70n, 170n; "The Life of Agesilaus," I, 140n; "The Life of Phocion," II, 337n; "The Life of Timoleon," I, 154n; *Lives*, I, 94n, 140n, 389n; II, 329–330, 368n; III, 386n; "The Lives of Ten Orators," I, 198n; "The Lives of Tiberius and Caius Gracchus," III, 354n; *Morals*,

I, 14n, 94n, 179n, 389n; II, 368n; III, 386n; "Of Banishment," II, 154n; "Of Brotherly Love," III, 253n; "Of Garrulity," II, 258n; "Of Isis and Osiris," II, 353; III, 279n; "Of Large Acquaintance," II, 288n; "Of Love," II, 264n, 275n; III, 59n; *On the Opinions of the Philosophers*, II, 38n; "Plutarch's Symposiacs," II, 72n, 324n; III, 126n; *Placita Philosophorum*, II, 38; "Whether an aged Man ought to meddle in State Affairs," III, 369n; "Why the Oracles cease to give Answers," III, 159n; "Why the Pythian Priestess Ceases her Oracles in Verse," I, 360n; III, 41n, 169n

Plymouth, Mass., I, xv, xxii, 88n, 98n; Emerson lectures in, III, xiii, 1n, 23n, 68n, 341n

Pocock(e), Edward, I, 357

Poet(s), I, 79, 81, 132–134, 143, 149, 160–162, 215, 221, 224, 226–229, 239, 243, 259, 262, 271–274, 284, 289–293, 296–299, 302, 305, 318, 340–341, 353, 356, 372; II, 37, 38, 39, 49, 55, 61, 97, 168–169, 274; III, 9, 17–18, 21, 45–46, 75, 77, 80, 81, 82, 83, 158, 198, 213–222 *passim*, 231–232, 252, 262, 266, 298–299, 348–365, 372–373, 510–511; American, I, 215; III, 82; Dream of, III, 263; Silent, I, 153; Soul of, III, 75

Poetical Works of Coleridge, Shelley, and Keats, The, III, 218

Poetic Treatment of All Subjects, III, 239–240

Poetry, I, 72–73, 79, 100, 115, 143, 148, 153, 160–163, 167, 215, 221–224, 227–228, 239–241, 243–248, 262–319, 338–353, 356–357, 372–374, 379, 382; II, 12, 36, 45, 47, 49, 51, 58–59, 99, 169; III, 17–18, 41, 46, 57, 60, 75, 93, 95, 133, 138–139, 202–237 *passim*, 299, 300, 307–308, 313, 330, 348–365, 372–373; Divine, III, 262; Genius of, III, 362–363; Silent, II, 51; Stock, III, 226, 359

Polarity, I, 74, 78; III, 52; in Writers, I, 161; II, 61–62; Law of Dualism or, III, 40; Principle of, I, 48; *see also* Dualism

Polarization, Laws of, I, 78

Polini, Marchese, I, 109

Politics, I, 189–190, 201; II, 20, 42, 69–82, 94, 98, 171, 181, 197, 214, 338, 362; III, 25, 63, 135–136, 238–247, 251, 276, 291, 303, 353, 441

Pollitt, J. D., "Ralph Waldo Emerson's Debt to John Milton," I, 145n

Pollok, Robert, I, 212; II, 65; III, 206

Pomeranus or Pommer (Johann Bugenhagen), I, 123–124n, 139

Pompeii, Italy, II, 159, 222

Pons Palatinus (The Broken Bridge), Rome, I, 106

Poor Richard, II, 317

Pope, Alexander, I, 4n, 149, 213, 274, 283, 284, 310, 384; II, 67; "Epistle to Dr. Arbuthnot," III, 309n; *An Essay on Criticism*, III, 380n; *An Essay on Man*, I, 42n; III, 207n; "The First Epistle of the Second Book of Horace," I, 148n; *The Works*, II, 75n

Pope, The, I, 121–141 *passim*, 180; III, 191, 275, 276; *see also individual names*

Porcellians, Harvard College, III, 483

Po River, I, 43

Porphyry, I, 299; II, 91; *Life of Plotinus*, I, 299n

Porson, Richard, I, 357; II, 164

Portsmouth, N.H., I, xxii, 419

Portugal, II, 81

Potidaea, Greece, II, 91

Poverty, II, 214, 215, 241, 270, 277; III, 33, 90, 104, 131–133, 399–400; *see also* Want(s)

Power(s), I, 24, 148, 330, 333–334, 370; II, 14, 76–78, 80–81, 85, 102, 105, 123–124, 127, 138–139, 142, 144, 181, 307, 309, 355; III, 11, 24, 37, 40, 41, 43, 62, 70, 139, 146, 154, 171, 189–190, 191, 195, 224, 280–282, 301, 312, 314, 363, 441, 450–451, 454, 455; Active, II, 229; III, 190; Civil, III, 265; Contemplative, II, 83; Demoniacal, III, 160–170; Divine, III, 252, 369; Ecclesiastical, III, 80, 265; Human, I, 34–42, 48, 242, 326, 335; II, 167, 221–222; III, 110; Idea of, II, 86; Imaginative, I, 289–293, 301–302, 305; Immaterial over Material, I, 143; Intellectual, I, 261; Latent, II, 215; Limits of Executive, III, 257; Lord's, II, 293, 351; III, 377; Mechanical, III, 306; Moral, II, 167, 263; III,

162, 164; New and Preternatural, III, 476; of Calculation, III, 15; of Comparison, III, 15; of Conscience, I, 231; of Custom, I, 231; of Faith, I, 231; of Fear, I, 231; of God, I, 175; of Love, I, 231; III, 52, 57; of Memory, III, 15; of Mind, I, 330; of Mind over Body, I, 178; of Nature, II, 225; of Science, I, 260; of Senses, III, 52; of Thought over Language, I, 350; Political, III, 80; Practical, II, 263; Reflective, I, 301, 305; Spiritual or Real, III, 442; Universal, III, 40, 48, 254

Practical Men, *see* Common Sense

Predestination, II, 145; III, 105

Presbyterians, I, 174; II, 94

Presence, II, 30–31, 33; Divine, II, 90; III, 20; Doctrine of, II, 30–31

Present, The, I, 187, 200, 380, 384; II, 2n, 19–20, 157–159, 225, 274; III, 182n, 250, 277, 280, 283–285, 313

Present Age, The, I, 131, 219; II, 19–20, 54, 60–62, 80–81, 157–173, 195–199, 213–215, 228, 337–338, 361; III, xv, 5–10, 24, 177n–182n, 186–315 *passim*, 337n–340n, 361–365, 367–382 *passim*, 451–462, 522; Education of, III, 286–301, 302, 304; Genius of, III, 188, 194, 200, 237, 303, 308, 362–364; Literature of, I, 372–385; III, 8–9, 202–237, 251, 281, 286, 302, 303, 307–308, 361–365, 374–375; Mind of, III, 229, 257, 277, 278, 285, 286; Philosophy of, II, 169; III, 303, 307–308; Politics of, III, 238–247, 303; Reforms of, I, 219; III, 256–270; 302, 303–304; Religion of, II, 169; III, 272–285, 287, 302, 304; Soul of, III, 187; Spirit of, II, 168–169; III, 187, 191, 377

Presentiments, III, 156, 169, 283, 287, 363

Prester John, II, 68

Priam, I, 283

Pride, I, 171, 180; II, 53, 153, 244, 347; III, 248–249; of Opinion, III, 50

Principle(s), I, 120, 165–167, 177, 189, 196, 216, 228, 358, 366, 382; II, 110, 112, 166, 172, 179, 181, 198, 199, 218, 254, 255, 292, 346–347, 362; III, 9, 25–26, 31, 48–49, 66,

144, 150, 197, 199, 217, 237, 249, 266, 290, 303, 307, 329, 379; Demonological, III, 163–165; First, I, 216; Healing, I, 138; Moral, II, 58; of Association, III, 29; of Life, II, 183; One, II, 187; Philosophical, I, 378; Republican, I, 378; III, 304; Selecting, III, 36; Universal, I, 65

Printing, I, 130–131; Invention of, I, 255; II, 165

Prior, Sir James, *Memoir of the Life and Character of the Rt. Hon. Edmund Burke*, I, 183n, 185n, 191n, 197n, 198n, 391n

Prior, Matthew, I, 357

Prison Discipline, I, 182; II, 106

Profitable, The, II, 87, 311

Progress, I, 6, 187; II, 13–14, 80, 81–82, 112, 145, 147, 159, 160, 167, 173–176, 185, 213, 248, 250–251, 254–255, 258, 291, 343, 362; III, 20, 29–31, 141, 171, 233, 241, 251, 253, 274, 285, 291, 315, 381; of Science, I, 10, 26; II, 225; of the Soul, III, 63–67

Prometheus, I, 257–259

Prony, Gaspard Ciair François Marie Riche de, I, 43n

Property, II, 70–82, 94, 98, 105, 124, 142, 160–161, 201, 223, 239–240, 285, 318; III, 11, 21, 32, 35, 64, 91, 92, 94, 118, 133, 197, 199, 314; Institution of, III, 485–487; Laws for, II, 72–74

Prophecy, II, 90, 99; III, 190; Spirit of, III, 280

Prophets(s), I, 274; III, 49, 124, 159, 205, 243, 280

Proportion, I, 49, 101–102, 190; II, 226–228, 265

Proserpine, I, 154, 222

Prosperity, I, 177; III, 149, 188, 329, 349, 369, 374

Protest, The, III, 85–102, 170

Protestants, I, 128, 174; II, 94; III, 187

Proteus, I, 259; II, 15

Provençal Language, I, 270

Provençal Literature, I, 284; III, 250

Proverbs, I, 230, 290, 358–359; II, 124, 126, 144, 152–153, 233–234, 312; III, 286–287, 329–330

Providence, I, 128, 210, 225, 259, 333; II, 215; Divine, II, 89, 199; III, 114, 139, 147, 285; Eternal Law of, I, 380

Providence, R.I., II, 195; Emerson lectures at, I, xxii; II, xi, 189n–194n; III, xiv, xv, 1n–2n, 5n, 23n, 51n, 175n–176n, 185n, 238n, 248n (?), 256n (?), 271n (?), 321n, 341n, 342n, 347n, 366n, 367n

Prudence, I, 156; II, 97, 229, 243, 249, 310–326, 330–332; III, 15, 62, 149, 162, 190, 239, 272, 311

Ptolemaic Vortices, III, 306

Ptolemy, II, 8; III, 474

Pückler-Muskau, Prince Hermann Ludwig Heinrich von, III, 211; *Semilasso in Africa*, III, 211n

Punishment, III, 145, 149; Corporal, III, 290; *see also* Capital Punishment; Compensation(s); Retribution

Pure, The, III, 283

Puritan(s), II, 93, 128; English, I, 157–158, 360

Purity, I, 313; II, 277

Pym, John, I, 353; II, 480

Pyramid(s), I, 47, 310; II, 59, 178; III, 30; of Ghizeh, III, 157

Pyrrho, I, 299

Pyrrhonism, III, 292, 307

Pythagoras, I, 79, 224, 359; III, 279, 311, 451

Pythoness, I, 318

Quakers, I, 94n, 164–182 *passim*; II, 91, 94, 214, 345–346, 351; III, 141, 187, 243, 267, 377, 388, 490

Quantocks, The, III, 98

Quarterly Review, The, I, 39n

Quietist, II, 92, 345

Rabelais, François, I, 366; III, 81, 511

Rachel, III, 144

Radical, II, 70

Radici, Signor, I, 115; "Review of the *Rime*," I, 113n–116n *passim*, 390n

Raleigh, Sir Walter, I, 263, 264, 315, 323, 353, 355; *History of the World*, I, 355; "The Soul's Errand," I, 264–265

Rameau, Jean-François, III, 133

Randolph, John, *Letters of John Randolph to a Young Relative*, I, 278

Raphael Sanzio, I, 8, 109, 152, 421; II, 51, 54, 225, 271, 315; III, 45–46, 88, 133, 237, 413; "Expulsion of Heliodorus from the Temple," III, 133; "Madonna di S. Sisto," II, 315;

"Transfiguration," I, 73 (?), 421; II, 271

Rapture(s), I, 169; II, 90–92; III, 45, 127, 180n–181n, 279; Celestial, III, 56; in Nature, III, 98; of the Intellect, III, 144; *see also* Ecstasy; Enthusiasm

Rationalism, II, 93

Rawley, William, *The Life of . . . Bacon*, I, 323n

Reading, *see* Books

Real, The, I, 10; II, 62, 67, 217, 294, 307; *see also* Ideal

Realism, I, 300–302, 346–347; II, 423; III, 220, 225–226

Realist, I, 168, 174–175

Reality, I, 175, 291, 381; II, 305–308, 312; III, 62, 201, 289, 314, 340n, 377–378, 382

Real World, I, 299; II, 313

Reason, I, xviii, 42, 81, 93n, 166, 206n, 216, 231, 238, 291, 296–297, 341, 342, 378–379, 381, 384, 385, 454; II, 9, 12–13, 33–34, 50–51, 58–59, 62–63, 67–68, 71, 78, 83–99, 106–112, 126, 141–147, 152, 158, 176, 179–184, 198, 219–220, 223, 247–249, 252, 259, 267, 272, 291, 303, 305, 353, 355, 362, 364; III, 89, 116, 123–125, 151, 153, 159, 189–190, 199, 304, 381, 454, 459; Common, II, 147; Divine, I, 378; II, 180; Pure, I, 134; II, 280; III, 462; Speculative, II, 238; Supreme, I, 40; II, 93; Unconscious, II, 57, 99; Universal, III, 199

Réaumur, René Antoine Ferchault de, I, 20

Receptiveness, III, 344n, 376, 520

Recreation, III, 25; *see also* Diversion

Red River, I, 215

Redwald, King of East Anglia, I, 250

Reed, Caleb, "The Nature and Character of True Wisdom and Intelligence," III, 17n, 386n

Reed, Sampson, I, 96n, 211n; *Observations on the Growth of the Mind*, II, 210n; "Oration on Genius," I, 365n

Reflection, I, 224, 226, 304, 385; II, 144, 158, 171, 173, 183–184, 251; III, 9–10, 106, 116, 200; Age of, II, 168–171, 180–181

Reform(s), I, 174–175; II, 15, 157, 199, 217, 219, 220; III, 16, 90–91, 196, 256–270, 275, 303–304, 325n, 376, 460; The Great, II, 220

Reformation, The, I, 94n, 119–143 *passim*, 360–362; II, 213, 224; III, 243

Reform Bill, II, 68, 80n

Reformer(s), I, 119, 174, 190, 195; II, 157; III, 20, 91, 187, 259–260, 339n–340n

Reisenpusch, Dr., I, 141

Relation of Man to Animals, I, 10, 27, 33, 34–35, 42–43, 79–81; II, 253; Relation of Man to Nature, I, 27–49; II, 22–40 *passim*, 253

Relief(s), III, 114–119, 121; *see also* Asylum; Compensation(s)

Religion, I, 119–182 *passim*, 211, 280, 361–362; II, 12, 20, 37, 42, 54, 63, 81, 83–98, 123, 130, 143, 169, 181, 197, 217, 223, 305, 338, 341, 345–346, 354; III, 6, 11, 19, 48, 90, 92, 94, 97, 127–129, 140–141, 151, 165, 190, 191–194, 196, 197, 203, 227, 233, 237, 242–243, 251, 263, 266, 271–285, 286–288, 302, 304, 310, 315, 324n–325n, 327–331, 357, 360, 455, 479; Evangelical, II, 341

Religious Sentiment, *see* Sentiment(s), Religious

Rembrandt van Rijn, II, 225

Report of the Experiments on Animal Magnetism, Made by a Committee of . . . the French Royal Academy, trans. John C. Colquhoun, I, 10, 332; III, 169

Republic, The, II, 362; Mind's, II, 70; Pure, II, 217

Republican Principle, III, 304

Reputation, I, 186, 369; III, 229–230; Literary, I, 212, 231, 271, 305–307; II, 65–66; III, 205–206, 510–511; *see also* Fame

Resources, III, 62, 105, 116–120, 288; of Being, III, 250

Resurrection, The, II, 228; III, 192

Retribution, III, 112, 148–149; *see also* Compensation(s); Punishment

Retrospective Review, I, 113n–116n, 390n

Retrospective Reviews, III, 198

Revelation, I, 132; II, 92–93, 181, 346; III, 276–277; Identity of, II, 180

Reverence, III, 477

Revolution(s), I, 123, 167, 177, 190, 212, 370; II, 15, 70, 81, 167, 179,

220; III, 9, 15, 97, 139, 188, 198, 243, 251, 273, 291, 308, 442; American, I, 75, 186; III, 225; Commercial, II, 161, 195–196; English, II, 213; French, I, 162, 183n, 184–185, 186, 195, 196, 201; II, 74, 175–176; III, 108, 133, 222, 225, 304, 307, 459; French (July 1830), II, 80n; in Character, III, 35; in Custom, Law, Opinion, III, 113; in Man, III, 52, 58; in Reading, I, 366; Moral, I, 361; Natural, II, 161; of Nature, I, 68; III, 28; Philosophical, II, 10–11, 167; Political, I, 181; II, 195–196; Religious, I, 143, 177; II, 10–11; Right of, I, 175; Spiritual, I, 127

Reynolds, Sir Joshua, I, 109, 191, 193; III, 132n–133n

Rhetoric, I, 102, 200; II, 45, 65; III, 126

Rhine River, I, 43; III, 246

Rhyme, III, 358–359

Rhythm, I, 305, 308–310; III, 358–359

Rialto, Bridge of the, Venice, I, 104

Ricciarelli, Daniele, *see* Volterra, Daniele da

Richard I, King of England, I, 254; II, 140

Richard II, King of England, I, 275

Richard III, King of England, II, 315

Riches, *see* Wealth

Richter, Jean Paul Friedrich, I, 123; II, 480; III, 60, 218

Ridiculous, The, *see* Comedy

Right(s), I, 147; II, 70–71; III, 125, 139–140, 143, 281, 485, 490; Cause of, II, 155; Higher, II, 361; Idea of, III, 247; Ideal of, II, 219–220; III, 124–125; Ideal Track of, III, 297; Sense of, II, 111; Spiritual, I, 167; Vision of, III, 139

Ripley, Ezra, II, 137n; III, 131n, 156n

Ripley, George, III, 325n, 339n

Ritho, I, 256

Ritson, Joseph, I, 257

Ritter, Heinrich, *Geschichte der Philosophie,* II, 249n, 368n

Roaring Thunders, III, 128

Robert I, Duke of Normandy ("Robert the Devil"), II, 108

Robert of Gloucester, *Chronicle of English History,* I, 265

Roberts, James Russell, "Emerson's Debt to the Seventeenth Century," I, 145n, 337n

Robertson, William, I, 147; *The History of Scotland,* I, 147n

Robin Hood, III, 210

Robinson, F. N., ed., *The Works of Geoffrey Chaucer,* I, 270n

Robinson, William, I, 179

Robinson Crusoe, III, 258

Rockingham, Charles Watson Wentworth, Second Marquis of, I, 184

Rocky Mountains, I, 54; II, 225

Rodanini Palace, Rome, I, 104

Roland, III, 282

Roman(s), I, 71, 237, 280; II, 14, 15, 44, 53, 73, 76, 131–135, 257, 269, 335; III, 69, 104, 112, 289, 354

Roman Age, II, 168

Roman Arch, III, 84

Roman Architecture, II, 44, 53, 269–270

Roman Art, II, 269–270

Roman Catholic Church, I, 119–143 *passim,* 174; II, 47, 94, 268, 351; III, 187, 191, 274, 276; Clergy, II, 53, 154; Hierarchy, I, 135; II, 178

Roman Catholicism, I, 119–143 *passim;* II, 25, 346

Romance(s), I, 254–263, 382, 384; II, 13; III, 516; Arabian, I, 257, 260; French, I, 316; Italian, I, 316; *see also* Fable(s)

Roman Empire, I, 188, 237; III, 7, 188, 242; Fall of, I, 250; *see also* Rome

Roman Law, III, 240

Roman Literature, *see* Latin Literature

Roman Painters, II, 264; III, 69

Romantic School, II, 187; *see also* Romance(s)

Rome, I, 90, 103–115 *passim,* 123, 136, 151, 236, 251, 271, 353, 420–421; II, 8, 11, 17, 50, 53, 74, 102, 134–135, 161, 163, 180, 226, 228, 270, 309; III, 13, 30, 162, 211, 243, 269, 276, 284, 340n, 399, 474

Roscoe, Thomas, "The Life of Michael Angelo Buonaroti," I, 109n, 112n, 113n, 114n, 117n; II, 66n

Ross, Sir John, II, 318; *Narrative of a Second Voyage of Discovery,* II, 319n, 368n

Rotch, Mary, I, 164n

Rouget de Lisle, Claude Joseph, III, 511

Rousseau, Jean Jacques, I, 132, 150, 189, 359n, 376; II, 67; III, 11n, 511
Routine, II, 218, 296, 362–363; Men of, III, 48; Parrots of, III, 288; Puppets of, III, 265
Rowe, Nicholas, trans., Lucan's *Pharsalia*, III, 159n
Rowland, III, 282
Roxburgh Clubs, III, 198
Roxbury, Mass., I, xxii
Rumford, Benjamin Thompson, Count, I, 12
Russell, William, Lord Russell, II, 87
Russell, William (1798–1873), I, xx
Russia, II, 123, 227; III, 187, 211, 374
Rutland, Charles Manners, Fourth Duke of, I, 193

Sabbath(s), II, 93; III, 325n
Sachs, Hans, III, 210
Sac Indians, II, 227
Sacred Band, III, 189
Sadducee, III, 291
Sailor, The, II, 116–117; III, 121
Saint(s), II, 341; III, 31, 88, 162, 249, 283
St. Elmo's Light, III, 191
Saint-Évremond, Charles de Marguetel de Saint-Denis, Seigneur de, *The Works*, III, 57n
St. George, Cardinal, I, 136
St. George (statue), Florence, I, 117
St. Gotthard Pass, III, 221
Saint-Hilaire, Geoffroy, *see* Geoffroy Saint-Hilaire, Étienne
St. Peter's Church, Rome, I, 73, 99, 108, 109, 111, 112, 114, 122, 318; III, 93
Saint-Pierre, *see* Bernardin de Saint-Pierre, Jacques-Henri
Saladin, II, 140
Salem, Mass., I, xxii; III, 353; Emerson lectures at, I, 207n; II, xi, 207n; III, xiv, 175n, 185n
Salem (Mass.) Lyceum, I, xx; Emerson lectures at, III, xiv, 175n, 185n
Salisbury, Earl of, *see* Cecil, Robert
Sallust (Caius Sallustius Crispus), *Bellum Catilinae*, II, 13
Salmasius, Claudius (Claude de Saumaise), I, 146n, 147
Salvian, I, 234–235
Sampson, Hillman B., II, 374; III, xii
Samson, I, 129
Samson (Coadjutor of Tetzel), I, 121

San Borgo, Italy, I, 106
Sandels, Samuel, "Emanuel Swedenborg," I, 25n, 389n
Sandwich Islanders, *see* Hawaiians
San Gallo, Antonio di (1485–1546), I, 106, 111
Sanity, I, 139–140; III, 85, 87, 126
San Miniato, Italy, I, 105
San Pietro in Vincoli, Church of, Rome, I, 108
Sanscrit, II, 234; III, 205
Santa Croce, Church of, Florence, I, 117
Santa Maria Novella, Church of, Florence, I, 117
Santa Maria sopra Minerva, Church of, Rome, I, 103, 108
Sappho, I, 360; II, 336
Saracens, II, 77
Sardanapalus, I, 311; II, 324
Sarpi, Paolo, I, 353
Satan, I, 132–133, 136; *see also* Devil(s)
Satire, I, 313, 314; III, 128–129, 131, 135
Saturn, III, 390, 420
Saturn (planet), I, 18
Saturnian Age, III, 264
Saul, II, 115
Saumaise, *see* Salmasius, Claudius
Saumaise, Madame de, I, 147
Saurin, Jacques, II, 184n
Savage, Richard, II, 316
Savage(s), I, 45–46, 76, 220–221; III, 454, 455; *see also* Noble Savage; Wild Man
Saxon Age, I, 138
Saxon Laws, I, 213
Saxons, *see* Anglo-Saxons
Scaliger, Joseph Justus, II, 164; III, 81, 194, 216, 375; *Scaligerana*, III, 81n, 216n
Scaliger, Julius Caesar, III, 253
Scandinavian Race, I, 360
Scarlett, James, First Baron Abinger, III, 82–83
Schelling, Friedrich Wilhelm Joseph von, I, 173; II, 260, 307; III, 48
Schiller, Johann Christoph Friedrich von, II, 68, 169, 185; III, 323n; *The Robbers*, I, 230; II, 185
Schlegel, August Wilhelm von, II, 64 (?), 68 (?); *A Course of Lectures on Dramatic Art and Literature*, III, 72n, 386n

Schlegel, Karl Wilhelm Friedrich von, II, 64 (?), 68 (?), 304; *Geschichte der alten und neuen Literatur*, II, 304n; *The Philosophy of History*, II, 3n

Schleiermacher, Friedrich Ernst Daniel, *Reden über die Religion*, II, 341n

Schlemel, *see* Peter Schlemihl

Scholar(s), I, 210–211, 215–216, 381; II, 258–259; III, 56, 129, 221, 234, 370, 458

Schönemann, Anna Elisabeth ("Lili"), III, 118n

School, The, III, 34–50; *see also* Education

Schuyler, General Philip John, III, 231

Science(s), I, 5–83, 225, 228, 260, 327–333; II, 12, 22–40, 42, 73, 94, 112, 114, 167, 172, 181–187, 200–201, 214–215, 221, 252, 253, 343; III, 30, 42, 81, 129–131, 145, 206, 228, 252, 281, 300, 314, 502; Absolute, III, 56; Highest Moral of, II, 39; Human, II, 311; Humanity of, II, 22–40; in Education, I, 70–71, 76; Joyous, III, 368; Moral, I, 360; Progress of, II, 225; of the Mind, II, 167; *see also* Anatomy; Astronomy; Botany; Chemistry; Geology; Natural History; Physics; Physiology; Zoology

Sciolists, I, 211

Scipio Africanus, Publius Cornelius ("the Elder"), II, 140 (?), 329, 334; III, 12 (?), 69 (?), 88, 243 (?)

Scoffer, III, 16

Scoresby, William, *An Account of the Arctic Regions*, I, 64, 390n

Scotland, III, 23n, 186n

Scots, I, 234

Scott, John, *Luther and the Lutheran Reformation*, I, 118n–139n *passim*, 390n

Scott, Sir Walter, I, 213, 268, 274, 313, 371n, 375–376, 384; II, 126, 232, 307, 321, 329; III, 1n, 107, 162, 198, 218, 459; *The Betrothed*, II, 232n; *The Bride of Lammermoor*, I, 260–261; *The Fair Maid of Perth*, I, 241n; *The Heart of Mid-Lothian*, II, 317n; *The Lady of the Lake*, III, 152n, 375; *Letters on Demonology and Witchcraft*, I, 332; *The Monastery*, I, 339; III, 162–163; *Old Mor-*

tality, II, 329n; *Peveril of the Peak*, II, 150n; *Redgauntlet*, II, 308

Scougal, Henry, II, 93; III, 502

Scripture(s), I, 212, 273; II, 89; III, 202, 236; *see also* Bible

Scudder, Townsend, III, "A Chronological List of Emerson's Lectures on his British Lecture Tour of 1847–1848," III, 23n, 186n

Sculpture, I, 99–117 *passim;* II, 10, 36, 45–46, 49, 50–51, 61, 133, 265; III, 73, 112; Greek, II, 269–270; III, 72, 93, 112; Laws of, II, 64; Oriental, II, 352

Scythian, III, 516

Seamen's Bethel, Boston, (Father Taylor's), III, 362–363n

Seckendorf, Veit Ludwig von, I, 127; *Commentarius Historicus et Apologeticus de Lutheranismo*, I, 127n, 131, 390n

Second Church, Boston, I, xv, 1n, 118n; III, 319n, 322n, 324n

Second Church, Concord, II, xvii

Second Thoughts, *see* Thought(s), Second

Sect, II, 102, 108–109

Sectarian, III, 477

Seeming, *see* Being, and Seeming

Selden, John, I, 306, 338, 357, 365; II, 164; *Selden's Table-Talk*, II, 164n, 368n

Self, III, 21, 75, 215, 314; Idea of, I, 218; Truth to, II, 151–152

Self-Command, III, 450

Self-Denial, II, 216, 256, 258, 277, 316; III, 88

Self-Esteem, I, 154–155

Self-Government, III, 245–246

Selfishness, I, 325; II, 40; III, 63, 214–216

Self-Made Men, III, 195

Self-Possession, II, 319–320; III, 43, 254, 298

Self-Reliance, I, 136; II, 260; III, 77–79, 232, 308–312, 382, 487; *see also* Self-Trust; Trust

Self-Respect, II, 344

Self-Sacrifice, II, 85

Self-Sufficiency, II, 280; of the Mind, II, 146–147

Self-Trust, II, 151–152, 199–200, 308, 330–331; III, 77–78, 93, 99–102, 103, 161, 248–249, 264–265, 423, 487; *see also* Self-Reliance; Trust

Self-Union, II, 145, 168

Semiramis, II, 179

Seneca, Lucius Annaeus, I, 279, 316, 341, 359; II, 135, 150; III, 289n; *De Providentia*, I, 359n; *De Vita Beata*, III, 149n; *Morals*, I, 359

Sense(s), I, 6, 11, 18, 40–41, 44–45, 49, 178, 220, 228, 300, 341; II, 94, 96, 141, 160, 196–199, 228, 248, 262, 275, 304, 310–312, 346, 362–364; III, 22, 38, 40, 48, 52, 78, 87–90, 95, 99, 109, 144, 166, 216, 249, 279, 355, 454; Law of, II, 316; Moral, I, 243, 340, 384; II, 73; of Benevolence, II, 344; of Duty, II, 338, 361; of Right, II, 111; of Veracity, II, 344; *see also* Body; Common Sense; Good Sense

Sentiment(s), I, 165, 194, 199, 214, 230, 341, 353, 359; II, 87, 352; III, 34–35, 39, 48, 62, 127, 140, 145, 168–169, 189–190, 236, 242, 272, 278; Guiding, III, 43; High, II, 338; Higher, II, 347; Highest, III, 127, 190, 191; Inward, III, 144; Laws of, I, 215; Laws of Moral, II, 353; Moral, I, 149, 154, 214, 285, 352, 360, 364, 376; II, 36, 75, 89, 199, 249, 340–341, 344–346, 352; III, 6, 81, 108, 124, 135, 145, 207, 249, 250, 252, 259, 272, 276, 277, 372, 460; of Duty, II, 84, 86, 355; III, 277, 308; of Freedom, III, 6; of Good, Beautiful, True, III, 190; of Heart, II, 342; of Hope, III, 39; of Humility, III, 272; of Justice, III, 6, 277; of Love, III, 53–55, 194, 277; of Patriotism, III, 135, 188; of Piety, I, 360; of Reverence to Virtue, I, 188; of Truth, III, 277, 455; of Unity, III, 41, 188; of Virtue, I, 190; III, 144; of World, III, 249; Parental, III, 190; Religious, I, 157, 165–168, 173, 177–178, 252; II, 50, 77, 93, 96, 350, 353; III, 76, 106, 127–129, 169, 190, 191–194, 274, 454; Social, III, 188; Spontaneous, III, 136, 249; Universal, II, 151

Separatists, I, 360

Serampore, India, II, 147

Seraphim, II, 281

Sermon on the Mount, II, 90

Servant(s), Freedom of, III, 91, 264, 275, 325n

Servetus, Michael, I, 234

Seven Champions of Christendom, The, see Johnson, Richard

Seven Sleepers of Ephesus, The, I, 256

Seven Whistlers, The, III, 194

Seven Wise Masters of Greece, The, I, 358

Sévigné, Marie de Rabutin-Chantal, Marquise de, II, 336

Seville, Spain, II, 118

Sewel, William, *The History of the Rise, Increase, and Progress of the Christian People Called Quakers*, I, 164n–182n *passim*, 391n, 459; II, 293n, 351n, 368n; III, 7n, 377n, 386n, 388

Shaftesbury, Anthony Ashley Cooper, Third Earl of, III, 230

Shakespeare, William, I, xix, xx, 4n, 35, 149, 153, 161, 162, 184, 196, 212, 213, 214, 215, 230, 251, 263, 271, 274, 275, 284, 287–319, 321, 326, 334, 335, 338, 339, 344, 353, 354, 360, 369, 384, 510–512; II, 48, 49, 51, 52, 60, 61, 63, 66, 67, 185, 186, 216, 225, 232, 254, 306–307, 319; III, 1n, 8, 17, 18, 21, 45, 69–70, 80, 81, 125, 161, 205, 208, 211n, 218, 221, 222, 233, 234, 361, 372, 417, 418, 502, 507; *All's Well That Ends Well*, I, 315; *Antony and Cleopatra*, I, 311–312, 314–315n; III, 161n; *As You Like It*, I, 302; *Coriolanus*, I, 271, 305, 316, 512; *Cymbeline*, I, 298n; II, 150n; Epitaph, I, 301; *Hamlet*, I, 293, 297–298n, 299n, 305, 309n, 314–315, 318, 334, 512; II, 63, 180; III, 18, 84, 116, 136n, 168n, 328n; *I Henry IV*, I, 309n; II, 148n; III, 109n; *II Henry IV*, I, 298n; II, 332n; *Henry V*, I, 314–315n; *I Henry VI*, II, 18; *III Henry VI*, I, 510–511; *Henry VIII*, I, 287n, 309, 316; *Julius Caesar*, I, 311, 313–315n; II, 316n, 319n; *King Lear*, I, 224, 264, 291, 293n, 310–311n, 314–315n, 318; II, 299n; III, 18, 109; *Love's Labor's Lost*, I, 264, 295n; *Macbeth*, I, 298n, 312, 314–315n; *Measure for Measure*, I, 223n, 292, 293n, 298n; *The Merchant of Venice*, I, 223n, 293n, 309n, 511; *A Midsummer Night's Dream*, I, 35n, 296n, 309n; *Much Ado About Nothing*, I, 301; *Othello*, I, 309n, 310–311n; III, 113n; *The Passionate*

Pilgrim, I, 295n; *The Rape of Lucrece*, I, 301; *Richard II*, II, 316n; *Richard III*, I, 291; *Romeo and Juliet*, I, 223n; *Sonnets*, I, 223n, 293–296, 299n, 301; *The Taming of the Shrew*, II, 223n; *The Tempest*, I, 292–293n, 298n; *Troilus and Cressida*, I, 315; *Twelfth Night*, I, 264; III, 126n; *Venus and Adonis*, I, 301; *The Winter's Tale*, I, 44n; II, 35n; *allusions to characters only, excluding citations above:* Ariel, I, 313; Beatrice, I, 313; Caliban, I, 310, 313; Cassius, III, 375; "Cato's daughter Portia," I, 313; Cleopatra, I, 313; Cordelia, I, 313; Coriolanus, I, 302; Desdemona, I, 313; Falstaff, I, 302, 311; II, 62; III, 125; Gloster ("feudal baron"), I, 312; Prince Hal, I, 313; III, 125; Hamlet, I, 306, 307, 313, 375; III, 95; Henry V, I, 302, 313; Henry VI, I, 302, 313; Imogen, I, 313; Isabel, I, 313; King John, I, 302; Juliet, I, 313; III, 64; Lear, I, 302, 375; Macbeth, I, 299; Lady Macbeth, I, 313; Northumberland, I, 312; Oberon, III, 118; Ophelia, I, 306, 307; Othello, I, 302, 307; Puck, III, 118; Richard, I, 375; Richard II, I, 313; Richard III, II, 315; Romeo, III, 64; Salisbury, I, 312; Shylock, I, 302; Titania, I, 313; Warwick, I, 312; The Witches, I, 313

Shakespeare Societies, III, 197

Shame, I, 243; III, 19, 137

Shaster, II, 95

Sheffield, Eng., I, 236

Sheking, I, 280; II, 283

Shelley, Percy Bysshe, III, 17, 196, 217; *The Poetical Works of Coleridge, Shelley, and Keats*, III, 218; "To a Skylark," III, 82

Sheridan, Richard Brinsley, I, 184, 186, 195, 200; II, 301

Shih king or Shih Ching, *see* Sheking

Show(s) of Things, I, 162, 168, 260; III, 251; of Nature, II, 249; *see also* Appearance(s)

Siberia, II, 57

Sicily, I, 90

Sickness, II, 177, 298; III, 40, 42, 106, 370; *see also* Disease

Sidney, Algernon, I, 361; II, 87, 140 (?), 335 (?); III, 88 (?), 97 (?), 116 (?)

Sidney, Sir Philip, I, 276, 306, 315, 337n, 338, 353, 354, 355, 361, 382; II, 140 (?), 335 (?); III, 88 (?), 97 (?), 116 (?); *The Arcadia*, I, 355; II, 67; *Defence of Poesie*, I, 306, 355

Sign(s), *see* Symbol(s), Symbolism

Silsbee, William, III, 321n

Simplicity, I, 156, 177; III, 137, 171, 291–292, 300, 302

Sin(s), II, 95, 330, 354; III, 93, 114, 155, 204, 264, 277, 296, 369, 370, 382, 423; Fear of, II, 108; Original, II, 145

Sinbad the Sailor, III, 258

Sistine Chapel, I, 106–108, 111; III, 100

Skeptic(s), I, 297, 305; II, 228; III, 16, 237

Skepticism, II, 97; III, 117, 274, 377–379; Idea of, I, 219

Slavery, I, 158; II, 72, 73, 154, 160, 176, 287; III, 91, 109, 114–115, 234, 256–257, 264, 354, 371, 477; Abolition of, I, 182; II, 68, 106, 151, 167; III, 243, 265, 267, 275, 299, 325n; Anti-, I, 219; II, 214; III, 199, 264

Slave-Trade, III, 114–115, 256–257

Sleep, II, 298, 322–323, 357n; III, 11, 40, 122–123, 152–156, 160–161, 235

Smeaton, John, II, 43n, 44

Smith, Adam, I, 196, 213; II, 60, 321; *The Theory of the Moral Sentiments*, I, 5n, 399; II, 321

Smith, Henry Nash, "Emerson's Problem of Vocation," I, 95n–96n

Smith, Captain John, III, 128; *Advertisements for the Unexperienced Planters of New-England, or Any Where*, III, 128n

Smith, John (1618–1652), I, 361, 365

Smith, Seba, *Letters . . . by Myself, Major Jack Downing*, I, 222n

Smollett, Tobias, I, 275

Socialists, The, III, 441

Society, I, 142, 168, 180, 200, 216, 219, 221; II, 18, 69–72, 75–80, 90, 97, 98–112, 124, 142, 156, 161–162, 171, 174–176, 180–181, 185–187, 195–200, 218–220, 240, 242, 279, 285, 288, 291, 294, 296, 304–312, 325, 344, 352, 354, 358, 362; III, 11, 19, 20, 22, 24, 35, 39, 85–102 *passim*, 112–114, 118, 138, 141, 144,

187, 190, 201, 203, 240, 255, 263–264, 269, 281, 288, 293, 296, 297, 300, 304–305, 307, 314, 369, 379–380, 395, 441, 454–455, 479, 482; Laws of, II, 111–112, 292

Society for Christian Union and Progress, III, 325n

Society for the Diffusion of Useful Knowledge, Boston, I, xvi, xx, 93n–94n, 205n; II, 207n

Socrates, I, 350, 358, 359; II, 78, 87, 90–91, 175, 178, 334; III, 69, 144, 247, 311, 441, 501; Daemon of, I, 172; II, 284

Sogd, Bukharia, II, 332

Solitude, I, 113, 215; II, 86, 105, 152, 279–280; III, 73, 96, 107, 118, 234–235, 254, 370, 380

Solomon, II, 16, 311; III, 105–106; Proverbs of, I, 335

Solon, I, 250, 358; II, 118

Sömmering, Samuel Thomas von, II, 461

Sophocles, I, 359; II, 60; III, 250; *Trachiniae*, III, 483n

Sorcery, III, 168

Sorrow, III, 103–119 *passim*, 145, 236, 293, 367–368

Sortilege, III, 151

Soul(s), I, 44, 79, 100, 110, 115, 116, 121, 122, 128, 133, 142, 160, 165, 166, 168, 174, 181, 221, 225, 230, 299, 300, 303, 350, 353, 354, 358, 359, 368; II, 16, 36–37, 40, 84–86, 89–94, 97, 100, 103, 107–108, 111–112, 132, 139, 143, 145, 149–150, 170, 172, 181–187, 197–200, 216, 220, 222–223, 225, 245–248, 251, 257, 260, 263–266, 271, 276–280, 283, 288, 290, 307–312, 318, 331, 340–342, 345–346, 351, 355–356, 361–362; III, 5–22, 24–33, 34–50, 51–52, 53, 59, 60–67, 70, 71–72, 73, 74, 77, 78, 79–80, 84, 85, 86, 87, 88, 89–90, 91, 92, 94, 95, 99, 102, 103, 106, 108, 109, 111, 112, 113, 118, 119, 121, 122, 125, 127, 141–143, 145, 148, 156, 158, 160–161, 166, 169, 170, 187, 188–191, 195, 196–197, 199, 203, 204, 207, 209, 214, 215, 216, 218, 224, 226, 229, 232–233, 236, 243, 248, 249–253, 254, 259, 260, 262, 267, 269, 273, 275, 276, 277, 278, 279, 280–285, 292, 296, 298, 300, 302–304, 307, 310, 313, 314, 325n, 328, 349, 350, 353, 354, 359, 368, 378, 381, 454, 461, 474, 483, 489, 507, 508; Central, II, 311; Common, II, 96, 247, 281, 285; III, 73, 253; Divine, II, 249; III, 28; Doctrine of the, III, 5–22, 24, 170; Eternal, III, 89, 300, 462; General, II, 147; Great, II, 252; III, 42, 232, 253; Health of, II, 145, 271; III, 25; Homesickness of, III, 30; Identity of, II, 187; Immortality of, II, 188; III, 277; Individual, II, 92; Internal, III, 77; Law(s) of, I, 381; II, 102, 150–151, 221, 345; III, 278; Living, III, 35; of Nature, II, 247; III, 215, 230; of Poet, III, 75; of the Age, III, 187; of the Whole, III, 280; of Universe, III, 204; of World, II, 154–155, 346; One, II, 159, 181; III, 35, 233; Over-, III, 280, 285; Procession of, III, 62–67; Social, II, 289; Substance of, III, 68; Supreme, III, 278, 330; Transmigration of, I, 79; III, 154, 354; Unity of, II, 86; III, 47; Universal, II, 15, 44, 48, 92, 159, 198, 288; III, 86, 300; Uprise of, III, 189, 214, 224, 325n; Voice of, III, 70; World of the, III, 89

South, Robert, I, 369; II, 60

South, The (U.S.), II, 138; III, 378

South America, I, 31, 42; II, 81, 138; III, 211, 225

Southampton, Henry Wriothesley, Third Earl of, I, 306

Southern Cross, I, 41

Southerner, The (U.S.), I, 214; II, 314; III, 371

Southey, Robert, I, 213, 257, 357; *The Curse of Kehama*, III, 105

South Sea, II, 100, 106; III, 128n, 143

South Sea Islander, II, 161

Space, II, 32; III, 170; Idea of, I, 218; Temple of, II, 96; Time and, I, 297; II, 172, 184–185, 208n; III, 11, 38–40, 143, 145, 152, 228, 233, 250; *see also* Place

Spain, I, 381; II, 17, 76, 81; III, 53, 210

Spalatin (George Burkhardt), I, 125, 131, 136, 139

Spaniards, I, 212

Spanish Historians, II, 56

Spanish Keys, I, 237

Spanish Proverb, II, 288

Sparta, III, 147–148

Spartan(s), II, 73, 131, 133, 241; III, 144

Spartan Maxim, II, 72

Spectator, I, 366, 483n; II, 141n

Speech(es), II, 42, 55, 163, 224; III, 244, 284, 314, 357–358; Forms of, III, 20; True, III, 300; *see also* Eloquence; Orator

Spenser, Edmund, I, 213, 216, 241, 274, 276, 287n, 288, 306, 315, 337n, 338, 354, 357, 361; II, 47, 67, 264; III, 17, 250; *Faerie Queene*, I, 315; "An Hymne in Honour of Beautie," II, 264n

Sphinx, The, I, 224; III, 48, 112

Spinoza, Baruch, I, 132; II, 260–261

Spires, Diet of, I, 127

Spirit(s), I, 166–167, 173, 224–225, 228, 231–232, 320, 370; II, 29–33, 36–37, 43, 55, 57, 63, 93–96, 132, 144, 155, 181, 184, 247, 263, 312, 346–347, 351; III, 10, 18, 19, 20, 27–28, 32, 38, 73, 92, 104, 111, 148–149, 155, 156, 216, 236, 272, 295, 314, 353, 374, 381, 477; Animal, III, 111, 136; Divine, II, 65, 102; III, 141; Eternal, I, 157; II, 54; Higher, III, 20, 331; Human, I, 300; II, 182, 318; III, 140; New, III, 522; of Man, II, 271; of the World, III, 191; Social, III, 516

Spiritualists, Pseudo-, III, 451

Spiritual Laws, *see* Law(s), Spiritual

Spontaneity, II, 250; III, 70; of Genius, III, 70–81; of the Will, III, 144

Sprague, Charles, "Ode Pronounced at the Centennial Celebration of the Settlement of Boston, September, 1830," I, 68n

Spurzheim, Kaspar, II, 97, 258; III, 140

Stability, III, 26–28; in Society, II, 344

Staël-Holstein, Anne Louise Germaine Necker, Baronne de, (Mme. de Staël), I, 97n, 207n, 263–264, 287n, 308, 312, 341, 424; II, 141, 336; III, 196, 217; *Germany*, I, 376; II, 16n, 99n, 368n; III, 154n, 158n, 386n; *The Influence of Literature upon Society*, I, 308n, 312n, 341n, 389n; II, 47n, 141n, 333n, 368n

Stanley, Thomas, *History of Philosophy*, I, 97n

State, II, 69–82, 102, 105, 143, 169, 217, 310; III, 187, 197, 199, 225, 228–229, 238–247, 258, 266, 314, 375, 441, 521; Idea of, I, 379

Staten Island, III, xiii

State Street, Boston, II, 226, 241; Unitarianism of, III, 325n

Statius, Publius Papinius, I, 284

Staupitz, John von, I, 128

Steam, I, 13–14, 67–68, 260; III, 158; Battery, II, 286; III, 306, 450

Steele, Sir Richard, *Spectator*, No. 75, I, 483n; II, 141n

Stentor, II, 13

Stephen, King of England, I, 134, 248

Sterne, Laurence, I, 275; III, 222

Stevenson, Marmaduke, I, 179

Stewart, Dugald, I, 371n, 374–375; *Elements of the Philosophy of the Human Mind*, I, 374; *A General View of the Progress of Metaphysical, Ethical, and Political Philosophy*, I, 190n, 323n, 325n, 374–375, 376, 389n; *The Philosophy of the Active and Moral Powers of Man*, I, 374; *Works*, II, 103n, 288n, 368n; III, 106n, 386n

Stoic(s), I, 186; II, 175; III, 292

Stoicism, II, 93, 152, 330

Stonehenge, I, 238, 256; II, 166; III, 30

Strasburg Cathedral, II, 59

Strode, William, "A Song in Praise of Melancholy," III, 58n

Stuarts, The, I, 157

Sturgis, Caroline, III, xii, 1n

Subjective, Subjectiveness, II, 57, 100; III, 26–27, 155, 200, 214–216, 218, 220–221, 284

Sublime, The, II, 200; III, 195; Moral, I, 214, 352

Success, II, 239; III, 287, 370

Suckling, Sir John, I, 357

Suffering, I, 156, 173; III, 112, 114–115, 145

Suffrage, III, 10; Universal, II, 214

Suicide, II, 39, 161, 198; III, 154

Sumatra, I, 41; II, 57

Supernatural, The, I, 80, 132; II, 323; III, 162, 167, 169, 194, 329; *see also* Demonology

Superstition, I, 156, 332; II, 167, 169, 343, 355; III, 106, 127, 129, 162, 169, 212–213, 266, 357, 454, 455; *see also* Demonology; Magic

Supreme Being, I, 170; II, 43, 307, 335; III, 76; *see also* God

Supreme Cause, *see* Cause, Supreme
Supreme Critic, III, 280
Supreme Mind, *see* Mind, Supreme
Supreme Reason, *see* Reason, Supreme
Supreme Soul, *see* Soul(s), Supreme
Sweden, II, 180
Swedenborg, Emanuel, I, 25n, 79, 96n, 164n, 173, 224, 384, 389n; II, 13, 25, 92, 172, 211n, 258, 300, 346; III, 16–17, 223, 225, 234, 275, 287, 361, 451, 513; *The Apocalypse Revealed*, II, 300n, 368n; III, 361; Celestial Secrets (*Arcana Coelestia*), III, 361; *The Doctrine of Marriage*, III, 361; *The Doctrine of the New Jerusalem Respecting the Sacred Scripture*, III, 17n; *Heaven and Hell*, II, 13n; III, 361
Swedenborgian(s), I, 208n; II, 346
Swedenborgianism (Church of the New Jerusalem), II, 25, 94, 172, 174, 346; III, 141, 275, 287
Swift, Jonathan, I, 146, 213, 274, 275; II, 65n, 67, 75n, 325; III, 206n, 511
Swinford, Lady Catherine, I, 270
Swiss, I, 43; II, 77
Switzerland, III, 221, 275, 407
Symbol(s), Symbolism, I, 24–26, 132, 220–221, 224, 289–292; II, 132, 148, 202, 219, 220–221, 311–312, 353; III, 28, 37–38, 157–158, 170, 251, 278, 349–354, 358, 378, 513–514; *see also* Allegory; Analogy; Correspondence
Symmons, Charles, ed., *The Prose Works of John Milton; with a Life of the Author*, I, 144n–163n *passim*, 390n; III, 27n, 386n
Symposium, The (Transcendental Club), *see* Hedge's Club
Synthesis, I, 318; III, 195
Syracuse, Sicily, I, 21
Syria, I, 42; II, 161
Syrtaeus, III, 511

Tacitus, Cornelius, I, 234; *Germania*, I, 38n; II, 320n
Taglioni, Maria (?), III, 350
Tahitian, II, 112
Talbot, John, First Earl of Shrewsbury, II, 17
Talent(s), I, 119, 154, 379; II, 361; III, 20, 80, 197, 216, 218, 281, 287, 297, 354, 368, 378, 450, 483, 490;

Man (Men) of, II, 62, 361; III, 235, 375, 460, 483
Taliessin, "Gall from the Bards," I, 239–240
Talleyrand-Périgord, Charles Maurice de, II, 136
Tamerlane, II, 68; III, 134–135, 231
Tamlane, Ballad of, I, 261
Tappan, Caroline Sturgis, *see* Sturgis, Caroline
Tariff(s), II, 108; III, 257
Tartars, II, 52, 68
Tartary, I, 42; III, 187
Tasso, Torquato, I, 357; II, 315–316
Taste, I, 101–102, 154, 190–191, 263, 273, 358, 372, 374, 383; II, 36, 204, 223, 225, 241, 249, 267, 278, 311; III, 81, 281, 287, 356; American, I, 381; III, 196; in Literature, I, 210–216; Woman's, III, 63
Tate, Nahum, I, 357
Taylor, Edward Thompson ("Father Taylor"), III, 363n
Taylor, Sir Henry, *Philip van Artevelde*, I, 223; II, 61; III, 152n
Taylor, Jeremy, I, 213, 214, 215, 361, 362, 369; II, xiv, 60, 93; III, 192; *Holy Dying*, I, xx; *Titles of the Ten Sermons*, III, 191n; *Twenty-Seven Sermons*, III, 254n; *The Whole Works*, III, 386n
Taylor, Thomas, "Introduction," *Select Works of Plotinus*, II, 91n, 332n, 368n
Teacher(s), I, 172, 211–214, 231–232, 273, 340; II, 148, 204, 258; III, 34–50 *passim*, 141, 229, 290, 501–503
Teaching, I, 210–216; II, 62, 203–204, 423–424; III, 34–50 *passim*, 282, 286–301 *passim*, 501–503
Tecumseh, III, 165
Teleboas River, II, 134
Telemachus, I, 150
Tell, William, II, 241
Temperament, I, 190; III, 41, 110–111, 114–115, 156, 287
Temperance, I, 160, 177, 182, 363; II, 155, 277, 292, 333, 337; III, 10, 257, 261–263, 265, 275, 303, 325n, 477; Idea of, I, 219; Meeting, III, 299; Reform, II, 287; Society of, II, 106–107; Universal, II, 299
Temple School, Boston, II, 192n
Temporary, The, II, 217

INDEX

Tennyson, Alfred, Lord, "A Dirge," II, 338n–339n

Terence (Publius Terentius Afer), I, 316

Terrific, The, I, 304

Terror(s), III, 105, 106, 110–113, 136, 194, 299; Ground of, III, 106; of Day of Doom, III, 194; of Finite Nature, III, 117; Physical and Metaphysical, III, 100

Tetzel, Johann, I, 120–123 passim

Texas, II, 68

Thales, I, 358

Theagenes, II, 154

Theanor, II, 284

Theban Phalanx, III, 189

Thebes, Egypt, II, 228; III, 30, 250

Theism, I, xvii, 134, 383; II, 354; III, 377

Thelwall, John, III, 98

Themis, II, 336

Themistocles, II, 111

Thénard, Louis Jacques, I, 2n

Theocracy, III, 246; The True, III, 276, 479

Theodosius II, Emperor, I, 256

Theology, II, 215; III, 159, 167; Dogmatic, III, 238; Natural, III, 286; Popular, I, 134; Shadow of, III, 170

Thermopylae, Greece, I, 384

Theseus, I, 283; III, 483

Theseus (sculpture), III, 73

Thesians, II, 154

Theurgists, The, III, 368n

Thibaudeau, Comte Antoine Clair, *Mémoirs sur le consulat . . .* and *Le Consulat et l'empire . . .* , II, 37n, 368n; III, 13n, 386n

Thing(s), I, 291, 303, 336, 376, 381, 382; II, 74, 75, 153, 155, 224, 228, 250, 260, 343; III, 35, 38, 55, 71–73, 74, 78, 109, 111, 141–142, 157, 190, 204–205, 266, 289, 314, 352, 361, 382, 455; Constitution of, II, 51, 276; Divine, III, 59, 483; Flux in, I, 221, 289; II, 27, 32; III, 27–28, 510; Forms of, II, 276; Law from, II, 218; Light of, III, 456; Moral, III, 72; Nature of, I, 370; II, 95, 144, 145; III, 86, 205; Plastic World of, III, 354; Shadows of Real, III, 60–61; Show(s) of, I, 162, 168, 260; III, 251; Simplicity and Identity of All, III, 291; Unity at Heart of, III, 41

Thinker(s), I, 226, 228, 229, 340; III, 7, 188, 242; Solitary, I, 191

Thomas à Becket, III, 81

Thomas à Kempis, II, 59, 93–94; III, 192; *On the Imitation of Christ,* I, xx

Thompson, Benjamin, Count Rumford, I, 12

Thompson, Frank T., "Emerson's Indebtedness to Coleridge," I, 371n

Thomson, James (1700–1748), I, 212, 308

Thoreau, Henry David, I, 208n; III, xii, 1n, 92n, 94n, 339n

Thought(s), I, 110, 190, 218–221, 224–230, 285, 290–292, 296, 299, 300, 304, 308, 318–319, 325, 333–334, 350, 378–379, 380, 385; II, 4n, 13, 35, 42, 55–59, 63, 86, 93, 98, 100, 146–148, 151–152, 170–171, 182, 224, 245–261 passim, 263, 271, 278, 284, 292, 297, 343, 355, 360–361, 364; III, 17, 32, 37–47 passim, 55, 66–67, 73, 75, 77, 78, 82, 89, 93, 101, 141, 143–144, 146, 153, 155, 156, 194, 199, 200, 203, 215, 222, 225, 226, 228, 230, 235, 236, 239–240, 241, 243, 249, 250, 254, 260, 266, 267, 272–273, 276, 279, 280, 282, 285, 286–287, 301, 307, 311, 312, 327–328, 349–350, 352, 355, 357–358, 376, 380, 381, 458, 507; and Matter, I, 24–26; Causal, III, 71, 144; First, I, 341; II, 168, 284; Kingdom of, III, 209; Law(s) of, I, 224, 291, 307, 311, 383; II, 318; New, II, 213–214; III, 5–10; of the Thought, III, 329; Popular, III, 273; Region of Pure, III, 115; Second, II, 64, 152, 168, 284; III, 87; Unity of, III, 43; Wood-, III, 235

Thrace, II, 91

Thucydides, III, 72

Thugs, II, 227

Tiber River, I, 106

Tillotson, John, I, 369; II, xiv

Time, I, 75, 110, 185, 231, 384; II, 2n, 32, 80, 146, 157, 171, 188, 313, 314, 318, 335; III, 22, 27, 47–48, 113, 114, 116, 141, 170, 203, 250–253; and Place, II, 159, 198, 224, 249, 335; III, 54–55, 123, 239; and Space, I, 297; II, 172, 184–185, 208n; III, 11, 38–40, 143, 145, 152, 228, 233, 250; Deeps of Infinite, III, 75; Idea of, I, 218; Kingdom of, III, 54–55,

585

75, 116; Ocean of, I, 250; III, 179; Shows of, I, 299; Stream of, I, 336; Temple of, II, 182; True Economy of, II, 146, 147; Urn of, III, 377

Times, The, *see* Present Age, The

Timoleon, I, 154; II, 140

Timur, *see* Tamerlane

Tindal, William, *see* Tyndale, William

Tiraboschi, Girolamo, II, 304; *History of Italian Literature,* II, 304n

Titans, I, 231

Tithes, III, 238

Titian (Tiziano Vecellio), I, 114; II, 46, 54; III, 220, 413

Tocqueville, Alexis Charles Henri Maurice Clérel de, III, 367–368; *Democracy in America,* III, 368n

Toland, John, I, 158

Tolles, Frederick B., "Emerson and Quakerism," I, 164n

Tooke, Horne, III, 98n

Tory, II, 70

Toulouse, France, II, 276

Toussaint L'Ouverture, Pierre Dominique, III, 477

Townshend, Charles (?), I, 201

Trade, I, 262; II, 42, 68, 81, 128, 132, 142, 160–161, 165–168, 201–202, 362; III, 6, 19, 25, 96, 190–191, 196, 237, 245, 305, 370, 454, 477; Free, II, 108; *see also* Commerce; Trades and Professions

Trades and Professions, I, 78, 370; II, 113–131, 137–138, 144, 181, 215, 230–245 *passim,* 296–297; III, 8, 24–25, 287; *see also* Commerce; Labor; Trade; Vocation

Tradition(s), I, 283–286, 316–317; II, 47, 342, 358; III, 91, 197–198, 259, 325n; Religious, III, 199, 274, 275; *see also* Convention(s); Custom(s); Usage(s)

Tragedy, I, 382; II, 54, 110–111; III, 103–120; Antique, III, 106; French, II, 60–61; Greek, II, 60–61; III, 105; of Life, III, 86; of Limitation and Inner Death, III, 297; of More and Less, III, 44

Tragic, The, III, 123; Elements, II, 9; III, 121, 171; *see also* Tragedy

Tramps, III, 451

Trance, I, 169; II, 90–92; *see also* Ecstasy; Enthusiasm; Rapture(s)

Tranquillity, II, 182; III, 112–114, 143

Transactions of the Royal Society of Edinburgh, I, 58n

Transcendental Club, The, *see* Hedge's Club

Transcendentalism, III, 307n, 339n–340n

Transcendentalist(s), III, 176n, 339n–340n, 483

Transcendental Philosophy, I, 173

Transmigration of Soul, I, 79; III, 154, 354

Transmission, III, 520

Travel, I, 89–90; II, 178–179; III, 22, 31, 228, 400–401

Trial by Jury, I, 243; II, 14; III, 240

Troglodyte, III, 516

Troilus, I, 283

Trojans, III, 12

Trojan War, I, 254; II, 276

Troubadours, I, 284; III, 118, 250

Troy, III, 12

True, The, I, 102, 110; II, 67, 354–355; III, 189–190, 483

Trust, II, 39, 144, 251, 300–304; III, 39, 77–78, 116, 145, 171, 199, 272, 281, 302, 304, 312, 439; Doctrine of, III, 328–330; *see also* Self-Trust

Truth(s), I, 75, 79, 83, 100, 101, 119, 127–128, 131, 153, 156, 176, 177, 180, 186, 187, 210–211, 226, 228, 232, 265, 274, 278, 280, 285, 299–300, 303, 304, 307, 326–327, 333, 354, 369, 375–376, 382–383; II, 50, 54, 57, 62, 85–87, 90, 92, 98–99, 102, 110, 188, 197–198, 227–228, 245–261, 264, 269, 271, 279, 301–307, 322, 336–337, 344, 355, 358, 362; III, 16–17, 19, 22, 29, 36, 39, 48, 54–55, 62, 71, 73, 81, 112, 124–125, 133, 137, 139–140, 143, 146, 164, 171, 196, 219, 222, 228, 235, 240, 245, 250, 251, 253, 259, 277, 278, 287, 289, 312, 328, 359–360, 369, 377, 381, 400, 419, 516, 525; Absolute, I, 159, 376; II, 42, 219, 354; III, 189–190, 299; Eternal Sentiment of, III, 455; Ethical, I, 360; First, II, 344; Highest, II, 344; Ideal, II, 59; III, 73; Ideal of, III, 124–125; Moral, I, 25, 290; Pure, II, 248; Sense of, III, 313–314; Spiritual, I, 297; II, 354; III, 359; to Self, II, 151–152

Tubal-cain, II, 226

Tucker, Ellen Louisa, *see* Emerson, Ellen Tucker (first wife)
Tucker, Elizabeth, I, xix
Tucker Estate, I, xvi; III, 321n
Tuke, Henry, *Memoirs of the Life of Fox*, I, 164n
Turk(s), I, 130, 134; II, 15, 160; III, 112, 290; Predestination of the, III, 105
Turkey, II, 74; III, 187, 211
Turner, Sharon, I, 276; II, 34; III, 123, 225; *The History of the Anglo-Saxons*, I, 205n, 207n, 233n–250n *passim*, 276n, 391n; II, 131n, 132n, 368n; III, 31n, 386n; *The Sacred History of the World*, II, 34n, 368n; III, 123n, 386n
Turpie, Mary C., "A Quaker Source for Emerson's Sermon on the Lord's Supper," I, 164n
Tuscan Painters, II, 269
Tuscany, Duke of, I, 112
Tuscany, II, 54
Twisden, Judge, I, 176
Tyndale, William, I, 360

Ulysses, III, 12
Unbelief, II, 96–97, 197, 300, 354; Age of, II, 96–97
Unconscious, The, II, 56, 135; III, 10
Unconsciousness, II, 58, 168, 170, 281; III, 19, 20, 74, 123, 167
Underconsciousness, I, 219
Understanding, I, xviii, 71, 93n, 101, 161, 188, 206n, 321, 325, 365, 378–379, 454; II, 68, 83, 90, 96, 141–142, 179, 223, 249, 303; III, 17, 19, 38, 48, 62, 73, 124–125, 135, 166–167, 169, 189–190, 219, 354, 454, 455
Unitarianism, I, xvi–xvii; II, 2n, 346; III, xi, 319n–326n
Unitarian Review, The, III, 271n
Unity, I, 334–335; III, 28, 29–30, 214, 228, 280; at Heart of Things, III, 41; in Nature, II, 25; Multitude in, I, 101; II, 264; of Cause, III, 72; of Men, II, 12; of Mind, II, 17, 25, 83; III, 39; of Soul, II, 86; III, 47; of Thought, III, 43; Sentiment of, III, 41, 188
Universal, The, III, 28, 234, 297–298, 381–382
Universal Being, III, 234; *see also* Being
Universal Humanity, II, 110

Universalist, The, II, 108–109
Universal Law(s), *see* Law(s), Universal
Universal Man, I, 226, 272; II, 12, 68, 74; III, 370
Universal Mind, *see* Mind, Universal
Universal Order, *see* Order, Universal
Universal Soul, *see* Soul, Universal
Universe, I, 166, 225, 327; II, 26, 144, 302–303; III, 36, 84, 93, 103, 141, 149, 168, 214, 252, 292, 353, 364; External, II, 266; Law(s) of, III, 166, 368; of Light and Love, I, 384; Order of, I, 74; Soul of, III, 204; *see also* World
Uranus (planet), I, 29
Urbino (servant of Michelangelo), I, 114
Urien Reged, I, 241
Urituco, I, 39
Usage(s), I, 180; III, 11, 89, 197, 240–241, 257, 262, 273, 303, 308–309, 490; *see also* Convention(s); Custom(s); Tradition(s)
Use, II, 245
Useful Knowledge, Society of, II, 106; *see also* Society for the Diffusion of Useful Knowledge, Boston
Uses of Natural History, I, 5–26, 46–48, 70–83
Utica, III, 268
Utilitarianism, II, 67
Utility, I, 233, 249, 265

Valais, Switzerland, III, 221
Valerius Maximus, I, 279
Van Buren, Martin, III, 135–136n
Vane, Sir Henry, I, 353, 365; II, 87
Varchi, Benedetto, I, 115
Vasari, Giorgio, I, 106, 107, 113, 116; *Vite de' Più Excellenti Pittori, Scultori, e Architetti*, I, 103n–116n *passim*, 390n
Vast, The, III, 169, 206, 287, 288–289; Love of, III, 196, 217
Vatican, The, II, 222; Museum, II, 43, 270–271
Vauban, Sébastien Le Prestre de, I, 106
Veda(s), II, 88–89, 124
Venetian Painters, II, 269; III, 69
Venice, Italy, I, 76, 104, 105; II, 74, 180; Music of, III, 220
Venus, II, 224, 269; of the Père la Chaise, III, 134
Venus (planet), I, 18

Venus (statue), III, 76

Vermont, III, 264

Veronese, Paul (Paolo Cagliari), III, 220

Verse, see Poetry

Very, Jones, III, 1n

Vesuvius, Mt., II, 27

Vice(s), I, 142, 336; II, 11, 95, 305; III, 65, 87, 104, 109, 112, 122, 148–149 252, 268, 273, 308, 370, 441

Vienna, Austria, II, 139

Vieta, François, I, 353

Viguier, Paule de, II, 276

Virgil (Publius Vergilius Maro), I, 262, 342; II, 424; III, 82; *Aeneid,* I, 184; *Eclogues,* III, 264n

Virginia Company of London, III, 128

Virgin Mary, see Mary, Virgin

Virtue(s), I, 68, 115, 148, 154, 159, 201, 316, 325, 334, 340–342, 363, 381; II, 75–76, 84–89, 93–95, 124, 127, 140, 162, 175, 195, 229, 249, 264, 272, 275–277, 287, 289, 291, 299, 305, 312, 322, 333–334, 337–338, 341, 346, 351, 360; III, 13, 16, 62, 65, 67, 76, 81, 87–91, 96, 108, 124, 133, 139–145, 149, 166, 171, 251, 252, 278–279, 280, 285, 298, 308, 311, 370, 374, 381, 483, 488; Idea of, I, 219; III, 144; Law of, II, 256–257; Sentiment of, I, 190; III, 144; Sentiment of Reverence to, I, 188; Wild, II, 306

Visconti, Galeazzo II, Duke of Milan, I, 270

Visconti, Violante, I, 270

Vision, II, 92, 202, 343; III, 143, 249, 340; Higher, III, 239; of Living Light, III, 280; of Perfect, III, 313; of Right, III, 139

Vocation, I, 100, 199; II, 147–148, 230–246, 296–297; III, 35, 287; see also Labor; Trades and Professions

Volkmann, Johann Jacob, II, 119

Voltaire, François Marie Arouet de, I, 2n, 341; II, 67; III, 224, 511; *Socrate,* I, 341n

Volterra, Daniele da (Daniele Ricciarelli), I, 111

Vopiscus, Flavius, I, 234–235n

Voss, Johann Heinrich, II, 164n

Vossius (Voss), Gerardus Johannes (?), II, 164

Vulcan, I, 107, 258; II, 234; III, 24

Wace, *Roman de Brut,* I, 241

Walden Pond, III, 94n

Walk the Waters (Walk-in-the-Water or My-ee-rah ?), III, 128

Wall, William, I, 87n, 278n (?)

Waller, Edmund, I, 357

Walpole, Horace, II, 65; III, 13n, 206, 213, 391; *Catalogue of Royal and Noble Authors,* II, 65n; III, 206n

Walpole, Sir Robert, III, 13

Waltham, Mass., I, xxii; III, xiv, 336n

Walton, Izaak, I, 353, 355, 357; "Life of Mr. George Herbert," I, 352n, 353n; "The Life of Sir Henry Wotton," I, 354n; II, 324n; *Lives,* I, 391n; II, 368n

Wandering Jew, The Tale of the, I, 256

Want(s), II, 54, 114–115; III, 11, 39–40, 106–108, 111, 119, 210, 400; and Have, II, 114; III, 427; see also Poverty

War, I, 129, 190, 216, 254–256, 262, 370; II, 14, 40, 63, 72, 81–82, 105, 165, 214, 215, 285–286, 330; III, 6, 42, 91, 198, 199, 203, 239, 370, 450, 474; Age of, I, 254–256; Idea of, I, 231

Warburton, William, II, 169n

Ward, Anna Barker, III, xii

Ward, Robert Plumer, *Tremaine,* II, 358n

Ward, Samuel Gray, III, xii, 248n

Wardlaw, Elizabeth, Lady, "Hardyknute," III, 214n

Wartburg, Eisenach, Germany, I, 126, 137; III, 101

Warton, Thomas, I, 257, 263, 357; II, 304; *History of English Poetry,* I, 205n, 207n, 209n, 233n, 241n, 244n, 253n, 256n, 260–269 *passim,* 276n, 284n, 337n, 391n; II, 304n

Washington, George, I, 112, 138, 211; II, 51, 75, 80, 132, 140, 151, 228, 241, 335, 338; III, 231, 311, 477

Washington, D.C., I, 419; II, 22n; Capitol, II, 54

Water, I, 13–14, 50–68, 259–260

Watertown, Mass., I, xxii

Waterville College, Me., I, xxii; III, xiv, xx, 336n–337n

Watt, James (1736–1819), I, 13, 57–58, 260; II, 18, 51; III, 158

Watt, James (1769–1848), I, 57–58

Wealth, I, 100, 251; II, 137–139; III, 21, 40, 107–108, 119, 146–147, 349
Webster, Daniel, I, xx, 79, 183n; II, 60
Wells, William C., *An Essay on Dew* . . . , I, 64n, 390n
Welsh Language, I, 238
Welsh Poetry, I, 239–241
Wesley, John, III, 243
West, The, I, 236
West, The (U.S.), I, 215; III, 378; Emerson lectures in, I, xxii; III, xv, 345n
West Indies, I, 42; III, 132, 370
Westminster Abbey, I, 117, 235
Whicher, Stephen E., *Freedom and Fate*, I, 96n; II, 1n
Whiggery, Universal, III, 341n
Whig Party (American), III, 187, 309
Whig Party (English), I, 184, 196, 367; II, 70
White, Gilbert, *Natural History and Antiquities of Selborne*, I, 5n, 19n, 390n, 399
White Mountains, I, 164; II, 222
Whiting, B. J., I, 269n
Whittemore, Amos, II, 18
Whole, The, I, 101, 103, 146, 229, 296; II, 5n; III, 123–124, 144, 237, 284, 380; Good of, III, 106; Soul of, III, 280; *see also* All, The
Wicliffe, John, *see* Wycliffe, John
Wieland, Christoph Martin, III, 220, 221
Wilberforce, William, II, 172; III, 140
Wild Man, I, 45–46; II, 56, 136, 306; *see also* Noble Savage; Savage(s)
Wiley, John, I, 216n
Will, I, 99, 124, 136, 162, 225, 242, 253, 291, 376; II, 43, 48, 129–131, 137–139, 143, 149–150, 152, 154, 171, 229, 241, 268, 282, 297–298, 310, 323, 336, 343, 358–359; III, 10, 15–16, 27, 33, 35, 37, 45, 74, 82, 85, 106, 108, 144, 146, 156, 218, 240, 241, 243, 258, 280–282, 295, 312, 329–330, 352, 356, 454; Abdication of, III, 178n, 201, 325n; Individual, II, 84, 86, 171, 298; Law of, II, 181; of God, I, 124, 126, 290; of Heaven, III, 41; Private, II, 149, 355; III, 282; Renunciation of, III, 312; Spontaneity of, III, 144
William the Conqueror, King of England, II, 108
Will's Coffeehouse, London, I, 216

Wilson, Alexander, I, 11; *The American Ornithology*, I, 11n
Winckelmann, Johann Joachim, I, 348; II, 226; III, 72n; *Geschichte der Kunst des Alterthums*, I, 348n
Winebago Indians, II, 8
Winkelried, Arnold von, I, 385
Wisdom, I, 140, 156, 190, 201, 251, 253, 303, 310, 383; II, 96, 103, 158, 162, 166, 195, 312, 314, 317, 355, 361; III, 16, 19, 33, 36, 41, 50, 67, 93, 123, 126, 136, 139, 153, 171, 229, 279, 280, 288, 292, 298, 312, 363, 441; Divine, III, 284; Law of, II, 256–257; of God, I, 171; of Humanity, III, 16, 218; Primary, III, 35; Proverbial, I, 313; Spirit of, III, 50
Wise (Man), The, I, 159, 199, 214, 229, 272, 274, 307, 383; II, 251, 257, 259–260; III, 19–21, 33, 119, 149, 242–244, 268, 284, 292, 441, 490
Wit(s), I, 272, 306, 315–316, 330, 336, 340, 356, 382; II, 35, 214; III, 17, 126–127, 130, 136, 137, 374, 375, 465; Law of, I, 214
Witan, III, 31
Wittenberg, Germany, I, 118–137 *passim*; College Church, I, 122; University of, I, 120, 123
Wolf, Friedrich August, II, 226; III, 225
Woman, I, 249, 280–282; II, 23, 102, 281–283, 302, 336; III, 62–65
Wood, Anthony (Anthony à Wood), I, 151
Worcester, Edward Somerset, Second Marquess of, *Century of the Names and Scantlings of such Inventions as at present I can call to mind to have tried and perfected*, I, 358
Worcester, Mass., I, xxii; III, xiv, 336n
Word(s), I, 128, 175, 220–221, 303, 310, 382; III, 171, 289, 310, 314–315, 369; Age of, III, 289; Made Flesh, I, 378; of God, I, 72, 128–129, 137, 170; III, 86
Wordsworth, William, I, xix, 3n, 4n, 153, 278, 283, 308, 371n, 376, 381n; II, 97, 211n, 272, 329; III, 1n, 9, 17, 196, 217–218, 222n, 226; "Dion," II, 107n, 329; III, 297n; *The Excursion*, II, 333n; "I grieved for Bonaparté," I, 140; "Influence of Natural Objects . . . ," III, 77–78n; "Laodamia,"

II, 329; "Lines Composed a Few Miles above Tintern Abbey," III, 9n, 218n; "London, 1802," I, 156–157n; "Ode, composed on May Morning," III, 52–53n; "Ode: Intimations of Immortality," II, 85n; "Ode to Duty," II, 168; "On the Extinction of the Venetian Republic," I, 236n; "Peter Bell," II, 272n; III, 194n; *Poems Dedicated to National Independence and Liberty*, Part II, Sonnet XII, II, 145n; Sonnet XXXIII, II, 198n; *The Poetical Works*, III, 78n; "The Prioress' Tale," I, 283; "The Recluse," I, 379n; II, 273n; *The River Duddon*, Sonnet XXXIV, I, 104n; "Rob Roy's Grave," I, 177; "Say, what is honour . . . ," I, 278n; "She was a Phantom of delight," III, 60n; "The Tables Turned," III, 457n; "To the Same" ["Poems of Sentiment and Reflection," XXVI], III, 57n; "When to the attractions of the busy world," I, 153n; "Written upon a Blank Leaf in 'The Complete Angler'," I, 20n

Work(s), III, 101–102, 200, 218, 259, 281, 309; and Faith, I, 120–121; Good, III, 308; Intellectual, III, 93, 146; *see also* Labor

World, I, 6, 28–29, 142, 224–226, 290, 297, 299, 326; II, 29–33, 39–40, 85, 114–116, 128, 132, 142, 143, 156, 177, 200, 201, 214–215, 219–224, 230, 261, 277, 301; III, 27, 34, 39, 41, 43, 54, 60–61, 89, 95, 119, 140, 240, 252, 301; Actual, I, 162, 300, 305; II, 310; Apparent, I, 299, 300; II, 67; Great Sentiment of, III, 249; Ideal, I, 162; II, 316, 362; Inner, I, 24, 175; II, 84, 313; Intellectual, III, 45; Invisible, I, 24–25, 143, 229, 290; Law(s) of, I, 214; II, 114, 301; III, 40, 106; Man of the, II, 258; III, 96–98, 149, 217; Material, I, 224, 289, 291, 300, 332; Moral, III, 269; of Events, II, 59; of Experience, I, 162; of the Soul, III, 89; of Thought, I, 162, 300; of Senses, I,

300; Order of, III, 41; Other, III, 60; Outer, I, 24, 175, 300; II, 84, 181; Physical and Metaphysical, III, 522; Real, I, 299; II, 313; Sensible, I, 143; Social, III, 269; Soul of, II, 154–155, 346; Spiritual, I, 332; Upper, III, 62; Visible, I, 24–25, 290; *see also* Earth; Globe; Universe

Worms, Diet of, I, 124–126, 132

Worship, III, 275–276

Wotton, Sir Henry, I, 337n, 353–355; II, 324; "The Character of a Happy Life," I, 354; *Reliquiae Wottonianae*, I, 207n, 354n, 355; II, 138n, 367n

Wren, Sir Christopher, II, 51; III, 76–77

Wycliffe, John, I, 124n, 269, 270, 286, 288, 356, 360

Xenophon, I, 150, 366; II, 134, 335; III, 72, 140n, 231; *Anabasis*, II, 134; III, 221; *Banquet*, I, 359

Xerxes, II, 151

Yankee, III, 362

Ygdrasil, II, 35

York, Me., III, 193–194n, 456

York Minster, I, 235

Young, Edward, I, 212, 308; *Night Thoughts*, II, 352n

Youth, II, 97, 145, 156, 170, 198–199, 217, 240, 242, 245, 261, 296–297, 299, 312, 335–336; III, 5, 9, 26, 43, 55–56, 58, 59, 76, 86, 88, 90–100, 104, 144–145, 166, 228, 234–235, 236, 261, 264–265, 274, 288, 291–293, 295–297, 303, 304–305, 373–374, 375, 376–377, 488; Perpetual, I, 258, 260, 369; III, 291–292

Zend-Avesta, II, 95

Zeno, I, 359; III, 299

Zodiac, The, II, 16; III, 233, 278, 369

Zoology, I, 46

Zoroaster, I, 166; II, 226; III, 144, 299, 368n; "The Oracles of Zoroaster, the Founder of the Persian Magi," III, 368n

Zwingli, Huldreich, I, 132